Praise for Ne *...* omation

Jason, Scott, and Matt have been key contributors in educating network engineers about both network automation and Linux networking. They have written and talked extensively about the importance of automation, on how automation impacts network engineers, and on the mechanics of automating networking devices.

—Kirk Byers
Creator of the Netmiko Python Library

Network automation is no longer just a proof of concept: it represents both the present and the future! Network Programmability and Automation provides the needed background for modern engineers, by widening the toolset for more consistent, stable and reliable networks.

—Mircea Ulinic
Network Systems Engineer, Cloudflare

Network automation is not hype anymore; it is a means to do your job faster, more consistently and more reliably. However, network automation is not just a single discipline; it is a collection of protocols, tools, and processes that can be overwhelming to the uninitiated. This book does a great job covering everything you will need to get your automation up and running.

—David Barroso
creator of NAPALM

Network Programmability and Automation

Skills for the Next-Generation Network Engineer

Jason Edelman, Scott S. Lowe, and Matt Oswalt

Beijing · Boston · Farnham · Sebastopol · Tokyo

Network Programmability and Automation

by Jason Edelman, Scott S. Lowe, and Matt Oswalt

Copyright © 2018 Jason Edelman, Scott S. Lowe, Matt Oswalt. All rights reserved.

Printed in the United States of America.

Published by O'Reilly Media, Inc., 1005 Gravenstein Highway North, Sebastopol, CA 95472.

O'Reilly books may be purchased for educational, business, or sales promotional use. Online editions are also available for most titles (*http://oreilly.com/safari*). For more information, contact our corporate/institutional sales department: 800-998-9938 or *corporate@oreilly.com*.

Editors: Virginia Wilson and Courtney Allen	**Interior Designer:** David Futato
Production Editor: Colleen Cole	**Cover Designer:** Karen Montgomery
Copyeditor: Dwight Ramsey	**Illustrator:** Rebecca Demarest
Proofreader: Rachel Monaghan	**Technical Reviewers:** Patrick Ogenstad, Akhil Behl,
Indexer: Judy McConville	Eric Chou, Sreenivas Makam

February 2018:   First Edition

Revision History for the First Edition

2018-02-02:   First Release

See *http://oreilly.com/catalog/errata.csp?isbn=9781491931257* for release details.

The O'Reilly logo is a registered trademark of O'Reilly Media, Inc. *Network Programmability and Automation*, the cover image, and related trade dress are trademarks of O'Reilly Media, Inc.

While the publisher and the authors have used good faith efforts to ensure that the information and instructions contained in this work are accurate, the publisher and the authors disclaim all responsibility for errors or omissions, including without limitation responsibility for damages resulting from the use of or reliance on this work. Use of the information and instructions contained in this work is at your own risk. If any code samples or other technology this work contains or describes is subject to open source licenses or the intellectual property rights of others, it is your responsibility to ensure that your use thereof complies with such licenses and/or rights.

978-1-491-93125-7

[M]

I dedicate this book to all network engineers starting their network automation journey. I sincerely hope it provides each of you with the knowledge needed to further enhance your career. I'd also like to thank Scott, Matt, and the whole O'Reilly team—I know it was a much longer process than we all planned, but we ultimately got through it! Thanks to everyone for making it a reality.

Jason Edelman

I'd like to dedicate this book to the Lord, who granted me the wisdom and understanding I needed to write this book (Exodus 31:3 NIV). I'd also like to dedicate it to my wife, Crystal, without whose support things like this wouldn't be possible.

Scott S. Lowe

I dedicate this book to anyone with a hunger and a passion for learning—every word was written with you in mind. I'd also like to thank my wife Jamie, who keeps me motivated and upbeat when life gets a little too crazy.

Matt Oswalt

Table of Contents

Preface

Welcome to *Network Programmability and Automation*!

The networking industry is changing dramatically. The drive for organizations and networking professionals to embrace the ideas and concepts of network programmability and automation is greater now than perhaps it has ever been, fueled by a revolution in new protocols, new technologies, new delivery models, and a need for businesses to be more agile and more flexible in order to compete. But what *is* network programmability and automation? Let's start this book with a quick look at how to answer that question.

What This Book Covers

As its title implies, this book is focused on network programmability and automation. At its core, network programmability and automation is about simplifying the tasks involved in configuring, managing, and operating network equipment, network topologies, network services, and network connectivity. There are many, many different components involved—including operating systems that are now seeing far broader use in networking than in the past, the use of new methodologies like Continuous Integration, and the inclusion of tools that formerly might have fallen only in the realm of the system administrator (tools like source code control and configuration management systems). We feel like all of these play a part in the core definition of what network programmability and automation is, so we cover all these topics. Our goal for this book is to enable readers to establish a foundation of knowledge around network programmability and automation.

How This Book Is Organized

This book isn't necessarily intended to be read from start to end; instead, we've broken the topics up so that you can easily find the topics in which you're most interested. You may find it useful to start out sequentially reading the first three chapters, as they provide background information and set the stage for the rest of the book. From there, you're welcome to jump to whatever topic or topics are most useful or interesting to you. We've tried to keep the chapters relatively standalone, but—as with any technology—that's not always possible. Wherever we can, we provide cross-references to help you find the information you need.

Here's a quick look at how we've organized the topics:

Chapter 1, Network Industry Trends

Provides an overview of the major events and trends that launched Software Defined Networking (SDN). As you'll see in Chapter 1, SDN was the genesis for an increased focus on network programmability and automation.

Chapter 2, Network Automation

Takes the SDN discussion from Chapter 1 and focuses specifically on network automation—the history of network automation, types of automation, tools and technologies involved in automation, and how automation affects operational models (and how operational models affect automation).

Chapter 3, Linux

Provides an overview of the Linux operating system. By no means a comprehensive discussion of Linux, this chapter aims to get networking professionals up to speed on Linux, basic Linux commands, and Linux networking concepts.

Chapter 4, Learning Python in a Network Context

Introduces networking professionals to the Python development language (*http://python.org*). Python is frequently used in network programmability and automation contexts, and this chapter covers many of the basics of programming with Python: data types, conditionals, loops, working with files, functions, classes, and modules.

Chapter 5, Data Formats and Data Models

Introduces common data formats that are often seen in network automation projects. JavaScript Object Notation (JSON), eXtensible Markup Language (XML), and YAML Ain't Markup Language (YAML) are all discussed. The chapter then introduces the concepts of data modeling and provides a light introduction to YANG, a common data modeling language for networking.

Wondering what a "data format" is?

If you're new to some of this stuff, don't let the terminology throw you off. A *data format* is nothing more than how data is encoded or encapsulated when being transferred between two points (for example, when data is returned in response to an API call). Chapter 5 breaks it all down for you.

Chapter 6, Network Configuration Templates

Looks at the use of templating languages to create network device configurations. The primary focus of this chapter is on the Jinja templating language, as it integrates natively with Python. We'll also discuss Mako and ERB, two other templating languages. Mako integrates with Python, while ERB is primarily used with Ruby.

Chapter 7, Working with Network APIs

Will take a look at the role of application programming interfaces (APIs) in network programmability and automation. We'll explore key terms and technologies pertaining to APIs, and use some popular vendor-specific APIs—both device APIs and controller APIs—as examples to see how they can be used for network programmability and automation.

Chapter 8, Source Control with Git

Introduces Git (*https://git-scm.com*), a very popular and widely used tool for source code control. We'll talk about why source code control is important, how it is used in a network programmability and automation context, and how to work with popular online services such as GitHub (*https://github.com*).

Chapter 9, Automation Tools

Explores the use of open source automation tools such as Ansible (*http://www.ansible.com/home*), Salt (*http://saltstack.com*), and StackStorm (*https://stackstorm.com/*), and how these tools can be used specifically for network programmability and automation.

Chapter 10, Continuous Integration

Examines the concepts of Continuous Integration (CI) and the key tools and technologies that are involved. We'll discuss the use of test-driven development (TDD), explore tools and frameworks like Jenkins and Gerrit, and take a look at a sample network automation workflow that incorporates all these CI elements.

Chapter 11, Building a Culture for Network Automation

Examines why a good culture is a crucial and foundational element for network automation, and shows how to nurture such a culture.

Appendix A, Advanced Networking in Linux

Continues the discussion started in Chapter 3, but dives much deeper into networking with macvlan interfaces, networking with virtual machines (VMs), working with network namespaces, networking with Linux containers (including Docker (*https://www.docker.com*) containers), and using Open vSwitch (OVS) (*http://openvswitch.org*).

Appendix B, Using NAPALM

Provides an introduction to using the NAPALM (Network Automation and Programmability Abstraction Layer with Multi-vendor support) Python library. This section explores the use of NAPALM for both vendor-neutral configuration management and retrieving data from network devices. Finally, we take a look at how NAPALM integrates with tools such as Ansible, Salt, and StackStorm, all covered in Chapter 9.

Who Should Read This Book

As we mentioned earlier, the goal of the book is to equip readers with foundational knowledge and a set of baseline skills in the areas of network programmability and automation. We believe that members of several different IT disciplines will benefit from reading this book.

Network Engineers

Given the focus on network programmability and automation, it's natural that one audience for this book is the "traditional" network engineer, someone who is reasonably fluent in network protocols, configuring network devices, and operating and managing a network. We believe this book will enable today's network engineers to be more efficient and more productive through automation and programmability.

Prerequisites

Network engineers interested in learning more about network programmability and automation don't need any previous knowledge in software development, programming, automation, or DevOps-related tools. The only prerequisite is an open mind and a willingness to learn about new technologies and how they will affect you—the networking professional—and the greater networking industry as a whole.

Systems Administrators

Systems administrators, who are primarily responsible for managing the systems that connect to the network, may already have previous experience with some of the tools that are discussed in this book (notably, Linux, source code control, and configuration management systems). This book, then, could serve as a mechanism to help them expand their knowledge and understanding of such tools by presenting them in a different context (for example, using Ansible to configure a network switch as opposed to using Ansible to configure a server running a distribution of Linux).

Prerequisites

What this book *doesn't* provide is any coverage or explanation of core networking protocols or concepts. However, as a result of managing network-connected systems, we anticipate that many systems administrators also have a basic knowledge of core networking protocols. So most experienced systems administrators should be fine. If you're a bit weak on your networking knowledge, we'd recommend supplementing this book with a book that focuses on core networking concepts and ideas. For example, *Packet Guide to Core Network Protocols* (O'Reilly) may be a good choice.

Software Developers

Software developers may also benefit from reading this book. Many developers will have prior experience with some of the programming languages and developer tools discussed in this book (such as Python and/or Git). Like systems administrators, developers may find it useful to see developer tools and languages used in a networking-centric context (for example, seeing how Python could be used to retrieve and store networking-specific data).

Prerequisites

We do assume that readers have a basic understanding of core network protocols and concepts, and all the examples we provide are networking-centric examples. As with systems administrators, software developers who are new to networking will probably find it necessary to supplement the material in this book with a book that focuses on core networking concepts.

Tools Used in this Book

As with any field of technology, there are many different versions and variations of the technologies and tools found in the network programmability and automation space. Therefore, we standardized on a set of tools in this book that we feel best represent the tools readers will find in the field. For example, there are many different distributions of Linux, but we will only be focusing on Debian, Ubuntu (which is itself a derivative of Debian), and CentOS (a derivative of Red Hat Enterprise Linux [RHEL]). To help make it easy for readers, we call out the specific version of the various tools in each tool's specific chapter.

Online Resources

We realize that we can't possibly cover *all* the material we'd like to cover regarding network automation and network programmability. Therefore, throughout the book we'll reference additional online resources that you may find helpful and useful in understanding the concepts, ideas, and skills being presented.

Conventions Used in This Book

The following typographical conventions are used in this book:

Italic

> Indicates new terms, URLs, email addresses, filenames, and file extensions.

`Constant width`

> Used for program listings, as well as within paragraphs to refer to program elements such as variable or function names, databases, data types, environment variables, statements, and keywords.

`Constant width bold`

> Shows commands or other text that should be typed literally by the user.

`Constant width italic`

> Shows text that should be replaced with user-supplied values or by values determined by context.

> This element signifies a tip or suggestion.

> This element signifies a general note.

> This element indicates a warning or caution.

O'Reilly Safari

 *Safari* (formerly Safari Books Online) is a membership-based training and reference platform for enterprise, government, educators, and individuals.

Members have access to thousands of books, training videos, Learning Paths, interactive tutorials, and curated playlists from over 250 publishers, including O'Reilly

Media, Harvard Business Review, Prentice Hall Professional, Addison-Wesley Professional, Microsoft Press, Sams, Que, Peachpit Press, Adobe, Focal Press, Cisco Press, John Wiley & Sons, Syngress, Morgan Kaufmann, IBM Redbooks, Packt, Adobe Press, FT Press, Apress, Manning, New Riders, McGraw-Hill, Jones & Bartlett, and Course Technology, among others.

For more information, please visit *http://oreilly.com/safari*.

How to Contact Us

Please address comments and questions concerning this book to the publisher:

> O'Reilly Media, Inc.
> 1005 Gravenstein Highway North
> Sebastopol, CA 95472
> 800-998-9938 (in the United States or Canada)
> 707-829-0515 (international or local)
> 707-829-0104 (fax)

We have a web page for this book, where we list errata, examples, and any additional information. You can access this page at *http://bit.ly/network-programmability-and-automation*.

To comment or ask technical questions about this book, send email to *bookquestions@oreilly.com*.

For more information about our books, courses, conferences, and news, see our website at *http://www.oreilly.com*.

Find us on Facebook: *http://facebook.com/oreilly*

Follow us on Twitter: *http://twitter.com/oreillymedia*

Watch us on YouTube: *http://www.youtube.com/oreillymedia*

Acknowledgments

This book would not have been possible without the help and support of a large community of people.

First, we'd like to extend our thanks to the vibrant network automation community. There are too many folks to name directly, but these are the folks who have created open source projects like NAPALM and Netmiko, who have helped lead the charge in educating folks about network automation, and who have tirelessly contributed their knowledge and experience for the benefit of others. Thank you all for your efforts and your contributions.

Our contributing authors helped make this book more complete and comprehensive than we would have been able to without their assistance, and we are deeply grateful for their help. Mircea Ulinic contributed the SaltStack section in the chapter on configuration management tools, and Jere Julian contributed some Puppet content that we unfortunately could not get included in this version of the book. Our thanks go to both Mircea and Jere.

Our technical reviewers were critical in ensuring that the content was both technically accurate and easily consumable by readers. We'd like to extend our thanks to Patrick Ogenstad, Akhil Behl, Eric Chou, and Sreenivas Makam. Thanks for helping make sure this book is the best it could be!

Finally, our thanks would not be complete without including the staff of O'Reilly Media: Virginia Wilson and Courtney Allen, our editors; Dwight Ramsey, our copy editor; Rachel Monaghan, our proofreader; Judy McConville, our indexer; Colleen Cole, our production editor; Randy Comer, the cover designer; and Rebecca Demarest, the illustrator. The importance of their efforts in helping us take this book from concept to production cannot be understated, and we thank them for their dedication and commitment.

## CHAPTER 1

Network Industry Trends

Are you new to Software Defined Networking (SDN)? Have you been hung up in the SDN craze for the past several years? Whichever bucket you fall into, do not worry. This book will walk you through foundational topics to start your network programmability and automation journey starting with the rise of SDN. This chapter provides insight to trends in the network industry focused around SDN, its relevance, and its impact in today's world of networking. We'll get started by reviewing how Software Defined Networking made it into the mainstream and ultimately led to trends around network programmability and automation.

The Rise of Software Defined Networking

If there was one person that could be credited with all the change that is occurring in the network industry, it would be Martin Casado, who is currently a General Partner and Venture Capitalist at Andreessen Horowitz. Previously, Casado was a VMware Fellow, Senior Vice President, and General Manager in the Networking and Security Business Unit at VMware. He has had a profound impact on the industry, not just from his direct contributions (including OpenFlow and Nicira), but by opening the eyes of large network incumbents and showing that network operations, agility, and manageability must change. Let's take a look at this in a little more detail.

OpenFlow

For better or for worse, OpenFlow served as the first major protocol of the Software Defined Networking (SDN) movement. OpenFlow is the protocol that Martin Casado worked on while he was earning his PhD at Stanford University under the supervision of Nick McKeown. OpenFlow is only a protocol that allows for the de-coupling of a network device's control plane from the data plane (see Figure 1-1). In simplest terms, the control plane can be thought of as the *brains* of a network device and the data plane can be thought of as the *hardware* or *application-specific integrated circuits* (ASICs) that actually perform packet forwarding.

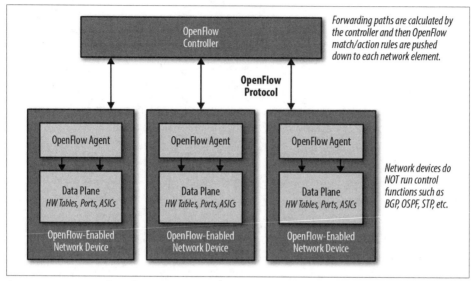

Figure 1-1. Decoupling the control plane and data plane with OpenFlow

Running OpenFlow in Hybrid Mode

Figure 1-1 depicts the network elements having no control plane. This represents a pure OpenFlow-only deployment. Many devices also support running OpenFlow in a hybrid mode, meaning OpenFlow can be deployed on a given port, virtual local area network (VLAN), or within a normal packet-forwarding pipeline such that if there is not a match in the *OpenFlow table*, then the existing forwarding tables (MAC, Routing, etc.) are used, making it more analogous to Policy Based Routing (PBR).

What this means is OpenFlow is a low-level protocol that is used to directly interface with the hardware tables (e.g., Forwarding Information Base, or FIB) that instruct a network device how to forward traffic (for example, "traffic to destination 192.168.0.100 should egress port 48").

 OpenFlow is a low-level protocol that manipulates flow tables, thus directly impacting packet forwarding. OpenFlow was not intended to interact with management plane attributes like authentication or SNMP parameters.

Because the tables OpenFlow uses support more than the destination address as compared to traditional routing protocols, there is more granularity (matching fields in the packet) to determine the forwarding path. This is not unlike the granularity offered by Policy Based Routing. Like OpenFlow would do many years later, PBR allows network administrators to forward traffic based on "non-traditional" attributes, like a packet's source address. However, it took quite some time for network vendors to offer equivalent performance for traffic that was forwarded via PBR, and the final result was still very vendor-specific. The advent of OpenFlow meant that we could now achieve the same granularity with traffic forwarding decisions, but in a vendor-neutral way. It became possible to enhance the capabilities of the network infrastructure without waiting for the next version of hardware from the manufacturer.

History of Programmable Networks

OpenFlow was not the first protocol or technology used to decouple control functions and intelligence from network devices. There is a long history of technology and research that predates OpenFlow, although OpenFlow is the technology that started the SDN revolution. A few of the technologies that predated OpenFlow include *Forwarding and Control Element Separation* (ForCES), Active Networks, Routing Control Platform (RCP), and Path Computation Element (PCE). For a more in-depth look at this history, take a look at the paper "The Road to SDN: An Intellectual History of Programmable Networks" (*https://www.cs.princeton.edu/courses/archive/fall13/cos597E/papers/sdnhistory.pdf*) by Jen Rexford, Nick Feamster, and Ellen Zegura.

Why OpenFlow?

While it's important to understand what OpenFlow is, it's even more important to understand the reasoning behind the research and development effort of the original OpenFlow spec that led to the rise of Software Defined Networking.

Martin Casado had a job working for the national government while he was attending Stanford. During his time working for the government, there was a need to react to security attacks on the IT systems (after all, this is the US government). Casado quickly realized that he was able to program and manipulate the computers and servers as he needed. The actual use cases were never publicized, but it was this type of control over endpoints that made it possible to react, analyze, and potentially reprogram a host or group of hosts when and if needed.

When it came to the network, it was near impossible to do this in a clean and programmatic fashion. After all, each network device was *closed* (locked from installing third-party software, as an example) and only had a command-line interface (CLI).

Although the CLI was and is still very well known and even preferred by network administrators, it was clear to Casado that it did not offer the flexibility required to truly manage, operate, and secure the network.

In reality, the way networks were managed had *never* changed in over 20 years except for the addition of CLI commands for new features. The biggest change was the migration from Telnet to SSH, which was a joke often used by the SDN company Big Switch Networks in their slides, as you can see in Figure 1-2.

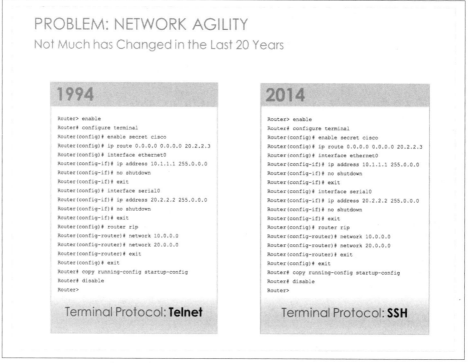

Figure 1-2. What's changed? From Telnet to SSH (source: Big Switch Networks)

All joking aside, the management of networks has lagged behind other technologies quite drastically, and this is what Casado eventually set out to change over the next several years. This lack in manageability is often better understood when other technologies are examined. Other technologies almost always have more modern ways of managing a large number of devices for both configuration management and data gathering and analysis—for example, hypervisor managers, wireless controllers, IP PBXs, PowerShell, DevOps tools, and the list can go on. Some of these are tightly coupled from vendors as commercial software, but others are more loosely aligned to allow for multi-platform management, operations, and agility.

If we go back to the scenario while Casado was working for the government, was it possible to redirect traffic based on application? Did network devices have an API? Was there a single point of communication to the network? The answers were largely *no* across the board. How could it be possible to *program* the network to dynamically control packet forwarding, policy, and configuration as easily as it was to write a program and have it execute on an end host machine?

The initial OpenFlow spec was the result of Martin Casado experiencing these types of problems firsthand. While the hype around OpenFlow has died down since the industry is starting to finally focus more on use cases and solutions than low-level protocols, this initial work was the catalyst for the entire industry to do a rethink on how networks are built, managed, and operated. Thank you, Martin.

This also means if it weren't for Martin Casado, this book would probably not have been written, but we'll never know now!

What Is Software Defined Networking?

We've had an introduction to OpenFlow, but what is Software Defined Networking (SDN)? Are they the same thing, different things, or neither? To be honest, SDN is just like Cloud was nearly a decade ago, before we knew about different types of Cloud, such as Infrastructure as a Service (IaaS), Platform as a Service (PaaS), and Software as a Service (SaaS).

Having reference examples and designs streamlines the understanding of what Cloud was and is, but even before these terms did exist, it could be debated that when you saw Cloud, you knew it. That's kind of where we are with Software Defined Networking. There are public definitions that exist that state white-box networking is SDN or that having an API on a network device is SDN. Are they *really* SDN? Not really.

Rather than attempt to provide a definition of SDN, we will cover the technologies and trends that are very often thought of as SDN, and included in the SDN conversation. They include:

- OpenFlow
- Network Functions Virtualization
- Virtual switching
- Network virtualization
- Device APIs
- Network automation
- Bare-metal switching
- Data center network fabrics
- SD-WAN
- Controller networking

We are intentionally not providing a definition of SDN in this book. While SDN is mentioned in this chapter, our primary focus is on general trends that are often categorized as SDN to ensure you're aware of each of these trends more specifically.

Of these trends, the rest of the book will focus on network automation, APIs, and peripheral technologies that are critical in understanding how all of the pieces come together in network devices that expose programmatic interfaces with modern automation tools and instrumentation.

OpenFlow

Even though we introduced OpenFlow earlier, we want to highlight a few more key points you should be aware of related to OpenFlow.

One of the major benefits that was supposed to be an outcome of using a protocol like OpenFlow between a controller and network devices was that there would be true vendor independence from the controller software, sometimes referred to as a network operating system (NOS), and the underlying virtual and physical network devices. What has actually happened, though, is that vendors who use OpenFlow in their solution (examples include Big Switch Networks, HP, and NEC) have developed OpenFlow extensions due to the pace of standards and the need to provide unique value-added features that the *off-the-shelf* version of OpenFlow does not offer. It is yet to be seen if all of the extensions end up making it into future versions of the Open-Flow *standard*.

When OpenFlow is used, you do gain the benefit to getting more granular with how traffic traverses the network, but with great power comes great responsibility. This is great if you have a team of developers. For example, Google rolled out an OpenFlow-based WAN called B4 that increases efficiency of their WAN to nearly 100%. For most other organizations, the use of OpenFlow or any other given protocol will be less important than what an overall solution offers to the business being supported.

While this particular section is called *OpenFlow*, architecturally it's about decoupling the control plane from the data plane. OpenFlow is just the main protocol being used to accomplish this functionality.

Network Functions Virtualization

Network Functions Virtualization, known as NFV, isn't a complex concept. It refers to taking functions that have traditionally been deployed as hardware, and instead deploying them as software. The most common examples of this are virtual machines that operate as routers, firewalls, load balancers, IDS/IPS, VPN, application firewalls, and any other service/function.

With NFV, it becomes possible to break down a monolithic piece of hardware that may have cost tens or hundreds of thousands of dollars, with hundreds to thousands of lines of commands, to get it configured into *N* pieces of software, namely virtual appliances. These smaller devices become much more manageable from an individual device perspective.

 The preceding scenario uses virtual appliances as the form factor for NFV-enabled devices. This is merely an example. Deploying network functions as software could come in many forms, including embedded in a hypervisor, as a container, or as an application running atop an x86 server.

It's not uncommon to deploy hardware that *may* be needed in three to five years just in case, because it's too complicated and even more expensive to have gradual upgrades. So not only is hardware an intensive capital cost, it's only used for the what-if scenarios *if* growth occurs. Deploying software-based, or NFV, solutions offers a better way to scale out and minimize the failure domain of a network or particular application while using a *pay-as-you-grow model*. For example, rather than purchasing a single large Cisco ASA, you can gradually deploy Cisco ASAv appliances and pay as you grow. You can also scale out load balancers easily with newer technologies from a company like Avi Networks.

If NFV could offer so much benefit, why haven't there been more solutions and products that fit into this category deployed in production? There are actually a few different reasons. First, it requires a rethink in how the network is architected. When there is a single monolithic firewall (as an example), everything goes through that firewall —meaning all applications and all users, or if not all, a defined set that you are aware of. In the modern NFV model where there could be many virtual firewalls deployed, there is a firewall per application or tenant as opposed to a single big-box FW. This makes the failure domain per firewall, or any other services appliances, fairly small, and if a change is being made or a new application is being rolled out, no change is required for the other per-application (per-tenant) based firewalls.

On the other hand, in the more traditional world of having monolithic devices, there is essentially a single pane of management for security policy—single CLI or GUI. This could make the failure domain immense, but it does offer administrators streamlined policy management since it's only a single device being managed. Based on the team or staff supporting these devices, they may opt still for a monolithic approach. That is the reality, but hopefully over time with improved tools that can help with the consumption and management of software-centric solutions, as an industry, we'll see more deployments leveraging this type of technology. In fact, in a world with modern automated network operations and management, it'll matter less which architecture is chosen from an operational efficiency perspective as you'll be able to manage either a single device or a larger quantity of devices in a much more efficient manner.

Aside from management, another factor that plays into this is that many vendors are not actively selling their *virtual appliance* edition. We're not saying they don't have virtual options, but they are usually not the preferred choice of many traditional equipment manufacturers. If a vendor has had a hardware business for the past several years, it's a drastic shift to a software-led model from a sales and compensation perspective. Because of this, many of these vendors are limiting the performance or features on their virtual appliance-based technology.

As will be seen in many of these technology areas, a major value of NFV is in agility too. Eliminating hardware decreases the time to provision new services by removing the time needed to rack, stack, cable, and integrate into an existing environment. Leveraging a software approach, it becomes as fast as deploying a new virtual machine into the environment, and an inherent benefit of this approach is being able to clone and back up the virtual appliance for further testing, for example in disaster recovery (DR) environments.

Finally, when NFV is deployed, it eliminates the need to route traffic through a specific physical device in order to get the required service.

Virtual switching

The more common virtual switches on the market these days include the VMware standard switch (VSS), VMware distributed switch (VDS), Cisco Nexus 1000V, Cisco Application Virtual Switch (AVS), and the open source Open vSwitch (OVS).

These switches every so often get wrapped into the SDN discussion, but in reality they are software-based switches that reside in the hypervisor kernel providing local network connectivity between virtual machines (and now containers). They provide functions such as MAC learning and features like link aggregation, SPAN, and sFlow just like their physical switch counterparts have been doing for years. While these virtual switches are often found in more comprehensive SDN and network virtualization solutions, by themselves they are a switch that just happens to be running in software. While virtual switches are not a solution on their own, they are extremely important as we move forward as an industry. They've created a new access layer, or new edge, within the data center. No longer is the network edge the physical top-of-rack (TOR) switch that is hardware-defined with limited flexibility (in terms of feature/function development). Since the new edge is software-based through the use of virtual switches, it offers the ability to more rapidly create new network functions in software, and thus, it is possible to distribute policy more easily throughout the network. As an example, security policy can be deployed to the virtual switch port that is nearest to the actual endpoint, be it a virtual machine or container, to further enhance the security of the network.

Network virtualization

Solutions that are categorized as network virtualization have become synonymous with SDN solutions. For purposes of this section, network virtualization refers to software-only overlay-based solutions. The popular solutions that fall into this category are VMware's NSX, Nuage's Virtual Service Platform (VSP), and Juniper's Contrail.

A key characteristic of these solutions is that an overlay-based protocol such as Virtual eXtensible LAN (VxLAN) is used to build connectivity between hypervisor-based virtual switches. This connectivity and tunneling approach provides Layer 2 adjacency between virtual machines that exist on different physical hosts independent of the physical network, meaning the physical network could be Layer 2, Layer 3, or a combination of both. The result is a virtual network that is decoupled from the physical network and that is meant to provide choice and agility.

It's worth pointing out that the term *overlay network* is often used in conjunction with the term *underlay network*. For clarity, the underlay is the underlying physical network that you physically cable up. The overlay network is built using a network virtualization solution that dynamically creates tunnels between virtual switches within a data center. Again, this is in the context of a software-based network virtualization solution. Also note that many hardware-only solutions are now being deployed with VxLAN as the overlay protocol to establish Layer 2 tunnels between top-of-rack devices within a Layer 3 data center.

While the overlay is an implementation detail of network virtualization solutions, these solutions are much more than just virtual switches being stitched together by overlays. These solutions are usually comprehensive, offering security, load balancing, and integrations back into the physical network all with a single point of management (i.e., the controller). Oftentimes these solutions offer integrations with the best-of-breed Layer 4–7 services companies as well, offering choice as to which technology could be deployed within network virtualzation platforms.

Agility is also achieved thanks to the central controller platform, which is used to dynamically configure each virtual switch, and services appliances as needed. If you recall, the network has lagged behind operationally due to the CLI that is pervasive across all vendors in the physical world. In network virtualization, there is no need to configure virtual switches manually, as each solution simplifies this process by providing a central GUI, CLI, and also an API where changes can be made programmatically.

Device APIs

Over the past several years, vendors have begun to realize that just offering a standard CLI was not going to cut it anymore and that using a CLI has severely held back operations. If you have ever worked with any programming or scripting language, you can probably understand that. For those that haven't, we'll talk more about this in Chapter 7.

The major pain point is that scripting with legacy or CLI-based network devices does not return structured data. This meant data would be returned from the device to a script in a raw text format (i.e., the output of a *show version*) and then the individual writing the script would need to parse that text to extract attributes such as uptime or operating system version. When the output of show commands changed even slightly, the scripts would break due to incorrect parsing rules. While this approach is all administrators have had, automation was technically possible, but now vendors are gradually migrating to API-driven network devices.

Offering an API eliminates the need to parse raw text, as structured data is returned from a network device, significantly reducing the time it takes to write a script. Rather than parsing through text to find the uptime or any other attribute, an object is returned providing exactly what is needed. Not only does it reduce the time to write a script, lowering the barrier to entry for network engineers (and other non-programmers), but it also provides a cleaner interface such that professional software developers can rapidly develop and test code, much like they operate using APIs on non-network devices. "Test code" could mean testing new topologies, certifying new network features, validating particular network configurations, and more. These are all things that are done manually today and are very time consuming and error prone.

One of the first more popular APIs in the network scene was that by Arista Networks. Its API is called eAPI, which is HTTP-based API that uses JSON-encoded data. Don't worry, HTTP-based APIs and JSON will be covered in chapters to follow, starting with Chapter 5. Since Arista, we've seen Cisco announce APIs such as Nexus NX-API and NETCONF/RESTCONF on particular platforms and a vendor like Juniper, which has had an extensible NETCONF interface all along but hasn't publicly drawn too much attention to it. It's worth noting that nearly every vendor out there has some sort of API these days.

This topic will be covered in much more detail in Chapter 7.

Network automation

As APIs in the network world continue to evolve, more interesting use cases for taking advantage of them will also continue to emerge. In the near term, network automation is a prime candidate for taking advantage of the programmatic interfaces being exposed by modern network devices that offer an API.

To put it in greater context, network automation is *not* just about automating the configuration of network devices. It is true that is the most common perception of network automation, but using APIs and programmatic interfaces can automate and offer much more than pushing configuration parameters.

Leveraging an API streamlines the access to all of the data bottled up in network devices. Think about data such as flow level data, routing tables, FIB tables, interface statistics, MAC tables, VLAN tables, serial numbers—the list can go on and on. Using modern automation techniques that in turn leverage an API can quickly aid in the day-to-day operations of managing networks for data gathering and automated diagnostics. On top of that, since an API is being used that returns structured data, as an administrator, you will have the ability to display and analyze the exact data set you want and need, even coming from various show commands, ultimately reducing the time it takes to debug and troubleshoot issues on the network. Rather than connecting to N routers running BGP trying to validate a configuration or troubleshoot an issue, you can use automation techniques to simplify this process.

Additionally, leveraging automation techniques leads to a more predictable and uniform network as a whole. You can see this by automating the creation of configuration files, automating the creation of a VLAN, or automating the process of troubleshooting. It streamlines the process for all users supporting a given environment instead of having each network administrator having *their own* best practice.

The various types of network automation will be covered in Chapter 2 in much greater depth.

Bare-metal switching

The topic of bare-metal switching is also often thought of as SDN, but it's not. Really, it isn't! That said, in our effort to give an introduction to the various technology trends that are *perceived* as SDN, it needs to be covered. If we rewind to 2014 (and even earlier), the term used to describe bare-metal switching was *white-box or commodity switching*. The term has changed, and not without good reason.

Before we cover the change from white-box to bare-metal, it's important to understand what this means at a high level since it's a massive change in how network devices are thought of. Network devices for the last 20 years were always bought as a physical device—these physical devices came as hardware appliances, an operating system, and features/applications that you can use on the system. These components all came from the same vendor.

In the white-box and bare-metal network devices, the device looks more like an x86 server (see Figure 1-3). It allows the user to disaggregate each of the required components, making it possible to purchase hardware from one vendor, purchase an operating system from another, and then load features/apps from other vendors or even the open source community.

White-box switching was a hot topic for a period of time during the OpenFlow hype, since the intent was to commoditize hardware and centralize the brains of the network in an OpenFlow controller, otherwise now known as an SDN controller. And in 2013, Google announced they had built their own switches and were controlling them with OpenFlow! This was the topic of a lot of industry conversations at the time, but in reality, not every end user is Google, so not every user will be building their own hardware and software platforms.

In parallel to these efforts, we saw the emergence of a few companies that were solely focused on providing solutions around white-box switching. They include Big Switch Networks, Cumulus Networks, and Pica8. Each of them offers software-only solutions, so they still need hardware that their software will run on to provide an end-to-end solution. Initially, these white-box hardware platforms came from Original Direct Manufacturers (ODM) such as Quanta, Super Micro, and Accton. If you've been in the network industry, more than likely you've never even heard of those vendors.

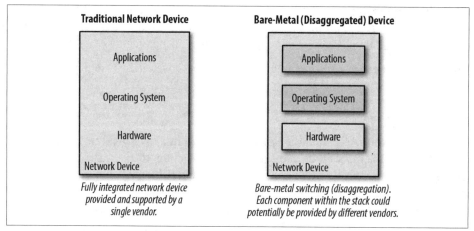

Figure 1-3. A look at traditional and bare-metal switching stacks

It wasn't until Cumulus and Big Switch announced partnerships with companies including HP and Dell that the industry started to shift from calling this trend white-box to bare-metal, since now name-brand vendors were supporting third-party operating systems from the likes of Big Switch and Cumulus Networks on their hardware platforms.

There still may be confusion on why bare-metal is technically not SDN, since a vendor like Big Switch plays in both worlds. The answer is simple. If there is a controller integrated with the solution using a protocol such as OpenFlow (it does not *have* to be OpenFlow), and it is programmatically communicating with the network devices, that gives it the flavor of Software Defined Networking. This is what Big Switch does —they load software on the bare-metal/white-box hardware running an OpenFlow agent that then communicates with the controller as part of their solution.

On the other hand, Cumulus Networks provides a Linux distribution purpose-built for network switches. This distribution, or operating system, runs traditional protocols such as LLDP, OSPF, and BGP, with no controller requirement whatsoever, making it more comparable, and compatible, to non-SDN based network architectures.

With this description it should be evident that Cumulus is a network operating system company that runs their software on bare-metal switches while Big Switch is a bare-metal-based SDN company requiring the use of their SDN controller, but also leverages third-party, bare-metal switching infrastructure.

In short, bare-metal/white-box switching is about disaggregation and having the ability to purchase network hardware from one vendor and load software from another, should you choose to do so. In this case, administrators are offered the flexibility to change designs, architectures, and software, without swapping out hardware, just the underlying operating system.

Data center network fabrics

Have you ever faced the situation where you could not easily interchange the various network devices in a network even if they were all running standard protocols such as Spanning Tree or OSPF? If you have, you are not alone. Imagine having a data center network with a collapsed core and individual switches at the top of each rack. Now think about the process that needs to happen when it's time for an upgrade.

There are many ways to upgrade networks like this, but what if it was just the top-of-rack switches that needed to be upgraded and in the evaluation process for new TOR switches, it was decided a new vendor or platform would be used? This is 100% normal and has been done time and time again. The process is simple—interconnect the new switches to the existing core (of course, we are assuming there are available ports in the core) and properly configure 802.1Q trunking if it's a Layer 2 interconnect or configure your favorite routing protocol if it's a Layer 3 interconnect.

Enter *data center network fabrics*. This is where the thought process around data center networks has to change.

Data center network fabrics aim to change the mindset of network operators from managing individual boxes one at a time to managing a system in its entirety. If we use the earlier scenario, it would not be possible to swap out a TOR switch for another vendor, which is just a single component of a data center network. Rather, when the network is deployed and managed as a system, it needs to be thought of as a system. This means the upgrade process would be to migrate from system to system, or fabric to fabric. In the world of fabrics, fabrics can be swapped out when it's time for an upgrade, but the individual components within the fabric cannot be—at least most of the time. It *may* be possible when a specific vendor is providing a migration or upgrade path and when bare-metal switching (only replacing hardware) is being used. A few examples of data center network fabrics are Cisco's Application Centric Infrastructure (ACI), Big Switch's Big Cloud Fabric (BCF), or Plexxi's fabric and hyper-converged network.

In addition to treating the network as a system, a few other common attributes of data center networking fabrics are:

- They offer a single interface to manage or configure the fabric, including policy management.
- They offer distributed default gateways across the fabric.
- They offer multi-pathing capabilities.
- They use some form of SDN controller to manage the system.

SD-WAN

One of the hottest trends in Software Defined Networking over the past two years has been Software Defined Wide Area Networking (SD-WAN). Over the past few years, a growing number of companies have been launched to tackle the problem of Wide Area Networking. A few of these vendors include Viptela (most recently acquired by Cisco), CloudGenix, VeloCloud, Cisco IWAN, Glue Networks, and Silverpeak.

The WAN had not seen a radical shift in technology since the migration from Frame Relay to MPLS. With broadband and internet costs being a fraction of what costs are for equivalent private line circuits, there has been an increase in leveraging site-to-site VPN tunnels over the years, laying the groundwork for the next big thing in WAN.

Common designs for remote offices typically include a private (MPLS) circuit and/or a public internet connection. When both exist, internet is usually used as backup only, specifically for guest traffic, or for general data riding back over a VPN to corporate while the MPLS circuit is used for low-latency applications such as voice or video communications. When traffic starts to get divided between circuits, this increases the complexity of the routing protocol configuration and also limits the granularity of how to route to the destination address. The source address, application, and real-time performance of the network is usually not taken into consideration in decisions about the best path to take.

A common SD-WAN architecture that many of the modern solutions use is similar to that of network virtualization used in the data center, in that an overlay protocol is used to interconnect the SD-WAN edge devices. Since overlays are used, the solution is agnostic to the underlying physical transport, making SD-WAN functional over the internet or a private WAN. These solutions often ride over two or more internet circuits at branch sites, fully encrypting traffic using IPSec. Additionally, many of these solutions constantly measure the performance of each circuit in use being able to rapidly fail over between circuits for specific applications even during brownouts. Since there is application layer visibility, administrators can also easily pick and choose which application should take a particular route. These types of features are often not found in WAN architectures that rely solely on destination-based routing using traditional routing protocol such as OSPF and BGP.

From an architecture standpoint, the SD-WAN solutions from the vendors mentioned earlier like Cisco, Viptela, and CloudGenix also typically offer some form of zero touch provisioning (ZTP) and centralized management with a portal that exists on premises or in the cloud as a SaaS-based application, drastically simplifying management and operations of the WAN going forward.

A valuable by-product of using SD-WAN technology is that it offers more *choice* for end users since basically any carrier or type of connection can be used on the WAN and across the internet. In doing so, it simplifies the configuration and complexity of carrier networks, which in turn will allow carriers to simplify their internal design and architecture, hopefully reducing their costs. Going one step further from a technical perspective, all logical network constructs such as Virtual Routing and Forwarding (VRFs) would be managed via the controller platform user interface (UI) that the SD-WAN vendor provides, again eliminating the need to wait weeks for carriers to respond to you when changes are required.

Controller networking

When it comes to several of these trends, there is some overlap, as you may have realized. That is one of the confusing points when you are trying to understand all of the new technology and trends that have emerged over the last few years.

For example, popular network virtualization platforms use a controller, as do several solutions that fall into the data center network fabric, SD-WAN, and bare-metal switch categories too. Confusing? You may be wondering why controller-based networking has been broken out by itself. In reality, it oftentimes is just characteristic and a mechanism to deliver modern solutions, but not all of the previous trends cover all of what controllers can deliver from a technology perspective.

For example, a very popular open source SDN controller is OpenDaylight (ODL), as shown in Figure 1-4. ODL, as with many other controllers, is a platform, not a product. They are platforms that can offer specialized applications such as network virtualization, but they can also be used for network monitoring, visibility, tap aggregation, or any other function in conjunction with applications that sit on top of the controller platform. This is the core reason why it's important to understand what controllers can offer above and beyond being used for more traditional applications such as fabrics, network virtualization, and SD-WAN.

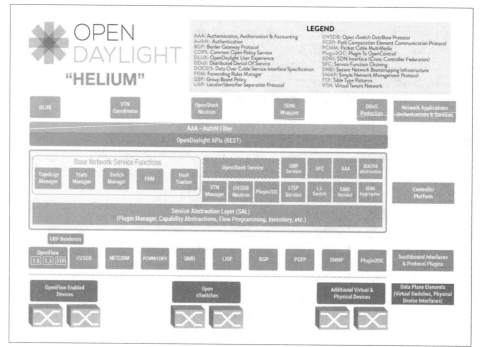

Figure 1-4. OpenDaylight architecture

Summary

There you have it: an introduction to the trends and technologies that are most often categorized as Software Defined Networking, paving the path into better network operations through network programmability and automation. Dozens of SDN startups were created over the past seven years, millions in VC money invested, and billions spent on acquisitions of these companies. It's been unreal, and if we break it down one step further, it's all with the common goal of leveraging software principles and technology to offer greater power, control, agility, and choice to the users of the technology while increasing the operational efficiencies.

In Chapter 2, we'll take a look at network automation and dive deeper into the various types of automation, some common protocols and APIs, and how automation has started to evolve in the last several years.

## CHAPTER 2

Network Automation

In this chapter, we're focused on providing a baseline of high-level network automation concepts so that you are better equipped to get the most out of each individual chapter going forward.

To accomplish this, the following sections are included in this chapter:

Why Network Automation?
> Examines various reasons to adopt automation and increase the efficiencies of network operations while proving there is much more to automation than delivering configurations faster to network devices.

Types of Network Automation
> Explores various types of automation from traditional configuration management to automating network diagnostics and troubleshooting, proving once again, there is more to automation than decreasing the time it takes to make a change.

Evolving the Management Plane from SNMP to Device APIs
> Provides a brief introduction to a few different API types found on network devices of the past and present.

Network Automation in the SDN Era
> Provides a short synopsis of why network automation tooling is still valuable when SDN, specifically referring to controller-based architectures, solutions are deployed.

This chapter is not meant to be a deep technical chapter, but rather an introduction to the ideas and concepts of network automation. It simply lays the foundation and provides context for the chapters that follow.

Why Network Automation?

Network automation, like most types of automation, is thought of as a means of doing things faster. While doing things more quickly is nice, reducing the time for deployments and configuration changes isn't always a problem that needs solving for many IT organizations.

Including speed, we'll take a look at a few of the reasons that IT organizations of all shapes and sizes should be looking at gradually adopting network automation. You should note that the same principles apply to other types of automation as well (application, systems, storage, telephony, etc.).

Simplified Architectures

Today, most network devices are configured as unique snowflakes (having many one-off non-standard configurations), and network engineers take pride in solving transport and application issues with one-off network changes that ultimately make the network not only harder to maintain and manage, but also harder to automate.

Instead of network automation and management being treated as a secondary project or an "add-on," it needs to be included from the outset as new architectures are being created. This includes ensuring there is the proper budget for personnel and/or tooling. Unfortunately, tooling is often the first item that gets cut when there is a shortage of budget.

The end-to-end architecture and associated day 2 operations need to be one and the same. You need to think about the following questions as architectures are created:

- Which features work across vendors?
- Which extensions work across platforms?
- What type of API or automation tooling works with particular network device platforms?
- Is there solid API documentation?
- What libraries exist for a given product?

When these questions get answered early on in the design process, the resulting architecture becomes simpler, repeatable, and easier to maintain *and* automate, all with fewer vendor-proprietary extensions enabled throughout the network.

Even after the simplified architecture gets deployed with the right management and automation tooling, remember it's still a necessity to minimize one-off changes to ensure the network configurations don't become snowflakes again.

Deterministic Outcomes

In an enterprise organization, change review meetings take place to review upcoming changes on the network, the impact they have on external systems, and rollback plans. In a world where a human is touching the CLI to make those upcoming changes, the impact of typing the wrong command is catastrophic. Imagine a team with 3, 4, 5, or 50 engineers. Every engineer may have his or her own way of making that particular upcoming change. Moreover, the ability to use a CLI and even a GUI does not eliminate or reduce the chance of error during the control window for the change.

Using proven and tested network automation to make changes helps achieve *more predictable* behavior than making changes manually, and gives the executive team a *better chance* at achieving deterministic outcomes, moving one step closer to having the assurance that the task at hand will get done right the first time without human error. This could be any task from a virtual local area network (VLAN) change to onboarding a new customer that requires several changes throughout the network.

Business Agility

We know that network automation offers speed and agility for deploying changes, but it does the same for retrieving data from network devices as fast as the business demands, or more practically, as fast as needed to dynamically troubleshoot a network issue.

Since the advent of server virtualization, server and virtualization administrators have had the ability to deploy new applications almost instantaneously. And the faster applications are deployed, the more questions are raised as to why it takes so long to configure network resources such as VLANs, routes, firewall (FW) policies, load-balancing polices, or all of the above, if deploying a new three-tier application.

It should be fairly obvious that by adopting network automation, the network engineering and operations teams can react faster to their IT counterparts for deploying applications, but more importantly, it helps the business be more agile. From an adoption perspective, it's critical to understand the existing, and often manual, workflows before attempting to adopt automation of any kind, no matter how good your intentions are for making the business more agile.

If you don't know what you want to automate, it'll complicate and prolong the process. Our *number one* recommendation as you start your network automation journey is to always understand existing manual workflows, document them, and understand the impact they have to the business. Then, the process to deploy automation technology and tooling becomes much simpler.

From simplified architectures to business agility, this section introduced some of the high-level points on why you should consider network automation. In the next section, we take a look at different types of network automation.

Types of Network Automation

Automation is commonly equated with speed, and considering that some network tasks don't require speed, it's easy to see why some IT teams don't see the value in automation. VLAN configuration is a great example because you may be thinking, "How *fast* does a VLAN really need to get created? Just how many VLANs are being added on a daily basis? Do *I* really need automation?" And they are all valid questions.

In this section, we are going to focus on several other tasks where automation makes sense, such as device provisioning, data collection, troubleshooting, reporting, and compliance. But remember, as we stated previously, automation is much more than speed and agility; it also offers you, your team, and your business more predictable and more deterministic outcomes.

Device Provisioning

One of the easiest and fastest ways to get started with network automation is to automate the creation of the device configuration files that are used for initial device provisioning and pushing them to network devices.

If we take this process and break it down into two steps, the first step is creating the configuration file, and the second is pushing the configuration onto the device.

In order to automate the creation of configuration files, we first need to decouple the *inputs* (configuration parameters) from the underlying vendor-proprietary syntax (CLI) of the configuration. This means we'll end up with separate files with values for the configuration parameters such as VLANs, domain information, interfaces, routing, and everything else being configured, and then, of course, a configuration template. This is something we cover in great detail in Chapter 6.

For now, think of the configuration template as the equivalent of a standard golden template that's used for all devices getting deployed. By leveraging a technique called *network configuration templating*, you are quickly able to produce consistent network configuration files specifically for your network. What this also means is you'll never have to use Notepad ever again, copying and pasting configs from file to file—isn't it about time for that?

Two tools that streamline using configuration templates with variables (data inputs) are Ansible and Salt. In less than a few seconds, these tools can generate hundreds of configuration files predictably and reliably.

 Building and generating configuration files from templates is covered in much more detail in Chapter 6, while performing the templating process with Ansible and Salt is covered in Chapter 9. This section is merely showing a high-level basic example.

Let's look at an example of taking a current configuration and decomposing it into a template and separate variables (inputs) file to articulate the point we're making.

Here is an example of a configuration file snippet:

```
hostname leaf1
ip domain-name ntc.com
!
vlan 10
    name web
!
vlan 20
    name app
!
vlan 30
    name db
!
```

If we decouple the data from the CLI commands, this file is transformed into two files: a template and a data (variables) file.

First let's look at the YAML (we cover YAML in depth in Chapter 5) variables file:

```
---
hostname leaf1
domain_name: ntc.com
vlans:
  - id: 10
    name: web
  - id: 20
    name: app
  - id: 30
    name: db
```

Note the YAML file is only our *data*.

 For this example, we're showing the Python-based Jinja templating language. Jinja is covered in detail in Chapter 6.

The resulting template that'll be rendered with the data file looks like this and is given the filename *leaf.j2*:

```
!
hostname {{ inventory_hostname }}
ip domain-name {{ domain_name }}
!
!
{% for vlan in vlans %}
vlan {{ vlan.id }}
  name {{ vlan.name }}
{% endfor %}
!
```

In this example, the *double curly braces* denote a Jinja variable. In other words, this is where the data variables get inserted when a template is rendered with data. Since the double curly braces denote variables, and we see those values are not in the template, they need to be stored somewhere. Again, we stored them in a YAML file. Rather than use flat YAML files, you could also use a script to fetch this type of information from an external system such as a network management system (NMS) or IP address management (IPAM) system.

In this example, if the team that controls VLANs wants to add a VLAN to the network devices, no problem. They just need to change it in the variables file and regenerate a new configuration file using Ansible or the rendering engine of their choice (Salt, pure Python, etc.).

 In Chapter 6, we also cover how you use native Python with Jinja templates, showing how you can create a Python script that can be used as a basic rendering engine.

At this point in our example, once the configuration is generated, it needs to be *pushed* to the network device. The *push* and *execution* process is not covered here, as there are plenty of ways to do this, including vendor-proprietary zero touch provisioning solutions as well as a few other methods that we look at Chapters 7 and 9.

Additionally, this was only meant to be a high-level introduction to templates; do not worry if it's not 100% clear yet. As we've said, working with templates is covered in far greater detail in Chapter 6.

Aside from building configurations and pushing them to devices, something that is arguably more important is data collection, which happens to be the next topic we cover.

Data Collection

Monitoring tools typically use the Simple Network Management Protocol (SNMP)—these tools poll certain management information bases (MIBs) and return data to the monitoring tool. Based on the data being returned, it may be more or less than you actually need. What if interface stats are being polled? You may get back every counter that is displayed in a show interface command, but what if you only needed *interface resets* and not *CRC errors, jumbo frames, output errors*, etc. Moreover, what if you want to see the interface resets correlated to the interfaces that have CDP/LLDP neighbors on them, and you want to see them *now*, not on the next polling cycle? How does network automation help with this?

Given that our focus is giving you more power and control, you can leverage open source tools and technology to customize exactly what you get, when you get it, how it's formatted, and how the data is used after it's collected, ensuring you get the most value from the data.

Here is a *very* basic example of collecting data from an IOS device using the Python library netmiko, which we cover in more detail in Chapter 7.

```
from netmiko import ConnectHandler

device = ConnectHandler(device_type='cisco_ios', ip='csr1',username='ntc',
                        password='ntc123')
output = device.send_command('show version')

print(output)
```

The great part is that output contains the show version response and you have the ability to parse it as you see fit based on your requirements.

 In the example given, we are describing *pulling* the data off the devices, which may not be ideal for all environments, but still suitable for many. Be aware that newer devices are starting to support a *push* model, often referred to as streaming telemetry, where the device itself streams real-time data such as interface stats to an application server of your choice.

Of course, any of this may require some up-front custom work but is totally worth it in the end, because the data being gathered is what you need, not what a given tool or vendor is providing you. Plus, isn't that why you're reading this book?

Network devices have an enormous amount of static and ephemeral data buried inside, and using open source tools or building your own gets you access to this data. Examples of this type of data include active entries in the BGP table, OSPF adjacencies, active neighbors, interface statistics, specific counters and resets, and even counters from application-specific integrated circuits (ASICs) themselves on newer platforms. Additionally, there are more general facts and characteristics of devices that can be collected too, such as serial number, hostname, uptime, OS version, and hardware platform, just to name a few. The list is endless.

 Always consider these questions as you start an automation project: "Does it make sense to build, buy, or customize?" and "Does it make sense to consume or operate?"

Migrations

Migrating from one platform to the next is never an easy task. This may involve platforms from the same vendor or from different vendors. Vendors may offer a script or a tool to help with migrations to *their* platform, but various forms of automation can be used to build out configuration templates, just like our example earlier, for all types of network devices and operating systems in such a way that you could generate a configuration file for all vendors given a defined and common set of inputs (common data model).

Of course, if there are vendor-proprietary extensions, they'll need to be accounted for too. The beautiful thing is that a migration tool such as this is much simpler to build on your own than have a vendor do it because the vendor needs to account for all features the device supports as compared to an individual organization that only needs a finite number of features. In reality, this is something vendors don't care much about; they are concerned with their equipment, not making it easier for you, the network operator, to manage a multi-vendor environment.

Having this type of flexibility helps with not only migrations, but also disaster recovery (DR), as it's very common to have different switch models in the production and DR data centers, and even different vendors. If a device fails for any reason and its replacement has to be a different platform, you'd be able to quickly leverage your common data model (think parameter inputs) and generate a new configuration immediately. We're starting to use the term *data model* loosely, but rest assured, we spend more time on describing and highlighting what data models are in Chapter 5.

Thus, if you are performing a migration, think about it at a more abstract level and think through the tasks necessary to go from one platform to the next. Then, see what can be done to automate those tasks, because only you, not the large networking vendors, have the motivation to make multi-vendor automation a reality. For example, think about adding a VLAN as an abstract step—then you can worry about the lower-level commands per platform. The point is, as you start adopting automation, it's extremely important to think about tasks and document them in human-readable format that is vendor-neutral, before putting hands to keyboard typing in CLI commands or writing code (per platform).

Configuration Management

As stated, configuration management is the most common type of automation, so we aren't going to spend too much time on it here. You should be aware that when we mention configuration management we are referring to deploying, pushing, and managing the configuration state of the device. This includes anything as basic as VLAN provisioning to more complex workflows that configure top-of-rack switches, firewalls, load balancers, and advanced security infrastructure, to deploy three-tier applications.

As you can see already through the different forms of automation that are *read-only*, you do not need to start your automation journey by pushing configurations. That said, if you are spending countless hours pushing the same change across a given number of routers or switches, you may want to!

The reality is that there are so many ways to start a network automation journey, but when you start automating configuration management, remember, with great power comes great responsibility. More importantly, don't forget to test before rolling out new automation tools into production environments.

The next few types of network automation we cover stem from automating the process of data collection. We've broken a few of them out to provide more context, and first up is automating compliance checks.

Compliance

As with many forms of automation, making configuration changes with any type of automation tool is seen as a risk. While making manual changes could arguably be riskier, as you've read and may have experienced firsthand, you have the option to start with data collection, monitoring, and configuration building, which are all *read-only* and *low-risk* actions. One low-risk use case that uses the data being gathered is configuration compliance checks and configuration validation. Does the deployed configuration meet security requirements? Are the required networks configured? Is protocol XYZ disabled? When you have control over the tools being deployed, it is more than possible to verify if something is True or False. It's easy enough to start small with one compliance check and then gradually add more as needed.

Based on the compliance of what you are checking, it's up to you to determine what happens next—maybe it just gets logged, or maybe a complex operation is performed, making your application capable of auto-remediation. These are forms of event-driven automation that we also touch upon when we cover StackStorm and Salt in Chapter 9. Our recommendation is that it's always best to start simple with network automation, but being aware of what's possible adds significant value as well. For example, if you just log or print messages to see what an interface maximum transmission unit (MTU) is, you're already prepared should you want to automatically reconfigure it to the right value if it is not the desired MTU. You'd just have to have a few more lines underneath your existing log/print messages. Again, the point is to start small, but think through what else you may need in the future.

Reporting

Once you start automating the collection of data, you may want to start building out custom and dynamic reports too. Maybe the data being returned becomes input to other configuration management tasks (event-driven again or more basic conditional configuration), or maybe you just want to create reports.

Given that reports can also be easily generated from templates combined with the actual ephemeral data from the device that'll be inserted into the template, the process to create and use reporting templates is the same process used to create configuration templates that we touched upon earlier in the chapter (remember, we'll explore templates in much more depth in Chapter 6).

Because of the simple nature of using text-based templates, it is possible to produce reports in any format you wish, including but not limited to:

- Simple text files
- Markdown files that can be easily viewed on GitHub, or some other Markdown viewer
- HTML reports that are deployed to a web server for easy viewing

It all depends on your requirements. The great thing is that the *network automator* has the power to create the exact type of report they need. In fact, you can use one set of data to generate different types of reports, maybe some technical and some higher-level for management.

Next up, we take a look at the value of automated troubleshooting.

Troubleshooting

Who enjoys getting consistently pulled into break/fix problems, especially when you should be sleeping or focused on other things?

Once you have access to real-time data and don't need to do any manual parsing on that data, automated troubleshooting becomes a reality.

Think about *how* you troubleshoot. Do you have a personal methodology? Is that methodology consistent across all members on your team? Does everyone check Layer 2 before troubleshooting Layer 3? What steps do you take to troubleshoot a given problem?

Let's take troubleshooting OSPF as an example:

- Do you know what it takes to form an OSPF adjacency between two devices?
- Can you rattle off the same answers at 2 a.m. or while on vacation at the beach?
- Maybe you remember some like devices need to be on the same subnet, have the same MTU, and have consistent timers, but forget they need to be the same OSPF network type.
- Do we really need to remember all of this and the associated commands to run on the CLI to get back each piece of data?

And these questions are only a *few* of the things that need to match for OSPF.

In any given environment, these types of compatibility checks need to be performed. Can you fathom running a script or using a tool for OSPF neighbor validation versus performing that process manually? Which would you prefer?

Again, OSPF is only the tip of the iceberg. Think about these other questions, still just being the tip:

- Can you correlate particular log messages to known conditions on the network?
- What about BGP neighbor adjacencies? How is a neighbor formed?
- Are you seeing all of the routes you think you should in the routing table?
- What about VPC and MLAG configuration?
- What about port-channels? Are there any inconsistencies?
- Do neighbors match the port-channel configuration (going down to the vSwitch)?
- What about cabling? Are all of the cables plugged in properly?

Even with these questions, we are just scratching the surface with what is possible when it comes to automated diagnostics and troubleshooting.

As you start to consider all of the types of automation possible, start to imagine a closed-loop system such that data is collected in an automated fashion, the data is then processed and analyzed in an automated fashion, and then you use advanced analytics to troubleshoot in an automated fashion. As these start to happen together in a uniform fashion, this becomes a closed loop, fully changing the way operations are managed within an organization.

If you are the rock star network engineer on your team, you may want to think about partnering up with a developer, or at the very least, start documenting your work-flows, so it's easier to share the knowledge you possess and it becomes easier to *codify*.

Better yet, start your own personal automation journey so you can sleep in every so often and empower everyone else to troubleshoot using some of your automated diagnostic workflows.

As you can see, network automation is much more than deploying configurations faster. After looking at several different types of automation, we are going to shift topics now and look at a few different ways automation tools and applications communicate with network devices, starting with SSH and ending with NETCONF and HTTP-based RESTful APIs.

Evolving the Management Plane from SNMP to Device APIs

If you want to improve the way networks are managed and operated day-to-day, improvements must begin with how you interface with the underlying devices being managed. This interface is how you and, more importantly, automation tools communicate with devices to perform the various types of network automation, such as data collection and configuration management.

In this section, we provide an overview of the different methods available to connect to the management plane of network devices starting with SNMP and then move on to more modern ways such as NETCONF and RESTful APIs. We then look at the impact of the *open networking* movement as it pertains to network operations and automation.

Application Programming Interfaces (APIs)

As a network engineer, you need to embrace APIs going forward, and not fear them. Remember that an API is just a mechanism that is used for computer software on one device to talk to computer software on another device. APIs are used nearly everywhere on the internet today—they just happen to finally be getting the focus they deserve from the network vendors. We'll soon see that APIs will become the primary means of managing network devices.

While we cover specific network APIs in more detail in Chapter 7, this section provides a high-level overview of a few different types of APIs that you'll find on network devices today.

SNMP

SNMP has been widely deployed for over 20 years on network devices. It shouldn't be new to anyone reading this book, but SNMP is a protocol that is used quite commonly for polling network devices for information such as up/down status and CPU, memory, and interface utilization.

In order to use SNMP, there must be an SNMP agent on a managed device and a network management station (NMS), which is the device that functions as a *server* that monitors and/or controls the managed devices.

Each network device being managed exposes a set of data that can be collected and configured via the SNMP agent. This set of data that is managed through SNMP is described and modeled through management information bases, or MIBs. Only if there is a MIB exposing a certain feature can it be monitored or managed. This includes making configuration changes through SNMP. Often overlooked, SNMP not only supports GetRequests for monitoring, but also supports SetRequests for manipulating objects and variables exposed through MIBs. The issue is that not many vendors offer full support for configuration management via SNMP; when they do, they often use custom MIBs, slowing down the integration process to network management platforms.

As mentioned, SNMP has been around for decades, but it was not built to be a real-time programmatic interface to network devices. We are already seeing vendors claim the gradual death of SNMP as it pertains to next-generation management and automation tooling. That said, SNMP does exist on nearly every network device, and Python libraries for SNMP also exist—so, if you need to collect basic information from a vast amount of device types, it may still make sense to use SNMP.

Just like SNMP has been used for years to perform network monitoring, SSH/Telnet and the CLI has been used for configuration management. Let's take a look now at SSH/Telnet and the CLI.

SSH/Telnet and the CLI

If you have ever managed a network device, you've definitely used the CLI to issue commands to perform some action on a device. You probably entered commands through the console and over Telnet and SSH sessions. As we stated in Chapter 1, the reality is that the migration from Telnet to SSH is arguably the biggest shift we've had in network operations over the past decade, and that shift wasn't about operations; it was about security ensuring that communications to network devices were encrypted.

The most important thing to realize as it pertains to managing devices via the CLI is that the CLI was built for humans. It was put on devices to improve usability for human operators. The CLI was *not* meant to be used for machine-to-machine communication (i.e., network scripting and automation).

If you issue a show command on the CLI of a device, you get raw text back. There is no structure to it. The best options to *parse* the response are to use the *pipe* (|) and keywords such as grep, include, and begin to look for particular lines of configuration. An example of that would be to check the description of an interface with the command show interface Eth1 | include description. This means if you needed to know how many CRC errors were on an interface after issuing a show interface in a script, you'd be forced to use some type of regular expression or manual parsing to figure it out. This is unacceptable.

However, when all we have is the CLI, CLI is what gets used. This is why there are plenty of network management platforms and custom scripts that have been built over the past two decades that perform management and automated operations using the CLI over SSH dealing with expect scripts and manual parsing. It's not that SSH/CLI makes it impossible to automate; rather, it makes automation extremely error prone and tedious.

The network vendors started to realize this, and now most newer device platforms have some type of API that simplifies machine-to-machine communication (many are incomplete, so be sure to test your favorite device's API), yielding a much simpler approach to automation that is also more in line with general software development principles.

After a brief look at common protocols such as SSH and SNMP, we'll look at NETCONF, an API that is becoming quite popular as it pertains to network automation.

NETCONF

NETCONF is a network management layer protocol. At the highest level, it can be compared to SNMP, as they are both protocols used to make configuration changes and retrieve data from networking devices.

The differences come in the details, of course. We cover a few high-level points here, but spend more time on NETCONF in Chapter 7.

- NETCONF is a connection-oriented protocol and commonly leverages SSH as its transport.
- Data sent between a NETCONF client (automation tool/script) and NETCONF server (network device) is encoded in XML. Don't worry if you aren't familiar with XML; we cover it in Chapter 5.
- Remote procedure calls (RPCs) are encoded in the XML document sent to the device and the device processes these RPCs. The <rpc> element is used to enclose a NETCONF request sent from the client to the server. In this context, think of these remote procedure calls as performing a prearranged operation on the device. RPCs are a way for a client to communicate to the server what structure and what type of request is being made.
- Supported RPCs map directly to supported NETCONF *operations* and *capabilities* for particular devices. For example, if you are making a change on a device you use the edit-config operation. If you are retrieving configuration data, you

use the `get` or `get-config` operation. These operations are wrapped inside the XML document within the `<rpc>` element sent to the device.

Additionally, NETCONF offers value in that it supports transaction-based changes. This means that if you are making more than one change in a given NETCONF session, or single XML document, and one of those changes fails, the complete change is *not* applied to the device (of course, these types of settings can usually be overridden too). This is in contrast to sending CLI commands sequentially and ending up with a partial configuration due to a typo or invalid command.

This was a short introduction to NETCONF, and as mentioned, we dive into NET-CONF in more detail later on in Chapter 7.

 It's worth pointing out that just because two different device platforms support NETCONF (or any common transport method) does not mean they are compatible from a tooling and developer's perspective. Even with the assumption that both devices support the same NETCONF features and capabilities, how the data is modeled is, more often than not, vendor specific. Data modeling is how the device represents state and configuration data. We'll learn more about data representation in JSON and XML and YANG, a common data modeling language, in Chapter 5.

RESTful APIs

REST stands for REpresentational State Transfer and is a style used to design and develop networked applications. Thus, systems that implement and adhere to a REST-based architecture are said to be RESTful.

Keeping this in context from a network perspective, the most common devices that expose APIs and adhere to the architectural style of REST are network controllers. That said, there are network devices that expose RESTful and general HTTP-based APIs too.

While the terms *REST* and *RESTful APIs* are new from a network standpoint, you're already interacting with many RESTful systems on a daily basis as you browse the internet using a web browser. We said that REST is a style used to develop networked applications. That style relies on a stateless client-server model in which the client keeps track of the session and no client state or context is held on the server. And best yet, the underlying transport protocol used is most commonly HTTP. Doesn't this sound like most systems found on the internet?

This means that RESTful APIs operate just like HTTP-based systems. First, you need a web server accessible via a URL (i.e., *SDN controller* or *network device* to communicate with), and second, you need to send the associated HTTP request to that URL.

For example, if you need to retrieve a list of devices from an SDN controller, you just need to send an HTTP GET to the given URL of the device, which could look something like this: `http://1.1.1.1/v1/devices`. The response that comes back would be some type of structured data like XML or JSON (which we cover in Chapter 5).

There are a few other things that we didn't touch upon, such as authentication, data encoding, and how to send an HTTP request if you're making a configuration change (HTTP PUT/POST/PATCH). As this section was just a short high-level introduction to REST and RESTful APIs, we cover more of those details in Chapter 7.

Next up is a short look at the impact *open networking* is having on the overall management of network devices.

Impact of Open Networking

There is a growing trend of all things *open*—open source, open networking, Open APIs, OpenFlow, Open Compute, Open vSwitch, OpenDaylight, OpenConfig, and the list goes on. While the definition of *open* can be debated, there is one thing that is certain: the *open networking* movement is improving what is possible when it comes to network operations and automation.

With this movement, we are seeing drastic changes in network devices, and this is a primary reason for writing this book.

First, many devices now support Python on-box. This means that you are able to drop into the Python Dynamic Interpreter and execute Python scripts locally on each network device. We cover Python in much more detail in Chapter 4, and you'll see what we mean firsthand.

Second, many devices now support a more robust API other than SNMP and SSH. For example, we just looked at NETCONF and RESTful HTTP-based APIs. One or both of those APIs are supported on many of the newer device operating systems that have emerged in the past 18 to 24 months. Remember, we cover device APIs in more detail in Chapter 7.

Finally, network devices are exposing more of the Linux internals that have been hidden from network operators in the past. You can now drop into a *bash* shell on network devices and issue commands such as `ifconfig`, write bash scripts, and install monitoring and configuration management tools via package managers such as `apt` and `yum`. You'll learn about all of these things in Chapter 3.

While *open networking* doesn't always mean interoperability, it is evident that network devices and controllers are opening themselves up to be operated in a much more programmatic manner better suited for enhanced network automation. There are a number of APIs on network devices that didn't exist a few years ago, ranging from Cisco's NX-API, Arista's eAPI, and Cisco's IOS-XE RESTCONF/NETCONF to any new SDN controllers that have APIs. The net result, for you as operators, is that you can take control of your networks and reduce the number of operational inefficiencies that exist today as you start using these APIs.

Network Automation in the SDN Era

We'll now take a look at the continued importance of network automation even when controller solutions are being deployed such as OpenDaylight or even commercial offerings like Cisco ACI or VMware NSX. The operations that the controllers perform on the network, such as acting as the control plane or managing policy and configuration, are irrelevant for this section.

The fact is that controllers are becoming common in next-gen architectures. Vendors such as Cisco, Juniper, VMware, Big Switch, Plexxi, Nuage, Viptela, and many others all offer controller platforms for their next-gen solutions, not to mention open source controllers such as OpenDaylight and OpenContrail.

Almost every controller on the market exposes northbound RESTful APIs, making controllers extremely easy to automate. While controllers themselves inherently simplify management and visibility through a single pane of glass, you can still end up making manual and error-prone changes through the GUI of a controller. If there are several pods or controllers deployed, from the same or different vendors, the problems of manual changes, troubleshooting, and data collection do not go away.

As we start to wrap up this chapter, it's important to note that even in the new era of SDN architectures and controller-based network solutions, the need for automation, better operations, and more predictable outcomes does not go away.

Summary

This chapter provided an overview of the value of network automation and various types of network automation; an introduction to common device APIs including SNMP, CLI/SSH, and more importantly NETCONF and RESTful; and a brief mention of YANG, a network modeling language that we'll cover in more detail in Chapter 5.

The chapter closed with a brief look at the impact that the open networking movement is having on network operations and automation. Finally, we touched on the value of network automation even when SDN controllers are deployed.

In each subsequent chapter, we dive deeper into each technology, providing hands-on practical examples whenever possible, but at the same time reviewing the importance of the people, process, and culture required to adopt comprehensive automation frameworks and pipelines. In fact, we focus significantly on people and culture in Chapter 11.

## CHAPTER 3

Linux

·

This chapter aims to help readers become familiar with the basics of Linux, an operating system that is becoming increasingly common in networking circles. You might wonder why we've included a chapter about Linux in this book. After all, what in the world does Linux, a UNIX-like operating system, have to do with network automation and programmability?

Examining Linux in a Network Automation Context

In looking at Linux from a network automation perspective, there are several reasons why we felt this content was important.

First, several modern network operating systems (NOSes) are based on Linux, although some use a custom command-line interface (CLI) that means they don't look or act like Linux. Others, however, do expose the Linux internals and/or use a Linux shell such as *bash*.

Second, some new companies and organizations are bringing to market full Linux distributions that are targeted at network equipment. For example, the OpenCompute Project (OCP) recently selected Open Network Linux (ONL) as a base upon which to build Linux-powered NOSes (Big Switch's Switch Light is an example Linux-based NOS built on ONL). Cumulus Networks is another example, offering their Debian-based Cumulus Linux as a NOS for supported hardware platforms. As a network engineer, you're increasingly likely to need to know Linux in order to configure your network.

Third, and finally, many of the tools that we discuss in this book have their origins in Linux, or require that you run them from a Linux system. For example, Ansible (a tool we'll discuss in Chapter 9) requires Python (a topic we'll discuss in Chapter 4). For a few different reasons we'll cover in Chapter 9, when automating network equipment with Ansible you'll typically run Ansible from a network-attached system running Linux, and *not* on the network equipment directly. Similarly, when you're using Python to gather and/or manipulate data from network equipment, you'll often do so from a system running Linux.

For these reasons, we felt it was important to include a chapter that seeks to accomplish the following goals:

- Provide a bit of background on the history of Linux
- Briefly explain the concept of Linux distributions
- Introduce you to bash, one of the most popular Linux shells available
- Discuss Linux networking basics
- Dive into some advanced Linux networking functionality

Keep in mind that this chapter is not intended to be a comprehensive treatise on Linux or the bash shell; rather, it is intended to get you "up and running" with Linux in the context of network automation and programmability. Having said that, let's start our discussion of Linux with a very brief look at its history and origins.

A Brief History of Linux

The story of Linux is a story with a couple of different threads.

One thread started out in the early 1980s, when Richard Stallman launched the GNU Project as an effort to provide a free UNIX-like operating system. GNU, by the way, stands for "GNU's Not UNIX," a recursive acronym Stallman created to describe the free UNIX-like OS he was attempting to create. Stallman's GNU General Public License (GPL) came out of the GNU Project's efforts. Although the GNU Project was able to create free versions of a wide collection of UNIX utilities and applications, the kernel—known as GNU Hurd—for the GNU Project's new OS never gained momentum.

A second thread is found in Linus Torvalds' efforts to create a MINIX clone in 1991 as the start of Linux. Driven by the lack of a free OS kernel, his initial work rapidly gained support, and in 1992 was licensed under the GNU GPL with the release of version 0.99. Since that time, the kernel he wrote (named Linux) has been the default OS kernel for the software collection created by the GNU Project.

Because Linux originally referred only to the OS kernel and needed the GNU Project's software collection to form a full operating system, some people suggested that the full OS should be called "GNU/Linux," and some organizations still use that designation today (Debian, for example). By and large, however, most people just refer to the entire OS as Linux, and so that's the convention that we will follow in this book.

Linux Distributions

As you saw in the previous section, the Linux operating system is made up of the Linux kernel plus a large collection of open source tools primarily developed as part of the GNU Project. The bundling together of the kernel plus a collection of open source software led to the creation of Linux *distributions* (also known as Linux *distros*). A distribution is the combination of the Linux kernel plus a selection of open source utilities, applications, and software packages that are bundled together and distributed together (hence the name *distribution*). Over the course of Linux's history, a number of Linux distributions have risen and fallen in popularity (anyone remember Slackware?), but as of this writing there are two major branches of Linux distributions: the Red Hat/CentOS branch and the Debian and Debian derivative branch.

Red Hat Enterprise Linux, Fedora, and CentOS

Red Hat was an early Linux distributor who became a significant influencer and commercial success in the Linux market, so it's perfectly natural that one major branch of Linux distributions is based on Red Hat.

Red Hat offers a commercial distribution, known as Red Hat Enterprise Linux (RHEL), in addition to offering technical support contracts for RHEL. Many organizations today use RHEL because it is backed by Red Hat, focuses on stability and reliability, offers comprehensive technical support options, and is widely supported by other software vendors.

However, the fast-moving pace of Linux development and the Linux open source community is often at odds with the slower and more methodical pace required to maintain stability and reliability in the RHEL product. To help address this dichotomy, Red Hat has an upstream distribution known as Fedora. We refer to Fedora as an "upstream distribution" because much of the development of RHEL and RHEL-based distributions occurs in Fedora, then flows "down" to these other products. In coordination with the broader open source community, Fedora sees new kernel versions, new kernel features, new package management tools, and other new developments first; these new things are tested and vetted in Fedora before being migrated to the more enterprise-focused RHEL distribution at a later date. For this reason, you may see Fedora used by developers and other individuals who need the "latest and greatest," but you won't often see Fedora used in production environments.

Although RHEL and its variants are only available from Red Hat through a commercial arrangement, the open source license (the GNU GPL) under which Linux is developed and distributed *requires* that the source of Red Hat's distribution be made publicly available. A group of individuals who wanted the stability and reliability of RHEL but without the corresponding costs imposed by Red Hat took the RHEL sources and created CentOS. (CentOS is a named formed out of "Community Enterprise

OS.") CentOS is freely available without cost, but—like many open source software packages—does not come with any form of technical support. For many organizations and many use cases, the support available from the open source community is sufficient, so it's not uncommon to see CentOS used in a variety of environments, including enterprise environments.

One of the things that all of these distributions (RHEL, Fedora, and CentOS) share is a common *package format*. When Linux distributions first started emerging, one key challenge that had to be addressed was the way in which software was packaged with the Linux kernel. Due to the breadth of free software that was available for Linux, it wasn't really effective to ship *all* of it in a distribution, nor would users necessarily *want* all of the various pieces of software installed. If not all of the software was installed, though, how would the Linux community address dependencies? A *dependency* is a piece of software required to run another piece of software on a computer. For example, some software might be written in Python, which of course would require Python to be installed. To install Python, however, might require other pieces of software to be installed, and so on. As an early distributor, Red Hat came up with a way to combine the files needed to run a piece of software along with additional information about that software's dependencies into a single package—a *package format*. That package format is known as an RPM, perhaps so named after the tool originally used to work with said packages: RPM Manager (formerly Red Hat Package Manager), whose executable name was simply rpm. All of the Linux distributions we've discussed so far—RHEL, CentOS, and Fedora—leverage RPM packages as their default package format, although the specific tool used to work with such packages has evolved over time.

RPM's successors

We mentioned that RPM originally referred to the actual package manager itself, which was used to work with RPM packages. Most RPM-based distributions have since replaced the rpm utility with newer package managers that do a better job of understanding dependencies, resolving conflicts, and installing (or removing) software from a Linux installation. For example, RHEL/CentOS/Fedora moved first to a tool called yum (short for "Yellowdog Updater, Modified"), and are now migrating again to a tool called dnf (which stands for "Dandified YUM").

Other distributions also leverage the RPM package format, such as Oracle Linux, Scientific Linux, and various SUSE Linux derivatives.

RPM portability

You might think that, because a number of different Linux distributions all leverage the same package format (RPM), RPM packages are portable across these Linux distributions. In theory, this is possible, but in practice it rarely works. This is usually due to slight variations in package names and package versions across the distributions, which makes resolving dependencies and conflicts practically impossible.

Debian, Ubuntu, and Other Derivatives

Debian GNU/Linux is a distribution produced and maintained by the Debian Project. The Debian Project was officially founded by Ian Murdock on August 16, 1993, and the creation of Debian GNU/Linux was funded by the Free Software Foundation's GNU Project from November 1994 through November 1995. To this day, Debian remains the only major distribution of Linux that is not backed by a commercial entity. All Debian GNU/Linux releases since version 1.1 have used a code name taken from a character in one of the *Toy Story* movies. Debian GNU/Linux 1.1, released in June 1996, was code-named "Buzz." The most recent stable version of Debian GNU/Linux, version 9.0, was released in June 2017 and is code-named "Stretch."

Debian GNU/Linux offers three branches: stable, testing, and unstable. The testing and unstable branches are rolling releases that will, eventually, become the next stable branch. This approach results in a typically very high-quality release, and could be one of the reasons that a number of other distributions are based on (*derived* from) Debian GNU/Linux.

One of the more well-known Debian derivatives is Ubuntu Linux, started in April 2004 and funded in large part by Canonical Ltd., a company founded by Mark Shuttleworth. The first Ubuntu, released in October 2004, was released as version 4.10 (the "4" denotes the year, and the "10" denotes the month of release), and was code-named "Warty Warthog." All Ubuntu codenames are cmposed of an adjective and an animal with the same first letter (Warty Warthog, Hoary Hedgehog, Breezy Badger, etc.). Ubuntu was initially targeted as a usable desktop Linux distribution, but now offers both desktop-, server-, and mobile-focused versions. Ubuntu uses time-based releases, releasing a new version every six months and a long-term support (LTS) release every two years. LTS releases are supported by Canonical and the Ubuntu community for a total of five years after release. All releases of Ubuntu are based on packages taken from Debian's unstable branch, which is why we refer to Ubuntu as a Debian derivative.

Speaking of packages: like RPM-based distributions, the common thread across the Debian and Debian derivatives—probably made clear by the term *Debian derivatives* used to describe them—is that they share a common package format, known as the

Debian package format (and denoted by a *.deb* extension on the files). The founders of the Debian Project created the DEB package format and the dpkg tool to solve the same problems that Red Hat attempted to solve with the RPM package format. Also like RPM-based distributions, Debian-based distributions evolved past the use of the dpkg tool directly, first using a tool called dselect and then moving on to the use of the apt tool (and programs like apt-get and aptitude).

Debian package portability

Just as with RPM packages, the fact that multiple distributions leverage the Debian package format doesn't mean that Debian packages are necessarily portable between distributions. Slight variations in package names, package versions, file paths, and other details will typically make this very difficult, if not impossible.

A key feature of the apt-based tools is the ability to retrieve packages from one or more remote *repositories*, which are online storehouses of Debian packages. The apt tools also feature better dependency determination, conflict resolution, and package installation (or removal).

Other Linux Distributions

There are other distributions in the market, but these two branches—the Red Hat/Fedora/CentOS branch and the Debian/Ubuntu branch—cover the majority of Linux instances found in organizations today. For this reason, we'll focus only on these two branches throughout the rest of this chapter. If you're using a distribution not from one of these two major branches—perhaps you're working with SUSE Enterprise Linux, for example—keep in mind there may be slight differences between the information contained here and your specific distribution. You should refer to your distribution's documentation for the details.

Now that we've provided an overview of the history of Linux and Linux distributions, let's shift our focus to interacting with Linux, focusing primarily on interacting via the shell.

Interacting with Linux

As a very popular server OS, Linux can be used in a variety of ways across the network. For example, you could receive IP addresses via a Linux-based DHCP server, access a Linux-powered web server running the Apache HTTP server or Nginx, or utilize a Domain Name System (DNS) server running Linux in order to resolve domain names to IP addresses. There are, of course, *many* more examples; these are just a few. In the context of our discussion of Linux, though, we're going to focus primarily on interacting with Linux via the *shell*.

The shell is what provides the command-line interface by which most users will interact with a Linux system. Linux offers a number of shells, but the most common shell is bash, the Bourne Again Shell (a play on the name of one of the original UNIX shells, the Bourne Shell). In the vast majority of cases, unless you've specifically configured your system to use a different shell, when you're interacting with Linux you're using bash. In this section, we're going to provide you with enough basic information to get started interacting with a Linux system's console, and we'll assume that you're using bash as your shell. If you are using a different shell, please keep in mind that some of the commands and behaviors we describe might be slightly different.

A good bash reference

Bash is a topic about which an entire book could be written. In fact, one already has—and is now in its third edition. If you want to learn more about bash than we have room to talk about in this book, we *highly* recommend O'Reilly's *Learning the bash Shell*, Third Edition.

We've broken our discussion of interacting with Linux into four major areas:

- Navigating the filesystem
- Manipulating files and directories
- Running programs
- Working with background services, known as *daemons*

This is introductory-level content

This section is primarily targeting users who are new to Linux (a lot of network engineers and IT professionals are mostly familiar with Microsoft Windows). If you're familiar with Linux, feel free to skip ahead.

Let's start with navigating the filesystem.

Navigating the Filesystem

Linux uses what's known as a *single-root* filesystem, meaning that all of the drives and directories and files in a Linux installation fall into a single namespace, referred to quite simply as /. (When you see / by itself, say "root" in your head.) This is in stark contrast to an OS like Microsoft Windows, where each drive typically has its own root (the drive letter, like *C:* or *D:*). Note that it *is* possible to mount a drive in a folder under Windows, but the practice isn't as common.

Everything is treated like a file

Linux follows in UNIX's footsteps in treating everything like a file. This includes storage devices (which are treated as block devices), ports on the computer (like serial ports), or even input/output devices. Thus, the importance of a single-root filesystem—which encompasses devices as well as storage—becomes even greater.

Like most other OSes, Linux uses the concept of directories (known as *folders* in some other OSes) to group files in the filesystem. Every file resides in a directory, and therefore every file has a unique *path* to its location. To denote the path of a file, you start at the root and list all the directories it takes to get to that file, separating the directories with a forward slash. For example, the command ping is often found in the *bin* directory off the root directory. The path, therefore, to ping would be noted like this: */bin/ping*.

In other words, start at the root directory (/), continue into the *bin/* directory, and find the file named *ping*. Similarly, on Debian Linux 8.1, the arp utility for viewing and manipulating Address Resolution Protocol (ARP) entries is found at (in other words, its *path* is) */usr/sbin/arp*.

This concept of path becomes important when we start considering that bash allows you to navigate, or move around, within the filesystem. The *prompt*, or the text that bash displays when waiting for you to input a command, will tell you where you are in the filesystem. Here's the default prompt for a Debian 8.1 system:

```
vagrant@jessie:~$
```

Do you see it? Unless you're familiar with Linux, you may have missed the tilde (~) following vagrant@jessie: in this example prompt. In the bash shell, the tilde is a shortcut that refers to the user's *home directory*. Each user has a home directory that is their personal location for storing files, programs, and other content for only that user. To make it easy to refer to one's home directory, bash uses the tilde as a shortcut. So, looking back at the sample prompt, you can see that this particular prompt tells you a few different things:

1. The first part of the prompt, before the @ symbol, tells you the current user (in this case, vagrant).

2. The second part of the prompt, directly after the @ symbol, tells you the current hostname of the system on which you are currently operating (in this case, jessie is the hostname).

3. Following the colon is the current directory, noted in this case as ~ meaning that this user (vagrant) is currently in his or her home directory.

4. Finally, even the $ at the end has meaning—in this particular case, it means that the current user (vagrant) does not have root permissions. The $ will change to a hash sign (the # character, also known as an octothorpe) if the user has root permissions. This is analogous to the way that the prompt for a network device, such as a router or switch, may change depending on the user's privilege level.

About the Environments We're Using

Throughout this chapter, you'll see various Linux prompts similar to ones we just showed you. We're using a tool called Vagrant (*http://www.vagrantup.com*) to simplify the creation of multiple different Linux environments—in this case, Debian GNU/Linux 8.1 (also known as "Jessie"), Ubuntu Linux 14.04 LTS (named "Trusty Tahr"), and CentOS 7.1.

The default prompt on a CentOS 7.1 system looks like this:

```
[vagrant@centos ~]$
```

As you can see, it's very similar, and it conveys the same information as the other example prompt we showed, albeit in a slightly different format. Like the earlier example, this prompt shows us the current user (vagrant), the hostname of the current system (centos), the current directory (~), and the effective permissions of the logged-in user ($).

The use of the tilde is helpful in keeping the prompt short when you're in your home directory, but what if you don't know the path to your home directory? In other words, what if you don't know where on the system your home directory is located? In situations like this where you need to determine the full path to your current location, bash offers the pwd (print working directory) command, which will produce output something like this:

```
vagrant@jessie:~$ pwd
/home/vagrant
vagrant@jessie:~$
```

The pwd command simply returns the directory where you're currently located in the filesystem (the working directory).

Now that you know where you are located in the filesystem, you can begin to move around the filesystem using the cd (change directory) command along with a path to a destination. For example, if you were in your home directory and wanted to change into the *bin* subdirectory, you'd simply type **cd bin** and press Enter (or Return).

Note the lack of the leading slash here. This is because /bin and bin might be two *very* different locations in the filesystem:

- Using `bin` (no leading slash) tells bash to change into the *bin* subdirectory of the current working directory.

- Using `/bin` (with a leading slash) tells bash to change into the *bin* subdirectory of the root (/) directory.

See how, therefore, `bin` and `/bin` might be very different locations? This is why understanding the concept of a single-root filesystem and the path to a file or directory is important. Otherwise, you might end up performing some action on a different file or directory than what you intended! This is particularly important when it comes to manipulating files and directories, which we'll discuss in the next section.

Before moving on, though, there are a few more navigational commands we need to discuss.

To move up one level in the filesystem (for example, to move from */usr/local/bin/* to */usr/local/*), you can use the `..` shortcut. Every directory contains a special entry, named `..` (two periods), that is a shortcut entry for that directory's parent directory (the directory one level above it). So, if your current working directory is */usr/local/bin*, you can simply type **cd ..** and press Enter (or Return) to move up one directory.

```
vagrant@jessie:/usr/local/bin$ cd ..
vagrant@jessie:/usr/local$
```

Note that you can combine the `..` shortcut with a directory name to move laterally between directories. For example, if you're currently in */usr/local* and need to move to */usr/share*, you can type **cd ../share** and press Enter. This moves you to the directory whose path is up one level (`..`) and is named *share*.

```
vagrant@jessie:/usr/local$ cd ../share
vagrant@jessie:/usr/share$
```

You can also combine multiple levels of the `..` shortcut to move up more than one level. For example, if you are currently in */usr/share* and need to move to / (the root directory), you could type **cd ../../** and press Enter. This would put you into the root directory.

```
vagrant@jessie:/usr/share$ cd ../..
vagrant@jessie:/$
```

All these examples are using *relative paths*—that is, paths that are relative to your current location. You can, of course, also use *absolute paths*—that is, paths that are anchored to the root directory. As we mentioned earlier, the distinction is the use of the forward slash (/) to denote an absolute path starting at the root versus a path relative to the current location. For example, if you are currently located in the root directory (/) and need to move to */media/cdrom*, you don't need the leading slash (because *media* is a subdirectory of /). You can type **cd media/cdrom** and press Enter. This will move you to */media/cdrom*, because you used a relative path to your destination.

```
vagrant@jessie:/$ cd media/cdrom
vagrant@jessie:/media/cdrom$
```

From here, though, if you needed to move to */usr/local/bin*, you'd want to use an absolute path. Why? Because there is no (easy) relative path between these two locations that doesn't involve moving through the root (see the following sidebar for a bit more detail). Using an absolute path, anchored with the leading slash, is the quickest and easiest approach.

```
vagrant@jessie:/media/cdrom$ cd /usr/local/bin
vagrant@jessie:/usr/local/bin$
```

More Than One Path

If you're thinking that you could have also used the command cd ../../usr/local/bin to move from */media/cdrom* to */usr/local/bin*, you've mastered the relationship between relative paths and absolute paths on a Linux system.

Finally, there's one final navigation trick we want to share. Suppose you're in */usr/local/bin*, but you need to switch over to */media/cdrom*. So you enter **cd /media/cdrom**, but after switching directories realize you needed to be in */usr/local/bin* after all. Fortunately, there is a quick fix. The notation cd - (using a hyphen after the cd command) tells bash to switch back to the last directory you were in before you switched to the current directory. (If you need a shortcut to get back to your home directory, just enter cd with no parameters.)

```
vagrant@jessie:/usr/local/bin$ cd /media/cdrom
vagrant@jessie:/media/cdrom$ cd -
/usr/local/bin
vagrant@jessie:/usr/local/bin$ cd -
/media/cdrom
vagrant@jessie:/media/cdrom$ cd -
/usr/local/bin
vagrant@jessie:/usr/local/bin$
```

Here are all of these filesystem navigation techniques in action.

```
vagrant@jessie:/usr/local/bin$ cd ..
vagrant@jessie:/usr/local$ cd ../share
vagrant@jessie:/usr/share$ cd ../..
vagrant@jessie:/$ cd media/cdrom
vagrant@jessie:/media/cdrom$ cd /usr/local/bin
vagrant@jessie:/usr/local/bin$ cd -
/media/cdrom
vagrant@jessie:/media/cdrom$ cd -
/usr/local/bin
vagrant@jessie:/usr/local/bin$
```

Now you should have a pretty good grasp on how to navigate around the Linux file-system. Let's build on that knowledge with some information on manipulating files and directories.

Manipulating Files and Directories

Armed with a basic understanding of the Linux filesystem, paths within the filesystem, and how to move around the filesystem, let's take a quick look at manipulating files and directories. We'll cover four basic tasks:

- Creating files and directories
- Deleting files and directories
- Moving, copying, and renaming files and directories
- Changing permissions

Let's start with creating files and directories.

Creating files and directories

To create files or directories, you'll work with one of two basic commands: touch, which is used to create files, and mkdir (make directory), which is used—not surprisingly—to create directories.

Other ways to create files

There are other ways of creating files, such as echoing command output to a file or using an application (like a text editor, for example). Rather than trying to cover all the possible ways to do something, we want to focus on getting you enough information to get started.

The touch command just creates a new file with no contents (it's up to you to use a text editor or appropriate application to add content to the file after it is created). Let's look at a few examples:

```
[vagrant@centos ~]$ touch config.txt
```

Here's an equivalent command (we'll explain why it's equivalent in just a moment):

```
[vagrant@centos ~]$ touch ./config.txt
```

Why this command is equivalent to the earlier example may not be immediately obvious. In the previous section, we talked about the .. shortcut for moving to the parent directory of the current directory. Every directory also has an entry noted by a single period (.) that refers to the *current directory*. Therefore, the commands touch `config.txt` and `touch ./config.txt` will *both* create a file named *config.txt* in the current working directory.

If both syntaxes are correct, why are there two different ways of doing it? In this case, both commands produce the same result—but *this isn't the case for all commands*. When you want to be sure that the file you're referencing is the file in the current working directory, use `./` to tell bash you want the file in the current directory.

```
[vagrant@centos ~]$ touch /config.txt
```

In this case, we're using an absolute path, so this command creates a file named *config.txt* in the root directory, assuming your user account has permission. (We'll talk about permissions in "Changing permissions" on page 51.)

When ./ is useful

One thing we haven't discussed in detail yet is the idea of bash's *search paths*, which are paths (locations) in the filesystem that bash will automatically search when you type in a command. In a typical configuration, paths such as */bin*, */usr/bin*, */sbin*, and similar locations are included in the search path. Thus, if you specify a filename from a file in one of those directories without using the full path, bash will find it for you by searching these paths. This is one of the times when being specific about a file's location (by including ./ or the absolute path) might be a good idea, so that you can be sure which file is the file being found and used by bash.

The `mkdir` command is very simple: it creates the directory specified by the user. Let's look at a couple quick examples.

```
[vagrant@centos ~]$ mkdir bin
```

This command creates a directory named *bin* in the current working directory. It's different than this command (relative versus absolute paths!):

```
[vagrant@centos ~]$ mkdir /bin
```

Like most other Linux commands, `mkdir` has a lot of options that modify its behavior, but one you'll use frequently is the `-p` parameter. When used with the `-p` option, `mkdir` will not report an error if the directory already exists, and will create parent directories along the path as needed.

For example, let's say you had some files you needed to store, and you wanted to store them in */opt/sw/network*. If you were in the */opt* directory and entered `mkdir sw/network` when the *sw* directory didn't already exist, the `mkdir` command would report an error. However, if you simply added the `-p` option, `mkdir` would then create the *sw* directory if needed, then create *network* under *sw*. This is a *great* way to create an entire path all at once without failing due to errors if a directory along the way already exists.

Creating files and directories is one half of the picture; let's look at the other half (deleting files and directories).

Deleting files and directories

Similar to the way there are two commands for creating files and directories, there are two commands for deleting files and directories. Generally, you'll use the rm command to delete (remove) files, and you'll use the rmdir command to delete directories. There is also a way to use rm to delete directories, as we'll show you in this section.

To remove a file, you simply use rm *filename*. For example, to remove a file named *config.txt* in the current working directory, you'd use one of the two following commands (do you understand why?):

```
vagrant@trusty:~$ rm config.txt
vagrant@trusty:~$ rm ./config.txt
```

You can, of course, use absolute paths (/home/vagrant/config.txt) as well as relative paths (./config.txt).

To remove a directory, you use rmdir *directory*. Note, however, that the directory has to be empty; if you attempt to delete a directory that has files in it, you'll get this error message:

```
rmdir: failed to remove 'src': Directory not empty
```

In this case, you'll need to first empty the directory, then use rmdir. Alternately, you can use the -r parameter to the rm command. Normally, if you try to use the rm command on a directory and you fail to use the -r parameter, bash will respond like this (in this example, we tried to remove a directory named *bin* in the current working directory):

```
rm: cannot remove 'bin': Is a directory
```

When you use rm -r *directory*, though, bash will remove the entire directory tree. Note that, by default, rm *isn't* going to prompt for confirmation—it's simply going to delete the whole directory tree. No Recycle Bin, no Trash Can…it's gone. (If you want a prompt, you can add the -i parameter.)

 The same goes for the mv and cp commands we'll discuss in the next section—without the -i parameter, these commands will simply overwrite files in the destination without any prompt. Be sure to exercise the appropriate level of caution when using these commands.

Creating and deleting files and directories aren't the only tasks you might need to do, though, so let's take a quick look at moving (or copying) files and directories.

Moving, copying, and renaming files and directories

When it comes to moving, copying, and renaming files and directories, the two commands you'll need to use are cp (for copying files or directories) and mv (for moving and renaming files and directories).

Check the man pages!

The basic use of all the Linux commands we've shown you so far is relatively easy to understand, but—as the saying goes—the devil is in the details. If you need more information on any of the options, parameters, or the advanced usage of just about any command in Linux, use the man (manual) command. For example, to view the manual page for the cp command, type **man cp**. The manual pages show a more detailed explanation of how to use the various commands.

To copy a file, it's just cp *source destination*. Similarly, to move a file you would just use mv *source destination*. Renaming a file, by the way, is consider moving it from one name to a new name (typically in the same directory).

Moving a directory is much the same; just use mv *source-dir destination-dir*. This is true whether the directory is flat (containing only files) or a tree (containing both files as well as subdirectories).

Copying directories is only a bit more complicated. Just add the -r option, like cp -r *source-dir destination-dir*. This will handle most use cases for copying directories, although some less common use cases may require some additional options. We recommend you read and refer to the man (manual) page for cp for additional details (see the "Check the man pages!" tip earlier).

The final topic we'd like to tackle in our discussion of manipulating files and directories is permissions.

Changing permissions

Taking a cue from its UNIX predecessors (keeping in mind that Linux rose out of efforts to create a free UNIX-like operating system), Linux is a multiuser OS that incorporates the use of permissions on files and directories. In order to be considered a multiuser OS, Linux had to have a way to make sure one user couldn't view/see/modify/remove other users' files, and so file- and directory-level permissions were a necessity.

Linux permissions are built around a couple of key ideas:

- Permissions are assigned based on the user (the user who owns the file), group (other users in the file's group), and others (other users not in the file's group).
- Permissions are based on the action (read, write, and execute).

Here's how these two ideas come together. Each of the actions (read, write, and execute) is assigned a value; specifically, read is set to 4, write is set to 2, and execute is set to 1. (Note that these values correspond exactly to binary values.) To allow multiple actions, add the values for each underlying action. For example, if you wanted to allow both read and write, the value you'd assign is 6 (read = 4, write = 2, so read +write = 6).

These values are then assigned to user, group, and others. For example, to allow the file's owner to read and write to a file, you'd assign the value 6 to the user's permissions. To allow the file's owner to read, write, and execute a file, you'd assign the value 7 to the user's permissions. Similarly, if you wanted to allow users in the file's group to read the file but not write or execute it, you'd assign the value 2 to the group's permissions. User, group, and other permissions are listed as an octal number, like this:

644 (user = read+write, group = read, others = read)

755 (user = read+write+execute, group = read+execute, others = read+execute)

600 (user = read+write, group = none, others = none)

620 (user = read+write, group = write, others = none)

You may also see these permissions listed as a string of characters, like rxwr-xr-x. This breaks down to the read (r), write (w), and execute (x) permissions for each of the three entities (user, group, and others). Here are the same examples as earlier, but written in alternate format:

644 = rw-r--r--

755 = rwxr-xr-w

600 = rw-------

620 = rw--w----

The read and write permissions are self-explanatory, but execute is a bit different. For a file, it means just what it says: the ability to execute the file as a program (something we'll discuss in more detail in the next section, "Running Programs" on page 54). For a directory, though, it means the ability to look into and list the contents of the directory. Therefore, if you want members of a directory's group to see the contents of that directory, you'll need to grant the execute permission.

A couple of different Linux tools are used to view and modify permissions. The ls utility, used for listing the contents of a directory, will show permissions when used with the -l option, and is most likely the primary tool you'll use to view permissions. Figure 3-1 contains the output of ls -l /bin on a Debian 8.1 system, and clearly shows permissions assigned to the files in the listing.

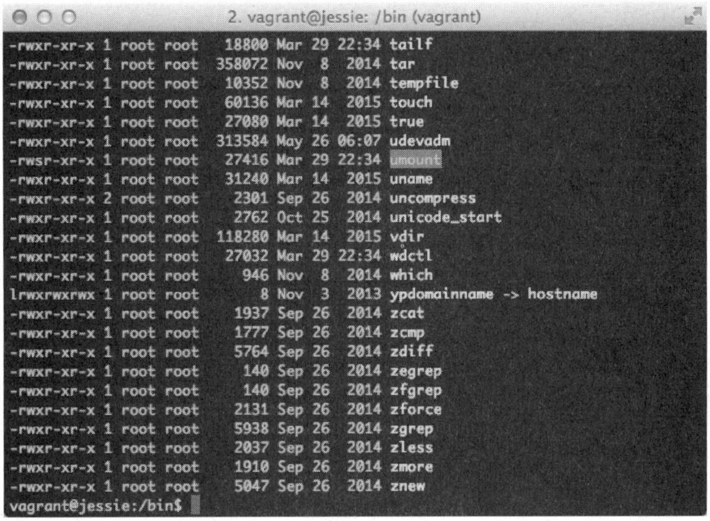

Figure 3-1. Permissions in a file listing

To change or modify permissions, you'll need to use the chmod utility. This is where the explanation of octal values (755, 600, 644, etc.) and the rwxr-wr-w notation (typically referred to as *symbolic notation*) comes in handy, because that's how chmod expects the user to enter permissions. As with relative paths versus absolute paths, the use of octal values versus symbolic notation is really a matter of what you're trying to accomplish:

- If you need (or are willing) to set all the permissions at the same time, use octal values. Even if you omit some of the digits, you'll still be changing the permissions because chmod assumes missing digits are leading zeros (and thus you're setting permissions to none).

- If you need to set only one part (user, group, or others) of the permissions while leaving the rest intact, use symbolic notation. This will allow you to modify only one part of the permissions (for example, only the user permissions, or only the group permissions).

Here are a few quick examples of using chmod. First, let's set the *bin* directory in the current working directory to mode 755 (owner = read/write/execute, all others = read/execute):

```
[vagrant@centos ~]$ chmod 755 bin
```

Next, let's use symbolic notation to add read/write permissions to the user that owns the file *config.txt* in the current working directory, while leaving all other permissions intact:

```
[vagrant@centos ~]$ chmod u+rw config.txt
```

Here's an even more complex example—this adds read/write permissions for the file owner, but removes write permission for the file group:

```
[vagrant@centos ~]$ chmod u+rw,g-w /opt/share/config.txt
```

The chmod command also supports the use of the -R option to act *recursively*, meaning the permission changes will be propagated to files and subdirectories (obviously this works only when you're using chmod against a directory).

Modifying ownership and file group

Given that file ownership and file group play an integral role in file permissions, it's natural that Linux also provides tools to modify file ownership and file group (the ls command is used to view ownership and group, as shown earlier in Figure 3-1). You'll use the chown command to change ownership, and the chgrp command to change the file group. Both commands support the same -R option as chmod to act recursively.

We're now ready to move on from file and directory manipulation to our next major topic in interacting with Linux, which is running programs.

Running Programs

Running programs is actually pretty simple, given the material we've already covered. In order to run a program, here's what's needed:

- A file that is actually an executable file (you can use the file utility to help determine if a file is executable)
- Execute permissions (either as the file owner, as a member of the file's group, or with the execute permission given to others)

We discussed the second requirement (execute permissions) in the previous section on permissions, so we don't need to cover that again here. If you don't have execute permissions on the file, use the chmod, chown, and/or chgrp commands as needed to address it. The first requirement (an executable file) deserves a bit more discussion, though.

What makes up an "executable file"? It could be a binary file, compiled from a programming language such C or C++. However, it could also be an executable text file, such as a bash shell script (a series of bash shell commands) or a script written in a language like Python or Ruby. (We'll be talking about Python extensively in the next chapter.) The file utility (which may or may not be installed by default; use your Linux distribution's package management tool to install it if it isn't already installed) can help here.

Here's the output of the file command against various types of executable files.

```
vagrant@jessie:~$ file /bin/bash
/bin/bash: ELF 64-bit LSB executable, x86-64, version 1 (SYSV), dynamically
linked, interpreter /lib64/ld-linux-x86-64.so.2, for GNU/Linux 2.6.32, BuildID[
sha1]=a8ff57737fe60fba639d91d603253f4cdc6eb9f7, stripped
vagrant@jessie:~$ file docker
docker: ELF 64-bit LSB executable, x86-64, version 1 (GNU/Linux), statically
linked, for GNU/Linux 2.6.24, BuildID[
sha1]=3d4e8c5339180d462a7f43e62ede4f231d625f71, not stripped
vagrant@jessie:~$ file shellscript.sh
script.sh: Bourne-Again shell script, ASCII text executable
vagrant@jessie:~$ file testscript.py
script.py: Python script, ASCII text executable
vagrant@jessie:~$ file testscript-2.rb
script.rb: Ruby script, ASCII text executable
```

Scripts and the shebang

You'll note that the file command can identify text files as a Python script, a Ruby script, or a shell (bash) script. This might sound like magic, but in reality it's relying upon a Linux construct known as the *shebang*. The *shebang* is the first line in a text-based script and it starts with the characters !, followed by the path to the interpreter to the script (the *interpreter* is what will execute the commands in the script). For example, on a Debian 8.1 system the Python interpreter is found at */usr/bin/python*, and so the shebang for a Python script would look like !/usr/bin/python. A Ruby script would have a similar shebang, but pointing to the Ruby interpreter. A bash shell script's shebang would point to bash itself, of course.

Once you've satisfied both requirements—you have an executable file and you have execute permissions on the executable file—running a program is as simple as entering the program name on the command line. *That's it.* Each program may, of course, have certain options and parameters that need to be supplied. The only real "gotcha" here might be around the use of absolute paths; for example, if multiple programs named `testnet` exist on your Linux system and you simply enter `testnet` at the shell prompt, which one will it run? This is where an understanding of bash search paths (which we'll discuss next) and/or the use of absolute paths can help you ensure that you're running the intended program.

Let's expand on this potential "gotcha" just a bit. Earlier in this chapter, in "Navigating the Filesystem" on page 43, we covered the idea of relative paths and absolute paths. We're going to add to the discussion of paths now by introducing the concept of a *search path*. Every Linux system has a search path, which is a list of directories on the system that it will search when the user enters a filename. You can see the current search path by entering `echo $PATH` at your shell prompt, and on a CentOS 7 system you'd see something like this:

```
[vagrant@centos ~]$ echo $PATH
/usr/local/bin:/usr/bin:/usr/local/sbin:/usr/sbin:/home/vagrant/.local/bin:
/home/vagrant/bin
[vagrant@centos ~]$
```

What this means is that if you had a script named *testscript.py* stored in */usr/local/bin*, you could be in *any* directory on the system and simply enter the script's name (*testscript.py*) to execute the script. The system would search the directories in the search path (in order) for the filename you'd entered, and execute the first one it found (which, in this case, would typically be the one in */usr/local/bin* because that's the first directory in the search path).

You'll note, by the way, that the search path does *not* include the current directory. Let's say you've created a *scripts* directory in your home directory, and in that directory you have a shell script you've written called *shellscript.sh*. Take a look at the behavior from the following set of commands:

```
[vagrant@centos ~]$ pwd
/home/vagrant/scripts
[vagrant@centos ~]$ ls
shellscript.sh
[vagrant@centos ~]$ shellscript.sh
-bash: /home/vagrant/bin/shellscript.sh: No such file or directory
[vagrant@centos ~]$ ./shellscript.sh
This is a shell script.
[vagrant@centos ~]$
```

Because the shell script wasn't in the search path, we had to use an absolute path—in this case, the absolute path was telling bash (via the `./` notation) to look in the current directory.

Therefore, the "gotcha" with running programs is that any program you run—be it a compiled binary or an ASCII text script that will be interpreted by bash, Python, Ruby, or some other interpreter—needs to be in the search path, or you'll have to explicitly specify the absolute path (which may include the current directory) to the program. In the case of multiple programs with the same name in different directories, it also means that the program bash finds *first* will be the program that gets executed, and the search order is determined by the search path.

To help with this potential gotcha when you have multiple programs with the same name, you can use the which command. For example, suppose you have a Python script named uptime that gathers uptime statistics from your network devices. Most Linux distributions also ship with a command called uptime (it displays information about how long the Linux system has been up and running). By typing **which uptime**, you can ask the Linux system to tell you the full path to the first uptime executable it found when searching the search path. (This is the one that would be executed if you just typed **uptime** at the prompt.) Based on this information, you can either specify a full path to your Python script, or modify the search path (if needed).

 You can, of course, change and customize the search path. The search path is controlled by what is known as an *environment variable* whose name is PATH. (By convention, all environment variables are specified in uppercase letters.) Modifying this environment variable will modify the search order that bash uses to locate programs.

There's one more topic we're going to cover before moving on to a discussion of networking in Linux, and that's working with background programs, also known as daemons.

Working with Daemons

In the Linux world, we use the term *daemon* to refer to a process that runs in the background. (You may also see the term *service* used to describe these types of background processes.) Daemons are most often encountered when you're using Linux to provide network-based functionality. Examples—some of which we discussed earlier when we first introduced the section on interacting with Linux—might include a DHCP server, an HTTP server, a DNS server, or an FTP server. On a Linux system, each of these network services is provided by a corresponding daemon (or service). In this section, we're going to talk about how to work with daemons: start daemons, stop daemons, restart a daemon, or check on a daemon's status.

It used to be that working with daemons on a Linux system varied pretty widely between distributions. Startup scripts, referred to as *init scripts*, were used to start, stop, or restart a daemon. Some distributions offered utilities—often nothing more than bash shell scripts—such as the service command to help simplify working with daemons. For example, on Ubuntu 14.04 LTS and CentOS 7.1 systems, the service command (found in */usr/sbin*) allowed you to start, stop, or restart a daemon. Behind the scenes, these utilities are calling distribution-specific commands (such as `initctl` on Ubuntu or `systemctl` on CentOS) to actually perform their actions.

In recent years, though, the major Linux distributions have converged on the use of systemd as their init system: RHEL/CentOS 7.x Debian 8.0 and later, and Ubuntu 15.04 and later all use systemd. Therefore, working with daemons (background services) should become easier in the future, although there are (and probably will continue to be) slight differences in each distribution's implementation and use of systemd.

> If you are interested in more details on systemd, we recommend having a look at the systemd website (*http://freedesktop.org/wiki/Software/systemd/*).

In the meantime, though, let's look at working with daemons across the three major Linux distributions we've selected for use in this chapter: Debian GNU/Linux 8.1 ("Jessie"), Ubuntu "Trusty Tahr" 14.04 LTS, and CentOS 7.1. We'll start with Debian GNU/Linux 8.1.

There's much more to systemd

> There's a great deal more to systemd than we have room to discuss here. When we provide examples on how to start, stop, or restart a background service using systemd, we assume that the systemd unit file has already been installed and enabled, and that it is recognized by systemd.

Working with background services in Debian GNU/Linux 8.1

Starting with version 8.0, Debian GNU/Linux uses systemd as its init system, and therefore the primary means by which you'll work with background services is via the `systemctl` utility (found on the system as */bin/systemctl*). Unlike some other distributions, Debian does not offer any sort of "wrapper" commands that in turn call `systemctl` on the backend, instead preferring to have users use `systemctl` directly.

To start a daemon using systemd, you'd call `systemctl` with the `start` subcommand (by the way, we're using the term *subcommand* here to refer to the parameter supplied to `systemctl` that provides the action it should take—we'll also use this nomenclature later in this chapter when working with Linux networking):

```
vagrant@jessie:~$ systemctl start service-name
```

To stop a daemon using systemd, replace the `start` subcommand with `stop`, like this:

```
vagrant@jessie:~$ systemctl stop service-name
```

Similarly, use the `restart` subcommand to stop and then start a daemon:

```
vagrant@jessie:~$ systemctl restart service-name
```

Note that `systemctl` also supports a `reload` subcommand, which will cause a daemon to reload its configuration. This may be less disruptive than restarting a daemon (via `systemctl restart`, which will almost always be disruptive), but the exact behavior of how a daemon will respond to reloading its configuration will vary (in other words, not all daemons will apply the new configuration automatically or behave in the same fashion).

You can use the `status` subcommand to `systemctl` to check the current status of a daemon. Figure 3-2 shows the output of running `systemctl status` on a Debian 8.1 virtual machine.

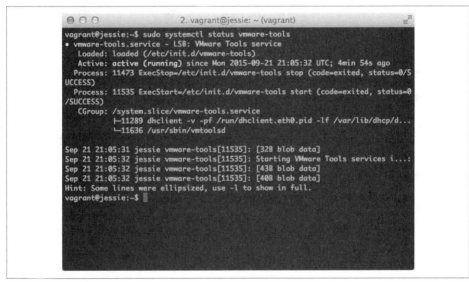

Figure 3-2. Output of a systemctl status command

What if you don't know the service name? `systemctl list-units` will give you a paged list of all the loaded and active units.

> Prior to version 8.0, Debian did not use systemd. Instead, Debian used an older init system known as *System V init* (or *sysv-rc*).

Now let's shift and take a look at working with daemons on Ubuntu Linux 14.04 LTS. Although Ubuntu Linux is a Debian derivative, you'll see that there are significant differences between Debian 8.x and this LTS release from Ubuntu.

Working with background services in Ubuntu Linux 14.04 LTS

Unlike Debian 8.x and CentOS 7.x, Ubuntu 14.04 LTS (recall that the LTS denotes a long-term support release that is supported for five years after release) does *not* use systemd as its init system. Instead, Ubuntu 14.04 uses a Canonical-developed system called Upstart. (The next major LTS release, Ubuntu 16.04, uses systemd. We're covering 14.04 here because it's quite likely you'll run into this LTS version in many production environments.)

The primary command you'll use to interact with Upstart for the purpose of stopping, starting, restarting, or checking the status of background services (also referred to as "jobs" in the Upstart parlance) is `initctl`, and it is used in a fashion very similar to `systemctl`.

For example, to start a daemon you'd use `initctl` like this:

```
vagrant@trusty:~$ initctl start service-name
service name start/running
```

Likewise, to stop a daemon you'd replace `start` in the previous command with `stop`, like this:

```
vagrant@trusty:~$ initctl stop service-name
service name stop/waiting
```

The `restart` and `status` subcommands to `initctl` work in much the same way. Here's an example of restarting and checking the status of the VMware Tools daemon (VMware Tools is a background service often installed in VMware-based virtual machines):

```
vagrant@trusty:~$ initctl restart vmware-tools
vmware-tools start/running
vagrant@trusty:~$ initctl status vmware-tools
vmware-tools start/running
```

And, as with `systemctl`, there is a way to get the list of service names, so that you know the name to supply when trying to start, stop, or check the status of a daemon:

```
vagrant@trusty:~$ initctl list
```

Ubuntu 14.04 LTS also comes with some shortcuts to working with daemons:

- There are commands named `start`, `stop`, `restart`, and `status` that are symbolic links to `initctl`. Each of these commands works as if you had typed `initctl` *subcommand*, so using `stop vmware-tools` would be the same as `initctl stop vmware-tools`. These symbolic links are found in the */sbin* directory.

- Ubuntu also has a shell script, named `service`, that calls `initctl` on the backend. The format for the `service` command is `service service subcommand`, where `service` is the name of the daemon (which you can obtain via `initctl list`) and `subcommand` is one of `start`, `stop`, `restart`, or `status`. Note that this syntax is opposite of `initctl` itself, which is `initctl subcommand service`, which may cause some confusion if you switch back and forth between using the `service` script and `initctl`.

 You may have noticed us mentioning something called a *symbolic link* in our discussion of managing daemons on Ubuntu 14.04. Symbolic links are pointers to a file that allow the file to be referenced multiple times (using different names in different directories) even though the file exists only once on the disk. Symbolic links are not unique to Ubuntu, but are common to all the Linux distributions we discuss in this book. Systemd also makes use of symbolic links when enabling systemd units.

Next, we'll look at working with background services in CentOS 7.1.

Working with background services in CentOS 7.1

CentOS 7.1 uses systemd as its init system, so it is largely similar to working with daemons on Debian GNU/Linux 8.x. In fact, the core `systemctl` commands are completely unchanged, although you will note differences in the unit names when running `systemctl list-units` on the two Linux distributions. Make note of these differences when using both CentOS 7.x and Debian 8.x in your environment.

One difference between Debian and CentOS is that CentOS includes a wrapper script named `service` that allows you to start, stop, restart, and check the status of daemons. It's likely that this wrapper script (we call it a "wrapper script" because it acts as a "wrapper" around `systemctl`, which does the real work on the backend) was included for backward compatibility, as previous releases of CentOS did *not* use systemd and also featured this same command. Note that although it shares a name with the `service` command from Ubuntu, the two scripts are *not* the same and are not portable between the distributions.

The syntax for the `service` command is `service service subcommand`. As on Ubuntu, where the syntax of the `service` script is opposite of `initctl`, you'll note that the `service` script on CentOS also uses a syntax that is opposite of `systemctl` (which is `systemctl subcommand service`).

Before we wrap up this section on working with daemons and move into a discussion of Linux networking, there are a few final commands you might find helpful.

Other daemon-related commands

We'll close out this section on working with daemons with a quick look at a few other commands that you might find helpful. For full details on all the various parameters for these commands, we encourage you to read the man pages (use `man` *command* at a bash prompt).

- To show network connections to a daemon, you can use the `ss` command. One particularly helpful use of this command is to show listening network sockets, which is one way to ensure that the networking configuration for a particular daemon (background service) is working properly. Use `ss -lnt` to show listening TCP sockets, and use `ss -lnu` to show listening UDP sockets.

- The `ps` command is useful for presenting information on the currently running processes.

Before we move on to the next section, let's take a quick moment and review what we've covered so far:

- We've provided some background and history for Linux.
- We've supplied information on basic filesystem navigation and paths.
- We've shown you how to perform basic file manipulations (create files and directories, move/copy files and directories, and remove files and directories).
- We've discussed how to work with background services, also known as daemons.

Our next major topic is networking in Linux, which will build on many of the areas we've already touched on so far in this chapter.

Networking in Linux

We stated earlier in this chapter that our coverage of Linux was intended to get you "up and running" with Linux in the context of network automation and programmability. You're very likely going to be using tools like Python, Ansible, or Jinja (covered in Chapters 4, 9, and 6, respectively) on Linux, and your Linux system is going to need to communicate across the network to various network devices. Naturally, this means that our discussion of Linux would not be complete without also discussing networking in Linux. This is, after all, a networking-centric book!

Working with Interfaces

The basic building block of Linux networking is the *interface*. Linux supports a number of different types of interfaces; the most common of these are physical interfaces, VLAN interfaces, and bridge interfaces. As with most other things in Linux, you configure these various types of interfaces by executing command-line utilities from the bash shell and/or using certain plain-text configuration files. Making interface configuration changes persistent across a reboot typically requires modifying a configuration file. Let's look first at using the command-line utilities, and then we'll discuss persistent changes using interface configuration files.

Interface configuration via the command line

Just as the Linux distributions have converged on systemd as the primary init system, most of the major Linux distributions have converged on a single set of command-line utilities for working with network interfaces. These commands are part of the iproute2 set of utilities, available in the major Linux distributions as either iproute or iproute2 (CentOS 7.1 uses iproute; Debian 8.1 and Ubuntu 14.04 use iproute2 for the package name). This set of utilities uses a command called ip to replace the functionality of earlier (and now deprecated) commands such as ifconfig and route (both Ubuntu 14.04 and CentOS 7.1 include these earlier commands, but Debian 8.1 does not).

More information on iproute2

If you're interested in more information on iproute2, visit the iproute2 Wikipedia page (*https://en.wikipedia.org/wiki/Iproute2*).

For interface configuration, two subcommands to the ip command will be used: ip link, which is used to view or set interface link status, and ip addr, which is used to view or set IP addressing configuration on interfaces. (We'll look at some other forms of the ip command later in this section.)

Let's look at a few task-oriented examples of using the ip commands to perform interface configuration.

Listing interfaces. You can use either the ip link or ip addr command to list all the interfaces on a system, although the output will be slightly different for each command.

If you want a listing of the interfaces along with the interface status, use ip link list, like this:

```
[vagrant@centos ~]$ ip link list
1: lo: <LOOPBACK,UP,LOWER_UP> mtu 65536 qdisc noqueue state UNKNOWN mode DEFAULT
    link/loopback 00:00:00:00:00:00 brd 00:00:00:00:00:00
2: ens32: <BROADCAST,MULTICAST,UP,LOWER_UP> mtu 1500 qdisc pfifo_fast state UP
    mode DEFAULT qlen 1000
    link/ether 00:0c:29:d7:28:17 brd ff:ff:ff:ff:ff:ff
3: ens33: <BROADCAST,MULTICAST,UP,LOWER_UP> mtu 1500 qdisc pfifo_fast state UP
    mode DEFAULT qlen 1000
```

```
    link/ether 00:0c:29:d7:28:21 brd ff:ff:ff:ff:ff:ff
[vagrant@centos ~]$
```

 The default "action," so to speak, for most (if not all) of the ip commands is to list the items with which you're working. Thus, if you
want to list all the interfaces, you can just use ip link instead of ip
link list, or if you wanted to list all the routes you can just use ip
route instead of ip route list. We will specify the full commands here for clarity.

As you can tell from the prompt, this output was taken from a CentOS 7.1 system.
The command syntax is the same across the three major distributions we're discussing in this chapter, and the output is largely identical (with the exception of interface
names).

You'll note that this output shows you the current list of interfaces (note that CentOS
assigns different names to the interfaces than Debian and Ubuntu), the current maximum transmission unit (MTU), the current administrative state (UP), and the ethernet media access control (MAC) address, among other things.

The output of this command also tells you the current state of the interface (note the
information in angle brackets immediately following the interface name):

- UP: Indicates that the interface is enabled.

- LOWER_UP: Indicates that interface link is up.

- NO_CARRIER (not shown): The interface is enabled, but there is no link.

If you're accustomed to working with network equipment, you're probably familiar
with an interface being "down" versus being "administratively down." If an interface is
down because there is no link, you'll see NO_CARRIER in the brackets immediately
after the interface name; if the interface is administratively down, then you won't see
UP, LOWER_UP, or NO_CARRIER, and the state will be listed as DOWN. In the next section
we'll show you how to use the ip link command to disable an interface (set an interface as administratively down).

You can also list interfaces using the ip addr list command, like this (this output is
taken from Ubuntu 14.04 LTS):

```
vagrant@trusty:~$ ip addr list
1: lo: <LOOPBACK,UP,LOWER_UP> mtu 65536 qdisc noqueue state UNKNOWN group default
    link/loopback 00:00:00:00:00:00 brd 00:00:00:00:00:00
    inet 127.0.0.1/8 scope host lo
       valid_lft forever preferred_lft forever
    inet6 ::1/128 scope host
       valid_lft forever preferred_lft forever
2: eth0: <BROADCAST,MULTICAST,UP,LOWER_UP> mtu 1500 qdisc pfifo_fast state UP
```

```
            group default qlen 1000
            link/ether 00:0c:29:33:99:f6 brd ff:ff:ff:ff:ff:ff
            inet 192.168.70.205/24 brd 192.168.70.255 scope global eth0
               valid_lft forever preferred_lft forever
            inet6 fe80::20c:29ff:fe33:99f6/64 scope link
               valid_lft forever preferred_lft forever
         3: eth1: <BROADCAST,MULTICAST,UP,LOWER_UP> mtu 1500 qdisc pfifo_fast state UP
            group default qlen 1000
            link/ether 00:0c:29:33:99:00 brd ff:ff:ff:ff:ff:ff
            inet 192.168.100.11/24 brd 192.168.100.255 scope global eth1
               valid_lft forever preferred_lft forever
            inet6 fe80::20c:29ff:fe33:9900/64 scope link
               valid_lft forever preferred_lft forever
      vagrant@trusty:~$
```

As you can see, the `ip addr list` command also lists the interfaces on the system, along with some link status information and the IPv4/IPv6 addresses assigned to the interface.

For both the `ip link list` and `ip addr list` commands, you can filter the list to only a specific interface by adding the interface name. The final command then becomes `ip link list` *interface* or `ip addr list` *interface*, like this:

```
vagrant@jessie:~$ ip link list eth0
2: eth0: <BROADCAST,MULTICAST,UP,LOWER_UP> mtu 1500 qdisc pfifo_fast state UP
    mode DEFAULT group default qlen 1000
    link/ether 00:0c:29:bf:af:1a brd ff:ff:ff:ff:ff:ff
vagrant@jessie:~$
```

Listing interfaces is very useful, of course, but perhaps even more useful is actually modifying the configuration of an interface. In the next section, we'll show you how to enable or disable an interface.

Enabling/disabling an interface. In addition to listing interfaces, you also use the `ip link` command to manage an interface's status. To disable an interface, for example, you set the interface's status to down using the `ip link set` command:

```
[vagrant@centos ~]$ ip link set ens33 down
[vagrant@centos ~]$ ip link list ens33
3: ens33: <BROADCAST,MULTICAST> mtu 1500 qdisc pfifo_fast state DOWN mode DEFAULT
    qlen 1000
    link/ether 00:0c:29:d7:28:21 brd ff:ff:ff:ff:ff:ff
[vagrant@centos ~]$
```

Note `state DOWN` and the lack of `NO_CARRIER`, which tells you the interface is administratively down (disabled) and not just down due to a link failure. (We've bolded the `state DOWN` in the preceding output to make it easier to spot.)

To enable (or re-enable) the ens33 interface, you'd simply use `ip link set` again, this time setting the status to "up":

```
[vagrant@centos ~]$ ip link set ens33 up
[vagrant@centos ~]$ ip link list ens33
3: ens33: <BROADCAST,MULTICAST,UP,LOWER_UP> mtu 1500 qdisc pfifo_fast state UP
    mode DEFAULT qlen 1000
    link/ether 00:0c:29:d7:28:21 brd ff:ff:ff:ff:ff:ff
[vagrant@centos ~]$
```

Setting the MTU of an interface.   If you need to set the MTU of an interface, you'd once again turn to the ip link command, using the set subcommand. The full syntax is ip link set mtu *MTU interface*.

As a specific example, let's say you wanted to run jumbo frames on the ens33 interface on your CentOS 7.x Linux system. Here's the command:

```
[vagrant@centos ~]$ ip link set mtu 9000 ens33
[vagrant@centos ~]$
```

As with all the other ip commands we've looked it, this change is immediate but not persistent—you'll have to edit the interface's configuration file to make the change persistent. We discuss configuring interfaces via configuration files in "Interface configuration via configuration files" on page 67.

Assigning an IP address to an interface.   To assign (or remove) an IP address to an interface, you'll use the ip addr command. We've already shown you how to use ip addr list to see a list of the interfaces and their assigned IP address(es); now we'll expand the use of ip addr to add and remove IP addresses.

To assign (add) an IP address to an interface, you'll use the command ip addr add *address* dev *interface*. For example, if you want to assign (add) the address 172.31.254.100/24 to the eth1 interface on a Debian 8.1 system, you'd run this command:

```
vagrant@jessie:~$ ip addr add 172.31.254.100/24 dev eth1
vagrant@jessie:~$
```

If an interface already has an IP address assigned, the ip addr add command simply *adds* the new address, leaving the original address intact. So, in this example, if the eth1 interface already had an address of 192.168.100.10/24, running the previous command would result in this configuration:

```
vagrant@jessie:~$ ip addr list eth1
3: eth1: <BROADCAST,MULTICAST,UP,LOWER_UP> mtu 1500 qdisc pfifo_fast state UP
    group default qlen 1000
    link/ether 00:0c:29:bf:af:24 brd ff:ff:ff:ff:ff:ff
    inet 192.168.100.10/24 brd 192.168.100.255 scope global eth1
       valid_lft forever preferred_lft forever
    inet 172.31.254.100/24 scope global eth1
       valid_lft forever preferred_lft forever
    inet6 fe80::20c:29ff:febf:af24/64 scope link
```

```
          valid_lft forever preferred_lft forever
vagrant@jessie:~$
```

To remove an IP address from an interface, you'd use ip addr del *address* dev *interface*. Here we are removing the 172.31.254.100/24 address we assigned earlier to the eth1 interface:

```
vagrant@jessie:~$ ip addr del 172.31.254.100/24 dev eth1
vagrant@jessie:~$ ip addr list eth1
3: eth1: <BROADCAST,MULTICAST,UP,LOWER_UP> mtu 1500 qdisc pfifo_fast state UP
    group default qlen 1000
    link/ether 00:0c:29:bf:af:24 brd ff:ff:ff:ff:ff:ff
    inet 192.168.100.10/24 brd 192.168.100.255 scope global eth1
        valid_lft forever preferred_lft forever
    inet6 fe80::20c:29ff:febf:af24/64 scope link
        valid_lft forever preferred_lft forever
vagrant@jessie:~$
```

As with the ip link command, the syntax for the ip addr add and ip addr del commands is the same across the three major Linux distributions we're discussing in this chapter. The output is also largely identical, although there may be variations in interface names.

So far, we've only shown you how to use the ip commands to modify the configuration of an interface. If you're familiar with configuring network devices (and since you're reading this book, you probably are), this could be considered analogous to modifying the running configuration of a network device. However, what we haven't done so far is make these configuration changes permanent. In other words, we haven't changed the startup configuration. To do that, we'll need to look at how Linux uses interface configuration files.

Interface configuration via configuration files

To make changes to an interface persistent across system restarts, using the ip commands alone isn't enough. You'll need to edit the interface configuration files that Linux uses on startup to perform those same configurations for you automatically. Unfortunately, while the ip commands are pretty consistent across Linux distributions, interface configuration files across different Linux distributions can be quite different.

For example, on RHEL/CentOS/Fedora and derivatives, interface configuration files are found in separate files located in */etc/sysconfig/network-scripts*. The interface configuration files are named ifcfg-*interface*, where the name of the interface (such as eth0 or ens32) is embedded in the name of the file. An interface configuration file might look something like this (this example is taken from CentOS 7.1):

```
NAME="ens33"
DEVICE="ens33"
ONBOOT=yes
```

```
NETBOOT=yes
IPV6INIT=yes
BOOTPROTO=dhcp
TYPE=Ethernet
```

Some of the most commonly used directives in RHEL/CentOS/Fedora interface configuration files are:

NAME

A friendly name for users to see, typically only used in graphical user interfaces (this name wouldn't show up in the output of ip commands).

DEVICE

This is the name of the physical device being configured.

IPADDR

The IP address to be assigned to this interface (if you're not using DHCP or BootP).

PREFIX

If you're statically assigning the IP address, this setting specifies the network prefix to be used with the assigned IP address. (You can use NETMASK instead, but the use of PREFIX is recommended.)

BOOTPROTO

This directive specifies how the interface will have its IP address assigned. A value of dhcp, as shown earlier, means the address will be provided via Dynamic Host Configuration Protocol (DHCP). The other value typically used here would be none, which means the address is statically defined in the interface configuration file.

ONBOOT

Setting this directive to yes will activate the interface at boot time; setting it to no means the interface will not be activated at boot time.

MTU

Specifies the default MTU for this interface.

GATEWAY

This setting specifies the gateway to be used for this interface.

There are many more settings, but these are the ones you're likely to see most often. For full details, check the contents of */usr/share/doc/initscripts-<version>/sysconfig.txt* on your CentOS system.

For Debian and Debian derivatives like Ubuntu, on the other hand, interface configuration is handled by the file */etc/network/interfaces*. Here's an example network interface configuration file from Ubuntu 14.04 LTS (we're using the `cat` command here to simply output the contents of a file to the screen):

```
vagrant@trusty:~$ cat /etc/network/interfaces
# This file describes the network interfaces available on your system
# and how to activate them. For more information, see interfaces(5).

# The loopback network interface
auto lo
iface lo inet loopback

# The primary network interface
auto eth0
iface eth0 inet dhcp

auto eth1
iface eth1 inet static
        address 192.168.100.11
        netmask 255.255.255.0
vagrant@trusty:~$
```

You'll note that Debian and Ubuntu use a single file to configure all the network interfaces; each interface is separated by a configuration stanza starting with `auto` *interface*. In each configuration stanza, the most common configuration options are (to view all the options for configuring interfaces on a Debian or Ubuntu system, run `man 5 interfaces`):

- Setting the address configuration method: You'll typically use either `inet dhcp` or `inet static` to assign IP addresses to interfaces. In the example shown earlier, the eth0 interface was set to use DHCP while eth1 was assigned statically.

- The `netmask` option provides the network mask for the assigned IP address (when the address is being assigned statically via `inet static`). However, you can also use the prefix format (like `192.168.100.10/24`) when assigning the IP address, which makes the use of the `netmask` directive unnecessary.

- The `gateway` directive in the configuration stanza assigns a default gateway when the IP address is being assigned statically (via `inet static`).

If you prefer using separate files for interface configuration, it's also possible to break out interface configuration into per-interface configuration files, similar to how RHEL/CentOS handle it, by including a line like this in the */etc/network/interfaces* file:

```
source /etc/network/interfaces.d/*
```

This line instructs Linux to look in the */etc/network/interfaces.d/* directory for per-interface configuration files, and process them as if they were directly incorporated into the main network configuration file. The */etc/network/interfaces* file on Debian

8.1 includes this line by default (but the directory is empty, and the interface configuration takes place in the */etc/network/interfaces* file). In the case of using per-interface configuration files, then it's possible that this might be the *only* line found in the */etc/network/interfaces* file.

A use case for per-interface configuration files

Per-interface configuration files may give you some additional flexibility when using a *configuration management* tool such as Chef, Puppet, Ansible, or Salt. These are important "tools of the trade" for managing systems, including Linux systems, and when using these tools it may be easier to generate per-interface configuration files instead of managing different sections within a single file. We will discuss using these tools for network automation in more detail in Chapter 9.

When you make a change to a network interface file, the configuration changes are *not* immediately applied. (If you want an immediate change, use the ip commands we described earlier in addition to making changes to the configuration files.) To put the changes into effect, you'll need to restart the network interface.

On Ubuntu 14.04, you'd use the initctl command, described in "Working with Daemons" on page 57 to restart the network interface:

    vagrant@trusty:~$ initctl restart network-interface INTERFACE=*interface*

On CentOS 7.1, you'd use the systemctl command:

    [vagrant@centos ~]$ systemctl restart network

And on Debian 8.1, you'd use a very similar command:

    vagrant@jessie:~$ systemctl restart networking

You'll note the systemd-based distributions (CentOS and Debian 8.x) lack a way to do per-interface restarts.

Once the interface is restarted, then the configuration changes are applied and in effect (and you can verify this through the use of the appropriate ip commands).

Everything we've shown you so far has involved physical interfaces, like eth0 or ens32. However, in much the same way that Linux treats many things as files, Linux networking also treats many things as interfaces. One such example is how Linux interacts with VLANs, a topic we explore in more detail in the following section.

Using VLAN interfaces

We mentioned in "Working with Daemons" on page 57 that the interface is the basic building block of Linux networking. In this section, we discuss *VLAN interfaces*, which are logical interfaces that allow an instance of Linux to communicate on multiple virtual local area networks (VLANs) simultaneously without having to have a dedicated physical interface for each VLAN. Instead, Linux uses the idea of logical VLAN interfaces that are associated with both a physical interface and a corresponding 802.1Q VLAN ID.

Chances are that you're already familiar with the idea of VLANs, so we won't bother covering this concept in any great detail. If you need a good reference to VLANs (or many other networking concepts), one good resource to consider is *Packet Guide to Routing and Switching*, by Bruce Hartpence, available from O'Reilly.

Creating, configuring, and deleting VLAN interfaces. To create a VLAN interface, you'll use the command ip link add link *parent-device* *vlan-device* type vlan id *vlan-id*. As you can see, this is simply an extension to the ip link command we've been discussing throughout the last several sections of this chapter.

There are a few different pieces to this command, so let's break it down a bit:

- The *parent-device* is the physical adapter with which the logical VLAN interface is associated. This would be something like eth1 on a Debian or Ubuntu system, or ens33 on a RHEL/CentOS/Fedora system.
- The *vlan-device* is the name to be given to the logical VLAN interface; the common naming convention is to use the name of the parent device, a dot (period), and then the VLAN ID. For a VLAN interface associated with eth1 and using VLAN ID 100, the name would be eth1.100.
- Finally, *vlan-id* is exactly that—the 802.1Q VLAN ID value assigned to this logical interface.

Let's look at an example. Suppose you want to create a logical VLAN interface on a Debian 8.x system. This logical interface is to be associated with the physical interface named eth2 and should use 802.1Q VLAN ID 150. The command would look like this:

```
vagrant@jessie:~$ ip link add link eth2 eth2.150 type vlan id 150
vagrant@jessie:~$
```

You can now verify that the logical VLAN interface was added using ip link list (note the eth2.150@eth2 as the name of the interface; you only need to use the portion before the @ symbol when working with the interface):

```
vagrant@jessie:~$ ip link list eth2.150
7: eth2.150@eth2: <BROADCAST,MULTICAST> mtu 1500 qdisc noqueue state DOWN
    mode DEFAULT group default
    link/ether 00:0c:29:5f:d2:15 brd ff:ff:ff:ff:ff:ff
vagrant@jessie:~$
```

To verify (aside from the name) that the interface is a VLAN interface, add the -d parameter to the `ip link list` command, like this:

```
vagrant@jessie:~$ ip -d link list eth2.150
7: eth2.150@eth2: <BROADCAST,MULTICAST> mtu 1500 qdisc noqueue state DOWN
    mode DEFAULT group default
    link/ether 00:0c:29:5f:d2:15 brd ff:ff:ff:ff:ff:ff
    vlan protocol 802.1Q id 150 <REORDER_HDR>
vagrant@jessie:~$
```

For the VLAN interface to be fully functional, though, you must also enable the interface and assign an IP address:

```
vagrant@jessie:~$ ip link set eth2.150 up
vagrant@jessie:~$ ip addr add 192.168.150.10/24 dev eth2.150
vagrant@jessie:~$
```

Naturally, this means you must also have a matching configuration on the physical switches to which this system is connected; specifically, the switch port must be configured as a VLAN trunk and configured to pass VLAN 150. The commands for this will vary depending on the upstream switch model and manufacturer.

Just like physical interfaces, a logical VLAN interface that is enabled and has an IP address assigned will add a route to the host's routing table:

```
vagrant@jessie:~$ ip route list
default via 192.168.70.2 dev eth0
192.168.70.0/24 dev eth0  proto kernel  scope link  src 192.168.70.243
192.168.100.0/24 dev eth1  proto kernel  scope link  src 192.168.100.10
192.168.150.0/24 dev eth2.150  proto kernel  scope link  src 192.168.150.10
vagrant@jessie:~$
```

To delete a VLAN interface, we recommend that you first disable the interface (set its status to down), then remove the interface:

```
vagrant@jessie:~$ ip link set eth2.150 down
vagrant@jessie:~$ ip link delete eth2.150
vagrant@jessie:~$
```

Naturally, as we discussed earlier in this chapter, the `ip` commands change the current (running) configuration but don't persist the changes—on a reboot, any VLAN interfaces you've created and configured will disappear. To make the changes persistent, you'll need to edit the interface configuration files.

On a Debian/Ubuntu system, it's a matter of simply adding a stanza to */etc/network/ interfaces* or adding a per-interface configuration file to */etc/network/interfaces.d* (and ensuring that file is sourced from */etc/network/interfaces*). The configuration stanza should look something like this:

```
auto eth2.150
iface eth2.150 inet static
  address 192.168.150.10/24
```

For RHEL/Fedora/CentOS systems, you'd create a per-interface configuration file in */etc/sysconfig/network-scripts* with a name like *ifcfg-eth2.150*. The contents would need to look something like this:

```
VLAN=yes
DEVICE=eth2.150
BOOTPROTO=static
ONBOOT=yes
TYPE=Ethernet
IPADDR=192.168.150.10
NETMASK=255.255.255.0
```

Use cases for VLAN interfaces. VLAN interfaces will be tremendously useful anytime you have a Linux host that needs to communicate on multiple VLANs at the same time *and* you wish to minimize the number of switch ports and physical interfaces required. For example, if you have a Linux host that needs to communicate on one VLAN to some web servers as well as communicate on another VLAN with some database servers, using a single physical interface with two logical VLAN interfaces (assuming there is enough bandwidth on a single physical interface) is an ideal solution.

Appendix A explores a few additional use cases for VLAN interfaces.

In addition to configuring and managing interfaces, another important aspect of Linux networking is configuring and managing the Linux host's IP routing tables. The next section provides more details on what's involved.

Routing as an End Host

In addition to configuring network interfaces on a Linux host, we also want to show you how to view and manage routing on a Linux system. Interface and routing configuration go hand-in-hand, naturally, but there are times when some tasks for IP routing need to be configured separately from interface configuration. First, though, let's look at how interface configurations affect host routing configuration.

Although the `ip route` command is your primary means of viewing and/or modifying the routing table for a Linux host, the `ip link` and `ip addr` commands may also affect the host's routing table.

First, if you wanted to view the current routing table, you could simply run `ip route list`:

```
vagrant@trusty:~$ ip route list
default via 192.168.70.2 dev eth0
192.168.70.0/24 dev eth0  proto kernel  scope link  src 192.168.70.205
192.168.100.0/24 dev eth1  proto kernel  scope link  src 192.168.100.11
vagrant@trusty:~$
```

The output of this command tells us a few things:

- The default gateway is 192.168.70.2. The eth0 device will be used to communicate with all unknown networks via the default gateway. (Recall from the previous section that this would be set via DHCP or via a configuration directive such as GATEWAY on a RHEL/CentOS/Fedora system or gateway on a Debian/Ubuntu system.)
- The IP address assigned to eth0 is 192.168.70.205, and this is the interface that will be used to communicate with the 192.168.70.0/24 network.
- The IP address assigned to eth1 is 192.168.100.11/24, and this is the interface that will be used to communicate with the 192.168.100.0/24 network.

If we disable the eth1 interface using `ip link set eth1 down`, then the host's routing table changes automatically:

```
vagrant@trusty:~$ ip link set eth1 down
vagrant@trusty:~$ ip route list
default via 192.168.70.2 dev eth0
192.168.70.0/24 dev eth0  proto kernel  scope link  src 192.168.70.205
vagrant@trusty:~$
```

Now that eth1 is down, the system no longer has a route to the 192.168.100.0/24 network, and the routing table updates automatically. This is all fully expected, but we wanted to show you this interaction so you could see how the `ip link` and `ip addr` commands affect the host's routing table.

For less automatic changes to the routing table, you'll use the `ip route` command. What do we mean by "less automatic changes"? Here are a few use cases:

- Adding a static route to a network over a particular interface
- Removing a static route to a network
- Changing the default gateway

Here are some concrete examples of these use cases.

Let's assume the same configuration we've been showing off so far—the eth0 interface has an IPv4 address from the 192.168.70.0/24 network, and the eth1 interface has an IPv4 address from the 192.168.100.0/24 network. In this configuration, the output of `ip route list` would look like this:

```
vagrant@trusty:~$ ip route list
default via 192.168.70.2 dev eth0
192.168.70.0/24 dev eth0  proto kernel  scope link  src 192.168.70.205
192.168.100.0/24 dev eth1  proto kernel  scope link  src 192.168.100.11
vagrant@trusty:~$
```

If we were going to model this configuration as a network diagram, it would look something like Figure 3-3.

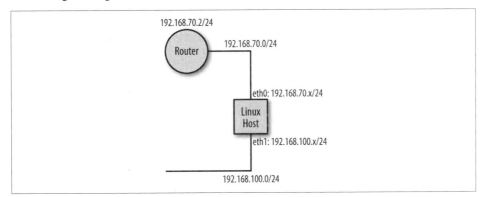

Figure 3-3. Sample network topology

Now let's say that a new router is added to the 192.168.100.0/24 network, and a network with which this host needs to communicate (using the subnet address 192.168.101.0/24) is placed beyond that router. Figure 3-4 shows the new network topology.

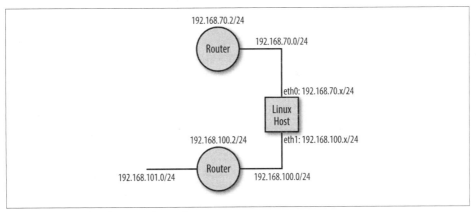

Figure 3-4. Updated network topology

The host's existing routing table won't allow it to communicate with this new network—since it doesn't have a route to the new network, Linux will direct traffic to the default gateway, which doesn't have a connection to the new network. To fix this, we add a route to the new network over the host's eth1 interface like this:

```
vagrant@jessie:~$ ip route add 192.168.101.0/24 via 192.168.100.2 dev eth1
vagrant@jessie:~$ ip route list
default via 192.168.70.2 dev eth0
192.168.70.0/24 dev eth0  proto kernel  scope link  src 192.168.70.204
192.168.100.0/24 dev eth1  proto kernel  scope link  src 192.168.100.10
```

```
192.168.101.0/24 via 192.168.100.2 dev eth1
vagrant@jessie:~$
```

The generic form for this command is `ip route add` *destination-net* via *gateway-address* dev *interface*.

This command tells the Linux host (a Debian system, in this example) that it can communicate with the 192.168.101.0/24 network via the IP address 192.168.100.2 over the eth1 interface. Now the host has a route to the new network via the appropriate router and is able to communicate with systems on that network. If the network topology were updated again with another router and another new network, as shown in Figure 3-5, we'd need to add yet another route.

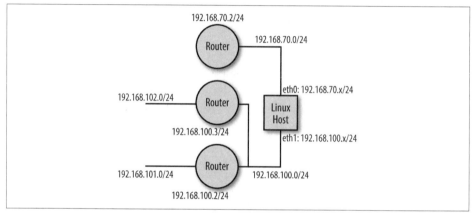

Figure 3-5. Final network topology

To address this final topology, you'd run this command:

```
vagrant@jessie:~$ ip route add 192.168.102.0/24 via 192.168.100.3 dev eth1
vagrant@jessie:~$ ip route list
default via 192.168.70.2 dev eth0
192.168.70.0/24 dev eth0  proto kernel  scope link  src 192.168.70.204
192.168.100.0/24 dev eth1  proto kernel  scope link  src 192.168.100.10
192.168.101.0/24 via 192.168.100.2 dev eth1
192.168.102.0/24 via 192.168.100.3 dev eth1
vagrant@jessie:~$
```

To make these routes persistent (remember that the `ip` commands *don't* typically make configuration changes persistent), you'd add these commands to the configuration stanza in */etc/network/interfaces* for the eth1 device, like this (or, if you were on a RHEL/Fedora/CentOS system, you'd edit */etc/sysconfig/network-scripts/ifcfg-eth1*):

```
auto eth1
iface eth1 inet static
        address 192.168.100.11
        netmask 255.255.255.0
```

```
up ip route add 192.168.101.0/24 via 192.168.100.2 dev $IFACE
up ip route add 192.168.102.0/24 via 192.168.100.3 dev $IFACE
```

The $IFACE listed on the commands in this configuration stanza refers to the specific interface being configured, and the up directive instructs Debian/Ubuntu systems to run these commands after the interface comes up. With these lines in place, the routes will automatically be added to the routing table every time the system is started.

If, for whatever reason, you need to *remove* routes from a routing table, then you can use the ip route command for that as well, this time using the delete subcommand:

```
[vagrant@centos ~]$ ip route del 192.168.103.0/24 via 192.168.100.3
```

The generic form of the command to remove (delete) a route is ip route del *destination-net* via *gateway-address*.

Finally, changing the default gateway is also something you might need to do using the ip route command. (We will note, however, that you can also change the default gateway—and make it persistent—by editing the interface configuration files. Using the ip route command will change it immediately, but the change will not be persistent.) To change the default gateway, you'd use a command somewhat like this (this assumes a default gateway is already present):

```
vagrant@trusty:~$ ip route del default via 192.168.70.2 dev eth0
vagrant@trusty:~$ ip route add default via 192.168.70.1 dev eth0
```

The default keyword is used in these commands to refer to the destination 0.0.0.0/0.

Linux also supports what is known as *policy routing*, which is the ability to support multiple routing tables along with rules that instruct Linux to use a specific routing table. For example, perhaps you'd like to use a different default gateway for each interface in the system. Using policy routing, you could configure Linux to use one routing table (and thus one particular gateway) for eth0, but use a different routing table (and a different default gateway) for eth1. Policy routing is a bit of an advanced topic so we won't cover it here, but if you're interested in seeing how this works read the man pages or help screens for the ip rule and ip route commands for more details (in other words, run **man ip rule** and **man ip route**).

The focus so far in this section has been around the topic of IP routing from a host perspective, but it's also possible to use Linux as a full-fledged IP router. As with policy routing, this is a bit of an advanced topic; however, we are going to cover the basic elements in the next section.

Routing as a Router

By default, virtually all modern Linux distributions have IP forwarding *disabled*, since most Linux users don't need IP forwarding. However, Linux has the ability to perform

IP forwarding so that it can act as a *router*, connecting multiple IP subnets together and passing (routing) traffic among multiple subnets. To enable this functionality, you must first enable IP forwarding.

To verify whether IP forwarding is enabled or disabled, you would run this command (it works on Debian, Ubuntu, and CentOS, although the command might be found at different paths on different systems):

```
vagrant@trusty:~$ /sbin/sysctl net.ipv4.ip_forward
net.ipv4.ip_forward = 0
vagrant@trusty:~$ /sbin/sysctl net.ipv6.conf.all.forwarding
net.ipv6.conf.all.forwarding = 0
vagrant@trusty:~$
```

In situations where a command is found in a different filesystem location among different Linux distributions, the which command mentioned earlier in this chapter can be helpful in that it will tell you where a particular command is located (assuming it is in the search path).

In both cases, the output of the command indicates the value is set to 0, which means it is disabled. You can enable IP forwarding on the fly without a reboot—but non-persistently, meaning it will disappear after a reboot—using this command:

```
[vagrant@centos ~]$ systcl -w net.ipv4.ip_forward=1
```

This is like the ip commands we discussed earlier in that the change takes effect immediately, but the setting will not survive a reboot of the Linux system. To make the change permanent, you must edit */etc/sysctl.conf* or put a configuration file into the */etc/sysctl.d* directory. Either way, add this value to either */etc/sysctl.conf* or to a configuration file in */etc/sysctl.d*:

```
net.ipv4.ip_forward = 1
```

Or, to enable IPv6 forwarding, add this value:

```
net.ipv6.conf.all.forwarding = 1
```

You can then either reboot the Linux host to make the changes effective, or you can run sysctl -p *<path to file with new setting>*.

Once IP forwarding is enabled, then the Linux system will act as a router. At this point, the Linux system is only capable of performing static routing, so you would need to use the `ip route` command to provide all the necessary routing instructions/information so that traffic could be routed appropriately. However, dynamic routing protocol daemons do exist for Linux that would allow a Linux router to participate in dynamic routing protocols such as BGP or OSPF. Two popular options for integrating Linux into dynamic routing environments are Quagga (*http://www.nongnu.org/quagga/*) and BIRD (*http://bird.network.cz*).

Using features like IPTables (or its successor, NFTables (*http://netfilter.org/projects/nftables/*)), you can also add functionality like Network Address Translation (NAT) and access control lists (ACLs).

In addition to being able to route traffic at Layer 3, Linux also has the ability to *bridge* traffic—that is, to connect multiple Ethernet segments together at Layer 2. The next section covers the basics of Linux bridging.

Bridging (Switching)

The Linux bridge offers you the ability to connect multiple network segments together in a protocol-independent way—that is, a bridge operates at Layer 2 of the OSI model instead of at Layer 3 or higher. Bridging—specifically, multiport transparent bridging—is widely used in data centers today in the form of network switches, but most uses of bridging in Linux are centered on various forms of virtualization (either via the KVM hypervisor or via other means like Linux containers). For this reason, we'll only briefly cover the basics of bridging here, and only in the context of virtualization.

Practical use case for bridging

Before we get into the details of creating and configuring bridges, let's look at a practical example of how a Linux bridge would be used.

Let's assume that you have a Linux host with two physical interfaces (we'll use eth0 and eth1 as the names of the physical interfaces). Immediately after you create a bridge (a process we'll describe in the following section), your Linux host looks something like Figure 3-6.

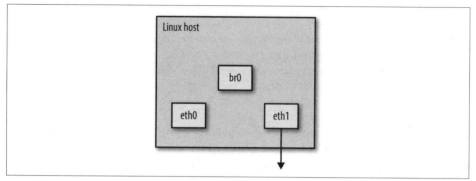

Figure 3-6. A Linux bridge with no interfaces

The bridge has been created and it exists, but it can't really *do* anything yet. Recall that a bridge is designed to join network segments—without any segments attached to the bridge, there's nothing it can (or will) do. You need to add some interfaces to the bridge.

Let's say you add the interface named eth1 to a bridge named br0. Now your configuration looks something like Figure 3-7.

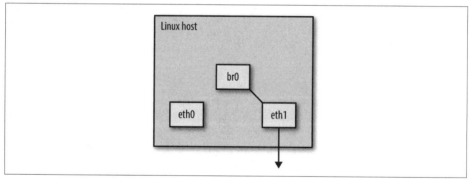

Figure 3-7. A Linux bridge with a physical interface

If we were now to attach a virtual machine (VM) to this bridge (Appendix A explores some specifics around using a bridge with a VM; this is typically accomplished via the use of KVM (*http://www.linux-kvm.org/page/Main_Page*) and Libvirt (*http://libvirt.org/*)), then your configuration would look something like Figure 3-8.

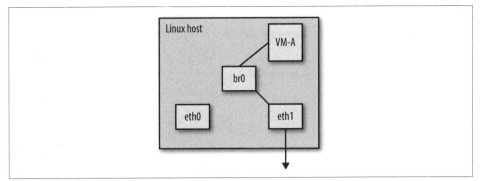

Figure 3-8. A Linux bridge with a physical interface and a VM

In this final configuration, the bridge named br0 connects—or *bridges*, if you prefer that term—the network segment to the VM and the network segment to the physical interface, providing a single Layer 2 broadcast domain from the VM to the NIC (and then on to the physical network). Providing network connectivity for VMs is a very common use case for Linux bridges, but not the only use case. You might also use a Linux bridge to join a wireless network (via a wireless interface on the Linux host) to an Ethernet network (connected via a traditional NIC).

Now that you have an idea of what a Linux bridge can do, let's take a look at creating and configuring Linux bridges.

Creating and configuring linux bridges

To configure Linux bridges, you'll use the same ip utility you've been using to configure and manage interfaces. Recall from the start of "Working with Interfaces" on page 62 we stated that interfaces are the basic building block of Linux networking. That statement holds true here, as bridges are treated as a type of interface by Linux.

What about brctl?

You may be familiar with an older command that is used to work with Linux bridges—specifically, the brctl command. Much in the same way that the ip command has superseded the older ifconfig command, the ip and bridge commands (the latter is discussed later in this section) supersede the older brctl. That being said, brctl is still available for most modern Linux distributions, and can still be used to manipulate Linux bridges. In this section, we'll focus on the newer commands that are part of the iproute2 packages.

To create a bridge, you'd use `ip link` with the `add` subcommand, like this:

```
vagrant@jessie:~$ ip link add name bridge-name type bridge
```

This would create a bridge that contains no interfaces (a configuration similar to Figure 3-7, earlier). You can verify this using the `ip link list` command. For example, if you had used the name br0 for *bridge-name* when you added the bridge, you'd use a command that looked something like this:

```
vagrant@jessie:~$ ip link list br0
5: br0: <BROADCAST,MULTICAST> mtu 1500 qdisc noqueue state DOWN mode DEFAULT
    group default
    link/ether 00:0c:29:5f:d2:15 brd ff:ff:ff:ff:ff:ff
vagrant@jessie:~$
```

You'll note that the new bridge interface is marked as DOWN; you'll need to use `ip link set` *bridge-name* up in order to bring the bridge interface up.

Once you've created the bridge, you can again use the `ip link` command to add a physical interface to the bridge. The general syntax for the command is `ip link set` *interface-name* set `master` *bridge-name*. So, if you wanted to add the eth1 interface to a bridge named br0, the command would look like this:

```
vagrant@jessie:~$ ip link set eth1 master br0
vagrant@jessie:~$
```

Your configuration now looks similar to Figure 3-8.

Once you have an interface added to a bridge, then the `bridge` command (part of the same iproute2 package that provides the `ip` command) becomes useful. As you've seen already in this chapter, different Linux distributions sometimes place the same command in different places. In this case, both Debian and Ubuntu put the `bridge` command in the */sbin* directory, while CentOS 7 puts it in the */usr/sbin* directory. Normally this isn't an issue, but in this case the default search path on Debian 8.1 does not include */sbin* (unless you're running as the root user, which is generally discouraged). This means you'll have to use the full path (*/sbin/bridge*) on Debian, or amend your search path to include the */sbin* directory. We'll assume that you've amended your search path and omit the full path to the `bridge` utility in our examples.

Using the `bridge` utility, you can show the interfaces that are part of a bridge with this command:

```
vagrant@trusty:~$ bridge link
3: eth1 state UP : <BROADCAST,MULTICAST,UP,LOWER_UP> mtu 1500 master br0 state
    forwarding priority 32 cost 4
vagrant@trusty:~$
```

The `bridge link` command shows all the interfaces that are part of the bridge; to see only a specific interface, you'd use `bridge link show dev` *interface-name*. The `bridge` command also enables you to edit specific properties of member interfaces, like enabling/disabling the processing of Bridge Protocol Data Units (BPDUs) or enabling/disabling whether traffic may be sent back out of the port on which it was received (hairpinning). We encourage you to have a look at the manual page for the `bridge` command for all the details (run `man bridge`).

To remove an interface from a bridge, you'll again use the `ip link` command, like this:

```
[vagrant@centos ~]$ ip link set interface-name nomaster
[vagrant@centos ~]$
```

Finally, to remove a bridge, the command is `ip link del` along with the name of the bridge to be removed. If you wanted to remove a bridge named `br0`, the command would look like this:

```
vagrant@trusty:~$ ip link del br0
vagrant@trusty:~$
```

Note that there is no need to remove interfaces from a bridge before removing the bridge itself.

All the commands we've shown you so far create nonpersistent configurations. In order to make these configurations persistent, you'll need to go back to "Interface configuration via the command line" on page 63. Why? Because Linux treats a bridge as a type of interface—in this case, a *logical* interface as opposed to a *physical* interface.

Because Linux treats bridges as interfaces, you'd use the same types of configuration files we discussed earlier: in RHEL/CentOS/Fedora, you'd use a file in */etc/sysconfig/network-scripts*, while in Debian/Ubuntu you'd use a configuration stanza in the file */etc/network/interfaces* (or a standalone configuration file in the */etc/network/interfaces.d* directory). Let's look at what a bridge configuration would look like in both CentOS and in Debian (Ubuntu will look very much like Debian).

In CentOS 7.1, you'd create an interface configuration file in */etc/sysconfig/network-scripts* for the bridge in question. So, for example, if you wanted to create a bridge named `br0`, you'd create a file named *ifcfg-br0*. Here's a sample interface configuration file for a bridge:

```
DEVICE=br0
TYPE=Bridge
ONBOOT=yes
BOOTPROTO=none
IPV6INIT=no
IPV6_AUTOCONF=no
DELAY=5
STP=yes
```

This creates a bridge named br0 that has Spanning Tree Protocol (STP) enabled. To add interfaces to the bridge, you'd have to modify the interface configuration files for the interfaces that should be part of the bridge. For example, if you wanted the interface named ens33 to be part of the br0 bridge, your interface configuration file for ens33 might look like this:

```
DEVICE=ens33
ONBOOT=yes
HOTPLUG=no
BOOTPROTO=none
TYPE=Ethernet
BRIDGE=br0
```

The BRIDGE parameter in this configuration file is what ties the interface named ens33 into the bridge br0.

Spanning Tree in Linux

You may have noticed that the example configuration file for a bridge under CentOS 7 has STP enabled. The Linux kernel has an STP implementation, but that implementation is being phased out in favor of implementations that live in userspace. For this reason, you can only use configuration files or the older brctl utility to manage the older in-kernel implementation.

One thing you'll note is that neither br0 nor ens33 has an IP address assigned. It's best, perhaps, to reason about this in the following way: on a typical network switch, a standard switch port that is configured for Layer 2 only isn't addressable via an IP address. That's the configuration we've replicated here: br0 is the switch, and ens33 is the Layer 2–only port that is part of the switch.

If you *did* want an IP address assigned (perhaps for management purposes, or perhaps because you also want to leverage Layer 3 functionality in Linux), then you can assign an IP address to the *bridge*, but *not* to the member interfaces in the bridge. Again, you can make an analogy to traditional network hardware here—it's like giving the switch a management IP address, but the individual Layer 2–only switch ports still aren't addressable by IP. To provide an IP address to the bridge interface, just add the IPADDR, NETMASK, and GATEWAY directives in the bridge's interface configuration file.

Debian (and therefore Ubuntu) are similar. In the case of setting up a bridge on Debian, you would typically add a configuration stanza to the */etc/network/interfaces* file to configure the bridge itself, like this:

```
iface br0 inet manual
    up ip link set $IFACE up
    down ip link set $IFACE down
    bridge-ports eth1
```

This would create a bridge named br0 with the eth1 interface as a member of the bridge. Note that no configuration is needed in the configuration stanzas for the interfaces that are named as members of the bridge.

If you want an IP address assigned to the bridge interface, simply change the inet manual to inet dhcp (for DHCP) or inet static (for static address assignment). When using static address assignment, you'd also need to include the appropriate configuration lines to assign the IP address (specifically, the address, netmask, and optionally the gateway directives).

Once you have configuration files in place for the Linux bridge, then the bridging configuration will be restored when the system boots, making it persistent. (You can verify this using ip link list.)

For more practical examples and details of how Linux bridges are used, refer to Appendix A.

Summary

In this chapter, we've provided a brief history of Linux, and why it's important to understand a little bit of Linux as you progress down the path of network automation and programmability. We've also supplied some basic information on interacting with Linux, working with Linux daemons, and configuring Linux networking. We discussed using Linux as a router and explored the functionality of the Linux bridge.

In our introduction to this chapter, we mentioned that one of the reasons we felt it was important to include some information on Linux was because some of the tools we'd be discussing have their roots in Linux or are best used on a Linux system. In the next chapter we'll be discussing one such tool: the Python programming language.

## CHAPTER 4

Learning Python in a Network Context

As a network engineer, there has never been a better time for you to learn to auto-mate and write code. As we articulated in Chapter 1, the network industry is funda-mentally changing. It is a fact that networking had not changed much from the late 1990s to about 2010, both architecturally and operationally. In that span of time as a network engineer, you undoubtedly typed in the same CLI commands hundreds, if not thousands, of times to configure and troubleshoot network devices. Why the madness?

It is specifically around the operations of a network that learning to read and write some code starts to make sense. In fact, scripting or writing a few lines of code to gather information on the network, or to make change, isn't new at all. It's been done for years. There are engineers who took on this feat—coding in their language of choice, learning to work with raw text using complex parsing, regular expressions, and querying SNMP MIBs in a script. If you've ever attempted this yourself, you know firsthand that it's possible, but working with regular expressions and parsing text is time-consuming and tedious.

Luckily, things are starting to move in the right direction and the barrier to entry for network automation is more accessible than ever before. We are seeing advances from network vendors, but also in the open source tooling that is available to use for automating the network, both of which we cover in this book. For example, there are now network device APIs, vendor- and community-supported Python libraries, and freely available open source tools that give you and every other network engineer access to a growing ecosystem to jump start your network automation journey. This ultimately means that you have to write less code than you would have in the past, and less code means faster development and fewer bugs.

Before we dive into the basics of Python, there is one more important question that we'll take a look at because it always comes up in conversation among network engineers: *Should network engineers learn to code?*

Should Network Engineers Learn to Code?

Unfortunately, you aren't getting a definitive *yes* or *no* from us. Clearly, we have a full chapter on Python and plenty of other examples throughout the book on how to use Python to communicate to network devices using network APIs and extend DevOps platforms like Ansible, Salt, and Puppet, so we definitely think learning the basics of any programming language is valuable. We also think it'll become an even more valuable skill as the network and IT industries continue to transform at such a rapid pace, and we happen to think Python is a pretty great first choice.

It's worth pointing out that we do not hold any technology religion to Python. However, we feel when it comes to network automation it is a great first choice for several reasons. First, Python is a dynamically typed language that allows you to create and use Python objects (such as variables and functions) where and when needed, meaning they don't need to be defined before you start using them. This simplifies the getting started process. Second, Python is also super readable. It's common to see conditional statements like `if device in device_list:`, and in that statement, you can easily decipher that we are simply checking to see if a device is *in* a particular list of devices. Another reason is that network vendors and open source projects are building a great set of libraries and tools using Python. This just adds to the benefit of learning to program with Python.

The real question, though, is *should every network engineer know how to read and write a basic script*? The answer to that question would be a definite *yes*. Now *should every network engineer become a software developer*? Absolutely not. Many engineers will gravitate more toward one discipline than the next, and maybe some network engineers do transition to become developers, but all types of engineers, not just network engineers, *should not* fear trying to read through some Python or Ruby, or even more advanced languages like C or Go. System administrators have done fairly well already with using scripting as a tool to allow them to do their jobs more efficiently by using bash scripts, Python, Ruby, and PowerShell.

On the other hand, this hasn't been the case for network administrators (which is a major reason for this book!). As the industry progresses and engineers evolve, it's very realistic for you, as a network engineer, to be more *DevOps oriented*, in that you end up somewhere in the middle—not as a developer, but also not as a traditional CLI-only network engineer. You could end up using open source configuration management and automation tools and then add a little code as necessary (and if needed) to accomplish and automate the workflows and tasks in your specific environment.

Unless your organization warrants it based on size, scale, compliance, or control, it's not common or recommended to write custom software *for everything* and build a home-grown automation platform. It's not an efficient use of time. What is recommended is that you understand the components involved in programming, software development, and especially fundamentals such as core data types that are common in all tools and languages, as we cover in this chapter focused on Python.

So we know the industry is changing, devices have APIs, and it makes sense to start the journey to learn to write some code. This chapter provides you with the building blocks to go from 0 to 60 to help you start your Python journey.

Throughout the rest of this chapter, we cover the following topics:

- Using the Python interactive interpreter
- Understanding Python data types
- Adding conditional logic to your code
- Understanding containment
- Using loops in Python
- Functions
- Working with files
- Creating Python programs
- Working with Python modules

Get ready—we are about to jump in and learn some Python!

This chapter's sole focus is to provide an introduction to Python foundational concepts for network engineers looking to learn Python to augment their existing skillsets. It is not intended to provide an exhaustive education for full-time developers to write production-quality Python software.

Additionally, please note the concepts covered in this chapter are heavily relevant outside the scope of Python. For example, you *must* understand concepts like loops and data types—which we'll explore here—in order to work with tools like Ansible, Salt, Puppet, and StackStorm.

Using the Python Interactive Interpreter

The Python interactive interpreter isn't always known by those just starting out to learn to program or even those who have been developing in other languages, but we think it is a tool that everyone should know and learn before trying to create stand-alone executable scripts.

The interpreter is a tool that is instrumental to developers of all experience levels. The Python interactive interpreter, also commonly known as the Python *shell*, is used as a learning platform for beginners, but it's also used by the most experienced developers to test and get real-time feedback without having to write a full program or script.

The Python shell, or interpreter, is found on nearly all native Linux distributions as well as many of the more modern network operating systems from vendors including, but not limited to, Cisco, HP, Juniper, Cumulus, and Arista.

To enter the Python interactive interpreter, you simply open a Linux terminal window, or SSH to a modern network device, type in the command `python`, and hit Enter.

All examples throughout this chapter that denote a Linux terminal command start with $. While you're at the Python shell, all lines and commands start with >>>. Additionally, all examples shown are from a system running Ubuntu 14.04 LTS and Python 2.7.6.

After entering the `python` command and hitting Enter, you are taken directly into the *shell*. While in the *shell*, you start writing Python code immediately! There is no text editor, no IDE, and no prerequisites to getting started.

```
$ python
Python 2.7.6 (default, Mar 22 2014, 22:59:56)
[GCC 4.8.2] on linux2
Type "help", "copyright", "credits" or "license" for more information.
>>>
```

Although we are jumping into much more detail on Python throughout this chapter, we'll take a quick look at a few examples right now to see the power of the Python interpreter.

The following example creates a variable called `hostname` and assigns it the value of ROUTER_1.

```
>>> hostname = 'ROUTER_1'
>>>
```

Notice that you did not need to declare the variable first or define that hostname was going to be of type string. This is a departure from some programming languages such as C and Java, and a reason why Python is called a dynamic language.

Let's print the variable hostname.

```
>>> print(hostname)
ROUTER_1
>>>
>>> hostname
'ROUTER_1'
>>>
```

Once you've created the variable you can easily print it using the print command, but while in the shell, you have the ability to also display the value of hostname or any variable by just typing in the name of the variable and pressing Enter. One difference to point out between these two methods is that when you use the print statement, characters such as the end of line (or \n) are interpreted, but are not when you're not using the print statement.

For example, using print interprets the \n and a new line is printed, but when you're just typing the variable name into the shell and hitting Enter, the \n is not interpreted and is just displayed to the terminal.

```
>>> banner = "\n\n   WELCOME TO ROUTER_1   \n\n"
>>>
>>> print(banner)


   WELCOME TO ROUTER_1


>>>
>>> banner
'\n\n   WELCOME TO ROUTER_1   \n\n'
>>>
```

Can you see the difference?

When you are validating or testing, the Python shell is a great tool to use. In the preceding examples, you may have noticed that single quotes and double quotes were both used. Now you may be thinking, could they be used together on the same line? Let's not speculate about it; let's use the Python shell to test it out.

```
>>> hostname = 'ROUTER_1"
  File "<stdin>", line 1
    hostname = 'ROUTER_1"
                        ^
SyntaxError: EOL while scanning string literal
>>>
```

And just like that, we verified that Python supports both single and double quotes, but learned they cannot be used together.

Most examples throughout this chapter continue to use the Python interpreter—feel free to follow along and test them out as they're covered.

We'll continue to use the Python interpreter as we review the different Python data types with a specific focus on networking.

Understanding Python Data Types

This section provides an overview of various Python data types including strings, numbers (integers and floats), booleans, lists, and dictionaries and also touches upon tuples and sets.

The sections on strings, lists, and dictionaries are broken up into two parts. The first is an introduction to the data type and the second covers some of its *built-in methods*. As you'll see, *methods* are natively part of Python, making it extremely easy for developers to manipulate and work with each respective data type.

For example, a method called `upper` that takes a string and converts it to all uppercase letters can be executed with the statement, `"router1".upper()`, which returns `ROUTER1`. We'll show many more examples of using methods throughout this chapter.

The sections on integers and booleans provide an overview to show you how to use mathematical operators and boolean expressions while writing code in Python.

Finally, we close the section on data types by providing a brief introduction to tuples and sets. They are more advanced data types, but we felt they were still worth covering in an introduction to Python.

Table 4-1 describes and highlights each data type we're going to cover in this chapter. This should act as a reference throughout the chapter.

Table 4-1. Python data types summary

Data Type	Description	Short Name (Type)	Characters	Example
String	Series of any characters surrounded by quotes	`str`	`""`	`hostname="nycr01"`
Integer	Whole numbers represented without quotes	`int`	n/a	`eos_qty=5`

Data Type	Description	Short Name (Type)	Characters	Example
Float	Floating point number (decimals)	`float`	n/a	`cpu_util=52.33`
Boolean	Either True or False (no quotes)	`bool`	n/a	`is_switchport=True`
List	Ordered sequence of values. Values can be of any data type.	`list`	`[]`	`vendors=['cisco', 'juniper', 'arista', 'cisco']`
Dictionary	Unordered list of key-value pairs	`dict`	`{}`	`facts={"vendor":"cisco", "platform":"catalyst", "os":"ios"}`
Set	Unordered collection of unique elements	`set`	`set()`	`set(vendors)=>['cisco', 'juniper', 'arista']`
Tuple	Ordered and unchangeable sequence of values	`tuple`	`()`	`ipaddr=(10.1.1.1, 24)`

Let's get started and take a look at Python strings.

Learning to Use Strings

Strings are a sequence of characters that are enclosed by quotes and are arguably the most well-known data type that exists in all programming languages.

Earlier in the chapter, we looked at a few basic examples for creating variables that were of type `string`. Let's examine what else you need to know when starting to use strings.

First, we'll define two new variables that are both strings: `final` and `ipaddr`.

```
>>> final = 'The IP address of router1 is: '
>>>
>>> ipaddr = '1.1.1.1'
>>>
```

You can use the built-in function called `type` to verify the data type of any given object in Python.

```
>>> type(final)
<type 'str'>
>>>
```

This is how you can easily verify the type of an object, which is often helpful in troubleshooting code, especially if it's code you didn't write.

Next, let's look at how to combine, add, or *concatenate* strings.

```
>>> final + ipaddr
'The IP address of router1 is: 1.1.1.1'
```

This example created two new variables: `final` and `ipaddr`. Each is a string. After they were both created, we *concatenated* them using the + operator, and finally printed them out. Fairly easy, right?

The same could be done even if `final` was not a predefined object:

```
>>> print('The IP address of router1 is: ' + ipaddr)
The IP address of router1 is: 1.1.1.1
>>>
```

Using built-in methods of strings

To view the available built-in methods for strings, you use the built-in `dir()` function while in the Python shell. You first create any variable that is a string or use the formal data type name of `str` and pass it as an argument to `dir()` to view the available methods.

`dir()` can be used on any Python object, not just strings, as we'll show throughout this chapter.

```
>>>
>>> dir(str)
# output has been omitted
['__add__', '__class__', '__contains__', '__delattr__', '__doc__',
'endswith', 'expandtabs', 'find', 'format', 'index', 'isalnum', 'isalpha',
'isdigit', 'islower', 'isspace', 'istitle', 'isupper', 'join', 'lower',
'lstrip', 'replace', rstrip', 'split', 'splitlines', 'startswith',
'strip', 'upper']
>>>
```

To reiterate what we said earlier, it's possible to also pass any string to the `dir()` function to produce the same output as above. For example, if you defined a variable such as hostname = 'ROUTER', hostname can be passed to dir()—that is, dir(hostname) —producing the same output as dir(str) to determine what methods are available for strings.

Using dir() can be a lifesaver to verify what the available methods are for a given data type, so don't forget this one.

Everything with a single or double underscore from the previous output is not reviewed in this book, as our goal is to provide a practitioner's introduction to Python, but it is worth pointing out those methods with underscores are used by the internals of Python.

Let's take a look at several of the string methods, including count, endswith, starts with, format, isdigit, join, lower, upper, and strip.

In order to learn how to use a given method that you see in the output of a dir(), you can use the built-in function called help(). In order to use the built-in help feature, you pass in the object (or variable) and the given method. The following examples show two ways you can use help() and learn how to use the upper method:

```
>>> help(str.upper)
>>>
>>> help(hostname.upper)
>>>
```

The output of each is the following:

```
Help on method_descriptor:

upper(...)
    S.upper() -> string

    Return a copy of the string S converted to uppercase.
(END)
```

When you're finished, enter **Q** to *quit* viewing the built-in help.

As we review each method, there are two key questions that you should be asking yourself. What value is returned from the method? And what action is the method performing on the original object?

Using the upper() and lower() methods. Using the upper() and lower() methods is helpful when you need to compare strings that do not need to be case-sensitive. For example, maybe you need to accept a variable that is the name of an interface such as

"Ethernet1/1," but want to also allow the user to enter "ethernet1/1." The best way to compare these is to use upper() or lower().

```
>>> interface = 'Ethernet1/1'
>>>
>>> interface.lower()
'ethernet1/1'
>>>
>>> interface.upper()
'ETHERNET1/1'
>>>
```

You can see that when you're using a method, the format is to enter the object name, or string in this case, and then append .methodname().

After executing interface.lower(), notice that ethernet1/1 was printed to the terminal. This is telling us that ethernet1/1 was *returned* when lower() was executed. The same holds true for upper(). When something is returned, you also have the ability to assign it as the value to a new or existing variable.

```
>>> intf_lower = interface.lower()
>>>
>>> print(intf_lower)
ethernet1/1
>>>
```

In this example, you can see how to use the method, but also assign the data being returned to a variable.

What about the original variable called interface? Let's see what, if anything, changed with interface.

```
>>> print(interface)
Ethernet1/1
>>>
```

Since this is the first example, it still may not be clear what we're looking for to see if something changed in the original variable interface, but we do know that it still holds the value of Ethernet1/1 and nothing changed. Don't worry, we'll see plenty of examples of when the original object is modified throughout this chapter.

Using the startswith() and endswith() methods.   As you can probably guess, starts with() is used to verify whether a string starts with a certain sequence of characters, and endswith() is used to verify whether a string ends with a certain sequence of characters.

```
>>> ipaddr = '10.100.20.5'
>>>
>>> ipaddr.startswith('10')
True
>>>
```

```
>>> ipaddr.startswith('100')
False
>>>
>>> ipaddr.endswith('.5')
True
>>>
```

In the previous examples that used the lower() and upper() methods, they returned a string, and that string was a modified string with all lowercase or uppercase letters.

In the case of startswith(), it does not return a string, but rather a boolean (bool) object. As you'll learn later in this chapter, boolean values are True and False. The startswith() method returns True if the sequence of characters being passed in matches the respective starting or ending sequence of the object. Otherwise, it returns False.

 Take note that boolean values are either True or False, no quotes are used for booleans, and the first letter must be capitalized. Booleans are covered in more detail later in the chapter.

Using these methods proves to be valuable when you're looking to verify the start or end of a string. Maybe it's to verify the first or fourth octet of an IPv4 address, or maybe to verify an interface name, just like we had in the previous example using lower(). Rather than assume a user of a script was going to enter the full name, it's advantageous to do a check on the first two characters to allow the user to input "ethernet1/1," "eth1/1," and "et1/1."

For this check, we'll show how to combine methods, or use the return value of one method as the base string object for the second method.

```
>>> interface = 'Eth1/1'
>>>
>>> interface.lower().startswith('et')
True
>>>
```

As seen from this code, we verify it is an Ethernet interface by first executing lower(), which returns eth1/1, and then the boolean check is performed to see whether "eth1/1" starts with "et". And, clearly, it does.

Of course, there are other things that could be invalid beyond the "eth" in an interface string object, but the point is that methods can be easily used together.

Using the strip() method. Many network devices still don't have application programming interfaces, or APIs. It is almost guaranteed that at some point if you want to write a script, you'll try it out on an older CLI-based device. If you do this, you'll be sure to encounter globs of raw text coming back from the device—this could be the result of any show command from the output of show interfaces to a full show running-config.

When you need to store or simply print something, you may not want any whitespace wrapping the object you want to use or see. In trying to be consistent with previous examples, this may be an IP address.

What if the object you're working with has the value of " 10.1.50.1 " including the whitespace. The methods startswith() or endswith() do not work because of the spaces. For these situations, strip() is used to remove the whitespace.

```
>>> ipaddr = '   10.1.50.1   '
>>>
>>>
>>> ipaddr.strip()
'10.1.50.1'
>>>
```

Using strip() returned the object without any spaces on both sides. Examples aren't shown for lstrip() or rstrip(), but they are two other built-in methods for strings that remove whitespace specifically on the left side or right side of a string object.

Using the isdigit() method. There) may be times you're working with strings, but need to verify the string object is a number. Technically, integers are a different data type (covered in the next section), but numbers can still be values in strings.

Using isdigit() makes it extremely straightforward to see whether the character or string is actually a *digit*.

```
>>> ten = '10'
>>>
>>> ten.isdigit()
True
>>>
>>> bogus = '10a'
>>>
>>> bogus.isdigit()
False
```

Just as with startswith(), isdigit() also returns a boolean. It returns True if the value is an integer, otherwise it returns False.

Using the count() method. Imagine working with a binary number—maybe it's to calculate an IP address or subnet mask. While there are some built-in libraries to do binary-to-decimal conversion, what if you just want to *count* how many 1's or 0's are in a given string? You can use count() to do this for you.

```
>>> octet = '11111000'
>>>
>>> octet.count('1')
5
```

The example shows how easy it is to use the count() method. This method, however, returns an int (integer) unlike any of the previous examples.

When using count(), you are not limited to sending a single character as a parameter either.

```
>>> octet.count('111')
1
>>>
>>> test_string = "Don't you wish you started programming a little earlier?"
>>>
>>> test_string.count('you')
2
```

Using the format() method. We saw earlier how to concatenate strings. Imagine needing to create a sentence, or better yet, a command to send to a network device that is built from several strings or variables. How would you *format* the string, or CLI command?

Let's use ping as an example and assume the command that needs to be created is the following:

```
ping 8.8.8.8 vrf management
```

 In the examples in this chapter, the network CLI commands being used are generic, as no actual device connections are being made. Thus, they map to no specific vendor as they are the "industry standard" examples that work on various vendors including Cisco IOS, Cisco NXOS, Arista EOS, and many others.

If you were writing a script, it's more than likely the target IP address you want to send ICMP echo requests to and the virtual routing and forwarding (VRF) will both be user input parameters. In this particular example, it means '8.8.8.8' and 'management' are the input arguments (parameters).

One way to build the string is to start with the following:

```
>>> ipaddr = '8.8.8.8'
>>> vrf = 'management'
>>>
>>> ping = 'ping' + ipaddr + 'vrf' + vrf
>>>
>>> print(ping)
ping8.8.8.8vrfmanagement
```

You see the spacing is incorrect, so there are two options—add spaces to your input objects or within the `ping` object. Let's look at adding them within `ping`.

```
>>> ping = 'ping' + ' ' + ipaddr + ' ' + 'vrf ' + vrf
>>>
>>> print(ping)
ping 8.8.8.8 vrf management
```

As you can see, this works quite well and is not too complicated, but as the strings or commands get longer, it can get quite messy dealing with all of the quotes and spaces. Using the `format()` method can simplify this.

```
>>> ping = 'ping {} vrf {}'.format(ipaddr, vrf)
>>>
>>> print(ping)
ping 8.8.8.8 vrf management
```

The `format()` method takes a number of arguments, which are inserted between the curly braces (`{}`) found within the string. Notice how the `format()` method is being used on a raw string, unlike the previous examples.

> It's possible to use any of the string methods on both variables or raw strings. This is true for any other data type and its built-in methods as well.

The next example shows using the `format()` method, with a pre-created string object (variable) in contrast to the previous example, when it was used on a raw string.

```
>>> ping = 'ping {} vrf {}'
>>>
>>> command = ping.format(ipaddr, vrf)
>>>
>>> print(command)
ping 8.8.8.8 vrf management
```

This scenario is more likely, in that you would have have a predefined command in a Python script with users inputting two arguments, and the output is the final command string that gets pushed to a network device.

Using the join() and split() methods.   These are the last methods for strings covered in this chapter. We saved them for last since they include working with another data type called `list`.

> Be aware that lists are formally covered later in the chapter, but we wanted to include a very brief introduction here in order to show the `join()` and `split()` methods for string objects.

Lists are exactly what they sound like. They are a *list* of objects—each object is called an *element*, and each element is of the same or different data type. Note that there is no requirement to have all elements in a list be of the same data type.

If you had an environment with five routers, you may have a list of hostnames.

```
>>> hostnames = ['r1', 'r2', 'r3', 'r4', 'r5']
```

You can also build a list of commands to send to a network device to make a configuration change. The next example is a list of commands to shut down an Ethernet interface on a switch.

```
>>> commands = ['config t', 'interface Ethernet1/1', 'shutdown']
```

It's quite common to build a list like this, but if you're using a traditional CLI-based network device, you might not be able to send a list object directly to the device. The device may require strings be sent (or individual commands).

join() is one such method that can take a list and create a string, but insert required characters, if needed, between them.

Remember that \n is the end of line (EOL) character. When sending commands to a device, you may need to insert a \n between commands to allow the device to render a new line for the next command.

If we take commands from the previous example, we can see how to leverage join() to create a single string with a \n inserted between each command.

```
>>> '\n'.join(commands)
'config t\ninterface Ethernet1/1\nshutdown'
>>>
```

Another practical example is when using an API such as NX-API that exists on Cisco Nexus switches. Cisco gives the option to send a string of commands, but they need to be separated by a semicolon (;).

To do this, you would use the same approach.

```
>>> ' ; '.join(commands)
'config t ; interface Ethernet1/1 ; shutdown'
>>>
```

In this example, we added a space before and after the semicolon, but it's the same overall approach.

> In the examples shown, a semicolon and an EOL character were used as the seperator, but you should know that you don't need to use any characters at all. It's possible to concatenate the elements in the list without inserting any characters, like this: ''.join(list).

You learned how to use join() to create a string out of a list, but what if you needed to do the exact opposite and create a list from a string? One option is to use the split() method.

In the next example, we start with the previously generated string, and convert it back to a list.

```
>>> commands = 'config t ; interface Ethernet1/1 ; shutdown'
>>>
>>> cmds_list = commands.split(' ; ')
>>>
>>> print(cmds_list)
['config t', 'interface Ethernet1/1', 'shutdown']
>>>
```

This shows how simple it is to take a string object and create a list from it. Another common example for networking is to take an IP address (string) and convert it to a list using split(), creating a list of four elements—one element per octet.

```
>>> ipaddr = '10.1.20.30'
>>>
>>> ipaddr.split('.')
['10', '1', '20', '30']
>>>
```

That covered the basics of working with Python strings. Let's move on to the next data type, which is numbers.

Learning to Use Numbers

We don't spend much time on different types of numbers such as floats (decimal numbers) or imaginary numbers, but we do briefly look at the data type that is denoted as int, better known as an integer. Quite frankly, this is because most people understand numbers and there aren't built-in methods that make sense to cover at this point. Rather than cover built-in methods for integers, we take a look at using mathematical operators while in the Python shell.

You should also be aware that decimal numbers in Python are referred to as *floats*. Remember, you can always verify the data type by using the built-in function type():

```
>>> cpu = 41.3
>>>
>>> type(cpu)
<type 'float'>
>>>
>>>
```

Performing mathematical operations

If you need to add numbers, there is nothing fancy needed: just add them.

```
>>> 5 + 3
8
>>> a = 1
>>> b = 2
>>> a + b
3
```

There may be a time when a counter is needed as you are looping through a sequence of objects. You may want to say `counter = 1`, perform some type of operation, and then do `counter = counter + 1`. While this is perfectly functional and works, it is more idiomatic in Python to perform the operation as `counter += 1`. This is shown in the next example.

```
>>> counter = 1
>>> counter = counter + 1
>>> counter
2
>>>
>>> counter = 5
>>> counter += 5
>>>
>>> counter
10
```

Very similar to addition, there is nothing special for subtraction. We'll dive right into an example.

```
>>> 100 - 90
10
>>> count = 50
>>> count - 20
30
>>>
```

When multiplying, yet again, there is no difference. Here is a quick example.

```
>>> 100 * 50
5000
>>>
>>> print(2 * 25)
50
>>>
```

The nice thing about the multiplication operator (*) is that it's also possible to use it on strings. You may want to format something and make it nice and pretty.

```
>>> print('*' * 50)
**************************************************
>>>
>>> print('=' * 50)
```

```
=======================================================
>>>
```

The preceding example is extremely basic, and at the same time extremely powerful. Not knowing this is possible, you may be tempted to print one line a time and print a string with the command `print(*******************)`, but in reality after learning this and a few other tips covered later in the chapter, pretty-printing text data becomes much simpler.

If you haven't performed any math by hand in recent years, division may seem like a nightmare. As expected, though, it is no different than the previous three mathematical operations reviewed. Well, sort of.

There is not a difference with how you enter what you want to accomplish. To perform an operation you still use `10 / 2` or `100 / 50`, and so on, like so:

```
>>> 100 / 50
2
>>>
>>> 10/ 2
5
>>>
```

These examples are probably what you expected to see.

The difference is what is returned when there is a remainder:

```
>>> 12 / 10
1
>>>
```

As you know, the number 10 goes into 12 *one* time. This is what is known as the *quotient*, so here the quotient is equal to 1. What is not displayed or returned is the *remainder*. To see the remainder in Python, you must use the `%`, or modulus operation.

```
>>> 12 % 10
2
>>>
```

This means to fully calculate the result of a division problem, both the `/` and `%` operators are used.

That was a brief look at how to work with numbers in Python. We'll now move on to booleans.

Learning to Use Booleans

Boolean objects, otherwise known as objects that are of type `bool` in Python, are fairly straightforward. Let's first review the basics of general boolean logic by looking at a *truth table* (Table 4-2).

Table 4-2. Boolean truth table

A	B	A and B	A or B	Not A
False	False	False	False	True
False	True	False	True	True
True	False	False	True	False
True	True	True	True	False

Notice how all values in the table are either `True` or `False`. This is because with boolean logic all values are reduced to either `True` or `False`. This actually makes booleans easy to understand.

Since boolean values can be only `True` or `False`, all expressions also evaluate to either `True` or `False`. You can see in the table that BOTH values, for A and B, need to be `True`, for "A and B" to evaluate to `True`. And "A or B" evaluates to `True` when ANY value (A or B) is `True`. You can also see that when you take the *NOT* of a boolean value, it calculates the inverse of that value. This is seen clearly as "NOT False" yields True and "NOT True" yields `False`.

From a Python perspective, nothing is different. We still only have two boolean values, and they are `True` and `False`. To assign one of these values to a variable within Python, you must enter it just as you see it, (with a capitalized first letter, and without quotes).

```
>>> exists = True
>>>
>>> exists
True
>>>
>>> exists = true
Traceback (most recent call last):
  File "<stdin>", line 1, in <module>
NameError: name 'true' is not defined
>>>
```

As you can see in this example, it is quite simple. Based on the real-time feedback of the Python interpreter, we can see that using a lowercase *t* doesn't work when we're trying to assign the value of `True` to a variable.

Here are a few more examples of using boolean expressions while in the Python interpreter.

```
>>> True and True
True
>>>
>>> True or False
True
>>>
```

```
>>> False or False
False
>>>
```

In the next example, these same conditions are evaluated, assigning boolean values to variables.

```
>>> value1 = True
>>> value2 = False
>>>
>>> value1 and value2
False
>>>
>>> value1 or value2
True
>>>
```

Notice that boolean expressions are also not limited to two objects.

```
>>> value3 = True
>>> value4 = True
>>>
>>> value1 and value2 and value3 and value4
False
>>>
>>> value1 and value3 and value4
True
>>>
```

When extracting information from a network device, it is quite common to use booleans for a quick check. Is the interface a routed port? Is the management interface configured? Is the device reachable? While there may be a complex operation to answer each of those questions, the result is stored as True or False.

The counter to those questions would be, is the interface a switched port or is the device not reachable? It wouldn't make sense to have variables or objects for each question, but we could use the not operator, since we know the not operation returns the inverse of a boolean value.

Let's take a look at using not in an example.

```
>>> not False
>>> True
>>>
>>> is_layer3 = True
>>> not is_layer3
False
>>>
```

In this example, there is a variable called is_layer3. It is set to True, indicating that an interface is a Layer 3 port. If we take the not of is_layer3, we would then know if it is a Layer 2 port.

We'll be taking a look at conditionals (`if-else` statements) later in the chapter, but based on the logic needed, you may need to know if an interface is in fact Layer 3. If so, you would have something like `if is_layer3:`, but if you needed to perform an action if the interface was Layer 2, then you would use `if not is_layer3:`.

In addition to using the and and or operands, the *equal to* == and *does not equal to* != expressions are used to generate a boolean object. With these expressions, you can do a comparison, or check, to see if two or more objects are (or not) equal to one another.

```
>>> True == True
True
>>>
>>> True != False
True
>>>
>>> 'network' == 'network'
True
>>>
>>> 'network' == 'no_network'
False
>>>
```

After a quick look at working with boolean objects, operands, and expressions, we are ready to cover how to work with Python lists.

Learning to Use Python Lists

You had a brief introduction to lists when we covered the string built-in methods called `join()` and `split()`. Lists are now covered in a bit more detail.

Lists are the object type called `list`, and at their most basic level are an ordered sequence of objects. The examples from earlier in the chapter when we looked at the `join()` method with strings are provided again next to provide a quick refresher on how to create a list. Those examples were lists of strings, but it's also possible to have lists of any other data type as well, which we'll see shortly.

```
>>> hostnames = ['r1', 'r2', 'r3', 'r4', 'r5']
>>> commands = ['config t', 'interface Ethernet1/1', 'shutdown']
>>>
```

The next example shows a list of objects where each object is a different data type!

```
>>> new_list = ['router1', False, 5]
>>>
>>> print(new_list)
['router1', False, 5]
>>>
```

Now you understand that lists are an ordered sequence of objects and are enclosed by brackets. One of the most common tasks when you're working with lists is to access an individual element of the list.

Let's create a new list of interfaces and show how to print a single element of a list.

```
>>> interfaces = ['Eth1/1', 'Eth1/2', 'Eth1/3', 'Eth1/4']
>>>
```

The list is created and now three elements of the list are printed one at a time.

```
>>> print(interfaces[0])
Eth1/1
>>>
>>> print(interfaces[1])
Eth1/2
>>>
>>> print(interfaces[2])
Eth1/3
>>>
```

To access the individual elements within a list, you use the element's *index* value enclosed within brackets. It's important to see that the index begins at 0 and ends at the "length of the list minus 1." This means in our example, to access the first element you use interfaces[0] and to access the last element you use interfaces[3].

In the example, we can easily see that the length of the list is four, but what if you didn't know the length of the list?

Luckily Python provides a built-in function called len() to help with this.

```
>>> len(interfaces)
4
>>>
```

Another way to access the last element in any list is: list[-1].

```
>>> interfaces[-1]
'Eth1/4'
>>>
```

Oftentimes, the terms *function* and *method* are used interchangeably, but up until now we've mainly looked at methods, not functions. The slight difference is that a function is called without referencing a parent object. As you saw, when you use a built-in method of an object, it is called using the syntax object.method(), and when you use functions like len(), you call it directly. That said, it is very common to call a method a function.

Using built-in methods of Python lists

To view the available built-in methods for lists, the dir() function is used just like we showed previously when working with string objects. You can create any variable that is a list or use the formal data type name of list and pass it as an argument to dir(). We'll use the interfaces list for this.

```
>>> dir(interfaces)
['append', 'count', 'extend', 'index', 'insert', 'pop', 'remove', 'reverse',
'sort']
```

In order to keep the output clean and simplify the example, we've removed all objects that start and end with underscores.

Let's take a look at a few of these built-in methods.

Using the append() method. The great thing about these method names, as you'll continue to see, is that they are human readable, and for the most part, intuitive. The append() method is used to *append* an element to an existing list.

This is shown in the next example, but let's start with creating an empty list. You do so by assigning empty brackets to an object.

```
>>> vendors = []
>>>
```

Let's append, or add vendors to this list.

```
>>> vendors.append('arista')
>>>
>>> print(vendors)
['arista']
>>>
>>> vendors.append('cisco')
>>>
>>> print(vendors)
['arista', 'cisco']
>>>
```

You can see that using append() adds the element to the *last* position in the list. In contrast to many of the methods reviewed for strings, this method is *not* returning anything, but modifying the original variable, or object.

Using the insert() method. Rather than just *append* an element to a list, you may need to *insert* an element at a specific location. This is done with the insert() method.

To use insert(), you need to pass it two arguments. The first argument is the position, or index, where the new element gets stored, and the second argument is the actual object getting inserted into the list.

In the next example, we'll look at building a list of commands.

```
>>> commands = ['interface Eth1/1', 'ip address 1.1.1.1/32']
```

 As a reminder, the commands in these examples are generic and do not map back to a specific vendor or platform.

Let's now assume we need to add two more commands to the list ['interface Eth1/1', 'ip address 1.1.1.1/32']. The command that needs to be added as the first element is config t and the one that needs to be added just before the IP address is no switchport.

```
>>> commands = ['interface Eth1/1', 'ip address 1.1.1.1/32']
>>>
>>> commands.insert(0, 'config t')
>>>
>>> print(commands)
['config t', 'interface Eth1/1', 'ip address 1.1.1.1/32']
>>>
>>> commands.insert(2, 'no switchport')
>>>
>>> print(commands)
['config t', 'interface Eth1/1', 'no switchport', 'ip address 1.1.1.1/32']
>>>
```

Using the count() method. If you are doing an inventory of types of devices throughout the network, you may build a list that has more than one of the same object within a list. To expand on the example from earlier, you may have a list that looks like this:

```
>>> vendors = ['cisco', 'cisco', 'juniper', 'arista', 'cisco', 'hp', 'cumulus',
'arista', 'cisco']
>>>
```

You can *count* how many instances of a given object are found by using the count() method. In our example, this can help determine how many Cisco or Arista devices there are in the environment.

```
>>> vendors.count('cisco')
4
>>>
>>> vendors.count('arista')
2
>>>
```

Take note that count() returns an int, or integer, and does not modify the existing object like insert(), append(), and a few others that are reviewed in the upcoming examples.

Using the pop() and index() methods. Most of the methods thus far have either modified the original object or returned something. pop() does both.

```
>>> hostnames = ['r1', 'r2', 'r3', 'r4', 'r5']
>>>
```

The preceding example has a list of hostnames. Let's pop (remove) r5 because that device was just decommissioned from the network.

```
>>> hostnames.pop()
'r5'
>>>
>>> print(hostnames)
['r1', 'r2', 'r3', 'r4']
>>>
```

As you can see, the element being popped is returned *and* the original list is modified as well.

You should have also noticed that no element or index value was passed in, so you can see by default, pop() pops the last element in the list.

What if you need to pop "r2"? It turns out that in order to *pop* an element that is not the last element, you need to pass in an index value of the element that you wish to pop. But how do you find the index value of a given element? This is where the index() method comes into play.

To find the index value of a certain element, you use the index() method.

```
>>> hostnames.index('r2')
1
>>>
```

Here you see that the index of the value "r2" is 1.

So, to pop "r2", we would perform the following:

```
>>> hostnames.pop(1)
'r2'
>>>
>>> print(hostnames)
['r1', 'r3', 'r4']
>>>
```

It could have also been done in a single step:

```
hostnames.pop(hostnames.index('r2'))
```

Using the sort() method. The last built-in method that we'll take a look at for lists is sort(). As you may have guessed, sort() is used to *sort* a list.

In the next example, we have a list of IP addresses in non-sequential order, and sort() is used to update the original object. Notice that nothing is returned.

```
>>> available_ips
['10.1.1.1', '10.1.1.9', '10.1.1.8', '10.1.1.7', '10.1.1.4']
>>>
>>>
>>> available_ips.sort()
>>>
>>> available_ips
['10.1.1.1', '10.1.1.4', '10.1.1.7', '10.1.1.8', '10.1.1.9']
```

 Be aware that the sort from the previous example sorted IP addresses as strings.

In nearly all examples we covered with lists, the elements of the list were the same type of object; that is, they were all commands, IP addresses, vendors, or hostnames. However, it would not be an issue if you needed to create a list that stored different types of contextual objects (or even data types).

A prime example of storing different objects arises when storing information about a particular device. Maybe you want to store the hostname, vendor, and OS. A list to store these device attributes would look something like this:

```
>>> device = ['router1', 'juniper', '12.2']
>>>
```

Since elements of a list are indexed by an integer, you need to keep track of which index is mapped to which particular attribute. While it may not seem hard for this example, what if there were 10, 20, or 100 attributes that needed to be accessed? Even if there were mappings available, it could get extremely difficult since lists are *ordered*. Replacing or updating any element in a list would need to be done very carefully.

Wouldn't it be nice if you could reference the individual elements of a list by *name* and not worry so much about the *order* of elements? So, rather than access the hostname using device[0], you could access it like device['hostname'].

As luck would have it, this is exactly where Python dictionaries come into action, and they are the next data type we cover in this chapter.

Learning to Use Python Dictionaries

We've now reviewed some of the most common data types, including strings, integers, booleans, and lists, which exist across all programming languages. In this section, we take a look at the dictionary, which is a Python-specific data type. In other languages, they are known as associative arrays, maps, or hash maps.

Dictionaries are *unordered* lists and their *values* are accessed by names, otherwise known as *keys*, instead of by index (integer). Dictionaries are simply a collection of unordered *key-value* pairs called *items*.

We finished the previous section on lists using this example:

```
>>> device = ['router1', 'juniper', '12.2']
>>>
```

If we build on this example and convert the list `device` to a dictionary, it would look like this:

```
>>> device = {'hostname': 'router1', 'vendor': 'juniper', 'os': '12.1'}
>>>
```

The notation for a dictionary is a curly brace ({), then key, colon, and value, for each key-value pair separated by a comma (,), and then it closes with another curly brace (}).

Once the `dict` object is created, you access the desired value by using *dict[key]*.

```
>>> print(device['hostname'])
router1
>>>
>>> print(device['os'])
12.1
>>>
>>> print(device['vendor'])
juniper
>>>
```

As already stated, dictionaries are unordered—unlike lists, which are ordered. You can see this because when `device` is printed in the following example, its key-value pairs are in a different order from when it was originally created.

```
>>> print(device)
{'os': '12.1', 'hostname': 'router1', 'vendor': 'juniper'}
>>>
```

It's worth noting that it's possible to create the same dictionary from the previous example a few different ways. These are shown in the next two code blocks.

```
>>> device = {}
>>> device['hostname'] = 'router1'
>>> device['vendor'] = 'juniper'
```

```
>>> device['os'] = '12.1'
>>>
>>> print(device)
{'os': '12.1', 'hostname': 'router1', 'vendor': 'juniper'}
>>>

>>> device = dict(hostname='router1', vendor='juniper', os='12.1')
>>>
>>> print(device)
{'os': '12.1', 'hostname': 'router1', 'vendor': 'juniper'}
>>>
```

Using built-in methods of Python dictionaries

Python dictionaries have a few built-in methods worth covering, so as usual, we'll dive right into them.

Just as with the other data types, we first look at all available methods minus those that start and end with underscores.

```
>>> dir(dict)
['clear', 'copy', 'fromkeys', 'get', 'has_key', 'items', 'iteritems', 'iterkeys',
'itervalues', 'keys', 'pop', 'popitem', 'setdefault', 'update', 'values',
'viewitems', 'viewkeys', 'viewvalues']
>>>
```

Using the get() method. We saw earlier how to access a key-value pair of a dictionary using the notation of *dict[key]*. That is a very popular approach, but with one caveat. If the key does not exist, it raises a KeyError since the key does not exist.

```
>>> device
{'os': '12.1', 'hostname': 'router1', 'vendor': 'juniper'}
>>>
>>> print(device['model'])
Traceback (most recent call last):
  File "<stdin>", line 1, in <module>
KeyError: 'model'
>>>
```

Using the get() method provides another approach that is arguably safer, unless you *want* to raise an error.

Let's first look at an example using get() when the key exists.

```
>>> device.get('hostname')
'router1'
>>>
```

And now an example for when a key doesn't exist:

```
>>> device.get('model')
>>>
```

As you can see from the preceding example, absolutely nothing is returned when the key isn't in the dictionary, but it gets better than that. get() also allows the user to define a value to return when the key does not exist! Let's take a look.

```
>>> device.get('model', False)
False
>>>
>>> device.get('model', 'DOES NOT EXIST')
'DOES NOT EXIST'
>>>
>>>
>>> device.get('hostname', 'DOES NOT EXIST')
'router1'
>>>
```

Pretty simple, right? You can see that the value to the right of the key is only returned if the key does not exist within the dictionary.

Using the keys() and values() methods. Dictionaries are an unordered list of key-value pairs. Using the built-in methods called keys() and values(), you have the ability to access the lists of each, individually. When each method is called, you get back a list of keys or values, respectively, that make up the dictionary.

```
>>> device.keys()
['os', 'hostname', 'vendor']
>>>
>>> device.values()
['12.1', 'router1', 'juniper']
>>>
```

Using the pop() method. We first saw a built-in method called pop() earlier in the chapter when we were reviewing lists. It just so happens dictionaries also have a pop() method, and it's used very similarly. Instead of passing the method an index value as we did with lists, we pass it a key.

```
>>> device
{'os': '12.1', 'hostname': 'router1', 'vendor': 'juniper'}
>>>
>>> device.pop('vendor')
'juniper'
>>>
>>> device
{'os': '12.1', 'hostname': 'router1'}
>>>
```

You can see from the example that pop() modifies the original object *and* returns the value that is being popped.

Using the update() method. There may come a time where you are extracting device information such as hostname, vendor, and OS and have it stored in a Python dictionary. And down the road you need to add or *update* it with another dictionary that has other attributes about a device.

The following shows two different dictionaries.

```
>>> device
{'os': '12.1', 'hostname': 'router1', 'vendor': 'juniper'}
>>>
>>> oper = dict(cpu='5%', memory='10%')
>>>
>>> oper
{'cpu': '5%', 'memory': '10%'}
>>>
```

The update() method can now be used to update one of the dictionaries, basically adding one dictionary to the other. Let's add oper to device.

```
>>> device.update(oper)
>>>
>>> print(device)
{'os': '12.1', 'hostname': 'router1', 'vendor': 'juniper', 'cpu': '5%',
'memory': '10%'}
>>>
```

Notice how nothing was returned with update(). Only the object being updated, or device in this case, was modified.

Using the items() method. When working with dictionaries, you'll see items() used *a lot*, so it is extremely important to understand—not to discount the other methods, of course!

We saw how to access individual values using get() and how to get a list of all the keys and values using the keys() and values() methods, respectively.

What about accessing a particular key-value pair of a given item at the same time, or iterating over all items? If you need to iterate (or loop) through a dictionary and simultaneously access keys and values, items() is a great tool for your tool belt.

 There is a formal introduction to loops later in this chapter, but because items() is commonly used with a for loop, we are showing an example with a for loop here. The important takeaway until loops are formally covered is that when using the for loop with items(), you can access a key and value of a given item at the same time.

The most basic example is looping through a dictionary with a for loop and printing the key *and* value for each item. Again, loops are covered later in the chapter, but this is meant just to give a basic introduction to items().

```
>>> for key, value in device.items():
...     print(key + ': ' + value)
...
os :  12.1
hostname :  router1
vendor :  juniper
cpu :  5%
memory :  10%
>>>
```

It's worth pointing out that in the for loop, key and value are user defined and could have been anything, as you can see in the example that follows.

```
>>> for my_attribute, my_value, in device.items():
...     print(my_attribute + ': ' + my_value)
...
os :  12.1
hostname :  router1
vendor :  juniper
cpu :  5%
memory :  10%
>>>
```

We've now covered the major data types in Python. You should have a good understanding of how to work with strings, numbers, booleans, lists, and dictionaries. We'll now provide a short introduction into two more data types, namely sets and tuples, that are a bit more advanced than the previous data types covered.

Learning About Python Sets and Tuples

The next two data types don't necessarily need to be covered in an introduction to Python, but as we said at the beginning of the chapter, we wanted to include a quick summary of them for completeness. These data types are set and tuple.

If you understand lists, you'll understand sets. Sets are a list of elements, but there can only be one of a given element in a set, and additionally elements cannot be indexed (or accessed by an index value like a list).

You can see that a set looks like a list, but is surrounded by set():

```
>>> vendors = set(['arista', 'cisco', 'arista', 'cisco', 'juniper', 'cisco'])
>>>
```

The preceding example shows a set being created with multiple elements that are the same. We used a similar example when we wanted to use the count() method for lists when we wanted to count how many of a given vendor exists. But what if you want to only know how many, and which, vendors exist in an environment? You can use a set.

```
>>> vendors = set(['arista', 'cisco', 'arista', 'cisco', 'juniper', 'cisco'])
>>>
>>> vendors
```

```
set(['cisco', 'juniper', 'arista'])
>>>
>>> len(vendors)
3
>>>
```

Notice how vendors only contains three elements.

The next example shows what happens when you try to access an element within a set. In order to access elements in a set, you must iterate through them, using a for loop as an example.

```
>>> vendors[0]
Traceback (most recent call last):
  File "<stdin>", line 1, in <module>
TypeError: 'set' object does not support indexing
>>>
```

It is left as an exercise for the reader to explore the built-in methods for sets.

The tuple is an interesting data type and also best understood when compared to a list. It is like a list, but cannot be modified. We saw that lists are *mutable*, meaning that it is possible to update, extend, and modify them. Tuples, on the other hand, are *immutable*, and it is not possible to modify them once they're created. Also, like lists, it's possible to access individual elements of tuples.

```
>>> description = tuple(['ROUTER1', 'PORTLAND'])
>>>
>>>
>>> description
('ROUTER1', 'PORTLAND')
>>>
>>>
>>> print(description[0])
ROUTER1
>>>
```

And once the variable object description is created, there is no way to modify it. You cannot modify any of the elements or add new elements. This could help if you need to create an object and want to ensure no other function or user can modify it. The next example shows that you cannot modify a tuple and that a tuple has no methods such as update() or append().

```
>>> description[1] = 'trying to modify one'
Traceback (most recent call last):
  File "<stdin>", line 1, in <module>
TypeError: 'tuple' object does not support item assignment
>>>
>>> dir(tuple)
['__add__', '__class__', '__contains__', '__delattr__', '__doc__', '__eq__',
'__format__', '__ge__', '__getattribute__', '__getitem__', '__getnewargs__',
'__getslice__', '__gt__', '__hash__', '__init__', '__iter__', '__le__',
```

```
'__len__', '__lt__', '__mul__', '__ne__', '__new__', '__reduce__',
'__reduce_ex__', '__repr__', '__rmul__', '__setattr__', '__sizeof__',
'__str__', '__subclasshook__', 'count', 'index']
>>>
```

To help compare and contrast lists, tuples, and sets, we have put this high-level summary together:

- Lists are mutable, they can be modified, individual elements they can be accessed directly, and can have duplicate values.

- Sets are mutable, they can be modified, individual elements cannot be accessed directly, and they cannot have duplicate values.

- Tuples are immutable, they cannot be updated or modified once created, individual elements can be accessed directly, and they can have duplicate values.

This concludes the section on data types. You should now have a good understanding of the data types covered, including strings, numbers, booleans, lists, dictionaries, sets, and tuples.

We'll now shift gears a bit and jump into using conditionals (*if then* logic) in Python.

Adding Conditional Logic to Your Code

By now you should have a solid understanding of working with different types of objects. The beauty of programming comes into play when you start to use those objects by applying logic within your code, such as executing a task or creating an object when a particular condition is true (or not true!).

Conditionals are a key part of applying logic within your code, and understanding conditionals starts with understanding the `if` statement.

Let's start with a basic example that checks the value of a string.

```
>>> hostname = 'NYC'
>>>
>>> if hostname == 'NYC':
...     print('The hostname is NYC')
...
The hostname is NYC
>>>
```

Even if you did not understand Python before starting this chapter, odds are you knew what was being done in the previous example. This is part of the value of working in Python—it tries to be as human readable as possible.

There are two things to take note of with regard to syntax when you're working with an `if` statement. First, *all* `if` statements end with a colon (`:`). Second, the code that gets executed *if* your condition is true is part of an indented block of code—this indentation *should be* four spaces, but technically does not matter. All that *technically* matters is that you are consistent.

 Generally speaking, it is good practice to use a four-space indent when writing Python code. This is widely accepted by the Python community as the norm for writing idiomatic Python code. This makes code sharing and collaboration much easier.

The next example shows a full indented code block.

```
>>> if hostname == 'NYC':
...     print('This hostname is NYC')
...     print(len(hostname))
...     print('The End.')
...
This hostname is NYC
3
The End.
>>>
```

Now that you understand how to construct a basic `if` statement, let's add to it.

What if you needed to do a check to see if the hostname was "NJ" in addition to "NYC"? To accomplish this, we introduce the *else if* statement, or `elif`.

```
>>> hostname = 'NJ'
>>>
>>> if hostname == 'NYC':
...     print('This hostname is NYC')
... elif hostname == 'NJ':
...     print('This hostname is NJ')
...
This hostname is NJ
>>>
```

It is very similar to the `if` statement in that it still needs to end with a colon and the associated code block to be executed must be indented. You should also be able to see that the `elif` statement must be aligned to the `if` statement.

What if NYC and NJ are the only valid hostnames, but now you need to execute a block of code if some other hostname is being used? This is where we use the `else` statement.

```
>>> hostname = 'DEN_CO'
>>>
>>> if hostname == 'NYC':
...     print('This hostname is NYC')
... elif hostname == 'NJ':
...     print('This hostname is NJ')
... else:
```

```
...        print('UNKNOWN HOSTNAME')
...
UNKNOWN HOSTNAME
>>>
```

Using else isn't any different than if and elif. It needs a colon (:) and an indented code block underneath it to execute.

When Python executes conditional statements, the conditional block is exited as soon as there is a match. For example, if hostname was equal to 'NYC', there would be a match on the first line of the conditional block, the print statement print('This hostname is NYC') would be executed, and then the block would be exited (no other elif or else would be executed).

The following is an example of an error that is produced when there is an error with indentation. The example has extra spaces in front of elif that should not be there.

```
>>> if hostname == 'NYC':
...        print('This hostname is NYC')
...    elif hostname == 'NJ':
  File "<stdin>", line 3
    elif hostname == 'NJ':
                        ^
IndentationError: unindent does not match any outer indentation level
>>>
```

And the following is an example of an error produced with a missing colon.

```
>>> if hostname == 'NYC'
  File "<stdin>", line 1
    if hostname == 'NYC'
                       ^
SyntaxError: invalid syntax
>>>
```

The point is, even if you have a typo in your code when you're just getting started, don't worry; you'll see pretty intuitive error messages.

You will continue to see conditionals in upcoming examples, including the next one, which introduces the concept of containment.

Understanding Containment

When we say *containment*, we are referring to the ability to check whether some object *contains* a specific element or object. Specifically, we'll look at the usage of in building on what we just learned with conditionals.

Although this section only covers in, it should not be underestimated how powerful this feature of Python is.

If we use the variable called vendors that has been used in previous examples, how would you check to see if a particular vendor exists? One option is to loop through the entire list and compare the vendor you are looking for with each object. That's definitely possible, but why not just use in?

Using containment is not only readable, but also simplifies the process for checking to see if an object has what you are looking for.

```
>>> vendors = ['arista', 'juniper', 'big_switch', 'cisco']
>>>
>>> 'arista' in vendors
True
>>>
```

You can see that the syntax is quite straightforward and a bool is returned. It's worth mentioning that this syntax is another one of those expressions that is considered writing idiomatic Python code.

This can now be taken a step a further and added into a conditional statement.

```
>>> if 'arista' in vendors:
...     print('Arista is deployed.')
...
'Arista is deployed.'
>>>
```

The next example checks to see if part of a string is *in* another string compared to checking to see if an element is in a list. The examples show a basic boolean expression and then show using the expression in a conditional statement.

```
>>> version = "CSR1000V Software (X86_64_LINUX_IOSD-UNIVERSALK9-M),
Version 16.3.1, RELEASE"
>>>
>>> "16.3.1" in version
True
>>>
>>> if "16.3.1" in version:
...     print("Version is 16.3.1!!")
...
Version is 16.3.1!!
>>>
>>>
```

As we previously stated, containment when combined with conditionals is a simple yet powerful way to check to see if an object or value exists within another object. In fact, when you're just starting out, it is quite common to build really long and complex conditional statements, but what you really need is a more efficient way to evaluate the elements of a given object.

One such way is to use loops while working with objects such as lists and dictionaries. Using loops simplifies the process of working with these types of objects. This will become much clearer soon, as our next section formally introduces loops.

Using Loops in Python

We've finally made it to loops. As objects continue to grow, especially those that are much larger than our examples thus far, loops are absolutely required. Start to think about lists of devices, IP addresses, VLANs, and interfaces. We'll need efficient ways to search data or perform the same operation on each element in a set of data (as examples). This is where loops begin to show their value.

We cover two main types of loops—the for loop and while loop.

From the perspective of a network engineer who is looking at automating network devices and general infrastructure, you can get away with almost always using a for loop. Of course, it depends on exactly what you are doing, but generally speaking, for loops in Python are pretty awesome, so we'll save them for last.

Understanding the while Loop

The general premise behind a while loop is that some set of code is executed *while* some condition is true. In the example that follows, the variable counter is set to 1 and then for as long as, or *while*, it is less than 5, the variable is printed, and then increased by 1.

The syntax required is similar to what we used when creating if-elif-else statements. The while statement is completed with a colon (:) and the code to be executed is also indented four spaces.

```
>>> counter = 1
>>>
>>> while counter < 5:
...     print(counter)
...     counter += 1
...
1
2
3
4
>>>
```

From an introduction perspective, this is all we are going to cover on the while loop, as we'll be using the for loop in the majority of examples going forward.

Understanding the for Loop

for loops in Python are awesome because when you use them you are usually loop-ing, or *iterating*, over a set of objects, like those found in a list, string, or dictionary. for loops in other programming languages require an index and increment value to always be specified, which is not the case in Python.

Let's start by reviewing what is sometimes called a *for-in* or *for-each* loop, which is the more common type of for loop in Python.

As in the previous sections, we start by reviewing a few basic examples.

The first is to print each object within a list. You can see in the following example that the syntax is simple, and again, much like what we learned when using conditionals and the while loop. The first statement or beginning of the for loop needs to end with a colon (:) and the code to be executed must be indented.

```
>>> vendors
['arista', 'juniper', 'big_switch', 'cisco']
>>>
>>> for vendor in vendors:
...     print('VENDOR: ' + vendor)
...
VENDOR:  arista
VENDOR:  juniper
VENDOR:  big_switch
VENDOR:  cisco
>>>
```

As mentioned earlier, this type of for loop is often called a *for-in* or *for-each* loop because you are iterating over *each* element *in* a given object.

In the example, the name of the object vendor is totally arbitrary and up to the user to define, and for each iteration, vendor is equal to that specific element. For example, in this example vendor equals arista during the first iteration, juniper in the second iteration, and so on.

To show that vendor can be named anything, let's rename it to be network_vendor.

```
>>> for network_vendor in vendors:
...     print('VENDOR: ' + network_vendor)
...
VENDOR:  arista
VENDOR:  juniper
VENDOR:  big_switch
VENDOR:  cisco
>>>
```

Let's now combine a few of the things learned so far with containment, conditionals, and loops.

The next example defines a new list of vendors. One of them is a *great* company, but just not cut out to be a network vendor! Then it defines approved_vendors, which is basically the proper, or approved, vendors for a given customer. This example loops through the vendors to ensure they are all approved, and if not, prints a statement saying so to the terminal.

```
>>> vendors = ['arista', 'juniper', 'big_switch', 'cisco', 'oreilly']
>>>
>>> approved_vendors = ['arista', 'juniper', 'big_switch', 'cisco']
>>>
>>> for vendor in vendors:
...     if vendor not in approved_vendors:
...         print('NETWORK VENDOR NOT APPROVED: ' + vendor)
...
NETWORK VENDOR NOT APPROVED:  oreilly
>>>
```

You can see that not can be used in conjunction with in, making it very powerful and easy to read what is happening.

We'll now look at a more challenging example where we loop through a dictionary, while extracting data from another dictionary, and even get to use some built-in methods you learned earlier in this chapter.

To prepare for the next example, let's build a dictionary that stores CLI commands to configure certain features on a network device:

```
>>> COMMANDS = {
...     'description': 'description {}',
...     'speed': 'speed {}',
...     'duplex': 'duplex {}',
... }
>>>
>>> print(COMMANDS)
{'duplex': 'duplex {}', 'speed': 'speed {}', 'description': 'description {}'}
>>>
```

We see that we have a dictionary that has three items (key-value pairs). Each item's key is a network feature to configure, and each item's value is the start of a command string that'll configure that respective feature. These features include speed, duplex, and description. The values of the dictionary each have curly braces ({}) because we'll be using the format() method of strings to insert variables.

Now that the COMMANDS dictionary is created, let's create a second dictionary called CONFIG_PARAMS that will be used to dictate which commands will be executed and which value will be used for each command string defined in COMMANDS.

```
>>> CONFIG_PARAMS = {
...     'description': 'auto description by Python',
...     'speed': '10000',
```

```
...     'duplex': 'auto'
... }
>>>
```

We will now use a for loop to iterate through CONFIG_PARAMS() using the items built-in method for dictionaries. As we iterate through, we'll use the key from CON FIG_PARAMS and use that to get the proper value, or command string, from COMMANDS. This is possible because they were prebuilt using the same key structure. The command string is returned with curly braces, but as soon as it's returned, we use the format() method to insert the proper value, which happens to be the value in CONFIG_PARAMS.

Let's a take a look.

```
>>> commands_list = []
>>>
>>> for feature, value in CONFIG_PARAMS.items():
...     command = COMMANDS.get(feature).format(value)
...     commands_list.append(command)
...
>>> commands_list.insert(0, 'interface Eth1/1')
>>>
>>> print(commands_list)
['interface Eth1/1', 'duplex auto', 'speed 10000',
  'description auto description by Python']
>>>
```

Now we'll walk through this in even more detail. Please take your time and even test this out yourself while on the Python interactive interpreter.

In the first line commands_list is creating an empty list []. This is required in order to append() to this list later on.

We then use the items() built-in method as we loop through CONFIG_PARAMS. This was covered very briefly earlier in the chapter, but items() is giving you, the network developer, access to both the key *and* value of a given key-value pair at the same time. This example iterates over three key-value pairs, namely description/auto description by Python, speed/10000, and duplex/auto.

During each iteration—that is, for each key-value pair that is being referred to as the variables feature and value—a command is being pulled from the COMMANDS dictionary. If you recall, the get() method is used to get the value of a key-value pair when you specify the key. In the example, this key is the feature object. The value being returned is description {} for description, speed {} for speed, and duplex {} for duplex. As you can see, all of these objects being returned are strings, so then we are able to use the format() method to insert the value from CONFIG_PARAMS because we also saw earlier that multiple methods can be used together on the same line!

Once the value is inserted, the command is appended to `commands_list`. Once the commands are built, we `insert()` `Eth1/1`. This could have also been done first.

If you understand this example, you are at a really good point already with getting a grasp on Python!

You've now seen some of the most common types of `for` loops that allow you to iterate over lists and dictionaries. We'll now take a look at another way to construct and use a `for` loop.

Using the enumerate() function

Occasionally, you may need to keep track of an index value as you loop through an object. We show this fairly briefly, since most examples that are reviewed are like the previous examples already covered.

`enumerate()` is used to enumerate the list and give an index value, and is often handy to determine the exact position of a given element.

The next example shows how to use `enumerate()` within a `for` loop. You'll notice that the beginning part of the `for` loop looks like the dictionary examples, only unlike `items()`, which returns a key and value, `enumerate()` returns an index, starting at 0, *and* the object from the list that you are enumerating.

The example prints both the index and value to help you understand what it is doing:

```
>>> vendors = ['arista', 'juniper', 'big_switch', 'cisco']
>>>
>>> for index, each in enumerate(vendors):
...     print(index + ' ' + each)
...
0 arista
1 juniper
2 big_switch
3 cisco
>>>
```

Maybe you don't need to print all of indices and values out. Maybe you only need the index for a given vendor. This is shown in the next example.

```
>>> for index, each in enumerate(vendors):
...     if each == 'arista':
...         print('arista index is: ' + index)
...
arista index is:  0
>>>
```

We've covered quite a bit of Python so far, from data types to conditionals to loops. However, we still haven't covered how to efficiently reuse code through the use of functions. This is what we cover next.

Using Python Functions

Because you are reading this book, you probably at some point have heard of functions, but if not, don't worry—we have you covered! Functions are all about eliminating redundant and duplicate code and easily allowing for the reuse of code. Frankly and generally speaking, functions are the opposite of what network engineers do on a daily basis.

On a daily basis network engineers are configuring VLANs over and over again. And they are likely proud of how fast they can enter the same CLI commands into a network device or switch over and over. Writing a script with functions eliminates writing the same code *over and over.*

Let's assume you need to create a few VLANs across a set of switches. Based on a device from Cisco or Arista, the commands required may look something this:

```
vlan 10
  name USERS
vlan 20
  name VOICE
vlan 30
  name WLAN
```

Imagine you need to configure 10, 20, or 50 devices with the same VLANs! It is very likely you would type in those six commands for as many devices as you have in your environment.

This is actually a perfect opportunity to create a function and write a small script. Since we haven't covered scripts yet, we'll still be working on the Python shell.

For our first example, we'll start with a basic print() function and then come right back to the VLAN example.

```
>>> def print_vendor(net_vendor):
...     print(net_vendor)
...
>>>
>>> vendors = ['arista', 'juniper', 'big_switch', 'cisco']
>>>
>>> for vendor in vendors:
...     print_vendor(vendor)
...
arista
juniper
big_switch
cisco
>>>
```

In the preceding example, print_vendor() is a function that is created and *defined* using def. If you want to pass variables (parameters) into your function, you enclose them within parentheses next to the function name. This example is receiving one parameter and is referenced as vendor while in the function called print_vendor(). Like conditionals and loops, function declarations also end with a colon (:). Within the function, there is an indented code block that has a single statement—it simply prints the parameter being received.

Once the function is created, it is ready to be immediately used, even while in the Python interpreter.

For this first example, we ensured vendors was created and then looped through it. During each iteration of the loop, we passed the object, which is a string of the vendor's name, to print_vendor().

Notice how the variables have different names based on where they are being used, meaning that we are passing vendor, but it's received and referenced as net_vendor from within the function. There is no requirement to have the variables use the same name while within the function, although it'll work just fine if you choose to do it that way.

Since we now have an understanding of how to create a basic function, let's return to the VLAN example.

We will create two functions to help automate VLAN provisioning.

The first function, called get_commands(), obtains the required commands to send to a network device. It accepts two parameters, one that is the VLAN ID using the parameter vlan and one that is the VLAN NAME using the parameter name.

The second function, called push_commands(), pushes the actual commands that were gathered from get_commands to a given list of devices. This function also accepts two parameters: device, which is the device to send the commands to, and commands, which is the list of commands to send. In reality, the push isn't happening in this function, but rather it is printing commands to the terminal to simulate the command execution.

```
>>> def get_commands(vlan, name):
...     commands = []
...     commands.append('vlan ' + vlan)
...     commands.append('name ' + name)
...
...     return commands
...
>>>
>>> def push_commands(device, commands):
...     print('Connecting to device: ' + device)
...     for cmd in commands:
...         print('Sending command: ' + cmd)
>>>
```

In order to use these functions, we need two things: a list of devices to configure and the list of VLANs to send.

The list of devices to be configured is as follows:

```
>>> devices = ['switch1', 'switch2', 'switch3']
>>>
```

In order to create a single object to represent the VLANs, we have created a list of dictionaries. Each dictionary has two key-value pairs, one pair for the VLAN ID and one for the VLAN name.

```
>>> vlans = [{'id': '10', 'name': 'USERS'}, {'id': '20', 'name': 'VOICE'},
{'id': '30', 'name': 'WLAN'}]
>>>
```

If you recall, there is more than one way to create a dictionary. Any of those options could have been used here.

The next section of code shows one way to use these functions. The following code loops through the vlans list. Remember that each element in vlans is a dictionary. For each element, or dictionary, the id and name are obtained by way of the get() method. There are two print statements, and then the first function, get_com mands(), is called—id and name are parameters that get sent to the function, and then a list of commands is returned and assigned to commands.

Once we have the commands for a given VLAN, they are executed on each device by looping through devices. In this process push_commands() is called for each device for each VLAN.

You can see the associated code and output generated here:

```
>>> for vlan in vlans:
...     id = vlan.get('id')
...     name = vlan.get('name')
...     print('\n')
...     print('CONFIGURING VLAN:' + id)
...     commands = get_commands(id, name)
...     for device in devices:
...         push_commands(device, commands)
...         print('\n')
...
>>>

CONFIGURING VLAN: 10
Connecting to device:  switch1
Sending command:  vlan 10
Sending command:  name USERS

Connecting to device:  switch2
Sending command:  vlan 10
Sending command:  name USERS
```

```
Connecting to device:  switch3
Sending command:  vlan 10
Sending command:  name USERS

CONFIGURING VLAN: 20
Connecting to device:  switch1
Sending command:  vlan 20
Sending command:  name VOICE

Connecting to device:  switch2
Sending command:  vlan 20
Sending command:  name VOICE

Connecting to device:  switch3
Sending command:  vlan 20
Sending command:  name VOICE

CONFIGURING VLAN: 30
Connecting to device:  switch1
Sending command:  vlan 30
Sending command:  name WLAN

Connecting to device:  switch2
Sending command:  vlan 30
Sending command:  name WLAN

Connecting to device:  switch3
Sending command:  vlan 30
Sending command:  name WLAN
>>>
```

 Remember, not all functions require parameters, and not all functions return a value.

You should now have a basic understanding of creating and using functions, understanding how they are called and defined with and without parameters, and how it's possible to call functions from within loops.

Next, we cover how to read and write data from files in Python.

Working with Files

This section is focused on showing you how to read and write data from files. Our focus is on the basics and to show enough that you'll be able to easily pick up a complete Python book from O'Reilly to continue learning about working with files.

Reading from a File

For our example, we have a configuration snippet located in the same directory from where we entered the Python interpreter.

The filename is called *vlans.cfg* and it looks like this:

```
vlan 10
  name USERS
vlan 20
  name VOICE
vlan 30
  name WLAN
vlan 40
  name APP
vlan 50
  name WEB
vlan 60
  name DB
```

With just two lines in Python, we can *open* and *read* the file.

```
>>> vlans_file = open('vlans.cfg', 'r')
>>>
>>> vlans_file.read()
'vlan 10\n  name USERS\nvlan 20\n  name VOICE\nvlan 30\n
name WLAN\nvlan 40\n  name APP\nvlan 50\n  name WEB\nvlan 60\n
  name DB'
>>>
>>> vlans_file.close()
>>>
```

This example read in the full file as a complete `str` object by using the `read()` method for file objects.

The next example reads the file and stores each line as an element in a list by using the `readlines()` method for file objects.

```
>>> vlans_file = open('vlans.cfg', 'r')
>>>
>>> vlans_file.readlines()
['vlan 10\n', '  name USERS\n', 'vlan 20\n', '  name VOICE\n', 'vlan 30\n',
'  name WLAN\n', 'vlan 40\n', '  name APP\n', 'vlan 50\n', '  name WEB\n',
'vlan 60\n', '  name DB']
>>>
>>> vlans_file.close()
>>>
```

Let's reopen the file, save the contents as a string, but then manipulate it, to store the VLANs as a dictionary similar to how we used the `vlans` object in the example from the section on functions.

```
>>> vlans_file = open('vlans.cfg', 'r')
>>>
>>> vlans_text = vlans_file.read()
>>>
>>> vlans_list = vlans_text.splitlines()
>>>
>>> vlans_list
['vlan 10', ' name USERS', 'vlan 20', ' name VOICE', 'vlan 30',
' name WLAN', 'vlan 40', ' name APP', 'vlan 50', ' name WEB',
'vlan 60', ' name DB']
>>>
>>> vlans = []
>>> for item in vlans_list:
...     if 'vlan' in item:
...         temp = {}
...         id = item.strip().strip('vlan').strip()
...         temp['id'] = id
...     elif 'name' in item:
...         name = item.strip().strip('name').strip()
...         temp['name'] = name
...         vlans.append(temp)
...
>>>
>>> vlans
[{'id': '10', 'name': 'USERS'}, {'id': '20', 'name': 'VOICE'},
{'id': '30', 'name': 'WLAN'}, {'id': '40', 'name': 'APP'},
{'id': '50', 'name': 'WEB'}, {'id': '60', 'name': 'DB'}]
>>>
>>> vlans_file.close()
>>>
```

In this example, the file is read and the contents of the file are stored as a string in
vlans_text. A built-in method for strings called splitlines() is used to create a list
where each element in the list is each line within the file. This new list is called
vlans_list and has a length equal to the number of commands that were in the file.

Once the list is created, it is iterated over within a for loop. The variable item is used
to represent each element in the list as it's being iterated over. In the first iteration,
item is 'vlan 10'; in the second iteration, item is ' name users'; and so on. Within
the for loop, a list of dictionaries is ultimately created where each element in the list
is a dictionary with two key-value pairs: id and name. We accomplish this by using a
temporary dictionary called temp, adding both key-value pairs to it, and then appending it to the final list only after appending the VLAN name. Per the following note,
temp is reinitialized *only* when it finds the next VLAN.

Notice how strip() is being used. You can use strip() to strip not only whitespace,
but also particular substrings within a string object. Additionally, we *chained* multiple
methods together in a single Python statement.

For example, with the value ' name WEB', when strip() is first used, it returns 'name WEB'. Then, we used strip('name'), which returns ' WEB', and then finally strip() to remove any whitespace that still remains to produce the final name of 'WEB'.

 The previous example is not the only way to perform an operation for reading in VLANs. That example *assumed* a VLAN ID and name for every VLAN, which is usually not the case, but is done this way for conveying certain concepts. It initialized temp only when "VLAN" was found, and only appended temp after the "name" was added (this would not work if a name did not exist for every VLAN and is a good use case for using Python error handling using try/except statements—which is out of scope in this book).

Writing to a File

The next example shows how to write data to a file.

The vlans object that was created in the previous example is used here too.

```
>>> vlans
[{'id': '10', 'name': 'USERS'}, {'id': '20', 'name': 'VOICE'},
{'id': '30', 'name': 'WLAN'}, {'id': '40', 'name': 'APP'},
{'id': '50', 'name': 'WEB'}, {'id': '60', 'name': 'DB'}]
```

A few more VLANs are created before we try to write the VLANs to a new file.

```
>>> add_vlan = {'id': '70', 'name': 'MISC'}
>>> vlans.append(add_vlan)
>>>
>>> add_vlan = {'id': '80', 'name': 'HQ'}
>>> vlans.append(add_vlan)
>>>
>>> print(vlans)
[{'id': '10', 'name': 'USERS'}, {'id': '20', 'name': 'VOICE'},
{'id': '30', 'name': 'WLAN'}, {'id': '40', 'name': 'APP'},
{'id': '50', 'name': 'WEB'}, {'id': '60', 'name': 'DB'},
{'id': '70', 'name': 'MISC'}, {'id': '80', 'name': 'HQ'}]
>>>
```

There are now eight VLANS in the vlans list. Let's write them to a new file, but keep the formatting the way it should be with proper spacing.

The first step is to open the new file. If the file doesn't exist, which it doesn't in our case, it'll be created. You can see this in the first line of code that follows.

Once it is open, we'll use the get() method again to extract the required VLAN values from each dictionary and then use the file method called write() to write the data to the file. Finally, the file is closed.

```
>>> write_file = open('vlans_new.cfg', 'w')
>>>
>>> for vlan in vlans:
...     id = vlan.get('id')
...     name = vlan.get('name')
...     write_file.write('vlan ' + id + '\n')
...     write_file.write('  name ' + name + '\n')
...
>>>
>>> write_file.close()
>>>
```

The previous code created the *vlans_new.cfg* file and generated the following contents in the file:

```
$ cat vlans_new.cfg
vlan 10
  name USERS
vlan 20
  name VOICE
vlan 30
  name WLAN
vlan 40
  name APP
vlan 50
  name WEB
vlan 60
  name DB
vlan 70
  name MISC
vlan 80
  name HQ
```

As you start to use file objects more, you may see some interesting things happen. For example, you may forget to close a file, and wonder why there is no data in the file that you know should have data!

> By default, what you are writing with the write() method is held in a buffer and only written to the file when the file is closed. This setting is configurable.

It's also possible to use the with statement, a context manager, to help manage this process.

Here is a brief example using with. One of the nice things about with is that it *automatically* closes the file.

```
>>> with open('vlans_new.cfg', 'w') as write_file:
...     write_file.write('vlan 10\n')
```

```
...     write_file.write('  name TEST_VLAN\n')
...
>>>
```

 When you open a file using open() as with open('vlans.cfg', 'r'), you can see that two parameters are sent. The first is the name of the file including the relative or absolute path of the file. The second is the *mode*, which is an optional argument, but if not included, is the equivalent of read-only, which is the r mode. Other modes include w, which opens a file only for writing (if you're using the name of a file that already exists, the contents are erased), a opens a file for appending, and r+ opens a file for reading and writing.

Everything in this chapter thus far has been using the dynamic Python interpreter. This showed how powerful the interpreter is for writing and testing new methods, functions, or particular sections of your code. No matter how great the interpreter is, however, we still need to be able to write programs and scripts that can run as a standalone entity. This is exactly what we cover next.

Creating Python Programs

Let's take a look at how to build on what we've been doing on the Python shell and learn how to create and run a standalone Python script, or program. This section shows how to easily take what you've learned so far and create a script within just a few minutes.

 If you're following along, feel free to use any text editor you are comfortable with, including, but not limited to vi, vim, Sublime Text, Notepad++, or even a full-blown Integrated Development Environment (IDE), such as PyCharm.

Let's look at a few examples.

Creating a Basic Python Script

The first step is to create a new Python file that ends with the *.py* extension. From the Linux terminal, create a new file by typing **touch net_script.py** and open it in your text editor. As expected, the file is completely empty.

The first script we'll write simply prints text to the terminal. Add the following five lines of text to *net_script.py* in order to create a basic Python script.

```
#!/usr/bin/env python

if __name__ == "__main__":
    print('^' * 30)
    print('HELLO NETWORK AUTOMATION!!!!!')
    print('^' * 30)
```

Now that the script is created, let's execute it.

To execute a Python script from the Linux terminal, you use the python command. All you need to do is append the script name to the command as shown here.

```
$ python net_script.py
^^^^^^^^^^^^^^^^^^^^^^^^^^^^^^
HELLO NETWORK AUTOMATION!!!!!
^^^^^^^^^^^^^^^^^^^^^^^^^^^^^^
```

And that's it! If you were following along, you just created a Python script. You might have noticed that everything under the if __name__ == "__main__": statement is the same as if you were on the Python interpreter.

Now we'll take a look at the two unique statements that are optional, but recommended, when you are writing Python scripts. The first one is called the shebang. You may also recall that we first introduced the shebang in Chapter 3.

Understanding the Shebang

The *shebang* is the first line in the script: #!/usr/bin/env python. This is a special and unique line for Python programs.

It is the only line of code that uses the # as the first character other than comments. We will cover comments later in the chapter, but note for now that # is widely used for commenting in Python. The shebang happens to be the exception and also needs to be the first line in a Python program, when used.

> Python linters used to perform checks on the code can also act upon the text that comes after comments starting with #.

The shebang instructs the system which Python interpreter to use to execute the program. Of course, this also assumes file permissions are correct for your program file (i.e., that the file is executable). If the shebang is not included, you must use the python keyword to execute the script, which we have in all of our examples anyway.

For example, if we had the following script:

```
if __name__ == "__main__":
    print('Hello Network Automation!')
```

we could execute using the statement $ python hello.py, assuming the file was saved as *hello.py*. But we could not be execute it using the statement $ ./hello.py. In order for the statement $ ./hello.py to be executed, we need to add the shebang to the program file because that's how the system knows how to execute the script.

The shebang as we have it, /usr/bin/env python, defaults to using Python 2.7 on the system we're using to write this book. But it is also possible if you have multiple versions of Python installed to modify the shebang to specifically use another version, such as /usr/bin/env python3 to use Python 3.

It's also worth mentioning that the shebang /usr/bin/env python allows you to modify the system's environment so that you don't have to modify each individual script, just in case you did want to test on a different version of Python. You can use the command which python to see which version will be used on your system.

For example, our system defaults to Python 2.7.6:

```
$ which python
/usr/bin/python
$
$ /usr/bin/python
Python 2.7.6 (default, Jun 22 2015, 17:58:13)
[GCC 4.8.2] on linux2
Type "help", "copyright", "credits" or "license" for more
information.
>>>
```

Next, we'll take a deeper look at the if __name__ == "__main__": statement. Based on the quotes, or lack thereof, you can see that __name__ is a variable and "__main__" is a string. When a Python file is executed as a standalone script, the variable name __name__ is automatically set to "__main__". Thus, whenever you do python <script>.py, everything underneath the if __name__ == "__main__" statement is executed.

At this point, you are probably thinking, when wouldn't __name__ be equal to "__main__"? That is discussed in "Working with Python Modules" on page 140, but the short answer is: when you are importing particular objects from Python files, but not necessarily using those files as a standalone program.

Now that you understand the shebang and the if __name__ == "__main__": statement, we can continue to look at standalone Python scripts.

Migrating Code from the Python Interpreter to a Python Script

This next example is the same example from the section on functions. The reason for this is to show you firsthand how easy it is to migrate from using the Python interpreter to writing a standalone Python script.

The next script is called *push.py*.

```python
#!/usr/bin/env python


def get_commands(vlan, name):
    commands = []
    commands.append('vlan ' + vlan)
    commands.append('name ' + name)
    return commands


def push_commands(device, commands):
    print('Connecting to device: ' + device)
    for cmd in commands:
        print('Sending command: ' + cmd)

if __name__ == "__main__":

    devices = ['switch1', 'switch2', 'switch3']

    vlans = [{'id': '10', 'name': 'USERS'}, {'id': '20', 'name': 'VOICE'},
            {'id': '30', 'name': 'WLAN'}]

    for vlan in vlans:
        vid = vlan.get('id')
        name = vlan.get('name')
        print('\n')
        print('CONFIGURING VLAN:' + vid)
        commands = get_commands(vid, name)
        for device in devices:
            push_commands(device, commands)
            print('\n')
```

The script is executed with the command `python push.py`.

The output you see is exactly the same output you saw when it was executed on the Python interpreter.

If you were creating several scripts that performed various configuration changes on the network, we can intelligently assume that the function called `push_commands()` would be needed in almost all scripts. One option is to copy and paste the function in all of the scripts. Clearly, that would not be optimal because if you needed to fix a bug in that function, you would need to make that change in *all* of the scripts.

Just like functions allow us to reuse code within a single script, there is a way to reuse and share code between scripts/programs. We do so by creating a Python module, which is what we'll cover next as we continue to build on the previous example.

Working with Python Modules

We are going to continue to leverage the *push.py* file we just created in the previous section to better articulate how to work with a Python module. You can think of a module as a type of Python file that holds information, (e.g., Python objects), that can be used by other Python programs, but is not a standalone script or program itself.

For this example, we are going to enter back into the Python interpreter while in the same directory where the *push.py* file exists.

Let's assume you need to generate a new list of commands to send to a new list of devices. You remember that you have this function called push_commands() in another file that already has the logic to push a list of commands to a given device. Rather than re-create the same function in your new program (or in the interpreter), you reuse the push_commands() function from within *push.py*. Let's see how this is done.

While at the Python shell, we will type in import push and hit Enter. This imports all of the objects within the *push.py* file.

```
>>> import push
>>>
```

Take a look at the imported objects by using dir(push).

```
>>> dir(push)
['__builtins__', '__doc__', '__file__', '__name__', '__package__', 'get_commands',
'push_commands']
>>>
```

Just as we saw with the standard Python data types, push also has methods that start and end with underscores, but you should also notice the two objects called get_com mands and push_commands, which are the functions from the *push.py* file!

If you recall, push_commands() requires two parameters. The first is a device and the second is a list of commands. Let's now use push_commands() from the interpreter.

```
>>> device = 'router1'
>>> commands = ['interface Eth1/1', 'shutdown']
>>>
>>> push.push_commands(device, commands)
Connecting to device:  router1
Sending command:  interface Eth1/1
Sending command:  shutdown
>>>
```

You can see that the first thing we did was create two new variables (device and com mands) that are used as the parameters sent to push_commands().

push_commands() is then called as an object of push with the parameters device and commands.

If you are importing multiple modules and there is a chance of overlap between function names, the method shown using import push is definitely a good option. It also makes it really easy to know where (in which module) the function exists. On the other hand, there are other options for importing objects.

One other option is to use from import. For our example, it would look like this: from push import push_commands. Notice in the following code, you can directly use push_commands() without referencing push.

```
>>> from push import push_commands
>>>
>>> device = 'router1'
>>> commands = ['interface Eth1/1', 'shutdown']
>>>
>>> push_commands(device, commands)
Connecting to device:  router1
Sending command:  interface Eth1/1
Sending command:  shutdown
>>>
```

It's recommended to make import statements as specific as possible and only import what's used in your code. You should *not* use wildcard imports, such as from push import *. Statements like this load all objects from the module, potentially overloading and causing namespace conflicts with objects you've defined. And it also complicates troubleshooting, as it makes it difficult to decipher where an object was defined or came from.

Another option is to rename the object as you are importing it, using from import as. If you happen to not like the name of the object or think it is too long, you can rename it on import. It looks like this for our example:

```
>>> from push import push_commands as pc
>>>
```

Notice how easy it is to rename the object and make it something shorter and or more intuitive.

Let's use it in an example.

```
>>> from push import push_commands as pc
>>>
>>> device = 'router1'
```

```
>>> commands = ['interface Eth1/1', 'shutdown']
>>>
>>> pc(device, commands)
Connecting to device:  router1
Sending command:  interface Eth1/1
Sending command:  shutdown
>>>
```

 In our examples, we entered the Python Dynamic Interpreter from the same directory where the module *push.py* was saved. In order to use this module, or any new module, from anywhere on your system, you need to put your module into a directory defined in your PYTHONPATH. This is a Linux environment variable that defines all directories your system will look in for Python modules and programs.

By now you should understand not only how to create a script, but also how to create a Python module with functions (and other objects) and how to use those reusable objects in other scripts and programs.

Passing Arguments into a Python Script

In the last two sections, we looked at writing Python scripts and using Python modules. Now we'll look at a module that's part of the Python standard library (i.e., comes with Python by default) that allows us to easily pass in arguments from the command line into a Python script. The module is called sys, and specifically we're going to use an attribute (or variable) within the module called argv.

Let's take a look at a basic script called *send_command.py* that only has a single print statement.

```
#!/usr/bin/env python

import sys

if __name__ == "__main__":
    print(sys.argv)
```

Now we'll execute the script, passing in a few arguments simulating data we'd need to log in to a device and issue a show command.

```
ntc@ntc:~$ python send-command.py username password 10.1.10.10 "show version"
['send-command.py', 'username', 'password', '10.1.10.10', 'show version']
ntc@ntc:~$
```

You should see that sys.argv is a list. In fact, it's simply a list of strings of what we passed in from the Linux command line. This is a standard Python list that has elements matching the arguments passed in. You can also infer what really happened:

Python did a split (str.split(" ")) on send-command.py username password 10.1.10.10 "show version" which created the list of five elements!

Finally, note that when you're using sys.argv the first element is always the script name.

If you'd like, you can assign the value of sys.argv to an arbitrary variable to simplify working with the parameters passed in. In either case, you can extract values using the appropriate index values as shown:

```
#!/usr/bin/env python

import sys

if __name__ == "__main__":
    args = sys.argv
    print("Username:  " + args[0])
    print("Password:  " + args[1])
    print("Device IP: " + args[2])
    print("Command:   " + args[3])
```

And if we execute this script:

```
ntc@ntc:~$ python send-command.py username password 10.1.10.10 "show version"
Username:    send-command.py
Password:    username
Device IP:   password
Command:     10.1.10.10
ntc@ntc:~$
```

You can continue to build on this to perform more meaningful network tasks as you continue reading this book. For example, after reading Chapter 7, you'll be able to pass parameters like this into a script that actually connects to a device using an API issuing a show command (or equivalent).

 When using sys.argv, you still need to account for error handling (at a minimum, check the length of the list). Additionally, the user of the script must know the precise order of the elements that need to be passed in. For more advanced argument handling, you should look at the Python module called argparse that offers a very user-intuitive way of passing in arguments with "flags" and a built-in help menu. This is out of the scope of the book.

Using pip and Installing Python Packages

As you get started with Python, it's likely you're going to need to install other software written in Python. For example, you may want to test automating network devices with netmiko, a popular SSH client for Python, that we cover in Chapter 7. It's most common to distribute Python software, including `netmiko`, using the Python Package Index (PyPI), pronounced "pie-pie." You can also browse and search the PyPI repository directly at *https://pypi.python.org/pypi*.

For any Python software hosted on PyPI such as `netmiko`, you can use the program called `pip` to install it on your machine directly from PyPI. `pip` is an installer that by default goes to PyPI, downloads the software, and installs it on your machine.

Using `pip` to install `netmiko` can be done with a single line on your Linux machine:

```
ntc@ntc:~$ sudo pip install netmiko
# output omitted
```

This will install `netmiko` in a system path (it'll vary based on the OS being used).

By default this will install the latest and greatest (stable release) of a given Python package. However, you may want to ensure you install a specific version—this is helpful to ensure you don't automatically install the next release without testing. This is referred to as *pinning*. You can *pin* your install to a specific release. In the next example, we show how you can pin the install of `netmiko` to version 1.4.2.

```
ntc@ntc:~$ sudo pip install netmiko==1.4.2
# output omitted
```

You can use `pip` to upgrade versions of software too. For example, you may have installed version 1.4.2 of `netmiko` and when you're ready, you can upgrade to the latest release by using the `--upgrade` or `-U` flag on the command line.

```
ntc@ntc:~$ sudo pip install netmiko --upgrade
# output omitted
```

It's also common to need to install Python packages from *source*. That simply means getting the latest release—for example, from GitHub, a version control system that we cover in Chapter 8. Maybe the software package on GitHub has a bug fix you need that is not yet published to PyPI. In this case, it's quite common to perform a `git clone`—something that we also show you how to do in Chapter 8.

When you perform a clone of a Python project from GitHub, there is a good chance you'll see two files in the root of the project: *requirements.txt* and *setup.py*. These can be used to install the Python package from source. The requirements file lists the requirements that are needed for the application to run. For example, here is the current *requirements.txt* for `netmiko`:

```
paramiko>=1.13.0
scp>=0.10.0
pyyaml
```

You can see that `netmiko` has three dependencies, commonly referred to as *deps*. You can also install these deps directly from PyPI using a single statement, again using the `pip` installer.

```
ntc@ntc:~$ sudo pip install -r requirements.text
# output omitted
```

To completely install `netmiko` (from source) including the requirements, you can also use execute the *setup.py* file that you'd see in the same directory after performing the Git clone.

```
ntc@ntc:~$ sudo python setup.py install
# output omitted
```

By default, installing the software with *setup.py* will also install directly into a system path. Should you want to contribute back to a given project on GitHub, and actively develop on the project, you can also install the application directly from where the files exist (directory where you cloned the project).

```
ntc@ntc:~$ sudo python setup.py develop
# output omitted
```

This makes it such that the files in your local directory are the ones running `netmiko`, for our example. Otherwise, if you use the `install` option when running *setup.py*, you'll need to modify the files in your system path to effect the local `netmiko` install (for troubleshooting as another example).

Learning Additional Tips, Tricks, and General Information When Using Python

We are going to close this chapter with what we call Python *tips, tricks, and general information*. It's useful information to know when working with Python—some of it is introductory and some of it is more advanced, but we want to really prepare you to continue your dive into Python following this chapter, so we're including as much as possible.

These tips, tricks, and general information are provided here in no particular order of importance:

- You may need to access certain parts of a string or elements in a list. Maybe you need just the first character or element. You can use the index of 0 for strings (not covered earlier), but also for lists. If there is a variable called `router` that is assigned the value of `'DEVICE'`, `router[0]` returns `'D'`. The same holds true for lists, which was covered already. But what about accessing the last element in the string or list? Remember, we learned that we can use the `-1` index for this. `router[-1]` returns `'E'` and the same would be true for a list as well.

- Building on the previous example, this notation is expanded to get the first few characters or last few (again, same for a list):

```
>>> hostname = 'DEVICE_12345'
>>>
```

```
>>> hostname[4:]
'CE_12345'
>>>
>>> hostname[:-2]
'DEVICE_123'
>>>
```

This can become pretty powerful when you need to parse through different types of objects.

- You can convert (or cast) an integer to a string by using str(10). You can also do the opposite, converting a string to an integer by using int('10').

- We used dir() quite a bit when learning about built-in methods and also mentioned the type() and help() functions. A helpful workflow for using all three together is as follows:

  — Check your data type using type()

  — Check the available methods for your object using dir()

  — After knowing which method you want to use, learn how to use it using help()

  Here is an example of that workflow:

```
>>> hostname = 'router1'
>>>
>>> type(hostname)
<type 'str'>
>>>
>>> dir(hostname)
>>> # output omitted; it would show all methods including "upper"
>>>
>>> help(hostname.upper)  # output omitted
>>>
```

- When you need to check a variable type within Python, error handling (try/except) can be used, but if you do need to explicitly know what type of an object something is, isinstance() is a great function to know about. It returns True if the variable being passed in is of the object type also being passed in.

```
>>> hostname = ''
>>> devices = []

>>> if isinstance(devices, list):
...     print('devices is a list')
...
devices is a list
>>>
>>> if isinstance(hostname, str):
...     print('hostname is a string')
```

```
...
hostname is a string
>>>
```

- We spent time learning how to use the Python interpreter and create Python scripts. Python offers the `-i` flag to be used when executing a script, but instead of exiting the script, it enters the interpreter, giving you access to all of the objects built in the script—this is *great* for testing.

Here's a sample file called *test.py*:

```
if __name__ == "__main__":
    devices = ['r1', 'r2', 'r3']

    hostname = 'router5'
```

Let's see what happens when we run the script with the `-i` flag set.

```
$ python -i test.py
>>>
>>> print(devices)
['r1', 'r2', 'r3']
>>>
>>> print(hostname)
router5
>>>
```

Notice how it executed, but then it dropped you right into the Python shell and you have access to those objects. Pretty cool, right?

- Objects are `True` if they are not null and `False` if they are null. Here are a few examples:

```
>>> devices = []
>>> if not devices:
...     print('devices is empty')
...
devices is empty
>>>
>>> hostname = 'something'
>>>
>>> if hostname:
...     print('hostname is not null')
...
hostname is not null
>>>
```

- In the section on strings, we looked at concatenating strings using the plus sign (+), but also learned how to use the `format()` method, which was a lot cleaner. There is another option to do the same thing using %. One example for inserting strings (s) is provided here:

```
>>> hostname = 'r5'
>>>
>>> interface = 'Eth1/1'
>>>
>>> test  = 'Device %s has one interface: %s ' % (hostname, interface)
>>>
>>> print(test)
Device r5 has one interface: Eth1/1
>>>
```

- We haven't spent any time on comments, but did mention the # (known as a hash tag, number sign, or pound sign) is used for inline comments.

```
def get_commands(vlan, name):
    commands = []

    # building list of commands to configure a vlan
    commands.append('vlan ' + vlan)
    commands.append('name ' + name)  # appending name
    return commands
```

- A docstring is usually added to functions, methods, and classes that help describe what the object is doing. It should use triple quotes (""") and is usually limited to one line.

```
def get_commands(vlan, name):
    """Get commands to configure a VLAN.
    """

    commands = []
    commands.append('vlan ' + vlan)
    commands.append('name ' + name)
    return commands
```

You learned how to import a module, namely *push.py*. Let's import it again now to see what happens when we use help on get_commands() since we now have a docstring configured.

```
>>> import push
>>>
>>> help(push.get_commands)

Help on function get_commands in module push:

get_commands(vlan, name)
    Get commands to configure a VLAN.
(END)
>>>
```

You see all docstrings when you use help. Additionally, you see information about the parameters and what data is returned if properly documented.

We've now added Args and Returns values to the docstring.

```python
def get_commands(vlan, name):
    """Get commands to configure a VLAN.

    Args:
        vlan (int): vlan id
        name (str): name of the vlan

    Returns:
        List of commands is returned.
    """

    commands = []
    commands.append('vlan ' + vlan)
    commands.append('name ' + name)
    return commands
```

These are now displayed when the help() function is used to provide users of this function much more context on how to use it.

```
>>> import push
>>>
>>> help(push.get_commands)

Help on function get_commands in module push:

get_commands(vlan, name)
    Get commands to configure a VLAN.

    Args:
        vlan (int): vlan id
        name (str): name of the vlan

    Returns:
        List of commands is returned.
(END)
```

- Writing your own classes wasn't covered in this chapter because classes are an advanced topic, but a very basic introduction of using them is shown here because they are used in subsequent chapters.

  We'll walk through an example of not only using a class, but also importing the class that is part of a Python package (another new concept). Please note, this is a mock-up and general example. This is not using a real Python package.

```
>>> from vendors.cisco.device import Device
>>>
>>> switch = Device(ip='10.1.1.1', username='cisco', password='cisco')
>>>
>>> switch.show('show version')
# output omitted
```

What is actually happening in this example is that we are importing the `Device` class from the module *device.py* that is part of the Python package called *vendors* (which is just a directory). That may have been a mouthful, but the bottom line is, the import should look very similar to what you saw in "Working with Python Modules" on page 140, and a Python package is just a collection of modules that are stored in different directories.

As you look at the example code and compare it to importing the `push_com mands()` function from "Working with Python Modules" on page 140, you'll notice a difference. The function is used immediately, but the class needs to be initialized.

The class is being initialized with this statement:

```
>>> switch = Device(ip='10.1.1.1', username='cisco', password='cisco')
>>>
```

The arguments passed in are used to construct an instance of `Device`. At this point, if you had multiple devices, you may have something like this:

```
>>> switch1 = Device(ip='10.1.1.1', username='cisco', password='cisco')
>>> switch2 = Device(ip='10.1.1.2', username='cisco', password='cisco')
>>> switch3 = Device(ip='10.1.1.3', username='cisco', password='cisco')
>>>
```

In this case, each variable is a separate instance of `Device`.

> Parameters are not always used when a class is initialized. Every class is different, but if parameters are being used, they are passed to what is called the constructor of the class; in Python, this is the method called __init__. A class without a constructor would be initialized like so: `demo = FakeClass()`. Then you would use its methods like so: `demo.method()`.

Once the class object is initialized and created, you can start to use its *methods*. This is just like using the built-in methods for the data types we learned about earlier in the chapter. The syntax is *class_object.method*.

In this example, the method being used is called `show()`. And in real time it returns data from a network device.

> As a reminder, using method objects of a class is just like using the methods of the different data types such as strings, lists, and dictionaries. While creating classes is an advanced topic, you should understand how to use them.

If we executed `show` for `switch2` and `switch3`, we would get the proper return data back as expected, since each object is a different instance of `Device`.

Here is a brief example that shows the creation of two `Device` objects and then uses those objects to get the output of `show hostname` on each device. With the library being used, it is returning XML data by default, but this can easily be changed, if desired, to JSON.

```
>>> switch1 = Device(ip='nycsw01', username='cisco', password='cisco')
>>> switch2 = Device(ip='nycsw02', username='cisco', password='cisco')
>>>
>>> switches = [switch1, switch2]
>>> for switch in switches:
...     response = switch.show('show hostname')[1]
...     print(response)
...
# output omitted
>>>
```

Summary

This chapter provided a grass-roots introduction to Python for network engineers. We covered foundational concepts such as working with data types, conditionals, loops, functions, and files, and even how to create a Python module that allows you to reuse the same code in different Python programs/scripts. Finally, we closed out the chapter by providing a few tips and tricks along with other general information that you should use as a reference as you continue on with your Python and network automation journey.

In Chapter 5 we introduce you to different data formats such as YAML, JSON, and XML, and in that process, we also build on what was covered in this chapter. For example, you'll take what you learned and start to use Python modules to simplify the process of working with these data types, and also see the direct correlation between YAML, JSON, and Python dictionaries.

## CHAPTER 5

Data Formats and Data Models

If you've done any amount of exploration into the world of APIs, you've likely heard about terms like JSON, XML, or YAML. Perhaps you've heard the terms XSD or YANG. You may have heard the term *markup language* when discussing one of these. But what are these things, and what do they have to do with networking or network automation?

In the same way that routers and switches require standardized protocols in order to communicate, applications need to be able to agree on some kind of syntax in order to exchange data between them. For this, applications can use standard *data formats* like JSON and XML (among others). Not only do applications need to agree on how the data is formatted, but also on how the data is structured. *Data models* define how the data stored in a particular data format is structured.

In this chapter, we'll discuss some of the formats most commonly used with network APIs and automation tools, and how you as a network developer can leverage these tools to accomplish tasks. We'll also briefly discuss data models and their role in network automation.

Introduction to Data Formats

A computer programmer typically uses a wide variety of tools to store and work with data in the programs they build. They may use simple variables (single value), arrays (multiple values), hashes (key-value pairs), or even custom objects built in the syntax of the language they're using.

This is all perfectly standard within the confines of the software being written. However, sometimes a more abstract, portable format is required. For instance, a non-programmer may need to move data in and out of these programs. Another program may have to communicate with this program in a similar way, and the programs may not even be written in the same language, as is often the case with something like traditional client-server communications. For example, many third-party user interfaces (UIs) are used to interface with public cloud providers. This is made possible (in a simplified fashion) thanks to standard data formats. The moral of the story is that we need a standard format to allow a diverse set of software to communicate with each other, and for humans to interface with it.

It turns out there are a few options. With respect to data formats, what we're talking about is text-based representation of data that would otherwise be represented as internal software constructs in memory. All of the data formats that we'll discuss in this chapter have broad support over a multitude of languages and operating systems. In fact, many languages, including Python, which we covered in Chapter 4, have built-in tools that make it easy to import and export data to these formats, either on the filesystem or on the network.

So as a network engineer, how does all this talk about software impact you? For one thing, this level of standardization is already in place from a raw network protocol perspective. Protocols like BGP, OSPF, and TCP/IP were conceived out of a necessity for network devices to have a single language to speak across a globally distributed system—the internet! The data formats in this chapter were conceived for a very similar reason—to enable computer systems to openly understand and communicate with each other.

Every device you have installed, configured, or upgraded was given life by a software developer that considered these very topics. Some network vendors saw fit to provide mechanisms that allow operators to interact with a network device using these widely supported data formats; others did not. The goal of this chapter is to help you understand the value of standardized and simplified formats like these, so that you can use them to your advantage on your network automation journey.

For example, some configuration models are friendly to automated methods, by representing the configuration model in these data formats like XML or JSON. It is very easy to see the XML representation of a certain data set in Junos, for example:

```
root@vsrx01> show interfaces | display xml
<rpc-reply xmlns:junos="http://xml.juniper.net/junos/12.1X47/junos">
    <interface-information xmlns="http://xml.juniper.net/junos/12.1X47/
    junos-interface" junos:style="normal">
        <physical-interface>
            <name>ge-0/0/0</name>
            <admin-status junos:format="Enabled">up</admin-status>
            <oper-status>up</oper-status>
            <local-index>134</local-index>
            <snmp-index>507</snmp-index>
            <link-level-type>Ethernet</link-level-type>
            <mtu>1514</mtu>
            <source-filtering>disabled</source-filtering>
            <link-mode>Full-duplex</link-mode>
```

```
<speed>1000mbps</speed>
```

```
... output truncated ...
```

Now, of course this is not very easy on the eyes, but that's not the point. From a programmatic perspective, this is ideal, since each piece of data is given its own easily parseable field. A piece of software doesn't have to guess where to find the name of the interface; it's located at the well-known and documented tag "name". This is key to understanding the different needs that a software system may have when interacting with infrastructure components, as opposed to a human being on the CLI.

When thinking about data formats at a high level, it's important to first understand exactly what we intend to do with the various data formats at our disposal. Each was created for a different use case, and understanding these use cases will help you decide which is appropriate for you to use.

Types of Data

Now that we've discussed the use case for data formats, it's important to briefly talk about what kind of data might be represented by these formats. After all, the purpose of these formats is to communicate things like words, numbers, and even complex objects between software instances. If you've taken any sort of programming course, you've likely heard of most of these.

 Note that since this chapter isn't about any specific programming languages, these are just generic examples. These data types may be represented by different names, depending on their implementation.

Chapter 4 goes over Python specifically, so be sure to go back and refer to that chapter for Python-specific definitions and usage.

String

Arguably, the most fundamental data type is the string. This is a very common way of representing a sequence of numbers, letters, or symbols. If you wanted to represent an English sentence in one of the data formats we'll discuss in this chapter, or in a programming language, you'd probably use a string to do so. In Python, you may see `str` or `unicode` to represent these.

Integer

There are actually a number (get it?) of data types that have to do with numerical values, but for most people the integer is the first that comes to mind when discussing numerical data types. The integer is exactly what you learned in math class: a whole number, positive or negative. There are other data types like float or decimal that you might use to describe non-whole values. Python represents integers using the int type.

Boolean

One of the simplest data types is boolean, a simple value that is either true or false. This is a very popular type used when a programmer wishes to know the result of an operation, or whether two values are equal to each other, for example. This is known as the bool type in Python.

Advanced data structures

Data types can be organized into complex structures as well. All of the formats we'll discuss in this language support a basic concept known as an *array*, or a *list* in some cases. This is a list of values or objects that can be represented and referenced by some kind of index. There are also key-value pairs, known by many names, such as dictionaries, hashes, hash maps, hash tables, or maps. This is similar to the array, but the values are organized according to key-value pairs, where both the key and the value can be one of several types of data, like string, integer, and so on. An array can take many forms in Python: sets, tuples, and lists are all used to represent a sequence of items, but are different from each other in what sort of flexibility they offer. Key-value pairs are represented by the dict type.

This is not a comprehensive list, but covers the vast majority of use cases in this chapter. Again, the implementation-specific details for these data types really depend on the context in which they appear. The good news is that all of the data formats we'll discuss in this chapter have wide and very flexible support for all of these and more.

Throughout the rest of this chapter, we'll refer to data types in monospaced fonts, like string or boolean, so that it's clear we're referring to a specific data type.

Now that we've established what data formats are all about, and what types of data may be represented by each of them, let's dive in to some specific examples and see these concepts written out.

YAML

If you're reading this book because you've seen some compelling examples of network automation online or in a presentation and you want to learn more, you may have heard of YAML. This is because YAML is a particularly human-friendly data format, and for this reason, it is being discussed before any other in this chapter.

 YAML stands for "YAML Ain't Markup Language," which seems to tell us that the creators of YAML didn't want it to become just some new markup standard, but a unique attempt to represent data in a human-readable way. Also, the acronym is recursive!

Reviewing YAML Basics

If you compare YAML to the other data formats that we'll discuss like XML or JSON, it seems to do much the same thing: it represents constructs like lists, key-value pairs, strings, and integers. However, as you'll soon see, YAML does this is an exceptionally human-readable way. YAML is very easy to read and write if you understand the basic data types discussed in the last section.

This is a big reason that an increasing number of tools (see Ansible) are using YAML as a method of defining an automation workflow, or providing a data set to work with (like a list of VLANs). It's very easy to use YAML to get from zero to a functional automation workflow, or to define the data you wish to push to a device.

At the time of this writing, the latest YAML specification is YAML 1.2, published at *http://www.yaml.org/*. Also provided on that site is a list of software projects that implement YAML, typically for the purpose of being read in to language-specific data structures and doing something with them. If you have a favorite language, it might be helpful to follow along with the YAML examples in this chapter, and try to implement them using one of these libraries.

Let's take a look at some examples. Let's say we want to use YAML to represent a list of network vendors. If you paid attention in the last section, you'll probably be thinking that we want to use a `string` to represent each vendor name—and you'd be correct! This example is very simple:

```
---
- Cisco
- Juniper
- Brocade
- VMware
```

You'll notice three hyphens (`---`) at the top of every example in this section; this is a YAML convention that indicates the beginning of our YAML document.

The YAML specification also states that an ellipsis (…) is used to indicate the end of a document, and that you can actually have multiple instances of triple hyphens to indicate multiple documents within one file or data stream. These methods are typically only used in communication channels (e.g., for termination of messages), which is not a very popular use case, so we won't be using either of these approaches in this chapter.

This YAML document contains four items. We know that each item is a `string`. One of the nice features of YAML is that we usually don't need quote or double-quote marks to indicate a string; this is something that is usually automatically discovered by the YAML parser (e.g., PyYAML). Each of these items has a hyphen in front of it.

Since all four of these strings are shown at the same level (no indentation), we can say that these strings compose a list with a length of 4.

YAML very closely mimics the flexibility of Python's data structures, so we can take advantage of this flexibility without having to write any Python. A good example of this flexibility is shown when we mix data types in this list (not every language supports this):

```
---
- Core Switch
- 7700
- False
- ['switchport', 'mode', 'access']
```

In this example, we have another list, again with a length of 4. However, each item is a totally unique type. The first item, Core Switch, is a string type. The second, 7700, is interpreted as an integer. The third is interpreted as a boolean. This "interpretation" is performed by a YAML interpreter, such as PyYAML. PyYAML, specifically, does a pretty good job of inferring what kind of data the user is trying to communicate.

YAML boolean types are actually very flexible, and accept a wide variety of values that really end up meaning the same thing when interpreted by a YAML parser.

For instance, you could write False, as in the above example, or you could write no, off, or even simply n. They all end up meaning the same thing: a false boolean value. This is a big reason that YAML is often used as a human interface for many software projects.

The fourth item in this example is actually itself a list, containing three string items. We've seen our first example of nested data structures in YAML! We've also seen an example of the various ways that some data can be represented. Our "outer" list is shown on separate lines, with each item prepended by a hyphen. The inner list is shown on one line, using brackets and commas. These are two ways of writing the same thing: a list.

Note that sometimes it's possible to help the parser figure out the type of data we wish to communicate. For instance, if we wanted the second item to be recognized as a string instead of an integer, we could enclose it in quotes ("7700"). Another reason to enclose something in quotes would be if a string contained a character that was part of the YAML syntax itself, such as a colon (:).

Refer to the documentation for the specific YAML parser you're using for more information on this.

Early on in this chapter we also briefly talked about key-value pairs (or dictionaries, as they're called in Python). YAML supports this structure quite simply. Let's see how we might represent a dictionary with four key-value pairs:

```
---
Juniper: Also a plant
Cisco: 6500
Brocade: True
VMware:
  - esxi
  - vcenter
  - nsx
```

Here, our keys are shown as `strings` to the left of the colon, and the corresponding values for those keys are shown to the right. If we wanted to look up one of these values in a Python program for instance, we would reference the corresponding key for the value we are looking for.

Similar to lists, dictionaries are very flexible with respect to the data types stored as values. In the above example, we are storing a myriad of data types as the values for each key-value pair.

It's also worth mentioning that YAML dictionaries—like lists—can be written in multiple ways. From a data representation standpoint, the previous example is identical to this:

```
---
{Juniper: Also a plant, Cisco: 6500, Brocade: True,
VMware: ['esxi', 'vcenter', 'nsx']}
```

Most parsers will interpret these two YAML documents precisely the same, but the first is obviously far more readable. That brings us to the crux of this argument: if you are looking for a more human-readable document, use the more verbose options. If not, you probably don't even want to be using YAML in the first place, and you may want something like JSON or XML. For instance, in an API, readability is nearly irrelevant—the emphasis is on speed and wide software support.

Finally, you can use a hash sign (#) to indicate a comment. This can be on its own line, or after existing data.

```
---
- Cisco      # ocsiC
- Juniper    # repinuJ
- Brocade    # edacorB
- VMware     # erawMV
```

Anything after the hash sign is ignored by the YAML parser.

As you can see, YAML can be used to provide a friendly way for human beings to interact with software systems. However, YAML is fairly new as far as data formats go.

With respect to communication directly between software elements (i.e., no human interaction), other formats like XML and JSON are much more popular and have much more mature tooling that is conducive to that purpose.

Working with YAML in Python

Let's narrow in on a single example to see how exactly a YAML interpreter will read in the data we've written in a YAML document. Let's reuse some previously seen YAML to illustrate the various ways we can represent certain data types:

```
---
Juniper: Also a plant
Cisco: 6500
Brocade: True
VMware:
  - esxi
  - vcenter
  - nsx
```

Let's say this YAML document is saved to our local filesystem as *example.yml*. Our objective is to use Python to read this YAML file, parse it, and represent the contained data as some kind of variable.

Fortunately, the combination of native Python syntax and the aforementioned third-party YAML parser, PyYAML, makes this very easy:

```
import yaml
with open("example.yml") as f:
    result = yaml.load(f)
    print(result)
    type(result)

{'Brocade': True, 'Cisco': 6500, 'Juniper': 'Also a plant',
'VMware': ['esxi', 'vcenter', 'nsx']}
<type 'dict'>
```

 The Python snippet used in the previous example uses the yaml module that is installed with the pyyaml Python package. This is easily installed using pip as discussed in Chapter 4.

This example shows how easy it is to load a YAML file into a Python dictionary. First, a context manager is used to open the file for reading (a very common method for reading any kind of text file in Python), and the load() function in the yaml module allows us to load this directly into a dictionary called result. The following lines show that this has been done successfully.

Data Models in YAML

In the introduction to this chapter, we mentioned that data models define the structure for how data is stored in a data format, such as YAML, XML, or JSON. Let's take a look at one of the YAML examples from the previous section and discuss it in the context of data models for YAML.

Let's say we had this data stored in YAML:

```
---
Juniper: vSRX
Cisco: Nexus
Brocade: VDX
VMware: NSX
```

Intuitively, we—as people—can look at this data in YAML and understand that it is a list of vendors and a network product from that vendor. We've mentally created a data model that says each entry in this YAML document should contain a pair of `string` values; the first `string` (the key) is the vendor name, and the second `string` (the value) is the product name. Together, these `strings` form a dictionary of key-value pairs.

However, what if we were working with this (implied) data model and supplied this data instead?

```
---
Juniper: vSRX
Cisco: 6500
Brocade: True
VMware:
  - esxi
  - vcenter
  - nsx
```

This is valid YAML, but it's invalid data. Even if Brocade had a product named "True," most YAML interpreters would (by default) read this data as a `boolean` value instead of a `string`. When our software went to do something with this data, it would expect a `string` and get a `boolean` instead—and that would very likely cause the software to produce incorrect results or even crash.

Data models are a way to define the structure and content of data stored in a data format such as YAML. Using a data model, we could explicitly state that the data in the YAML document must be a key-value list, and that each value must be a `string`.

Unfortunately, YAML does not provide any built-in mechanism for describing or enforcing data models. There are third-party tools (one such example is Kwalify (*http://www.kuwata-lab.com/kwalify/*)). This is one reason why YAML is very suitable for human-to-machine interaction, but not necessarily as well suited for machine-to-machine interaction.

YAML is considered a superset of JSON, a format we'll discuss later in this chapter. In theory, this means that tools for validating a JSON schema—the data model for a JSON document—could also validate a YAML document.

The next data format, XML, offers some features and functionality that make it more suitable for machine-to-machine interaction. Let's take a closer look.

XML

As mentioned in the previous section, while YAML is a suitable choice for human-to-machine interaction, other formats like XML and JSON tend to be favored as the data representation choice when software elements need to communicate with each other. In this section, we're going to talk about XML, and why it is suitable for this use case.

XML enjoys wide support in a variety of tools and languages, such as the LXML library (*http://lxml.de/*) in Python. In fact, the XML definition itself is accompanied by a variety of related definitions for things like schema enforcement, transformations, and advanced queries. As a result, this section will attempt only to whet your appetite with respect to XML. You are encouraged to try some of the tools and formats listed on your own.

Reviewing XML Basics

XML shares some similarities to what we've seen with YAML. For instance, it is inherently hierarchical. We can very easily embed data within a parent construct:

```
<device>
  <vendor>Cisco</vendor>
  <model>Nexus 7700</model>
  <osver>NXOS 6.1</osver>
</device>
```

In this example, the `<device>` element is said to be the root. While spacing and indentation don't matter for the validity of XML, we can easily see this, as it is the first and outermost XML tag in the document. It is also the parent of the elements nested within it: `<vendor>`, `<model>`, and `<osver>`. These are referred to as the *children* of the `<device>` element, and they are considered siblings of each other. This is very conducive to storing metadata about network devices, as you can see in this particular example. In an XML document, there may be multiple instances of the `<device>` tag (or multiple `<device>` elements), perhaps nested within a broader `<devices>` tag.

You'll also notice that each child element also contains data within. Where the root element contained XML children, these tags contain text data. Thinking back to the section on data types, it is likely these would be represented by `string` values in a Python program, for instance.

XML elements can also have attributes:

```
<device type="datacenter-switch" />
```

When a piece of information may have some associated metadata, it may not be appropriate to use a child element, but rather an attribute.

The XML specification has also implemented a namespace system, which helps to prevent element naming conflicts. Developers can use any name they want when creating XML documents. When a piece of software leverages XML, it's possible that the software would be given two XML elements with the same name, but those elements would have different content and purpose.

For instance, an XML document could implement the following:

```
<device>Palm Pilot</device>
```

This example uses the `<device>` element name, but clearly is being used for some purpose other than representing a network device, and therefore has a totally different meaning than our switch definition a few examples back.

Namespaces can help with this, by defining and leveraging prefixes in the XML document itself, using the `xmlns` designation:

```
<root>
  <e:device xmlns:c="http://example.org/enduserdevices">Palm Pilot</e:device>
  <n:device xmlns:m="http://example.org/networkdevices">
    <n:vendor>Cisco</n:vendor>
    <n:model>Nexus 7700</n:model>
    <n:osver>NXOS 6.1</n:osver>
  </n:device>
</root>
```

There is much more involved with writing and reading a valid XML document. We recommend you check out the W3Schools documentation on XML (*http://www.w3schools.com/xml/*).

Using XML Schema Definition (XSD) for Data Models

While YAML has some built-in constructs to help describe the data type within (the use of hyphens and indentation), XML doesn't have those same mechanisms. Many XML parsers don't make the same assumptions that PyYAML and other YAML parsers do, for example.

Recall from the beginning of this chapter that we described data formats as allowing applications—or devices, like network devices—to exchange information in standardized ways. XML is one of these standardized ways to exchange information. However, data formats like XML don't enforce what *kind* of data is contained in the various fields and values. To help ensure the right kind of data is in the right XML elements, we have *XML Schema Definition (XSD)*.

XML Schema Definition (*http://www.w3schools.com/schema/*) allows us to describe the building blocks of an XML document. Using this language, we're able to place constraints on where data should (or should not) be in our XML document. There were previous attempts to provide this functionality (e.g., DTD), but they were limited in their capabilities. Also, XSD is actually written in XML, which simplifies things greatly.

One very popular use case for XSD—or really any sort of schema or modeling language—is to generate source code data structures that match the schema. We can then use that source code to automatically generate XML that is compliant with that schema, as opposed to writing out the XML by hand.

For a concrete example of how this is done in Python, let's look once more at our XML example.

```
<device>
  <vendor>Cisco</vendor>
  <model>Nexus 7700</model>
  <osver>NXOS 6.1</osver>
</device>
```

Our goal is to print this XML to the console. We can do this by first creating an XSD document, then generating Python code from that document using a third-party tool. Then, that code can be used to print the XML we need.

Let's write an XSD schema file that describes the data we intend to write out:

```
<?xml version="1.0" encoding="utf-8"?>
<xs:schema elementFormDefault="qualified" xmlns:xs="http://www.w3.org/2001/
XMLSchema">
  <xs:element name="device">
  <xs:complexType>
    <xs:sequence>
      <xs:element name="vendor" type="xs:string"/>
      <xs:element name="model" type="xs:string"/>
      <xs:element name="osver" type="xs:string"/>
    </xs:sequence>
  </xs:complexType>
</xs:element>
</xs:schema>
```

In this schema document, we can see that we are describing that each <device> element can have three children, and that the data in each of these child elements must be a string. Not shown here but supported in the XSD specification is the ability to specify that child elements are required; in other words, you could specify that a <device> element *must* have a <vendor> child element present.

We can use a Python tool called pyxb to create a Python file that contains class object representations of this schema:

```
~$ pyxbgen -u schema.xsd -m schema
```

This will create *schema.py* in this directory. So, if we open a Python prompt at this point, we can import this schema file and work with it. In the below example, we're creating an instance of the generated object, setting some properties on it, and then rendering that into XML using the toxml() function:

```
import schema
dev = schema.device()
dev.vendor = "Cisco"
dev.model = "Nexus"
dev.osver = "6.1"
dev.toxml("utf-8")
'<?xml version="1.0" encoding="utf-8"?><device><vendor>Cisco</vendor><model>Nexus
</model><osver>6.1</osver></device>'
```

This is just one way of doing this; there are other third-party libraries that allow for code generation from XSD files. Also take a look at generateDS, located here: *https:// pypi.python.org/pypi/generateDS/*.

 Some RESTful APIs (see Chapter 7) use XML to encode data between software endpoints. Using XSD allows the developer to generate compliant XML much more accurately, and with fewer steps. So, if you come across a RESTful API on your network device, ask your vendor to provide schema documentation—it will save you some time.

There is much more information about XSD located on the W3Schools site at *https:// www.w3.org/standards/xml/schema*.

Transforming XML with XSLT

Given that the majority of physical network devices still primarily use a text-based, human-oriented mechanism for configuration, you might have to familiarize yourself with some kind of template format. There are a myriad of them out there, and templates in general are very useful for performing safe and effective network automation.

The next chapter in this book, Chapter 6, goes into detail on templating languages, especially Jinja. However, since we're talking about XML, we may as well briefly discuss Extensible Stylesheet Language Transformations (XSLT).

XSLT is a language for applying transformations to XML data, primarily to convert them into XHTML or other XML documents. As with many other languages related to XML, XSLT is defined on the W3Schools site, and more information is located here at *http://www.w3schools.com/xsl/*.

Let's look at a practical example of how to populate an XSLT template with meaningful data so that a resulting document can be achieved. As with our previous examples, we'll leverage some Python to make this happen.

The first thing we need is some raw data to populate our template. This XML document will suffice:

```
<?xml version="1.0" encoding="UTF-8"?>
<authors>
    <author>
        <firstName>Jason</firstName>
        <lastName>Edelman</lastName>
    </author>
    <author>
        <firstName>Scott</firstName>
        <lastName>Lowe</lastName>
    </author>
    <author>
        <firstName>Matt</firstName>
        <lastName>Oswalt</lastName>
    </author>
</authors>
```

This amounts to a list of authors, each with `<firstName>` and `<lastName>` elements. The goal is to use this data to generate an HTML table that displays these authors, via an XSLT document.

An XSLT template to perform this task might look like this:

```
<?xml version="1.0" encoding="UTF-8"?>

<xsl:stylesheet xmlns:xsl="http://www.w3.org/1999/XSL/Transform" version="1.0">
<xsl:output indent="yes"/>
<xsl:template match="/">
  <html>
  <body>
  <h2>Authors</h2>
    <table border="1">
      <tr bgcolor="#9acd32">
        <th style="text-align:left">First Name</th>
        <th style="text-align:left">Last Name</th>
      </tr>
      <xsl:for-each select="authors/author">
      <tr>
        <td><xsl:value-of select="firstName"/></td>
        <td><xsl:value-of select="lastName"/></td>
      </tr>
      </xsl:for-each>
    </table>
```

```
    </body>
    </html>
 </xsl:template>
 </xsl:stylesheet>
```

A few notes on the above XSLT document:

- First, you'll notice that there is a basic `for-each` construct embedded in what otherwise looks like valid HTML. This is a very standard practice in template language—the static text remains static, and little bits of logic are placed where needed. You'll see more of this in Chapter 6.

- Second, it's also worth pointing out that this `for-each` statement uses a "coordinate" argument (listed as `"authors/author"`) to state exactly which part of our XML document contains the data we wish to use. This is called XPath, and it is a syntax used within XML documents and tools to specify a location within an XML tree.

- Finally, we use the `value-of` statement to dynamically insert (like a variable in a Python program) a value as text from our XML data.

Assuming our XSLT template is saved as *template.xsl*, and our data file as *xmldata.xml*, we can return to our trusty Python interpreter to combine these two pieces and come up with the resulting HTML output.

```
from lxml import etree
xslRoot = etree.fromstring(open("template.xsl").read())
transform = etree.XSLT(xslRoot)
xmlRoot = etree.fromstring(open("xmldata.xml").read())
transRoot = transform(xmlRoot)
print(etree.tostring(transRoot))

<html><body><h2>Authors</h2><table border="1"><tr bgcolor="#9acd32">
<th style="text-align:left">First Name</th><th style="text-align:left">Last Name
</th></tr>
<tr><td>Jason</td><td>Edelman</td></tr>
<tr><td>Scott</td><td>Lowe</td></tr>
<tr><td>Matt</td><td>Oswalt</td></tr></table></body></html>
```

This produces a valid HTML table for us, seen in Figure 5-1.

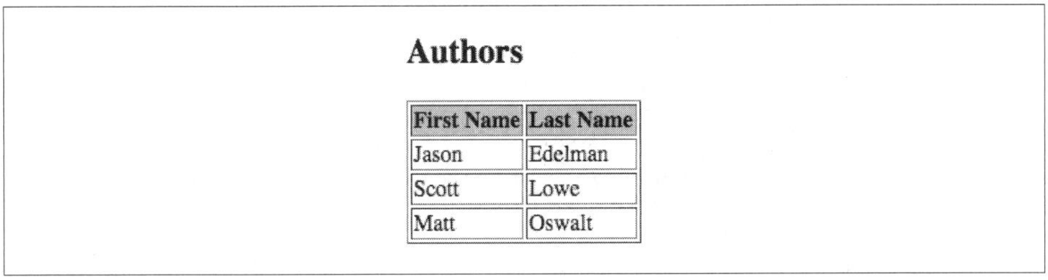

Figure 5-1. HTML table produced by XSLT

XSLT also provides some additional logic statements:

- `<if>`—only output the given element(s) if a certain condition is met
- `<sort>`—sorting elements before writing them as output
- `<choose>`—a more advanced version of the `if` statement (allows "else if" or "else" style of logic)

It's possible for us to take this example even further, and use this concept to create a network configuration template, using configuration data defined in XML, as shown in Examples 5-1 and 5-2:

Example 5-1. XML interface data

```
<?xml version="1.0" encoding="UTF-8"?>
<interfaces>
    <interface>
        <name>GigabitEthernet0/0</name>
        <ipv4addr>192.168.0.1 255.255.255.0</ipv4addr>
    </interface>
    <interface>
        <name>GigabitEthernet0/1</name>
        <ipv4addr>172.16.31.1 255.255.255.0</ipv4addr>
    </interface>
    <interface>
        <name>GigabitEthernet0/2</name>
        <ipv4addr>10.3.2.1 255.255.254.0</ipv4addr>
    </interface>
</interfaces>
```

Example 5-2. XSLT template for router config

```
<?xml version="1.0" encoding="UTF-8"?>
<xsl:stylesheet version="1.0" xmlns:xsl="http://www.example.org/routerconfig">

<xsl:template match="/">
    <xsl:for-each select="interfaces/interface">
      interface <xsl:value-of select="name"/><br />
          ip address <xsl:value-of select="ipv4addr"/><br />
    </xsl:for-each>
</xsl:template>
</xsl:stylesheet>
```

With the XML and XSLT documents shown in Examples 5-1 and 5-2, we can get a rudimentary router configuration in the same way we generated an HTML page:

```
interface GigabitEthernet0/0
ip address 192.168.0.1 255.255.255.0
interface GigabitEthernet0/1
```

```
ip address 172.16.31.1 255.255.255.0
interface GigabitEthernet0/2
ip address 10.3.2.1 255.255.254.0
```

As you can see, it's possible to produce a network configuration by using XSLT. However, it is admittedly a bit cumbersome. It's likely that you will find Jinja a much more useful templating language for creating network configurations, as it has a lot of features that are conducive to network automation. Jinja is covered in Chapter 6.

Searching XML Using XQuery

In the previous section, we alluded to using XPath in our XSLT documents to very particularly locate specific nodes in our XML document. However, if we needed to perform a more advanced lookup, we would need a bit more than a simple coordinate system.

XQuery leverages tools like XPath to find and extract data from an XML document. For instance, if you are accessing the REST API of a router or switch using Python, you may have to write a bit of extra code to get to the exact portion of the XML output that you wish to use. Alternatively, you can use XQuery immediately upon receiving this data to present only the data relevant to your Python program.

XQuery is a powerful tool, almost like a programming language unto itself. For more info on XQuery, check out the W3School specification (*https://www.w3.org/stand ards/xml/query.html*).

JSON

So far in this chapter, we've discussed YAML, a tool well suited for human interaction and easy import into common programming language data structures. We've also discussed XML, which isn't the most attractive format to look at, but has a rich ecosystem of tools and wide software support. In this section, we'll discuss JSON, which combines a few of these strengths into one data format.

Reviewing JSON Basics

JSON was invented at a time when web developers were in need of a lightweight communication mechanism between web servers and applets embedded within web pages. XML was around at this time, of course, but it proved a bit too bloated to meet the needs of the ever-demanding internet.

You may have also noticed that YAML and XML differ in a big way with respect to how these two data formats map to the data model of most programming languages like Python. With libraries like PyYAML, importing a YAML document into source code is nearly effortless. However, with XML there are usually a few more steps needed, depending on what you want to do.

For these and other reasons, JavaScript Object Notation (JSON) burst onto the scene in the early 2000s. It aimed to be a lightweight version of XML, more suited to the data models found within popular programming languages. It's also considered by many to be more human-readable, although that is a secondary concern for data formats.

 Note that JSON is widely considered to be a subset of YAML. In fact, many popular YAML parsers can also parse JSON data as if it were YAML. However, some of the details of this relationship are a bit more complicated. See the YAML specification section (*http://yaml.org/spec/1.2/spec.html#id2759572*) for more information.

In the previous section, we showed an example of how three authors may be represented in an XML document:

```
<authors>
    <author>
        <firstName>Jason</firstName>
        <lastName>Edelman</lastName>
    </author>
    <author>
        <firstName>Scott</firstName>
        <lastName>Lowe</lastName>
    </author>
    <author>
        <firstName>Matt</firstName>
        <lastName>Oswalt</lastName>
    </author>
</authors>
```

To illustrate the difference between JSON and XML, specifically with respect to JSON's more lightweight nature, here is an equivalent data model provided in JSON:

```
{
    "authors":[
        {
            "firstName": "Jason",
            "lastName": "Edelman"
        },
        {
            "firstName": "Scott",
            "lastName": "Lowe"
        },
        {
            "firstName": "Matt",
            "lastName": "Oswalt"
        }
    ]
}
```

This is significantly simpler than its XML counterpart. No wonder JSON was more attractive than XML in the early 2000s, when "Web 2.0" was just getting started!

Let's look specifically at some of the features. You'll notice that the whole thing is wrapped in curly braces {}. This is very common, and it indicates that JSON objects are contained inside. You can think of "objects" as key-value pairs, or dictionaries as we discussed in the section on YAML. JSON objects always use `string` values when describing the keys in these constructs.

In this case, our key is `"authors"`, and the value for that key is a JSON list. This is also equivalent to the list format we discussed in YAML—an ordered list of zero or more values. This is indicated by the square brackets [].

Contained within this list are three objects (separated by commas and a newline), each with two key-value pairs. The first pair describes the author's first name (key of `"firstName"`) and the second, the author's last name (key of `"lastName"`).

We discussed the basics of data types at the beginning of this chapter, but let's take an abbreviated look at the supported data types in JSON. You'll find they match our experience from YAML quite nicely:

Number
A signed decimal number.

String
A collection of characters, such as a word or a sentence.

Boolean
`True` or `False`.

Array
An ordered list of values; items do not have to be the same type (enclosed in square brackets, []).

Object
An unordered collection of key-value pairs; keys must be `strings` (enclosed in curly braces, {}).

Null
Empty value. Uses the word `null`.

Let's work with JSON in Python and see what we can do with it. This will be quite similar to what we reviewed when using Python dictionaries in Chapter 4.

Working with JSON in Python

JSON enjoys wide support across a myriad of languages. In fact, you will often be able to simply import a JSON data structure into constructs of a given language, simply with a one-line command. Let's take a look at some examples.

Our JSON data is stored in a simple text file:

```
{
  "hostname": "CORESW01",
  "vendor": "Cisco",
  "isAlive": true,
  "uptime": 123456,
  "users": {
    "admin": 15,
    "storage": 10,
  },
  "vlans": [
    {
      "vlan_name": "VLAN30",
      "vlan_id": 30
    },
    {
      "vlan_name": "VLAN20",
      "vlan_id": 20
    }
  ]
}
```

Our goal is to import the data found within this file into the constructs used by our language of choice.

First, let's use Python. Python has tools for working with JSON built right in to its standard library, aptly called the `json` package. In this example, we define a JSON data structure (borrowed from the Wikipedia entry on JSON) within the Python program itself, but this could easily also be retrieved from a file or a REST API. As you can see, importing this JSON is fairly straightforward (see the inline comments):

```python
# Python contains very useful tools for working with JSON, and they're
# part of the standard library, meaning they're built into Python itself.
import json

# We can load our JSON file into a variable called "data"
with open("json-example.json") as f:
    data = f.read()

# json_dict is a dictionary, and json.loads takes care of
# placing our JSON data into it.
json_dict = json.loads(data)

# Printing information about the resulting Python data structure
print("The JSON document is loaded as type {0}\n".format(type(json_dict)))
```

```
print("Now printing each item in this document and the type it contains")
for k, v in json_dict.items():
    print(
        "-- The key {0} contains a {1} value.".format(str(k), str(type(v)))
    )
```

Those last few lines are there so we can see exactly how Python views this data once imported. The output that results from running this Python program is as follows:

```
~ $ python json-example.py

The JSON document is loaded as type <type 'dict'>

Now printing each item in this document and the type it contains
-- The key uptime contains a <type 'int'> value.
-- The key isAlive contains a <type 'bool'> value.
-- The key users contains a <type 'dict'> value.
-- The key hostname contains a <type 'unicode'> value.
-- The key vendor contains a <type 'unicode'> value.
-- The key vlans contains a <type 'list'> value.
```

You might be seeing the unicode data type for the first time. It's probably best to just think of this as roughly equivalent to the str (string) type, discussed in Chapter 4.

In Python, the str type is actually just a sequence of bytes, whereas unicode specifies an actual encoding.

Using JSON Schema for Data Models

In the YAML section, we explained the idea behind data models, and mentioned that YAML doesn't have any built-in mechanisms for data models. In the XML section, we talked about XSD, which allows us to enforce a schema (or data model) within XML—that is, we can be very particular with the type of data contained within an XML document. What about JSON?

JSON also has a mechanism for schema enforcement, aptly named *JSON Schema*. This specification is defined at *http://json-schema.org/documentation.html*, but has also been submitted as an internet draft.

A Python implementation of JSON Schema (*https://pypi.python.org/pypi/jsonschema*) exists, and implementations in other languages can also be found.

Before we wrap up this chapter, we want to discuss a way of describing data models that is independent of a particular data format. XSD works only for XML, and JSON Schema works only for JSON. Is there a way to describe a data model that can be used with either XML or JSON? There is indeed, and the next section discusses this solution: YANG.

Data Models Using YANG

Throughout this chapter, we've been discussing data models in the context of specific data formats—for example, how to enforce a data model in XML or JSON. In this section, we'd like to take a step back and look at data models more generically, then conclude with a discussion of using YANG to describe networking-specific data models.

To help solidify the concepts of data models, let's quickly review some key facts about data models:

- Data models describe a constrained set of data in the form of a schema language (like XSD, for example).

- Data models use well-defined types and parameters to have a structured and standard representation of data.

- Data models do not transport data, and data models don't care about the underlying transport protocols in use (for example, you could use JSON over HTTP, or you could use XML over HTTP).

Now that you understand what data models are, we're going to shift focus to YANG specifically.

YANG Overview

YANG is a data modeling language defined in RFC 6020. It is analogous to what we mentioned with respect to XSD for generic XML data, but YANG is specifically focused on network constructs. YANG is used to model configuration and operational state data and also used to model general RPC data. General RPC data and tasks allow us to model generic tasks, such as upgrading a device.

YANG provides the ability to define syntax and semantics to more easily define data using built-in and customizable types. You can enforce semantics such that VLAN IDs must be between 1 and 4094. You can enforce the operational state of an interface in that it must be "up" or "down." The model defines these types of constructs and ultimately becomes the source of truth on what's permitted on a network device.

There are various types of YANG models. Some of these YANG models were created by end users; others were created by vendors or open working groups.

- There are industry standard models from groups like the IETF and the Open-Config Working Group. These models are vendor and platform neutral. Each model produced by an open standards group is meant to provide a base set of options for a given feature.

- Of course, there also are vendor-specific models. As you know, almost every vendor has their own solution for multichassis link aggregation (VSS, VPC, MC-LAG, Virtual Chassis). This means each vendor would need to have their own model if they adopt a model-driven architecture.

- Per vendor, you may even see differences in a given feature. Thus, there are also platform-specific models. Maybe OSPF operates differently on platform X versus platform Y from the same vendor. This would require a different model.

Taking a Deeper Dive into YANG

There is only so much that can be conveyed with words. If seeing a picture is worth a thousand words, then seeing how YANG maps to XML, JSON, and CLI must also be worth a thousand words. We're going to dive deep into YANG statements to make the point on how YANG translates into data that two systems use to communicate.

 Note that we are not showing how to create a custom YANG model, as that is out of scope for this book. But we are highlighting a few YANG statements to help you better understand YANG.

The YANG language includes the YANG leaf statement, which allows you to define an object that is a single instance, has a single value, and has no children.

```
leaf hostname {
    type string;
    mandatory true;
    config true;
    description "Hostname for the network device";
}
```

You can extrapolate from the YANG leaf statement what this code is doing. It's defining a construct that will hold the value of the hostname on a network device. It is called hostname, it must be a string, it is required, but it is also configurable.

You can also define operational data with YANG leaf statements, setting config to be **false**.

A YANG leaf is represented in XML and JSON as a single element or key-value pair.

```
<hostname>NYC-R1</hostname>
```

```
{
    "hostname": "NYC-R1"
}
```

Another YANG statement is the leaf-list statement. This is just like the leaf statement, but there can be multiple instances. Since it's a list object, there is a parameter called ordered-by that can be set to user or system based on whether ordering is important—that is, ACLs versus SNMP community strings versus name servers.

```
leaf-list name-server {
    type string;
    ordered-by user;
    description "List of DNS servers to query";
}
```

A YANG leaf-list statement is represented in XML and JSON as a single element, such as the following (first in XML, then in JSON):

```
<name-server>8.8.8.8</name-server>
<name-server>4.4.4.4</name-server>

{
    "name-server": [
        "8.8.8.8",
        "4.4.4.4"
    ]
}
```

The next YANG statement we'll look at is the YANG list. It allows you to create a list of leafs or leaf-lists. Here is an example of a YANG list definition.

```
list vlan {
    key "id";
    leaf id {
        type int;
        range 1..4094;
    }
    leaf name {
        type string;
    }
}
```

More importantly for our context is to understand how this is modeled in XML and JSON. Here are examples of how XML and JSON, respectively, would represent this YANG model.

```
<vlan>
    <id>100</id>
    <name>web_vlan></name>
</vlan>
<vlan>
    <id>200</id>
    <name>app_vlan></name>
</vlan>

{
    "vlan": [
```

```
    {
        "id": "100",
        "name": "web_vlan"
    },
    {
        "id": "200",
        "name": "app_vlan"
    }
  ]
}
```

It should be starting to make more sense how data is modeled in YANG and how it's sent over the wire as encoded XML or JSON.

One final YANG statement is the YANG `container`. Containers map directly to hierarchy in XML and JSON. In our previous example, we had a list of VLANs, but no outer construct or tag element in XML that contained all VLANs. We are going to add a container called `vlans` to depict this.

```
container vlans {
    list vlan {
        key "id";
        leaf id {
            type int;
            range 1..4094;
        }
        leaf name {
            type string;
        }
    }
}
```

The only difference from our last example was adding in the first `container` statement. Here are the final XML and JSON representations of that complete object:

```
<vlans>
  <vlan>
      <id>100</id>
      <name>web_vlan></name>
  </vlan>
  <vlan>
      <id>200</id>
      <name>app_vlan></name>
  </vlan>
</vlans>
{
    "vlans": {
        "vlan": [
            {
                "id": "100",
                "name": "web_vlan"
            },
```

```
                    {
                        "id": "200",
                        "name": "app_vlan"
                    }
                ]
            }
        }
```

The point of this section was not just to provide a brief introduction to a few different YANG statements, but to really show that YANG is simply a modeling language. It's a way to enforce constraints on data inputs, and these inputs when being used in an API are represented as XML and JSON. It could be any other data format as well. The device itself then performs checks to see if data adheres to the underlying model being used.

A modeling language like YANG allows you to define semantics and constraints for a given data set. How does a network device ensure VLANs are *between* 1 and 4094? How does a network device ensure the administrative state is either *shutdown* or *no shutdown*? You answer these types of questions by having proper definitions of data. These definitions are defined in a schema document or a specific modeling language. One option for this is to use XML Schema Definitions, which we reviewed earlier in this chapter. However, XSDs are generic. While they are a good way to define a schema for XML documents, XSDs are not *network smart*, and as a result the industry is seeing a shift with how schemas and models are written. YANG is a modeling language specifically built for networking; it understands networking constructs. As an example, it has built-in types to validate whether an input is a valid IPv4 address, BGP AS, or MAC address. YANG is also neutral to the encoding type. A model can be written in YANG and then be *represented* as either JSON or XML. This is what RESTCONF offers. RESTCONF is a REST API that uses XML- or JSON-encoded data that happens to represent data defined by YANG models. We'll discuss REST-CONF in more detail in Chapter 7.

Summary

In this chapter, we've discussed a few key concepts. *Data formats* such as YAML, XML, and JSON are used to format (or encode) data for exchange between applications, systems, or devices. These data formats specify how data is formatted (or encoded), but don't necessarily define the structure of the data. *Data models* define the structure of data formatted (or encoded) in a data format. Sometimes these data models are format-specific; for example, XSD is specific to XML, and JSON Schema is specific to JSON. Finally, YANG provides a format-independent way to describe a data model that can be represented in XML or JSON.

In the next chapter, we're going to talk in more depth about templates, and how they can be used for network automation.

## CHAPTER 6

Network Configuration Templates

Much of a network engineer's job involves the CLI, and much of this work involves syntax-specific keywords and phrases that are often repeated several times, depending on the change. This not only becomes inefficient over time, but is also very error-prone. It may be obvious how to configure a BGP neighbor relationship on Cisco IOS, for instance, but what's not obvious at times are the smaller, "gotcha" configurations, like remembering to append the right BGP community configuration. Often in networking, there are many different ways to do the same thing—and this may be totally dependent on your organization.

One of the key benefits of network automation is consistency—being able to predictably and repeatably make changes to production network infrastructure and achieve a desired result. One of the best ways to accomplish this is by creating templates for all automated interaction with the network.

Creating templates for your network configurations means that you can standardize those configurations per the standard for your organization, while also allowing network administrators and the *consumers* (Help Desk, NOC, IT Engineers) of the network to dynamically fill in some values when needed. You get the benefits of speed, requiring much less information to make a change, but also consistency, because the template contains all of the necessary configuration commands that your policies dictate.

We'll start this chapter with an introduction to template tools in general, and then look at some specific implementations, and how we can leverage these tools to create network configuration templates.

The Rise of Modern Template Languages

The reality is that template technologies have been around for a very, very long time. Just a basic search for "template languages" shows a multitude of these, most often several options just for every related programming language.

You may also notice that the vast majority of these languages have deep applications in the web development industry. This is because much of the web is based on templates! Instead of writing HTML files for every single user profile page a social media site may have, the developers will write one, and insert dynamic values into that template, depending on the data being presented by the backend.

In short, template languages have a wide variety of relevant use cases. There are the obvious roots in web development, and of course we'll be talking about using them for network configuration in this chapter, but they have applications in just about any text-based medium, including documentation and reports.

So it's important to remember that there are three pieces to using templates. First, the templates have to be written. You also have to remember that you need some form of data, that'll ultimately get rendered into the template, to produce something meaningful like a network configuration. This leads us to the third piece—something has to drive data into the template. This could be an automation tool like Ansible, which we cover in Chapter 9, or you could be doing it yourself with a language like Python, which we show later on in this chapter. Templates are not very useful on their own.

 Most template languages aren't full-on "programming languages" in the purest sense—most often, a template language will be closely tied to another language that will drive data into the templates that you've built. As a result, there will be several similarities between each template language and its "parent" language. A good example is one that we'll discuss in this chapter heavily: Jinja is a template language that came out of a very Python-centric community, so there are some very distinct similarities there.

So if you're wondering which template language to use, it's probably best to decide which "real" language you're aligned with (either through writing your own code, or by using an existing tool like Ansible), and go from there.

As mentioned previously in this chapter, template languages aren't necessarily a new concept, but we are seeing new ideas and even entire languages make it into the ecosystem all the time. If you look at the history of template languages, a very large number of them were created to serve as a crucial part of the web: dynamic content. This is easily taken for granted these days, but back when the web was just getting started, and most websites were built from fairly static content, dynamically loading pieces of data into a page was a big step forward for the web.

Using Templates for Web Development

Django (*https://www.djangoproject.com/*) is a Python-based web framework, and is a popular modern example of this concept. Django has a template language that allows the web developer to create web content in much the same way, but also offers a way to make portions of the page dynamic. Using Django's template language, the developer can designate portions of an otherwise static page to load dynamic data when the user requests a page.

Here's a very simple example—note that this looks very much like an HTML document, but with certain portions replaced with variables (indicated with the {{ }} notation):

```
<h1>{{ title }}</h1>

{% for article in article_list %}
<h2>
  <a href="{{ article.get_absolute_url }}">
    {{ article.headline|upper }}
  </a>
</h2>
{% endfor %}
```

This template can be rendered by Django when a user loads the page. At this time, the Django framework will populate the `title` and `article_list` variables, and the user will receive a page that's been fully populated with real data. The developer doesn't have to write a static HTML page for every possible thing the user wants to retrieve— this is managed by logic on the backend of this web application.

 The Django templating language is very similar (but not identical) to the templating language Jinja (*http://jinja.pocoo.org/docs/dev/*), which we'll be discussing in depth in this chapter. Don't worry about the syntax; we'll get into that. For now, just focus on the concepts and the value that templates provide: consistency.

There are a multitude of other template languages that we won't have time to get into in this chapter, but you should be aware that they exist. Python alone has several options, such as the aforementioned Django and Jinja languages, but also Mako (*http://www.makotemplates.org/*) and Genshi (*https://genshi.edgewall.org/*). Other languages like Go (*https://golang.org/pkg/text/template/*) and Ruby (*http://ruby-doc.org/ stdlib-2.3.0/libdoc/erb/rdoc/ERB.html*) have built-in template systems. Again, the thing to remember is that the important work of populating a template with data is the role of one of these languages, like Python or Go, so this is the number-one factor in deciding which template language to use. More often than not, it's best to go with a template system built for that language.

Expanding On the Use of Templates

Finally, it's important to note that the concepts of templating, especially those discussed in this chapter, are not really specific to any single use case, and can be applied to just about any text-based medium. We'll go into detail on using templates for network configurations in this chapter, but as we just explored, templates can also be used for building dynamic web pages. In fact, we can use templates for something even more generic, like a basic report. Perhaps you're just pulling data from a network device and simply wish to be able to produce a nice report on this data and email it to some coworkers. Example 6-1 shows an example Jinja template for producing a report containing a list of VLANs.

Example 6-1. Basic report with Jinja

```
| VLAN ID | NAME | STATUS |
| ------- |------| -------|
{% for vlan in vlans %}
| {{ vlan.get('vlan_id') }} | {{ vlan.get('name') }} | {{ vlan.get('status') }} |
{% endfor %}
```

Because we're really just working with text, we can build a template for it. Keep this in mind as you get into the details of template technologies like Jinja—templates have applications well beyond the narrow set of use cases we'll explore in this chapter.

The Value of Templates in Network Automation

At this point you might be wondering why we're talking about web development and how that could possibly help us on our network automation journey. It's very important to understand the value behind templates in general, whether they're used for the web or not. Templates get us consistency—instead of hand-crafting text files full of HTML tags or entering CLI commands, with templates we can declare which parts of our files need to remain static, and which parts should be dynamic.

Every network engineer that's worked on a network long enough has had to prepare a configuration file for a new piece of network gear, like a switch or router. Maybe this has to be done for many switches—perhaps for a new data center build. In order to make the best use of time, it's useful to build these configurations ahead of time, so that when the switch is physically racked and cabled, the network engineer needs only to paste the configuration into a terminal.

Let's say you're in charge of a rollout like this—it's your job to come up with configurations for all switches going into the new data center being built for your organization. Obviously each switch will need its own unique configuration file, but there's also a large portion of the configuration that will be similar between devices. For instance, you might have the same SNMP community strings, the same admin password, and the same VLAN configuration (at least for similar device types like TOR switches). Then again, there are also probably some parts of the configuration that are unique to a single device; things like management IPs and hostnames are a simple example, but what if it's a Layer 3 switch? You'll need a unique subnet configuration for that device, and probably some fairly unique routing protocol configurations, depending on where that device exists in the topology. Deciding what parameters go to which switches can be fairly time-consuming, and very likely to result in errors. Templates allow us to standardize on a common base configuration, and help ensure that the right values get filled in for each device. Separating the template from the data that populates it is one of the best ways to simplify this process.

The primary value of templates for network engineers is achieving configuration consistency. Appropriately implemented, templates can actually reduce the likelihood that a human error can cause issues while making changes to production network configurations. There seems to be a lot of fear that making complex changes in an automated way in production is a bad idea, but if you follow good discipline and properly test your templates, you really can improve network operations. Templates don't automatically remove human error, but when used properly, they can greatly reduce it, resulting in fewer outages.

Using templates to aid the rollout of new network devices is a simple example of the value of templates, since it has the added benefit of saving a lot of time for the network engineer. However, don't think that this is the only place where templates can be used. In many network automation projects, templates are not even used by humans, but by automation software like Ansible to push configuration changes to network devices—live, in production.

We'll show concrete examples of using Jinja templates through the remainder of this chapter.

Jinja for Network Configuration Templates

The rest of this chapter will focus on one template language in particular—Jinja. We'll start with some basics, and ramp up to more advanced topics, all while showing how these concepts can be used to generate consistent network device configurations.

Why Jinja?

We've mentioned Jinja in the introduction to this chapter, but we also mentioned several other template languages. Why are we only looking at Jinja for network template automation? In addition to keeping this chapter from growing out of control, we chose Jinja because it is closely aligned with many of the other technologies mentioned in this book, including Python (Chapter 4). In fact, Jinja is a template language built for Python. Jinja is also aligned and used heavily by Ansible and Salt, two automation tools written in Python, both of which we cover in Chapter 9. So, if you're familiar with Python by now, Jinja will look and feel very similar.

Could you build network templates with other template languages? Sure. However, if you're new to template languages, and especially if you're following this book's advice and picking up some Python skills, you will find Jinja a very powerful tool on your network automation journey.

Dynamically Inserting Data into a Basic Jinja Template

Let's start with a basic example and write a template to configure a single switch interface. Here's an actual switchport (using industry-standard CLI syntax) configuration that we want to convert to a template (so we can configure the hundreds of other switchports in our environment):

```
interface GigabitEthernet0/1
  description Server Port
  switchport access vlan 10
  switchport mode access
```

This kind of snippet is fairly easy to write a template for—we need only decide which parts of this configuration need to stay the same, and which need to be dynamic. In this next example, we've removed the specific interface name ("GigabitEthernet0/1") and converted it into a variable that we'll populate when we render the template into an actual configuration:

```
interface {{ interface_name }}
  description Server Port
  switchport access vlan 10
  switchport mode access
```

This means we can pass in the variable interface_name when rendering this template, and that spot will get filled in with the value associated with interface_name.

However, the previous example assumes that each network interface has an identical configuration. What if we wanted a different VLAN, or a different interface description on some of the interfaces? In that case, we should also convert some of the other parts of the configuration into their own variables:

```
interface {{ interface_name }}
  description {{ interface_description }}
  switchport access vlan {{ interface_vlan }}
  switchport mode access
```

These are simple examples, but they're not very namespace-friendly.

It's common to leverage concepts like classes and dictionaries in a language like Python when rendering a template. This allows us to store multiple instances of data like this, that we can loop over and write multiple times in our resulting configuration. We'll look at loops in a future section, but for now, here's that same template rewritten, and saved as *template.j2*, to take advantage of something like a Python class or dictionary:

```
interface {{ interface.name }}
  description {{ interface.description }}
  switchport access vlan {{ interface.vlan }}
  switchport mode access
```

This was a minor change, but an important one. The object `interface` is passed to the template as a whole. If `interface` was a Python class, then `name`, `description`, and `vlan` are all properties of that class. The same is true if `interface` was a dictionary—the only difference is that they are all keys of this dictionary, and not properties, so the rendering engine would automatically place the corresponding values for those keys when rendering this template.

Rendering a Jinja Template File in Python

In the previous example, we looked at a basic Jinja template for a switchport configuration, but we didn't explore how that template is actually rendered, and what drove data into our template, to result in the final product. We'll explore that now by using Python and the Jinja2 library.

While the templating language itself is known as "Jinja," the Python library for working with Jinja is called "Jinja2."

Let's use the same template snippet from the previous example, and use Python to populate those fields with real data. We'll use the Python interpreter for this example so you can walk through on your own machine.

The Jinja2 rendering engine in Python is not part of the standard library, so it is not installed by default. However, Jinja2 can be installed with `pip`, through the command `pip install jinja2`, the same as any other Python package found on PyPI, as we covered in Chapter 4.

Once the Jinja2 library is installed, we should first import the required objects that we'll need in order to render our templates.

```
>>> from jinja2 import Environment, FileSystemLoader
```

Next, we need to set up the environment, so the renderer knows where to find the template.

```
>>> ENV = Environment(loader=FileSystemLoader('.'))
>>> template = ENV.get_template("template.j2")
```

The first line sets up the `Environment` object, specifying a single dot (.) to indicate that the templates exist in the same directory in which we started the Python interpreter. The second line derives a template object from that environment by statically specifying the template name, *template.j2*. Again, the contents of this template file are identical to what we previously saved as *template.j2*.

Now that this is done, we need our data. For this example, we'll use a Python dictionary. Note that the keys for this dictionary correspond to the field names referenced in our template.

```
>>> interface_dict = {
...     "name": "GigabitEthernet0/1",
...     "description": "Server Port",
...     "vlan": 10,
...     "uplink": False
... }
```

 It's important to remember that very rarely will you need to manually create data structures in Python to populate a template with data. This is being done for illustrative purposes in this book, but you should always write your software to pull from other sources, rather than embed data into your software.

We now have everything we need to render our template. We'll call the `render()` function of our template object to pass data into the template engine, and use the `print()` function to output our rendered output to the screen.

```
>>> print(template.render(interface=interface_dict))
interface GigabitEthernet0/1
  description Server Port
  switchport access vlan 10
  switchport mode access
```

Note we passed an argument to the `render()` function of our template object. Pay close attention to the name—the keyword argument `interface` corresponds to the references to `interface` within our Jinja template. This is how we get our interface dictionary into the template engine—when the template engine sees references to `interface` or its keys, it will use the dictionary passed here to satisfy that reference.

As you can see, the rendered output is as we expected. However, we don't have to use a Python dictionary. It's not uncommon to drive data from other Python libraries into a Jinja template, and this may take the form of a Python class.

The next example shows a Python program that's similar to what we just went through, but instead of using a dictionary, we use a Python class.

```python
from jinja2 import Environment, FileSystemLoader

ENV = Environment(loader=FileSystemLoader('.'))

template = ENV.get_template("template.j2")


class NetworkInterface(object):

    def __init__(self, name, description, vlan, uplink=False):
        self.name = name
        self.description = description
        self.vlan = vlan
        self.uplink = uplink

interface_obj = NetworkInterface("GigabitEthernet0/1", "Server Port", 10)

print(template.render(interface=interface_obj))
```

The output from this program is identical to the previous output. Therefore, there really isn't one "right" way to populate a Jinja template with data—it depends on where that data comes from. Fortunately, the Python Jinja2 library allows for some flexibility here.

 In this book, we don't deal with Python classes that much. This is because there are many other resources out there for learning how to implement these in your Python code, and often, the APIs that a network engineer will work with will map nicely to simple structures like lists or dictionaries. This book is meant to bridge the gap between software basics and the tools that exist in the next industry.

However, there are a lot of benefits to object-oriented programming and the use of things like classes. Used correctly, object-oriented code can be more readable, maintainable, and even more testable. Keep this in mind as you write your code and decide whether a full-fledged object definition is the way to go, or a simple dictionary will suffice.

Conditionals and Loops

It's time to really make our templates work for us. The previous examples are useful for understanding how to insert dynamic data into a text file, but that's just part of the battle of scaling network templates up to properly automate network configuration.

Jinja allows us to embed Python-esque logic into our template files in order to do things like make decisions or condense duplicate data into one chunk that is *unpacked* at render time via a `for` loop. While these tools are very powerful, they can also be a slippery slope.

It's important to not get too carried away with putting all kinds of advanced logic into your templates—Jinja has some really useful features, but it was never meant to be a full-blown programming language, so it's best to keep a healthy balance.

Read the Jinja FAQ (*http://jinja.pocoo.org/docs/dev/faq/*)—specifically the section titled "Isn't it a terrible idea to put Logic into Templates?" for some tips.

Using conditional logic to create a switchport configuration

Let's continue on our example of configuring a single switchport—but in this case, we want to make a decision about what to render by using a conditional in the template file itself.

Often, some switchport interfaces will be VLAN trunks, and others will be in "mode access." A good example is an access layer switch, where two or more interfaces are the "uplink" ports and need to be configured to permit all VLANs. Our previous examples showed an "uplink" boolean property, set to `True` if the interface was an uplink, and `False` if it was just an access port. We can check against this value in our template using a conditional:

```
interface {{ interface.name }}
 description {{ interface.description }}
{% if interface.uplink %}
 switchport mode trunk
{% else %}
 switchport access vlan {{ interface.vlan }}
 switchport mode access
{% endif %}
```

In short, if the `uplink` property of `interface` is `True`, then we want to make this interface a VLAN trunk. Otherwise, let's make sure that it's set up with the appropriate access mode.

In the previous example, we also see a new syntax—the {% ... %} braces are a special Jinja tag that indicates some kind of logic. This template is built to configure Gigabit Ethernet0/1 as a VLAN trunk, and any other interface will be placed in access mode, in vlan 10.

Using a loop to create many switchport configurations

We've only configured a single interface until this point, so let's see if we can use Jinja loops to create configurations for many switchports. For this, we use a for loop that's extremely similar to the syntax we would normally have in Python.

```
{% for n in range(10) %}
interface GigabitEthernet0/{{ n+1 }}
 description {{ interface.description }}
 switchport access vlan {{ interface.vlan }}
 switchport mode access
{% endfor %}
```

Note that we're again using the {% ... %} syntax to contain all logic statements. In this template, we're calling the range() function to give us a list of integers to iterate over, and for each iteration, we print the result of "n+1" because range() starts at 0, and normally, switchports start at 1.

Using a loop and conditionals to create switchport configurations

This gets us an identical configuration for 10 switchports—but what if we wanted a different configuration for some of them? Take the example we saw when we explored Jinja conditionals—perhaps the first port is a VLAN trunk. We can combine what we've learned about conditionals and loops to accomplish this:

```
{% for n in range(10) %}

interface GigabitEthernet0/{{ n+1 }}
 description {{ interface.description }}
{% if n+1 == 1 %}
 switchport mode trunk
{% else %}
 switchport access vlan {{ interface.vlan }}
 switchport mode access
{% endif %}

{% endfor %}
```

This results in GigabitEthernet0/1 being configured as a VLAN trunk, but GigabitEthernet0/2–10 are in access mode. Here is an example using simulated data for the interface descriptions:

```
interface GigabitEthernet0/1
 description TRUNK INTERFACE
 switchport mode trunk
interface GigabitEthernet0/2
 description ACCESS INTERFACE
 switchport mode access
interface GigabitEthernet0/3
 description ACCESS INTERFACE
```

```
switchport mode access
...
```

Looping over variables in a for loop to generate configurations

We were able to access keys in a dictionary in our Jinja template in the previous examples, but what if we wanted to actually iterate over things like dictionaries and lists by using a `for` loop?

Let's imagine that we're passing the following list to our template as `interface_list`. Here's the relevant Python for this:

```
intlist = [
    "GigabitEthernet0/1",
    "GigabitEthernet0/2",
    "GigabitEthernet0/3"
]
print(template.render(interface_list=intlist))
```

We would then reference `interface_list` in our loop so that we could access its members and generate a switchport configuration for each one. Note that the nested conditional has also been modified, since our counter variable n no longer exists:

```
{% for iface in interface_list %}

interface {{ iface }}
{% if iface == "GigabitEthernet0/1" %}
 switchport mode trunk
{% else %}
 switchport access vlan 10
 switchport mode access
{% endif %}

{% endfor %}
```

We now simply refer to `iface` to retrieve the current item of that list for every iteration of the loop.

We can also do the same thing with dictionaries. Again, here's a relevant Python snippet for constructing and passing in a dictionary to this Jinja template. We'll keep it simple this time, and just pass a set of interface names as keys, with the corresponding port descriptions as values:

```
intdict = {
    "GigabitEthernet0/1": "Server port number one",
    "GigabitEthernet0/2": "Server port number two",
    "GigabitEthernet0/3": "Server port number three"
}
print(template.render(interface_dict=intdict))
```

We can modify our loop to iterate over this dictionary in much the same way we'd do in native Python:

```
{% for name, desc in interface_dict.items() %}
interface {{ name }}
  description {{ desc }}
{% endfor %}
```

The `for name, desc...` means that at each iteration of the loop, `name` will be a key in our dictionary, and `desc` will be the corresponding value for that key. Don't forget to add the `.items()` notation as shown here, in order to properly unpack these values.

This allows us to simply refer to `name` and `desc` in the body of the template, and the result is shown here:

```
interface GigabitEthernet0/3
  description Server port number three

interface GigabitEthernet0/2
  description Server port number two

interface GigabitEthernet0/1
  description Server port number one
```

> You may have noticed the interfaces were out of order in the previous example output. This is due to the fact that dictionaries are unordered and we were iterating through the dictionary items using a for loop. You may have remembered this from when we first covered dictionaries in Chapter 4.

You may have noticed a few limitations in the previous examples. In a few examples, we iterated using the `range()` function, meaning we didn't have all of the valuable metadata about our interfaces like we do when we use classes or dictionaries. Even though we used a dictionary in a subsequent example, its structure was little more than storing an interface name with a description.

Generating interface configurations from a list of dictionaries

In this last example, we're going to combine usage of lists and dictionaries to really put this template to work for us. Each interface will have its own dictionary, where the keys will be attributes of each network interface, like `name`, `description`, or `uplink`. Each dictionary will be stored inside a list, which is what our template will iterate over to produce configuration.

First, here's the data structure in Python that was just described:

```
interfaces = [
    {
        "name": "GigabitEthernet0/1",
        "desc": "uplink port",
        "uplink": True
    },
    {
        "name": "GigabitEthernet0/2",
        "desc": "Server port number one",
        "vlan": 10
    },
    {
        "name": "GigabitEthernet0/3",
        "desc": "Server port number two",
        "vlan": 10
    }
]
print(template.render(interface_list=interfaces))
```

This will allow us to write a very powerful template that iterates over this list, and for each list item, simply refers to keys found within that particular dictionary. The next example makes use of all of the techniques we've learned about loops and conditionals.

```
{% for interface in interface_list %}
interface {{ interface.name }}
  description {{ interface.desc }}
  {% if interface.uplink %}
    switchport mode trunk
  {% else %}
    switchport access vlan {{ interface.vlan }}
    switchport mode access
  {% endif %}
{% endfor %}
```

 When accessing data in a dictionary when using Jinja, you can use the traditional Python syntax of dict['key'] or the shorthand form as we've been showing with dict.key. These two are identical and if you're trying to access a key that doesn't exist, a key error will be raised. However, you can also use the get() method in Jinja if it's an optional key or if you want to return some other value if the key doesn't exist—for example, dict.get(key, 'UNKNOWN').

As mentioned previously, it's bad form to embed data into our Python applications (see the interfaces list of dictionaries from the previous example). Instead of this, let's place that data into its own YAML file, and rewrite our application to import this data before using it to render the template. This is a very good practice, because it allows someone with no Python experience to edit the network configuration by simply changing this simple YAML file.

Here's an example of a YAML file that is written to be identical to our `interfaces` list in the previous example:

```
---
- name: GigabitEthernet0/1
  desc: uplink port
  uplink: true
- name: GigabitEthernet0/2
  desc: Server port number one
  vlan: 10
- name: GigabitEthernet0/3
  desc: Server port number two
  vlan: 10
```

As we explored in Chapter 5, importing a YAML file in Python is very easy. As a refresher, here's our full Python application, but instead of the static, embedded list of dictionaries, we're simply importing a YAML file to get that data:

```
from jinja2 import Environment, FileSystemLoader
import yaml

ENV = Environment(loader=FileSystemLoader('.'))

template = ENV.get_template("template.j2")

with open("data.yml") as f:
    interfaces = yaml.load(f)
    print(template.render(interface_list=interfaces))
```

We can reuse the same template we previously created and achieve the same result—but this time, the data that we're using to populate our template comes from an external YAML file, which is easier for everyone to maintain. The Python file now only contains the logic of pulling in data, and rendering a template. This makes for a more maintainable template rendering system.

This covers the basics of loops and conditionals. In this section, we've really only explored a portion of what's possible. Explore these concepts on your own, and apply them to your own use cases.

Jinja Filters

Occasionally we need to apply some kind of manipulation to a variable within our template. A simple example might be to convert a snippet of text to be all uppercase characters.

Filters allow us to accomplish this goal. In the same way that we can pipe output from a command into another command in a terminal shell on a Linux distribution, we can take the result of a Jinja statement and pipe it into a filter. The resulting text will make it into the rendered output of our template.

Using the "upper" Jinja filter

Let's take our last template and use a built-in filter to capitalize the descriptions for each interface configuration:

```
{% for interface in interface_list %}
interface {{ interface.name }}
  description {{ interface.desc|upper }}
  {% if interface.uplink %}
    switchport mode trunk
  {% else %}
    switchport access vlan {{ interface.vlan }}
    switchport mode access
  {% endif %}
{% endfor %}
```

After the `interface.desc` variable name, but still within the curly braces, we can use the pipe (|) to filter the value of `desc` into the `upper` filter. This is a filter built in to the Jinja2 library for Python that capitalizes the text piped to it.

Chaining Jinja filters

We can also chain filters, in much the same way that we might chain pipes of commands in Linux, or methods in Python. Let's use the `reverse` filter to take our capitalized text and print it backward:

```
{% for interface in interface_list %}
interface {{ interface.name }}
  description {{ interface.desc|upper|reverse }}
  {% if interface.uplink %}
    switchport mode trunk
  {% else %}
    switchport access vlan {{ interface.vlan }}
    switchport mode access
  {% endif %}
{% endfor %}
```

This results in the following output:

```
interface GigabitEthernet0/1
  description TROP KNILPU
  switchport mode trunk

interface GigabitEthernet0/2
  description ENO REBMUN TROP REVRES
  switchport access vlan 10
  switchport mode access

interface GigabitEthernet0/3
```

```
description OWT REBMUN TROP REVRES
switchport access vlan 10
switchport mode access
```

To recap, our original description for GigabitEthernet0/1 was first "uplink port," and then it was "UPLINK PORT" because of the upper filter, and then the reverse filter changed it to "TROP KNILPU," before the final result was printed into the template instance.

Creating custom Jinja filters

This is all great, and there are tons of other great built-in filters, all documented within the Jinja specification. But what if we wanted to create our own filter? Perhaps there's something specific to network automation that we would like to perform in our own custom filter that doesn't come with the Jinja2 library?

Fortunately, the library allows for this. The next example shows a full Python script where we're defining a new function, get_interface_speed(). This function is simple—it looks for certain keywords like "gigabit" or "fast" in a provided string argument, and returns the current Mbps value. It also loads all of our template data from a YAML file as was shown in previous examples.

```
# Import Jinja2 library and PyYAML
from jinja2 import Environment, FileSystemLoader
import yaml

# Declare template environment
ENV = Environment(loader=FileSystemLoader('.'))


def get_interface_speed(interface_name):
    """ get_interface_speed returns the default Mbps value for a given
        network interface by looking for certain keywords in the name
    """

    if 'gigabit' in interface_name.lower():
        return 1000
    if 'fast' in interface_name.lower():
        return 100

# Filters are added to the ENV object after declaration. Note that we're
# actually passing in our "get_interface_speed" function and not running
# it--the template engine will execute this function when we call
# template.render()
ENV.filters['get_interface_speed'] = get_interface_speed
template = ENV.get_template("templatestuff/template.j2")

# We load our YAML file and pass it in to the template when rendering it.
with open("templatestuff/data.yml") as f:
```

```
    interfaces = yaml.load(f)
    print(template.render(interface_list=interfaces))
```

With a slight modification to our template, as shown in the next example, we can leverage this filter by passing `interface.name` into the `get_interface_speed` filter. The resulting output will be whatever integer our function decided to return. Since all interface names are GigabitEthernet, the speed is set to 1000.

```
{% for interface in interface_list %}
interface {{ interface.name }}
  description {{ interface.desc|upper|reverse }}
  {% if interface.uplink %}
    switchport mode trunk
  {% else %}
    switchport access vlan {{ interface.vlan }}
    switchport mode access
  {% endif %}
  speed {{ interface.name|get_interface_speed }}
{% endfor %}
```

Using existing Python code as a Jinja filter

We don't always have to write our own functions in order to create a custom Jinja filter. Sometimes there's an existing Python function out there that would work really well as a Jinja filter. Using an existing Python function is fairly easy to do; just make sure you've imported it appropriately and pass it in as if you created it.

As an example, we can use a function from the `bracket_expansion` library to quickly produce a set of interface names without having to craft our own list or dictionary that contains these names. Read the following inline comments for more details on how this works:

```
# Import Jinja2 library
from jinja2 import Environment, FileSystemLoader

# bracket_expansion is also a third party library.
# Install through pip before running this.
from bracket_expansion import bracket_expansion

# Declare template environment
ENV = Environment(loader=FileSystemLoader('.'))

# Filters are added to the ENV object after declaration. "bracket_expansion"
# is a function that we're passing in--the template engine will actually
# execute this function when rendering the template.
ENV.filters['bracket_expansion'] = bracket_expansion
template = ENV.get_template("template.j2")

# The bracket_expansion function we've passed in as a filter requires a
# text pattern to work against. We'll pass this in as "iface_pattern"
print(template.render(iface_pattern='GigabitEthernet0/0/[0-3]'))
```

This is a tremendously powerful tool—and you could absolutely write your own Python functions to take this to the next level. Experiment with other text manipulation functions and libraries, or perhaps write your own.

Template Inheritance in Jinja

As you create bigger, more capable templates for your network configuration, you may want to be able to break templates up into smaller, more specialized pieces. It's quite common to have a template for VLAN configuration, one for interfaces, and maybe another for a routing protocol. This kind of organizational tool, while optional, can allow for much more flexibility. The question is, how do you link these templates together in a meaningful way to form a full configuration?

Jinja allows you to perform inheritance in a template file, which is a handy solution to this problem. For instance, you may have a *vlans.j2* file that contains only the VLAN configuration, and you can inherit this file to produce a VLAN configuration in another template file. You might be writing a template for interface configuration, and you wish to also produce a VLAN configuration from another template. The next example shows how this is done using the `include` statement:

```
{% include 'vlans.j2' %}

{% for name, desc in interface_dict.items() %}
interface {{ name }}
  description {{ desc }}
{% endfor %}
```

This would render *vlans.j2*, and insert the resulting text into the rendered output for the template that included it. Using the `include` statement, template writers can compose switch configurations made up of modular parts. This is great for keeping things organized.

Another inheritance tool in Jinja is the `block` statement. This is a powerful, but more complicated, method of performing inheritance, as it mimics object inheritance in more formal languages like Python. Using blocks, you can specify portions of your template that may be overridden by a child template, if present. If a child template is not present, it will still contain some default text.

This shows an example where `blocks` may be used in a parent template:

```
{% for interface in interface_list %}
interface {{ interface.name }}
  description {{ interface.desc }}
{% endfor %}
!
{% block http %}
  no ip http server
```

```
      no ip http secure-server
  {% endblock %}
```

We'll call this template *no-http.j2*, indicating that we'd like to normally turn off the embedded HTTP server in our switch. However, we can use blocks to give us some greater flexibility here. We can create a child template called *yes-http.j2* that is designed to override this block, and output the configuration that enables the HTTP server if that's what we want.

```
  {% extends "no-http.j2" %}
  {% block http %}
    ip http server
    ip http secure-server
  {% endblock %}
```

This allows us to enable the HTTP server simply by rendering the child template. The first line in the previous example extends the parent template *no-http.j2* so all of the interface configurations will still be present in the rendered output. However, because we've rendered the child template, the `http` block of the child overrides that of the parent. Using blocks in this way is very useful for portions of the configuration that may need to change but aren't properly served by traditional variable substitution.

The Jinja documentation on template inheritance (*http://jinja.pocoo.org/docs/dev/templates/#template-inheritance*) goes into much more detail, and would be a great resource to keep bookmarked.

Variable Creation in Jinja

Jinja allows us to actually create variables within a template itself. We do so using the `set` statement. A common use case for this is variable shortening. Sometimes you have to go through several nested dictionaries or Python objects to get what you want, and you may want to reuse this value several times in your template. Rather than repeat a long string of properties or keys, use the `set` statement to represent a particular value using a much smaller name:

```
  {% set int_desc = switch01.config.interfaces['GigabitEthernet0/1']['description'] %}
  {{ int_desc }}
```

Summary

After this deep dive into Jinja, it's important to take a step back and think about where templates can/should be used in a network automation context. By reading the previous examples, it's easy to get the impression that you have to write Python to make use of templates.

While it's true that this is a very powerful way to use templates to drive network configuration, it's certainly not the only option. As we'll discuss in Chapter 9, tools like

Ansible and Salt allow us to define configuration data in a simple YAML format and insert this data into a template without ever writing any code. Certainly, if the template is simple enough and you're really only looking for a way to create templates from an existing configuration, this is a very simple way of generating templates.

Here are a few parting thoughts on using templates for network automation:

- Keep the templates simple. Leveraging loops and conditionals to enhance your templates is fine, but don't go overboard here. Jinja isn't as robust as a fully featured, general-purpose programming like Python, so keep the more advanced stuff out of the template.

- Leverage template inheritance to reuse portions of configurations that don't need to be duplicated

- Remember, syntax and data should be handled separately. For instance, keep VLAN IDs in their own data file (maybe YAML), and the CLI syntax to implement those VLANs in a dedicated template.

- Use version control (i.e., Git) to store all of your templates.

If you follow these, you'll be able to put templates to work for you in your network automation journey.

## CHAPTER 7

Working with Network APIs

From Python and data formats to configuration templating with Jinja, we've explored key foundational technologies and skills that will make you a better network engineer. In this chapter, we're going to put these skills to practical use and start to consume and communicate to different types of network device APIs.

In order to best help you understand how to start automating networks, this chapter is organized into three sections:

Understanding Network APIs
We examine the architecture and foundation of different APIs, including RESTful HTTP-based APIs, non-RESTful HTTP-based APIs, and NETCONF.

Exploring Network APIs
We introduce tools commonly used for testing and learning how to use each API type.

Automating Using Network APIs
Finally, we look at Python libraries that allow you to start automating your networks. We'll look at the Python requests library for consuming HTTP-based APIs, ncclient for interacting with NETCONF devices, and netmiko for automating devices using SSH.

As you read this chapter, please keep in mind one thing—this chapter is *not* a comprehensive guide on any particular API, and it should not serve as API documentation. We will provide examples using different vendor implementations of a given API, as it's very common to be working in a multi-vendor environment. It's also important to see the common patterns and unique contrasts between different implementations of the same API type.

Understanding Network APIs

Our focus is on two of the most common types of APIs you'll find on network devices, HTTP-based APIs and NETCONF-based APIs. We're going to start by looking at foundational concepts for each type of API; once we review them, we explore the consumption of these APIs with hands-on examples using specific vendor implementations.

Let's get started by diving into HTTP-based RESTful APIs.

Getting Familiar with HTTP-Based APIs

There are two types of HTTP-based APIs to understand in the context of network APIs. They are RESTful HTTP-based APIs and non-RESTful HTTP-based APIs. In order to better understand them and what the term *RESTful* means, we are going to start by examining RESTful APIs. Once you understand RESTful architecture and principles, we'll move on and compare them with non-RESTful HTTP-based APIs.

Understanding RESTful APIs

RESful APIs are becoming more popular and more commonly used in the networking industry, although they've been around since the early 2000s. Most of the APIs that exist today within network infrastructure are HTTP-based RESTful APIs. This means that when you hear about a RESTful API on a network device or SDN controller, it is an API that will be communicating between a client and a server.

The client would be an application such as a Python script or web UI application and the server would be the network device or controller. Moreover, since HTTP is being used as transport, you'd be performing some operation using URLs just as you do already as you browse the World Wide Web. Thus, if you understand that when you're browsing to a website, HTTP GETs are performed, and when you're filling out a web form and clicking submit, an HTTP POST is performed, you already understand the basics of working with RESTful APIs.

Let's look at examples of retrieving data from a website and retrieving data from a network device via a RESTful API. In both instances, an HTTP GET request is sent to the web server (see Figure 7-1).

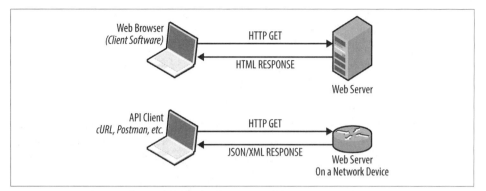

Figure 7-1. Understanding REST by looking at HTTP GET responses

In Figure 7-1, one of the primary differences is the data that is sent to and from the web server. When browsing the internet, you receive HTML data that your browser will interpret so that it is able to display the website properly. On other hand, when issuing an HTTP GET request to a web server that is exposing a RESTful API (remember, it's exposing it via a URL), you receive data back that is mostly encoded using JSON or XML. This is where we'll use what we reviewed in Chapter 5. Since you receive data back in JSON/XML, the client application must understand how to interpret JSON and/or XML. Let's continue with the overview so we have a more complete picture before we start to explore the use of RESTful HTTP APIs.

Now that we've covered a high-level overview of RESTful APIs, let's take it one step deeper and look at the origins of RESTful APIs. It's worth noting that the birth and structure of modern web-based RESTful APIs came from a PhD dissertation (*http://www.ics.uci.edu/~fielding/pubs/dissertation/top.htm*) by Roy Fielding in 2000. In this dissertation titled *Architectural Styles and the Design of Network-based Software Architectures*, he defined the intricate detail of working with networked systems on the internet that use the architecture defined as REST.

There are six architectural constraints that an interface must conform to in order to be considered RESTful. For the purposes of this chapter, we'll look at three of them.

Client-Server

This is a requirement to improve the usability of systems while simplifying the server requirements. Having a client-server architecture allows for portability and changeability of client applications without the server components being changed. This means you could have different API clients (web UI, CLI) that consume the same server resources (backend API).

Stateless

The communication between the client and server must be stateless. Clients that use stateless forms of communication must send all data required for the server to understand and perform the requested operation in a single request. This is in contrast to interfaces such as SSH where there is a persistent connection between a client and a server.

Uniform interface

Individual resources in scope within an API call are identified in HTTP request messages. For example, in RESTful HTTP-based systems, the URL used references a particular resource. In the context of networking, the resource maps to a network device construct such as a hostname, interface, routing protocol configuration, or any other *resource* that exists on the device. The uniform interface also states that the client should have enough information about a resource to create, modify, or delete a resource.

These are just three of the six core constraints of the REST architecture, but we can already see the similarity between RESTful systems and how we consume the internet through web browsing on a daily basis. Keep in mind that HTTP is the primary means of implementing RESTful APIs, although the transport type could in theory be something else. In order to really understand RESTful APIs, then you must also understand the basics of HTTP.

Understanding HTTP request types. It's important to understand that while every RESTful API we look at is an HTTP-based API, we will eventually look at HTTP-based APIs that do not adhere to the principles of REST, and therefore are not RESTful. However, in either case, the APIs require an understanding of HTTP. Because these APIs are using HTTP as transport, we're going to be working with the same HTTP request types and response codes that are used on the internet already.

For example, common HTTP request types include GET, POST, PATCH, PUT, and DELETE. As you can imagine, GET requests are used to request data from the server, DELETE requests are used to delete a resource on the server, and the three P's (POST, PATCH, PUT) are used to make a change on the server.

In the context of networking, we can think of these request types as the following:

- GET: obtaining configuration or operational data
- PUT, POST, PATCH: making a configuration change
- DELETE: removing a particular configuration

Table 7-1 depicts these request types. We'll use each of these in real examples later in the chapter.

Table 7-1. HTTP request types

Request Type	Description
GET	Retrieve a specified resource
PUT	Create or replace a resource
PATCH	Create or update a resource object
POST	Create a resource object
DELETE	Delete a specified resource

Understanding HTTP response codes.   Just as the request types are the same if you're using a web browser on the internet or using a RESTful API, the same is true for response codes.

Ever see a "401 Unauthorized" message when you were trying to log in to a website and used invalid credentials? Well, you would receive the same response code if you were trying to log in to a system using a RESTful API and you sent the wrong credentials. The same is true for successful messages or if the server has an error of its own. Table 7-2 depicts a list of the common types of response codes you see when working with HTTP-based APIs. Please note that this list is not exclusive—others exist too.

Table 7-2. HTTP response codes

Response Code	Description
2XX	Successful
4XX	Client error
5XX	Server error

Remember, the response code types for HTTP-based APIs are no different than standard HTTP response codes. We are merely providing a table for the series of response codes and will leave it as an exercise for the reader to learn about individual responses.

Now that we have an understanding of the principles of REST and HTTP, it's important to also take note of non-RESTful HTTP-based APIs.

Understanding non-RESTful HTTP-based APIs

While RESTful APIs are preferred, you may come across non-RESTful HTTP-based APIs too. In the network industry, this is most commonly seen on APIs that *sit above* CLIs, meaning the API call actually sends a command to the device versus sending native structured data. The preferred approach is to have any modern network platform's CLI or web UI use the underlying API, but for "legacy" or pre-existing systems that were built using commands, it is in fact common to see the use of non-RESTful

APIs, as it was easier to add an API this way rather than rearchitect the underlying system.

There are two major differences between RESTful HTTP-based APIs and non-RESTful HTTP-based APIs. We previously introduced the concept of HTTP request types that map to a particular verb such as GET, POST, PATCH, PUT, and DELETE. RESTful APIs use particular verbs to dictate the type of change being requested of the target server. For example, in the context of networking, a configuration change would never occur if you're doing an HTTP GET, since you're simply retrieving data. However, systems that are HTTP-based but do not follow RESTful principles could use the same HTTP verb for every API call. This means if you're retrieving data or making a configuration change, all API calls could be using a POST request. If you see this in a given API type, it is still an HTTP-based API, but not a RESTful HTTP-based API.

Another common difference to be aware of brings the focus to the URL being used in individual API calls. If you are using an HTTP-based API that always uses the same URL and does not allow you to access a specific resource by a URL change, the API is a RESTful HTTP-based API.

Having HTTP-based APIs on network infrastructure is a great step in the right direction for the industry, but ideally, all HTTP APIs would follow the principles of REST.

While you do use the same tools to consume RESTful and non-RESTful HTTP-based APIs, it is important to be conscious of these differences for network APIs, as non-RESTful HTTP-based APIs are usually not as flexible as their RESTful counterparts.

Now that we've introduced HTTP-based APIs, let's shift our focus and introduce the NETCONF API.

Diving into NETCONF

NETCONF is a network management protocol, defined in RFC 6241, designed from the ground up for configuration management and retrieving configuration and operational state data from network devices. In this respect, NETCONF has a clear delineation between configuration and operational state; API requests are used to perform different operations such as retrieving configuration state, retrieving operational state, and making configuration changes.

We stated in the previous section that RESTful APIs aren't new; they are merely new for network devices and SDN controllers. As we transition to looking at the NETCONF API, it's worth noting that NETCONF is also not new. NETCONF has been around for over a decade. In fact, it's an industry-standard protocol with its original RFC having been written in 2005. It's even been on various network devices for years, although often as a limited API rarely being used.

One of the core attributes of NETCONF is its ability to utilize different configuration datastores. Most network engineers are familiar with running configurations and startup configurations. These are thought of as two configuration files, but they are two configuration datastores in the context of NETCONF. NETCONF implementations often tend to use a third datastore called a candidate configuration. The candidate configuration datastore holds configuration objects (CLI commands if you're using CLI for configuration) that are not yet applied to the device. As an example, if you enter a configuration on a device that supports candidate configurations, they do not take action immediately. Instead, they are held in the candidate configuration and only applied to the device when a *commit* operation is performed. When the commit is executed, the candidate configuration is written to the running configuration.

Candidate configuration datastores have been around for years as originally defined in the NETCONF RFC over a decade ago. One of the issues the industry has faced is having usable implementations of NETCONF that offered this functionality. However, not all implementations have been unused—there have, in fact, been successful implementations. Juniper's Junos has had a robust NETCONF implementation for years, along with the capability of a candidate configuration; more recently, Cisco IOS-XR added increased support for NETCONF along with support of a candidate configuration. Operating systems like HPE's Comware 7 and Cisco IOS-XE support NETCONF, but do not yet support a candidate configuration datastore.

Always check your hardware and software platforms even if they are from the same vendor. It is likely that the capabilities supported between them are different. The support of a candidate configuration is just one example of this.

We stated that with a candidate configuration you enter various configurations and they aren't yet applied until a commit operation is performed. This leads us to another core attribute of NETCONF-enabled devices—configuration changes as a transaction. In our same example, it means that all configuration objects (commands) are committed as a transaction. All commands succeed, or they are *not* applied. This is in contrast to the more common scenario of entering a series of commands and having a command somewhere in the middle fail, yielding a partial configuration.

The support of a candidate configuration is just one attribute of NETCONF. Let's now take a deeper dive into the underlying NETCONF protocol stack.

Learning the NETCONF protocol stack

We've covered several attributes of NETCONF, but it's time to dive a little deeper into the protocol stack NETCONF uses to communicate between a client and server. In our examples, the client is going to be a Python application or SSH client and the server is a target network device we're going to be automating.

There are four core layers of the NETCONF protocol stack (Table 7-3). We are going to review each and show concrete examples of what they mean for the XML object being sent between the client and server.

Table 7-3. NETCONF protocol stack

Layer	Example
Transport	SSHv2, SOAP, TLS
Messages	`<rpc>`, `<rpc-reply>`
Operations	`<get-config>`, `<get>`, `<copy-config>`, `<lock>`, `<unlock>`, `<edit-config>`, `<delete-config>`, `<kill-session>`, `<close-session>`
Content	Configuration/filers: XML representation of data models (YANG, XSD)

> NETCONF only supports XML for data encoding. On the other hand, remember that RESTful APIs *have the ability* to support JSON and/or XML.

Transport. NETCONF is commonly implemented using SSH as transport; it is its own SSH subsystem. While all of our examples use NETCONF over SSH, it is technically possible to implement NETCONF over SOAP, TLS, or any other protocol that meets the requirements of NETCONF. With the migration of SOAP to RESTful APIs, there has been limited further development on NETCONF over SOAP, and while NETCONF over TLS is possible, no platforms covered in the book currently support it.

A few of these requirements are:

- It must be a connection-oriented session, and thus there must be a consistent connection between a client and a server.
- NETCONF sessions must provide a means for authentication, data integrity, confidentiality, and replay protection.

- Although NETCONF can be implemented with other transport protocols, each implementation *must* support SSH at a minimum.

Messages. NETCONF messages are based on a remote procedure call (RPC)–based communication model and each message is encoded in XML. Using an RPC-based model allows the XML messages to be used independent of the transport type. NETCONF supports two message types, namely `<rpc>` and `<rpc-reply>`. Viewing the actual XML-encoded object helps elucidate NETCONF, so let's take a look at a NETCONF RPC request.

In simplest terms, the message types are always going to be `<rpc>` and `<rpc-reply>` and they will always be the outermost XML tag in the encoded object.

```
<rpc message-id="101">
    <!-- rest of request as XML... -->
</rpc>
```

Every NETCONF `<rpc>` includes a required attribute called `message-id`. You can see this in the previous example. It's an arbitrary string the client sends to the server. The server reuses this ID in the response header so the client knows which message the server is responding to.

The other message type is the `<rpc-reply>`. The NETCONF server responds with the `message-id` and any other attributes received from the client, (e.g., XML namespaces).

```
<rpc-reply message-id="101" xmlns="urn:ietf:params:xml:ns:netconf:base:1.0">
  <data>
    <!-- XML content/response... -->
  </data>
</rpc-reply>
```

This `<rpc-reply>` example above assumes that the XML namespace was in the `<rpc>` sent by the client. Note that the actual data response coming from NETCONF server is embedded within the `<data>` tag.

Next, we'll show how the NETCONF request dictates which particular NETCONF operation (RPC) it's requesting of the server.

Operations. The outermost XML element is always the type of message being sent (i.e., `<rpc>` or `<rpc-reply>`). When you are sending a NETCONF request from the client to the server, the next element, or the child of the message type, is the requested NETCONF (RPC) operation. You saw a list of NETCONF operations in Table 7-3, and now we'll take a look at each of them.

The two primary operations we review in this chapter are `<get>` and `<edit-config>`.

The `<get>` operation retrieves running configuration and device state information.

```
<rpc message-id="101" xmlns="urn:ietf:params:xml:ns:netconf:base:1.0">
  <get>
    <!-- XML content/response... -->
  </get>
</rpc>
```

Since `<get>` is the child element within the `<rpc>` message, this means the client is requesting a NETCONF `<get>` operation.

Within the `<get>` hierarchy, there are optional filter types that allow you to selectively retrieve a portion of the running configuration, namely *subtree* and *xpath* filters. Our focus is on *subtree* filters, which allow you to provide an XML document, which is a subtree of the complete XML tree hierarchy that you wish to retrieve in a given request.

In the next example, we reference a specific XML data object using the `<native>` element and *http://cisco.com/ns/yang/ned/ios* URL. This XML data object is the XML representation of a specific data model that exists on the target device. This data model represents a full running configuration as XML, but we're requesting just the `<interface>` configuration hierarchy.

As shown throughout this chapter, the actual JSON and XML objects sent between clients and servers are largely vendor- and OS-dependent.

The next two examples shown for the `<get>` operation are XML requests from a Cisco IOS-XE device running 16.3+ code.

```
<rpc message-id="101" xmlns="urn:ietf:params:xml:ns:netconf:base:1.0">
  <get>
    <filter type="subtree">
      <native xmlns="http://cisco.com/ns/yang/ned/ios">
      <interface>
      </interface>
      </native>
    </filter>
  </get>
</rpc>
```

We could add more elements to the filter's XML tree to narrow down the response that comes back from the NETCONF server. We will now add two elements to the filter—so instead of receiving the configuration objects for all interfaces, we'll receive the configuration of only GigabitEthernet1.

```
<rpc message-id="101" xmlns="urn:ietf:params:xml:ns:netconf:base:1.0">
  <get>
     <filter type="subtree">
       <native xmlns="http://cisco.com/ns/yang/ned/ios">
        <interface>
         <GigabitEthernet>
          <name>1</name>
         </GigabitEthernet>
        </interface>
       </native>
     </filter>
  </get>
</rpc>
```

The next most common NETCONF operation is the <edit-config> operation. This operation is used to make a configuration change. Specifically, this operation loads a configuration into the specified configuration datastore: running, startup, or candidate.

When the <edit-config> operation is used, you set the target configuration datastore with the <target> tag. If not specified, it'll default to the *running* configuration. Also within the <edit-config> hierarchy, the configuration elements that are to be loaded onto the target datastore are often enclosed within the <config> element. The XML elements within <config> map back to a specific data model.

```
<rpc message-id="101" xmlns="urn:ietf:params:xml:ns:netconf:base:1.0">
  <edit-config>
    <target>
      <running/>
    </target>
    <config>
      <configuration>
        <routing-options>
          <static>
            <route>
              <name>0.0.0.0/0</name>
              <next-hop>10.1.0.1</next-hop>
            </route>
          </static>
        </routing-options>
      </configuration>
    </config>
  </edit-config>
</rpc>
```

The <config> element is not mandatory when you're using the <edit-config> operation. What can be used within <config> is based on the NETCONF capabilities that are supported on a given device. If the :url capability is supported, you can use the <url> tag to specify a location of a file containing configuration data.

We cover more on NETCONF capabilities later in this section.

Additionally, vendors can implement platform-specific options. An example is what Juniper's Junos offers for <edit-config>. The previous example uses <config> and requires XML configuration objects for adding a static route to a Juniper Junos device. Juniper's Junos also supports <config-text> within <edit-config>, which allows you to include configuration elements using text format (curly brace or set syntax).

The <edit-config> operation also supports an attribute called operation that provides more flexibility as to how a device applies the configuration object. When the operation attribute is used, it can be set to one of five values: merge, replace, create, delete, or remove. The default value is merge. If you wanted to delete the route from the previous example, you could use delete or remove; the difference in these is that an error occurs if you use delete when the object doesn't exist. You could optionally use create, but an error is raised if the object already exists. Often, merge is used for making configuration changes for this reason.

Finally, you could use the replace operation if you wanted to replace a given XML hierarchy in the configuration data object. In the static route example, you would use replace if you wanted to end up with *just* the default static route on the device; it would automatically remove all other configured static routes.

 If this still seems a little confusing, do not worry. Once we start exploring and automating devices using NETCONF in the next two sections, you'll see even more examples that use various XML objects across different device types using operations such as the NETCONF merge and replace operations.

We've shown what XML documents look like when using the <get> and <edit-config> operations. The following list describes the other base NETCONF operations:

`<get-config>`

Retrieve all or part of a specified configuration (e.g., running, candidate, or startup).

`<copy-config>`

Create or replace a configuration datastore with the contents of another configuration datastore. Using this operation requires the use of a full configuration.

`<delete-config>`

Delete a configuration datastore (note that the running configuration datastore can't be deleted).

`<lock>`

Lock the configuration datastore system of a device that is being updated to be certain that no other systems (NETCONF clients) can make a change at the same time.

`<unlock>`

Unlock a previously issued lock on a configuration datastore.

`<close-session>`

Request a graceful termination of a NETCONF session.

`<kill-session>`

Forcefully and immediately terminate a NETCONF session.

The aforementioned list is not an exhaustive list of NETCONF operations, but rather the core operations that each device must support in a NETCONF implementation. NETCONF servers can also support extended operations such as `<commit>` and `<validate>`. In order to support extended operations like these, the device must support required dependencies called NETCONF capabilities.

The `<commit>` operation commits the candidate configuration as the device's new running configuration. In order to support the `<commit>` operation, the device must support the `:candidate` capability.

The `<validate>` operation validates the contents of the specified configuration (running, candidate, startup). Validation consists of checking a configuration for both syntax and semantics before applying the configuration to the device.

We've mentioned NETCONF capabilities twice already. We'll now provide a little more context into what they are. As you know now, NETCONF supports a base set of NETCONF RPC operations. However, these are implemented by the device supporting a base set of NETCONF *capabilities*. NETCONF capabilities are exchanged between client and a server during connection setup and the capabilities supported are denoted by a URL/URI. For example, every device that supports NETCONF should support the base operation and that URL is denoted as `urn:ietf:par ams:xml:ns:netconf:base:1.0`. Additional capabilities use the form `urn:ietf:params:netconf:capability:{`*name*`}:1.`*x* where *name* is the name of the capability and specific capabilities are usually referenced as `:name` as we showed by referencing the `:candi date` capability. When we start exploring the use of NETCONF from a hands-on perspective, you'll get to see all capabilities a given device supports.

Content. The last layer of the NETCONF protocol stack to understand is the *content*. The content refers to the actual XML document that gets embedded within the RPC operation tag elements. We already showed examples of what the content could be for particular NETCONF operations.

In our first example, we looked at content that selectively requested configuration elements for the interfaces on a Cisco IOS-XE device:

```
<native xmlns="http://cisco.com/ns/yang/ned/ios">
  <interface>
  </interface>
</native>
```

The most important point to understand about *content* is that it is the XML representation of a particular schema or data model that the device supports. We described and introduced schemas and data models in Chapter 5.

The IOS-XE device used in our examples supports models written in the YANG modeling language, and one of those models is a model that represents the full running configuration. While the model is written in YANG, it must be represented as XML between a NETCONF client and NETCONF server since NETCONF only supports XML encoding.

The next example highlights the *content* to add a static route to a Juniper device running Junos. Again, the critical part is to understand how to construct the proper XML document that the device OS requires; understanding the language, such as YANG or XML Schema Definitions (XSD), that the model or schema was written in is much less important. For example, do we know if this Juniper XML document maps to a schema written as an XSD or a model written in YANG? We'll leave that as an exercise for the reader.

```
<configuration>
  <routing-options>
    <static>
      <route>
        <name>0.0.0.0/0</name>
        <next-hop>10.1.0.1</next-hop>
      </route>
    </static>
  </routing-options>
</configuration>
```

Now that we've covered the types of APIs we'll discuss in this chapter, let's shift our focus to exploring these APIs.

Exploring Network APIs

As we start our journey of *consuming* and interacting with network APIs, the focus in this section is just like the focus we've had thus far throughout the book—on vendor-neutral tools and libraries. More specifically, we are going to look at tools such as cURL and Postman for working with HTTP-based APIs, and NETCONF over SSH for working with NETCONF APIs on network devices.

It's important to note that this section is strictly about *exploring* network APIs in that we showcase how to get started using and testing network APIs without writing any code. Our focus in this section is to start to put into use what we've learned thus far about particular API types. This section is *not* about the tools and techniques you would use for automating production networks. Those types of tools and libraries are covered in "Automating Using Network APIs" on page 231.

Exploring HTTP-Based APIs

We'll get started by exploring the use of HTTP-based APIs. Note the same tools can be used for both RESTful and non-RESTful HTTP-based APIs. The first tool we'll look at is called cURL.

cURL

cURL is a command-line tool for working with URLs. What this means is that from the Linux command line, we can send HTTP requests using the cURL program. While cURL uses URLs, it can communicate to servers using protocols besides HTTP including FTP, SFTP, TFTP, TELNET, and many more. You can use the command man curl from the Linux command line to get an in-depth look at all of the various options cURL supports.

We are going to look at using cURL with the Cisco ASA RESTful API. As we're just getting started with RESTful APIs, we'll begin with a simple HTTP GET request that retrieves all interfaces of a Cisco ASA security appliance.

 The Cisco ASA and ASAv platforms that support the RESTful API have built-in API documentation and a console for testing the API directly on the ASA. You can browse to *https://<asa-ip>/doc/*, log in, and then see and test every API that the ASA supports.

In order to make an API call to retrieve a list of interfaces and their configuration, we'll use the cURL statement shown in the following example:

```
$ curl -u ntc:ntc123 -k https://asav/api/interfaces/physical
```

The statement uses two flags and specifies the desired URL needed to retrieve the interfaces on the ASA. The first flag shown is -u, which denotes that the *user name:_password_* is going to follow. The second flag is -k, which explicitly allows cURL to perform *insecure* SSL connections, and in our case it's needed to permit the use of a self-signed certificate on the ASA. Finally, we specify the URL of the resource we want to query.

```
$ curl -u ntc:ntc123 -k https://asav/api/interfaces/physical
# response omitted
```

If you issue the previous cURL statement, you'll see large output word-wrapped on the terminal, making it hard to read. Alternatively, you can *pipe* the response to python -m json.tool to pretty print the response object, making it much more human readable.

```
$ curl -u ntc:ntc123 -k https://asav/api/interfaces/physical | python -m json.tool
  % Total    % Received % Xferd  Average Speed   Time    Time     Time  Current
                                 Dload  Upload   Total   Spent    Left  Speed
100  4114  100  4114    0     0  15819      0 --:--:-- --:--:-- --:--:-- 15884

{
    "kind":"collection#MgmtInterface",
    "selfLink":"https://asav/api/interfaces/physical",
    "rangeInfo":{
        "offset":0,
        "limit":4,
        "total":4
    },
    "items":[
        {
            "kind":"object#MgmtInterface",
            "selfLink":"https://asav/api/interfaces/physical/Management0_API_SLASH_0",
            "hardwareID":"Management0/0",
            "interfaceDesc":"",
            "channelGroupID":"",
            "channelGroupMode":"active",
            "duplex":"auto",
            # keys removed for brevity
            "managementOnly":true,
```

```
            "mtu":1500,
            "name":"management",
            "securityLevel":0,
            "shutdown":false,
            "speed":"auto",
            "ipAddress":{
                "kind":"StaticIP",
                "ip":{
                    "kind":"IPv4Address",
                    "value":"10.0.0.101"
                },
                "netMask":{
                    "kind":"IPv4NetMask",
                    "value":"255.255.255.0"
                }
            },,
            "objectId":"Management0_API_SLASH_0"
        },
        {
            "kind":"object#GigabitInterface",
            "selfLink":"https://asav/api/interfaces/physical/GigabitEthernet0_API_SLASH_0",
            "hardwareID":"GigabitEthernet0/0",
            "interfaceDesc":"",
            # keys removed for brevity
        },
        # other interface dictionaries removed for brevity
    ]
}
$
```

Take note of the object type received and printed to the terminal. You should have realized that it is a JSON object (or dictionary, in Python) since it begins and ends with curly braces. You could also see when viewing the response that the items key is a list of dictionaries where each dictionary represents an interface.

The Cisco ASA API only supports JSON encoding, but many RESTful APIs support both JSON *and* XML encoding. When systems or network devices support different encoding types, you need to specify the desired encoding type in the HTTP request message. This type of declaration happens in the HTTP headers that are part of the HTTP request.

Two common HTTP headers that we are going to use as we dive deeper into HTTP APIs are Accept and Content-Type. The Accept header is used to specify certain media types that are acceptable for the response, while the Content-Type is used to indicate the type of data being sent to the server in the case of resource changes. We review examples of using these HTTP headers in the next two sections.

We've looked at one basic example issuing a GET request to the ASA RESTful API using cURL. We're going to shift to a more user-friendly tool called Postman for exploring and testing HTTP-based APIs.

Exploring HTTP-based APIs with Postman

Postman is a Google Chrome application that provides a user-intuitive web GUI frontend to interact with HTTP-based APIs. As you'll see, Postman and tools alike make it much easier to learn and test HTTP APIs, as they put the focus on using the API without worrying about writing code.

Once Postman is installed and you launch it as a Chrome application, you'll see a screen similar to Figure 7-2.

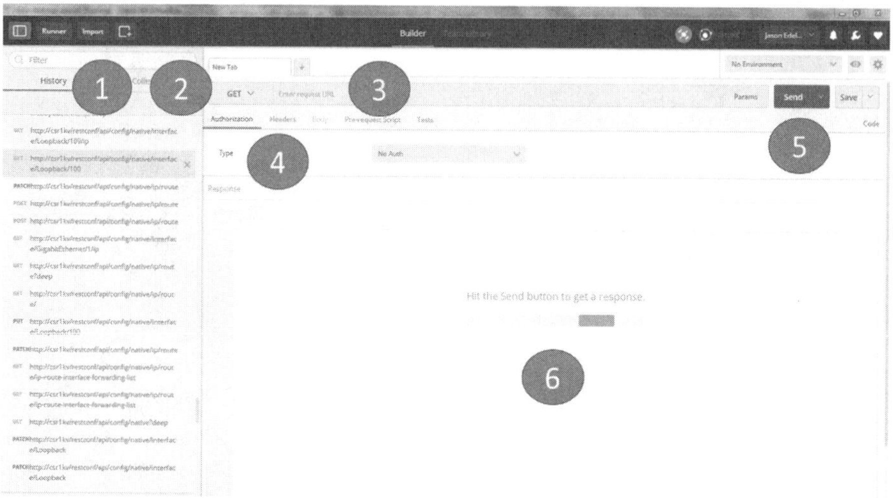

Figure 7-2. Introduction to Postman

Let's analyze what you see, using the numbers outlined in the figure.

1. The left pane has two tabs to be aware of, *History* and *Collections*. The History tab shows all previously executed API calls with Postman. Additionally, the history is easily accessible if you log in to Postman on another machine, as it's leveraging Chrome under the covers and is the same as accessing web browsing history. The Collections tab allows you to save a series of API requests as a *collection* and, once created, can be executed individually or as a collection that is analogous to a script.

2. In this drop-down, you are able to choose the appropriate HTTP Request method (e.g., GET, PUT, PATCH, POST, DELETE). The default when you log in to Postman is GET.

3. This is the URL required to perform a specific API request.

4. For this figure, we're focused on three tabs here: *Authorization*, *Headers*, and *Body*. In the Authorization tab, you select the proper form of authentication required by the server. We are going to be using *Basic Auth* for our examples with the Cisco ASA RESTful API. The Headers tab is where you define the request headers that are used in a given API request. For example, if you want to define the encoding type of the request, it is configured in this tab. Finally, the Body tab

is where you define the JSON or XML body that needs to be sent in the API request if you are making a change to a resource—for example, using a POST to create a loopback interface.

5. Once you've defined your HTTP method (2), typed in your URL (3), and configured the required parameters (4), you can click the Send button to issue the API call to the device.

6. When the API request is made, the result is displayed in this open text box.

For our first example with Postman, we show how to retrieve the list of interfaces on the Cisco ASA device using its RESTful API—this is the same example we showed already using cURL.

Figure 7-3 shows that the HTTP method has been set to GET, the URL has been entered, and credentials have been entered.

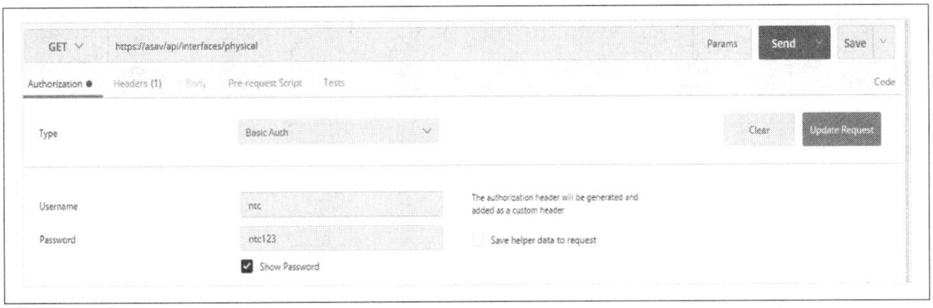

Figure 7-3. Performing a GET request with Postman

Notice that the Headers tab shows as Headers (1) in Figure 7-4. This is because we pressed the Update Request button. This automatically created a header called Authorization and set it to be equal to the base64-encoded string of the username and password.

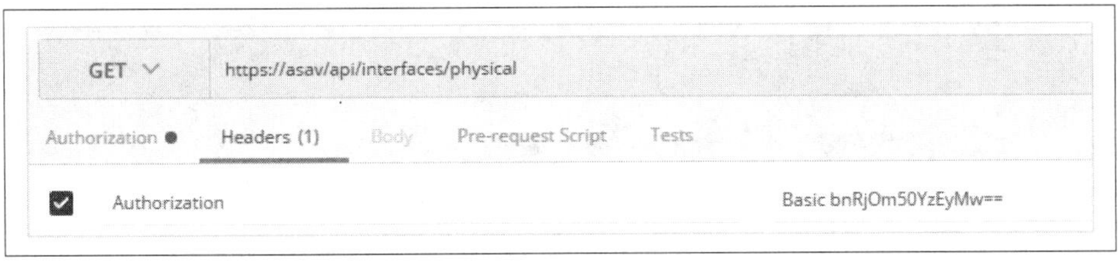

Figure 7-4. The Authorization request header

A base64-encoded string does *not* mean it has been encrypted. You can easily encode and decode base64-encoded strings with Python using the `base64` Python module.

```
>>> import base64
>>>
>>> encoded = base64.b64encode('ntc:ntc123')
>>> encoded
'bnRjOm50YzEyMw=='
>>>
>>> text = base64.b64decode(encoded)
>>> text
'ntc:ntc123'
>>>
```

Once the request is constructed, you send it to the device by clicking the blue Send button. Upon the server executing the request, the bottom portion of the screen displays the response and HTTP status code (Figure 7-5).

Figure 7-5. Viewing an HTTP GET response

Although it has no impact because the Cisco ASA device only supports JSON, the `Accept` HTTP request header can be explicitly defined in the Headers tab (Figure 7-6).

Figure 7-6. Setting the request header

Retrieving configuration data by issuing a GET request is quite straightforward, as you simply need to provide credentials and a URL. When making a configuration change, you need an HTTP Body to the underlying API request.

Since we just made a request that retrieved all physical interfaces, let's make a configuration change to one of the physical interfaces. Let's configure the interface description on GigabitEthernet0/0. To make this change we need to make three changes to our current API call in Postman.

1. Update the URL.
2. Update the HTTP request method.
3. Add the appropriate JSON body.

A fourth optional change would be to set the *Content-Type* header, but since the ASA only supports JSON, it's not required.

The new and resulting API can be defined like this:

1. HTTP Request Type: PATCH
2. URL: *https://asav/api/interfaces/physical/GigabitEthernet0_API_SLASH_0*
3. Body:

```
{
    "kind": "object#GigabitInterface",
    "interfaceDesc": "Configured by Postman"
}
```

After making these changes in Postman, we have the following in Figure 7-7.

Figure 7-7. Performing PATCH request with Postman

Once you click Send and make the request, voilà—the Cisco ASA device has a newly configured interface description.

Learning how to construct a proper API request requires getting familiar with API documentation. The API documentation (the API definition and spec) defines what a given URL must be, the HTTP request type, headers, and what the body needs to be for a successful API call.

For example, how did we know to use *GigabitEthernet0_API_SLASH_0* in the URL for making an interface change on the ASA, make it a PATCH request, and include the `kind` and `interfaceDesc` keys in the JSON body? The answer: *API documentation*. Luckily, the documentation for the ASA, as we said previously, is on the device at *https://<asa-ip-address>/doc/*. You can also glean information from performing GET requests, because oftentimes you need to use the same values in the body of a POST/PATCH/PUT, as we saw with the value of `object#GigabitInterface` for the `kind` key.

We've introduced two tools thus far that make it possible for us to interact with HTTP-based APIs without writing any code. We showed how to make the same API call using both cURL and Postman, as well as how to make a configuration with Postman. Next, we're going to shift our focus and explore using NETCONF.

Exploring NETCONF

As you learn new APIs, it's advantageous to learn about associated tooling that allows you to learn the API without writing any code. You saw this with Postman when learning how to use HTTP-based APIs. For NETCONF, we are going to cover how to use an SSH client that creates an interactive NETCONF session. You'll learn how to construct a proper NETCONF request while also seeing how the device responds to a given request without writing any code.

Using an interactive NETCONF over SSH session is not an ideal choice for learning NETCONF. It is not user-intuitive or user-friendly, but there are not any other tools that exist for *learning* and *exploring* the use of NETCONF. You should not in any way look to use an interactive SSH session as a valid operational model for automating network devices using NETCONF.

In our first example, we connect to a Cisco IOS-XE router via SSH on port 830, the default port number for NETCONF. In order to connect to the device, we'll use a standard Linux `ssh` command, but change the port to 830.

```
$ ssh -p 830 ntc@ios-csr1kv
```

As soon as we connect and authenticate, the NETCONF server (Cisco IOS-XE router) responds with a hello message that includes all of its supported NETCONF capabilities including supported NETCONF operations, capabilities, models/schemas, and a session ID.

The following is a subset of the response and capabilities from the Cisco IOS-XE device. We cleaned up the response because it responds with a few hundred lines due to the large quantity of models supported:

```xml
<?xml version="1.0" encoding="UTF-8"?>
<hello xmlns="urn:ietf:params:xml:ns:netconf:base:1.0">
<capabilities>
<capability>urn:ietf:params:netconf:base:1.0</capability>
<capability>urn:ietf:params:netconf:base:1.1</capability>
<capability>urn:ietf:params:netconf:capability:writable-running:1.0</capability>
<capability>urn:ietf:params:netconf:capability:xpath:1.0</capability>
<capability>urn:ietf:params:netconf:capability:validate:1.0</capability>
<capability>urn:ietf:params:netconf:capability:validate:1.1</capability>
<capability>urn:ietf:params:netconf:capability:rollback-on-error:1.0</capability>
<capability>urn:ietf:params:netconf:capability:notification:1.0</capability>
<capability>urn:ietf:params:netconf:capability:interleave:1.0</capability>
<capability>http://tail-f.com/ns/netconf/actions/1.0</capability>
<capability>http://tail-f.com/ns/netconf/extensions</capability>
<capability>urn:ietf:params:netconf:capability:with-defaults:1.0?basic-mode=
report-all</capability>
<capability>urn:ietf:params:xml:ns:yang:ietf-netconf-with-defaults?revision=
2011-06-01&amp;module=ietf-netconf-with-defaults</capability>
<capability>http://cisco.com/ns/example/enable?module=enable</capability>
<capability>http://cisco.com/ns/yang/ned/ios?module=ned&amp;revision=2016-07-01
</capability>
<capability>http://cisco.com/ns/yang/ned/ios/asr1k?module=ned-asr1k&amp;revision=
2016-04-07</capability>
<capability>http://cisco.com/yang/cisco-ia?module=cisco-ia&amp;revision=
2016-05-20</capability>
<!-- OUTPUT OMITTED -->
<capability>urn:ietf:params:xml:ns:yang:smiv2:VPN-TC-STD-MIB?module=
VPN-TC-STD-MIB&amp;revision=2005-11-15</capability>
</capabilities>
<session-id>324</session-id></hello>]]>]]>
```

Once we receive the server's capabilities, the NETCONF connection setup process has started. The next step is to send our (client) capabilities. A capabilities exchange is required to be able to send any NETCONF requests to the server.

We are going to limit the client's capabilities for this example to a few base operations and work with a single model on the IOS XE device.

The hello object we're going to send to the device to complete the capabilities exchange is the following:

```xml
<?xml version="1.0" encoding="UTF-8"?>
<hello xmlns="urn:ietf:params:xml:ns:netconf:base:1.0">
  <capabilities>
    <capability>urn:ietf:params:netconf:base:1.0</capability>
```

```
    <capability>urn:ietf:params:netconf:base:1.1</capability>
    <capability>http://cisco.com/ns/yang/ned/ios?module=ned&amp;revision=
2016-07-01</capability>
    <capability>http://cisco.com/ns/yang/ned/ios/asr1k?module=
ned-asr1k&amp;revision=2016-04-07</capability>
  </capabilities>
</hello>
]]>]]>
```

When the client sends its hello, it does *not* send the session ID attribute that's found in the server hello message.

Take note of the last six characters in the preceding XML documents above:]]>]]>. These characters are used to denote that the request is complete and it can be processed. They are required when you are using an interactive NETCONF session.

As you start working with the SSH client, you'll realize it's not like a familiar interactive CLI, although it is an interactive session. There is no help menu or question mark help available. There is no man page. It's quite common to think something is broken or the terminal is frozen. It's not. If you do not get any errors after you copy and paste XML documents into the session terminal, things are likely going well. In order to break out of the interactive session, you'll need to use the Control+C buttons on your keyboard—there is no way to safely exit the interactive NETCONF session.

Once the client responds with its capabilities, you're ready to start sending NET-CONF requests. You can use a text editor to preconstruct your XML documents.

If you're following along, after you've sent the client hello object and pasted it into the SSH session, you'd see the following output (the end of the server hello, and the complete client hello ending with]]>]]>):

```
<--- output truncated --->
<capability>urn:ietf:params:xml:ns:yang:smiv2:UDP-MIB?module=UDP-MIB&amp;revision=
2005-05-20</capability>
<capability>urn:ietf:params:xml:ns:yang:smiv2:VPN-TC-STD-MIB?module=
VPN-TC-STD-MIB&amp;revision=2005-11-15</capability>
</capabilities>
<session-id>1415</session-id></hello>]]>]]><?xml version="1.0"?>
<hello xmlns="urn:ietf:params:xml:ns:netconf:base:1.0">
    <capabilities>
        <capability>urn:ietf:params:netconf:base:1.0</capability>
        <capability>urn:ietf:params:netconf:capability:writable-running:1.0
        </capability>
        <capability>urn:ietf:params:netconf:capability:xpath:1.0</capability>
```

```
        <capability>urn:ietf:params:netconf:capability:validate:1.0
        </capability>
        <capability>urn:ietf:params:netconf:capability:rollback-on-error:1.0
        </capability>
        <capability>http://cisco.com/ns/yang/ned/ios?module=ned&amp;revision=
        2016-06-20</capability>
    </capabilities>
</hello>]]>]]>
```

At this point, we've now successfully connected to the device and exchanged capabilities, and we can now issue an actual NETCONF request. Our first example will query the device for its configuration on GigabitEthernet1.

This following XML document is constructed in a text editor and then copied and pasted into the interactive session:

```
<?xml version="1.0"?>
<rpc message-id="101" xmlns="urn:ietf:params:xml:ns:netconf:base:1.0">
  <get>
      <filter type="subtree">
        <native xmlns="http://cisco.com/ns/yang/ned/ios">
         <interface>
          <GigabitEthernet>
           <name>1</name>
          </GigabitEthernet>
         </interface>
        </native>
      </filter>
  </get>
</rpc>
]]>]]>
```

As soon as you hit Enter, the request is sent to the device. You'll see the XML RPC reply from the device in near real time.

```
<?xml version="1.0" encoding="UTF-8"?>
<rpc-reply xmlns="urn:ietf:params:xml:ns:netconf:base:1.0" message-id="101"
xmlns:nc="urn:ietf:params:xml:ns:netconf:base:1.0">
<data><native xmlns="http://cisco.com/ns/yang/ned/ios"><interface>
<GigabitEthernet><name>1</name><negotiation><auto>true</auto></negotiation>
<vrf><forwarding>MANAGEMENT</forwarding></vrf><ip><address><primary>
<address>10.0.0.51</address><mask>255.255.255.0</mask></primary></address></ip>
</GigabitEthernet></interface></native></data></rpc-reply>]]>]]>
```

You can optionally take the <rpc-reply> and use any XML formatter to make it more readable. Using an XML formatter on this data yields the following:

```
<rpc-reply message-id="101" xmlns="urn:ietf:params:xml:ns:netconf:base:1.0"
xmlns:nc="urn:ietf:params:xml:ns:netconf:base:1.0">
    <data>
        <native xmlns="http://cisco.com/ns/yang/ned/ios">
            <interface>
                <GigabitEthernet>
```

```
            <name>1</name>
            <negotiation>
                <auto>true</auto>
            </negotiation>
            <vrf>
                <forwarding>MANAGEMENT</forwarding>
            </vrf>
            <ip>
                <address>
                    <primary>
                        <address>10.0.0.51</address>
                        <mask>255.255.255.0</mask>
                    </primary>
                </address>
            </ip>
          </GigabitEthernet>
        </interface>
      </native>
    </data>
  </rpc-reply>
```

We've successfully made our first NETCONF request to a network device and received a response. The point here isn't to do anything with it, just like we didn't do anything with data returned with Postman. The value is that we've tested and validated an XML request retrieve configuration for GigabitEthernet1 and now know what the response looks like to ease us into automating devices with Python.

Let's take a look at another example using an interactive NETCONF over SSH session. This time, we'll use a Juniper vMX running Junos and obtain its configuration for interface fxp0.

We need to use the same process just covered. We need to connect to the NETCONF subsystem over SSH, receive the server capabilities in a hello message, and then respond with a hello that has our client capabilities.

```
$ ssh -p 830 ntc@junos-vmx -s netconf
Password:
<!-- No zombies were killed during the creation of this user interface -->
<!-- user ntc, class j-super-user -->
<hello xmlns="urn:ietf:params:xml:ns:netconf:base:1.0">
  <capabilities>
    <capability>urn:ietf:params:netconf:base:1.0</capability>
    <capability>urn:ietf:params:netconf:capability:candidate:1.0</capability>
    <capability>urn:ietf:params:netconf:capability:confirmed-commit:1.0
    </capability>
    <capability>urn:ietf:params:netconf:capability:validate:1.0</capability>
    <capability>urn:ietf:params:netconf:capability:url:1.0?scheme=
    http,ftp,file</capability>
    <capability>urn:ietf:params:xml:ns:netconf:base:1.0</capability>
    <capability>urn:ietf:params:xml:ns:netconf:capability:candidate:1.0
    </capability>
```

```
    <capability>urn:ietf:params:xml:ns:netconf:capability:confirmed-
    commit:1.0</capability>
    <capability>urn:ietf:params:xml:ns:netconf:capability:validate:1.0
    </capability>
    <capability>urn:ietf:params:xml:ns:netconf:capability:url:1.0?protocol=
    http,ftp,file</capability>
    <capability>http://xml.juniper.net/netconf/junos/1.0</capability>
    <capability>http://xml.juniper.net/dmi/system/1.0</capability>
  </capabilities>
  <session-id>4128</session-id>
</hello>
]]>]]>
```

 Based on the vendor implementation, you may need to supply -s
netconf as you SSH to the device. -s denotes the SSH subsystem
being used.

We then respond with our client hello message. We're just using base capabilities
since we aren't doing anything outside of what is supported in the NETCONF base
operations and capabilities.

```
<?xml version="1.0" encoding="UTF-8"?>
<hello xmlns="urn:ietf:params:xml:ns:netconf:base:1.0">
  <capabilities>
    <capability>urn:ietf:params:netconf:base:1.0</capability>
  </capabilities>
</hello>
]]>]]>
```

Once the capabilities exchange is complete, we then send the appropriate XML object
requesting the configuration for fxp0.

```
<?xml version="1.0"?>
<rpc message-id="101" xmlns="urn:ietf:params:xml:ns:netconf:base:1.0">
    <get>
        <filter type="subtree">
            <configuration>
                <interfaces>
                    <interface>
                        <name>fxp0</name>
                    </interface>
                </interfaces>
            </configuration>
        </filter>
    </get>
</rpc>
]]>]]>
```

The response returned is as follows:

```
<rpc-reply xmlns:junos="http://xml.juniper.net/junos/15.1F4/junos" message-id="101"
xmlns="urn:ietf:params:xml:ns:netconf:base:1.0">
<data>
<configuration xmlns="http://xml.juniper.net/xnm/1.1/xnm"
junos:changed-seconds="1482848933" junos:changed-localtime="2016-12-27 14:28:53 UTC">
    <interfaces>
        <interface>
            <name>fxp0</name>
            <unit>
                <name>0</name>
                <family>
                    <inet>
                        <address>
                            <name>10.0.0.31/24</name>
                        </address>
                    </inet>
                </family>
            </unit>
        </interface>
    </interfaces>
</configuration>
<database-status-information>
<database-status>
<user>ntc</user>
<terminal>p0</terminal>
<pid>4091</pid>
<start-time junos:seconds="1482857982">2016-12-27 16:59:42 UTC</start-time>
<idle-time junos:seconds="52">00:00:52</idle-time>
<edit-path>[edit]</edit-path>
</database-status>
<database-status>
<user>ntc</user>
<terminal></terminal>
<pid>4168</pid>
<start-time junos:seconds="1482858044">2016-12-27 17:00:44 UTC</start-time>
<edit-path></edit-path>
</database-status>
</database-status-information>
</data>
</rpc-reply>
]]>]]>
```

We've now seen two examples using NETCONF <get> operations to the device. Let's
take a look at one more example introducing how to use the <edit-config> operation, which is used to make a configuration change.

While our focus is now making a configuration change, in order to see the proper
way to construct an XML request for a configuration change, we are going to first
issue a get request since that will show us the structure of the complete object that
needs to get sent back to the device.

For this example, we are using an industry-standard data model for interfaces called *ietf-interfaces*, and supported by Cisco IOS-XE.

After we establish a NETCONF connection to the device, we can issue the following get request to obtain interface-related configurations:

```
<?xml version="1.0"?>
<rpc message-id="101" xmlns="urn:ietf:params:xml:ns:netconf:base:1.0">
    <get>
        <filter type="subtree">
            <interfaces xmlns="urn:ietf:params:xml:ns:yang:ietf-interfaces">
            </interfaces>
        </filter>
    </get>
</rpc>
]]>]]>
```

The cleaned-up and formatted response from the Cisco IOS-XE router is as follows:

```
<?xml version="1.0" encoding="UTF-8"?>
<rpc-reply message-id="101" xmlns="urn:ietf:params:xml:ns:netconf:base:1.0">
  <data>
    <interfaces xmlns="urn:ietf:params:xml:ns:yang:ietf-interfaces">
      <interface>
        <name>GigabitEthernet1</name>
        <type xmlns:ianaift="urn:ietf:params:xml:ns:yang:iana-if-type">
ianaift:ethernetCsmacd</type>
        <enabled>true</enabled>
        <ipv4 xmlns="urn:ietf:params:xml:ns:yang:ietf-ip">
          <address>
            <ip>10.0.0.51</ip>
            <netmask>255.255.255.0</netmask>
          </address>
        </ipv4>
        <ipv6 xmlns="urn:ietf:params:xml:ns:yang:ietf-ip"/>
      </interface>
      <interface>
        <name>GigabitEthernet4</name>
        <type xmlns:ianaift="urn:ietf:params:xml:ns:yang:iana-if-type">
ianaift:ethernetCsmacd</type>
        <enabled>true</enabled>
        <ipv4 xmlns="urn:ietf:params:xml:ns:yang:ietf-ip"/>
        <ipv6 xmlns="urn:ietf:params:xml:ns:yang:ietf-ip"/>
      </interface>
    </interfaces>
  </data>
</rpc-reply>
]]>]]>
```

We've shortened the response by removing GigabitEthernet2 and GigabitEthernet3 to make it more readable.

Notice how GigabitEthernet1 has an IP address configured. You can perform a get request, check the configuration objects returned, and use this as the foundation to modify the configurations on other interfaces to simplify the process.

Let's make a configuration change and configure the IP address of 10.4.4.1/24 on GigabitEthernet4.

In order to construct the object, we'll extract the required data from our get request. Two items to update as we do this are the following:

1. Our object returned in the <data> tag will get enclosed in a <config> tag when we want to make a configuration change using the NETCONF <edit-config> operation.

2. The constructed object needs to specify a *target* datastore (i.e., running, startup, or candidate) based on what the target node supports.

After we make these changes, the result is the following:

```
<?xml version="1.0"?>
<rpc message-id="101" xmlns="urn:ietf:params:xml:ns:netconf:base:1.0">
    <edit-config>
      <target>
        <running/>
      </target>
        <config>
          <interfaces xmlns="urn:ietf:params:xml:ns:yang:ietf-interfaces">
            <interface>
              <name>GigabitEthernet4</name>
              <type xmlns:ianaift="urn:ietf:params:xml:ns:yang:iana-if-type">
ianaift:ethernetCsmacd</type>
              <enabled>true</enabled>
              <ipv4 xmlns="urn:ietf:params:xml:ns:yang:ietf-ip">
                <address>
                  <ip>10.4.4.1</ip>
                  <netmask>255.255.255.0</netmask>
                </address>
              </ipv4>
            </interface>
          </interfaces>
        </config>
    </edit-config>
</rpc>
]]>]]>
```

Once this XML document is built in a text editor, it can easily be copied and pasted into an active NETCONF session.

Pasting this into an interactive NETCONF session, we'll see successful response as shown in the following output:

```
<?xml version="1.0" encoding="UTF-8"?>
<rpc-reply xmlns="urn:ietf:params:xml:ns:netconf:base:1.0" message-id="101">
  <ok/>
</rpc-reply>
]]>]]>
```

We've stated this a few times already, but we are going to restate it because it's extremely important. As you get started using NET-CONF APIs (or RESTful APIs), you need to be aware of how to construct the proper request object. This is often challenging as you get started, but the hope is there are *easy* ways to help figure out how to build these objects. This could come from API documentation, tooling built to interface with the underlying schema definitions files such as XSDs or YANG modules, or even CLI commands on the device. For example, Cisco Nexus and Juniper Junos have CLI commands that show you exactly what the XML document needs to be for a given request. We'll take a look at this soon.

Now that we've reviewed and explored HTTP-based APIs and the NETCONF, you must understand how to automate network devices using these APIs. We'll now take a look at using Python to automate devices using HTTP-based APIs, NETCONF, and SSH.

Automating Using Network APIs

As we've stated, there is a difference with the tools used to *explore* and *learn* to use an API and the tools used to *consume* an API that fits into more of a production operational model. Thus far, we've looked at cURL and Postman for exploring HTTP-based APIs and an interactive NETCONF over SSH session for exploring the use of NET-CONF. In this part of the chapter, we'll be looking at how to use Python to automate network devices. Our focus is on three different Python libraries.

requests
> An intuitive and popular HTTP library for Python. This is the library we use for automating devices and controllers with both RESTful HTTP-based APIs and non-RESTful HTTP-based APIs.

ncclient
> This is a NETCONF client for Python. This is the library we use for automating devices using NETCONF.

netmiko
> This is a network-first SSH client for Python. This is the library we use for automating devices via native SSH targeting devices without programmatic APIs.

Let's get started by looking at the requests library and communicating with HTTP-based APIs.

Using the Python requests Library

You've seen how to make HTTP-based API calls from the command line with cURL and from within a GUI with Postman. These are great mechanisms to explore using a given API, but realistically in order to write a script or a program that's helpful for automating network devices, you need to be able to make API calls from within a script or program. In this section, we introduce the Python requests library—it simplifies working with web-based APIs. While we provide an overview of different APIs in this section, such as the Arista eAPI, Cisco ASA RESTful API, Cisco NX-API, and Cisco IOS-XE RESTCONF API, it is meant to be read from start to finish, as the core focus is getting started with using the requests library.

 To install requests, you can use `pip`:

```
[sudo] pip install requests
```

Let's dive in and take a look at our first example using requests. This is a complete Python script used to retrieve the interface configuration of a Cisco ASA. It is the same GET request we've already executed with cURL and Postman.

```python
#!/usr/bin/env python

import json
import requests
from requests.auth import HTTPBasicAuth


if __name__ == "__main__":

    auth = HTTPBasicAuth('ntc', 'ntc123')
    headers = {
        'Accept': 'application/json',
        'Content-Type': 'application/json'
    }

    url = "https://asav/api/interfaces/physical"
    response = requests.get(url, auth=auth, headers=headers, verify=False)
```

Let's take a look at the script, now fully commented, to understand exactly what each line is doing.

```python
#!/usr/bin/env python

# The json module is imported so that we can encode and decode JSON
# objects over the wire. While we work with JSON objects in Python as
# dictionaries, they are sent over the wire as JSON strings in API calls.
# This means we need a way to convert dictionaries to strings so they are
# understood by the network device (web server).  The converse is true too.
# When you receive a response from a device using JSON encoding, a JSON
# string is received that needs to be converted to a dictionary in
# order to consume it in Python.  We use the json module for these actions.
import json

# The Python requests library is used to issue and work HTTP-based systems.
# We are also using a helper function from requests
# called `HTTPBasicAuth` to simplify authentication
import requests
from requests.auth import HTTPBasicAuth

# This executes if our script is being run directly.
if __name__ == "__main__":

    # An authentication object is created using the helper function
    # called HTTPBasicAuth. This works when the device supports
    # basic authentication. Note that the variable name auth
    # is arbitrary. All variables are. We just happen to
    # align our variable names to the parameter name used
    # by the requests library.
    # If you don't use the HTTPBasicAuth helper function
    # you can set the credentials in the get function
    # using a tuple such as auth=(ntc, ntc123).
    auth = HTTPBasicAuth('ntc', 'ntc123')

    # This statement creates a Python dictionary for the HTTP request
    # headers that are going to use in the API calls.  The two
    # headers we are setting are Content-Type and Accept.  These
    # are the same headers we reviewed and also set with Postman.
    headers = {
        'Accept': 'application/json',
        'Content-Type': 'application/json'
    }

    # The URL is saved as a variable called url to modularize our
    # code and simplify the next statement.
    url = "https://asav/api/interfaces/physical"

    # This last statement is when the API call is executed using requests.
    # In the requests library, there is a function per HTTP verb and in
    # this example we are issuing a GET request, so we are therefore
    # using the `get` function. We pass four objects into the `get` function.
```

```
# The first  object passed in must be the URL and the others should be
# keyword arguments (key=value pairs). We're using the three keyword
# arguments called auth, headers, and verify. We simply set the keywords
# auth and headers equal to the variables we previously created and
# then set verify equal to False since the Cisco ASA device is using
# a self-signed certificate and we aren't verifying it.
response = requests.get(url, auth=auth, headers=headers, verify=False)
```

If you run this script against a device that is using a self-signed certificate or unverified HTTPS connection, you will receive a warning message. When using the requests library, you can suppress
this using the following Python statement:

```
requests.packages.urllib3.disable_warnings()
```

Let's continue to build on this; we are now going to update an interface description
using requests, which is the same request we also showed with Postman.

In order to make a configuration change using the requests library, we need to make
the same three changes we showed in Postman: update the URL, update the HTTP
request type, and send data in the body of the request.

```
payload = {
  "kind": "object#GigabitInterface",
  "interfaceDesc": "Configured by Python"
}

url = "https://asav/api/interfaces/physical/GigabitEthernet0_API_SLASH_0"
response = requests.patch(url, data=json.dumps(payload), auth=auth,
                          headers=headers, verify=False)
```

Pay attention to the HTTP verb being used. This particular request
is using the patch() function as a resource is being updated. If we
were creating a resource, the post() function would be used, and if
we were replacing a resource, put() would be used. We'll look at
these functions in more examples later in the chapter.

Updating the URL and the request type are simple changes. You can see in this example, the url variable is updated in the last statement, and the patch() function is now
called.

Now we're going to focus on how to send data in the body of the HTTP request. This
is where we need to differentiate between a Python dictionary and JSON string.
While we work with dictionaries in Python to construct the required body, this is sent
over the wire as a JSON string. To convert the dictionary to a well-formed JSON
string, we use the dumps() function from the json module. This function takes a dic-

tionary and converts it to a JSON string. We finally take the string object and pass it over the wire by assigning it to the data key being passed to the patch() function.

After providing an introduction to using the Python requests library, we are going to continue to build on it while looking at three more HTTP-based APIs. Keep in mind, even though we cover different APIs in this chapter, it is meant to be read from start to finish and not as API documentation for any given API.

Getting familiar with Cisco NX-API

We are now going to look at the Cisco Nexus NX-API while diving a bit deeper into the requests library. As we show a few examples with NX-API, keep in mind a few things:

- The NX-API is a non-RESTful HTTP-based API. In other words, it's an HTTP-based API that doesn't follow all of the principles of REST. An HTTP POST is used no matter what operation is being performed—even if show commands are used, a POST is still used.
- Remember POST requests require data to be sent in the data payload of the request. This is where solid API tools and documentation come into play. Nexus switches have a built-in tool called the NX-API Developer Sandbox that we are going to leverage in order to learn the required structure of the payload object.
- The URL format for NX-API API calls is always *http(s)://<ip-address-nexus>/ins*

Using the NX-API Developer Sandbox. Before we dive into using NX-API in Python, let's take a quick look at the NX-API Developer Sandbox, as this is how you figure out how to structure a proper HTTP request with NX-API.

Once NX-API is enabled, you can browse to the Nexus switch in a web browser. Once you log in, you'll see the Cisco NX-API Developer Sandbox as shown in Figure 7-8.

This NX-API Sandbox is an on-box tool that enables you to test APIs and understand what the request and response objects look like without writing any code. This is similar in nature to what Postman offers, but the sandbox exists directly on each Nexus switch.

 An *on-box tool* is a tool that resides directly on the network device. Specifically, the NX-API Developer Sandbox is a web utility that resides on each and every Nexus switch.

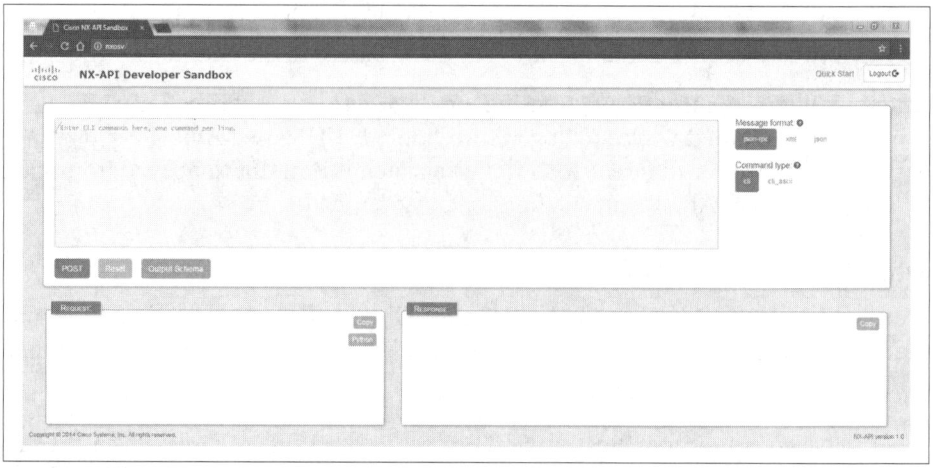

Figure 7-8. Cisco NX-API Developer Sandbox

As soon as a command is typed in the upper-left text box in the sandbox, a JSON-based request object is automatically generated in the bottom left (Figure 7-9).

Figure 7-9. JSON request in the NX-API Developer Sandbox

When the blue POST button is clicked, the API call is made to the switch and the HTTP response is shown in the bottom right. The response is the same object we'll get when API calls are made from Python too.

Let's extract the request object and save it as a variable so that we can use it in a Python script.

```
payload = {
    "ins_api": {
        "version": "1.0",
        "type": "cli_show",
        "chunk": "0",
        "sid": "1",
        "input": 'show version',
        "output_format": "json"
    }
}
```

Remember, payload is a dictionary and we need to convert it to a string before we send it across the wire. We'll do this again with the dumps() function in the json Python module. Additionally, remember that every API request with NX-API is a POST—this determines the function we need to use in the requests library.

Consuming NX-API in a Python script.   Let's look at a complete Python script, making an API call to execute the show version command.

```
import json
import requests
from requests.auth import HTTPBasicAuth

if __name__ == "__main__":

    auth = HTTPBasicAuth('ntc', 'ntc123')
    headers = {
        'Content-Type': 'application/json',
        'Accept': 'application/json'
    }
    url = 'http://nxos-spine1/ins'

    payload = {
        "ins_api": {
            "version": "1.0",
            "type": "cli_show",
            "chunk": "0",
            "sid": "1",
            "input": 'show version',
            "output_format": "json"
        }
    }

    response = requests.post(url, data=json.dumps(payload),
                             headers=headers, auth=auth)

    print(response)
```

There isn't much inside this script that we haven't covered already, but let's recap.

We are using the `json` module, as this is how we are serializing and de-serializing JSON objects (strings) to/from dictionaries. The requests library is imported since it's this library that will make the HTTP requests to the Nexus devices. The last object we're importing is called `HTTPBasicAuth` and we're using it to simplify authentication.

The first part of the script parameterizes the credentials, headers, and URL required to use NX-API. This isn't any different from what we did when using the ASA RESTful API.

```
auth = HTTPBasicAuth('ntc', 'ntc123')
headers = {
    'Content-Type': 'application/json',
    'Accept': 'application/json'
}
url = 'http://nxos-spine1/ins'
```

Here we can see what the credentials are—these are the same credentials you would use to log in to the Nexus switch via SSH (assuming correct permissions).

Now take note of the URL. This is a fixed URL for all NX-API communications. It is the IP/FQDN of the switch plus `/ins`, which happens to be the first three letters of Insieme, the company Cisco acquired in 2012 for data center networking and SDN solutions.

Last, we'll take a look at the remaining part of the script:

```
payload = {
    "ins_api": {
        "version": "1.0",
        "type": "cli_show",
        "chunk": "0",
        "sid": "1",
        "input": 'show version',
        "output_format": "json"
    }
}

response = requests.post(url, data=json.dumps(payload),
                        headers=headers, auth=auth)
print(response)
```

You should see that the variable we called `payload` was taken directly from NX-API Developer Sandbox, and in Python, this is a Python dictionary with a single key-value pair. The key is called `ins_api` and the value is a nested dictionary with six key-value pairs.

This all comes together on the next line, where we can finally execute the API call to the Nexus switch. You can see that the syntax of the Python statement is `requests.post()` and will be the same for whatever verb you need in your request. For example, if you were doing a GET request, it would be `requests.get()`.

We're subsequently passing in four Python objects to the post() function within the requests library. The first is a positional argument, which is the URL; the next three we are passing in as keyword arguments using keywords required by the post() function including data, headers, and auth.

As we've already said, do not forget to use data=json.dumps(<dict>) because we need to serialize the dictionary as a string over the wire to the Nexus switch.

In the last line of the script, we simply print the response.

Let's save this script as \nxapi-cli.py and run it from the command line.

```
ntc@ntc:~$ python nxapi-cli.py
<Response [200]>
ntc@ntc:~$
```

You can see we get an HTTP response of 200 back and everything worked as expected, but there is only one question that remains, *Where is the data we want to see from the* show version *command?*

Using NX-API from the Python interactive interpreter. We are going rerun this script using the -i flag on the command line, which automatically drops us into the Python interactive interpreter, but will allow us to access all objects from our script. We originally introduced the -i flag in Chapter 4. It is a great way to test and troubleshoot.

```
ntc@ntc:~$ python -i nxapi-cli.py
<Response [200]>
>>>
```

At this point, we're in the Python interactive interpreter and can see the objects from our script using the dir() function, which we also covered in Chapter 4.

```
>>> dir()
['HTTPBasicAuth', '__builtins__', '__doc__', '__name__', '__package__',
'auth', 'json', 'payload', 'requests', 'response', 'url']
>>>
```

Let's take it one step further and use dir() on response because dir() displays all attributes and methods of a given object.

```
>>> dir(response)
['__attrs__', '__bool__', '__class__', '__delattr__', '__dict__',
'__doc__', '__format__', '__getattribute__', '__getstate__', '__hash__',
'__init__', '__iter__', '__module__', '__new__', '__nonzero__', '__reduce__',
'__reduce_ex__', '__repr__', '__setattr__', '__setstate__', '__sizeof__',
'__str__',
'__subclasshook__', '__weakref__', '_content', '_content_consumed',
'apparent_encoding', 'close', 'connection', 'content', 'cookies',
'elapsed', 'encoding', 'headers', 'history', 'is_permanent_redirect',
'is_redirect', 'iter_content', 'iter_lines', 'json', 'links',
'ok', 'raise_for_status', 'raw', 'reason', 'request', 'status_code', 'text',
```

```
'url']
>>>
```

We are going to focus on two of the attributes—status_code and text.

The status_code attribute gives us access to the HTTP response code as an integer.

```
>>> print(response.status_code)
200
>>> type(response.status_code)
<type 'int'>
>>>
```

The text attribute stores the actual response we care about from the Nexus switch. This is the same data that you saw in the response window (bottom right) in the NX-API Developer Sandbox.

```
>>> print(response.text)
{
  "ins_api":  {
    "type": "cli_show",
    "version":  "1.2",
    "sid":  "eoc",
    "outputs":  {
      "output": {
        "input":  "show version",
        "msg":  "Success",
        "code": "200",
        "body": {
          "header_str": "Cisco Nexus Operating System (NX-OS) Software...",
          "loader_ver_str": "N/A",
          "kickstart_ver_str":  "7.3(1)D1(1) [build 7.3(1)D1(0.10)]",
          "sys_ver_str":  "7.3(1)D1(1) [build 7.3(1)D1(0.10)]",
          "kick_file_name": "bootflash:///titanium-d1-kickstart.7.3.1.D1.0...",
          "kick_cmpl_time": " 1/11/2016 16:00:00",
          "kick_tmstmp":  "02/22/2016 23:39:33",
          "isan_file_name": "bootflash:///titanium-d1.7.3.1.D1.0.10.bin",
          "isan_cmpl_time": " 1/11/2016 16:00:00",
          "isan_tmstmp":  "02/23/2016 01:43:36",
          "chassis_id": "NX-OSv Chassis",
          "module_id":  "NX-OSv Supervisor Module",
          "cpu_name": "Intel(R) Xeon(R) CPU @ 2.50G",
          "memory": 4002312,
          "mem_type": "kB",
          "proc_board_id":  "TM604E634FB",
          "host_name":  "nxos-spine1",
          "bootflash_size": 1582402,
          "kern_uptm_days": 0,
          "kern_uptm_hrs":  3,
          "kern_uptm_mins": 16,
          "kern_uptm_secs": 45,
          "manufacturer": "Cisco Systems, Inc."
        }
```

```
          }
        }
      }
    }
    >>>
```

Let's save it as a variable and extract the value of the host_name key from it.

```
>>> result = response.text
>>>
>>> print(result['ins_api']['outputs']['output']['body']['host_name'])
Traceback (most recent call last):
  File "<stdin>", line 1, in <module>
TypeError: string indices must be integers
>>>
```

What happened and what caused the error?

Understanding the JSON response of an HTTP-based API.   We stated a few times already that JSON strings are sent across the wire. We can prove this by checking the data type of result.

Earlier, we used json.dumps() to take a dictionary and encode it as a JSON string. However, now we need to do the opposite. We have to take a JSON string and convert it to a dictionary. To do this, we'll use json.loads(). This converts a JSON-formatted string to a dictionary.

```
>>> result_dict = json.loads(result)
>>>
>>> type(result_dict)
<type 'dict'>
>>>
>>> print(result_dict['ins_api']['outputs']['output']['body']['host_name'])
nxos-spine1
>>>
```

The main lesson here is to not forget to properly serialize and de-serialize dictionaries as strings and vice versa and to check your data types. As you see, this is quite easy to verify using the built-in type() function.

Exploring more NX-API examples with Python scripts.   At this point, we exit from the Python interactive interpreter and make a few changes to the script that allow for a little more flexibility in how it's used. We'll update the script so we can pass an arbitrary command and NX-API message format into the script.

```
import json
import sys
import requests
from requests.auth import HTTPBasicAuth
```

```python
if __name__ == "__main__":

    auth = HTTPBasicAuth('ntc', 'ntc123')

    url = 'http://nxos-spine1/ins'

    command = sys.argv[1]

    if len(sys.argv) > 2:
        command_type = sys.argv[2]
    else:
        command_type = 'cli_show'

    payload = {
        "ins_api": {
            "version": "1.0",
            "type": command_type,
            "chunk": "0",
            "sid": "1",
            "input": command,
            "output_format": "json"
        }
    }

    response = requests.post(url, data=json.dumps(payload),  auth=auth)

    print('STATUS CODE: ' + response.status_code)

    print('RESPONSE:')
    results = json.loads(response.text)
    print(json.dumps(results, indent=4))
```

There are a few changes to the script that you should note:

- The type and input keys in the dictionary are now parameterized. These keys are specific to NX-API. They are now variables that can be passed in from the terminal when you are executing the script.

- Remember we covered sys.argv in Chapter 4. Our use here will require us to pass in at least one argument, which is the command or argv[1]. The first argument, argv[0], is always the script name.

- The user can also now pass in and optionally change the type (argv[2]) based on the command(s) being executed or the response type desired. You can test this and visually see it in the NX-API Developer Sandbox, but valid type can be set to cli_show (to return JSON), cli_show_ascii (to return raw text), and cli_conf (to make pass configuration mode commands).

- The last change is that we are now printing the status_code and text attributes of the response.

Passing a show command into the script. Let's execute the modified script, passing `show version` as an argument.

```
ntc@ntc:~$ python nxapi-cli.py "show version"
STATUS CODE:  200
RESPONSE:
{
    "ins_api": {
        "outputs": {
            "output": {
                "msg": "Success",
                "input": "show version",
                "code": "200",
                "body": {
                    "kern_uptm_secs": 34,
                    "kick_file_name": "bootflash:///titanium-d1-kickstart.7.3.1.D1.0.10.bin",
                    "loader_ver_str": "N/A",
                    "module_id": "NX-OSv Supervisor Module",
                    "kick_tmstmp": "02/22/2016 23:39:33",
                    "isan_file_name": "bootflash:///titanium-d1.7.3.1.D1.0.10.bin",
                    "sys_ver_str": "7.3(1)D1(1) [build 7.3(1)D1(0.10)]",
                    "bootflash_size": 1582402,
                    "kickstart_ver_str": "7.3(1)D1(1) [build 7.3(1)D1(0.10)]",
                    "kick_cmpl_time": " 1/11/2016 16:00:00",
                    "chassis_id": "NX-OSv Chassis",
                    "proc_board_id": "TM604E634FB",
                    "memory": 4002312,
                    "kern_uptm_mins": 10,
                    "cpu_name": "Intel(R) Xeon(R) CPU @ 2.50G",
                    "kern_uptm_hrs": 4,
                    "isan_tmstmp": "02/23/2016 01:43:36",
                    "manufacturer": "Cisco Systems, Inc.",
                    "header_str": "Cisco Nexus Operating System (NX-OS) Software\nTAC support: ...",
                    "isan_cmpl_time": " 1/11/2016 16:00:00",
                    "host_name": "nxos-spine1",
                    "mem_type": "kB",
                    "kern_uptm_days": 0
                }
            }
        },
        "version": "1.2",
        "type": "cli_show",
        "sid": "eoc"
    }
}
ntc@ntc:~$
```

Since we can change the format of the response to plain text, let's now pass in the optional parameter and set it to `cli_show_ascii`. This is another parameter you can learn how to use while in the NX-API Developer Sandbox.

```
ntc@ntc:~$ python nxapi-cli.py "show version" "cli_show_ascii"
STATUS CODE:  200
RESPONSE:
{
    "ins_api": {
        "outputs": {
            "output": {
                "msg": "Success",
                "input": "show version",
                "code": "200",
```

```
                    "body": "Cisco Nexus Operating System (NX-OS) Software\nTAC support: ..."
                }
            },
            "version": "1.2",
            "type": "cli_show_ascii",
            "sid": "eoc"
        }
    }
    ntc@ntc:~$
```

When you set the `type` to `cli_show_ascii`, you receive the response as a string as opposed to structured data, just as if you were on the CLI and it's returned as a value in the body key.

Passing in configuration commands to the script.   If you did any further testing using the NX-API Developer Sandbox, you may have noticed when you send configuration parameters, they are passed as a string with a semicolon in between each command embedded in the `input` key when using the `json` message format.

We'll show one example using our same script.

```
ntc@ntc:~$ python nxapi-cli.py "vlan 10 ; vlan 20 ; exit ;" "cli_conf"

STATUS CODE:  200
RESPONSE:
{
    "ins_api": {
        "outputs": {
            "output": [
                {
                    "msg": "Success",
                    "body": {},
                    "code": "200"
                },
                {
                    "msg": "Success",
                    "body": {},
                    "code": "200"
                },
                {
                    "msg": "Success",
                    "body": {},
                    "code": "200"
                }
            ]
        },
        "version": "1.2",
        "type": "cli_conf",
        "sid": "eoc"
    }
}
ntc@ntc:~$
```

When you make configuration changes via NX-API, you receive a response element per command sent. Note that the response from the previous example contains a dictionary per successful executed command in the output key.

You've now seen how to use the requests library to make API calls against Cisco ASA and Nexus devices. You should realize that the same patterns were used in each. We are going to emphasize this even more as we use another API.

Getting familiar with Arista eAPI

We're now going to look at Arista's eAPI, which is very similar to Cisco's NX-OS NX-API. As we show a few examples with eAPI, keep in mind a few things:

- eAPI is a non-RESTful HTTP-based API. In other words, it's an HTTP-based API that doesn't follow all of the principles of REST. An HTTP POST is used no matter what operation is being performed—even if show commands are used, a POST is still used.

- Remember POST requests require data to be sent in the data payload of the request. This is where solid API tools and documentation come into play. Arista switches have a built-in tool called the *Command Explorer* that we are going to leverage in order to learn the required structure of the payload object.

- The URL format for eAPI API calls is always *http(s)://<ip-address-eos>/command-api*.

Using the eAPI Command Explorer. Before we dive into using eAPI in Python, let's take a quick look at the Command Explorer. This is how you figure out how to structure a proper HTTP request with eAPI. Once eAPI is enabled, you can browse to the Arista switch in a web browser and view the Command Explorer (Figure 7-10).

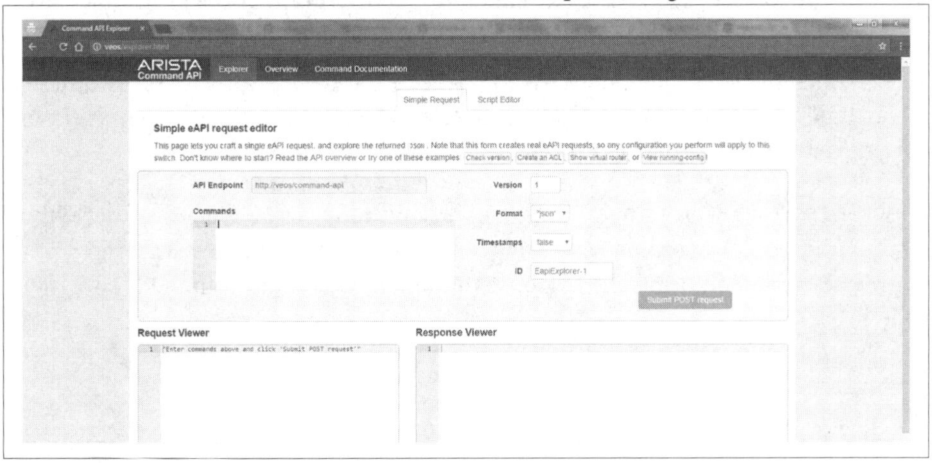

Figure 7-10. Arista eAPI Command Explorer

Similar to what we saw with the Cisco NX-API Developer Sandbox, the Arista eAPI Command Explorer is an on-box tool that enables you to test APIs and understand what the request and response objects look like without writing any code.

As soon as a command is typed in the Commands list in the center pane, you click the green "Submit POST request" button to make the API call, and then you can view the request and response objects in the bottom-left and -right panes, respectively.

Let's look at an example issuing the show version command on the Arista switch (Figure 7-11).

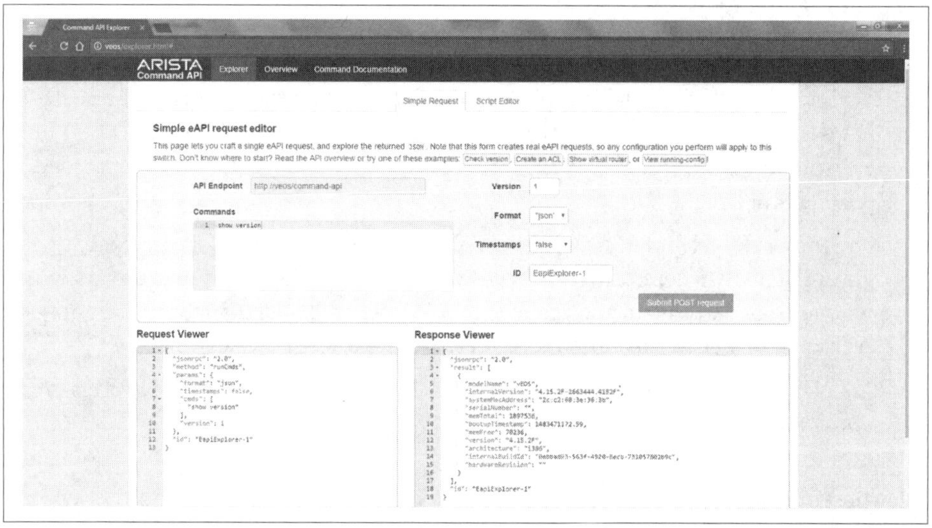

Figure 7-11. JSON request in the eAPI Command Explorer

The response object shown in the Command Explorer utility is the same object we'll get when API calls are made from Python.

You'll notice that the JSON object being sent to the device with Arista is different than with Cisco Nexus. It's quite typical for this to be the case with different APIs, but take special note of the data type of the commands being sent.

Consuming eAPI in a Python script. Let's take a look at a script that uses the Python requests library to communicate using eAPI. The script executes the show vlan brief command and prints the response to the terminal along with the HTTP status code.

```
import json
import sys
import requests
from requests.auth import HTTPBasicAuth
```

```python
if __name__ == "__main__":

    auth = HTTPBasicAuth('ntc', 'ntc123')

    url = 'http://eos-spine1/command-api'

    payload = {
        "jsonrpc": "2.0",
        "method": "runCmds",
        "params": {
            "format": "json",
            "timestamps": False,
            "cmds": [
                "show vlan brief"
            ],
            "version": 1
        },
        "id": "EapiExplorer-1"
    }

    response = requests.post(url, data=json.dumps(payload),  auth=auth)
    print('STATUS CODE: ' + response.status_code)

    print('RESPONSE:')
    results = json.loads(response.text)
    print(json.dumps(results, indent=4))
```

The script is saved as *eapi-requests.py* and, when executed, gives the following output:

```
ntc@ntc:~$ python eapi-requests.py
STATUS CODE:  200
RESPONSE:
{
    "jsonrpc": "2.0",
    "result": [
        {
            "sourceDetail": "",
            "vlans": {
                "1": {
                    "status": "active",
                    "interfaces": {},
                    "dynamic": false,
                    "name": "default"
                },
                "30": {
                    "status": "active",
                    "interfaces": {},
                    "dynamic": false,
                    "name": "VLAN0030"
                },
                "20": {
                    "status": "active",
```

```
                    "interfaces": {},
                    "dynamic": false,
                    "name": "VLAN0020"
                }
            }
        }
    ],
    "id": "EapiExplorer-1"
}
ntc@ntc:~$
```

As you can see, the response is a nested JSON object. The important key is `result`, which itself is a list of dictionaries. It's a list element for each command executed. Since we only sent the one command, we only have a single list element in the response.

Optimizing the eAPI script.   Let's improve this script a bit to build on what we covered in Chapter 4, so that it just prints the VLAN ID and name for each VLAN configured on the system. The resulting output we are aiming for is this:

```
VLAN ID    NAME
1          default
20         VLAN0020
30         VLAN0030
```

These changes are more about using Python than the API itself, but it's still good practice to go through this exercise. We'll save the result, extract the VLANs dictionary, and then loop through the dictionary, printing each VLAN as desired.

```
response = requests.post(url, data=json.dumps(payload), auth=auth)
rsp = json.loads(response.text)
vlans = rsp['result'][0]['vlans']
print('{:12}{:<10}'.format('VLAN ID', 'NAME'))
for vlan_id, config in vlans.items():
    print('{:<12}{:<10}'.format(vlan_id,  config['name']))
```

After running this new script, you'll see the following output:

```
ntc@ntc:~$ python eapi-requests.py
VLAN ID    NAME
1          default
30         VLAN0030
20         VLAN0020
ntc@ntc:~$
```

Using eAPI to autoconfigure interface descriptions based on LLDP data.   Let's continue to use eAPI to build something a little more useful. How about a Python script that auto-configures interface descriptions for Ethernet interfaces based on LLDP neighbors for two Arista spine switches?

In order to do this, we *should* modularize the script to support multiple devices as well as have a simple way to send multiple API calls without requiring multiple payload objects in the script.

Our goal is to autoconfigure interface descriptions such that they will look like the following:

```
interface Ethernet1
   description Connects to interface Ethernet1 on neighbor eos-spine2.ntc.com
   no switchport
!
interface Ethernet2
   description Connects to interface Ethernet2 on neighbor eos-spine2.ntc.com
   no switchport
!
```

It's an exercise for the reader to review the following script, but you can tell, it's just simply one function that makes the eAPI request to the Arista EOS switch. Everything else is Python programming that we covered in Chapter 4. The practice of writing modular code to easily reuse code within a script becomes more natural over time.

```python
import json
import sys
import requests
from requests.auth import HTTPBasicAuth


def issue_request(device, commands):
    """Make API request to EOS device returning JSON response
    """

    auth = HTTPBasicAuth('ntc', 'ntc123')
    url = 'http://{}/command-api'.format(device)
    payload = {
        "jsonrpc": "2.0",
        "method": "runCmds",
        "params": {
            "format": "json",
            "timestamps": False,
            "cmds": commands,
            "version": 1
        },
        "id": "EapiExplorer-1"
    }

    response = requests.post(url, data=json.dumps(payload),  auth=auth)

    return json.loads(response.text)

def get_lldp_neighbors(device):
    """Get list of neighbors
```

```
Sample response for a single neighbor:
{
    "ttl": 120,
    "neighborDevice": "eos-spine2.ntc.com",
    "neighborPort": "Ethernet2",
    "port": "Ethernet2"
}
"""
commands = ['show lldp neighbors']
response = issue_request(device, commands)
neighbors = response['result'][0]['lldpNeighbors']

# neighbors is returned as a list of dictionaries
return neighbors

def configure_interfaces(device, neighbors):
    """Configure interfaces in a single API call per device
    """

    command_list = ['enable', 'configure']
    for neighbor in neighbors:
        local_interface = neighbor['port']
        if local_interface.startswith('Eth'):
            # Excluding Management as it has multiple neighbors
            description = 'Connects to interface {} on neighbor {}'.format(
                neighbor['neighborPort'],
                neighbor['neighborDevice'])
            description = 'description ' + description

            interface = 'interface {}'.format(local_interface)
            cmds = [interface, description]
            command_list.extend(cmds)
    response = issue_request(device, command_list)

if __name__ == "__main__":
    # device names are FQDNs
    devices = ['eos-spine1', 'eos-spine2']
    for device in devices:
        neighbors = get_lldp_neighbors(device)
        configure_interfaces(device, neighbors)
        print('Auto-Configured Interfaces for {}'.format(device))
```

By now, you're probably feeling comfortable using the requests library after looking at using three different APIs. We've used a native RESTful API on the Cisco ASA, and the Nexus NX-API and Arista eAPI, which are both non-RESTful HTTP-based APIs. Remember, every request using NX-API or eAPI is an HTTP POST and the URL is the same for every request, whereas a true RESTful API using HTTP as transport has a different URL based on the resource in question (e.g., interface resource, routing resource, and routes).

Earlier in the chapter, we said we would make note of custom libraries when appropriate. It's worth pointing out that it is critical to understand how to use the requests library, but Arista does have an open source library called pyeapi. Like most libraries, it's an abstraction layer to simplify performing common tasks. When using pyeapi, you don't need to worry about them being HTTP POSTs or how to structure the payload of an object. That is all taken care of by the library.

The following script using pyeapi is equivalent to the one we wrote earlier using requests, although the one with pyeapi is just communicating to a single device. As you can see, the difference is with the underlying communication to the device. Once you have the response object, the code is identical. Note: this example script makes use of a pyeapi configuration file. Creating a proper eAPI configuration file is out of the scope of this book.

```
from pyeapi import connect_to

if __name__ =="__main__":

    device = connect_to('eos-spine1')
    rsp = device.enable('show vlan brief')
    vlans = rsp[0]['result']['vlans']

    print('{:12}{:<10}'.format('VLAN ID', 'NAME'))
    for vlan_id, config in vlans.items():
        print('{:<12}{:<10}'.format(vlan_id,  config['name']))
```

For more information on pyeapi, you can reference the code and its docs page.

Getting familiar with RESTCONF on IOS-XE

In order to show one more HTTP-based API that adheres to the principles of REST before we transition to automating devices with NETCONF APIs, we'll take a look at a newer device API for Cisco IOS-XE. It is called RESTCONF. The RESTCONF API on IOS-XE is a robust RESTful API that uses HTTP for transport and supports JSON *and* XML encoding. This means as the network developer, you have the choice to work with whichever data format you prefer.

RESTCONF is an IETF draft (*https://tools.ietf.org/html/draft-ietf-netconf-restconf-09*) and is a particular implementation of a RESTful API. It is an HTTP-based protocol that provides a programmatic interface for accessing data that is modeled in YANG.

The RESTCONF API can be enabled via the `restconf` global configuration command on IOS-XE 16.3.1 or later. Note you also need to configure the `ip http/s server` global configuration command. IMPORTANT: The `restconf` command is *not* supported by TAC until 16.6 or later. Based on your version, it may be a hidden command and may not be supported by TAC. You'll know it's supported when you see the command! Also note that specific API calls using NETCONF/RESTCONF are changing after 16.3 and instructions on how to convert 16.3 API calls (as shown in this section) to 16.5+ can be found on GitHub (*https://github.com/YangMo dels/yang/tree/master/vendor/cisco/xe/1651*).

The RESTCONF API supports the GET, PUT, PATCH, POST, and DELETE request types, making it extremely powerful to perform particular network operations, which we'll cover shortly.

Before we show how to use the RESTful API on IOS-XE, we need to point out one difference about using RESTCONF versus a traditional RESTful API. It pertains to the headers used in the HTTP request. In the previous examples for Cisco NX-API, Cisco ASA RESTful API, and Arista eAPI, the `Content-Type` and `Accept` headers were set to `application/json`. This is typical for HTTP-based APIs, but because RESTCONF is unique in that the API is generated from YANG models, the `Content-Type` and `Accept` headers are different. When you work with a RESTCONF API, there are different headers that can be used. For RESTCONF, we are primarily going to use `application/vnd.yang.data+json`. Note: it is possible to substitute out `json` for `xml`.

Executing an API call using RESTCONF.   The first API call we are going to execute retrieves a full running configuration modeled as JSON.

```
Method: GET
URL: 'http://ios-csr1kv/restconf/api/config/native'
Accept-Type: application/vnd.yang.data+json
```

Executing this API call in your tool of choice shows an output like what's in the next example, but you would see a full configuration (we are just showing a snippet):

```
{
    "ned:native": {
        # truncated for brevity
        "interface": {
            "GigabitEthernet": [
                {
                    "name": "1"
                },
```

```
        {
            "name": "2"
        },
        {
            "name": "3"
        },
        {
            "name": "4"
        }
    ]
},
# truncated for brevity
}
```

We can also add a query parameter to the URL to get back every child element that is part of the JSON hierarchy. Notice the preceding example only had a single key called name for each interface. Adding ?deep adds the full configuration per interface. You can see this in the next example.

```
Method: GET
URL: 'http://ios-csr1kv/restconf/api/config/native?deep'
Accept-Type: application/vnd.yang.data+json

{
    "ned:native": {
        # truncated for brevity
        "interface": {
            "GigabitEthernet": [
                {
                    "negotiation": {
                        "auto": true
                    },
                    "ip": {
                        "access-group": {},
                        "arp": {
                            "inspection": {}
                        },,
                        "verify": {
                            "unicast": {}
                        },
                        "authentication": {},
                        "address": {
                            "primary": {
                                "mask": "255.255.255.0",
                                "address": "10.0.0.51"
                            }
                        },
                        "dhcp": {
                            "snooping": {},
                            "relay": {
                                "information": {}
                            }
```

```
            },
            "rsvp": {},
            "ospf": {
                "dead-interval": {},
                "fast-reroute": {}
            },
            "igmp": {}
        },
        "standby": {},
        "bandwidth": {},
        "cdp": {},
        "wrr-queue": {},
        "bfd": {},
        "snmp": {
            "trap": {
                "link-status-capas": {
                    "link-status": {}
                }
            }
        },
        "power": {},
        "logging": {},
        "storm-control": {
            "broadcast": {}
        }
        "encapsulation": {},
        "name": "1",
    # truncated for brevity
    },
    # the above output is just for GigabitEthernet1
    # it repeats for each interface when using ?deep
}
```

While much of the output has been omitted in this example, the point is that when you add ?deep, you get back all child elements for the RESTCONF API on IOS-XE.

As you may have guessed, the Python script that was used to print the preceding outputs has the same structure as the other examples using the Python requests library.

Here is the sample script we used to output both JSON objects from the last two examples.

```
#!/usr/bin/env python

import json
import requests
from requests.auth import HTTPBasicAuth


if __name__ == "__main__":

    auth = HTTPBasicAuth('ntc', 'ntc123')
    headers = {
```

```
            'Accept': 'application/vnd.yang.data+json',
            'Content-Type': 'application/vnd.yang.data+json'
        }

        url = 'http://ios-csr1kv/restconf/api/config/native?deep'
        response = requests.get(url, headers=headers, auth=auth)

        response = json.loads(response.text)
        print(json.dumps(response, indent=4))
```

Navigating a RESTCONF API response. Now that we understand how to get the equivalent of a show run through an API call, we can get more granular with subsequent API calls by understanding the tree structure of the JSON object returned. You can see from the previous examples that we focused on showing the interface configuration.

Let's now issue an API request to retrieve the IP address configurations that exist on the GigabitEthernet1 interface. A simplified JSON structure is shown in the next example to depict specifically the JSON keys/values that represent the interface data we want.

```
{
    "ned:native": {
        "interface": {
            "GigabitEthernet": [
                    "name": "1",
                    "ip": {
                        "address": {
                            "primary": {
                                "mask": "255.255.255.0",
                                "address": "10.0.0.51"
                            }
                        }
                    }
            ]
        # truncated for brevity
```

It's the same output data that can be used to test and construct subsequent and more granular HTTP GET requests. To configure the address for GigabitEthernet1, you can see that it is the following path based on the previously gathered JSON output:

```
interface (dict) -> GigabitEthernet (list) -> ip (dict) -> address (dict)
```

Although the value of GigabitEthernet is a list, we use the value of the name key in the API call URL to extract a particular element. Let's take a look.

In order to perform this request, we still need to use an HTTP GET. The main change is in the URL since we are going to be accessing a different *resource* within the network device.

The following is the URL required to make this particular API request: *http://ios-csr1kv/restconf/api/config/native/interface/GigabitEthernet/1/ip/address.*

After we run the updated script, we see exactly what we wanted—just the IP address information for GigabitEthernet1. If there were secondary IP addresses, you would see them too.

```
cisco@cisco:~/netconf/xe$ python iosxe_restconf_GigE1.py
{
    "ned:address": {
        "primary": {
            "mask": "255.255.255.0",
            "address": "10.0.0.51"
        }
    }
}
```

Using HTTP verbs PUT and PATCH with RESTCONF on IOS-XE. So far in this chapter, we've made GET and POST requests using the Python requests library across NX-OS, EOS, and now IOS-XE. Since HTTP verbs such as PUT and PATCH can prove to be extremely valuable with how network devices are managed in the future, let's take a look at them while still working with the IOS-XE RESTCONF API.

First, we are going to use a PATCH request to add OSPF network statements to an existing OSPF configuration.

This is the current and complete OSPF configuration on our IOS-XE router.

```
ios-csr1kv#show run | begin router ospf
router ospf 10
 router-id 100.100.100.100
 network 10.0.1.10 0.0.0.0 area 0
 network 10.0.2.100 0.0.0.0 area 0
 !
```

What we want to do is add the following two network statements:

```
network 10.0.10.1 0.0.0.0 area 0
network 10.0.20.1 0.0.0.0 area 0
```

If we go back to our complete running configuration, we see that the following URL can be used to access the OSPF configuration: *http://ios-csr1kv/restconf/api/config/native/router*.

There is an `ospf` key inside the object returned. Based on viewing the output of a pre-configured router, we'd then be able to see that the OSPF object requires a list of dictionaries. There is a single list element per OSPF process ID.

The following example shows a summary of the JSON representation of the OSPF configuration that was taken from the full running configuration output:

```
"router": {
    "ospf": [
        {
            "id": 10,
```

```
        "router-id": "100.100.100.100",
        "network": [
            {
                "ip": "10.0.1.10",
                "mask": "0.0.0.0",
                "area": 0
            },
            {
                "ip": "10.0.2.100",
                "mask": "0.0.0.0",
                "area": 0
            }
        ]
        # truncated for brevity
    }
  ]
},
```

Remember, we're simply trying to add, or *Patch*, two more network statements into the OSPF configuration. There are various ways to structure the URL and body based on what level in the hierarchy we want to use. In order to show uniformity between the next two examples and to minimize the change in headers, we are going to use the following URL to add these network statements: *http://ios-csr1kv/restconf/api/config/native/router*.

The object we are going to send needs to be modeled just like the data we saw in the GET response.

 When using PATCH, you only need to include the key-value pairs you want to update/add.

In order to add these routes, we'll send the following JSON object to the device using this URL: *http://ios-csr1kv/restconf/api/config/native/router*:

```
{
    "ned:router": {
        "ospf": [
            {
                "id": 10,
                "network": [
                    {
                        "ip": "10.0.10.1",
                        "mask": "0.0.0.0",
                        "area": "0"
                    },
                    {
                        "ip": "10.0.20.1",
```

```
                    "mask": "0.0.0.0",
                    "area": "0"
                }
            ]
        }
    ]
}
}
```

In order to simplify the Python script and make it something more analogous to what would be used in a production environment, we are going to abstract away the OSPF configuration (inputs) and store them into a YAML file. The same JSON object just shown can easily be modeled in a YAML file. Take a look at the following example:

```
---
ospf:
  - id: 10
    network:
      - ip: 10.0.10.1
        mask: 0.0.0.0
        area: 0
      - ip: 10.0.20.1
        mask: 0.0.0.0
        area: 0
```

We saved this file as *ospf-config.yml* and used it as our inputs directly in the Python script. Note: this YAML object is equal to the object inside the ned:router key.

Using Python to consume the IOS-XE RESTCONF API.   Let's look at our new Python script that will add these two network statements to the existing OSPF configuration.

```
#!/usr/bin/env python

import json
import requests
from requests.auth import HTTPBasicAuth
import yaml


if __name__ == "__main__":

    auth = HTTPBasicAuth('ntc', 'ntc123')
    headers = {
        'Accept': 'application/vnd.yang.data+json',
        'Content-Type': 'application/vnd.yang.data+json'
    }

    url = 'http://ios-csr1kv/restconf/api/config/native/router'

    ospf_config = yaml.load(open('ospf-config.yml').read())

    ospf_object_to_send = {
```

```
        "ned:router": ospf_config
    }

    response = requests.patch(url, data=json.dumps(ospf_object_to_send),
                              headers=headers, auth=auth)

    print(response.status_code)
```

Upon executing this script and checking the router, you see the following new OSPF configuration:

```
router ospf 10
 router-id 100.100.100.100
 network 10.0.1.10 0.0.0.0 area 0
 network 10.0.2.100 0.0.0.0 area 0
 network 10.0.10.1 0.0.0.0 area 0
 network 10.0.20.1 0.0.0.0 area 0
 !
```

> If needed, please reference Chapter 4 for working with files in Python, and Chapter 5 for working with YAML objects.

Understanding declarative configuration management. When we think about managing network configurations with the CLI, it's quite trivial to add configurations. However, it is quite complex to remove or negate commands. For example, what if you had a single instance of OSPF running with 50 network statements, but due to a change in design, you only need 2 network statements? You would actually have to know which 48 statements need to be negated with a no command. This process is arduous and mundane as we extrapolate the effort for all types of configurations on a network device. For our example, wouldn't it be easier to take the opposite approach—focus on the configuration that *should* exist on the network device? This is a growing trend, becoming more possible due to newer APIs and ways of thinking. This is called *declarative configuration*.

Let's see how we can make the slightest change in our OSPF configuration and script to declaratively configure OSPF to yield the following commands.

```
router ospf 10
 router-id 10.10.10.10
 network 10.0.10.1 0.0.0.0 area 0
 network 10.0.20.1 0.0.0.0 area 0
 !
```

By declaratively configuring OSPF, we are are ensuring *no other OSPF config exists* other than what exists in the single API call.

The changes in the output reflect a new router ID, the removal of the two original network statements, and the addition of the new network statements.

First, we'll update the YAML file and add a key called `router-id` with its associated value of `10.10.10.10`. Remember, whatever we have in the YAML file will be the *only* OSPF configuration that exists after the API call.

```
---

ospf:
  - id: 10
    router-id: 10.10.10.10
    network:
      - ip: 10.0.10.1
        mask: 0.0.0.0
        area: 0
      - ip: 10.0.20.1
        mask: 0.0.0.0
        area: 0
```

Once the YAML file is updated and saved, the last change required is to update the API call to use an HTTP PUT instead of a PATCH.

```
response = requests.put(url, data=json.dumps(ospf_object_to_send),
                        headers=headers, auth=auth)
```

After these changes, we run the script, and voilà! This following output is our new OSPF configuration on the router:

```
router ospf 10
 router-id 10.10.10.10
 network 10.0.10.1 0.0.0.0 area 0
 network 10.0.20.1 0.0.0.0 area 0
 !
```

With RESTful APIs that offer this type of power and control, you need to ensure you have a good process for making changes. As you can see, if you are only trying to make a slight change and addition and happen to send a PUT request, there can be catastrophic consequences.

From an overall adoption perspective of this particular API, you may want to start using PATCH requests and gradually migrate to the point where you can indeed use PUTs to declaratively manage specific sections of configuration.

The example we showed using the PUT declaratively configures everything under the `router` key, not just OSPF configuration. If you execute this API in your environment, it would technically eliminate all other routing protocol configurations too. That's not a good thing. However, we chose to show that API to highlight its power and potential danger if it's not used and understood properly.

Another, slightly safer option is to declaratively manage just the OSPF process ID 10 configuration. To do this you can use the following URL and object:

```
METHOD: PUT
URL: http://ios-csr1kv/restconf/api/config/native/router/ospf/10
BODY:
{
    "ned:ospf": [
        {
            "id": 10,
            "network": [
                {
                    "ip": "10.0.10.1",
                    "mask": "0.0.0.0",
                    "area": "0"
                },
                {
                    "ip": "10.0.20.1",
                    "mask": "0.0.0.0",
                    "area": "0"
                }
            ]
        }
    ]
}
```

Now that we've shown how to start automating devices that have HTTP-based APIs, let's look at the same approach using the Python ncclient for automating devices using the NETCONF API.

Using the Python ncclient Library

The Python ncclient is the de facto NETCONF client for Python. It is client software that is built to communicate programmatically with NETCONF servers. Remember, in our case, a NETCONF server is going to be a network device. We are going to walk through several examples using the ncclient on Cisco IOS-XE, Cisco IOS-XR, and Juniper Junos devices.

To install the ncclient, you can use `pip`:

```
pip install ncclient
```

Once the ncclient is installed, you can start to issue NETCONF API calls to network devices. Let's walk through this while in the Python interactive interpreter.

When we enter the Python interpreter, the first step we need to perform is the import of the manager module within the ncclient Python package.

```
>>> from ncclient import manager
>>>
```

The main function we are going to use within the manager module is responsible for establishing the persistent connection to the device. Keep in mind that since NET-CONF runs over SSH it is a stateful and persistent connection (compared to what we discussed previously about RESTful APIs being stateless). This function is called con nect() and accepts a number of parameters such as hostname/IP address, port number, and credentials. You'll see in the following example that there are other parameters that will remain unchanged for our examples that map back to underlying SSH configuration and properties.

```
>>> device = manager.connect(host='ios-csr1kv', port=830, username='ntc',
...                          password='ntc123', hostkey_verify=False,
...                          device_params={}, allow_agent=False,
...                          look_for_keys=False)
...
>>>
```

As soon as the connect function is called, a NETCONF session is established to the network device and an object is returned of type ncclient.manager.Manager. You can see this by printing the variable that saved this object.

```
>>> print(device)
<ncclient.manager.Manager object at 0x7f0420059d90>
>>>
```

For our example, device is an instance of an ncclient Manager object. Let's explore this object from the Python interactive interpreter.

Understanding the Manager object

First, we'll look at the output of the dir() function on device and then use help() again on a specific object.

```
>>> dir(device)
['_Manager__set_async_mode', '_Manager__set_raise_mode', '_Manager__set_timeout',
'...methods removed for brevity... '_device_handler', '_raise_mode', '_session',
'_timeout', 'async_mode', 'channel_id', 'channel_name', 'client_capabilities',
'close_session', 'commit', 'connected', 'copy_config', 'delete_config',
'discard_changes', 'dispatch', 'edit_config', 'execute', 'get', 'get_config',
'get_schema', 'kill_session', 'lock', 'locked', 'poweroff_machine',
'raise_mode', 'reboot_machine', 'scp', 'server_capabilities', 'session',
'session_id', 'timeout', 'unlock', 'validate']
>>>
```

A few methods shown in the dir() output map back to connection setup and tear-down, but also notice methods that map directly back to specific NETCONF operations.

As you saw when we were constructing XML documents and sending them over an interactive NETCONF session, an XML tag within the <rpc> specified the operation. We looked at two operations: <get> and <edit-config>. In the output of the previous example above, you'll notice two methods called get and edit_config. If you look closer, you see methods that map back to other standard NETCONF operations we reviewed earlier as well: copy-config, get-schema, lock, unlock, validate, and so on.

Exploring the get method.   You now know that methods of our device object map back to NETCONF operations. Let's see how we can use them by using the built-in help() function.

```
>>>
>>> help(device.get)


Help on method wrapper in module ncclient.manager:

wrapper(self, *args, **kwds) method of ncclient.manager.Manager instance
    Retrieve running configuration and device state information.

    *filter* specifies the portion of the configuration to
            retrieve (by default entire configuration is retrieved)

    :seealso: :ref:`filter_params`
(END)
```

The text displayed when we use the help() function is automatically pulled from the docstring directly in the code. The help is only as good as what the ncclient author writes in there. If you're not happy with it, it's open source, so feel free to issue a pull request on GitHub.

In the help for the get() method, we see that they are using a variable amount of parameters and keyword arguments denoted by the * and **. The optional keyword that we can use is called filter. Certain devices support returning the entire configurations; our examples focus on using the filter parameter to selectively retrieve portions of the configuration as XML-encoded data.

Retrieving Cisco IOS-XE device configurations with ncclient

Earlier in the chapter when we were exploring the use of NETCONF, we used the following XML document as a way to query the Cisco IOS-XE router for its configuration on GigabitEthernet1:

```
<?xml version="1.0"?>
<rpc message-id="101" xmlns="urn:ietf:params:xml:ns:netconf:base:1.0">
  <get>
     <filter type="subtree">
        <native xmlns="http://cisco.com/ns/yang/ned/ios">
         <interface>
          <GigabitEthernet>
           <name>1</name>
          </GigabitEthernet>
         </interface>
        </native>
     </filter>
  </get>
</rpc>
]]>]]>
```

As stated earlier in this chapter, the IOS-XE version used for this book was 16.3.1. The device models have changed since 16.3 into 16.5 and 16.6. Instructions for how to convert 16.3 API calls (as shown in this section) to 16.5+ can be found on GitHub (*https://github.com/YangModels/yang/tree/master/vendor/cisco/xe/1651*).

This was a NETCONF RPC using the `<get>` operation to send the provided filter to the device. If we want to do this in Python, we need to build the same filter object. We'll do this as an XML string.

```
>>> get_filter = """
...     <native xmlns="http://cisco.com/ns/yang/ned/ios">
...       <interface>
...         <GigabitEthernet>
...           <name>1</name>
...         </GigabitEthernet>
...       </interface>
...     </native>
... """
>>>
```

Remember that triple quotes in Python denote a multiline comment and can be used to create a multiline string that can be used as a value of a variable.

Once the filter is created, we pass that as a parameter into the get() method.

```
>>> nc_get_reply = device.get(('subtree', get_filter))
>>>
```

All filters used in this book are *subtree* filters. NETCONF and the ncclient also support *xpath* filters. They rely on specific NETCONF capabilities that the network device must support.

The object we need to pass to the get() method must be a single object. It is a tuple that has two elements—the type of filter and the filter/expression.

Finally, while our examples use XML strings as the filters, it is also possible to use native XML objects (etree objects). We are using string objects, as they are much more human-readable and easier to use when getting started. You may want to use native etree objects if you need to dynamically build a filter object. We examine etree element objects in the next few examples too.

We issued a NETCONF request to the device and stored it in nc_get_reply.

Viewing an ncclient NETCONF reply

Let's print the response object, nc_get_reply.

```
>>> print(nc_get_reply)
<?xml version="1.0" encoding="UTF-8"?>
<rpc-reply xmlns="urn:ietf:params:xml:ns:netconf:base:1.0"
message-id="urn:uuid:e103ecdf-9713-46c0-8769-0e574d9b4489"
xmlns:nc="urn:ietf:params:xml:ns:netconf:base:1.0"><data>
<native xmlns="http://cisco.com/ns/yang/ned/ios"><interface>
<GigabitEthernet><name>1</name><negotiation><auto>true</auto>
</negotiation><vrf><forwarding>MANAGEMENT</forwarding></vrf>
<ip><address><primary><address>10.0.0.51</address><mask>255.255.255.0</mask>
</primary></address></ip></GigabitEthernet></interface></native>
</data></rpc-reply>
>>>
```

Let's also examine the data type of the return object.

```
>>> type(nc_get_reply)
<class 'ncclient.operations.retrieve.GetReply'>
>>>
```

You can view the XML response in the print output, but since this is an ncclient GetReply object and is not a native Python object like a string, dictionary, or list, we'll need to learn about this object's built-in attributes.

It just so happens that a GetReply object has a few built-in attributes that simplify working with NETCONF get replies. Let's examine a few of them.

The attributes data and data_ele return the same object, and this is the response represented as a native XML object. To verify these object types, you can use the type() function.

```
>>> type(nc_get_reply.data)
<type 'lxml.etree._Element'>
>>>
>>> type(nc_get_reply.data_ele)
<type 'lxml.etree._Element'>
>>>
```

When we refer to native XML objects, we are referring to lxml.etree._Element objects.

```
>>> print(nc_get_reply.data_ele)
<Element {urn:ietf:params:xml:ns:netconf:base:1.0}data at 0x7f041acbab48>
>>>
>>> print(nc_get_reply.data)
<Element {urn:ietf:params:xml:ns:netconf:base:1.0}data at 0x7f041acbab48>
>>>
```

Notice how it is exactly the same object. This is the same object type we mentioned earlier that could be used as a filter instead of an XML string. For the remainder of this section we use data, although you can use data_ele if you prefer as they are the same object.

In order to convert a native XML object to a string, you can use the lxml Python library and more specifically, the function called tostring(). Remember, we initially introduced the lxml library in Chapter 5.

```
>>> from lxml import etree
>>>
>>> as_string = etree.tostring(nc_get_reply.data)
>>>
>>> print(as_string)
<data xmlns="urn:ietf:params:xml:ns:netconf:base:1.0"
xmlns:nc="urn:ietf:params:xml:ns:netconf:base:1.0">
<native xmlns="http://cisco.com/ns/yang/ned/ios"><interface>
<GigabitEthernet><name>1</name><negotiation><auto>true</auto>
</negotiation><vrf><forwarding>MANAGEMENT</forwarding></vrf>
<ip><address><primary><address>10.0.0.51</address>
<mask>255.255.255.0</mask></primary></address></ip>
</GigabitEthernet></interface></native></data>
>>>
```

Notice how the output is not formatted so it can be easily read. You can use an optional parameter called pretty_print and set it to True to make the response more readable.

```
>>> as_string = etree.tostring(nc_get_reply.data, pretty_print=True)
>>>
>>> print(as_string)
<data xmlns="urn:ietf:params:xml:ns:netconf:base:1.0"
xmlns:nc="urn:ietf:params:xml:ns:netconf:base:1.0">
  <native xmlns="http://cisco.com/ns/yang/ned/ios">
    <interface>
```

```
        <GigabitEthernet>
          <name>1</name>
          <negotiation>
            <auto>true</auto>
          </negotiation>
          <vrf>
            <forwarding>MANAGEMENT</forwarding>
          </vrf>
          <ip>
            <address>
              <primary>
                <address>10.0.0.51</address>
                <mask>255.255.255.0</mask>
              </primary>
            </address>
          </ip>
        </GigabitEthernet>
      </interface>
    </native>
</data>

>>>
```

Exploring more attributes of the ncclient reply

We've reviewed the data and data_ele attributes; now let's look at another attribute called xml. The xml attribute returns the response as an XML string. You can verify this using the type() function.

```
>>> type(nc_get_reply.xml)
<type 'str'>
>>>
```

Finally, you can print and view the value as the XML string.

```
>>> print(nc_get_reply.xml)
<?xml version="1.0" encoding="UTF-8"?>
<rpc-reply xmlns="urn:ietf:params:xml:ns:netconf:base:1.0"
message-id="urn:uuid:e103ecdf-9713-46c0-8769-0e574d9b4489"
xmlns:nc="urn:ietf:params:xml:ns:netconf:base:1.0"><data>
<native xmlns="http://cisco.com/ns/yang/ned/ios"><interface>
<GigabitEthernet><name>1</name><negotiation><auto>true</auto>
</negotiation><vrf><forwarding>MANAGEMENT</forwarding></vrf><ip>
<address><primary><address>10.0.0.51</address><mask>255.255.255.0</mask>
</primary></address></ip></GigabitEthernet></interface>
</native></data></rpc-reply>
>>>
```

When you view the output as an XML string using the xml attribute, notice the outer-most XML tag is <rpc-reply> and all response data is nested under the XML tag of <data>.

Just like you can take an XML object and covert it to a string with `etree.tostring()`, you can take a string and convert it to an XML object with `etree.fromstring()`.

```
>>> as_object = etree.fromstring(nc_get_reply.xml)
>>>
>>> print(as_object)
<Element {urn:ietf:params:xml:ns:netconf:base:1.0}rpc-reply at 0x7fc33365f9e0>
>>>
```

Not worrying about the XML namespace yet, we can see the name of the XML object is `rpc-reply`. The name when you print an XML object is always what the outermost XML tag is, and in our case that's `rpc-reply`.

At this point, we've used the NETCONF `<get>` operation through the use of the `get()` method of the ncclient device object, but we still haven't shown how to parse and extract information from the XML RPC reply message.

We saw in the response that there is an IP address and mask configured on Gigabit Etheret1. Both of these elements are child elements of an XML object called `<address>`. Here is the object we are interested in:

```
<address>
  <primary>
    <address>10.0.0.51</address>
    <mask>255.255.255.0</mask>
  </primary>
</address>
```

This means there will always be more than one `<address>` object when there are primary and secondary addresses configured.

Let's extract the primary IP address and mask and save them in individual variables. We are going to do this in two steps. First, we'll extract the `<primary>` object, and once we have that, we'll extract the precise `<address>` and `<mask>` elements.

```
>>> primary = nc_get_reply.data.find(
    './/{http://cisco.com/ns/yang/ned/ios}primary')
>>>
```

In this example, we are introducing the `find()` method for `etree._Element` objects. The `find()` method is a simple way to search a full XML object for a given XML tag when using the expression denoted by `.//`. Since we want to extract the `<primary>` object and its children, we could have tried the following example first, but if we had, it wouldn't have worked:

```
>>> primary = nc_get_reply.data.find('.//primary')
>>>
```

This statement tries to extract the XML element with a tag of `<primary>`. The only caveat is that when XML namespaces are used, the actual tag name is equal to the namespace concatenated with the tag, or in other words, {*namespace*}*tag*. Alternatively, if an XML namespace alias is used it is *alias*:_tag_. In our case, there is no alias, so the <primary> object is {http://cisco.com/ns/yang/ned/ios}primary.

There are actually two namespaces in our example. Pay close attention to which one is used.

```
<data xmlns="urn:ietf:params:xml:ns:netconf:base:1.0"
 xmlns:nc="urn:ietf:params:xml:ns:netconf:base:1.0">
   <native xmlns="http://cisco.com/ns/yang/ned/ios">
```

You can gradually print one child object at a time to see which namespace is used. In our example, the default namespace is urn:ietf:params:xml:ns:netconf:base:1.0, but when we print a single object, we only see the one. The next namespace in the hierarchy is overriding the default namespace for all children of the <native> element.

In order to better understand this, let's print <primary> as a string.

```
>>> print(etree.tostring(primary, pretty_print=True))
<primary xmlns="http://cisco.com/ns/yang/ned/ios"
xmlns:nc="urn:ietf:params:xml:ns:netconf:base:1.0">
  <address>10.0.0.51</address>
  <mask>255.255.255.0</mask>
</primary>

>>>
```

Notice how this is the XML string starting at the <primary> tag. Let's now extract the values we want—the IP address and subnet. We'll use the same approach again using the find() method on the object we created called primary. This time we'll go one step further, showing that the text attribute of the XML object returned is the actual value of interest to us, which in our case is going to be an IP address and subnet mask.

```
>>> ipaddr = primary.find('.//{http://cisco.com/ns/yang/ned/ios}address')
>>> ipaddr.text
'10.0.0.51'
>>>
>>> mask = primary.find('.//{http://cisco.com/ns/yang/ned/ios}mask')
>>> mask.text
'255.255.255.0'
>>>
```

You may be thinking, "Extracting values based on the namespaces is tedious," and you are absolutely right. However, remember a few things:

- You already know the namespace from building the request object. You simply have to concatenate two strings.

- It is possible to build a function to strip namespaces from an XML object before doing XML parsing, further simplifying the process.

We've seen how to extract a single value such as those shown like a primary IP address and subnet mask, but what about extracting all objects if there were multiples? One example of this is an interface having multiple secondary IP addresses.

Adding to the query filter to minimize the response data

At this point, we've added a few secondary addresses *manually* to GigabitEthernet4 and will now perform the same steps in order to see what the response object looks like from a NETCONF <get> operation for just GigabitEthernet4.

```
>>> get_filter = """
...     <native xmlns="http://cisco.com/ns/yang/ned/ios">
...       <interface>
...        <GigabitEthernet>
...         <name>4</name>
...        </GigabitEthernet>
...       </interface>
...     </native>
... """
>>>
>>> nc_get_reply = device.get(('subtree', get_filter))
>>>
>>> print(etree.tostring(nc_get_reply.data, pretty_print=True))
<data xmlns="urn:ietf:params:xml:ns:netconf:base:1.0"
xmlns:nc="urn:ietf:params:xml:ns:netconf:base:1.0">
  <native xmlns="http://cisco.com/ns/yang/ned/ios">
    <interface>
      <GigabitEthernet>
        <name>4</name>
        <negotiation>
          <auto>true</auto>
        </negotiation>
        <ip>
          <address>
            <primary>
              <address>10.4.4.1</address>
              <mask>255.255.255.0</mask>
            </primary>
            <secondary>
```

```
            <address>20.2.2.1</address>
            <mask>255.255.255.0</mask>
            <secondary/>
          </secondary>
          <secondary>
            <address>22.2.2.1</address>
            <mask>255.255.255.0</mask>
            <secondary/>
          </secondary>
          <secondary>
            <address>24.2.2.1</address>
            <mask>255.255.255.0</mask>
            <secondary/>
          </secondary>
        </address>
      </ip>
    </GigabitEthernet>
  </interface>
 </native>
</data>

>>>
```

For this exercise, our goal is to print all secondary IP addresses and masks.

One option is to use a `for` loop to do this using a method called `iter()` of `etree` objects.

In the example that follows, we also clean up how we are using namespaces by building a variable called `xmlns` that we can then use to template a string using the `for mat()` method.

```
>>> xmlns = '{http://cisco.com/ns/yang/ned/ios}'
>>> address_container = nc_get_reply.data.find('.//{}address'.format(xmlns))
>>> for secondary in address_container.iter('{}secondary'.format(xmlns)):
...     if secondary:
...         print(secondary.find('.//{}address'.format(xmlns)).text)
...         print(secondary.find('.//{}mask'.format(xmlns)).text)
...         print('-' * 10)
...
20.2.2.1
255.255.255.0
----------
22.2.2.1
255.255.255.0
----------
24.2.2.1
255.255.255.0
----------
>>>
```

That is just one way to extract the secondary addresses (or any multiples). Let's take a look at a simpler approach. Since we already have `address_container` that contains all of our primary and secondary addresses, we'll use that to print each of them by first extracting all `address` elements using the `findall()` method of `etree._Element` objects.

```
>>> all_addresses = address_container.findall('.//{}address'.format(xmlns))
>>>
>>> for item in all_addresses:
...     print(item.text)
...
10.4.4.1
20.2.2.1
22.2.2.1
24.2.2.1
>>>
```

The `findall()` method proves to be valuable when you need to extract multiple elements of the same type.

By now, you should be getting the hang of issuing NETCONF `<get>` requests. Let's look at one more, but this time, we are going to use a Juniper Junos vMX router.

Retrieving Juniper vMX Junos device configurations with ncclient

On our Juniper vMX, we currently have two SNMP read-only community strings configured. For verification, this is the output after we issue the `show snmp` command while in configuration mode:

```
ntc@vmx1# show snmp
community public {
    authorization read-only;
}
community networktocode {
    authorization read-only;
}

[edit]
ntc@vmx1#
```

Our desire is to extract the name of each community string and the authorization level for each.

Juniper has functionality in its CLI such that you can see the expected XML response as well when you pipe the command to `display xml`.

```
ntc@vmx1# show snmp | display xml
<rpc-reply xmlns:junos="http://xml.juniper.net/junos/15.1F4/junos">
    <configuration junos:changed-seconds="1482848933"
junos:changed-localtime="2016-12-27 14:28:53 UTC">
        <snmp>
```

```
            <community>
                <name>public</name>
                <authorization>read-only</authorization>
            </community>
            <community>
                <name>networktocode</name>
                <authorization>read-only</authorization>
            </community>
        </snmp>
    </configuration>
    <cli>
        <banner>[edit]</banner>
    </cli>
</rpc-reply>

[edit]
ntc@vmx1#
```

Now that we know what's going to be returned from our NETCONF request, we can more easily write the associated Python code. Whenever you are issuing a NETCONF get request to a Junos device, <configuration> needs to be the outermost XML tag when you're collecting configuration state information. Within that element, you can build the appropriate filter, which can be gleaned from the XML text found while on the CLI. Our filter string to request SNMP configuration looks like this:

```
get_filter = """
<configuration>
  <snmp>
  </snmp>
</configuration>
"""
```

We're also going to instantiate a new device object and use the variable name vmx to connect to our Juniper vMX router.

```
>>> vmx = manager.connect(host='junos-vmx', port=830, username='ntc',
...                       password='ntc123', hostkey_verify=False,
...                       device_params={}, allow_agent=False,
...                       look_for_keys=False)
...
>>>
```

The next step is to make the request, just like we've done already. After the request is made, we'll verify the output, printing the XML string to the terminal using the xml attribute of the response.

```
>>> nc_get_reply = vmx.get(('subtree', get_filter))
>>>
>>> print(nc_get_reply.xml)
<rpc-reply xmlns="urn:ietf:params:xml:ns:netconf:base:1.0"
xmlns:junos="http://xml.juniper.net/junos/15.1F4/junos"
xmlns:nc="urn:ietf:params:xml:ns:netconf:base:1.0"
```

```
message-id="urn:uuid:29121999-68b8-4dc5-9374-63bab673677b">
<data>
<configuration xmlns="http://xml.juniper.net/xnm/1.1/xnm"
junos:changed-seconds="1482848933"
junos:changed-localtime="2016-12-27 14:28:53 UTC">
    <snmp>
        <community>
            <name>public</name>
            <authorization>read-only</authorization>
        </community>
        <community>
            <name>networktocode</name>
            <authorization>read-only</authorization>
        </community>
    </snmp>
</configuration>
<database-status-information>
<database-status>
<user>ntc</user>
<terminal>p0</terminal>
<pid>37551</pid>
<start-time junos:seconds="1483116118">2016-12-30 16:41:58 UTC</start-time>
<idle-time junos:seconds="684">00:11:24</idle-time>
<edit-path>[edit]</edit-path>
</database-status>
<database-status>
<user>ntc</user>
<terminal></terminal>
<pid>37643</pid>
<start-time junos:seconds="1483117954">2016-12-30 17:12:34 UTC</start-time>
<edit-path></edit-path>
</database-status>
</database-status-information>
</data>
</rpc-reply>
>>>
```

Juniper also responds with metadata about the request that you don't see on the CLI, such as the user who issued the request and the start time of the request.

As we stated, our goal is to parse the response, saving the community string and authorization type for each community. Rather than just print these to the terminal, let's save them as a list of Python dictionaries.

In order to do this, we'll follow the same steps we used earlier. The only difference is we're saving the data and not printing it. Remember, we need to either strip XML namespaces using custom code or note the namespace being used when we print the response object as an XML string.

```
>>> snmp_list = []
>>>
>>> xmlns = '{http://xml.juniper.net/xnm/1.1/xnm}'
>>>
>>> communities = nc_get_reply.data.findall('.//{}community'.format(xmlns))
>>>
>>> for community in communities:
...     temp = {}
...     temp['name'] = community.find('.//{}name'.format(xmlns)).text
...     temp['auth'] = community.find('.//{}authorization'.format(xmlns)).text
...     snmp_list.append(temp)
...
>>>
>>> print(snmp_list)
[{'name': 'public', 'auth': 'read-only'}, {'name': 'networktocode',
                                           'auth': 'read-only'}]
>>>
```

We've seen how to issue NETCONF requests to obtain configuration data, but now we are going to transition a bit and show how to make configuration changes via the NETCONF API using the `<edit-config>` operation.

Making Cisco IOS-XE configuration changes with ncclient

The `<edit-config>` NETCONF operation maps directly to the `edit_config()` method of our device object in the ncclient. If you recall, we already showed an example of using an `<edit-config>` operation when we were exploring the use of NET-CONF. There are two elements we need to be aware of and define when making a configuration change. The first element is called `<target>`, and this defines which configuration datastore is going to get modified in the request. Valid datastores are running, startup, and candidate. The second parameter is called <config> and needs to be an XML string or object that defines the requested configuration changes.

In our first example, we're going to configure a new SNMP community string using the network element driver (ned) YANG model that we used earlier, denoted by the namespace `http://cisco.com/ns/yang/ned/ios`. When using this particular model, we can use a single filter to return the XML object that will depict the hierarchy required for subsequent API calls. We already showed this when using the RESTful API on IOS-XE. The URL for the RESTful API was *http://ios-csr1kv/restconf/api/config/native*. The same `get` request filter for NETCONF is the following:

```
get_filter = """
    <native xmlns="http://cisco.com/ns/yang/ned/ios">
    </native>
"""
```

> If the device supports both NETCONF and RESTCONF, you can use tools such as Postman to interact with the RESTful HTTP API and use XML encoding to better understand the objects required for NETCONF.

When this filter is sent to the device, the device responds back nearly a full configuration. We aren't showing the output generated because it's a lengthy output, but if you try it, you'll see that `<snmp-server>` is a child element of `<data>`.

What this means is we can add `<snmp-server>` to the filter in order to selectively retrieve just the SNMP configuration.

```
get_filter = """
    <native xmlns="http://cisco.com/ns/yang/ned/ios">
      <snmp-server>
      </snmp-server
    </native>
"""
```

Even though our goal is to make a configuration change, we are performing a `get` request to see how the data needs to be structured when we send it back to the device in the `<edit-config>` request.

```
>>> nc_get_reply = device.get(('subtree', get_filter))
>>>
>>> print(etree.tostring(nc_get_reply.data, pretty_print=True))
<data xmlns="urn:ietf:params:xml:ns:netconf:base:1.0"
xmlns:nc="urn:ietf:params:xml:ns:netconf:base:1.0">
  <native xmlns="http://cisco.com/ns/yang/ned/ios">
    <snmp-server>
      <community>
        <name>networktocode</name>
        <RO/>
      </community>
      <community>
        <name>private</name>
        <RW/>
      </community>
      <community>
        <name>public</name>
        <RO/>
      </community>
    </snmp-server>
  </native>
</data>

>>>
```

Now that we can see how to *model* SNMP data as XML, we can construct a new XML configuration object. Let's add a new community string called `secure` that has read-write privileges. It is modeled as such:

```
<native xmlns="http://cisco.com/ns/yang/ned/ios">
  <snmp-server>
    <community>
      <name>secure</name>
      <RW/>
    </community>
  </snmp-server>
</native>
```

One final tag we need to encapsulate this document in is `<config>`. This is often required when you're using the `<edit-config>` operation, as covered in our discussion of the NETCONF protocol stack earlier in the chapter.

Finally, we create a new variable that represents our configuration object.

```
config_filter = """
    <config>
      <native xmlns="http://cisco.com/ns/yang/ned/ios">
        <snmp-server>
          <community>
            <name>secure</name>
            <RW/>
          </community>
        </snmp-server>
      </native>
    </config>
"""
```

IOS-XE doesn't currently support a candidate configuration, so we are going to make this change on the running-configuration datastore. We do so by using the `edit_con fig()` method and passing in two parameters, `target` and `config`.

```
>>> response = device.edit_config(target='running', config=config_filter)
>>>
```

If you check the configuration via the CLI or make a `get` request, you'll see there are now four community strings on the device, including the `secure` community string.

Performing a NETCONF delete operation with ncclient. We've seen how to make a configuration change on the device using the `<edit-config>` operation. The default operation as we stated earlier and depicted in Table 7-3 is a `merge` operation. We can change the type of operation using the XML attribute called `operation`.

We just added the SNMP community string called `secure` using the `merge` (default) operation. We are now going to show how to remove it using the `delete` operation.

In order to do this, only the XML configuration string (or object) needs to get updated. Take note of the new line in the new XML string: `operation="delete"`.

```
config_filter = """
    <config>
      <native xmlns="http://cisco.com/ns/yang/ned/ios">
        <snmp-server>
          <community operation="delete">
            <name>secure</name>
            <RW/>
          </community>
        </snmp-server>
      </native>
    </config>
"""
```

Making this request using the same `edit_config()` method results in the removal of the `secure` community string.

You now know how to add a configuration using `operation=merge` and how to remove a configuration using `operation=delete`, but how would you ensure that *only* the `secure` community exists?

Performing a NETCONF replace operation with ncclient. There are a few ways to go about *replacing* a given hierarchy of XML configuration. One option is to make an API call to configure all desired SNMP community strings, then retrieve all currently configured SNMP communities in another API call, loop over the response, and issue a delete per community if it's not desired. While it's not a terrible approach, NETCONF offers a better way—as you already know, of course.

With NETCONF, you can use the `replace` operation instead of `merge` or `delete`. This is the same as doing a PUT with RESTCONF.

We are going to update the XML configuration string, adding in `operation=replace` and see what the result is.

```
config_filter = """
    <config>
      <native xmlns="http://cisco.com/ns/yang/ned/ios">
        <snmp-server operation="replace">
          <community>
            <name>secure</name>
            <RW/>
          </community>
        </snmp-server>
      </native>
    </config>
"""
```

The same `<edit-config>` request is made to ensure the *only* `<snmp-server>` configuration is the single community string called `secure`. Pay special attention that the `operation="replace"` line is in a different location in the XML hierarchy than it was in the last example. Placing it as an attribute of `<snmp-server>` replaces the full configuration of SNMP. If you issued the API called with `operation="delete"` on the same line, it would *delete all* related SNMP configuration. As we said with REST-CONF PUTs, the same is true with NETCONF `replace` operations; be aware of their power.

> When you start experimenting with the `delete` and `replace` operations, you need to be extremely careful. The `merge` operation is the default for a very good reason—you would only ever add or update a configuration. More importantly, if you put the `operation="delete"` line at the wrong place in the XML hierarchy, it could have a catastrophic effect on the network. Please always make sure you test in a lab or sandbox environment first. Do *not* test this in production!

Making Juniper vMX Junos configuration changes with ncclient

We've seen a few examples of working with the ncclient and the Cisco IOS-XE NET-CONF API. Let's change things up and look at more examples using Juniper Junos.

Our Juniper vMX has four static routes configured.

Both of the following outputs were taken directly from the CLI using the `show` and `show | display xml` commands.

```
routing-options {
    static {
        route 0.0.0.0/0 next-hop 10.0.0.2;
        route 10.1.100.0/24 next-hop 10.254.1.1;
        route 10.2.200.0/24 next-hop 10.254.1.1;
        route 10.33.100.0/24 next-hop 192.168.1.1;
    }
}
```

In the XML output, there is a parent XML tag called `<configuration>`, not shown for conciseness in the output.

```
<routing-options>
    <static>
        <route>
            <name>0.0.0.0/0</name>
            <next-hop>10.0.0.2</next-hop>
        </route>
        <route>
            <name>10.1.100.0/24</name>
            <next-hop>10.254.1.1</next-hop>
```

```
        </route>
        <route>
            <name>10.2.200.0/24</name>
            <next-hop>10.254.1.1</next-hop>
        </route>
        <route>
            <name>10.33.100.0/24</name>
            <next-hop>192.168.1.1</next-hop>
        </route>
    </static>
</routing-options>
```

Let's add a new static route using the ncclient. From what we already learned, we can break it down into a few steps.

1. Instantiate a new device object using `manager.connect()`.

2. Choose the desired option, `merge`, `delete`, or `replace`. We only want to add a new static route, so using the default `merge` operation will work.

3. Generate the required XML string. Remember this always goes inside the `<config>` tag and since this example is for Junos, the pipe to XML (`| xml`) on the CLI is helpful to generate the desired XML string (or object).

4. Save the string as a new variable in Python.

5. Choose the target configuration datastore. Note that Juniper supports a candidate configuration. We can leverage that to see how it's different from modifying running configurations.

6. Issue the API call using the `edit_config()` method of the instantiated device object.

7. If the candidate configuration was used as the target datastore, commit the configuration.

The new static route we want to add has the prefix 172.16.20.0/24 with a next-hop value of 10.0.0.2.

```
>>> vmx = manager.connect(host='junos-vmx', port=830, username='ntc',
...                       password='ntc123', hostkey_verify=False,
...                       device_params={}, allow_agent=False,
...                       look_for_keys=False)
...
>>>
>>> configuration = """
...     <config>
...       <configuration>
...         <routing-options>
...           <static>
...             <route>
...               <name>172.16.20.0/24</name>
```

```
...                      <next-hop>10.0.0.2</next-hop>
...                   </route>
...                </static>
...             </routing-options>
...          </configuration>
...       </config>
...    """
>>>
>>> response = vmx.edit_config(target='candidate', config=configuration)
>>>
>>> vmx.commit()
<rpc-reply xmlns="urn:ietf:params:xml:ns:netconf:base:1.0"
xmlns:junos="http://xml.juniper.net/junos/15.1F4/junos"
xmlns:nc="urn:ietf:params:xml:ns:netconf:base:1.0"
message-id="urn:uuid:37c92cf6-f1d6-4af5-b813-1d3be0eccd99">
Setting up Virtual platform specific options
<ok/>
</rpc-reply>
>>>
```

The major difference in this example is we are highlighting the use of the candidate configuration datastore and subsequently committing the configuration to the running configuration.

If you want to clean up any unused static routes and just end up with a single default static route, simply use operation=replace at the correct location in the XML string.

```
>>> configuration = """
...    <config>
...       <configuration>
...          <routing-options operation="replace">
...             <static>
...                <route>
...                   <name>0.0.0.0/0</name>
...                   <next-hop>10.0.0.2</next-hop>
...                </route>
...             </static>
...          </routing-options>
...       </configuration>
...    </config>
...    """
>>>
>>> response = vmx.edit_config(target='candidate', config=configuration)
>>>
>>> vmx.commit()
<rpc-reply xmlns="urn:ietf:params:xml:ns:netconf:base:1.0"
xmlns:junos="http://xml.juniper.net/junos/15.1F4/junos"
xmlns:nc="urn:ietf:params:xml:ns:netconf:base:1.0"
message-id="urn:uuid:dbc0c58b-4b3b-488f-89f2-67608b28cc77">
Setting up Virtual platform specific options
<ok/>
```

```
</rpc-reply>
>>>
```

 Juniper also supports using the `<config-text>` XML tag in addition to `<config>` should you want to pass the text configuration in CLI curly brace notation.

Making Cisco IOS-XR configuration changes with ncclient

As we start to wrap up working with NETCONF, you probably noticed that you need to be aware of how to construct proper XML objects in order to succeed in getting data from a device or making a configuration change. This has been mentioned a few times already. This is similar to knowing different CLI commands between different operating systems and vendors. There are, however, committees and working groups developing vendor-neutral data models. One of these is the OpenConfig Working Group (WG) that is developing vendor-neutral data models. At the lowest level, this means that we can send the same XML object to devices from different vendors using the `<edit-config>` operation to make a configuration change.

At the time of this writing, several vendors are adding support for vendor-neutral models from the OpenConfig WG, but it's still early on overall. For example, both Juniper Junos and Cisco IOS-XR support the OpenConfig BGP data model. We are going to show this using Cisco IOS-XR.

Our Cisco IOS-XR router has the following *basic* BGP configuration:

```
!
router bgp 65512
 bgp router-id 1.1.1.1
 !
```

Using NETCONF and the OpenConfig BGP model represented as XML, we can extract the existing BGP configuration.

```
>>>
>>> get_filter = """
...     <bgp xmlns="http://openconfig.net/yang/bgp">
...       <global>
...         <config>
...         </config>
...       </global>
...     </bgp>
... """
>>>
>>> xr = manager.connect(host='ios-xrv', port=22, username='ntc',
...                       password='ntc123', hostkey_verify=False,
...                       device_params={}, allow_agent=False,
...                       look_for_keys=False)
```

```
>>>
>>> nc_get_reply = xr.get(('subtree', get_filter))
>>>
>>> print(etree.tostring(nc_get_reply.data, pretty_print=True))
<data xmlns="urn:ietf:params:xml:ns:netconf:base:1.0"
xmlns:nc="urn:ietf:params:xml:ns:netconf:base:1.0">
  <bgp xmlns="http://openconfig.net/yang/bgp">
   <global>
    <config>
     <as>65512</as>
     <router-id>1.1.1.1</router-id>
    </config>
   </global>
  </bgp>
 </data>


>>>
```

Now that we understand the object that's returned to us, let's use it as the foundation to build a <config> object that changes the router ID.

```
>>> config = """
...     <config>
...       <bgp xmlns="http://openconfig.net/yang/bgp">
...        <global>
...         <config>
...          <router-id>10.10.10.10</router-id>
...         </config>
...        </global>
...       </bgp>
...      </config>
...     """
>>>
>>> response = xr.edit_config(target='candidate', config=config)
>>>
>>> xr.commit()
<?xml version="1.0"?>
<rpc-reply message-id="urn:uuid:9e0f496b-0685-42ca-870b-6d0307b92641"
xmlns:nc="urn:ietf:params:xml:ns:netconf:base:1.0"
xmlns="urn:ietf:params:xml:ns:netconf:base:1.0">
 <ok/>
</rpc-reply>
```

As more vendors and operating systems support vendor-neutral data models, you'll be able to issue the same exact API call against those devices, simplifying working different device types. Until that point comes, you'll need to understand the XML objects required per network operation system.

Understanding vendor-specific NETCONF operations

In this section, we have focused on the two most commonly used methods in the ncclient, namely <edit-config> and <get>. However, as you may have noticed earlier in this chapter when we did a dir() on the device object, there are many more methods to be aware of as you pursue your network automation journey with NETCONF and the ncclient. Here are a few of those.

close_session
> Remember that NETCONF is using a persistent SSH connection. This method is used to disconnect from the device.

commit
> Used to commit a candidate configuration to the active running configuration.

connected
> Used to check and see if there is an active session to the device. This is an attribute, so its usage is device.connected and it returns a boolean value (True or False).

copy_config
> Creates or replaces an entire configuration datastore with the contents of another complete configuration datastore.

delete_config
> Deletes a configuration datastore.

lock and unlock
> For a production environment, you may want to lock the configuration datastore before changes are made so that no other person or system can make changes during your NETCONF session. When it's complete, you can unlock the configuration.

server_capabilities
> An object that you can loop over to view all supported capabilities on the server.

Everything we focused on with the Python-based ncclient was vendor-neutral and would work across vendors, assuming you understand how to build the proper XML objects. However, you should understand that not every vendor implements NETCONF the same way even though it is an industry-standard protocol. For example, particular vendors have created their own platform-specific NETCONF operations or created their own methods for ncclient to simplify performing common operations. This is in contrast to NETCONF standard operations such as <edit-config>, <get>, <lock>, <unlock>, and <commit>.

Here are a few examples to emphasize this point.

- HPE Comware 7 switches support standard NETCONF operations, but have a few custom operations to save configuration, roll back to another configuration, and issue raw CLI commands. These custom operations map back to built-in methods found in the ncclient. For example, to issue display commands you would use `cli_display()`; or to serialize configuration over a NETCONF session, you'd use the `cli_config()` method.

- Juniper has created custom methods within the ncclient such as `load_configuration()`, `get_configuration()`, `compare_configuration()`, and `command()`, just to name a few. Several of Juniper's are wrappers to simplify performing common tasks with standard NETCONF operations, and others use Juniper-specific NETCONF RPC operations.

- Cisco Nexus also supports the ability to send CLI commands using the method `exec_command()`, which maps to the Nexus-specific NETCONF operation called `exec-command`.

In order to use these vendor-specific options when using the ncclient, you need to specify the correct platform in the `device_params` parameter when instantiating a device object.

Every example we showed used `device_params={}` because we used industry-standard operations within the ncclient. If you choose the vendor-specific methods and operations, you would set the `device_params` parameter to its required value.

Here are a few examples using `device_params` to use vendor-specfic operations and methods.

```
vmx = manager.connect(host='junos-vmx', port=830, username='ntc',
                      password='ntc123', hostkey_verify=False,
                      device_params={'name': 'junos'},
                      allow_agent=False, look_for_keys=False)

nxos = manager.connect(host='nxos1', port=22, username='ntc',
                       password='ntc123', hostkey_verify=False,
                       device_params='name': 'nexus'},
                       allow_agent=False, look_for_keys=False)

hpe = manager.connect(host='hpe5930', port=830, username='ntc',
                      password='ntc123', hostkey_verify=False,
                      device_params={'name': 'hpcomware'},
                      allow_agent=False, look_for_keys=False)
```

We've now provided an introduction to both using the Python requests and ncclient libraries to communicate with modern programmatic network APIs. We are going to shift gears now and talk about using SSH in Python, as SSH is still the most widely deployed interface on network devices.

Using netmiko

Using CLI commands SSH is the de facto way network engineers and operators manage their infrastructure. Commands are passed over a persistent SSH connection to a network device, the device interprets them, and it responds with text that is viewable by a human on a terminal window. SSH does not use structured encoded data such as XML or JSON over the wire. While SSH is not a modern or a programmatic API, it is important to have an understanding of how to use Python to automate network operations with SSH for three reasons:

- Not all devices support a programmatic API.
- You may want to automate the turning on of the API.
- Even if you're automating a device with an API:
  — It's good to have a backup plan
  — Not all operations of a device may be supported with the API.

This is not ideal, as it shows immaturity in the underlying API.

In this section, we show how to get started with a popular open source SSH client for Python called netmiko.

Netmiko's purpose is to simplify SSH device management specifically for network devices. It is built on top of another library called paramiko.

We're focused on netmiko, as it provides a lower barrier to entry and already understands how to communicate with a large number of network device types. netmiko has varied support for over two dozen device types, including those from Arista, Brocade, Cisco, Dell, HPE, Juniper, Palo Alto Networks, and many more. The great part about netmiko is that its overall usage is the same across vendors. This is similar to what we saw with ncclient. With the ncclient, the only difference per platform was the XML object sent to the device; with netmiko, the only difference is the commands sent to the device.

Let's get started with netmiko.

To install netmiko, you can use pip:

```
pip install netmiko
```

The first thing you need to do is import the proper netmiko device object. This object handles the SSH connection setup, teardown, and the sending of commands to the device. We saw the same approach with ncclient.

```
>>> from netmiko import ConnectHandler
>>>
```

We're now ready to establish an SSH connection to the network device and create a netmiko device object. The `ConnectHandler` object handles the SSH connection to the network device.

```
>>> device = ConnectHandler(host='veos', username='ntc', password='ntc123',
                            device_type='arista_eos')
>>>
```

At this point, there is an active SSH connection from Python using netmiko with our Arista switch. Because each platform supports different commands and handles SSH differently, we are required to provide the `device_type` parameter when instantiating an instance of the `ConnectHandler` object.

Let's check the available methods for our new device object called `device` using the `dir()` function.

```
>>> dir(device)
[...methods removed for brevity...,'check_config_mode', 'check_enable_mode',
'cleanup', 'clear_buffer', 'commit', 'config_mode', 'device_type',
'disable_paging', 'disconnect', 'enable', 'establish_connection',
'exit_config_mode', 'exit_enable_mode', 'find_prompt', 'global_delay_factor',
'host', 'key_file', 'key_policy', 'normalize_cmd', 'normalize_linefeeds',
'password', 'port', 'protocol', 'read_channel', 'read_until_pattern',
'read_until_prompt', 'read_until_prompt_or_pattern', 'remote_conn',
'remote_conn_pre', 'secret', 'select_delay_factor', 'send_command',
'send_command_expect', 'send_command_timing', 'send_config_from_file',
'send_config_set', 'session_preparation', 'set_base_prompt', 'set_terminal_width',
'special_login_handler', 'ssh_config_file', 'strip_ansi_escape_codes',
'strip_backspaces', 'strip_command', 'strip_prompt', 'system_host_keys',
'telnet_login', 'timeout', 'use_keys', 'username', 'verbose', 'write_channel']
>>>
```

As a network engineer, you should feel pretty comfortable with many of the attributes shown from the `dir()` function, as they are very network-centric. We'll walk through a few of them now.

Verify the device prompt

Use the `find_prompt()` method to check the prompt string of the device.

```
>>> device.find_prompt()
u'eos-spine1#'
>>>
>>> output = device.find_prompt()
>>>
>>> print(output)
eos-spine1#
>>>
```

Enter configuration mode

Because netmiko understands different vendors and what configuration mode means, it has a method to go into configuration mode that works across vendors; of course, the command netmiko uses under the covers may be different per OS.

```
>>> output1 = device.config_mode()
>>>
>>> output2 = device.find_prompt()
>>>
>>> print(output2)
eos-spine1(config)#
>>>
```

Send commands

The most common operation you're going to perform with netmiko is sending commands to a device. Let's look at a few methods to do this.

To simply send a single command to a device, you can use one of three methods:

send_command_expect()
:   This method is used for long-running commands that may take a while for the device to process (show run on a larger chassis, show tech, etc.). By default, this method waits for the same prompt string to return before completing. Optionally, you can pass what the new prompt string is going to be should it change based on the commands being sent.

send_command_timing()
:   This method is used for short-running commands; this method is timing-based and does not check the prompt string.

send_command()
:   This is an older method in netmiko, which now acts as a wrapper for simply calling send_command_expect(). Thus, send_command() and send_command_expect() perform the same operation.

Let's look at a few examples.

Here we're gathering a show run and printing out the first 165 characters for verification:

```
>>> output = device.send_command('show run')
>>>
>>> print(output[:165])
! Command: show running-config
! device: eos-spine1 (vEOS, EOS-4.15.2F)
!
! boot system flash:vEOS-lab.swi
!
```

```
transceiver qsfp default-mode 4x10G
!
hostname eos-spine
>>>
```

Send a command that changes the prompt string (remember we're still in configuration mode when we entered output1 = device.config_mode()) as follows:

```
>>> output = device.send_command_expect('end')
Traceback (most recent call last):
  File "<stdin>", line 1, in <module>
  File "/usr/local/lib/python2.7/dist-packages/netmiko/base_connection.py",
line 681, in send_command_expect
    return self.send_command(*args, **kwargs)
  File "/usr/local/lib/python2.7/dist-packages/netmiko/base_connection.py",
line 673, in send_command
    search_pattern))
IOError: Search pattern never detected in
send_command_expect: eos\-spine1\(config\)\#
>>>
```

The stack trace shown is expected, as send_command_expect() expects to see the same prompt string by default. Since we are in config mode with the current prompt string of eos-spine1(config)#, when we type the command end, the new prompt string is going to be eos-spine1#.

In order to execute a command that changes the prompt string, you have two options. First, you can use the expect_string parameter that defines the new and expected prompt string.

```
>>> output = device.send_command_expect('end', expect_string='eos-spine1#')
>>>
```

Second, you can use the send_command_timing() method, which is timing-based, and doesn't expect a particular prompt string to be found again.

```
>>> output = device.send_command_timing('end')
>>>
```

We've seen three methods thus far on how to send commands with netmiko. Let's look at two more useful ones, as you may want to send several commands at once versus one at a time.

netmiko also supports a method called send_config_set() that takes a parameter that must be an iterable. We'll show this using a Python list, but you can also use a Python set.

```
>>> commands = ['interface Ethernet5', 'description configured by netmiko',
    'shutdown']
>>>
>>> output = device.send_config_set(config_commands=commands)
>>>
```

```
>>> print(output)
config term
eos-spine1(config)#interface Ethernet5
description configured by netmiko
eos-spine1(config-if-Et5)#description configured by netmiko
eos-spine1(config-if-Et5)#shutdown
eos-spine1(config-if-Et5)#end
eos-spine1#
>>>
```

This method checks to see if you're already in configuration mode. If you aren't, it goes into config mode, executes the commands, and by default, exits configuration mode. You can verify this by viewing the returned output as shown in the previous example.

Finally, there is a method that can execute commands from a file. This allows you to do something like create a Jinja template, render it with variable data, write the data to file, and then execute those commands from the file with the netmiko method send_config_from_file( ). Building on what we covered in Chapters 4 and 6, let's see how to perform this workflow.

```
>>> from netmiko import ConnectHandler
>>> from jinja2 import Environment, FileSystemLoader
>>>
>>> device = ConnectHandler(host='veos', username='ntc', password='ntc123',
                            device_type='arista_eos')
>>>
>>> interface_dict = {
...     "name": "Ethernet6",
...     "description": "Server Port",
...     "vlan": 10,
...     "uplink": False
... }
>>>
>>> ENV = Environment(loader=FileSystemLoader('.'))
>>> template = ENV.get_template("config.j2")
>>> commands = template.render(interface=interface_dict)
>>>
>>> with open('veos.conf', 'w') as config_file:
...     config_file.writelines(commands)
...
>>> output = device.send_config_from_file('veos.conf')
>>>
>>> verification = device.send_command('show run interface Eth6')
>>>
>>> print(verification)
interface Ethernet6
   description Server Port
   switchport access vlan 10
>>>
```

Everything shown in the previous example was covered in prior chapters. Note that *config.j2* must be created for this to work, and for this example, that Jinja template was stored in the same directory from where we entered in the Python interpreter. The contents of the template were from the same example shown in Chapter 6, and are as follows:

```
interface {{ interface.name }}
  description {{ interface.description }}
  switchport access vlan {{ interface.vlan }}
  switchport mode access
```

Once you're done working with netmiko, you can gracefully disconnect from the device using the `disconnect()` method.

```
>>> device.disconnect()
>>>
```

Netmiko is also used as the primary SSH driver for different devices within NAPALM, a robust and multi-vendor network Python library for configuring devices and retrieving data, which is covered in Appendix B.

This concludes automating SSH-based network devices using netmiko. You've now seen how to automate various types of network devices across a range of API types with the goal of helping you on your automation journey no matter the device or API type you need to work with.

Summary

This chapter focused on two core types of APIs, HTTP-based APIs and NETCONF, specifically in the context of networking. We introduced APIs, we explored APIs through the use of command-line and GUI-based tools, and we automated network devices using those same APIs in Python. We examined both RESTful and non-RESTful HTTP-based APIs. As you start to use different types of HTTP-based APIs on network devices, keep in mind the following points:

- Not all HTTP APIs are RESTful, but the tools you use for RESTful and non-RESTful APIs are the same.
- Every RESTful API we reviewed used HTTP as transport.
- HTTP APIs can use XML or JSON for data encoding, but the device may only implement one or the other. The API's author determines what gets supported.
- RESTCONF is an implementation of a RESTful API that uses HTTP to access and manipulate data defined by YANG models.

- Tools such as cURL and Postman are helpful as you get started with APIs, but to write code to interact with HTTP APIs, you need a library that *speaks* HTTP, such as the Python requests library.

- Pay close attention to the HTTP verbs used when making configuration changes—using the wrong verb can have unintended consequences.

- You need to use API documentation or device tooling (Arista Command Explorer, NX-API Developer Sandbox, ASA API Documentation & Console) to better understand how to construct a proper API request: URL, headers, HTTP method, and body.

 While we did not cover a specific implementation of an SDN Controller's API, learning to use a new API is always the same process. You need to use the API documentation, understand how that platform structured and built its API, and then you need to *explore* it, using either Postman or Python. Our goal was to use example platforms to communicate how to use APIs more generally, but by now, you should be able to continue your journey exploring APIs on other network (physical or virtual) devices, controllers, or even cloud platforms that also use HTTP APIs.

We also spent time exploring NETCONF and using NETCONF with the Python ncclient. As your NETCONF takeaways, please also keep in mind the following points:

- NETCONF is a connection-oriented and session-based protocol that commonly uses SSH as transport.

- NETCONF requires a capabilities exchange between the client and server before the client can perform a given request.

- NETCONF supports only XML encoding.

- NETCONF is used independently of how the data being transported is modeled.

- The XML documents and resulting objects are XML representations of data that adhere to a device's schema or data model. NETCONF can use XML-encoded data that adheres to data modeled by XML Schema Definitions (XSDs), YANG, or any other language/definition.

Finally, we provided an introduction to automating devices using SSH with netmiko.

As you continue your journey automating network devices with different types of APIs, remember that there is no magic here—you need to perform due diligence to understand how to use any given API.

## CHAPTER 8

Source Control with Git

So far in this book, we've shown you lots of ways to add automation to your toolbox, whether via scripting languages like Python (see Chapter 4) or via templating languages like Jinja (see Chapter 6). The increased use of Python-based scripts or Jinja templates means that managing these artifacts (and by *artifacts* we mean the files that make up these scripts, templates, and other automation tools you're employing) is very important. In particular, managing the *changes* to these artifacts has significant value (we'll explain why shortly).

In this chapter, we're going to show you how to use a *source control* tool—that is, a tool that is designed to manage the artifacts you're creating and using in your network automation processes. The use of a source control tool lets you avoid messy and error-prone approaches like appending date- and timestamps to the end of filenames, and keeps you from running into accidentally deleted or overwritten files.

To start things out, let's take a closer look at the idea of source control. We're going to keep the discussion fairly generic for now; we'll delve into a specific source control tool known as Git later in the chapter. The generic qualities discussed in the next section are not specific to any particular source control tool, however.

Use Cases for Source Control

Simply put, *source control* is a way of tracking files and the changes made to those files over time (source control is also known as *version control* or *revision control*). We know that's a really generic description, so let's look at some specific use cases:

- If you're a developer writing code as part of a larger software development project, you could track the code you're writing using source control tools. This use case is probably the most well-known use case, and the one most people immediately think about when we mention the idea of source control.

- Let's say you're part of a team of administrators managing network devices. You could take the device configuration files and track them using source control tools.

- Suppose you're responsible for maintaining documentation for portions of your organization's Information Technology (IT) infrastructure. You could track the documentation using source control tools.

In each of these cases, source control is tracking files (network configurations, documentation, software source code). By *tracking* these files, we mean that the source control tool is keeping a record of the files, the changes made to the files over time, and who made each set of changes to the files. If a change to one of the files being tracked breaks something, you can revert or roll back to a previous version of the file, undoing the changes and getting back to a known good state. In some cases (depending on the tool being used), source control tools might enable you to more easily collaborate with coworkers in a distributed fashion.

Benefits of Source Control

The previous section indirectly outlined some of the benefits of using a source control tool, but let's pull out a few specific benefits that come from the use of source control.

Change Tracking

First, you're able to track the changes to the files stored in the source control tool over time. You can see the state of the files at any given point in time, and therefore you're able to relatively easily see exactly *what* changed. This is an often overlooked benefit. When you're working with lengthy network configuration files, wouldn't it be helpful to be able to see *exactly* what changed from one version to the next? Further, most source control tools also have the ability to add metadata about the change, such as why a change was made or a reference back to an issue or trouble ticket. This additional metadata can also prove quite useful in troubleshooting.

Accountability

Not only do the source control tools track changes over time, but they also track *who* made the changes. Every change is logged with who made that particular change. In a team environment where multiple team members might be working together to manage network configurations or server configuration files, this is extraordinarily useful. Never again will you have to ask, "Who made this change?" The source control tool will already have that information.

Process and Workflow

Using source control tools also helps you and your organization enforce a healthy process and workflow. We'll get into this more in Chapter 10, but for now think about the requirement that all changes be logged in source control first *before* being pushed into production. This gives you a linear history of changes along with a log of the individual responsible for each set of changes, and enables you to enforce things like review (having someone else review your changes before they get put into production) or testing (having automated tests performed against the files in the source control system).

Benefits of Source Control for Networking

Although source control is most typically associated with software development, there are clear benefits for networking professionals. Here are just a few examples:

- Python scripts (such as the ones readers will be able to write after reading this book!) that interact with network devices can be placed in source control, so that versions of the script can be more easily managed.

- Network device configurations can be placed in source control, enabling you to see the state of a network device configuration at any point in time. A really well-known tool called RANCID uses this approach for storing network device configuration backups.

- It's easy to highlight the changes between versions of network device configurations, allowing you and your team to easily verify that only the desired changes are in place (e.g., that you didn't accidentally prune a VLAN from the wrong 802.1Q trunk).

- Configuration templates can be placed in source control, ensuring that you and your team can track changes to these templates *before* they are used to generate network device configurations or reports.

- You can use source control with network documentation.

- All changes to any of these types of files are captured along with the person responsible for the changes—no more "playing the blame game."

Now that you have an idea of the benefits that source control can bring to you, your organization, and your workflow, let's take a look at a specific source control tool that is widely used: Git (*https://git-scm.com/*).

Enter Git

Git is the latest in a long series of source control tools, and has emerged as the de facto source control tool for most open source projects. (It doesn't hurt that Git manages the source code for the Linux kernel.) For that reason, we'll focus our discussion of source control tools on Git, but keep in mind that other source control tools do exist. They are, unfortunately, out of the scope of this book.

Let's start with a brief history of how and why Git appeared.

Brief History of Git

As we mentioned earlier, Git is the source control tool used to manage the source code for the Linux kernel. Git was launched by Linus Torvalds, the creator of the Linux kernel, in early April 2005 in response to a disagreement between the Linux kernel developer community and the proprietary system they were using at the time (a system called BitKeeper).

Torvalds had a few key design goals when he set out to create Git:

Speed
   Torvalds needed Git to be able to rapidly apply patches to the Linux source code.

Simplicity
   The design for Git needed to be as simple as possible.

Strong support for nonlinear development
   The Linux kernel developers needed a system that could handle lots of parallel branches. Thus, this new system (Git) needed to support rapid branching and merging, and branches needed to be as lightweight as possible.

Support for fully distributed operation
   Every developer needed a full copy of the entire source code and its history.

Scalability
   Git needed to be scalable enough to handle large projects, like the Linux kernel.

Development of Git was fast. Within a few days of its launch, Git was self-hosted (meaning that the source code for Git was being managed by Git). The first merge of multiple branches occurred just a couple weeks later. At the end of April—just a few weeks after its launch—Git was benchmarked at applying patches to the Linux kernel tree at 6.7 patches per second. In June 2005, Git managed the 2.6.12 release of the Linux kernel, and the 1.0 release of Git occurred in late December 2005.

As of this writing, the most recent release of Git was version 2.13.1, and versions of Git were available for all major desktop operating systems (Linux, Windows, and macOS). Notable open source projects using Git include the Linux kernel (as we've already mentioned), Perl, the Gnome desktop environment, Android, the KDE Project, and the X.Org implementation of the X Window System. Additionally, some very popular online source control services are based on Git, including services like GitHub (*https://github.com*), BitBucket (*https://bitbucket.org*), and GitLab (*http://about.gitlab.com*). Some of these services also offer on-premises implementations. You'll get the opportunity to look more closely at GitLab in Chapter 10, when we discuss Continuous Integration.

Git Terminology

Before we progress any further, let's be sure that we've properly defined some terminology. Some of these terms we may have used before, but we'll include them here for the sake of completeness.

Repository

In Git, a repository is the name given to the database that contains all of a project's information (files and metadata) and history. (We're using the term *project* here just to refer to an arbitrary grouping of files for a particular purpose or effort.) A repository is a complete copy of all of the files and information associated with a project throughout the lifetime of the project. It's important to note that once data is added to a repository it is immutable; that is, it can't be changed once added. This *isn't* to say that you can't make changes to files stored in a repository, just that the repository stores and tracks these files in such a way that changes to a file create a new entry in the repository (specifically, Git uses SHA hashes to create content-addressable objects in the repository).

Working directory

This is the directory where you, as the user of Git, will modify the files contained in the repository. The working directory is *not* the same as the repository. Note that the term *working directory* is also used for other purposes on Linux/UNIX/macOS systems (to refer to the current directory, as output by the `pwd` command). Git's working directory is *not* the same as the current directory, and very specifically refers to the directory where the *.git* repository is stored.

Index

The index describes the repository's directory structure and contents at a point in time. The index is a dynamic binary file maintained by Git and modified as you stage changes and commit them to the repository.

Commit

A commit is an entry in the Git repository recording metadata for each change introduced to the repository. This metadata includes the author, the date of the commit, and a commit message (a description of the change introduced to the repository). Additionally, a commit captures the state of the entire repository at the time the commit was performed. Keep in mind when we say "a change to the repository" this might mean multiple changes to multiple files; Git allows you to lump changes to multiple files together as a single commit. (We'll discuss this in a bit more detail later in this chapter.)

Overview of Git's Architecture

With the terminology from the previous section in mind, we can now provide an overview of Git's architecture. We'll limit our discussion of Git's architecture to keep it relatively high-level, but detailed enough to help with your understanding of how Git operates.

 For a more in-depth discussion of Git's architecture, we recommend *Version Control with Git*, Second Edition (O'Reilly).

As we described earlier, a Git *repository* is a database that contains all of the information about a project: the files contained in the project, the changes made to the project over time, and the metadata about those changes (who made the change, when the change was made, etc.). By default, this information is stored in a directory named *.git* in the root of your working directory (this behavior can be changed). For example, here's a file listing of a newly initialized Git repository's working directory, showing the *.git* directory where the actual repository data is found:

```
relentless:npab-examples slowe (master)$ ls -la
total 0
drwxr-xr-x   3 slowe   staff   102 May 11 15:37 .
drwxr-xr-x  16 slowe   staff   544 May 11 15:37 ..
drwxr-xr-x  10 slowe   staff   340 May 11 15:37 .git
relentless:npab-examples slowe (master)$
```

As you can tell from this prompt, this directory listing is from the directory *npab-examples*. In this example, the *working directory* is the *npab-examples* directory, and the Git *repository* is in *npab-examples/.git*. This is why we said earlier that the working directory and the repository aren't the same. It's common for new users to refer to the working directory as the repository, but keep in mind that the actual repository is in the *.git* subdirectory.

Within the *.git* directory you'll find all the various components that make up a Git repository:

- The index—which we defined earlier as representing the repository's directory structure and contents at a given point in time—is found at *.git/index*.

- The files contained within a Git repository are treated as content-addressable objects and stored in subdirectories in *.git/objects.*

- Any repository-specific configuration details are found in *.git/config.*

- Metadata about the repository, the changes stored in the repository, and the objects in the repository can be found in *.git/logs.*

All of the information stored in the *.git* directory is maintained by Git—you should never need to directly interact with the contents of this directory. Over the course of this chapter, we'll share with you the various commands that are needed to interact with the repository to add files, commit changes, revert changes, and more. In fact, that leads us directly into our next section, which will show you how to work with Git.

Working with Git

Now that you have an idea of what Git's architecture looks like, let's shift our focus to something a bit more practical: actually *working* with Git.

Throughout our discussion of working with Git, we're going to use a (hopefully) very practical example. Let's assume that you are a network engineer reponsible for rolling out some network automation tools in your environment. During this process, you're going to end up creating Python scripts, Jinja templates, and other files. You'd like to use Git to manage these files so that you can take advantage of all the benefits of source control.

The following sections walk you through each of the major steps in getting started using Git to manage the files created as part of your network automation effort.

Installing Git

The steps for installing Git are extremely well documented, so we won't go through them here. Git is often preinstalled in various distributions of Linux; if not, Git is almost always available to install via the Linux distribution's package manager (such as `dnf` for RHEL/CentOS/Fedora, or `apt` for Debian/Ubuntu). Installers are available for macOS and Windows that make it easy to install Git. Detailed instructions and options for installing Git are also available on the Git website (*https://git-scm.com/book/en/v2/Getting-Started-Installing-Git*).

Creating a Repository

Once Git is installed, the first step is to create a repository. First, you'll create a directory where the repository will be stored. Assuming you're using an Ubuntu Linux system, it might look something like this (the commands would be very similar, if not identical, on other Linux distributions or on macOS):

```
vagrant@trusty:~$ mkdir ~/net-auto
vagrant@trusty:~$
```

Then you can change into this directory and create the empty repository using the
git init command:

```
vagrant@trusty:~$ cd net-auto
vagrant@trusty:~/net-auto$ git init
Initialized empty Git repository in /home/vagrant/net-auto/.git
vagrant@trusty:~/net-auto$
```

The git init command is responsible for initializing, or creating, a new Git repository. This involves creating the *.git* directory and all of the subdirectories and contents found within them.

> The various git commands we describe throughout this chapter
> should be very nearly identical across all systems on which Git
> runs. We'll use various Linux distributions (and this will be reflec-
> ted in the shell prompts in the examples we show), but using Git on
> macOS should be the same as on Linux. Using Git on Windows
> should be similar, but there may be syntactical differences here and
> there due to the differences in the underlying operating systems.

If you were now to run ls -la in the *net-auto* directory, you'd see the *.git* directory
that stores the empty Git repository created by the git init command. The repository is now ready for you to start adding content. You'd add content to a repository by
adding files.

Adding Files to a Repository

Adding files to repository is a multistage process:

1. Add the files to the repository's working directory.

2. Stage the files to the repository's index.

3. Commit the staged files to the repository.

Let's go back to our example. You've created your new Git repository to store files created as part of your network automation project, and some of the first files you'd like
to add to the repository are the current configuration files from your network devices. You already have three configuration files: *sw1.txt*, *sw2.txt*, and *sw3.txt*, that contain the current configurations for three switches.

First, copy the files into the working directory (in our example, */home/vagrant/net-
auto*). More generically, remember the working directory is the parent directory of
the *.git* directory (which holds the actual Git repository). On a Linux or macOS sys-

tem, copying files into the working directory would involve the `cp` command; on a Windows-based machine, you'd use the `copy` command.

The files are now in the working directory but are *not* in the repository itself. This means that Git is not tracking the files or their content, and therefore you can't track changes, know who made the changes, or roll back to an earlier version.

You can verify this by running the `git status` command, which in this example would produce some output that looks like this:

```
vagrant@trusty:~/net-auto$ git status
On branch master

Initial commit

Untracked files:
  (use "git add <file>..." to include in what will be committed)

    sw1.txt
    sw2.txt
    sw3.txt

nothing added to commit but untracked files present (use "git add" to track)
```

The output of the `git status` command tells you that untracked files are present in the working directory and nothing has been added to the repository. As the output indicates, you'll need to use the `git add` command to add these untracked files to the repository, like this:

```
vagrant@trusty:~/net-auto$ git add sw1.txt
vagrant@trusty:~/net-auto$ git add sw2.txt
vagrant@trusty:~/net-auto$ git add sw3.txt
vagrant@trusty:~/net-auto$
```

You could also use shell globbing to add multiple files at the same time. For example, you could use `git add sw*.txt` to add all three switch configurations with a single command.

After you've used `git add` to add the files to the staging area, you can run `git status` again to see the current status:

```
vagrant@trusty:~/net-auto$ git status
On branch master

Initial commit

Changes to be committed:
  (use "git rm --cached <file>..." to unstage)

    new file:   sw1.txt
    new file:   sw2.txt
```

```
        new file:    sw3.txt

vagrant@trusty:~/net-auto$
```

At this point, the files have been *staged* into Git's index. This means that Git's index and the working directory are in sync. Technically speaking, the files have been added as objects to Git's object store as well, but there is no "point in time" reference to these objects. In order to create that point-in-time reference, you must first *commit* the staged changes.

Committing Changes to a Repository

Before you're ready to commit changes to a repository, there are a couple of things you'll need to be sure you've done. Recall that one of the benefits of using Git as a source control tool is not only that you're able to track the changes made to the files stored in the repository, but that you're also able to know who made each set of changes. In order to have that information, you'll first need to provide that information to Git. (You could also do this right after installing Git; it's not necessary to create a repository first.)

Providing user information to Git

Git has a series of configuration options; some of these configuration options are repository-specific, some are user-specific, and some are system-wide. Recall from earlier that Git stores repository-specific configuration information in *.git/config*. In this particular case—where we need to provide the user's name and email address so that Git can track who made each set of changes—it's the user-specific configuration we need to modify, not the repository-specific configuration.

So where are these values stored? These settings are found in the *.gitconfig* file in your home directory. This file is an INI-style file, and you can edit it either using your favorite text editor or using the `git config` command. In this case, we'll show you how to use the `git config` command to set this information.

To set your name and email address, use the following commands:

```
vagrant@jessie:~/net-auto$ git config --global user.name "John Smith"
vagrant@jessie:~/net-auto$ git config --global user.email
"john.smith@networktocode.com"
vagrant@jessie:~/net-auto$
```

We used the `--global` option here to set it as a user-specific value; if you wanted to set a different user name and/or email address as a repository-specific value, just omit the `--global` flag (but be sure you are in the working directory of an active repository first; Git will report an error otherwise). With the `--global` flag, `git config` modifies the *.gitconfig* file in your home directory; without it, `git config` modifies the *.git/config* file of the current repository.

Committing changes

When Git has been configured with your identity, you're ready to *commit* the changes you've made to the files into the repository. Remember that before you can commit changes into the repository you must first *stage* the files using the git add command; this is true both for newly created files as well as modified files that were already in the repository (we'll review that scenario shortly). Since you've already staged the changes (via the git add command earlier) and verified it (via the git status command, which shows the files are staged), then you're ready to commit.

Committing changes to a repository is as simple as using the git commit command:

```
vagrant@jessie:~/net-auto$ git commit -m "First commit to new repository"
[master (root-commit) 9547063] First commit to new repository
 3 files changed, 24 insertions(+)
 create mode 100644 sw1.txt
 create mode 100644 sw2.txt
 create mode 100644 sw3.txt
vagrant@jessie:~/net-auto$
```

If you omit the -m parameter to git commit, then Git will launch the default text editor so you can provide a commit message. The text editor that Git launches is configurable (via git config or editing *.gitconfig* in your home directory). You could, for example, configure Git to use Sublime Text (*https://www.sublimetext.com/*), Atom (*https://atom.io/*), or some other graphical text editor.

So what's happening when you commit the changes to the repository? When you added the files via git add, objects representing the files (and the files' content) were added to Git's object database. Specifically, Git created *blobs* (binary large objects) to represent the files' content and *tree objects* to represent the files and their directory structure. When you commit the changes via git commit, you're adding another type of object to the Git database (a *commit object*) that references the tree objects, which in turn reference the blobs. With a commit object, you now have a "point in time" reference to the entire state of the repository.

At this point, your repository has a single commit, and you can see that commit using the git log command:

```
vagrant@jessie:~/net-auto$ git log
commit 95470631aba32d6823c80fdd3c6f923824dde470
Author: John Smith <john.smith@networktocode.com>
Date:   Thu May 12 17:37:22 2016 +0000

    First commit to new repository
vagrant@jessie:~/net-auto$
```

The `git log` command shows the various commits—or checkpoints, if you will—you created over the lifetime of the repository. Every time you commit changes, you create a commit object, and that commit object references the state of the repository at the time it was created. This means you can only view the state of the repository and its contents at the time of a commit. Commits, therefore, become the "checkpoints" by which you can move backward (or forward) through the history of the repository.

Recommendations for committing changes

Understanding how commits work leads to a few recommendations around committing your changes to a repository:

Commit frequently
> You can only view the state of the repository at the time when changes are committed. If you make changes, save the files, make more changes, then save and commit, you won't be able to view the state of the repository at the first set of changes (because you didn't commit).

Commit at logical points
> Don't commit every time you save changes to a file in the repository. We know this sounds like a contradiction to the previous bullet, but it really only makes sense to commit changes when the changes are complete. For example, committing changes when you're only halfway through updating a switch's configuration doesn't make sense; you wouldn't want to roll back to a half-completed switch configuration. Instead, commit when you've finished the switch configuration.

Use helpful commit messages
> As you can see from the previous `git log` output, commit messages help you understand the changes that were contained in that commit. Try to make your commit messages helpful and straightforward—it's likely that in six months, the commit message will be the only clue to help you decipher what you were doing at that point in time.

Before we move on to the next section, there's one more topic we need to discuss. We've explained that objects in a Git repository are immutable, and that changes to an object (like a file) result in the creation of a new object (addressed by the SHA hash of the object's content). This is true for all objects in the Git repository, including blobs (file content), tree objects, and commit objects.

What if, though, you made a commit and realized the commit contained errors? Maybe you have some typos in your network configuration, or the commit message is wrong. In this case, Git allows you to modify (or *amend*) the last commit.

Amending commits

In a situation where the last commit is incorrect for some reason, it is possible to *amend* the commit through the use of the --amend flag to git commit. Note that you could just make another commit instead of amending the previous commit; both approaches are valid and each approach has its advantages and disadvantages, which we'll discuss shortly. First, though, let's show you how to amend a commit.

To amend a commit, you'd follow the same set of steps as with a "normal" commit:

1. Make whatever changes you need to make.

2. Stage the changes.

3. Run git commit --amend to commit the changes, marking it as an amendment.

Under the hood, Git is actually creating new objects—which is in line with Git's philosophy and approach of content-addressable immutable objects—but in the history of the repository, you'll see *only* the amended commit, not the original commit. This results in a "cleaner" history, although some purists may argue that simply making another commit (instead of using --amend) would be the best approach.

Which approach is best? That is mostly decided by you, the user, but there are a couple considerations. If you're collaborating with others via Git and a shared repository, using --amend to amend commits already sent to the shared repository is generally a bad idea. The one exception to this would be in an environment using Gerrit, where amended commits are used extensively. We'll talk more about Gerrit in Chapter 10, and we'll cover collaborating with Git later in this chapter in the section "Collaborating with Git" on page 336.

Changing and Committing Tracked Files

You've created a repository, added some new files, and committed changes to the repository. Now, though, you need to make some changes to the files that are already in the repository. How does that work?

Fortunately, the process for committing modified versions of files into a repository looks pretty much identical to what we've shown you already:

1. Modify the file(s) in the working directory.

2. Stage the change(s) to the index using git add. This puts the index in sync with the working directory.

3. Commit the changes using git commit. This puts the repository in sync with the index, and creates a point-in-time reference to the state of the repository.

Let's review this in a bit more detail. Suppose you needed to modify one of the files, *sw1.txt*, because the switch's configuration has changed (or perhaps because you're enforcing that configurations can only be deployed *after* they've been checked into source control). After a tracked file (a file about which Git already knows and is tracking) is modified, `git status` will show that changes are present:

```
vagrant@trusty:~/net-auto$ git status
On branch master
Changes not staged for commit:
  (use "git add <file>..." to update what will be committed)
  (use "git checkout -- <file>..." to discard changes in working directory)

    modified:   sw1.txt

no changes added to commit (use "git add" and/or "git commit -a")
vagrant@trusty:~/net-auto$
```

Note the difference between this status message and the status message we showed you earlier. In this case, Git knows about the *sw1.txt* file (it's already been added to the repository), so the status message is different. Note how the status message changes if you were to add another switch configuration file, *sw4.txt*, to the working directory:

```
vagrant@trusty:~/net-auto$ git status
On branch master
Changes not staged for commit:
  (use "git add <file>..." to update what will be committed)
  (use "git checkout -- <file>..." to discard changes in working directory)

    modified:   sw1.txt

Untracked files:
  (use "git add <file>..." to include in what will be committed)

    sw4.txt

no changes added to commit (use "git add" and/or "git commit -a")
vagrant@trusty:~/net-auto$
```

Again, Git provides a clear distinction between tracking changes to an already known file and detecting untracked (not previously added) files to the working directory. Either way, though, the process for getting these changes (modified file and new file) into the repository is exactly the same, as you can see in the output of the `git status` command: just use the `git add` command, then the `git commit` command.

```
vagrant@trusty:~/net-auto$ git add sw1.txt
vagrant@trusty:~/net-auto$ git add sw4.txt
vagrant@trusty:~/net-auto$ git status
On branch master
Changes to be committed:
  (use "git reset HEAD <file>..." to unstage)
```

```
    modified:    sw1.txt
    new file:    sw4.txt

vagrant@trusty:~/net-auto$ git commit -m "Update sw1, add sw4"
[master 679c41c] Update sw1, add sw4
 2 files changed, 9 insertions(+)
 create mode 100644 sw4.txt
vagrant@trusty:~/net-auto$
```

In the output of the `git status` commands, you may have noticed a reference to `git commit -a`. The `-a` option simply tells Git to add all changes from all known files. If you're only committing changes to known files *and* you are OK with committing all the changes together in a single commit, then using `git commit -a` allows you to avoid using the `git add` command first.

If, however, you want to break up changes to multiple files into separate commits, then you'll need to use `git add` followed by `git commit` instead. Why might you want to do this?

- You might want to limit the scope of changes in a single commit so that it's less impactful to revert to an earlier version.

- You may want to limit the scope of changes in a single commit so that others can review your changes more easily. (This is something we'll discuss in more detail in Chapter 10.)

- When collaborating with others, it's often considered a "best practice" to limit commits to a single logical change, which means you may include some changes in a commit but not others. We'll discuss some general guidelines for collaborating with Git later in this chapter in the section "Collaborating with Git" on page 336.

You'll also notice that we've been using `git commit -m` in our examples here. The `-m` option allows the user to include a commit message on the command line. If you don't include the `-m`, then Git will open your default editor so that you can supply a commit message. Commit messages are required, and as we mentioned earlier we recommend that you make your commit messages as informative as possible. (You'll be thankful for informative commit messages when reviewing the output of `git log` in the future.) You can also combine both the `-a` and `-m` options, as in `git commit -am "Committing all changes to tracked files"`.

For more information on the various options to any of the git commands, just type **git help <command>**, like git help commit or git help add. This will open the man page for that part of Git's documentation. If you like to use the man command instead, you can do that too; just put a dash into the git command. Thus, to see the man page for git commit, you'd enter **man git-commit**.

Now that you've committed another set of changes to the repository, let's look at the output of git log:

```
vagrant@trusty:~/net-auto$ git log
commit 679c41c13ceb5b658b988fb0dbe45a3f34f61bb3
Author: John Smith <john.smith@networktocode.com>
Date:   Thu May 12 20:41:19 2016 +0000

    Update sw1, add sw4

commit 95470631aba32d6823c80fdd3c6f923824dde470
Author: John Smith <john.smith@networktocode.com>
Date:   Thu May 12 17:37:22 2016 +0000

    First commit to new repository
vagrant@trusty:~/net-auto$
```

Your repository now has two commits. Before we explore how to view a repository at a particular point in time (at a particular commit), let's first review a few other commands and make some additional commits to the repository.

Unstaging Files

If you've been following along, your repository now has four switch configuration files (*sw1.txt* through *sw4.txt*) and two commits. Let's say you need to add a fifth switch configuration file (named *sw5.txt*, of course). You know already the process to follow:

1. Copy the file *sw5.txt* into the working directory.
2. Use git add to stage the file from the working directory into the index.

At this point, running git status will report that *sw5.txt* has been staged and is ready to commit to the repository:

```
vagrant@jessie:~/net-auto$ git status
On branch master
Changes to be committed:
  (use "git reset HEAD <file>..." to unstage)

    new file:   sw5.txt
```

```
vagrant@jessie:~$
```

However, you realize after staging the file that you aren't ready to commit the file in its current state. Maybe the file isn't complete, or perhaps the file doesn't accurately reflect the actual configuration of "sw5" on the network. In such a situation, the best approach would be to *unstage* the file.

The command to unstage the file—that is, to remove it from the index so the working directory and the index are no longer synchronized—has already been given to you by Git. If you refer back to the output of `git status` shared just a couple paragraphs ago, you'll see Git telling you how to unstage the file. The command looks like this:

```
git reset HEAD file
```

In order to explain what's happening with this command, we first need to explain what *HEAD* is. HEAD is a pointer referencing the last commit you made (or the last commit you checked out into the working directory, but we haven't gotten to that point yet). Recall that when you stage a file (using `git add`), you are taking content from the working directory into the index. When you commit (using `git commit`), you are creating a point-in-time reference—a commit—to the content. Every time you commit, Git updates HEAD to point to the latest commit.

 HEAD also plays a strong role when you start working with multiple Git branches. We haven't discussed branches yet (they're covered later in this chapter in the section "Branching in Git" on page 323), but when we do get to branches we'll expand our discussion of HEAD at that time.

Here's a quick way to help illustrate this. If you've been following along with the examples we've been using in this chapter, then you can use these commands as well (just keep in mind that the SHA checksums shown here will differ from your own SHA checksums).

First, use `cat` to show the contents of *.git/HEAD*:

```
vagrant@jessie:~/net-auto$ cat .git/HEAD
ref: refs/heads/master
vagrant@jessie:~/net-auto$
```

You'll see that HEAD is a pointer to the file *refs/heads/master*. If you `cat` that file, you'll see this:

```
vagrant@jessie:~/net-auto$ cat .git/refs/heads/master
679c41c13ceb5b658b988fb0dbe45a3f34f61bb3
vagrant@jessie:~/net-auto$
```

The contents of *.git/refs/heads/master* is a SHA checksum. Now run `git log`, and compare the SHA checksum of the latest commit against that value:

```
vagrant@jessie:~/net-auto$ git log
commit 679c41c13ceb5b658b988fb0dbe45a3f34f61bb3
Author: John Smith <john.smith@networktocode.com>
Date:   Thu May 12 20:41:19 2016 +0000

    Update sw1, add sw4

commit 95470631aba32d6823c80fdd3c6f923824dde470
Author: John Smith <john.smith@networktocode.com>
Date:   Thu May 12 17:37:22 2016 +0000

    First commit to new repository
vagrant@jessie:~/net-auto$
```

You'll note that the SHA checksum of the last commit matches the value of HEAD (which points to *refs/heads/master*), illustrating how HEAD is a pointer to the latest commit. Later in this chapter, we'll show how HEAD also incorporates branches and how it changes when you check out content to your working directory.

For now, though, let's get back to `git reset`. The `git reset` command is a powerful command, but fortunately it has some sane defaults. When used in this way—that is, without any flags and when given a filename or path—the only thing `git reset` will do is make the index look like the content referenced by HEAD (which we now know references a particular commit, by default the latest commit).

Recall that `git add` makes the index look like the working directory, which is how you stage a file. The `git reset HEAD` *file* command is the exact opposite, making the index look like the content referenced by HEAD. It *undoes* changes to the index made by `git add`, thus *unstaging* files.

Let's see it in action. You've already staged *sw5.txt* in preparation for committing it to the repository, so `git status` shows the file listed in the "Changes to be committed:" section. Now run `git reset`:

```
vagrant@trusty:~/net-auto$ git reset HEAD sw5.txt
vagrant@trusty:~/net-auto$ git status
On branch master
Untracked files:
  (use "git add <file>..." to include in what will be committed)

    sw5.txt

nothing added to commit but untracked files present (use "git add" to track)
vagrant@trusty:~/net-auto$
```

You can see that *sw5.txt* is no longer listed as a change to be committed, and is instead shown as an untracked file (it's no longer in the index). Now you can continue working on the content of *sw5.txt*, committing a version of it to the repository when you're ready.

We've shown you how to create a repository, add files (both new and existing files), commit changes, and unstage files. What if you had files that need to be co-located with other files in the repository, but shouldn't be tracked by Git? This is where file exclusions come into play.

Excluding Files from a Repository

There may be occasions where there are files you need to store in the working directory—the "scratch space" for a Git repository—that you don't want included in the repository. Fortunately, Git provides a way to exclude certain files or filename patterns from inclusion in the repository.

Going back to our example, you've created a repository in which to store network automation artifacts. Let's suppose that you have a Python script that connects to your network switches in order to gather information from the switches. An example of one such Python script—in this case, one written to connect to an Arista switch and gather information—might look like this:

```python
#!/usr/bin/env python

from pyeapi.client import Node as EOS
from pyeapi import connect
import yaml


def main():

    creds = yaml.load(open('credentials.yml'))

    un = creds['username']
    pwd = creds['password']

    conn = connect(host='eos-npab', username=un, password=pwd)
    device = EOS(conn)

    output = device.enable('show version')
    result = output[0]['result']

    print('Arista Switch Summary:')
    print('--------------------')
    print('OS Version:' + result['version'])
    print('Model:' + result['modelName'])
    print('System MAC:' + result['systemMacAddress'])

if __name__ == "__main__":
    main()
```

Part of how this script operates is via the use of authentication credentials stored in a separate file (in this case, a YAML file named *credentials.yml*). Now, you need these credentials to be stored with the Python script, but you wouldn't necessarily want the credentials to be tracked and managed by the repository.

To Include or Exclude Secrets?

Including secrets—information like passwords, SSH keys, or the like—into a Git repository will depend greatly on how the repository is being used. For a strictly private repository where per-user secrets are not needed, including secrets in the repository is probably fine. For repositories where per-user secrets should be used or for repositories that may at some point be shared publicly, you'll likely want to exclude secrets from the repository using the mechanisms outlined in this section.

Fortunately, Git provides a couple ways to exclude files from being tracked as part of a repository. Earlier in this chapter in the section "Committing Changes to a Repository" on page 302, we discussed how Git configuration can be handled on a repository-specific, user-specific, or system-wide basis. Excluding files from Git repositories is similar, in that there are ways to exclude files on a per-repository basis or on a per-user basis.

Excluding files per-repository

Let's start with the per-repository method. The most common way of excluding (or ignoring) files is to use a *.gitignore* file stored in the repository itself. Like any other content in the repository, the *.gitignore* file must be staged into the index and committed to the repository any time changes are made. The advantage of this approach is that the *.gitignore* file is then distributed as part of the repository, which is very useful when you are part of a team whose members are all using Git as a distributed version control system (DVCS).

The contents of the *.gitignore* file are simply a list of filenames or filename patterns, one on each line. To create your own list of files for Git to ignore, you'd simply create the file named *.gitignore* in the working directory, edit it to add the filenames or filename patterns you want ignored, and then add/commit it to the repository.

Looking at our Python script from earlier, you can see that it looks for its credentials in the file named *credentials.yml*. Let's create *.gitignore* (if you don't already have one) to ignore this file:

1. Create an empty file using `touch .gitignore`.

2. Edit *.gitignore*, using the text editor of your choice, to add *credentials.yml* on a single line in the file.

At this point, if you run `git status` you'll see that Git has noticed the addition of the *.gitignore* file, but the *credentials.yml* file is *not* listed:

```
vagrant@trusty:~/net-auto$ git status
On branch master
Untracked files:
  (use "git add <file>..." to include in what will be committed)

    .gitignore

nothing added to commit but untracked files present (use "git add" to track)
vagrant@trusty:~/net-auto$
```

You can now stage and commit the *.gitignore* file into the repository using `git commit -am "Adding .gitignore file"`.

Now, if you create the *credentials.yml* file for the Python script, Git will politely ignore the file. For example, here you can see the file exists in the working directory, but `git status` reports no changes or untracked files:

```
[vagrant@centos net-auto]$ ls -la
total 40
drwxrwxr-x 3 vagrant vagrant 4096 May 31 16:32 .
drwxr-xr-x 5 vagrant vagrant 4096 May 12 17:18 ..
drwxrwxr-x 8 vagrant vagrant 4096 May 31 16:34 .git
-rw-rw-r-- 1 vagrant vagrant    8 May 31 16:27 .gitignore
-rw-rw-r-- 1 vagrant vagrant   15 May 31 16:32 credentials.yml
-rwxrwxr-x 1 vagrant vagrant    0 May 31 16:32 script.py
-rw-rw-r-- 1 vagrant vagrant   98 May 12 20:22 sw1.txt
-rw-rw-r-- 1 vagrant vagrant   84 May 12 17:17 sw2.txt
-rw-rw-r-- 1 vagrant vagrant   84 May 12 17:17 sw3.txt
-rw-rw-r-- 1 vagrant vagrant   84 May 12 20:33 sw4.txt
-rw-rw-r-- 1 vagrant vagrant  135 May 31 14:56 sw5.txt
[vagrant@centos net-auto]$ git status
On branch master
nothing to commit, working directory clean
[vagrant@centos net-auto]$
```

Now, if you're really paying attention you might note that the fact Git reported nothing to commit isn't necessarily a guarantee the file has been ignored. Let's use a few more `git` commands to verify it. First, we'll use `git log` to show the history of commits:

```
vagrant@jessie:~/net-auto$ git log --oneline
ed45c95 Adding .gitignore file
5cd13a8 Add Python script to talk to network switches
2a656c3 Add configuration for sw5
679c41c Update sw1, add sw4
```

```
9547063 First commit to new repository
vagrant@jessie:~/net-auto$
```

Now, let's interrogate Git to see the contents of the repository at these various points in time. To do this, we'll use the `git ls-tree` command along with the SHA hash of the commit we'd like to inspect. You've probably noticed by now that Git often uses just the first seven characters of a SHA hash, like in the preceding output of the `git log --oneline` command (Git will automatically use more characters to keep the hashes unique as needed). In almost every case (there may be an exception out there somewhere!), that's true for commands you enter that require a SHA hash. For example, to see what was in the repository at the time of the next-to-last commit (whose SHA hash starts with 5cd13a8), you could just do this:

```
vagrant@trusty:~/net-auto$ git ls-tree 5cd13a8
100755 blob e69de29bb2d1d6434b8b29ae775ad8c2e48c5391    script.py
100644 blob 2567e072ca607963292d73e3acd49a5388305c53    sw1.txt
100644 blob 02df3d404d59d72c98439f44df673c6038352a27    sw2.txt
100644 blob 02df3d404d59d72c98439f44df673c6038352a27    sw3.txt
100644 blob 02df3d404d59d72c98439f44df673c6038352a27    sw4.txt
100644 blob 88b23c7f60dc91f7d5bfeb094df9ed28996daeeb    sw5.txt
vagrant@trusty:~/net-auto$
```

You can see that *credentials.yml* does not exist in the repository as of this commit. What about the latest commit?

```
vagrant@jessie:~/net-auto$ git ls-tree ed45c95
100644 blob 2c1817fdecc27ccb3f7bce3f6bbad1896c9737fc    .gitignore
100755 blob e69de29bb2d1d6434b8b29ae775ad8c2e48c5391    script.py
100644 blob 2567e072ca607963292d73e3acd49a5388305c53    sw1.txt
100644 blob 02df3d404d59d72c98439f44df673c6038352a27    sw2.txt
100644 blob 02df3d404d59d72c98439f44df673c6038352a27    sw3.txt
100644 blob 02df3d404d59d72c98439f44df673c6038352a27    sw4.txt
100644 blob 88b23c7f60dc91f7d5bfeb094df9ed28996daeeb    sw5.txt
vagrant@jessie:~/net-auto$
```

(We'll leave it as an exercise for the reader to review the rest of the commits to verify that the *credentials.yml* file is *not* present in any commit.)

Excluding files globally

In addition to excluding files on a per-repository basis using a *.gitignore* file in the repository's working directory, you can also create a global file for excluding files for all repositories on your computer. Just create a *.gitignore_global* file in your home directory and add exclusions to that file. You may also want to run this command to ensure that Git is configured to use this new *.gitignore_global* file in your home directory:

```
git config --global core.excludesfile /path/to/.gitignore_global
```

If you placed *.gitignore_global* in your home directory, then the path to the file would typically be noted as *~/.gitignore_global*.

The use of the `git log` and `git ls-tree` commands naturally leads us into a discussion of how to view more information about a repository, its history, and its contents.

Viewing More Information About a Repository

When it comes to viewing more information about a repository, we've already shown you one command that you'll use quite a bit: the `git log` command. The `git log` command has already been used on a number of occasions, which should give you some indicator of just how useful it is.

Viewing basic log information

The most basic form of `git log` shows the history of commits up to HEAD, so just running `git log` will show you all the commits over the history of the repository. Here's the output of `git log` for the example repository we've been using in this chapter:

```
[vagrant@centos net-auto]$ git log
commit ed45c956da4b7e38b61b96ae050c4da77337f7ad
Author: John Smith <john.smith@networktocode.com>
Date:   Tue May 31 16:34:26 2016 +0000

    Adding .gitignore file

commit 5cd13a84de0e01f358636dee98da2df7d95e17ea
Author: John Smith <john.smith@networktocode.com>
Date:   Tue May 31 16:33:41 2016 +0000

    Add Python script to talk to network switches

commit 2a656c3288d5a324fba1c2cbfccbc0e29db73969
Author: John Smith <john.smith@networktocode.com>
Date:   Tue May 31 14:56:56 2016 +0000

    Add configuration for sw5

commit 679c41c13ceb5b658b988fb0dbe45a3f34f61bb3
Author: John Smith <john.smith@networktocode.com>
Date:   Thu May 12 20:41:19 2016 +0000

    Update sw1, add sw4

commit 95470631aba32d6823c80fdd3c6f923824dde470
Author: John Smith <john.smith@networktocode.com>
Date:   Thu May 12 17:37:22 2016 +0000
```

```
    First commit to new repository
[vagrant@centos net-auto]$
```

Viewing brief log information

The `git log` command has a number of different options; there are too many for us
to cover all of them here. One of the more useful options that we've already shown
you, the `--oneline` option, would produce the following output for the same example repository:

```
[vagrant@centos net-auto]$ git log --oneline
ed45c95 Adding .gitignore file
5cd13a8 Add Python script to talk to network switches
2a656c3 Add configuration for sw5
679c41c Update sw1, add sw4
9547063 First commit to new repository
[vagrant@centos net-auto]$
```

As you can see from the example output, the `--oneline` option abbreviates the SHA
hash and lists only the commit message. For repositories with a lengthy history, it
may be most helpful to start with `git log --oneline`, then drill into the details of a
specific commit.

> Disabling Git's default behavior to pipe output through a pager can
> make finding things via the use of `grep` possible. To disable Git's
> pager functionality, use the `--no-pager` option, as in `git --no-
> pager log --oneline`.

To drill into the details of a specific commit, there are a few different options. First,
you can use the `git log` command and supply a range of commits to show. The syntax is `git log start SHA..end SHA`. So, if we wanted to show more details on the
last couple of commits in our example repository, we'd run a command that looks like
this (if you're wondering where the SHA values came from, refer to the output of `git
log --oneline` from earlier in this section, and recall that you only need to supply
the first seven characters of the SHA hash):

```
vagrant@trusty:~/net-auto$ git log 5cd13a8..ed45c95
commit ed45c956da4b7e38b61b96ae050c4da77337f7ad
Author: John Smith <john.smith@networktocode.com>
Date:   Tue May 31 16:34:26 2016 +0000

    Adding .gitignore file
vagrant@trusty:~/net-auto$
```

Git also has some symbolic names that you can use in commands like `git log` (and
others). We've already reviewed HEAD. If you wanted to use the commit just before
HEAD, you'd reference that symbolically as `HEAD~1`. If you wanted to refer to the

commit two places back from HEAD, you'd use HEAD~2; for three commits back, it's HEAD~3. (You can probably spot the pattern.) In this case, with this particular repository, this command produces the same results as the previous command we showed you:

```
vagrant@trusty:~/net-auto$ git log HEAD~1..HEAD
commit ed45c956da4b7e38b61b96ae050c4da77337f7ad
Author: John Smith <john.smith@networktocode.com>
Date:   Tue May 31 16:34:26 2016 +0000

        Adding .gitignore file
vagrant@trusty:~/net-auto$
```

When we expand our discussion of HEAD later in this chapter, you'll understand why we said "in this particular case, with this particular repository" that the two git log commands would produce the same output.

Drilling into information on specific commits

Another way to drill into the details of a particular commit would be to use the git cat-file command. Git, like so many other UNIX/Linux tools, treats everything as a file. Thus, commits can be treated as a file, and their "contents" shown on the screen. This is what the git cat-file command does. So, taking the abbreviated SHA from a particular commit, you can look at more details about that commit with a command like this:

```
vagrant@jessie:~/net-auto$ git cat-file -p 2a656c3
tree 9f955969460fe47cb3b22d44e497c7a76c7a8db2
parent 679c41c13ceb5b658b988fb0dbe45a3f34f61bb3
author John Smith <john.smith@networktocode.com> 1464706616 +0000
committer John Smith <john.smith@networktocode.com> 1464706616 +0000

Add configuration for sw5
vagrant@jessie:~$
```

(The -p option to git cat-file, by the way, just does some formatting of the output based on the type of file. The man page for git cat-file will provide more details on this and other switches.)

You'll note this output contains a couple pieces of information that the default git log output doesn't show: the parent commit SHA and the tree object SHA. You can use the parent commit SHA to see this commit's "parent" commit. Every commit has a parent commit that lets you follow the chain of commits all the way back to the initial one, which is the only commit in a repository without a parent. The tree object SHA captures the files that are in the repository at the time of a given commit; we used this earlier with the git ls-tree command, like this:

```
vagrant@jessie:~/net-auto$ git ls-tree 9f9559
100644 blob 2567e072ca607963292d73e3acd49a5388305c53     sw1.txt
```

```
100644 blob 02df3d404d59d72c98439f44df673c6038352a27    sw2.txt
100644 blob 02df3d404d59d72c98439f44df673c6038352a27    sw3.txt
100644 blob 02df3d404d59d72c98439f44df673c6038352a27    sw4.txt
100644 blob 88b23c7f60dc91f7d5bfeb094df9ed28996daeeb    sw5.txt
vagrant@jessie:~/net-auto$
```

Using the SHA checksums listed here, you could then use the `git cat-file` command to view the contents of one of these files at that particular time (as of that particular commit).

Let's see how that works. In the following set of commands, we'll first use `git log --oneline` to show the history of commits to a repository. Then we'll use `git cat-file` and `git ls-tree` with the appropriate seven-character SHA hashes to display the contents of a particular file at two different points in time (as of two different commits).

```
vagrant@trusty:~/net-auto$ git log --oneline
ed45c95 Adding .gitignore file
5cd13a8 Add Python script to talk to network switches
2a656c3 Add configuration for sw5
679c41c Update sw1, add sw4
9547063 First commit to new repository
vagrant@trusty:~/net-auto$ git cat-file -p 9547063
tree fdad0ff90745deb944a430e2151d085aebc68d00
author John Smith <john.smith@networktocode.com> 1463074642 +0000
committer John Smith <john.smith@networktocode.com> 1463074642 +0000

First commit to new repository
vagrant@trusty:~/net-auto$ git ls-tree fdad0f
100644 blob 02df3d404d59d72c98439f44df673c6038352a27    sw1.txt
100644 blob 02df3d404d59d72c98439f44df673c6038352a27    sw2.txt
100644 blob 02df3d404d59d72c98439f44df673c6038352a27    sw3.txt
vagrant@trusty:~/net-auto$ git cat-file -p 02df3d
interface ethernet0

interface ethernet1

interface ethernet2

interface ethernet3

vagrant@trusty:~/net-auto$
```

This shows us the contents of *sw1.txt* as of the initial commit. Now, let's repeat the same process for the second commit:

```
vagrant@trusty:~/net-auto$ git log --oneline
ed45c95 Adding .gitignore file
5cd13a8 Add Python script to talk to network switches
2a656c3 Add configuration for sw5
679c41c Update sw1, add sw4
9547063 First commit to new repository
```

```
vagrant@trusty:~/net-auto$ git cat-file -p 679c41c
tree a093d5f26677d345cb274ceb826e70bdb31ffd6f
parent 95470631aba32d6823c80fdd3c6f923824dde470
author John Smith <john.smith@networktocode.com> 1463085679 +0000
committer John Smith <john.smith@networktocode.com> 1463085679 +0000

Update sw1, add sw4
vagrant@trusty:~/net-auto$ git ls-tree a093d5
100644 blob 2567e072ca607963292d73e3acd49a5388305c53    sw1.txt
100644 blob 02df3d404d59d72c98439f44df673c6038352a27    sw2.txt
100644 blob 02df3d404d59d72c98439f44df673c6038352a27    sw3.txt
100644 blob 02df3d404d59d72c98439f44df673c6038352a27    sw4.txt
vagrant@trusty:~/net-auto$ git cat-file -p 2567e0
interface ethernet0
  duplex auto

interface ethernet1

interface ethernet2

interface ethernet3

vagrant@trusty:~/net-auto$
```

Ah, note that the contents of the *sw1.txt* file have changed! However, this is a bit laborious—wouldn't it be nice if there were an easier way to show the differences between two versions of a file within a repository? This is where the `git diff` command comes in handy.

Distilling Differences Between Versions of Files

We mentioned at the start of this chapter that one of the benefits of using version control for network automation artifacts (switch configurations, Python scripts, Jinja templates, etc.) is being able to see the differences between versions of files over time. In the previous section, we showed you a very manual method of doing so; now we're going to show you the easy way: the `git diff` command.

 Note that Git also supports integration with third-party diff tools, including graphical diff tools. In such cases, you would use `git difftool` instead of `git diff`.

Examining differences between commits

The `git diff` command shows the differences between versions of a file (the differences between a file at two different points in time). You just need to supply the two commits and the file to be compared. Here's an example. First, we list the history using `git log`, then we use `git diff` to compare two versions of a file.

```
[vagrant@centos net-auto]$ git log --oneline
ed45c95 Adding .gitignore file
5cd13a8 Add Python script to talk to network switches
2a656c3 Add configuration for sw5
679c41c Update sw1, add sw4
9547063 First commit to new repository
[vagrant@centos net-auto]$ git diff 9547063..679c41c sw1.txt
diff --git a/sw1.txt b/sw1.txt
index 02df3d4..2567e07 100644
--- a/sw1.txt
+++ b/sw1.txt
@@ -1,4 +1,5 @@
 interface ethernet0
+  duplex auto

 interface ethernet1

[vagrant@centos net-auto]$
```

The format in which `git diff` shows the differences between the files can be a bit
confusing at first. The key in deciphering the output lies in the lines just after the
`index...` line. There, `git diff` tells us that dashes will be used to represent file *a*
(`--- a/sw1.txt`), and pluses will be used to represent file *b* (`+++ b/sw1.txt`). Following that is the representation of the differences in the files—lines that exist in file *a* are
preceded by a dash, while lines that exist in file *b* are preceded by a plus. Lines that
are the same in both files are preceded by a space.

Thus, in this example, we can see that the later commit, represented by the hash
`679c41c`, the line `duplex auto` was added. Obviously, this is a very simple example,
but hopefully you can begin to see just how useful this is.

Omitting the Filename in Commands

If you omit the filename with the `git diff` command (for example, if you entered `git diff start SHA..end SHA`), then Git will
show a diff for *all* the files changed in that commit, rather than just
a specific file referenced on the command line. Adding the filename to the `git diff` command allows you to focus on the
changes a specific file.

Viewing other types of differences

Let's make some changes to the configuration file for *sw1.txt* so that the diff is a bit
more complex, and along the way we'll also show how you can use `git diff` in other
ways.

First, we'll make some changes to *sw1.txt* using the text editor of your choice. It
doesn't really matter what the changes are; we'll run `git status` to provide that

changes exist in the working directory. However, *before* you stage the changes, let's see if we can use git diff again.

```
vagrant@trusty:~/net-auto$ git status
On branch master
Changes not staged for commit:
  (use "git add <file>..." to update what will be committed)
  (use "git checkout -- <file>..." to discard changes in working directory)

    modified:   sw1.txt

no changes added to commit (use "git add" and/or "git commit -a")
vagrant@trusty:~/net-auto$ git diff
diff --git a/sw1.txt b/sw1.txt
index 2567e07..7005dc6 100644
--- a/sw1.txt
+++ b/sw1.txt
@@ -1,9 +1,11 @@
 interface ethernet0
-  duplex auto
+  switchport mode access vlan 101

 interface ethernet1
+  switchport mode trunk

 interface ethernet2
+  switchport mode access vlan 102

 interface ethernet3
-
+  switchport mode trunk
vagrant@trusty:~/net-auto$
```

Running git diff like this—without any parameters or options—shows you the differences between your working tree and the index. That is, it shows you the changes that have not yet been staged for the next commit.

Now, let's stage the changes in preparation for the next commit, then see if there's another way to use git diff:

```
vagrant@jessie:~/net-auto$ git add sw1.txt
vagrant@jessie:~/net-auto$ git status
On branch master
Changes to be committed:
  (use "git reset HEAD <file>..." to unstage)

    modified:   sw1.txt

vagrant@jessie:~/net-auto$ git diff
vagrant@jessie:~/net-auto$ git diff --cached
diff --git a/sw1.txt b/sw1.txt
index 2567e07..f3b5ad5 100644
```

```
--- a/sw1.txt
+++ b/sw1.txt
@@ -1,9 +1,11 @@
 interface ethernet0
- duplex auto
+ switchport mode access vlan 101

 interface ethernet1
+ switchport mode trunk

 interface ethernet2
+ switchport mode access vlan 102

 interface ethernet3
-
+ switchport mode trunk
vagrant@jessie:~/net-auto$
```

You can see that the first `git diff` command returned no results, which makes sense
—there are no changes that *aren't* staged for the next commit. However, when we add
the `--cached` parameter, it tells `git diff` to show the differences between the index
and HEAD. In other words, this form of `git diff` shows the differences between the
index and the last commit.

Once we finally commit this last set of changes, we can circle back around to our
original use of `git diff`, which allows us to see the changes between two arbitrary
commits.

```
[vagrant@centos net-auto]$ git commit -m "Defined VLANs on sw1"
[master 3588c31] Defined VLANs on sw1
 1 file changed, 4 insertions(+), 2 deletions(-)
[vagrant@centos net-auto]$ git status
On branch master
nothing to commit, working directory clean
[vagrant@centos net-auto]$ git log --oneline
3588c31 Defined VLANs on sw1
ed45c95 Adding .gitignore file
5cd13a8 Add Python script to talk to network switches
2a656c3 Add configuration for sw5
679c41c Update sw1, add sw4
9547063 First commit to new repository
[vagrant@centos net-auto]$ git diff 679c41c..3588c31 sw1.txt
diff --git a/sw1.txt b/sw1.txt
index 2567e07..f3b5ad5 100644
--- a/sw1.txt
+++ b/sw1.txt
@@ -1,9 +1,11 @@
 interface ethernet0
- duplex auto
+ switchport mode access vlan 101
```

```
    interface ethernet1
+    switchport mode trunk

    interface ethernet2
+    switchport mode access vlan 102

    interface ethernet3
-
+    switchport mode trunk
[vagrant@centos net-auto]$
```

Before we move on to our next topic—we'll discuss branches in Git next—let's take a moment to review what you've done so far:

- Staged changes (using `git add`) and committed them to the repository (using `git commit`)

- Modified the configuration of Git (using `git config`)

- Unstaged changes that weren't yet ready to be committed (using `git reset`)

- Excluded files from inclusion in the repository (using `.gitignore`)

- Reviewed the history of the repository (using `git log`)

- Compared different versions of files within the repository to see the changes in each version (using `git diff`)

In the next section, we'll expand our discussion of Git to cover what is, arguably, one of Git's most powerful features: branching.

Branching in Git

If you refer back to "Brief History of Git" on page 296, you'll see that one of the primary design goals for Git was strong support for nonlinear development. That's a fancy way of saying that Git needed to support multiple developers working on the same thing at the same time. So how is this accomplished? Git does it through the use of *branches*.

A *branch* in Git is a pointer to a commit. Now, that might not sound too powerful, so let's use some figures to help better explain the concept of a branch, and why nonlinear development in Git can be powerful.

First, recall from the section "Overview of Git's Architecture" on page 298 that Git uses a series of objects: blobs (representing the content of files in the repository), trees (representing the file and directory structure of the repository), and commits (representing a point-in-time snapshot of the repository, its structure, and its content). You can visualize this as shown in Figure 8-1.

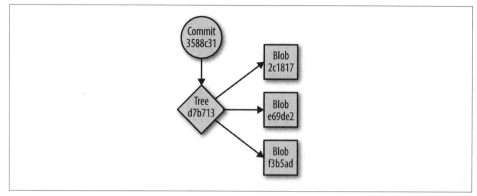

Figure 8-1. Objects in a Git repository

Each of these objects is identified by the SHA-1 hash of its contents. You've seen how commits are referenced via their SHA-1 hash, and you've seen how to use the `git ls-tree` or `git cat-file` commands to see the contents of tree and blob objects, respectively, by referencing their SHA-1 hash.

As you make changes and commit them to the repository, you create more commit objects (more snapshots), each of which points back at the previous commit (referred to as its "parent" commit; you saw this in the section "Viewing More Information About a Repository" on page 315). After a few commits, you can visualize it like Figure 8-2 (we've omitted the blobs to simplify the diagram).

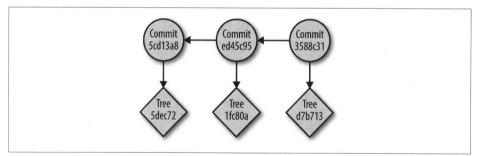

Figure 8-2. A chain of commits in a Git repository

Each commit points to a tree object, and each tree object points to blobs that represent the contents of the repository at the time of the commit. Using the reference to the tree object and the associated blobs, you can re-create the state of the repository at any given commit—hence why we refer to commits as point-in-time snapshots of the repository.

This is all well and good—and helps to explain Git's architecture a bit more fully—but what does it have to do with branching in Git? To answer that question (and we *will* answer it, we promise!), we need to revisit the concept of HEAD. In the section

"Unstaging Files" on page 308, we defined HEAD as a pointer that points to the latest commit, or to the commit we've checked out into the working directory. You visualize HEAD as something like Figure 8-3.

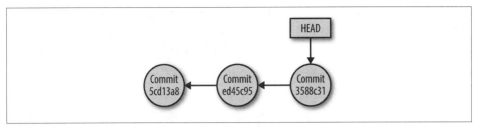

Figure 8-3. HEAD pointing to the latest commit

You can verify this using a procedure we outlined earlier in this chapter (this assumes you haven't checked out a different branch or different commit, something we'll discuss shortly):

1. From the repository's working directory, run **cat .git/refs/heads/master**. Note the value displayed.

2. Compare the value of the previous command to the value of the last commit from the output of `git log --oneline`. You should see the same value in both places, indicating that HEAD points to the latest commit.

By default, *every* Git repository starts out with a single branch, named *master*. As a branch is just a reference to a commit, this is illustrated graphically in Figure 8-4.

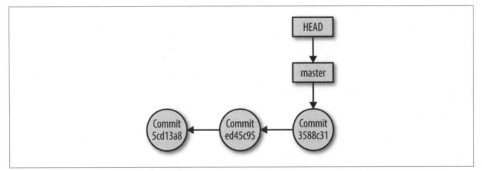

Figure 8-4. HEAD pointing to the latest commit in the master branch

You can see that the branch reference points to a commit, and that HEAD points to the branch reference.

However, you're not limited to only a single branch in a Git repository. In fact, because branches are so lightweight (a reference to a commit), you're strongly encouraged to use multiple branches. So, when you create a new branch—let's call this new branch *testing*, though the name doesn't really matter—the organization of the Git objects now looks something like Figure 8-5.

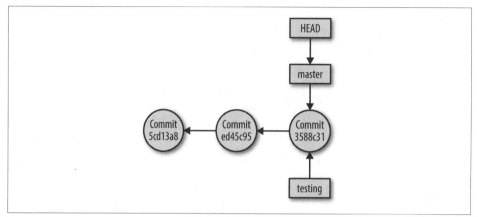

Figure 8-5. New branch created in a Git repository

So, you've created the new branch—we'll show you the commands to do that shortly —and the new branch now references a particular commit. However, HEAD hasn't moved. HEAD gets moved when you check out content into the repository, so in order to move HEAD to the new branch, you first have to *check out* the new branch. Similarly, if you wanted to work with the repository at an earlier point in time (at an earlier commit) you'd need to check out that particular commit. Once you check out a branch, HEAD now points to the new branch, as in Figure 8-6.

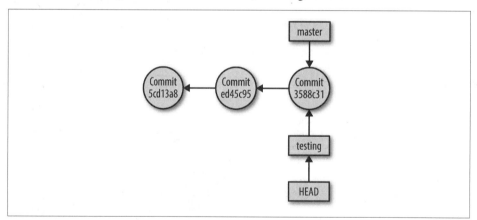

Figure 8-6. HEAD pointing to a checked-out branch

At this point, you can now start making changes and committing them to the repository. This is where branches start to really show their power: they *isolate new changes from the master branch*. Let's assume you've made some changes to the testing branch and have committed those changes to the repository. The graphical view of the objects and relationships inside the repository now looks like Figure 8-7.

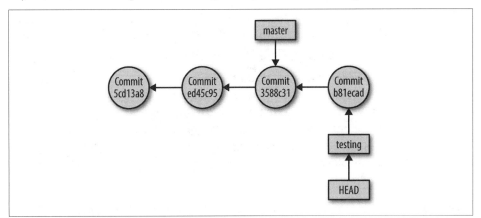

Figure 8-7. Adding a commit to a branch

You'll note that the testing branch—and HEAD—move forward to represent the latest commit, but the master branch remains *untouched*. At any point, you can check out the master branch and be right back where you were before you created the new branch and made the changes. This diagram shows an example of how multiple branches can evolve over time and allow for the development of hotfixes, new features, and new releases without affecting the master branch.

Figure 8-8 is a complicated example of branches, but it gives an idea of how branches *might* be used in a typical software development environment.

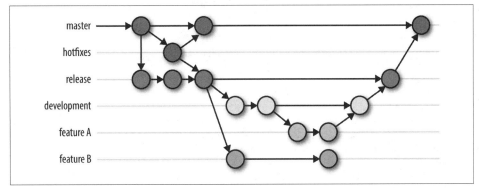

Figure 8-8. Multiple branches in a development cycle

Hopefully, the wheels in your head are turning and you're starting to think about the possibilities that branches create:

- You can create a new branch when you want to try something new or different, without affecting what's in the master branch. If it doesn't work out, no big deal— the content in the master branch remains untouched.

- Branches form the basis by which you can collaborate with other authors on the same repository. If you're working in branch A and your coworker is working in branch B, then you're assured that you won't affect each other's changes. (Now, you might have some issues when it comes time to bring the changes from the two branches together when you *merge*, but that's a different story—one we'll tackle later in this chapter in the section "Merging and Deleting Branches" on page 331.)

Let's turn our attention now to the practical side of working with Git branches, where we can see the theory we've been describing in practice.

Creating a Branch

To create a Git branch—which, again, is just a reference to a commit—you'll use the `git branch` command. So, to create the testing branch we discussed in the previous section, you'd simply run `git branch testing`. The command doesn't produce any output, but there *is* a way you can verify that it actually did something.

First, look in the *.git/refs/heads* directory, and you'll see a new entry there named after your newly created branch. If you run `cat` on that new file, you'll see that it points to the commit referenced by HEAD when you created the branch. Let's see that in action:

```
vagrant@trusty:~/net-auto$ git branch testing
vagrant@trusty:~/net-auto$ ls -la .git/refs/heads
total 16
drwxrwxr-x 2 vagrant vagrant 4096 Jun  4 19:16 .
drwxrwxr-x 4 vagrant vagrant 4096 May 12 14:52 ..
-rw-rw-r-- 1 vagrant vagrant   41 Jun  4 19:16 master
-rw-rw-r-- 1 vagrant vagrant   41 Jun  4 19:13 testing
vagrant@trusty:~/net-auto$ cat .git/refs/heads/testing
3588c31cbf958fe1a28d5e1f19ace669de99bb8c
vagrant@trusty:~/net-auto$ git log --oneline
3588c31 Defined VLANs on sw1
ed45c95 Adding .gitignore file
5cd13a8 Add Python script to talk to network switches
2a656c3 Add configuration for sw5
679c41c Update sw1, add sw4
9547063 First commit to new repository
vagrant@trusty:~/net-auto$
```

The presence of the *testing* file in *.git/refs/heads*, along with the content of the file referencing the latest commit as of the time of creation, shows that the branch has been created. You can also verify this by simply running `git branch`, which will output the list of branches. The active branch—the branch that is *checked out* for use in the working directory—will have an asterisk before it (and, if colors are enabled in your terminal, may be listed in a different color). This shows you that your testing branch has been created, but not checked out—the master branch is still active.

To switch the active branch, you must first check out the branch.

Checking Out a Branch

To *check out* a branch means to make it the active branch, and the branch that will be available in the working directory for you to edit/modify. To check out a branch, use the `git checkout` command, supplying the name of the branch you'd like to check out:

```
vagrant@jessie:~/net-auto$ git branch
* master
  testing
vagrant@jessie:~/net-auto$ git checkout testing
Switched to branch 'testing'
vagrant@jessie:~/net-auto$
```

> You can create a branch and check it out at the same time using `git checkout -b <branch name>`.

Let's make a simple change to the repository—say, let's add a file—then switch back to the "master" branch to see how Git handles this. First, we'll stage *sw6.txt* to the repository and commit it to the testing branch:

```
[vagrant@centos net-auto]$ git add sw6.txt
[vagrant@centos net-auto]$ git commit -m "Add sw6 configuration"
[testing b45a2b1] Add sw6 configuration
 1 file changed, 12 insertions(+)
 create mode 100644 sw6.txt
[vagrant@centos net-auto]$
```

Note that the response from Git when you commit the change includes the branch name and the SHA hash of the commit (`[testing b45a2b1]`). A quick `git log --oneline` will verify that the latest commit has the same hash as reported by the `git commit` command. Likewise, a quick `cat .git/HEAD` will show that you're on the testing branch (because it points to *.git/refs/heads/testing*), and `cat .git/refs/heads/`

`testing` will also show the latest commit SHA hash. This shows that HEAD points to the latest commit in the checked-out branch.

Viewing Git Branch Information in the Prompt

When you're working with multiple branches in a Git repository, it can sometimes be challenging to know *which* branch is currently active (checked out). To help address this, most distributions of Git since version 1.8 have included support to allow bash—the shell most Linux distributions use by default—to display the currently active Git branch in the bash prompt. On Ubuntu 14.04 and Debian 8.x, this file is named *git-sh-prompt* and is found in the */usr/lib/git-core* directory. On CentOS 7 (and presumably on RHEL 7), the file is named *git-prompt.sh* and is found in the */usr/share/git-core/contrib/completion* directory. On macOS, the file is installed as part of the XCode command-line tools, is named *git-prompt.sh*, and is found in the */Library/Developer/CommandLineTools/usr/share/git-core* directory. The instructions for using this functionality are found at the top of the appropriate file for your OS.

Now, let's switch back to the master branch and see what the working directory looks like:

```
vagrant@trusty:~/net-auto$ git checkout master
Switched to branch 'master'
vagrant@trusty:~/net-auto$ ls -la
total 40
drwxrwxr-x 3 vagrant vagrant 4096 Jun  7 16:49 .
drwxr-xr-x 5 vagrant vagrant 4096 May 12 17:18 ..
drwxrwxr-x 8 vagrant vagrant 4096 Jun  7 16:49 .git
-rw-rw-r-- 1 vagrant vagrant    8 May 31 16:27 .gitignore
-rw-rw-r-- 1 vagrant vagrant   15 May 31 16:32 pw.txt
-rwxrwxr-x 1 vagrant vagrant    0 Jun  7 16:34 script.py
-rw-rw-r-- 1 vagrant vagrant  200 Jun  3 20:47 sw1.txt
-rw-rw-r-- 1 vagrant vagrant   84 May 12 17:17 sw2.txt
-rw-rw-r-- 1 vagrant vagrant   84 May 12 17:17 sw3.txt
-rw-rw-r-- 1 vagrant vagrant   84 May 12 20:33 sw4.txt
-rw-rw-r-- 1 vagrant vagrant  135 May 31 14:56 sw5.txt
vagrant@trusty:~/net-auto$
```

Wait—the *sw6.txt* file is *gone!* What happened? Not to worry, you haven't lost anything. Recall that checking out a branch makes it the active branch, and therefore the branch that will be present in the working directory for you to modify. The *sw6.txt* file isn't in the master branch, it's in the testing branch, so when you switched to master using `git checkout master`, that file was removed from the working directory. Recall also that the working directory *isn't* the same as the repository—even though the file has been removed from the working directory, it's *still* in the repository, as you can easily verify:

```
vagrant@jessie:~/net-auto$ git checkout testing
Switched to branch 'testing'
vagrant@jessie:~/net-auto$ ls -la
total 44
drwxrwxr-x 3 vagrant vagrant 4096 Jun  7 16:53 .
drwxr-xr-x 5 vagrant vagrant 4096 May 12 17:18 ..
drwxrwxr-x 8 vagrant vagrant 4096 Jun  7 16:53 .git
-rw-rw-r-- 1 vagrant vagrant    8 May 31 16:27 .gitignore
-rw-rw-r-- 1 vagrant vagrant   15 May 31 16:32 pw.txt
-rwxrwxr-x 1 vagrant vagrant    0 Jun  7 16:34 script.py
-rw-rw-r-- 1 vagrant vagrant  200 Jun  3 20:47 sw1.txt
-rw-rw-r-- 1 vagrant vagrant   84 May 12 17:17 sw2.txt
-rw-rw-r-- 1 vagrant vagrant   84 May 12 17:17 sw3.txt
-rw-rw-r-- 1 vagrant vagrant   84 May 12 20:33 sw4.txt
-rw-rw-r-- 1 vagrant vagrant  135 May 31 14:56 sw5.txt
-rw-rw-r-- 1 vagrant vagrant  221 Jun  7 16:53 sw6.txt
vagrant@jessie:~/net-auto$
```

This illustrates how branches help isolate changes from the master branch, a key benefit of using branches. Using a branch, you can make some changes, test those changes, and then discard them if necessary—all while knowing that your master branch remains safe and untouched.

However, what if the changes you made in a branch were changes you wanted to keep? Perhaps you tried out a new Jinja template, it worked perfectly in your testing, and now you'd like to make that a permanent part of your repository? This is where *merging* branches comes into play.

Merging and Deleting Branches

Before we get into merging branches, let's revisit the contents of a commit object in Git. In our example repository, we'll examine the contents of the latest commit object for the testing branch:

```
vagrant@jessie:~/net-auto$ git checkout testing
Switched to branch 'testing'
vagrant@jessie:~/net-auto$ git cat-file -p b45a2b1
tree f6b5dfbfdbf6bc29f04300c9a82c6936397d9b27
parent 3588c31cbf958fe1a28d5e1f19ace669de99bb8c
author John Smith <john.smith@networktocode.com> 1465317796 +0000
committer John Smith <john.smith@networktocode.com> 1465317796 +0000

Add sw6 configuration
vagrant@jessie:~/net-auto$
```

What does this tell us?

1. This particular commit references the tree object with the hash f6b5df.

2. The author and committer of this commit is John Smith.

3. The commit message indicates that this commit captures the addition of the configuration for sw6.

4. Finally, note that this commit has a parent commit with a hash of 3588c31.

We've mentioned before that every commit (except the very first commit) has a pointer to a parent commit. This is illustrated in Figures 8-2 through 8-7, where the commit objects point "backward in time" to the previous commit.

When we merge branches, Git is going to create a new commit object—called a *merge commit* object—that will actually have *two* parents. Each of these parents represents the two branches that were brought together as part of the merge process. In so doing, Git maintains the link back to previous commits so that you can always "roll back" to previous versions.

At a high level, the merge process looks like this:

1. Switch to the branch into which the other branch should be merged. If you're merging back into master, check out (switch to) master.

2. Run the `git merge` command, specifying the name of the branch to be merged into master.

3. Supply a message (a commit message for the merge commit) describing the changes being merged.

Reviewing fast-forward merges

Let's see this in action. Let's take the testing branch, which has a new switch configuration (*sw6.txt*) that isn't present in the master branch, and merge it back into master.

First, let's ensure you are on the master branch:

```
[vagrant@centos net-auto]$ git branch
  master
* testing
[vagrant@centos net-auto]$ git checkout master
Switched to branch 'master'
[vagrant@centos net-auto]$
```

Next, let's actually merge the testing branch into the master branch:

```
[vagrant@centos net-auto]$ git merge testing
Updating 3588c31..b45a2b1
Fast-forward
 sw6.txt | 12 ++++++++++++
 1 file changed, 12 insertions(+)
 create mode 100644 sw6.txt
[vagrant@centos net-auto]$
```

Note the "Fast-forward" in the response from Git; this indicates that it was possible to merge the branches by simply replaying the same set of changes to the master branch as was performed on the branch being merged. In situations like this—a simple merge—you won't see an additional merge commit:

```
vagrant@trusty:~/net-auto$ git log --oneline
b45a2b1 Add sw6 configuration
3588c31 Defined VLANs on sw1
ed45c95 Adding .gitignore file
5cd13a8 Add Python script to talk to network switches
2a656c3 Add configuration for sw5
679c41c Update sw1, add sw4
9547063 First commit to new repository
vagrant@trusty:~/net-auto$ ls -la sw6.txt
-rw-rw-r-- 1 vagrant vagrant 221 Jun  7 20:53 sw6.txt
vagrant@trusty:~/net-auto$
```

Deleting a branch

Once a branch (and its changes) have been merged, you can delete the branch using **git branch -d *branch-name***. Note that you generally don't want to delete a branch before it's been merged; otherwise, you'll lose the changes stored in that branch (Git will prompt you if you try to delete a branch that hasn't been merged). Once a branch has been merged, though, its changes are safely stored in another branch (typically the master branch, but not always), and it's therefore now safe to delete.

Reviewing merges with a merge commit

Now, let's look at a more complex example. First, let's create a new branch to store some changes we'll make relative to the configuration for sw4. To do that, we'll simply run `git checkout -b sw4`. This creates the new branch *and* checks it out so it's the active branch. Once you've made some changes to *sw4.txt*, use `git add` and `git commit` to stage and commit the changes.

Next, let's switch back to master (using `git checkout master`) and make some changes to a *different* switch configuration. Stage and commit the changes to the master branch. Now what happens when we try to merge the sw4 branch into master?

Before we answer that question, let's explore the commit objects a bit. Here are the contents of the last commit object in the sw4 branch:

```
vagrant@jessie:~/net-auto$ git checkout sw4
Switched to branch 'sw4'
vagrant@jessie:~/net-auto$ git log --oneline HEAD~2..HEAD
40e88b8 Add port descriptions for sw4
b45a2b1 Add sw6 configuration
vagrant@jessie:~/net-auto$ git cat-file -p 40e8b8
tree 845b53f6715d73c36d90b3fe3224bfb494853ba5
parent b45a2b162334376f2100974687742de1a23c2594
```

```
author John Smith <john.smith@networktocode.com> 1465333657 +0000
committer John Smith <john.smith@networktocode.com> 1465333657 +0000

Add port descriptions for sw4
vagrant@jessie:~/net-auto$
```

The `git log --oneline HEAD~2..HEAD` command just shows the last two commits leading up to HEAD (which points to the last commit on the active branch). As you can see, this commit object points to a parent commit of b45a2b1.

Here's the last commit on the master branch:

```
vagrant@jessie:~/net-auto$ git checkout master
Switched to branch 'master'
vagrant@jessie:~/net-auto$ git log --oneline HEAD~2..HEAD
183b8fe Fix sw3 configuration for hypervisor
b45a2b1 Add sw6 configuration
vagrant@jessie:~/net-auto$ git cat-file -p 183b8fe
tree 42a59b4058f927ef5af049e581480cd5530bd3b1
parent b45a2b162334376f2100974687742de1a23c2594
author John Smith <john.smith@networktocode.com> 1465333836 +0000
committer John Smith <john.smith@networktocode.com> 1465333836 +0000

Fix sw3 configuration for hypervisor
vagrant@jessie:~/net-auto$
```

This commit, the latest in the master branch, *also* points to the same parent commit —showing that the two branches diverge.

Now let's run the merge:

```
vagrant@jessie:~/net-auto$ git branch
* master
  sw4
vagrant@jessie:~/net-auto$ git merge sw4
(default Git editor opens to allow user to provide commit message)
Merge made by the 'recursive' strategy.
 sw4.txt | 4 ++++
 1 file changed, 4 insertions(+)
vagrant@jessie:~/net-auto$ git log --oneline HEAD~3..HEAD
81f5963 Merge branch 'sw4'
183b8fe Fix sw3 configuration for hypervisor
40e88b8 Add port descriptions for sw4
b45a2b1 Add sw6 configuration
vagrant@jessie:~/net-auto$
```

In this instance, changes on *both* branches needed to be reconciled when merging the branches. It wasn't possible to just "replay" the changes from the sw4 branch to master, because master had some changes of its own. Thus, Git creates a *merge commit*. Let's look at that file real quick:

```
[vagrant@centos net-auto]$ git cat-file -p 81f5963
tree e71cfa26549241b609fa39e69dc51fdafd1d7cb4
```

```
parent 183b8fe2d02bbd6b2b7a19ecc39dc9e792fe2e75
parent 40e88b88271b535cceb311bb904d6afac20c15c3
author John Smith <john.smith@networktocode.com> 1465334492 +0000
committer John Smith <john.smith@networktocode.com> 1465334492 +0000

Merge branch 'sw4'
[vagrant@centos net-auto]$
```

Note the presence of *two* parent commits, which—if you look—represent the commits we made to each branch before merging the sw4 branch into master. This is how Git knows that the branches have converged, and how Git maintains the relationship between commits over time.

Now that the commits in the sw4 branch have been merged into the master branch, you can just delete the branch using git branch -d sw4:

```
[vagrant@centos net-auto]$ git branch -d sw4
Deleted branch sw4 (was 40e88b8).
[vagrant@centos net-auto]$ git branch
* master
[vagrant@centos net-auto]$
```

Deleting an Unmerged Branch

Note that it's possible to delete an unmerged branch using git branch -D *branch*. However, in such situations, you will *lose* the changes in that branch, so tread carefully.

So, to recap:

- To create a branch, use git branch *new branch name*.
- To check out a branch, use git checkout *branch*.
- To create a new branch and check it out in one step, use git checkout -b *new branch name*.
- To merge a branch into master, run git merge *branch* while the master branch is checked out.
- To delete a branch after its changes have been merged, use git branch -d *branch name*.

Let's now turn our attention to using Git's distributed nature to collaborate with others via Git.

Collaborating with Git

As we discussed in the section "Brief History of Git" on page 296, one of the key design goals for Git was that it was a fully distributed system. Thus, every developer needed to be able to work from a full copy of the source code stored in the repository as well as the repository's full history. When you combine this fully distributed nature with Git's other key design goals—speed, simplicity, scalability, and strong support for non-linear development via lightweight branches—you can see why Git has become a leading option for users needing a collaborative version control system.

On its own, Git can act as a "server" and provides mechanisms for communications between systems running Git. Git supports a variety of transport protocols, including Secure Shell (SSH), HTTPS, and Git's own protocol (using TCP port 9418). If you're simply using Git on a couple of different systems and need to keep repositories in sync, you can do this with no additional software.

Further, Git's distributed nature has enabled a number of online services based on Git to appear. Many Git users take advantage of online Git-based services such as GitHub (*https://github.com/*) or BitBucket (*https://bitbucket.org/*). There's also a wide variety of open source projects to facilitate collaboration via Git, such as GitLab (*https:// about.gitlab.com/*), Gitblit (*http://gitblit.com/index.html*), or Djacket (*http:// djacket.github.io/*) (which, somewhat ironically, is hosted on GitHub). As you can see, there's no shortage of ways by which you can collaborate with others using Git and Git-based tools.

In this section, we'll explore how to collaborate using Git. That collaboration might be as simple as keeping repositories in sync on multiple systems, but we'll also cover using public Git-based services (focusing on GitHub). Along the way, you'll learn about cloning repositories; Git remotes; pushing, fetching, and pulling changes from other repositories; and using branches when collaborating.

Let's start with exploring a simple scenario involving multiple systems running Git, where you need to share/sync one or more repositories between these systems.

Collaborating Between Multiple Systems Running Git

So far in this chapter, you've been building your collection of network configurations, scripts, and templates in a Git repository on a single system. What happens when you need or want to be able to access this repository from a separate system? Maybe you have a desktop system at work and a laptop that you use for travel and at home. How do you use your network automation repository from both systems? Fortunately, because of Git's fully distributed design, this is pretty straightforward.

Can it be as simple as copying files? Let's see what happens when we simply copy a repository and its working directory to a new location on the same system. First, we'll run `git log --oneline HEAD~2..HEAD` in the existing repository:

```
vagrant@trusty:~/net-auto$ git log --oneline HEAD~2..HEAD
81f5963 Merge branch 'sw4'
183b8fe Fix sw3 configuration for hypervisor
40e88b8 Add port descriptions for sw4
vagrant@trusty:~/net-auto$
```

Now, let's copy the repository and working directory to a new location on the same system, run the same `git log` command, and see what we get:

```
vagrant@trusty:~$ cp -ar net-auto netauto2
vagrant@trusty:~$ cd netauto2
vagrant@trusty:~/netauto2$ git log --oneline HEAD~2..HEAD
81f5963 Merge branch 'sw4'
183b8fe Fix sw3 configuration for hypervisor
40e88b8 Add port descriptions for sw4
vagrant@trusty:~/netauto2$
```

Looks like the contents are identical! If you were to continue to explore the contents of the repository at *~/netauto2* using `git ls-tree`, `git cat-file`, or other commands, you'd find that the two repositories are, in fact, identical. Why is this? Recall that Git uses SHA1 hashes to identify all content: blobs, tree objects, and commit objects. A key property of the SHA1 hashes is that *identical content produces identical hashes*. Recall also that we stated that the contents of the Git repository are immutable (once created, they can't be modified). The combination of these attributes and Git's architecture means that it's possible to copy a repository using simple tools like `cp` and end up with an intact version of the repository. It's this ability to copy repositories—with all data and metadata intact—that is a key factor in Git's fully distributed nature.

Note there's no link between the copies, so changes made in one copy *won't* be automatically reflected in the other copy, or vice versa. (You can verify this, if you'd like, by making a commit in either copy, then using `git log` in both repositories.) In order to create a link between the copies, we have to explore something known as a *remote*.

Linking repositories with remotes

A Git *remote* is really nothing more than a reference to another repository. Git uses lightweight references pretty extensively—you've seen this already in the use of branches and HEAD—and in this case remotes are very similar. A remote is a lightweight reference to another repository, specified by a location.

Let's add a remote to the *netauto2* repository that refers back to the original repository in *net-auto*. To do this, we'll use the `git remote` command:

```
vagrant@jessie:~/netauto2$ git remote
vagrant@jessie:~/netauto2$ git remote add first ~/net-auto
vagrant@jessie:~/netauto2$ git remote
first
vagrant@jessie:~/netauto2$
```

When you use `git remote` with no parameters, it simply lists any existing remotes. In this case, there are none (yet). So you next run the `git remote add` command, which takes two parameters:

- The name to use for the remote repository. This name is purely symbolic—it can be whatever makes sense to you. In this case, we used `first` as the name for the remote.

- The location of the remote repository. In this case, the remote repository is on the same system (for now), so the location is simply a filesystem path.

Finally, running `git remote` again shows that the new remote has been added.

With the remote in place, you now have an asymmetric link between the two remotes. That is, *netauto2* has a reference to *net-auto*, but the reverse is *not* true. Via this asymmetric link, we can exchange information between Git repositories. Let's see how this works.

First, let's list the branches available in our *netauto2* repository. We'll add the `-a` parameter here, which we'll explain in more detail shortly:

```
vagrant@trusty:~/netauto2$ git branch -a
* master
vagrant@trusty:~/netauto2$
```

Now, let's fetch—and we're using the term *fetch* here intentionally, for reasons that will be evident later in this section—information from the remote repository, which you configured earlier. We'll update the information using the `git remote update` command, then run `git branch -a` again:

```
vagrant@trusty:~/netauto2$ git remote update first
Fetching first
From /home/vagrant/net-auto
 * [new branch]      master       -> first/master
vagrant@trusty:~/netauto2$ git branch -a
* master
  remotes/first/master
vagrant@trusty:~/netauto2$
```

Note there's now a new branch listed here. This is a special kind of branch known as a *remote tracking branch*. You won't make changes or commits to this branch, as it is only a reference to the branch that exists in the remote repository. You'll notice the `first` in the name of the branch; this refers back to the symbolic name you gave the

Git remote when you added it. We had to use the -a parameter to git branch in order to show remote tracking branches, which aren't listed by default.

 Instead of the two-step git remote add followed by git remote update, you can fetch information from a remote repository when you add the remote using the syntax **git remote add -f *name* *location***.

So what does this new remote tracking branch allow us to do? It allows us to *transfer* information between repositories in order to keep two repositories up-to-date. We'll show you how this works in the next section.

Fetching and merging information from remote repositories

Once a remote has been configured for a repository, information has been retrieved from the configured remote, and remote tracking branches have been created, it's possible to start to transfer information between remotes using various git commands. You could use these commands to keep branches of repositories or entire repositories in sync.

To see this in action, we'll want to change one of the two repositories on your system (the *net-auto* repository) and see how to get that information into the *netauto2* repository.

First, in the *net-auto* repository, let's make a change to the *sw2.txt* configuration file and commit that change to the repository. (We won't go through all the steps here, as we've covered that previously. Need a hint? Edit the file, use git add, then git commit.)

Verify that you can see the new commit in the *net-auto* directory using git log --oneline HEAD~1..HEAD, then switch to the *netauto2* repository and run the same git log command. The commit(s) listed will be different.

To get the updated information from *net-auto* over to *netauto2*, you have a few options:

- You can run **git remote update *name***, which updates *only* the specified remote.

- You can run **git remote update** (without a remote's name), which updates *all* remotes for this repository.

- You can run **git fetch *name***, which will update (or *fetch*) information from the specified remote repository. In this respect, git fetch is a lot like git remote update, although the syntax is slightly different (again we refer you to the man pages or the help screens for specific details). Note that git fetch is considered the "conventional" way of retrieving information from a remote, as opposed to using git remote update as we did earlier.

So, let's run git fetch first, which will pull information from the repository named *first*. You'll see output that looks something like this (the SHA hashes will differ, of course):

```
remote: Counting objects: 5, done.
remote: Compressing objects: 100% (3/3), done.
remote: Total 3 (delta 1), reused 0 (delta 0)
Unpacking objects: 100% (3/3), done.
From /home/vagrant/net-auto
   81f5963..7c2a3e6  master     -> first/master
```

OK, so we've retrieved information from *first/master* (the master branch of the remote named *first*). Why, then, does git log in netauto2 not show this? This is because you've only *fetched* (updated) the information from the remote repository; you haven't actually made it part of the current repository.

We caution you against using the word "pull" when referring to simply retrieving information from a remote repository. In Git, the idea of "pulling" from a remote repository has a very specific meaning and its own command (both of which we'll discuss shortly). Try to train yourself to use "fetching" or "retrieving" when referring to the act of getting information from a remote repository.

So if you've only fetched the changes across but not made them a part of the current repository, how do you do that? That is, how do you make them part of the current repository? The changes in the remote repository are stored in a branch, which means they are kept separate from the default master branch of the current repository. How do we get changes from one branch to another branch? That's right—you *merge* the changes:

```
vagrant@jessie:~/netauto2$ git checkout master
Already on 'master'
vagrant@jessie:~/netauto2$ git merge first/master
Updating 81f5963..7c2a3e6
Fast-forward
 sw2.txt | 7 +++++++
 1 file changed, 7 insertions(+)
vagrant@jessie:~/netauto2$
```

As you can see from Git's output, it has taken the changes applied to *first/master* (the master branch of the remote repository named *first*) and merged them—via a fast-forward—into the master branch of the current repository. Because this is a fast-forward, there will not be a merge commit, and now both repositories are in sync.

If you noted that the use of `git fetch` and `git merge` on the master branch of two repositories doesn't necessarily keep the repositories in sync, then you are *really* paying attention! In fact, only the master branches of the two repositories are in sync. To keep the entire repositories in sync, you'd need to perform this operation on all branches.

Pulling information from remote repositories

Why the two-step process of first `git fetch` and then `git merge`? The primary reason is you might want to be able to review the changes from the remote repository *before* you merge them, in the event that you aren't ready for those changes to be applied to the current repository.

As with so many things in Git, though, there is a shortcut. If you'd like to fetch changes and merge them in a single operation, you can use **git pull *name***, where *name* is the name of the remote from which you'd like to get and merge changes into the current branch. The `git pull` command is simply combining the `git fetch` and `git merge` operations.

So you've seen how to get changes from *net-auto* to *netauto2*, but what about the reverse? We mentioned that adding a remote to *netauto2* is an asymmetric relationship in that *netauto2* now knows about *net-auto*, but the reverse is not true. In a situation such as we've described here—where you, as a single user, want to keep repositories in sync on separate systems—the best approach would be to add a remote from *net-auto* to *netauto2*, and then use `git fetch` and `git merge` to move changes in either direction. Graphically, this would look something like Figure 8-9.

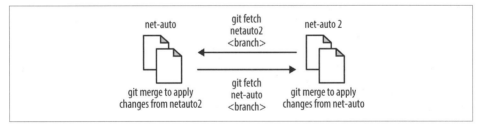

Figure 8-9. Using git fetch and git merge between repositories

 Git almost always offers multiple ways to do something, which can be both useful (in that it is very flexible) and frustrating (in that there's no "one way" to do something). Two-way transfer of information between Git repositories as we've described in this section is one of these areas where there's more than one way to get the job done. For new users of Git, this is probably the easiest way to handle it.

We started this section asking the question, "How do I use my network automation repository from multiple systems?" We've shown you how to make a copy of a repository, how to use Git remotes to link repositories, and how to use various Git commands to transfer data between repositories. In the next two sections, we're going to show you a simpler, easier way of copying and linking repositories, and we'll extend our working model across multiple systems, respectively.

Cloning repositories

In the previous sections, we showed you that you could simply copy a repository from one location to another and then use `git remote` to create a remote that would allow you to transfer information between repositories.

This process isn't difficult, but what if there were an even easier way? There is, and it's called *cloning* a repository via the `git clone` command. Let's see how this works.

The general syntax of this command is **git clone *repository directory***.

In this command, *repository* is the location of the repository you're cloning, and *directory* is the (optional) directory where you'd like to place the cloned repository. If you omit *directory*, then Git will place the cloned repository into a directory with the same name as the repository. Adding the *directory* parameter to the `git clone` command gives you some flexibility in where you'd like to place the cloned repository.

To illustrate how `git clone` works, let's kill the *netauto2* repository. It shouldn't have any changes in it, but if it does then you should know how to get those changes back into the original *net-auto* repository. (Need a hint? Add a remote, fetch changes, and merge the changes.)

```
vagrant@trusty:~$ rm -rf netauto2
vagrant@trusty:~$ git clone ~/net-auto na-clone
Cloning into 'na-clone'...
done.
vagrant@trusty:~$ cd na-clone
vagrant@trusty:~/na-clone$ git log --oneline HEAD~2..HEAD
7c2a3e6 Update sw2 configuration
81f5963 Merge branch 'sw4'
40e88b8 Add port descriptions for sw4
vagrant@trusty:~/na-clone$
```

As you can see, `git clone` makes a copy of the repository, just like we did manually in the previous section. There's more, though—now run `git remote` in this new cloned repository:

```
vagrant@trusty:~/na-clone$ git remote -v
origin
vagrant@trusty:~/na-clone$
```

Here's the advantage of using `git clone` over the manual steps we showed you earlier —it *automatically* creates a remote pointing back to the original repository from which this repository was cloned. Further, it *automatically* creates remote tracking branches for you (you can verify this using `git branch -a` or `git branch -r`). Because it handles these extra steps for you, `git clone` should be your preferred mechanism for cloning a repository.

Before we move on, let's talk a bit about the "origin" branch that was automatically created by `git clone`. While the name of a remote is strictly symbolic, origin does have some special significance for Git. You can think of it as a default remote name. In cases where you have multiple remotes (yes, this is definitely possible!) and you run a `git fetch` without specifying a remote, Git will default to origin. Aside from this behavior, though, there are no special attributes given to the remote named origin.

As an example of using multiple remotes, this book itself was written using Git and multiple Git remotes. One Git remote was GitHub; the other was O'Reilly's repository. Here's the output of `git remote -v` from one author's repository:

```
oreilly    git@git.atlas.oreilly.com:oreillymedia/network-automation.git (fetch)
oreilly    git@git.atlas.oreilly.com:oreillymedia/network-automation.git (push)
origin     https://github.com/jedelman8/network-automation-book.git (fetch)
origin     https://github.com/jedelman8/network-automation-book.git (fetch)
```

Now we're finally ready to tackle the last step, which is taking everything we've learned so far and applying it to extend our Git working model with repositories across multiple systems.

Extending our working model across multiple systems

When we discussed the idea of creating a Git remote (see the section "Linking repositories with remotes" on page 337), we said that a remote had two attributes: the name (symbolic in nature) and the location. So far you've only seen remotes on the same system, but Git natively supports remotes on *different* systems across a variety of protocols.

For example, a remote on the same system uses a location like this:

```
/path/to/git/repository
file:///path/to/git/repository
```

However, a remote could also use various network protocols to reach a repository on a separate system:

```
git://host.domain.com/path/to/git/repository
ssh://[user@]host.domain.com/path/to/git/repository
http://host.domain.com/path/to/git/repository
https://host.domain.com/path/to/git/repository
```

The `git://` syntax references Git's native protocol, which is unauthenticated and therefore used for anonymous access (generally read-only access). The `ssh://` syntax refers to Secure Shell; this is actually Git's protocol tunneled over SSH for authenticated access. Finally, you have HTTP and HTTPS variants as well.

This means that you could take the working model we've described throughout this section and *easily* extend it to multiple systems using whatever network protocol best suits your needs. In this section, we're going to focus on the use of SSH, and later in this chapter we'll show you some examples of using HTTPS with public Git hosting services.

Going back to our example, let's say you need to be able to work on your network automation repository from both your desktop system and a laptop that you take with you. Let's assume that both systems support SSH (i.e., they are running Linux, macOS, or some other UNIX variant). The first step would be to configure password-less authentication for SSH, generally using SSH keys. This will allow the various `git` commands to work without prompting for a password. Configuring SSH falls outside the scope of this book, but it's very well documented online.

The next step is then to create the necessary Git remotes. The repository already exists on your desktop (for the purposes of this example, we'll use our Ubuntu "Trusty Tahr" system to represent your desktop), but it doesn't exist on your laptop (which we'll represent with our Debian "Jessie" system). So, the first thing to do would be to clone the repository over to the laptop:

```
vagrant@jessie:~$ git clone ssh://trusty.domain.com/~/net-auto net-auto
Cloning into 'net-auto'...
remote: Counting objects: 32, done.
remote: Compressing objects: 100% (30/30), done.
remote: Total 32 (delta 12), reused 0 (delta 0)
Receiving objects: 100% (32/32), 2.99 KiB | 0 bytes/s, done.
Resolving deltas: 100% (12/12), done.
Checking connectivity... done.
vagrant@jessie:~$
```

This copies the repository from your desktop (*trusty.domain.com*) to your laptop (placing it in the directory specified; in this case, *net-auto*), creates a Git remote named origin pointing back to the original, and creates remote tracking branches. You can verify all this by using `git remote` to see the remote, and `git branch -r` to see remote tracking branches.

If you'd prefer to have a remote name that more clearly identifies where the remote is found, you can rename the remote from the default name, origin. Let's rename the remote to reflect that it's coming from our Ubuntu-based desktop:

```
vagrant@jessie:~/net-auto$ git remote
origin
vagrant@jessie:~/net-auto$ git remote rename origin trusty
```

```
vagrant@jessie:~/net-auto$ git remote
trusty
vagrant@jessie:~/net-auto$
```

Now, back on the Ubuntu system, we need to create a remote to the repository on the Debian laptop. The repository already exists here, so we can't use `git clone`; instead, we'll need to add the remote manually, and then fetch information from the remote to create the remote tracking branches:

```
vagrant@trusty:~/net-auto$ git remote add jessie ssh://jessie.domain.com/~/net-auto
vagrant@trusty:~/net-auto$ git remote
jessie
vagrant@trusty:~$ git fetch jessie
From ssh://jessie.domain.com/~/net-auto
 * [new branch]      master      -> jessie/master
vagrant@trusty:~/net-auto$ git branch -r
  jessie/master
vagrant@trusty:~/net-auto$
```

Great—now you have the repository on both systems, a remote on each system pointing back to the other, and remote tracking branches created on each side. From here, the workflow is exactly like we described in earlier sections:

1. Make changes on either system (not both at the same time!) and commit those changes to the repository. Ideally, you should work *exclusively* in branches other than the master branch.

2. When you get back to the other system, run a `git fetch` and `git merge` to fetch and merge changes from remote branches into local branches. (If you don't care to review the changes before merging, you can use `git pull`.) Be sure to do this *before* you get started working!

3. Repeat as needed to keep branches on both systems up-to-date with each other.

This approach works fairly well for a single developer on two systems, but what about more than one developer? While it's possible to build a "full mesh" of Git remotes and remote tracking branches, this can quickly become very unwieldy. Using a shared repository in cases like this greatly simplifies how things work, as you'll see in the next section.

Using a shared repository

If you've been poking around Git remotes with the `git remote` command, you may have discovered the `-v` switch, which enables more verbose output. For example, running `git remote -v` from one of the two systems configured in the previous section shows this:

```
trusty  ssh://trusty.domain.com/~/net-auto (fetch)
trusty  ssh://trusty.domain.com/~/net-auto (push)
```

This is useful, as it shows the full location of the remote repository. We've discussed the use of `git fetch` to retrieve information from the remote repository, but what's this idea of push?

So far we've only discussed the idea of retrieving information from a remote repository to your local repository through the use of commands like `git remote update`, `git fetch`, and `git pull`. It is possible, though, to send (Git uses the term *push*) changes to a remote repository from your local repository. However, in such cases, it is strongly recommended that the remote repository should be a *bare repository*.

What is a *bare repository*? Put simply, a bare repository is a Git repository without a working directory. (Recall that the term *working directory* has a very'specific definition in Git, and shouldn't be taken to mean the same as the current directory.) All the discussions of Git repositories so far have assumed the presence of a working directory, because someone—a user like you—was going to be working on the repository. You, as the user of the repository, had to have some way of interacting with the content in the repository, and the working directory was how Git provided that method of interaction.

The reason you are strongly recommended against pushing to a non-bare repository (a repository with a working directory) is that a push doesn't reset the working directory. Let's go back to our previous example—two systems configured with remotes and remote tracking branches pointing to the other system—and see how this might cause problems:

1. Let's say you're being a really good Git citizen and you're working from a branch. We'll call this branch *new-feature*. You've got new-feature checked out on your first system, so it's the contents of the new-feature branch that are in the working directory. As the day ends, you still have a few unfinished changes left in the working directory, but you commit a few other changes.

2. From your second system, you fetch the changes, review them, merge them into the local new-feature branch, and continue working. You know that you can't see the uncommitted changes in the working directory on your first system, but that's no problem. All is well so far.

3. It's the end of the evening now, and you've just completed some work. You decide to push your changes to your work system's new-feature branch.

4. The next day, you come into work and decide to get started. Your uncommitted changes are still in the working directory, but you don't see the changes you pushed last night. What's going on here?

This is the issue with pushing to a non-bare repository: the changes were pushed to the remote repository, but the working directory was not updated. That's why you can't see the changes. In order to be able to see the changes, you'll have to run `git` reset --hard HEAD, which will *throw away* the changes in the working directory in order to show the pushed changes. Not a good situation, right?

Using a bare repository eliminates these problems, but it also eliminates the possibility of being able to interactively work with the repository. This is probably perfectly fine for a shared repository being used by multiple developers, though.

To create a new, bare repository, simply add the --bare option to git init:

```
vagrant@trusty:~$ git init --bare shared-repo.git
Initialized empty Git repository in /home/vagrant/shared-repo.git/
vagrant@trusty:~$ git init non-bare-repo
Initialized empty Git repository in /home/vagrant/non-bare-repo/.git/
```

Note the difference in the output of Git when --bare is used and when it is not used. In a non-bare repository, the actual Git repository is in the *.git* subdirectory, and Git's response indicates this. In a bare repository, though, there's no working directory, so the Git repository sits *directly* at the root of the directory specified.

 Although not required, it is accepted convention to end the name of a bare repository in *.git*.

In our case, though, we have an *existing* repository, and we need to somehow transition that into a bare repository that we can now share among multiple users. Git is prepared for such a scenario: we can use git clone to clone an existing repository into a new bare repository.

```
vagrant@trusty:~$ git clone --bare net-auto na-shared.git
Cloning into bare repository 'na-shared.git'...
done.
vagrant@trusty:~$
```

When you use git clone --bare, Git does not add any remotes or remote tracking branches. This makes sense, if you think about it; generally, remotes and remote tracking branches are useful only when you are interacting with the repository directly. With a bare repository, you aren't interacting with the repository directly; you'll use a clone on another system, which will have remotes and remote tracking branches.

Let's take our two-system setup (with the repository on Trusty and Jessie and remotes pointing back to each other) and transition it into a shared, bare repository on a third system. We'll introduce our third system, a CentOS system, to serve as the shared repository.

First, we need to get the repository onto the CentOS system. Here's where `git clone --bare` will come into play:

```
[vagrant@centos ~]$ git clone --bare ssh://trusty.domain.com/~/net-auto
na-shared.git
Cloning into bare repository 'na-shared.git'...
remote: Counting objects: 32, done.
remote: Compressing objects: 100% (30/30), done.
Receiving objects: 100% (32/32), done.
remote: Total 32 (delta 12), reused 0 (delta 0)
Resolving deltas: 100% (12/12), done.
[vagrant@centos ~]$
```

Now we can clone this bare repository onto our two work systems. First, the Ubuntu system:

```
vagrant@trusty:~$ git clone ssh://centos.domain.com/~vagrant/na-shared.git
na-shared
Cloning into 'na-shared'...
remote: Counting objects: 32, done.
remote: Compressing objects: 100% (18/18), done.
remote: Total 32 (delta 12), reused 32 (delta 12)
Receiving objects: 100% (32/32), done.
Resolving deltas: 100% (12/12), done.
Checking connectivity... done.
vagrant@trusty:~$ cd na-shared
vagrant@trusty:~/na-shared$ git remote -v
origin  ssh://centos.domain.com/~vagrant/na-shared.git (fetch)
origin  ssh://centos.domain.com/~vagrant/na-shared.git (push)
vagrant@trusty:~/na-shared$ git branch -r
  origin/HEAD -> origin/master
  origin/master
vagrant@trusty:~/na-shared$ git log --oneline HEAD~2..HEAD
7c2a3e6 Update sw2 configuration
81f5963 Merge branch 'sw4'
40e88b8 Add port descriptions for sw4
vagrant@trusty:~/na-shared$
```

You can see that the `git clone` into the bare repository and subsequently back down to your Ubuntu system preserved all the data and metadata in the repository, and automatically created Git remotes and remote tracking branches. (You can verify the Git history, if you'd like, by running `git log` in the new `na-shared` repository as well as in the old `net-auto` repository still on your system.)

Next, we perform the same steps on the Debian system:

```
vagrant@jessie:~$ git clone ssh://centos.domain.com/~vagrant/na-shared.git
na-shared
Cloning into 'na-shared'...
remote: Counting objects: 32, done.
remote: Compressing objects: 100% (18/18), done.
remote: Total 32 (delta 12), reused 32 (delta 12)
```

```
Receiving objects: 100% (32/32), done.
Resolving deltas: 100% (12/12), done.
Checking connectivity... done.
vagrant@jessie:~$ cd na-shared
vagrant@jessie:~/na-shared$ git remote -v
origin  ssh://centos.domain.com/~vagrant/na-shared.git (fetch)
origin  ssh://centos.domain.com/~vagrant/na-shared.git (push)
vagrant@jessie:~/na-shared$ git branch -r
  origin/HEAD -> origin/master
  origin/master
vagrant@jessie:~/na-shared$
```

Now that you have the new *na-shared* repository on all your systems, you can simply remove the old *net-auto* repository with `rm -rf net-auto`.

What does the workflow look like now?

1. You'll still want to work almost exclusively in branches other than the master branch. This becomes particularly important when working with other users in the same shared repository.

2. Before starting work on the local clone on any system, run `git fetch` to retrieve any changes present on the shared repository but not in your local clone. Merge the changes into local branches as needed with `git merge`.

3. Make changes in the local repository and commit them to your local clone.

4. Push the changes up to the shared repository using `git push`.

We haven't talked about the `git push` command before, so it probably deserves a bit of explanation.

Pushing changes to a shared repository

Now that you have a bare repository, you can push changes to the remote using `git push`. The general syntax is **git push *remote branch***, where *remote* is the name of the Git remote and *branch* is the name of the branch to which these changes should be pushed.

To illustrate this in action, let's make some changes to the network automation repository on our Debian system. We'll add a Jinja template, *hv-tor-config.j2*, that represents the base configuration for a top-of-rack switch to which hypervisors are connected.

First, because we don't want to work off the master branch, we create a new branch to hold our changes:

```
vagrant@jessie:~/na-shared$ git checkout -b add-sw-tmpl
Switched to a new branch 'add-sw-tmpl'
vagrant@jessie:~/na-shared$
```

After we add the file to the working directory (by creating it from scratch or by copying it in from elsewhere), we'll stage and commit the changes:

```
vagrant@jessie:~/na-shared$ git add hv-tor-config.j2
vagrant@jessie:~/na-shared$ git commit -m "Add Jinja template for TOR config"
[add-sw-tmpl 8cbbe6f] Add Jinja template for TOR config
 1 file changed, 15 insertions(+)
 create mode 100644 hv-tor-config.j2
vagrant@jessie:~/na-shared$
```

Now, we'll push the changes to the origin remote, which points to our shared (bare) repository:

```
vagrant@jessie:~/na-shared$ git push origin add-sw-tmpl
Counting objects: 3, done.
Compressing objects: 100% (3/3), done.
Writing objects: 100% (3/3), 423 bytes | 0 bytes/s, done.
Total 3 (delta 1), reused 0 (delta 0)
To ssh://centos.domain.com/~vagrant/na-shared.git
 * [new branch]      add-sw-tmpl -> add-sw-tmpl
vagrant@jessie:~/na-shared$
```

This allows coworkers and others with whom we are collaborating to then fetch the changes on their systems. They would just use `git fetch` to retrieve the changes, make a local branch corresponding to the remote tracking branch, then review the changes using whatever methods they wanted. Here, we'll show `git diff`, which isn't terribly useful considering the only change is adding a single new file.

```
vagrant@trusty:~/na-shared$ git fetch origin
remote: Counting objects: 4, done.
remote: Compressing objects: 100% (3/3), done.
remote: Total 3 (delta 1), reused 0 (delta 0)
Unpacking objects: 100% (3/3), done.
From ssh://centos.domain.com/~vagrant/na-shared
 * [new branch]      add-sw-tmpl -> origin/add-sw-tmpl
vagrant@trusty:~/na-shared$ git checkout --track -b add-sw-tmpl origin/add-sw-tmpl
Branch add-sw-tmpl set up to track remote branch add-sw-tmpl from origin.
Switched to a new branch 'add-sw-tmpl'
vagrant@trusty:~/na-shared$ git diff master..HEAD
diff --git a/hv-tor-config.j2 b/hv-tor-config.j2
new file mode 100644
index 0000000..989d723
--- /dev/null
+++ b/hv-tor-config.j2
@@ -0,0 +1,15 @@
+interface ethernet0
+  switchport mode access vlan {{ mgmt_vlan_id }}
+
+interface ethernet1
+  description Connected to {{ server_uplink_1 }}
+  switchport mode trunk
+
```

```
+interface ethernet2
+  description Connected to {{ server_uplink_2 }}
+  switchport mode trunk
+
+interface ethernet3
+  description Connected to {{ server_uplink_3 }}
+  switchport mode trunk
+
vagrant@trusty:~/na-shared$
```

Once everyone agrees that the changes are OK, then you can merge the changes into the master branch. First, perform the merge locally:

```
vagrant@jessie:~/na-shared$ git checkout master
Switched to branch 'master'
Your branch is up-to-date with 'origin/master'
vagrant@jessie:~$ git merge add-sw-tmpl
Updating 7c2a3e6..8cbbe6f
Fast-forward
 hv-tor-config.j2 | 15 +++++++++++++++
 1 file changed, 15 insertions(+)
 create mode 100644 hv-tor-config.j2
vagrant@jessie:~/na-shared$
```

This a fast-forward, so there's no commit merge. Now push the changes to the shared repository:

```
vagrant@jessie:~/na-shared$ git push origin master
Total 0 (delta 0), reused 0 (delta 0)
To ssh://centos.domain.com/~vagrant/na-shared.git
   7c2a3e6..8cbbe6f  master -> master
vagrant@jessie:~/na-shared$
```

Finally, delete your branch (also frequently referred to as a *feature branch* or a *topic branch*) and push that change to the shared repository:

```
vagrant@jessie:~/na-shared$ git branch -d add-sw-tmpl
Deleted branch add-sw-tmpl (was 8cbbe6f).
vagrant@jessie:~/na-shared$ git push origin --delete add-sw-tmpl
To ssh://centos.domain.com/~vagrant/na-shared.git
 - [deleted]         add-sw-tmpl
vagrant@jessie:~/na-shared$
```

Your collaborators can then get the changes that were merged into the master branch, delete the local branch they created, then delete the remote tracking branch that is no longer needed using the `git fetch --prune` command:

```
vagrant@trusty:~/na-shared$ git pull origin master
From ssh://centos.domain.com/~vagrant/na-shared
 * branch            master      -> FETCH_HEAD
   7c2a3e6..8cbbe6f  master      -> origin/master
Updating 7c2a3e6..8cbbe6f
Fast-forward
```

```
hv-tor-config.j2 | 15 +++++++++++++++
1 file changed, 15 insertions(+)
create mode 100644 hv-tor-config.j2
vagrant@trusty:~/na-shared$ git fetch --prune origin
From ssh://192.168.100.12/~vagrant/na-shared
 x [deleted]        (none)     -> origin/add-sw-tmpl
vagrant@trusty:~/na-shared$ git branch -d add-sw-tmpl
Deleted branch add-sw-tmpl (was 8cbbe6f).
vagrant@trusty:~/na-shared$
```

The `git fetch --prune` command is new; it's used to delete a remote tracking branch when the branch no longer exists on the remote. In this particular case, we're removing the remote tracking branch for *origin/add-sw-tmpl*, as noted in the output of the command.

Be Patient When Learning Git

We know that all this may sound really complicated if you're new to Git. It's OK—everyone was new to Git at some point (except maybe Linus). Take it slow, and be patient with yourself. After a little while of using Git, the commands will start to feel more natural. Until then, you might find it handy to have a Git "cheat sheet" nearby to remind you of some of the commands and their syntax.

Before we move on to our final topic—collaborating using Git-based online services —let's recap what we've discussed in this section:

- Git uses the concept of *remotes* to create links between repositories. You'll use the `git remote` command to manipulate remotes. A remote can point to a filesystem location as well as a location across the network, such as another system via SSH.

- To retrieve changes from a remote repository into your local repository, use `git fetch remote`.

- Git relies heavily on branches when working with remote repositories. Special branches known as remote tracking branches are automatically created when you use `git fetch` to retrieve changes.

- Changes retrieved from a remote repository can be merged into your local repository just like any other branch merge using `git merge`.

- If you don't want to follow the two-step `git fetch` followed by `git merge`, you can use `git pull`.

- You'll use `git push` to push changes to a remote repository, but this remote repository should be a bare repository.

- Using a bare repository as a central, shared repository can enable multiple users to collaborate on a single repository. Changes are exchanged via branches and through the use of `git push`, `git fetch`, `git merge`, and `git pull`.

Our last section in this chapter builds on everything we've shown you so far, and focuses on using Git-based online services to collaborate with other users.

Collaborating Using Git-Based Online Services

Fundamentally, collaborating with other users using a Git-based online services will look and feel very much like what we described in the previous section. All the same concepts apply—using clones to make copies of repositories, using remotes and remote tracking branches, and working in branches to exchange changes with other users in the same repository. You'll even continue to use the same commands: `git fetch`, `git push`, `git merge`, and `git pull`.

All that being said, there are a few differences that we'd like to cover. For the sake of brevity, we'll focus here on the use of GitHub as the Git-based online service by which you are collaborating. The topics we'll cover in this section are:

- Forking repositories
- Pull requests

Ready? Let's start with forking repositories.

Forking repositories

Forking a GitHub project is essentially the same as *cloning* a Git repository. (We'll use the terms *project* and *repository* somewhat interchangeably in this section.) When you fork a GitHub repository, you are issuing a command to GitHub's servers to clone the repository into your user account. At the time of creation, your fork will be a full and complete copy of the original repository, including all the content and the commit history. Once the repository has been forked into your account, it's just as if you'd issued a `git clone` from the command line—links are maintained back to the original project, much like a Git remote. (These remotes are not exposed to the user, though.) The key difference here is that forking a repository on GitHub does *not* create a local copy of the repository; you'll still need to use `git clone` to clone the forked copy down to your local system, as we'll show you shortly.

So why fork a repository? In the case of a large online service such as GitHub, there are hundreds of thousands of repositories hosted there. Each of these repositories is associated with a GitHub user ID, and that user ID is allowed to control who may or may not contribute to the repository. What if you found a repository to which you wanted to contribute? The owner of that repository may not know you (a very likely situation), and may not trust your ability to contribute to his or her repository. However, if you had your own copy of the repository, you could make the contributions you wanted to make and then let the owner of the original decide if such contributions were worthwhile. So, instead of trying to get approval to contribute directly to a repository, you instead *fork* (clone) the repository to your own account, where you can work with it. At some point later, you can (optionally) see if the original repository wants to include your changes moving forward (we'll discuss this in the section "Pull requests" on page 356).

To fork a GitHub repository, just follow these steps:

1. Log into GitHub using your security credentials.
2. Locate the repository you'd like to fork into your own account, and click the Fork button in the upper-right corner of the screen.
3. If you are a member of any GitHub organizations, you may be prompted for the user account or organization where you'd like this repository to be forked. Choose your own user account unless you know you need a different option.

That's it! GitHub will fork (clone) the repository into your user account.

Because GitHub repositories are bare repositories, you'll generally need to then clone this bare repository down to your local system to work with it. (Note that GitHub provides some web-based tools to create files, edit files, make commits, and similar.) To clone a GitHub repository out of your account, you'd just use the `git clone` command, followed by the URL of the GitHub repository. For example, here's the URL of one of the authors' GitHub repositories: *https://github.com/lowescott/learning-tools.git*

Let's say your GitHub username is npabook (this user did not exist at the time of this writing). If you were to fork the preceding repository, it would make a full and complete copy of the repository into your user account, just as if you'd used `git clone`. At this point, the URL for your forked repository would be: *https://github.com/npabook/learning-tools.git*

If you ran `git clone https://github.com/npabook/learning-tools.git` from your local system, Git would clone the repository down to your local system, create a remote named origin that points back to your forked repository on GitHub, and create remote tracking branches—just as `git clone` worked in our earlier examples.

Once you have a clone of the repository on your local system, working with your forked GitHub repository is *exactly* like we described in the previous section:

1. Create new feature/topic branches locally to isolate changes away from the master branch.
2. Use `git push` to push those changes to the remote GitHub repository.

3. Merge the changes into the master branch using `git merge` whenever you're ready.

4. Use `git fetch` followed by `git merge` to pull down the changes to the master branch, or combine those steps using `git pull`.

5. Delete the local feature/topic branch and the remote branch on the GitHub repository.

So far, this should all seem pretty straightforward to you—we haven't really seen anything different from what we described earlier. There is one situation, though, that requires some discussion: how do you keep your fork in sync with the original?

Keeping forked repositories in sync

Although GitHub maintains links back to the original repository when you fork it into your user account, GitHub does not provide a way to keep the two repositories synchronized. Why would it be important to keep your fork synchronized with the original? Suppose you wanted to contribute to an ongoing project. Over time, your forked copy would fall hopelessly behind the original as development continued, branches were merged, and changes committed to the original. In order for your fork to be useful for you to use to contribute changes, it needs to be up-to-date with the original.

To keep your forked repository up-to-date, you're going to need to use multiple remotes. (We did say earlier that multiple remotes is definitely something you might need to use with Git.) Let's walk through how this would work. We'll assume you've already forked the repository in GitHub.

First, clone the forked repository down to your system using `git clone`. The command would look something like this:

```
git clone https://username@github.com/username/repository-name.git
```

This will clone the repository down to your local system, create a remote named origin that points back to the URL specified before, and creates remote tracking branches. At this point, if you ran `git remote` in this repository, you'd see a single remote named origin (remember that `git remote -v` will also show the location of the remote—in this case, the HTTPS URL).

Next, add a *second* remote that points to the original repository. The command would look something like this:

```
git remote upstream add https://github.com/original-user/repository-name.git
```

The name "upstream" here is strictly symbolic, but we like to use it, as this reminds us that the remote points to the upstream (or original) project. (We've also found that "upstream" is commonly used, so it may make sense to use the same remote name that others use for consistency.) Your local repository now has two remotes: origin, which points to your forked repository, and upstream, which points to the original repository.

Now, to keep your repository up-to-date with the original (all these steps are taken from within the cloned Git repository on your local system):

1. Check out the master branch using `git checkout master`.

2. Get the changes from the original repository. You can use a combination of `git fetch upstream master` followed by `git merge upstream/master`, or you can use `git pull upstream master` (which combines the steps). Your local, cloned repository is now in sync with the original repository.

3. Push the changes from your local repository to the forked repository using `git push origin master`. Now your forked repository is up-to-date with the original repository.

This process doesn't keep any feature/topic branches up-to-date, but that's generally not a problem—most of the time you'll only want to keep master synchronized between the original and the forked repository.

The next section talks about how to let the owner of a repository know that you have changes you'd like her to consider including in her repository.

Pull requests

Let's quickly recap the recommended process for working with a shared repository such as that offered by GitHub:

1. Create a local branch—called a feature or topic branch—in which to store the changes you're going to make.

2. Stage and commit the changes to the new local branch.

3. Push the local branch to the remote repository using `git push remote branch`.

That gets the changes into your forked repository, but how does the owner of the original repository know that you've pushed some changes up to your forked copy? In short: he or she *doesn't*. Why? Well, for one, it's entirely possible that you are truly forking—creating a divergent codebase—and don't want or need the original author(s) to know about your changes. Second, what if the changes you committed don't contain all the changes you want the original authors to consider? How would Git or GitHub know when you are ready? In short: it *can't*. Only you can know when your code is ready for the original authors to review for inclusion, and that's the purpose of a pull request.

A *pull request* is a notification to the authors of the original repository that you have changes you'd like them to consider including in their repository. Creating a pull request comes after step 3 in the preceding list. Once you've pushed your changes into a branch in your forked repository, you can create a pull request against the original repository. (Note that other Git-based platforms, such as GitLab, may use terms like *merge request* instead of pull request. The basic idea and workflow are much the same.)

To create a pull request after pushing a branch up to GitHub, go to the original repository. Just under the line listing the commits, branches, releases, and contributors, a new line will appear with a button labeled "Compare & pull request." This is illustrated in Figure 8-10.

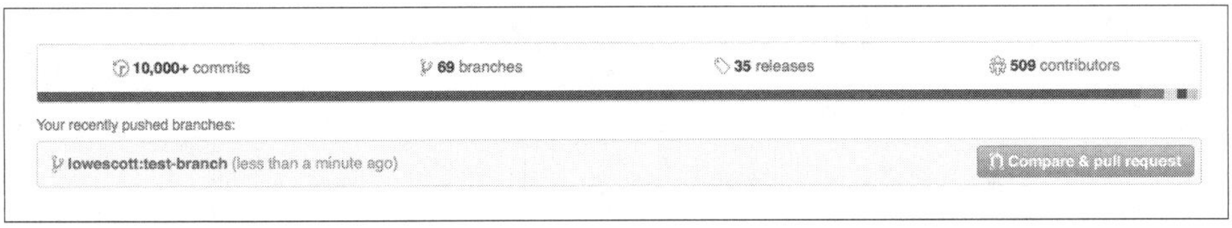

Figure 8-10. Creating a new pull request in GitHub

Click that button, and GitHub will open a screen to create the pull request. The base fork, base branch, head fork, and comparison branch will all be automatically filled in for you, and the notes in the pull request will be taken from the last commit message. Make any changes as needed, then click the green "Create pull request" button.

The owners of the original repository then have to decide if the changes found in your branch can and should be merged into their repository. If they agree—or if you are the one receiving the pull request—then you can merge the changes in GitHub's web interface.

Once the changes have been merged into the original repository, you can update your fork's master branch from the original (using `git fetch` and `git merge`, or the one-step `git pull`). Since the changes from your feature/topic branch are now found in the master branch, you can then delete the branch (as well as any remote tracking branches for your forked repository), as it is no longer needed.

As you can see, aside from a few minor differences, the general workflow for collaborating via GitHub is very similar to the workflow for collaborating using only a shared (bare) repository. By and large, the same terms, concepts, and commands are used in both cases, which makes it easier for you to collaborate with others using Git.

Summary

In this chapter, we've provided an introduction to Git, a very widely used version control system. Git is a fully distributed version control system that provides strong support for nonlinear development with branches. Like other version control systems, Git offers accountability (who made what changes) and change tracking (knowing the changes that were made). These attributes are just as applicable in networking-centric use cases as they are in developer-centric use cases. Branches are a key part of collaborating with Git. To help with Git collaboration, a number of online services (such as GitHub or BitBucket) have appeared, allowing users across organizations to collaborate on repositories with relative ease.

## CHAPTER 9

Automation Tools

No discussion of network automation would be complete without evaluating the role that automation tools—tools like Ansible, Chef, Puppet, StackStorm, and Salt—play in a network automation context.

Traditionally, these tools have been more focused on the server automation use case. This was an understandable focus given that most, if not all, of these tools had their origins in automating server operating systems and managing operating system (OS) and/or application configuration. In recent years, though, there has been a great deal of effort by a number of companies to enhance the network automation functionality of their products. These enhancements make these products much more useful and powerful in a network automation use case.

In this chapter, we'll discuss how to use some major automation tools for network automation. The tools we'll cover in this chapter are:

- Ansible
- Salt
- StackStorm

Before we get into the details and examples of how to use these tools for network automation, let's first take a quick look at an overview of the various tools we're going to discuss.

Reviewing Automation Tools

While all of these tools are focused on automation, each tool has its own architecture and approaches automation in a slightly different way. This gives each tool its own set of strengths and weaknesses. In this section, we'd like to quickly review each of the tools so that you can begin to see how these tools might be used in their environment.

At a high level, some of the major architectural differences between the tools include:

Agent-based versus agentless

Some tools require an agent—a piece of software—to be running on the system or device being managed. In a network automation use case, this could prove to be a problem, as not every network operating system (NOS) supports running agents on a network device. In situations where the NOS doesn't support running an agent natively on the device, there are sometimes workarounds involving a "proxy agent." Agentless tools, obviously, don't require an agent, and may be more applicable in network automation use cases.

Centralized versus decentralized

Agent-based architectures often also require a centralized "master server." Some agentless products also leverage a master server, but most agentless products are decentralized.

Custom protocol versus standards-based protocol

Some tools have a custom protocol they use; this is often tied to agent-based architectures. Other tools leverage SSH as the transport protocol. Given the ubiquity of SSH in network devices, tools leveraging SSH as their transport protocol may be better suited to network automation use cases.

Domain-specific language (DSL) versus standards-based data formats and general-purpose languages

Some tools have their own DSL; to use this tool, users must create the appropriate files in that DSL to be consumed by the automation tool. A DSL is a language purpose-built for a specific domain (or tool). For organizations that aren't already familiar with the DSL, this might create an additional learning curve. Other tools leverage YAML, which is considered a general-purpose language in this context. Remember, we discussed YAML in Chapter 5.

Language for extensibility

Most of these automation tools support the ability to add or extend functionality using a high-level scripting language. Some tools use Ruby as their language of choice for extending functionality; others leverage Python.

Push versus pull versus event-driven

Some automation tools operate in a "push" model; that is, information is pushed from one place out to the devices or systems being managed. Others operate in a pull model, typically pulling configuration information or instructions (often on some sort of scheduled basis). Finally, there are also event-driven tools, which perform an action in response to some other event or trigger.

With this high-level set of architectural differences in mind, let's take a quick look at the three tools we're going to discuss in this chapter.

Ansible

> Ansible uses a decentralized, agentless architecture with SSH as the underlying transport protocol. It is typically operated in a push model, though it also supports a pull model. Ansible is built using Python and leverages Python for extensibility. Ansible supports templating using the Jinja templating language. Ansible originally targeted a way to run ad hoc commands on servers, but has since evolved into task orchestration using "playbooks" that perform idempotent tasks on target systems. Playbooks can be written in standard YAML or an Ansible derivation of YAML.

Salt

> Salt can use either an agent-based architecture or an agentless architecture. In an agent-based architecture, Salt agents communicate with the Salt master over a message bus; in the agentless architecture, they communicate via SSH or other third-party libraries such as NAPALM (covered later). Salt is built using Python, and can be extended with Python. Jinja provides default templating functionality. Salt started out as a tool for remote server management, much like Ansible, and has since gained idempotent configuration management via Salt States, which are written in YAML. One distinction to make with Salt is that it is also a platform for event-driven automation beyond general configuration management.

StackStorm

> StackStorm takes a dramatically different approach than the other tools listed here. StackStorm focuses solely on event-driven automation; that is, tasks are performed in response to events. StackStorm leverages Python to build sensors that emit events or actions that perform a task. StackStorm uses YAML in several places to provide metadata for sensors or actions, or to define a workflow.

Now, let's dive a bit deeper into each of the products we're going to discuss and take a more in-depth look at how each product can be used for network automation. We've arranged the in-depth discussion of the products in alphabetical order, so we'll start with Ansible.

Using Ansible

Most tools we're covering in this chapter take months (or more) to master. Our goal in this chapter, and specifically now with respect to Ansible, is to provide a jump start with enough information so you can start automating common tasks immediately. In order to do this, we've broken this section into six major areas:

- Understanding how Ansible works

- Constructing an inventory file
- Executing an Ansible playbook
- Understanding variable files
- Writing Ansible playbooks for network automation
- Using third-party modules

By the time you complete this section, you'll have a solid foundation on Ansible, the different types of network automation you can accomplish using Ansible, and most importantly, enough to continue on your automation journey.

We'll start by looking at how Ansible works.

Ansible is an open source platform by Red Hat. In this section, we only cover Ansible core—the open source platform. However, it's worth noting that Red Hat does sell a commercial offering, Ansible Tower, that sits above Ansible core and offers Enterprise features such as Role Based Access Control (RBAC), secure storage for network credentials, and a number of other features such as a RESTful API so you can programmatically execute Ansible playbooks (just to name a few).

Understanding How Ansible Works

The first thing we're to going review is how Ansible works from an architectural perspective when automating not only network devices, but also Linux servers. It is important to differentiate, as there is a subtle but important difference, and this ultimately is reflected when we're creating automation workflows with Ansible.

Automating Linux servers

When Ansible is used to automate Linux servers, it operates in a distributed fashion. The Ansible control host, the machine that has Ansible installed, connects to each server being automated via SSH. The control host subsequently copies Python code to each server—this code is what performs the automation task at hand. This includes anything from restarting a Linux process and installing Linux packages to updating text files, pulling updates down from a Git repository, or simply running a bash script on the target Linux hosts being automated. If 100 Linux servers were being automated, 100 servers execute the Ansible "code" (or modules) to perform the task.

Ansible can also be used to automate Windows servers, but the context here is to describe the origins and most common use of Ansible, and how that compares to automating networking devices.

Automating network devices

How Ansible works when automating network devices is a little different. Ansible works in a local, or centralized, fashion when automating network devices. When automating network devices, the Ansible control host gets configured to run in *local* mode. When Ansible runs in local mode, Ansible does not connect to each device via SSH *and* copy Python code to each network device. In fact, when running in local mode, Ansible actually connects to itself and executes the Python code *locally*. The Python code that runs locally may still connect to the network device via SSH, but it may also be via an API (or Telnet or SNMP). However, even when Ansible connects via SSH for network devices, Python files are not copied to the device and CLI commands are simply sent over a SSH connection. From an extremely high-level view, this becomes analogous to executing Python scripts on a server and automating some number of network devices in parallel.

 It is possible to have network modules not operate in local mode, but it requires updates to many network operating systems. In order to support this, the network device must currently permit you to SSH into the device, copy Python files to a temp directory, and then execute those files with a Python execution engine. This, of course, works natively with Cumulus Linux. Two other operating systems that currently support this are Cisco IOS-XR and Arista EOS.

Now that you understand how Ansible operates differently for network devices as compared to Linux hosts (which is what Ansible was initially built for), let's review some Ansible vernacular that's critical to getting started and using Ansible.

Constructing an Inventory File

The first Ansible file we're going to look at is the Ansible inventory file. The inventory file is one of two files required in order to start automating network devices with Ansible. The second, which we'll cover next, is the playbook. The inventory file is an *ini*-like file that contains the devices that will be automated with Ansible.

The following is a basic example of an Ansible inventory file:

```
10.1.100.10
10.5.10.10
nyc-lf01
```

This example is one of the simplest inventory files you can have. The file literally has three lines in it, one per device. As you can see, by default you can use either IP addresses or hostnames (that are fully qualified domain names).

While an inventory file can seem very basic, you can gradually add more structure and data to it as you start doing more with Ansible. If you're only testing and getting started with three devices, the previous example may suffice. However, you need to consider more realistic scenarios such as having larger quantities of devices, having different types of devices, and deploying those devices in different parts of a network (e.g., data center, DMZ, WAN, or access, just to name a few). In the upcoming examples, we'll introduce how to create groups and define variables in the inventory file.

Let's walk through building out an inventory file that will represent the devices for two regions, *EMEA* and *AMERS*, and two device roles, *dc* and *cpe* (see Figure 9-1). Each device role per region comprises different types of network equipment as you can see in the diagram.

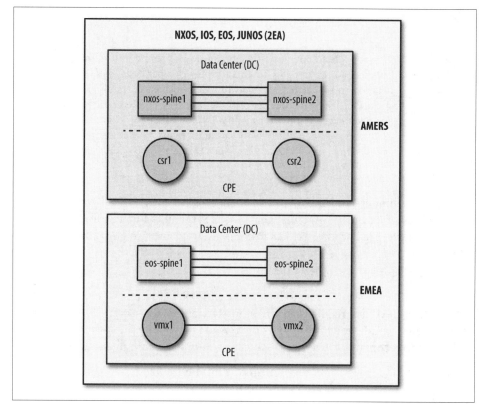

Figure 9-1. Network topology diagram

 The devices in Figure 9-1 were used for both the Ansible and Salt sections in this chapter. The AMERS region has Cisco routers being used as CPE edge devices and Nexus switches in the DC, while the EMEA region has Juniper routers being used as CPE edge devices and Arista switches in the DC.

Working with inventory groups

As you can see, there are two core geographic locations with different device types in the AMERS and EMEA regions. We'll want to create different groups such that we can easily automate all devices of a certain type, for a certain operating system, or within a given location.

To do this, we'll start by creating two groups for the devices in the AMERS region called `amers-cpe` and `amers-dc`. Each group will have two devices. The `cpe` group will have two Cisco CSR 1000V devices and the `dc` group will have two Nexus switches.

```
[amers-cpe]
csr1
csr2

[amers-dc]
nxos-spine1
nxos-spine2
```

The bracket [ ] syntax is how you're able to create logical groups within the inventory file. You'll see later how we can reference these groups in a playbook so they are easily automated.

Using nested groups in an inventory file

You can also create groups of groups, or nested groups, in an inventory file. For example, you may want to automate all devices in the AMERS region. To do this, we'll add a group called `amers` that contains `amers-cpe` and `amers-dc`.

```
[amers:children]
amers-cpe
amers-dc

[amers-cpe]
csr1
csr2

[amers-dc]
nxos-spine1
nxos-spine2
```

When creating nested groups, you must use `:children` in the group name definition. After we've added the `amers` group, there are three explicitly defined groups in our inventory file: `amers`, `amers-cpe`, and `amers-dc`.

Using the same approach, we can build out the inventory for the EMEA region as shown in the next example:

```
[emea:children]
emea-cpe
emea-dc
```

```
[emea-cpe]
vmx1
vmx2

[emea-dc]
eos-spine1
eos-spine2
```

You may also want to create groups to automate all devices of a particular role in the network such as all CPE devices or all DC devices. To do this, you can create additional groups.

```
[all-cpe:children]
amers-cpe
emea-cpe

[all-dc:children]
amers-dc
emea-dc
```

As you're seeing, inventory files can be extremely basic when you're just getting started, but can quickly expand based on how you want to automate your network devices.

After getting your group structure defined and into your desired state, it's good to know that you can even define variables within your inventory file.

Using variables in Ansible

There are two types of variables that you can define in your Ansible inventory file:

- Group-based variables
- Host-based variables

Managing group variables.   Group variables are assigned at the group level. For example, you may define a variable such as the NTP Server IP address to use for all devices in the AMERS and then another NTP IP address for devices in EMEA.

This is reflected in an inventory like this:

```
[amers:vars]
ntp_server=10.1.200.11

[emea:vars]
ntp_server=10.10.200.11
```

When defining group variables, you create a new section in the inventory file with the name of the group and append :vars. In this section, you define group-based variables. Our example created a single variable called ntp_server. When you're automating devices in the AMERS group and reference this variable, the value of 10.1.200.11 is used and when automating devices in the EMEA group, the value of 10.10.200.11 is used.

 There is no specific requirement around the ordering of groups and variables in your inventory file. You can have all groups and then all variables, or group 1, group 1 variables, group 2, group 2 variables, and so on.

Managing host variables.   You can also define host-based variables that are specific to a given device in the inventory file. To define a host variable, you put the variable on the same line as the host. One scenario, given our NTP example, is that there is a dedicated NTP server per region. But what if there is a device called nxos-spine1 that *must* use a different address?

This is accomplished as shown here:

```
[amers-dc]
nxos-spine1  ntp_server=10.1.200.200
nxos-spine2
```

Adding a variable=value on the same line as the device is how you add host-specific variables within the inventory file. You can also add multiple variables on the same line, such as the following:

```
[amers-dc]
nxos-spine1  ntp_server=10.1.200.200  syslog_server=10.1.200.201
nxos-spine2
```

Understanding variable priority.   It's important to understand that more specific variables have priority, meaning that if you have nested groups such as amers and amers-cpe, a group variable in amers-cpe will override the same variable if defined as an amers group variable. If there was a host-specific variable for a device in amers-cpe, that would then have higher priority and override the amers-cpe group variable.

There are many more ways to use variables than this book outlines, and variable priority may not seem like an issue when you're getting started, but it's a much larger topic to consider in large Ansible projects. The priority of Ansible variables is well defined on Ansible's website.

Getting familiar with the all group.   Be aware that there is an implicit group that always exists called all. This group is used to automate all devices in an inventory file. You can also assign group variables in the all group like this:

```
[all:vars]
ntp_server=10.1.200.199
syslog_server=10.1.200.201
```

Variables defined in the `all` group end up being "defaults" and are only used if the given variable isn't defined in a more specific group or as a host-based variable.

 You need to know how group and host-based variables work, but the inventory file is not the proper place to define all of your variables for a given project. Dedicated files are recommended for defining variables—these files are covered in "Managing host variables" on page 367.

If you're testing along as you're reading, you'll want to add a few more groups and variables to the inventory file as shown here:

```
[nxos]
nxos-spine1
nxos-spine2

[nxos:vars]
os=nxos

[eos]
eos-spine1
eos-spine2

[eos:vars]
os=eos

[iosxe]
csr1
csr2

[iosxe:vars]
os=ios

[junos]
vmx1
vmx2

[junos:vars]
os=junos
```

The reason we've added groups and group-based variables for each OS is that in many cases this information is required to automate a given device because many modules either (a) only work for a particular device OS, or (b) are multi-vendor and still require knowing the OS up front.

After constructing the complete inventory, we end up with the following:

```
[all:vars]
ntp_server=10.1.200.199
syslog_server=10.1.200.201

[amers-cpe]
csr1
csr2

[amers-dc]
nxos-spine1
nxos-spine2

[amers:children]
amers-cpe
amers-dc

[amers-cpe]
csr1
csr2

[amers-dc]
nxos-spine1   ntp_server=10.1.200.200   syslog_server=10.1.200.201
nxos-spine2

[emea:children]
emea-cpe
emea-dc

[emea-cpe]
vmx1
vmx2

[emea-dc]
eos-spine1
eos-spine2

[all-cpe:children]
amers-cpe
emea-cpe

[all-dc:children]
amers-dc
emea-dc

[amers:vars]
ntp_server=10.1.200.11

[emea:vars]
ntp_server=10.10.200.11

[nxos]
```

```
nxos-spine1
nxos-spine2

[nxos:vars]
os=nxos

[eos]
eos-spine1
eos-spine2

[eos:vars]
os=eos

[iosxe]
csr1
csr2

[iosxe:vars]
os=ios

[junos]
vmx1
vmx2

[junos:vars]
os=junos
```

The easiest and most common way to get started with inventory is to use the inventory file. However, if you happen to work in a very dynamic or large environment, or have an existing CMDB or network management system that contains inventory data, Ansible can be integrated with those systems. Ansible supports dynamic inventory scripts such that an inventory file is replaced with a script. The script queries your CMDB/NMS, normalizes the data, and then returns valid JSON in the structure Ansible requires as defined in their docs (out of scope for this book). You can also return variables in the dynamic inventory script such that if you're a large enterprise, all you'd manage are playbooks—all inventory and variables are then returned dynamically as you execute your playbook.

Earlier we stated that the Ansible inventory file was one of two files required in order to start automating network devices with Ansible. The second file is the Ansible playbook—this is what we'll dive into next.

Executing an Ansible Playbook

The playbook is a file that contains your automation instructions. In other words, playbooks contain the individual tasks and workflows that you want to use to automate your network. The playbook itself is written in YAML. This is when being familiar with YAML, as covered in Chapter 5, will come in handy.

The term *playbook* comes from a sports analogy, and thus each playbook file contains one or more plays. And if we expand on that, each play contains one or more tasks.

Let's take a look at an example playbook to better understand its structure and associated terminology. We are going to review plays, tasks, modules, and using variables in a playbook, as well as the link from the playbook to the inventory file.

```
---

- name: PLAY 1 - ISSUE SNMP COMMANDS
  hosts: iosxe
  connection: local
  gather_facts: no

  tasks:

    - name: TASK1 - DEPLOY SNMP COMMANDS
      ios_command:
        commands:
          - show run | inc snmp
        provider:
          username: ntc
          password: ntc123
          host: "{{ inventory_hostname }}"

    - name: TASK 2- DEPLOY SNMP COMMANDS
      ios_config:
        commands:
          - snmp-server community public RO
        provider:
          username: ntc
          password: ntc123
          host: "{{ inventory_hostname }}"
```

Our example playbook includes a single play and two tasks. You should already be familiar with the basics of YAML and indentation from Chapter 5. What is ultimately required is a YAML list of plays and a YAML list of tasks as the value of the `tasks` key. If your indentation is off even slightly, you'll receive error messages from Ansible when you try to run your playbook, so you must be careful.

Let's start reviewing this playbook going top-down:

- YAML files always start with three hyphens `---` and since the playbooks are written using YAML, we need them.
- The next few lines are our play definition. Notice the keys `name`, `hosts`, `connection`, and `gather_facts`.

name

> This is optional, but recommended. This is used to define what the play is for and what task is being performed. In other words, it's arbitrary text.

hosts

> This is how you specify which devices you want to automate. You can specify a host, group, multiple of each, or even expressions that refer back to names in your inventory file. For example, if you wanted to automate all devices in EMEA using our previous inventory file, you can use hosts: emea or for devices that are IOS and NXOS groups, you could do hosts: iosxe,nxos denoting a comma-separated list.

connection

> This is used to define the connection type a play uses. *Most* networking devices require setting the connection to local. This directly maps to the architecture of Ansible, which we originally covered in "Automating network devices" on page 363 earlier in the chapter.

gather_facts

> Since we're automating network devices and running in local mode, we're simply saying do not collect facts on the machine running Ansible. If you were running Ansible out of the box automating Linux servers, Ansible would by default collect *facts* from each node, including items such as OS type, OS version, vendor, IPv4 addresses, and much more.

Next, we'll take a look at tasks, what they are, and how they relate to modules.

Understanding tasks in an Ansible playbook

After you define the high-level attributes of your play, such as the connection type and the hosts you want to automate, you need to define tasks. Each task runs an Ansible module, which is performing some form of automation. In our example there are two tasks, denoted by the task names.

Just like the play definition using name, it's common practice to have a name key used and defined for each task to better identify tasks as they're running in real time when the playbook is executed.

Getting familiar with Ansible modules

On the same indent level as name in both tasks, you'll see ios_command and ios_config. These are called Ansible *modules*. Ansible modules perform a specific operation. In particular, ios_command is used to issue exec-level commands to Cisco IOS devices and ios_config is used to send configuration-level commands to Cisco IOS devices.

We'll cover many more modules in this section as we walk through example play-books.

 Ansible has over 700+ modules that allow you to automate Linux servers, network devices, Windows servers, public cloud environments, and much more.

Let's look at the task again that uses the ios_command module:

```
- name: TASK1 - DEPLOY SNMP COMMANDS
  ios_command:
    commands:
      - show run | inc snmp
    provider:
      username: ntc
      password: ntc123
      host: "{{ inventory_hostname }}"
```

You'll notice that there is more data indented under ios_command, specifically the words *commands* and *provider*. These words are parameters and are being passed into the module. You can think of this process as being similar to passing variables or key-value pairs into a Python function.

Understanding YAML data types is extremely important as you use Ansible. For example, the commands parameter accepts a *list* and the provider parameter accepts a *dictionary*. Both of these data types were covered in Chapters 4 and 5.

As a network engineer, sending a list of commands to a network device probably makes sense, so let's focus on the provider parameter. The provider parameter is a dictionary that is used to pass in connection information, such as credentials and the host (device) being automated, as well as port and protocol information. In our example, the value of provider has three key-value pairs—namely, username, password, and host. Note: many more keys are supported within the provider top-level object based on you using SSH keys, setting enable passwords, and changing port/protocol information.

In this case, we are passing in the username and password values as clear text to define and demonstrate how tasks, modules, and parameters are related to one another. The last key host is assigned the value of {{ inventory_hostname }}. You need to understand two things about this value.

The first is that this is the syntax of a variable within Ansible. More specifically, this is a Jinja variable. You should recognize this from covering Jinja configuration templates in Chapter 6. This particular variable, inventory_hostname, is a built-in Ansible variable that is equal to the device name as defined in the inventory file. In our example playbook, we're automating all devices in the group called iosxe, which is two Cisco routers: csr1 and csr2. For all devices in that group, both tasks are executed by Ansible. When the device being automated is csr1, inventory_hostname is equal to csr1; when the device being automated is csr2, inventory_hostname is equal to csr2.

We've now provided a high-level overview of how to construct a playbook. As this section progresses, we'll continue to dive into more detail on how certain modules work, including ios_command and ios_config, and cover much more about Ansible and automating network devices.

Executing a playbook

As we've stated, the two files required to get started with Ansible are the inventory file and playbook. We've reviewed both and are ready to execute a playbook against a set of network devices.

> In our example, we saved the inventory file as *inventory* and the playbook as *snmp-intro.yml*. Both filenames are arbitrary and user-defined.

In order to execute a playbook, you use the ansible-playbook Linux program using the -i flag to reference the inventory file and then the name of the playbook:

```
$ ansible-playbook -i inventory snmp-intro.yml

PLAY [PLAY 1 - ISSUE SNMP COMMANDS] *****************************************

TASK [TASK1 - DEPLOY SNMP COMMANDS] *****************************************
ok: [csr2]
ok: [csr1]

TASK [TASK 2- DEPLOY SNMP COMMANDS] *****************************************
ok: [csr2]
ok: [csr1]

PLAY RECAP *****************************************************
csr1                       : ok=2    changed=0    unreachable=0    failed=0
csr2                       : ok=2    changed=0    unreachable=0    failed=0
```

You also have the option to not specify the inventory file every time you execute a playbook. To do this, you can either use the default inventory file */etc/ansible/hosts*, set the ANSIBLE_INVENTORY environment variable, or define it in the *ansible.cfg* file. For example, you can do the following:

```
$ export ANSIBLE_INVENTORY=inventory
$
$ ansible-playbook snmp-intro.yml
$
```

Using Variable Files

If you understand how to construct an inventory file with groups and variables and
the basics of writing playbooks, you can accomplish quite a bit with Ansible. However, using the inventory file is not the recommended place to keep large amounts of
variables. It's quick and easy for testing, but when managing a production implementation, you should use variable files (when not using dynamic inventory and CMDB).

Understanding variable files requires that you understand the naming necessary to
use them. The concept of using variables is no different than group- and host-based
variables in the inventory file—the only difference is that they are stored in YAML
files.

Group-based variable files

In order to store group variables in YAML files, you must store them in a directory
called *group_vars*, often in the same directory as your playbooks for basic projects.
This is a special and unique name for Ansible—this directory *must* be called
group_vars.

In the *group_vars* directory, you have two options.

The first and most common for getting started with Ansible is to have YAML files
that are equal to the group names as they're defined in the inventory file. When constructing our inventory file, we had explicitly defined groups such as `emea`, `amers`, and
`iosxe`, but also the implicitly defined group called `all`. To define variables in these
files, we'd need files named *emea.yml*, *amers.yml*, *iosxe.yml*, and *all.yml*. These files
are only required if you need to define group variables for that specific group.

This is an example of defining group variables for the `amers` group:

```
ntc@ntc:~/testing$ more group_vars/amers.yml
---

snmp:
  contact: Joe Smith
  location: AMERICAS-NJ
  communities:
    - community: public
      type: ro
    - community: public123
      type: ro
    - community: private
      type: rw
```

```
        - community: secure
            type: rw
ntc@ntc:~/testing$
```

You would do the same for each group you need to define variables for.

As you define more variables for a given group, it may seem logical to want to have particular variables in their own files—for example, AAA variables in their own, NTP in their own, and so on. This is the second option.

In the second option, you create a subdirectory equal to the group name, and in it, you put multiple files named whatever you like. Here is an example showing both options:

```
ntc@ntc:~/testing/group_vars$ tree
.
├── all.yml
├── amers.yml
├── apac
│   ├── aaa.yml
│   ├── interfaces.yml
│   └── ntp.yml
└── emea.yml

1 directory, 6 files
```

Using host-based variable files

Using host-based variable files is exactly like using group variables, but the directory is called *host_vars* and files (or directories) need to match the the device name as defined in the inventory file.

Here is an example highlighting both options, analogous to what we showed earlier in the group variables example:

```
cisco@cisco:~/testing/host_vars$ tree
.
├── csr1.yml
├── csr2.yml
└── vmx1
    ├── interfaces.yml
    └── ntp.yml

1 directory, 4 files
```

Now that we've covered variables and how to use them in a more robust manner, it's time to move on to writing more useful Ansible playbooks.

Writing Ansible Playbooks for Network Automation

At this point, we've taken a look at the Ansible architecture, reviewed the Ansible inventory file, and playbook, and also introduced common Ansible terminology such as plays, tasks, modules, parameters, and variables. In this section, we are going to introduce more Ansible modules and specific Ansible functionality while highlighting what is possible with Ansible, specifically for network automation. Our focus is on showing how Ansible is used to automate the following tasks:

- Creating multi-vendor configuration templates and autogenerating configurations
- Deploying configurations and ensuring a given configuration exists
- Gathering data from network devices
- Performing compliance checks
- Generating reports

Breaking down common core network modules

Before we walk through the aforementioned tasks and examples, we need to review the common set of core modules that Ansible has for a large set of network vendors and operating systems. It's critical to understand these, as they are the *core* modules that ship with Ansible and they all operate in a similar fashion. Three types of common core network modules are:

command
> Used to send exec-level commands to network devices. These are implemented and named as *xos_command* (i.e., `ios_command`, `nxos_command`, `junos_command`, and so on).

config
> Used to send configuration commands to network devices. These are implemented and named as *xos_config* (i.e., `ios_config`, `nxos_config`, `junos_config`, and so on).

facts
> Used to gather information from network devices such as OS version, hardware platform, serial number, hostname, neighbors, and much more. These are implemented and named as *xos_facts* (i.e., `ios_facts`, `nxos_facts`, `junos_facts`, and so on).

With these three modules per network OS, you can accomplish quite a bit with Ansible for network automation. Each of these modules does have parameters, such as commands and `provider`, which we previously looked at (as well as a number of others). We'll review a few more of these in our upcoming examples.

> In order to see which parameters a given module supports along with a few examples, you can use the `ansible-doc` utility. For example, in order to learn how to use `ios_config`, you can enter the following command at your Linux bash prompt:
>
> ```
> $ ansible-doc ios_config
> ```

Now that you understand more about the common core modules, we're going to review our first real network example.

Creating and using configuration templates

In our first example, the goal is to show you can use Ansible to auto-generate SNMP configurations provided you have SNMP configuration templates and the associated input data.

The following SNMP CLI commands for IOS are what we want to deploy for IOS, but the goal is to deploy the same *data* across Arista EOS, Cisco NXOS, and Juniper Junos too. You need to consider this when building out an Ansible project.

```
snmp-server location AMERICAS-NJ
snmp-server contact Joe Smith
snmp-server community public RO
snmp-server community public123 RO
snmp-server community private RW
snmp-server community secure RW
```

At this point, we need to deconstruct the CLI commands into configuration templates using Jinja and YAML files that will store our inputs as variables, more specifically group-based variable files.

Since the goal is to support four operating systems, we're going to need a Jinja template per network OS. We also need to consider that there could be different input data for a given geography, which our example happens to have. We are going to show how to use the same template, but use different data since we have different SNMP community strings, contact, and location per region.

Creating variable files.   First, we'll show our data variables in each respective group variables file. The first is the SNMP data that is getting used for the devices in the Americas region:

```
ntc@ntc:~/testing$ more group_vars/amers.yml
---

snmp:
```

```
   contact: Joe Smith
   location: AMERICAS-NJ
   communities:
     - community: public
       type: ro
     - community: public123
       type: ro
     - community: private
       type: rw
     - community: secure
       type: rw
ntc@ntc:~/testing$
```

Next, we'll use the same structure for the data required for the EMEA region.

```
$ more group_vars/emea.yml
---

snmp:
   contact: Scott Grady
   location: EMEA-IE
   communities:
     - community: public123
       type: ro
     - community: supersecure
       type: rw
cisco@cisco:~/testing$
```

 We aren't spending time covering the details or data types of a given YAML variable and how to consume that in Jinja, as this has already been covered in Chapters 5 and 6.

We've also chosen to define our connection and credential information, which we'll use in upcoming playbooks in the all group variables file.

```
ntc@ntc:~/testing$ more group_vars/all.yml
---

base_provider:
   username: ntc
   password: ntc123
   host: "{{ inventory_hostname }}"

ntc@ntc:~/testing$
```

Creating Jinja templates.   The SNMP data is now defined that'll be used for configuration inputs. Now the associated Jinja templates need to get created. Ansible automatically looks for templates in the directory your playbooks are executed from and in a directory called *templates* relative to the same path. We are going to store the SNMP templates in *./templates/snmp*.

We can prebuild our files as shown here:

```
ntc@ntc:~/testing$ tree templates/
templates/
├── snmp
        ├── eos.j2
        ├── ios.j2
        ├── junos.j2
        ├── nxos.j2
```

The following is the template that was constructed in *ios.j2*:

```
snmp-server location {{ snmp.location }}
snmp-server contact {{ snmp.contact }}
{% for community in snmp.communities %}
snmp-server community {{ community.community }} {{ community.type | upper }}
{% endfor %}
```

The IOS template is straightforward; however, it does show the use of the Jinja filter called upper, which capitalizes the type we've defined as ro or rw in the YAML data file. While both work on the IOS CLI, it translates to RO and RW when entered into the configuration. It will become more apparent why this is important after deploying these configurations.

This following is the Juniper template to configure the same SNMP data on a Junos device:

```
set snmp location {{ snmp.location }}
set snmp contact {{ snmp.contact | replace(' ', '_') }}
{% for community in snmp.communities %}
{% if community.type | lower == "rw" %}
set snmp community {{ community.community }} authorization read-write
{% elif community.type | lower == "ro" %}
set snmp community {{ community.community }} authorization read-only
{% endif %}
{% endfor %}
```

There are a few things to point out about the Junos template:

- The replace filter was used since Junos doesn't support spaces in their contact. The other option is to change the data itself, but we wanted to show how a template for one OS compares to a template for another OS.

- A conditional was added because ro and rw aren't used in Junos commands and we needed to map our data to the right Junos commands.

Here is also what the EOS and NXOS templates look like:

```
snmp-server location {{ snmp.location }}
snmp-server contact {{ snmp.contact }}
{% for community in snmp.communities %}
snmp-server community {{ community.community }} {{ community.type }}
{% endfor %}

snmp-server location {{ snmp.location }}
snmp-server contact {{ snmp.contact }}
{% for community in snmp.communities %}
{% if community.type | lower == "rw" %}
snmp-server community {{ community.community }} group network-admin
{% elif community.type | lower == "ro" %}
snmp-server community {{ community.community }} group network-operator
{% endif %}
{% endfor %}
```

Generating network configuration files.   Now that the data variables and templates are in place, the final step prior to deployment is to generate the SNMP configuration files. In order to do this, we'll use the Ansible module called `template`. The `template` module automates the creation of files rendering input data (variables) with Jinja templates.

The next example shows how to use the `template` module. It uses the `src` and `dest` parameters. The `src` parameter references the proper template you want to use, and the `dest` parameter points to the location where you want the final rendered config to be stored.

```
---

- name: PLAY 1 - GENERATE SNMP CONFIGURATIONS
  hosts: all
  connection: local
  gather_facts: no

  tasks:

    - name: GENERATE CONFIGS FOR EACH OS
      template:
        src: "./snmp/{{ os }}.j2"
        dest: "./configs/snmp/{{ inventory_hostname }}.cfg"
```

> In our test environment, we manually created the *configs* directory and the *snmp* subdirectory. You could have also automated this with Ansible using the `file` module.

Note in the previous example that you can also use variables within paths, values, or anywhere else within a playbook. This makes it so that within a single task in a playbook, you can auto-generate the required configurations for any number of devices regardless of OS type.

 Remember that we added a variable called os as a group-based variable when constructing the inventory file earlier in this section.

At this point, the playbook is ready to be executed to generate the desired configs. This is shown in the following example:

```
cisco@cisco:~/testing$ ansible-playbook -i inventory snmp.yml
```

After the playbook is executed, we end up with the following files automatically created by inserting the proper data variables into the respective Jinja templates.

```
ntc@ntc:~/testing$ tree configs/snmp/
configs/snmp/
├── csr1.cfg
├── csr2.cfg
├── eos-spine1.cfg
├── eos-spine2.cfg
├── nxos-spine1.cfg
├── nxos-spine2.cfg
├── vmx1.cfg
└── vmx2.cfg

0 directories, 8 files
```

To validate that each of the YAML data variables was inserted correctly, let's see the outputs for one device in AMERS and one device in EMEA:

```
ntc@ntc:~/testing$ cat configs/snmp/csr1.cfg
snmp-server location AMERICAS-NJ
snmp-server contact Joe Smith
snmp-server community public RO
snmp-server community public123 RO
snmp-server community private RW
snmp-server community secure RW
ntc@ntc:~/testing$

ntc@ntc:~/testing$ cat configs/snmp/vmx1.cfg
set snmp location EMEA-IE
set snmp contact Scott_Grady
set snmp community public123 authorization read-only
set snmp community supersecure authorization read-write
ntc@ntc:~/testing$
```

Creating templates, variables, and a single task playbook is one of the common ways to get started with Ansible, as it doesn't require any network devices. It allows you to gradually hone your Jinja and YAML skills while building and standardizing network device configurations.

Ensuring a configuration exists

In the previous example, there were eight configurations developed and automatically generated. In this example, we are going to deploy those configurations and ensure they exist on each device.

Understanding idempotency. As we go through this example, pay attention to the words and phrases being used, such as *configuring SNMP* versus *ensuring the SNMP configuration exists*. In a traditional Python script, it may send the SNMP commands every time you execute the script. With Ansible, like many DevOps configuration management tools, the approach for configuration management is to be idempotent, meaning only make the change if needed. In the context of networking modules, each module has added intelligence to ensure that configuration commands are only sent to the device if they are needed to get the device into its desired state.

From a high level, modules accomplish this by always first collecting the existing configuration of the device. The commands that you want to ensure exist on the device are compared against the current state (running configuration). Only if the desired commands do not exist in the current configuration are they sent to the device. This is safer in that the module runs a playbook *N* times and sends the commands to the device only once.

This is exactly how the `config` modules work within Ansible. By default, they obtain a `show run` and the commands within the playbook are only sent to the device if they don't exist within the `show run`.

Using the config module. Let's see how to use the `eos_config` module to deploy the SNMP configuration file for the Arista EOS devices.

```
- name: PLAY 2 - ENSURE EOS SNMP CONFIGS ARE DEPLOYED
  hosts: eos
  connection: local
  gather_facts: no

  tasks:

    - name: DEPLOY CONFIGS FOR EOS
      eos_config:
        src: "./configs/snmp/{{ inventory_hostname }}.cfg"
        provider: "{{ base_provider }}"
```

This play was added to the existing playbook that generated the configurations as we're showing here, denoted by PLAY 2; we also could have created a new playbook strictly for deploying configurations.

The `config` modules accept a number of different parameters while the previous task simply uses two of them: `provider` and `src`. We're referencing `base_provider`, which we defined in `group_vars` for the `all` group, and passing that into the module as the `provider` value. This simplifies all tasks within a playbook such that you don't need to define the provider dictionary *N* times if you have *N* tasks in the playbook.

The `src` parameter can reference a config file or a Jinja template directly. As you can see, we're referencing the exact file that was generated in the first play.

Other common parameters used in the `config` modules are:

commands
> Mutually exclusive with `src`; rather than reference a template or configuration file, it allows you to embed a list of commands directly in the playbook.

parents
> List of parent commands that identify the hierarchy that commands should be evaluated against (required when you're using `commands` and configuring a device with commands that go outside of global configuration mode). For example, an example parent is `['interface Eth1']` and the commands list is `['duplex full']` when you're trying to configure duplex on Eth1.

There are even more parameters for the `config` modules, such as those that allow you to issue a particular command before and after issuing the commands from `parents` and `commands`. Remember to use `ansible-doc <os>_config` to see all parameters supported and even more examples.

Understanding check mode, verbosity, and limit.   Before we execute the playbook that'll create the configurations and deploy them, let's review a few other features you need to know when running Ansible playbooks:

Check mode
> This is the ability to run playbooks in "dry run" mode—the ability of knowing if changes *will* occur. It does everything as you'd expect when running a task, but does not actually make the given change. To use check mode, add the `--check` flag when executing your playbook. Note: check mode is a feature of individual modules.

Verbosity
> Every module returns JSON data. This JSON data contains metadata about the task at hand. For the `config` modules, it contains the commands being sent to the

device; and for `command` modules, it contains the response from the device. To run a playbook in verbose mode and see the JSON data returned from each module, add the -v flag when executing the playbook. You can use use up to four v's (-vvvv) when troubleshooting.

Limit

The common place to change the devices being automated is in the play definitions of a playbook using `hosts` such as `hosts: all`. If you wanted to automate just `junos` devices, one option is to change it to `hosts: junos`. Of course, this depends on having the `junos` defined in your inventory file. Another option is to use the `--limit` flag when executing a playbook such as `--limit junos`. Note: what you pass in with the `--limit` flag must be *in* the group or groups defined already within the `hosts` key in the playbook. Note that you can also pass in a single device, group, or multiple of each as such: `--limit junos,eos,csr1`.

The next example shows how you can use all three of these flags when running a single playbook. Using check mode in conjunction with verbose mode is valuable when deploying configurations because it shows exactly which commands *will* get sent to the device, but does not actually deploy them.

```
ntc@ntc:~/testing$ ansible-playbook -i inventory snmp.yml --limit eos-spine1
--check -v
Using /etc/ansible/ansible.cfg as config file

PLAY [PLAY 1 - GENERATE SNMP CONFIGURATIONS] **********************************

TASK [GENERATE CONFIGS FOR EACH OS] ******************************************
ok: [eos-spine1] => {"changed": false, "gid": 1000, "group": "cisco",
"mode": "0664", "owner": "cisco", "path": "./configs/snmp/eos-spine1.cfg",
"size": 133, "state": "file", "uid": 1000}

PLAY [PLAY 2 - ENSURE EOS SNMP CONFIGS ARE DEPLOYED] *************************

TASK [DEPLOY CONFIGS FOR EOS] ************************************************

changed: [eos-spine1] => {"changed": true, "commands": ["snmp-server location
EMEA-IE",
"snmp-server contact Scott Grady", "snmp-server community public123 ro",
"snmp-server community supersecure rw"], "session": "ansible_1497404657",
"updates": ["snmp-server location EMEA-IE", "snmp-server contact Scott Grady",
"snmp-server community public123 ro", "snmp-server community supersecure rw"]}

PLAY RECAP ******************************************************************
eos-spine1                 : ok=2    changed=1    unreachable=0    failed=0

ntc@ntc:~/testing$
```

As you can see in the example, there is much more output displayed because it was executed in verbose mode—this allows us to see the JSON data returned by each task and module. One other important point on reading playbook output is to understand what ok and changed are referring to. In the previous example, the last line states ok=2 changed=1. This tells us that two tasks were ok and successfully executed; however, only one of those tasks would have made a change (since this was run in check mode). If you are running a fully idempotent playbook for the second or more time, you'll always have changed=0 as no changes would occur.

You can now easily add subsequent plays that'll deploy the SNMP per OS. Here is one more for Junos:

```
- name: PLAY 3 - ENSURE JUNOS SNMP CONFIGS ARE DEPLOYED USING SET COMMANDS
  hosts: junos
  connection: local
  gather_facts: no

  tasks:

    - name: DEPLOY CONFIGS FOR JUNOS
      junos_config:
        src: "./configs/snmp/{{ inventory_hostname }}.cfg"
        provider: "{{ base_provider }}"
```

As you can see, the only difference is the module being used. Nothing else changes from the previous play.

Gathering and viewing network data

Ansible, like many automation tools, is used often to deploy configurations. However, Ansible also makes it possible to automate the collection of data from network devices. We're going to focus on two key methods for gathering data: using the core facts modules and issuing arbitrary show commands with the command module.

Using the core facts modules.   We'll first look at using the facts module. Core facts modules return the following data as JSON:

Table 9-1. Core facts modules used to automate the collection of data from network devices

Core facts module	Result
ansible_net_model	The model name returned from the device.
ansible_net_serialnum	The serial number of the remote device.
ansible_net_version	The operating system version running on the remote device.
ansible_net_hostname	The configured hostname of the device.
ansible_net_image	The image file the device is running.
ansible_net_filesystems	All filesystem names available on the device.
ansible_net_memfree_mb	The available free memory on the remote device in Mb.
ansible_net_memtotal_mb	The total memory on the remote device in Mb.

Core facts module	Result
ansible_net_config	The current active config from the device.
ansible_net_all_ipv4_addresses	All IPv4 addresses configured on the device.
ansible_net_all_ipv6_addresses	All IPv6 addresses configured on the device.
ansible_net_interfaces	A hash of all interfaces running on the system.
ansible_net_neighbors	The list of LLDP neighbors from the remote device.

After running a task to gather facts, we can access each of the previous keys directly in a playbook or a Jinja template just like any other variable (usually with double curly braces).

Let's take a look at an example.

```
---

- name: PLAY 1 - COLLECT FACTS FOR IOS
  hosts: iosxe
  connection: local
  gather_facts: no

  tasks:

    - name: COLLECT FACTS FOR IOS
      ios_facts:
        provider: "{{ base_provider }}"
```

You could optionally add more plays to gather facts per device type based on OS.

Using the debug module. In order to view the facts that are being returned from the module, you can run the playbook in verbose mode or simply use the debug module with the var parameter while referencing a valid facts key, as shown here:

```
# play definition omitted
  tasks:

    - name: COLLECT FACTS FOR IOS
      ios_facts:
        provider: "{{ base_provider }}"


    - name: DEBUG OS VERSION
      debug:
        var: ansible_net_version

    - name: DEBUG HOSTNAME
      debug:
        var: ansible_net_hostname
```

You usually reference variables with double curly braces within a playbook and Jinja template. Using the debug module with the var parameter is one of the times you do not use the curly brace notation! And remember, any variable in the playbook is also accessible in a Jinja template.

Running the tasks shown in the previous example produces the following output:

```
TASK [COLLECT FACTS FOR IOS] *************************************************
ok: [csr1]

TASK [DEBUG OS VERSION] ******************************************************
ok: [csr1] => {
    "ansible_net_version": "16.3.1",
    "changed": false
}

TASK [DEBUG HOSTNAME] ********************************************************
ok: [csr1] => {
    "ansible_net_hostname": "csr1",
    "changed": false
}
```

Note the playbook output and how you see the exact variables being referenced in the debug statements.

Issuing show commands and writing data to a file

You now know how to gather facts and debug the data being returned. In this section, we examine performing the same operation, but with the core command module. We'll show how to issue show commands, debug the response, and then subsequently write the show command output to a file.

Remember that one way to view the JSON response data from a task is simply executing the playbook in verbose mode. There is another way that allows you to use the debug module—to use this approach, you must first save the JSON response from the module as a variable and then debug that variable. Note: you don't need to save facts as a variable since facts are available to use natively within Ansible.

Using the register task attribute.   In order to save the JSON output that is returned from a module, you use the register task attribute. This allows you to save the JSON response data as a variable of the dictionary data type.

A task attribute gets inserted on the same indent level as the module name. In this example, we'll use the ios_command module, and thus we'll use the register attribute as a key on the same indent level as ios_command; register's associated value is the variable you want to save the data in. This is shown in the following example:

```
    - name: ISSUE SHOW COMMAND
      ios_command:
        commands:
          - show run | inc snmp-server community
        provider: "{{ base_provider }}"
      register: snmp_data
```

After the playbook is executed, the value of snmp_data is the JSON object returned by ios_command, which you also see when running the playbook in verbose mode.

Since the snmp_data variable is now created, or *registered*, the debug module can be used to view the data. The next example shows the playbook output for the previous task after the playbook was executed.

```
TASK [DEBUG COMPLETE SNMP RESPONSE] ********************************************
ok: [csr1] => {
    "changed": false,
    "snmp_data": {
        "changed": false,
        "stdout": [
            "snmp-server community ntc RO\nsnmp-server
            community public RO\nsnmp-server community public123 RO\nsnmp-server
            community private RW\nsnmp-server community secure RW"
        ],
        "stdout_lines": [
            [
                "snmp-server community ntc RO",
                "snmp-server community public RO",
                "snmp-server community public123 RO",
                "snmp-server community private RW",
                "snmp-server community secure RW"
            ]
        ]
    }
}
```

As you can see, using register along with the debug module provides a way to save and view the response data. After you view it, you need to understand the data structure to know how to access the data desired. For example, command modules return keys such as stdout and stdout_lines. Each of those respective values is a list—stdout is a list of command responses with a list length equal to the quantity of commands sent to the device and each element is the command response for that particular ordered command; stdout_lines is a nested object where the outer object is a list and the inner object changes based on the transport being used: list for CLI/SSH or dictionary for API (such as NX-API and eAPI). Our focus is on using stdout.

This means if you wanted to debug *only* the actual response as a string, you'd need to use one of the following debug statements:

```
- name: DEBUG COMMAND STRING RESPONSE WITH JINJA SHORTHAND SYNTAX
  debug:
    var: snmp_data.stdout.0

- name: DEBUG COMMAND STRING RESPONSE WITH STANDARD PYTHON SYNTAX
  debug:
    var: snmp_data['stdout'][0]
```

Additionally, as we've said, any variable in a playbook is also accessible in a template, so if you want to write the data to a file, you can use the `template` module with a basic template like the following:

```
{{ snmp_data['stdout'][0] }}
```

You can then use a single task to write the data to a file using the previously defined template:

```
- name: WRITE DATA TO FILE
  template:
    src: basic.j2
    # this template was saved in the templates directory
    dest: ./commands/snmp/{{ inventory_hostname }}.txt
    # the commands and snmp directories were created manually
```

It's critical to understand that every module returns JSON, and that data is saved with the `register` task attribute. Not only is this approach used for debugging data or writing data to file, but it's also used for performing compliance checks and generating reports, which we cover next.

Performing compliance checks

Compliance checks are quite often done manually by SSH'ing into devices and verifying something is either enabled or disabled, or configured or not configured, in order to satisfy a given network or security requirement. Automating these types of checks streamlines the process of ensuring the configuration and operational state is always as expected. These checks are always helpful for security engineers too—for example, when they're looking to validate that devices are hardened per requirements.

In order to perform compliance checks with Ansible, we need to first cover two more concepts within Ansible.

set_fact
> This is a module that creates an ad hoc variable out of some other complex set of data. For example, if you already registered a new variable that is a large dictionary, you may only care about a single key-value pair in that object. Using set_fact allows you to save one of those values as a new fact, or variable.

assert

It's quite common in software development to use `assert` statements for testing to ensure that a given condition is `True` or `False`. In Ansible, you can use the `assert` module to ensure that a condition is `True` or `False`.

Let's take a look at an example of *asserting* that VLAN 20 is configured on our two Arista EOS switches. The example consists of the following tasks:

1. Gather VLAN data.

2. Save VLAN data as `vlan_data`.

3. Print (debug) all VLAN data to see what's being returned.

4. Extract just the VLAN IDs from the full response.

5. Print just the VLAN IDs (validate that the extraction worked as expected).

6. Finally, perform the assertion that VLAN 20 is in the list of VLANs.

Here is the associated playbook:

```
---

- name: PLAY 1 - ISSUE SHOW COMMANDS
  hosts: eos
  connection: local
  gather_facts: no

  tasks:

    - name: RETRIEVE VLANS JSON RESPONSE
      eos_command:
        commands:
          - show vlan brief | json
        provider: "{{ base_provider }}"
      register: vlan_data

    - name: DEBUG VLANS AS JSON
      debug:
        var: vlan_data

    - name: CREATE EXISTING_VLANS FACT TO SIMPLIFY ACCESSING VLANS
      set_fact:
        existing_vlan_ids: "{{ vlan_data.stdout.0.vlans.keys() }}"

    - name: DEBUG EXISTING VLAN IDs
      debug:
        var: existing_vlan_ids

    - name: PERFORM COMPLIANCE CHECKS
      assert:
```

```
        that:
          - "'20' in existing_vlan_ids"
```

Running this playbook produces the following output for the last task, showing that VLAN is configured on eos-spine1, but not on eos-spine2.

```
TASK [PERFORM COMPLIANCE CHECKS] *********************************************
fatal: [eos-spine2]: FAILED! => {
    "assertion": "'20' in existing_vlan_ids",
    "changed": false,
    "evaluated_to": false,
    "failed": true
}
ok: [eos-spine1] => {
    "changed": false,
    "msg": "All assertions passed"
}
```

Once you understand what data is being returned from a given task and show command, you can perform an endless amount of assertions based on your exact need.

Next, we'll show how we can auto-generate reports from data coming back from devices too.

Generating reports

This section continues to build on the topic of gathering data. We first showed how to gather facts data, issue show commands, register the data, write the data to file, and finally perform assertions. In this section, we are going to refocus on writing data to a file, but in the context of generating a report.

Earlier, we showed how to gather facts using the core facts modules. We fully built out three plays in a single playbook that gathers facts using ios_facts, eos_facts, and nxos_facts. In the next example, we've added a fourth play to the playbook that autogenerates a facts report.

 While our report is for device facts, the same approach can be taken for *any* data returned from show commands or from any other variable that exists in an Ansible project.

```
- name: PLAY 4 - CREATE REPORTS
  hosts: "iosxe,eos,nxos"
  connection: local
  gather_facts: no

  tasks:

    - name: GENERATE DEVICE SPECIFIC REPORTS
```

```
    template:
      src: ./reports/facts.j2
      # these sub-directories were created manually
      dest: ./reports/facts/{{ inventory_hostname }}.md

  - name: CREATE MASTER REPORT
    assemble:
      src: ./reports/facts/
      dest: ./reports/master-report.md
      delimiter: "---"
    run_once: true
```

There are a few things to take note of in this playbook:

- This example is automating three groups of devices from the inventory file as denoted with hosts: "iosxe,eos,nxos".

- The template task generates a Markdown-based (*.md*) report per device.

- The assemble module assembles all of the individual reports into a single master report. This task also introduces another task attribute called run_once. Technically, it's not needed; but remember, we have several hosts being automated in this play, and only need *one* master report. So we simply tell Ansible to run it for the *first* device that happens to get automated—since the module is idempotent, even if you ran it *N* times without run_once, it wouldn't adversely impact the system. To build on this, you could also include the task attribute called dele gate_to and use the line delegate_to: localhost so it's run for the system (localhost) versus running once on the first host automated. At this point, it's semantics because both options work and solve the problem.

- The --- in Markdown is a horizontal bar across the page. This is being used as a device delimeter as the individual reports are combined into the master report.

The following shows the template used to generate the facts report:

```
# {{ inventory_hostname }}

## Facts

Serial Number: {{ ansible_net_serialnum }}

OS Version:   {{ ansible_net_version }}


## Neighbors

| Device | Local Interface | Neighbor | Neighbor Interface |
|--------|-----------------|----------|--------------------|
{% for interface, neighbors in ansible_net_neighbors.items() %}
{% for neighbor in neighbors %}
| {{ inventory_hostname }} | {{ interface }} | {{ neighbor.host }} |
```

```
{{ neighbor.port }} |
{% endfor %}
{% endfor %}

## Interface List
{% for interface in ansible_net_interfaces.keys() %}
  - {{ interface }}
{% endfor %}
```

This syntax is how you can build a Markdown-based table. This renders as an HTML-like table if you push it to GitHub or use a Markdown viewer. Most web browsers have plug-ins for viewing Markdown files; you can also easily try a Markdown editor such as SlackEdit (*https://stackedit.io/editor*).

Viewing the rendered text output for a single device looks like this:

```
# csr1

## Facts

Serial Number: 9KXI0D7TVFI

OS Version:   16.3.1


## Neighbors

| Device | Local Interface | Neighbor | Neighbor Interface |
|-----------------|----------|-------|-------------|
| csr1 | Gi4 | csr2.ntc.com | Gi4 |
| csr1 | Gi1 | csr2.ntc.com | Gi1 |
| csr1 | Gi1 | eos-spine1.ntc.com | Management1 |
| csr1 | Gi1 | vmx1 | fxp0 |
| csr1 | Gi1 | eos-spine2.ntc.com | Management1 |
| csr1 | Gi1 | vmx2 | fxp0 |

## Interface List
  - GigabitEthernet4
  - GigabitEthernet1
  - GigabitEthernet2
  - GigabitEthernet3
```

After pushing the rendered Markdown file to GitHub, you can see how it renders when viewing it online on GitHub (see Figure 9-2).

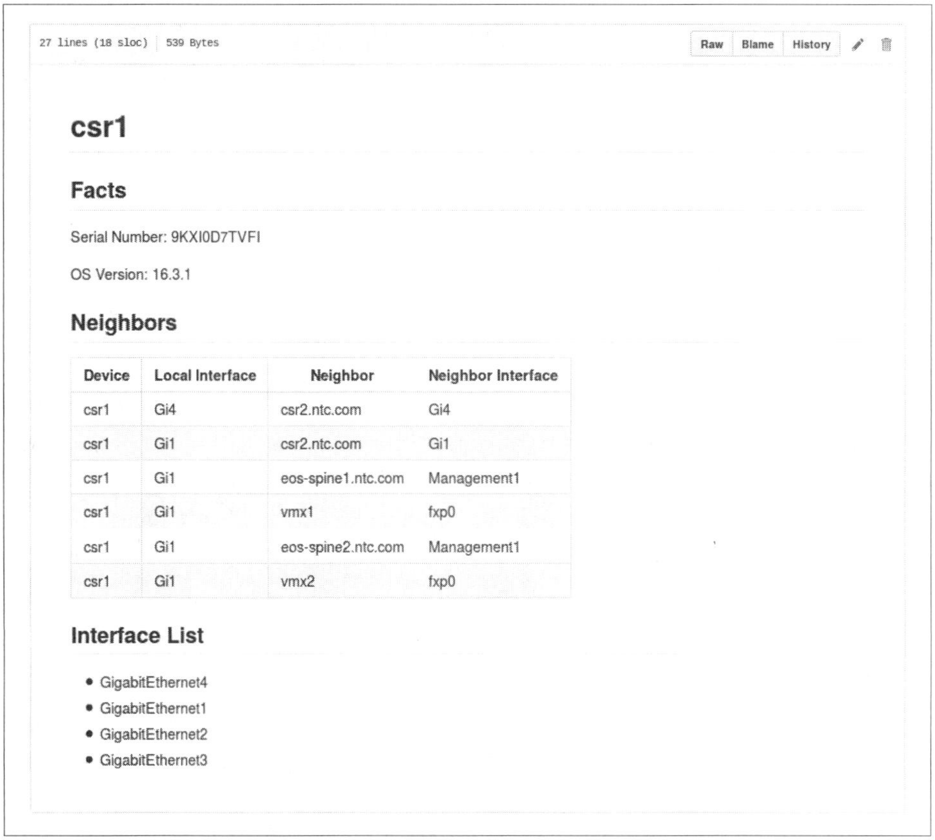
27 lines (18 sloc) | 539 Bytes

Raw Blame History

csr1

Facts

Serial Number: 9KXI0D7TVFI

OS Version: 16.3.1

Neighbors

Device	Local Interface	Neighbor	Neighbor Interface
csr1	Gi4	csr2.ntc.com	Gi4
csr1	Gi1	csr2.ntc.com	Gi1
csr1	Gi1	eos-spine1.ntc.com	Management1
csr1	Gi1	vmx1	fxp0
csr1	Gi1	eos-spine2.ntc.com	Management1
csr1	Gi1	vmx2	fxp0

Interface List

- GigabitEthernet4
- GigabitEthernet1
- GigabitEthernet2
- GigabitEthernet3

Figure 9-2. Viewing the facts generated report on GitHub

You can create any kind of templates desired: we've looked at configuration templates and Markdown templates, but you can just as easily create HTML templates too for ever greater customization.

Using Third-Party Ansible Modules

All of the examples we've reviewed in this chapter have used Ansible core modules—these are modules you can use right after installing Ansible. You can accomplish a tremendous amount with these modules from configuration to compliance checks to generating reports, as you've seen. However, there is an active community for third-party Ansible modules relevant for network automation. In this section, we'll review two core sets of open source third-party modules and how to manage installing third-party modules on your Ansible control host.

Many of the open source modules complement what is in Ansible core. It's also worth noting that many of these third-party modules predate any networking modules now in Ansible core.

Getting familiar with NTC modules

The company Network to Code open sourced several multi-vendor Ansible modules two years ago, now often referred to as NTC modules (*https://github.com/networkto code/ntc-ansible*).

This suite of modules is most commonly used for three primary reasons:

- Automatic parsing of raw text output from *legacy* devices using prebuilt TextFSM templates. TextFSM simplifies performing regular expressions on command output. All templates are also open sourced on GitHub (*https://github.com/networkto code/ntc-templates*). This parsing is accomplished with the `ntc_show_command` module, which is merely a wrapper for netmiko + TextFSM. The module also has an offline mode that allows you to use `command` modules, write the data to a file, and still parse that data with this module.

- Issuing commands on devices not yet supported in Ansible core. Because the `ntc_show_command` and `ntc_config_command` are using netmiko internally, you can automate any device netmiko supports (all via SSH). The netmiko library supports over two dozen device types, so the support for these modules is quite robust.

- Handling device OS management. There are a few modules within the NTC suite that allow you to back up config files, save configs, copy files to devices, upgrade OS images, and reboot them. These modules are quite commonly used for IOS and NXOS upgrades, but there is also some support for EOS and Junos.

Getting familiar with NAPALM modules

The Network Automation and Programmability Abstraction Layer with Multi-vendor Support (NAPALM) Project (*https://napalm-automation.net*) is a growing open source community developing multi-vendor network automation integrations.

There is deeper dive on NAPALM in Appendix B, but over the past two years, there have been two primary reasons that the NAPALM Ansible modules (*https:// github.com/napalm-automation/napalm-ansible*) have been used:

Declarative configuration management
  NAPALM focuses on the desired state configuration. It offers a common mechanism, using intelligence mostly found on network devices, to apply a desired state configuration file. When managing *full* configuration files in this fashion, you

simply deploy the new configuration—the configuration you want applied. You do *not* send command negations ("no" commands). NAPALM abstracts away how this operates per vendor and makes it so you don't have to micromanage device configurations. There is an option to send partial configurations as well, and based on network OS support. Still, only the commands that do not exist yet on the device are applied to it. You accomplish all of this by using the `napalm_install_config` module.

Obtaining configuration and operational state from devices

NAPALM also has a module called `napalm_get_facts` that is used to obtain a base set of facts as well as other information such as route entries, MAC table, BGP neighbors, LLDP neighbors, and much more. The benefit of using this module is that the data is preparsed and normalized for all vendors supported, eliminating the need for you to do that elsewhere in your playbook.

> Both NTC and NAPALM modules are multi-vendor and the modules themselves have a parameter that dictates the OS of the device being automated. There is not a module per OS as there is within Ansible core.

Being aware of non-core vendor modules

When you do not find modules of a given vendor in Ansible core, you should always check their GitHub page. There are a few companies that haven't yet contributed their modules to core. A few of them include:

- HPE for Comware7 switches
- Juniper for Junos devices
- Citrix for Netscaler devices
- Palo Alto for PAN Security appliances

So, remember to always check GitHub and with your vendor if you're looking for modules to manage a certain platform.

Installing third-party modules

The installation for third-party open source or custom modules is quite straightforward. There are only a few steps required.

1. Choose a path on your Linux system where you want to store all of your third-party modules.
2. Navigate to that path and perform a `git clone` on each repository that has modules you want to use.

3. Open your Ansible config vile (*ansible.cfg*) and update your module path with the directory where you performed your clones.

4. If you don't know where your *ansible.cfg* is, simply do an `ansible --version` on your system. You'll see an output like the following:

```
ntc@ntc:~/testing$ ansible --version
ansible 2.3.0.0
  config file = /etc/ansible/ansible.cfg
  configured module search path = [u'/etc/ntc/ansible/']
  python version = 2.7.6 (default, Jun 22 2015, 17:58:13) [GCC 4.8.2]
ntc@ntc:~/testing$
```

You'll see a line that states `library =`. This is where you'll update with the directory that has all of your cloned repos (e.g., `library = /etc/ntc/ansible/`). Once it's updated properly, you'll see the output of `ansible --version` update accordingly.

5. Finally, you still need to install any dependencies the modules have. These should be documented on each project's GitHub site and probably require a few packages to be installed via `pip`. Note: if you're using Python virtualenvs or a system with several Python versions, you may need to use the `ansible_python_inter preter` variable within Ansible.

Ansible Summary

As you've now seen, Ansible is quite robust and versatile with what can be achieved with respect to network automation, from compliance checks and reports to more general configuration management and automation. Its agentless architecture is what makes Ansible have a lower barrier to entry for network automation. Note that we only scratched the surface with showing what's possible when using Ansible. For more information on Ansible, check out *http://docs.ansible.com*.

Next, we are going to transition and take a look at Salt, which takes a different approach to automation.

Automating with Salt

Salt is a robust framework designed as an extremely fast and lightweight communication bus that offers capabilities such as automated configuration management, cloud provisioning, network automation, and event-driven automation, allowing you to achieve modern network operations of your infrastructure.

Salt is very flexible, and allows you to automate a wide variety of network devices and components, as do other tools in this chapter. Despite its somewhat perceived complexity, Salt can be set up in minutes so you can start automating network devices.

Similar to what we did in the previous section on Ansible, our goal is to provide a jump start with enough information so you can use Salt to start automating common network tasks immediately. In order to do this, we've divided this section into six major areas:

- Understanding the Salt architecture
- Getting familiar with Salt
- Managing network configurations with Salt
- Executing Salt functions remotely
- Diving into Salt's event-driven infrastructure
- Diving into Salt a bit further

Understanding the Salt Architecture

From an architectural perspective, Salt is designed as a simple core with pluggable interfaces. As you will see throughout this section, *everything* in Salt is pluggable and extensible, including the creation of new device drivers to automate network devices that use different APIs. To that end, Salt can be used to automate any type of network device.

Salt was initially developed to be an agent-based architecture, which wasn't well suited for network automation because, as we know, it's not easy to load software agents on all types of network devices. In fact, it's very hard or even impossible on traditional network equipment. Due to the demand for agentless automation solutions, Salt updated their architecture to offer both agentless and agent-based solutions. Additionally, in either deployment option, Salt facilitates event-driven network automation, which is covered later in this section.

At its core and default setup, Salt is a hub-and-spoke architecture. The hub, or central server, is referred to as the *Salt master* (running software called `salt-master`) and manages the spokes, which are referred to as *Salt minions* (running software called `salt-minion`), which in essence are the nodes being automated. The Salt master has the ability to manage thousands of *minions*. The communication between the master and minions is persistent and uses lightweight protocols to enable real-time communication—this approach allows Salt to scale and manage more than 30,000 minions using a single master server. For even larger designs, it's possible to distribute the minions to multiple master servers, which are eventually managed by a higher-level master.

This is how Salt operates quite commonly when automating servers. To understand how Salt operates when automating network devices, we need to review how Salt operates in an agentless architecture.

Using Salt in an agentless architecture with salt-ssh

The Salt architecture was extended to operate in an agentless mode of operation. In this mode of operation, the target nodes being automated do not have the `salt-minion` software package installed. Rather, another package called `salt-ssh` is used instead and can be installed directly on the master, or distributed on other nodes, as Salt provides a communication bus between all Salt-related processes.

In this design, the master connects to the target device using SSH, which is why this architecture is sometimes compared to Ansible. It's also worth noting that when using `salt-ssh`, you are still able to leverage the full functionality of Salt when automating your infrastructure.

> The `salt-ssh` subsystem is just another process used within the Salt architecture and can be installed on the master or another system.

Even the agentless mode of operation with `salt-ssh`, however, it hasn't particularly helped yet with automating network devices due to various transport types, APIs, and network operating systems. This is largely due to the lack of SSH-based integrations that have been built thus far for Salt.

This leads us to the next option that is most applicable to automating network devices, which is using Salt *proxy minions*.

Using Salt in an agentless architecture with proxy minions

Another approach Salt uses for agentless automation uses the concept of a Salt *proxy minion*. A proxy minion is a superset of the minion, thus offering all the features of the regular minions. For all intents and purposes, it is a virtual minion. This virtual minion is not installed on the devices you are automating—they simply proxy access to the devices you are automating. Proxy minions are extensible, offering you the ability to create (or choose) the preferred communication channel from a given proxy minion to the target devices being automated. This is how network automation is performed today with Salt.

A device managed, or minion, has a proxy process associated with it on the proxy minion, each consuming about 40 MB RAM. Using the proxy architecture, each proxy minion is capable of managing 100 devices from a proxy machine having only 4 GB RAM available. These characteristics make the proxy minion a solid choice for network automation. The proxy processes are controlled by the master, and very often, they run on the same physical server, but can also be placed in a distributed architecture, improving Salt's scaling capabilities for managing network devices. For example, Salt can automate a network consisting of 10,000 nodes by distributing the proxy minions on 10 machines, with each server running 1,000 proxy minion processes, thus managing 1,000 nodes each.

Automating network devices with Salt

Salt supports network automation through the use proxy minions. Four core proxy minions exist specifically for networking. They include:

NAPALM
> This natively offers multi-vendor network automation using the NAPALM open source Python library, which we cover in Appendix B.

Cisco Network Services Orchestrator (NSO)
> A commercial solution from Cisco that offers multi-vendor model-driven network automation primarily using NETCONF.

Juniper
> Used to manage Juniper Junos devices and developed by Juniper.

Cisco NX-OS
> Used to manage Cisco NXOS devices and developed by SaltStack.

For all of our examples going forward in this chapter, we're going to be strictly focused on using the NAPALM proxy minion to interact with various devices, including Cisco IOS, Cisco NXOS, Arista EOS, and Juniper Junos devices. This was our choice as it's open source, multi-vendor, and actively being developed.

Remember, we also used the devices and topology shown in Figure 9-3 (repeated from Figure 9-1) for the examples within this section (in addition to the Ansible section).

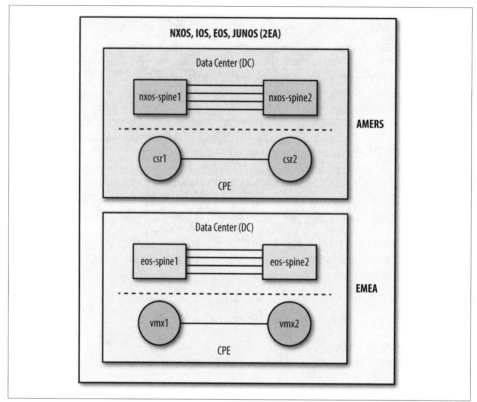

Figure 9-3. Network topology diagram

Again, Salt is very extensible and custom proxy minions can be written for different devices that have unique APIs or legacy interfaces, such as SNMP or Telnet.

Getting Familiar with Salt

There are many terms you should be aware of in order to start using Salt. In order to understand and use the system, you must have an idea of what these concepts are and how they fit into the overall Salt framework. We'll walk through a few of them now. First, we'll look at the SLS file format.

Understanding the SLS file format

Throughout this book, you've learned about Jinja templates and YAML files. In both cases, Jinja is just one type of templating language and YAML is just one way to structure data in a very human-readable format. Imagine using a single file that understands Jinja (and other templating languages) and YAML (and other data formats) in order to create different sets of data (the process of inserting data into the template). This is exactly what SLS files are.

SLS is a Salt-specific file format and it stands for SaLt State. It is a mixture of data representation and templating languages that can be used within the same file.

By default, an SLS file is YAML + Jinja. However, due to the flexibility of Salt and SLS, it can be easily switched to a different combination. This is an example of Salt's pluggability—you are not limited to Jinja and YAML only, but you're able to choose from a variety of options. For example, for data representation you can pick one of the following: YAML, YAMLEX, JSON, JSON5, HJSON, or even pure Python, and for templating, you can pick one of the following: Jinja, Mako, Genshi, Cheetah, Wempy, or, again, pure Python. The list of options can also be extended based on your requirements and preferences.

One case for supporting different types of data representations and templating engines is that it eases migrations from other tools. For example, if you had an internal (or custom) tool using Mako templates, another Python-based templating engine, you could easily use them with Salt—not being forced to use Jinja, as an example.

Here is a very basic SLS file that can be written as a pure YAML data file:

```
ntp_peers:
  - 10.10.10.1
  - 10.10.10.2
  - 10.10.10.3
```

You can add a Jinja for loop inside the same file to make it more dynamic:

```
ntp_peers:
  {%- for peer_id in range(1, 4) %}
  - 10.10.10.{{ peer_id }}
  {%- endfor %}
```

Showing the power of using SLS data files and other data and template types, the following is an example of using an HJSON data format with a Mako template.

```
#!hjson|mako
ntp_peers: [
  % for peer_id in range(1, 4):
  ${peer_id},
  % endfor
]
```

These three examples represent exactly the same data—a list of three NTP peers. The last one is a combination of HJSON and Mako—note the shebang at the top of the file specifying this. HJSON is a syntax extension to JSON, making it potentially more human-readable and less error-prone.

As stated earlier, you can also create SLS data files in pure Python. Here is another example that represents the same data:

```
#!py
def run():
    return [
        '10.0.10.{}'.format(peer_id) for peer_id in range(1, 4)
    ]
```

While all of these examples are SLS files, they are *data* files. They contain data that we'll eventually want to use to perform network automation tasks such as creating configuration files and configuring devices.

Please note that all of the SLS files noted here would be saved with a *.sls* extension.

Next we'll take a look at what *pillars* are and how they map back to SLS data files.

Understanding pillars

A pillar is a data *resource* that can either be a file that is an SLS file or data pulled from an external service such as a CMDB or another network management platform.

 When working with pillar files, keep in mind that the Salt master configuration file, which we cover in the next section, needs to have the proper paths defined for where you will store your pillars.

Within pillar files, you store all data required to manage network devices. This includes any common information such as authentication credentials, but also includes the actual configuration data for anything you wish to configure on the device, from interface configuration and protocols configuration to the BGP or NTP configuration.

The following is an example pillar file using the SLS file format:

```
proxy:
  proxytype: napalm
  driver: nxos
  fqdn: nxos-spine1.dc.amers
  username: ntc
  password: ntc123
hostname: nxos-spine1
openconfig-bgp:
  bgp:
    global:
      config:
        as: 65001
        router_id: 172.17.17.1
```

For our deployment, this pillar is added to the master. It is then distributed to all proxy minions, and in our case, we only have one proxy minion that is installed directly on the master server.

In the preceding pillar file, there are three keys defined. The first is called `proxy`, which is a special Salt keyword that requires key-value pairs that map to the specific proxy minion being used. The other keys, `hostname` and `openconfig-bgp`, are arbitrary user-defined keys that we're defining as they contain data values we want to configure and send to the network device.

In our example, this pillar was saved as */etc/salt/pillar/nxos_spine1_pillar.sls*. This particular pillar is device-specific, but as we'll see later in this section, they can also be broader for storing data used across a set of devices.

To avoid exposing sensitive data, you can encrypt the data using GPG and Salt will decrypt it during runtime (*https://docs.salt stack.com/en/latest/ref/renderers/all/salt.renderers.gpg.html*), or you can store it in a secured external pillar (for example, Vault).

For large deployments, you may want to retrieve data from some external system that already exists internal to your organization rather than manage large quantities of pillar files. For these use cases, it's possible to have external pillars. External pillars can be any external services including, but not limited to, databases, Git repositories, HTTP APIs, or even Excel files. The complete reference can be found at *https://docs.saltstack.com/en/latest/topics/devel opment/external_pillars.html*.

A common use case for network automation is fetching the data from an IP address management (IPAM) solution. Considering that most IPAM solutions expose data through an HTTP-based API, the next three lines could also be added to a pillar file:

```
ext_pillar:
  - http_yaml:
      url: https://my-ipam.org/api/<node>
```

In this case, all data returned from the IPAM can be data leveraged in some fashion when executing a Salt task such as rendering data into a template that'll be used to generate configurations.

Understanding the top file

We're now aware of the SLS file format and pillar data files that leverage the SLS file format. Another type of file in Salt that uses the SLS file format is called the *top file*.

The top file, often referred to simply as *the top*, defines the mapping between a minion or groups of minions and the data (through the use of pillars) that should be applied to them. To a certain extent, you can look at the top file as being similar to an Ansible inventory file, which we covered in the last section, but there are in fact many differences that you'll see.

Within the top file, you have the ability to specify which pillar(s) are assigned to which device(s). When new devices are added to Salt management, they are identified by a unique minion ID—this ID is assigned by you, the user. You can then reference this ID and map specific pillars (data) to the new device, or create broader groups based on device type, site, or region.

> The top file is commonly defined as *top.sls*. Our file was saved as */srv/pillar/top.sls*.

Here is a basic example of a top file that uses exact matches based on the minion ID and matches each device to a pillar data file.

```
base:
  csr1:  # minion id
    - csr1_pillar  # pillar mapped to csr1
  vmx1:
    - vmx1_pillar
  nxos-spine1:
    - nxos_spine1_pillar
  eos-spine1:
    - eos_spine1_pillar
```

In this basic example, the minion with the ID nxos-spine1 uses the *nxos_spine1_pillar.sls* pillar.

> Take notice of the base keyword as the root key in the top file. In Salt, base is a reserved keyword indicating that this is the *default* environment being managed by this Salt system. Thus, as you can imagine, you can manage different environments (prod, test, DR, QA) with Salt and reference them using different keys in your top file. We are using the default, or "base," environment for our examples.

As we alluded to, you may want to map a single pillar data file that contains certain configuration inputs for a certain device type to more than one device. In this case, you don't use the minion ID. You can use more advanced methods such as shell-like globbing and regular expressions, or even use device characteristics including grains, which we cover in an upcoming section, or pillar data.

Let's take a look at a few more examples of more realistic and advanced top files that leverage shell-like globbing and regular expressions.

The following example maps pillars to devices using characteristics about a device, called Salt grains, including vendor and OS version:

```
base:
  'G@vendor:juniper':
    - junos
  'G@os:ios and G@version:16*':
    - ios_16
  'E@(.*)-spine(\d)':
    - spine
```

In this example, the *junos.sls* pillar is loaded only for devices that are identified as manufactured by Juniper using the vendor characteristic. Again, these characteristics are called *grains*, which we cover in the next section. For now, you can see the G@, which indicates grains are being used. Similarly, the *ios_16.sls* pillar is mapped and loaded for all devices that are IOS and are version 16.X. Finally, you can also see in the last example, the spine pillar is loaded for any spine device (e.g., nxos-spine1 or eos-spine2). In this example, regular expressions are being used—note the E@ (expression). The minion ID must contain any characters (.*), followed by -spine, then followed by a single digit (\d) to match the spine devices in our topology.

You can also have default pillars that you want to apply to all devices. For example, to load a pillar, which we defined previously, called *ntp_peers.sls*, you can add the following to the top file:

```
'*':
  - ntp_peers
```

In this case, you can ensure that the entire network uses the same set of NTP peers.

You can also define custom groups based on your own business logic. To map a custom group of devices identified by a user-defined name (and a little more analogous to what's defined with Ansible), we need to use the nodegroups key in the Salt master configuration file—ours is stored at */etc/salt/master*:

```
nodegroups:
  amers:
    - 'csr*'
    - 'or'
    - 'nxos-spine*'
  emea:
    - 'vmx* and G@os:junos'
    - 'or'
    - 'eos-spine*'
```

Don't worry, we cover the Salt master configuration file in more detail in an upcoming section too.

There are now groups defined called amers and emea, such that the amers groups all devices whose minion ID starts with *csr* or *nxos-spine*, while emea groups devices whose ID starts with *eos-spine*, or running Junos and their ID starts with *vmx*.

Once these groups are defined in the master configuration file, they can be referenced in the top file. In the next example, pay attention to the two new keys called N@emea and N@amers. They are referencing the node groups (N@) that were just defined in the master configuration file.

```
base:
  'G@vendor:juniper':
    - junos
  'G@os:ios and G@version:16*':
    - ios_16
  'E@(.*)-spine(\d)':
    - spine
  'N@emea':
    - communities_emea
  'N@amers':
    - communities_amers
```

This assumes two pillars for BGP communities were created, *communities_amers.sls* and *communities_emea.sls*.

Don't forget that the top file is still SLS, thus Jinja + YAML by default, which can be leveraged to generate dynamic mappings. For example, if we have a longer list of regions, the last example could be written like this:

```
base:
  'G@vendor:juniper':
    - junos
  'G@os:ios and G@version:16*':
    - ios_16
  'E@(.*)-spine(\d)':
    - spine
{% for region in ['emea', 'amers', 'apac'] -%}
  'N@{{ region }}':
    - communities_{{ region }}
{% endfor -%}
```

While our focus is on getting started with Salt, you should be aware that you can integrate Salt to use external systems that offer more *dynamic tops*. Rather than a top file, you'd use an external service. This is helpful if you already have inventory and groupings in some other internal system or tool.

Understanding grains

We've already alluded to grains, but now we'll cover them in a little more detail. Remember that we've already defined pillars in SLS files. Thus, pillars are data provided by the user. In contrast, grains represent data gathered by Salt.

Grains are information that Salt collects about a given device such as device vendor, model, serial number, OS version, kernel, DNS, disks, GPUs, and uptime. You don't need to do anything with this data, but you should be aware that this data exists because it has *many* uses. For example, we've already shown how you can leverage grains in top files. You can also use this data in templates, conditional statements, and reports.

Grains is a Salt-specific term, but in other tools, this type of data is often referred to as *facts*. However, please note that they are not quite equivalent—grains are purely static data and they are cached. Dynamic details (such as interfaces details, BGP configuration, LLDP neighbors) is retrieved on runtime, via Salt *execution modules*.

Additionally, you have the ability to create your own grains either by using custom Salt integrations in the form of execution modules or by statically defining them in files. One option is to statically store grains data in the proxy minion configuration file as shown here:

```
grains:
  role: spine
  production: true
```

Before adding a new grain, it is recommended that you evaluate how dynamic the information is. Grains are more suitable for data very unlikely to change; otherwise, storing the data in a pillar is the preferred option.

In the next section, we'll look at using execution modules to view grains for one or more devices using the `salt` command.

Using execution modules

Salt uses execution modules, more commonly referred to as modules, in order to retrieve either data that's stored under Salt management or data directly from the device.

 We only review a handful of modules in this book. For a complete list of modules, please view them at *https://docs.saltstack.com/en/latest/salt-modindex.html*.

First, we'll review common modules and associated functions that are used to view both grains and pillar data. We'll show this using the `salt` command, but as you'll see later, you can also leverage these modules directly within SLS files that are used for templates, pillars, and other software artifacts within Salt.

In the first example, we'll simply print the grain called `model` for `csr1` using the `get` function within the `grains` execution module.

```
$ sudo salt csr1 grains.get model
csr1:
    CSR1000V
```

To see the complete list of grains available for a minion, you'd use `grains.items` instead, without passing any arguments.

You can also access specific data from a pillar while using the `salt` CLI command. In the next example, we check to see what the `ntp_peers` value is specifically for `csr1`. Similar to grains, `pillar.get` returns the value of specific pillar data.

```
$ sudo salt csr1 pillar.get ntp_peers
csr1:
    - 10.10.10.1
    - 10.10.10.2
    - 10.10.10.3
```

To retrieve a value from a more complex data structure in a pillar file, you use the `:` delimiter to navigate through key-value hierarchies. Using the previously defined structure from *nxos_spine1_pillar.sls* and shown here again, you can print just the BGP ASN for `nxos-spine1`:

```
# sample object in a pillar data file: nxos_spine1_pillar.sls
openconfig-bgp:
  bgp:
    global:
      config:
        as: 65001
        router_id: 172.17.17.1
```

```
$ sudo salt nxos-spine1 pillar.get openconfig-bgp:bgp:global:config:as
nxos-spine1:
    65001
```

As you start using the salt command, be aware of the general syntax:

```
$ sudo salt [options] <target> <function> [arguments]
```

In this case, target is used to specify the minions that are going to be automated with the arguments specified.

You can use salt --help for added assistance as you continue to use salt. We'll continue showing various examples using the salt command throughout this section.

Collecting device data using network modules

The previous examples used the grains and pillar modules. Those modules were simply accessing data that was predefined or cached data that was previously collected.

Salt also has over a dozen modules for retrieving feature-specific data from network devices including, but not limited to, NTP configuration, NTP peers, BGP, routes, SNMP, and users. There are even more advanced modules for extracting data from devices and representing it in YAML such that it maps to YANG models.

Remember all of this functionality, such as retrieving grains or configuration data from devices, while exposed to Salt, is occurring through the use of the NAPALM Python library.

The following are a few examples using modules on the CLI.

Retrieve the ARP table from the device with a minion ID of csr1:

```
$ sudo salt csr1 net.arp
# output omitted
```

Retrieve the MAC address table from the device with a minion ID of vmx1:

```
$ sudo salt vmx1 net.mac
# output omitted
```

Retrieve NTP statistics from the device with a minion ID of vmx1:

```
$ sudo salt vmx1 ntp.stats
# output omitted
```

Retrieve the active BGP neighbors from the device with a minion ID of vmx1:

```
$ sudo salt vmx1 bgp.neighbors
# output omitted
```

Retrieve the BGP configuration from the device with a minion ID of eos-spine1:

```
$ sudo salt eos-spine1 bgp.config
# output omitted
```

 In these examples, specific network functions are being executed within an execution module. In these examples, net, ntp, and bgp are the execution modules and what follows is the function inside the module (e.g., bgp.neighbors and bgp.config).

Understanding targeting and compound matching

In the previous examples, we were automating only a single device. Salt offers the ability to use *targeting* to automate more than one device. Targeting can be very simple, but can become as complex as required by the business logic. Let's look at a few examples.

Using the -L command line flag, you can explicitly define a list of devices you want to target:

```
$ sudo salt -L csr1,vmx1,nxos-spine1 net.mac
```

Using what's called *globbing*, you can use expressions such as a wildcard:

```
$ sudo salt 'vmx*' ntp.stats
```

Additionally, you can use grain data with the -G flag and target devices based on grains.

```
$ sudo salt -G 'os:junos' bgp.neighbors
```

You can even match devices using their static pillar data using the -I flag:

```
$ sudo salt -I 'bgp:as_number:65512' bgp.config
```

For the previous example to work, it would require the BGP configuration data to have the following equivalent YAML structure in a pillar file:

```
bgp:
  as_number: 65512
```

Now that you know how to automate a single minion or a group of minions based on a variety of options, it's worth understanding *compound matching*. Compound matching allows you to perform conditional-like logic, adding more flexibility to target the devices being automated.

In order to retrieve the BGP configuration from minions whose IDs start with vmx, running 15.1x, and have a predefined ASN of 65512 in the pillar file, you can use the following statement:

```
$ sudo salt -C 'vmx* and G@version:15.1* and I@bgp:as_number:65512' bgp.config
```

When using compound matching, you use the -C flag and then reference the other flags we previously covered using the flag and the @ symbol.

As compound matchers can get very complex at times, they can be defined in the master config file under nodegroups:

```
nodegroups:
    vmx-15-bgp: 'vmx* and G@os:junos and G@version:15.1* and I@bgp:as_number:65512'
```

You can then access and reference the node group on the CLI:

```
$ sudo salt -N vmx-15-bgp bgp.config
```

Verifying minions are up with the test module

In any size deployment, verifying minions are up and functional is a critical step in troubleshooting. You can accomplish this using the test module and more specifically the test.ping function.

```
$ sudo salt vmx1 test.ping
vmx1:
    True
```

test.ping is a simple function that only returns True. It is used to check if the minion is up and accepted by the master. Note: this is not an ICMP ping.

Viewing module and function docstrings

When just getting started with Salt, you may not be aware of how a particular function within a module works. In this case, you use the sys.doc option in the command being executed. sys.doc without any arguments returns the documentation for all modules.

Optionally, you can specify to return the docstring for a particular module or execution function:

```
$ sudo salt vmx1 sys.doc test.ping
test.ping:

    Used to make sure the minion is up and responding. Not an ICMP ping.

    Returns `True`.

    CLI Example:

        salt '*' test.ping
```

Understanding different output options for modules

The `salt` command permits a significant number of options. One of the most common is `--out`, which returns the output in the format specified. By default, the structure is displayed on the command line, in a human-readable and colorful format called `nested`:

```
$ sudo salt vmx1 ntp.peers
vmx1:
    ----------
    comment:
    out:
        - 1.2.3.4
        - 5.6.7.8
    result:
        True
```

Using the `--out` option, we can elect to return the structure in YAML, in JSON, or even as a table:

```
$ sudo salt --out=json vmx1 net.arp
{
    "vmx1": {
        "comment": "",
        "result": true,
        "out": [
            {
                "interface": "fxp0.0",
                "ip": "10.0.0.2",
                "mac": "2C:C2:60:FF:00:5F",
                "age": 1424.0
            },
            {
                "interface": "em1.0",
                "ip": "128.0.0.16",
                "mac": "2C:C2:60:64:28:01",
                "age": null
            }
        ]
    }
}
```

Next is an example of outputting the data to a table:

```
$ sudo salt --out=table vmx1 net.arp
vmx1:
----------
    comment:
    ----------
    out:
    ----------
        ----------------------------------------------------
        | Age  | Interface |    Ip    |       Mac       |
```

```
-----------------------------------------------------
| 991.0 |   fxp0.0  |   10.0.0.2  | 2C:C2:60:FF:00:5F |
-----------------------------------------------------
| None  |   em1.0   | 128.0.0.16  | 2C:C2:60:64:28:01 |
-----------------------------------------------------
result:
----------
```

There are several output types available and many others can be added. Although the --out option is for CLI usage, we are able to take the output in the format displayed on the screen and reuse it as-is in different services, including passing data to an external service.

While data can be passed to an external service, it can also be returned to an external service, which we cover next.

Sending data to external services

As you've seen, data is easily returned and viewed on the command line. However, you may also need to send this data to an external service. Using the --return CLI option, you define where to send the data, but you need to specify the name of a *returner*.

The list of available returners is diverse, some of the most usual being Slack, HipChat, Redis, SMS, SMTP, Kafka, and MySQL.

For example, we can configure the Slack returner by adding in the (proxy) minion or master configuration:

```
slack.channel: Network Automation
slack.api_key: d4735e3a265e16eee03f59718b
slack.username: salt
```

At this point, we can execute a command with the --return flag and the typical stdout is sent to Slack.

Here is an example:

```
$ sudo salt --return slack test.ping
# output omitted
```

 The output is still displayed on the command line, in the shape we want, while it is also forwarded to the selected service. If you do not want to return anything at all on the CLI, you can use the --out=quiet option.

While the outputters make sense only on the command line, returners can be used in other applications. For example, using the Salt scheduler, we can execute a job at specific intervals and its output is then sent to the designated returner. Similarly, when a task is performed as a result of a trigger, we may need to see its result from a monitoring tool.

Understanding states, state SLS files, and state modules

Salt states are modules used to manage, maintain, and enforce configuration. They are a declarative or imperative representation of a system configuration. Having the source of truth in the pillar, the state compares it with the current configuration, then decides what is required to be removed and what has to be added. Given modern network devices able to apply atomic configurations, it is even easier. In that case, we only need to generate the expected configuration and let the device compute the difference. In cases where the device does not have such capabilities, or it's more optimal to determine the difference ourselves, we need one additional step, as illustrated in the previous example.

Understanding the state SLS. The state SLS is a descriptor that defines which states will be executed when the state is applied. Each state is identified by a unique `state_name` that you define, which invokes a state function (built into Salt) passing a list of arguments.

```
<state_name>:
  <state_function>:
    - list of state arguments
```

Remember the following when you start working with state SLS files.

- `state_name` is an arbitrary name assigned.
- `state_function` is the state function we want to execute.

> Do not conflate the state SLS with the state module: the latter is a Python module that processes the arguments, executes the code, and produces the result, while the state SLS invokes one or more state functions.

State modules for network automation. For network automation needs, there are several state modules available, including `netyang`, `netconfig`, `netacl`, `netntp`, `netsnmp`, or `netusers`.

One of the most flexible is `netconfig`, which manages and deploys configurations on network devices using arbitrary user-defined templates. Our focus is on `netconfig`.

In this example, we use the `netconfig.managed` state function:

```
ntp_peers_example:
  netconfig.managed:
    - template_name: salt://ntp_template.j2
    - debug: true
```

Here is an overview of the various uses of the word `state` within the previous file:

- The file is a state SLS file.
- `ntp_peers_example` is a state name that we defined.
- `netconfig` is a built-in state module that manages configurations.
- `managed` or `netconfig.managed` is a built-in function that's part of the `netconfig` state module that specifically deploys the configurations onto network devices.

Additionally, remember that *ntp_template.j2* is a template that can leverage SLS functionality, and data inserted into the template could come from pillar data files that are SLS files. The main point is to remember that SLS is a file type.

Updating the master configuration file

We've made reference to various files that are used within Salt, such as pillars and templates. These types of files need to be stored in particular locations on your master server. You define these locations within the master configuration file.

The master configuration file is a YAML file that is preconfigured with default options as soon as Salt is installed. The default path for the master configuration file is either */etc/salt/master* or */srv/master*.

The list of options that can be configured in the master configuration file is long, but two of the most important are configuring `file_roots` and `pillar_roots`. These are *keys* in the config file—remember the file is YAML based.

Within `file_roots` you specify the paths local to the master server, where different files are stored, such as templates, states, pillars, and extension modules. The structure used is also flexible enough to allow you to have different environments on the same machine (e.g., production, test, and DR).

Here is a snippet from our sample configuration file that configures the `file_roots`:

```
file_roots:
  base:
    - /etc/salt/pillar
    - /etc/salt/templates
    - /etc/salt/states
    - /etc/salt/reactors
```

Note `base`, the special keyword in Salt we mentioned earlier. When used, it designates the respective paths that map to the *default* environment (since you can define multiple environments each as a different key). For example, if you wanted to define an environment called dev used for development only, the structure would be the following:

```
file_roots:
  dev:
    - /home/admin/pillar
    - /home/admin/states
```

The structure of `pillar_roots` is very similar to that of the `file_roots`, pointing to the directory where the pillar files are stored:

```
pillar_roots:
  base:
    - /etc/salt/pillar
```

You could subsequently update `pillar_roots` to support a development environment too:

```
pillar_roots:
  dev:
    - /home/admin/pillar
```

 It is not required to define templates within a flat directory such as */etc/salt/template*. There are designs where the templates are actually stored under each state, grouped more logically by how they're used and what devices are using them.

Once you have a base configuration on the master, the next step will be to perform similar tasks on the proxy minion, specifically when automating network devices.

Updating the minion and proxy minion configuration file

The minion has its own configuration file. The default paths supported are */etc/salt/minion* and */srv/minion*. As the proxy minion is a superset of the regular minion, it inherits all the options (YAML keys) supported by the minion configuration.

The proxy configuration file is stored either at */etc/salt/proxy* or */srv/proxy* (depending on the OS).

We did not make any changes or updates to the default proxy minion configuration file.

Next, we'll look at a few workflows that build and deploy network configurations.

Managing Network Configurations with Salt

We've seen how flexible SLS files are and what can be done with the `salt` command, but another unique capability of Salt is that any function available on the CLI can also be executed inside SLS files, including templates.

We're now going to walk through the process of auto-generating configurations through the use of templates.

Accessing data within templates

There are also a number of built-in *identifiers* (almost like variables) available, such as grains pillar opts (the dictionary of configuration options) or env (provides the environment variables). These can also be used directly inside a template similar to how they're used on the CLI (e.g., grains.get os). This adds value as you start templating out network configurations, as you'll see in the next few examples.

Execution functions can be accessed with the salt reserved keyword. While on the CLI we just execute ntp.peers; inside the template we only need to prepend salt:

```
{%- set configured_peers = salt.ntp.peers()['out'] -%}
```

configured_peers is a variable created in the template via the set statement in Jinja. configured_peers is a Jinja variable and when this template is executed, it'll be assigned the list of active NTP peers configured on the device through the ntp execution module.

In Salt as in many other tools, it's good practice to move the complexity of the Jinja templates into the actual functions such that the data or task can be eventually reused in other applications. This provides major benefits: making templates more readable, opening the gate to reusability, and providing a great way to reintroduce data into the system.

Custom execution modules take just a short time to write in Python and are automatically distributed to minions (or proxy minions). They can then be used within templates, other SLS files, or from the command line.

When using the grains, pillar, and opts keywords within a template, you can define high-level business logic and design templates in a vendor-agnostic manner, in such a way that the same template can be executed against different platforms, and it is intelligent enough to identify what configuration changes to load.

Creating Jinja network configuration templates

For example, you can define the Salt template to generate the configuration for the NTP peers, using the input data from the pillar defined earlier with a Jinja template that looks like this:

```
{%- if grains.os == 'junos' %}
system {
 replace:
```

```
    ntp {
        {%- for peer in pillar.ntp_peers %}
        peer {{ peer }};
        {%- endfor %}
    }
}
{%- elif grains.vendor | lower == 'cisco' %}
no ntp
    {%- for peer in pillar.ntp_peers %}
ntp peer {{ peer }}
    {%- endfor %}
{%- endif %}
```

The unique piece here is the use of the `pillar` keyword directly in the template. This allows you to access data defined in the pillar files.

If your goal was to ensure that a specific feature is configured exactly as desired in a declarative manner (with no extra peers still on the device), you can perform a `replace` operation on the device. On Junos, you do this using the `replace` keyword, while with other more traditional operating systems, command negations ("no" commands) are required.

 The `replace` keyword here for Junos maps back to the NETCONF `replace` operation that we covered in Chapter 7 and allows you to *replace* a full hierarchy within a configuration.

In this example, we saved the template as *ntp_template.j2* within the */etc/salt/templates* directory, as this was one of the `file_roots` defined originally in the master configuration file.

We can then reference this template as `salt://ntp_template.j2` when using it from the command line or from within Salt state files.

At this point, we've simply built out the Jinja template—we haven't yet rendered it with data, or created a configuration file.

To highlight what's possible using of the `salt` directive inside the template, we're able to determine the NTP peers to be added or removed based on retrieving in real time the existing peers using the statement `salt.ntp.peers`.

The following template creates the configuration for both IOS and Junos for configuring NTP peers. This template has the logic required to ensure only the peers defined in the pillar end up configured on the device, meaning any unwanted peers will be purged from the device (when the configuration is deployed).

```
{%- set configured_peers = salt.ntp.peers()['out'] -%}
{%- set add_peers = pillar.ntp_peers | difference(configured_peers) -%}
```

```
{%- set rem_peers = configured_peers | difference(pillar.ntp_peers) -%}
{%- if grains.os == 'junos' -%}
 {%- for peer in rem_peers -%}
delete system ntp peer {{ peer }}
 {% endfor -%}
 {%- for peer in add_peers -%}
set system ntp peer {{ peer }}
 {% endfor -%}
{%- elif grains.vendor | lower == 'cisco' %}
 {%- for peer in rem_peers -%}
no ntp peer {{ peer }}
 {% endfor -%}
 {%- for peer in add_peers -%}
ntp peer {{ peer }}
 {% endfor -%}
{%- endif -%}
```

For devices such as Juniper that provide support for partial configuration replace capabilities, this is quite a nice solution. For others, it could seem tedious due to the logic required to determine which "no" commands are needed to purge the unwanted peers. However, this is the best way to handle those scenarios where there isn't a native way for *partial* configuration replace operations.

Deploying network configurations with netconfig

Next, we need to define a state that can be executed to insert the data from the NTP pillar(s) into the NTP template to generate the required commands that'll send commands to the devices.

Here is where we'll use the netconf.managed state function. This renders the desired configuration and deploys the commands to the network device.

```
ntp_peers_example:
  netconfig.managed:
    - template_name: salt://ntp_template.j2
    - debug: true
```

This SLS state file was saved under one of the file_roots paths (e.g., */etc/salt/states*) as *ntp.sls*.

To execute this SLS state file, we need to call the execution function state.apply or state.sls with the name of the state file as an argument:

```
$ sudo salt vmx1 state.apply ntp
vmx1:
----------
          ID: ntp_peer_example
    Function: netconfig.managed
      Result: True
     Comment: Configuration changed!
     Started: 10:48:16.160777
```

```
       Duration: 4331.08 ms
        Changes:
                    ----------
                 diff:
                     [edit system ntp]
                     +     peer 10.10.10.1;
                     +     peer 10.10.10.3;
                     +     peer 10.10.10.2;
                     -     peer 1.2.3.4;
                     -     peer 5.6.7.8;
                 loaded_config:
                     delete system ntp peer 1.2.3.4
                     delete system ntp peer 5.6.7.8
                     set system ntp peer 10.10.10.1
                     set system ntp peer 10.10.10.3
                     set system ntp peer 10.10.10.2

Summary for vmx1
------------
Succeeded: 1 (changed=1)
Failed:    0
------------
Total states run:     1
Total run time:    4.331 s
```

Note that in a single execution, the commands were generated in memory and deployed to a network device. This example did not create a config file first.

The format of the output displayed in the previous example on the CLI is called *high-state*, but the object returned is still a Python object (we can verify using `--out=raw`); hence, it can be reused and define complex workflows.

Note the `loaded_config` key returned as we specified `debug: true` in the state SLS, having the configuration generated as required by the business logic.

The execution time is quite fast here given all the steps performed: it retrieved the current configuration, determined the difference, generated the configuration (all within the template), and subsequently loaded the commands onto the device, generated a diff, and then committed the configuration to memory on the device, all within 4.3 seconds.

We can also run the same exact state file, `ntp.sls`, against `csr1`. The state will process the same template, which knows from the grains that `csr1` is a Cisco IOS device and will generate the appropriate configuration to be loaded on the device:

```
$ sudo salt csr1 state.apply ntp
csr1:
    ----------
          ID: ntp_peer_example
    Function: netconfig.managed
      Result: True
```

```
         Comment: Configuration changed!
         Started: 11:38:14.609398
         Duration: 3414.471 ms
         Changes:
                  ----------
                  diff:
                      + ntp peer 10.10.10.1
                      + ntp peer 10.10.10.3
                      + ntp peer 10.10.10.2
                  loaded_config:
                      ntp peer 10.10.10.1
                      ntp peer 10.10.10.3
                      ntp peer 10.10.10.2

Summary for csr1
------------
Succeeded: 1 (changed=1)
Failed:    0
------------
Total states run:     1
Total run time:  3.414 s
```

Using state dependencies

Another important feature you can leverage within state files is creating state dependencies.

When you need to apply several states that depend on each other, you will find *state requisites (https://docs.saltstack.com/en/develop/ref/states/requisites.html)* very helpful. For example, if you need the `ntp_peer_example` state to be executed only if another state (such as `bgp_neighbors_example`) has been successfully executed, you only need to add two more lines:

```
ntp_peers_example:
  netconfig.managed:
    - template_name: salt://ntp_template.j2
    - require:
      - bgp_neighbors_example
```

Generating network configuration files

We also have the ability to decouple the configuration generation and deployment into separate steps—similar to what we showed in the Ansible section too. This is often helpful if you want to version or view the commands before you try doing any deployments.

In order to accomplish this, we'll use the `file.managed` state function. As arguments, we'll specify the template type and location of the template. Once the data is rendered in the template, we'll save it as *ntp_generated.conf* using the `name` key:

```
build_config:
  file.managed:
    - name: /home/admin/ntp_generated.conf
    - source: salt://ntp_template.j2
    - template: jinja
```

If we saved this *build-ntp.sls*, we could just build the configuration as follows:

```
$ sudo salt csr1 state.apply build-ntp
```

Generating and deploying network configurations from files

Another option if you did want to build the config and deploy within a single work-flow, but still wanted to generate a config file on the server first, would be to have both of these states in the same SLS file.

```
generate_config:
  file.managed:
    - name: /home/admin/ntp_generated.conf
    - source: salt://ntp_template.j2
    - template: jinja
ntp_peer_example:
  netconfig.managed:
    - template_name: /home/admin/ntp_generated.conf
    - require:
      - file: /home/admin/ntp_generated.conf
```

If we saved this as *ntp-build-deploy.sls* and executed it, we'd see the following output:

```
$ sudo salt vmx1 state.sls ntp-build-deploy
vmx1:
----------
          ID: /home/admin/ntp_generated.conf
    Function: file.managed
      Result: True
     Comment: File /home/admin/ntp_generated.conf updated
     Started: 12:17:25.544779
    Duration: 141.895 ms
     Changes:
              ----------
              diff:
                  ---
                  +++
                  @@ -0,0 +1,4 @@
                  + set system ntp peer 10.10.10.1
                  + set system ntp peer 10.10.10.3
                  + set system ntp peer 10.10.10.2
                  +
----------
          ID: ntp_peer_example
    Function: netconfig.managed
      Result: True
     Comment: Configuration changed!
```

```
       Started: 12:17:25.687279
      Duration: 4189.027 ms
       Changes:
                 ----------
                 diff:
                     [edit system]
                     +   ntp {
                     +       peer 10.10.10.1;
                     +       peer 10.10.10.3;
                     +       peer 10.10.10.2;
                     +   }

Summary for vmx1
------------
Succeeded: 2 (changed=2)
Failed:    0
------------
Total states run:     2
Total run time:    4.331 s
```

Parameterizing configuration filenames

In both previous examples when config files were generated, the filename used was /
home/admin/ntp_generated.conf. This is not scalable, as the filename is static. To
avoid hardcoding the filename, but generate the name depending on the device or
minion ID, we can specify this using the id field from the opts SLS special variable:

```
generate_config:
  file.managed:
    - name: /home/admin/{{ opts.id }}_ntp_generated.conf
    - source: salt://ntp_template.j2
    - template: jinja
```

The state above generates a file called *home/admin/vmx1_ntp_generate.conf* for the
vmx1 minion, *home/admin/csr1_ntp_generate.conf* for csr1, and so on.

Scheduling state execution

In Salt, it is very important to distinguish between jobs executed on the master and
jobs executed on the minion. While the minions run execution functions, the master
executes runners (covered in the next paragraphs). This is significantly important
when we are scheduling jobs: if we want to schedule an execution function, we add
the instructions in the (proxy) minion configuration file, while we schedule a runner
by adding the options in the master configuration file. In both cases, the syntax is the
same. For example, if we need to schedule the preceding state to be applied every
Monday at 11 a.m., we'd only need the following lines in the (proxy) minion configuration file:

```
schedule:
  ntp_state_weekly:
```

```
function: state.sls
args:
  - ntp
kwargs:
  test: true
ret: smtp
when:
  - Monday 11:00am
```

Under kwargs we configured `test: true`, which means the state is going to execute a dry run, but it will return the configuration difference. Moreover, we have subtly introduced another feature with the field `ret: smtp`. This tells Salt to take the output of the state and forward it to the *returner* called `smtp` (*https://docs.saltstack.com/en/develop/ref/returners/all/salt.returners.smtp_return.html*). This returner takes the data from the output of the state and sends an email with the configuration diff.

Generating reports

Generating reports is even more useful when they are also consumed by a process or a human. For this, the *returners* are very handy and easy to use. In the previous example, the NTP state is executed, and then its output is processed via the SMTP returner —this is basically sending the execution report as email.

To send the email with the content as-is, we only need to configure the following options on the minion:

```
smtp.from: ping@mirceaulinic.net
smtp.to: jason@networktocode.com
smtp.host: localhost
smtp.subject: NTP state report
```

We can customize the subject body using a template, as follows:

```
smtp.template: salt://ntp_state_report.j2
```

Where *ntp_state_report.j2* is found in the Salt filesystem, for example under the */etc/salt/templates* directory:

```
NTP consistency check
--------------------

Running on {{ id }}, which is a {{ grains.vendor }} {{ grains.model }} device,
running {{ grains.os }} {{ grains.version }}:

{{ result }}
```

When the scheduler is executed, it will send an email with the following body:

```
NTP consistency check
--------------------

Running on vmx1, which is a Juniper VMX device,
```

```
running junos 15.1F4.15:

vmx1:
----------
          ID: ntp_peer_example
    Function: netconfig.managed
      Result: None
     Comment: diff:
              [edit system]
              +   ntp {
              +       peer 10.10.10.1;
              +       peer 10.10.10.3;
              +       peer 10.10.10.2;
              +   }

              Configuration discarded.
     Started: 15:14:09.911816
    Duration: 969.945 ms
     Changes:

Summary for vmx1
------------
Succeeded: 1 (unchanged=1)
Failed:    0
------------
Total states run:     1
Total run time: 969.945 ms
```

With this setup, we can ensure that Salt periodically executes the NTP state in test mode, then generates and sends an email with the report.

From the CLI, we could achieve this by manually executing:

```
`$ sudo salt vmx1 state.sls ntp test=True --return smtp`.
```

In a very similar way, we can set this up to send reports with the result from multiple devices at a time, using a runner instead of an execution function. While the execution function is run by the minion process, a runner function is executed by the master process, which gives visibility over the entire network. In Python language, the result is a dictionary whose keys are the minion IDs matched, while the values are the actual result of each device.

Available from both CLI and scheduled process, returners are a very powerful tool for post-processing and data transformation. Later, we will see they can be reused when reacting to events, or to monitor the entire Salt activity.

Executing Salt Functions Remotely

We've covered quite a bit thus far on Salt, but one of the most important components to understand is the architecture employed by Salt for network devices. However, as you've learned a lot in this section, be aware that Salt offers two primary ways you can interact with Salt, and execute any command or tasks remotely from another machine. They are the built-in RESTful API and an external Python package called `pepper` that remotely executes `salt` commands on the master.

Using the Salt API

This RESTful API is included with Salt and can be used to perform any operation you can when using the `salt` command-line programs within the Linux shell.

A core feature of the RESTful API is that it allows you to pick one of three web servers supported *out of the box*. They include CherryPy, uWSGI, or Tornado.

The following is how you'd enable CherryPy by editing the master configuration file:

```
rest_cherrypy:
  port: 8001
  ssl_crt: /etc/nginx/ssl/my_certificate.pem
  ssl_key: /etc/nginx/ssl/my_key.key
```

This configures the server to listen on port 8001 and use the certificate and the key for secured requests.

Afterward, you can start executing Salt functions remotely through the use of custom scripts, Postman, or cURL. The following example shows the use of cURL to retrieve the ARP table for vmx1.

```
curl -sSk https://salt-master-ns-or-ip:8001/run \
    -H 'Content-type: application/json' \
    -d '[{
        "client": "local",
        "tgt": "vmx1",
        "fun": "net.arp",
        "username": "ntc",
        "password": "ntc123",
        "eauth": "pam"
    }]'
```

For configuration-related requests, the function is then replaced by `state.sls` or `state.apply` and the name of the state is specified in the `args` field:

```
curl -sSk https://salt-master-ns-or-ip:8001/run \
    -H 'Content-type: application/json' \
    -d '[{
        "client": "local",
        "tgt": "vmx1",
        "fun": "state.sls",
        "args": ["ntp"],
        "username": "ntc",
        "password": "ntc123",
        "eauth": "pam"
    }]'
```

This example, when executed, would run the NTP state that was defined earlier in the chapter.

Shaking it up with salt and pepper

Using the API is one option, and the preferred choice if you need to integrate Salt with third-party systems. However, another option is pepper—a Python library in which you can execute CLI commands, from a personal machine, directly on the Salt master server.

 pepper is installed from PyPI via pip like so: pip install salt-pepper.

pepper only requires you to configure the credentials as environment variables or in a configuration file *$HOME/.pepperrc*:

```
[main]
SALTAPI_URL=https://salt-master-ns-or-ip:8001/
SALTAPI_USER=my_username
SALTAPI_PASS=my_password
SALTAPI_EAUTH=pam
```

Pepper comes with a command-line binary (pepper) that can be used exactly like the master salt command. For example, we can execute NTP state from *our* machine and it'll run directly on the master:

```
$ pepper 'vmx1' state.sls ntp
# output omitted
```

Diving into Salt's Event-Driven Infrastructure

Salt is built around an event bus, which is an open system, based on ZeroMQ, used to notify Salt and other systems about operations. ZeroMQ is a cross-platform high-performance asynchronous messaging toolkit that focuses on handling tasks very efficiently, without additional overheads.

To watch the events in real time, we execute the following command on the master:

```
$ sudo salt-run state.event pretty=True
```

If we looked at using a module with the salt command, we'd see that there are three individual events that take place when the command is executed. For example, a command such as $ sudo salt -G os:nxos test.ping executes the following three events.

First, there is a Job ID, a way to uniquely reference any given event that is mapped to target minions. The event is described and shown as follows:

```
20170619145155855122  {
    "_stamp": "2017-06-19T14:51:55.855336",
    "minions": [
        "nxos-spine1"
    ]
}
```

Next, the job is executed on the appropriate minions. This event is described and shown as follows:

```
salt/job/20170619145155855122/new {
    "_stamp": "2017-06-19T14:51:55.855656",
    "arg": [],
    "fun": "test.ping",
    "jid": "20170619145155855122",
    "minions": [
        "nxos-spine1"
    ],
    "tgt": "os:nxos",
    "tgt_type": "grain",
    "user": "sudo_admin"
}
```

The final event for this command is the response and status for each minion that was in the target scope.

```
salt/job/20170619145155855122/ret/nxos-spine1 {
    "_stamp": "2017-06-19T14:51:55.867958",
    "cmd": "_return",
    "fun": "test.ping",
    "fun_args": [],
    "id": "nxos-spine1",
    "jid": "20170619145155855122",
    "retcode": 0,
    "return": true,
    "success": true
}
```

Note that in the final event there is a unique tag pattern for each minion. As you can see, the preceding example is showing the tag of salt/job/20170619145155855122/ret/nxos-spine1.

Next, we'll take a look at several items that have very specific meaning within Salt for event-driven network automation.

Watching external processes with beacons

In Salt, beacons are used to watch external processes that are not related to Salt and to import and return events onto the Salt bus.

For example, the `inotify` beacon is used to monitor when a file is changed. If we want to monitor when the *ntp_peers.sls* file is updated, the following lines need to be added in the (proxy) minion configuration:

```
beacons:
  inotify:
    - /etc/salt/pillar/ntp_peers.sls:
        mask:
          - modify
      disable_during_state_run: True
```

This instructs Salt to start monitoring the file */etc/salt/pillar/ntp_peers.sls* and push events onto the bus. Modifying the contents, we will see events with the following structure:

```
salt/beacon/vmx1/inotify//etc/salt/pillar/ntp_peers.sls {
    "_stamp": "2017-06-20T10:17:49.651695",
    "change": "IN_IGNORED",
    "id": "vmx1",
    "path": "/etc/salt/pillar/ntp_peers.sls"
}
```

This may be valuable for you to track data as it changes in the system. Since you can use modules within pillars (as an example), the data is dynamic, often getting pulled from the devices in real time. You'd be able to see this data change in real time using beacons.

Forwarding events with engines

Engines are another subsystem interfacing with the event bus. While beacons only listen to external processes and transform them into Salt events, engines can be bidirectional. Although their main scope is the forwarding of events, there are also engines able to inject messages on the bus. And that is the main difference between beacons and engines: *beacons* poll the service at specific intervals (default: 1 second), while the *engines* can fire and forward events on immediate occurrence.

A very good application could be logging Salt events to a syslog server such as Logstash, using the *http-logstash* engine. This would be defined on the master like so:

```
engines:
  - http_logstash:
      url: https://logstash.elastic.co/salt
      tags:
        - salt/job/*/new
        - salt/job/*/ret/*
```

The YAML configuration on the master configures the master to send events to Logstash. However, it's configured to send the events only matching the tags `salt/job/*/new` and `salt/job/*/ret/*`. For reference, if `tags` is not configured or empty, the engine would forward all events.

Listening to the salt bus with reactors

The reactor system listens to the event bus and executes an action when an event occurs. The reactors are configured on the master, the global syntax being:

```
reactor:
  - <tag match>:
    - <list of SLS descriptors to execute>
```

The tag match describes the pattern to be matched against the event tag.

```
reactor:
  - 'salt/beacon/*/inotify//etc/salt/pillar/ntp_peers.sls':
    - salt://run_ntp_state_on_pillar_update.sls
```

This example instructs Salt to execute the *run_ntp_state_on_pillar_update.sls* data file when the `inotify` beacon injects the corresponding event on the bus, on file update.

The reactor SLS, *run_ntp_state_on_pillar_update.sls*, can have any structure you'd like. For our example, we're using the following:

```
run_ntp_state:
  local.state.sls:
    - tgt: {{ data['id'] }}
    - arg:
      - ntp
    - ret: mongo
```

This executes the execution function `state.sls` with the argument `ntp` against the minion whose ID is extracted from the event body, under the field `id`.

The following events are what you'd see on the event bus. First, you'd see the pillar file, *ntp_peers.sls*, being changed.

```
salt/beacon/vmx1/inotify//etc/salt/pillar/ntp_peers.sls {
    "_stamp": "2017-06-20T10:57:24.651644",
    "change": "IN_IGNORED",
    "id": "vmx1",
    "path": "/etc/salt/pillar/ntp_peers.sls"
}
20170620105724736722  {
    "_stamp": "2017-06-20T10:57:24.737525",
    "minions": [
        "vmx1"
    ]
}
salt/job/20170620105724736722/new {
    "_stamp": "2017-06-20T10:57:24.737804",
    "arg": [
        "ntp"
    ],
    "fun": "state.sls",
    "jid": "20170620105724736722",
    "minions": [
```

```
          "vmx1"
      ],
      "tgt": "vmx1",
      "tgt_type": "glob",
      "user": "sudo_admin"
}
# followed also by the result of the state execution, omitted here due to size
# limits further output omitted
```

The first event is fired by the `inotify` beacon; then, the reactor kicks in and creates a new job and identifies the minions, then sends the task to the minions (only `vmx1` in this case).

Note the `ret` field in the reactor SLS: the mongo *returner* is invoked, which means Salt will forward the state results into MongoDB. This statement is optional and not required.

Suppose we have the pillar files maintained in Git. Configuring the local clone to track the remote origin server, the previous example is an excellent orchestration example: a pull request merged triggers automatic configuration deployment of the NTP peers for the entire network, without any manual work. Note also the difference between configuration management only and event-driven automation: beacon, reactor setup, and SLS—15 lines in total, and the results are sent into a structured database service. Moreover, we maintain vendor-agnostic entities of data, not pseudo-formatted files.

Adding business logic using Thorium

The reactor has the limitation that we are able to trigger actions only to individual events. Thorium is the next step: it is a complex system that can define business logic based on aggregate data and multiple events.

As with any other Salt system, Thorium has its own file roots, pointing by default to */srv/thorium*, and can be changed in the master configuration:

```
thorium_roots:
  base:
    - /etc/salt/thorium
```

Under the Thorium file roots, we have a dedicated *top.sls* file to include the Thorium descriptors.

For example, let's say we want to push a HipChat notification after we commit (executing the function `net.commit`) three times.

In the first place, as we need to count, we need to define a register that matches the `net.commit` function and counts:

```
commits:
  reg.list:
```

```
      - add: fun
      - match: salt/job/*/new
    check.contains:
      - value:
          fun: net.commit
      - count_gte: 3
```

In the `commits` register we store the function names extracted from the events having the tag matching `salt/job/*/new`. Then, `check.contains` ensures that the register contains the `net.commit` function and there are at least three occurrences.

The second part is pushing the HipChat notification:

```
too_many_commits:
  runner.cmd:
    - fun: salt.cmd
    - arg:
      - hipchat.send_message
    - kwargs:
      - room_id: 1717
      - message: too many commits
      - from_name: ''
      - api_key: Ag56uXGGB6jTh1Lc8sEpZOgX6rMCm7M5wN6dPLFd
      - api_version: v2
    - require:
      - check: commits
```

This configuration instructs Thorium to execute the `salt.cmd` runner to invoke the `hipchat.send_message` execution function with the necessary details, but *only* when the `commits` register defined earlier is matched.

Save the preceding configurations in an SLS file—say, *too_many_commits.sls*— under */etc/salt/thorium*, and include it in the corresponding top file (*/etc/salt/ thorium/top.sls*):

```
base:
  '*':
    - too_many_commits
```

After three commits, the Thorium complex reactor will push a HipChat notification.

Although this example is very minimalist, there are no complexity boundaries.

> You can do quite a lot with Salt without event-driven network automation. Our recommendation is to first start using the `salt` command and start creating relevant SLS data files in the form of pillars and templates. Once you've mastered the basics, you'll be ready to start exploring the event-driven capabilities of Salt and have a much greater grasp on what it offers.

Diving into Salt a Bit Further

The community has built a document of best practices to secure the Salt environment, hosted under the official documentation (*https://docs.saltstack.com/en/latest/topics/hardening.html*).

One good practice we'll point out now is restricting users from having the ability to use any command they want. Using the Publisher ACL system, you can define what permissions each user has:

```
publisher_acl:
  mircea:
    - .*
  jason:
    - csr*:
      - ntp.*
      - test.*
```

In this example, `mircea` is allowed to execute anything, while `jason` is allowed to use the execution functions from the `ntp` and `test` modules, but only on the `csr*` minions.

To restrict the access through the REST API, you can configure the External Authentication system (eAuth):

```
external_auth:
  pam:
    matt:
      - 'vmx*':
        - ntp.*
        - napalm_yang.*
    scott:
      - '@runner'
```

The configuration structure is very similar to the Publisher ACL system, where the authentication is PAM (Pluggable Authentication Modules): `matt` can execute the functions from the `ntp` and `napalm_yang` modules, while `scott` can invoke any runner. Note that PAM is just one option to use as the authentication system.

Understanding small database queries (SDB)

The SDB interface is designed to store and retrieve data that, unlike pillars and grains, is not necessarily minion-specific, through small database queries (hence the name SDB) using a compact URI. This allows users to reference a database value quickly inside a number of Salt configuration areas, without a lot of overhead. The basic format of an SDB URI is: *sdb://<profile>/<args>*.

There are a number of SDB modules available, including: SQLite3, CouchDB, Consul, Keyring, Memcached, REST API calls, Vault, or environment variables. For Vault, the configuration becomes as simple as the following.

/etc/salt/minion or */etc/salt/master*:

```
myvault:
  driver: vault
```

Once this is configured on the minion, we can access data from any configuration file (*/etc/salt/master, /etc/salt/minion,* or */etc/salt/proxy*), using a URI such as:

```
password: sdb://myvault/secret/passwords?get_pass
```

where *myvault* is the configuration profile, *secret/passwords* is the path where data is available, and `get_pass` is the key of the data to return.

SDB proves to be a nice way to manage sensitive data and avoid repeating the same configuration in multiple places by referencing it using a basic URI.

Understanding the Salt cache

Salt is caching a variety of details, mainly for performance improvements, but not limited to that. One of the most important is the job cache—after a job is executed, the results are stored, by default on the local filesystem—*/var/cache/salt/master/jobs/*—for 24 hours. We can turn off the job cache by configuring `job_cache: false`, or adjusting the caching period using the `keep_jobs` (in hours) option on the master. Additionally, we can forward everything to a third-party service. We can reuse the returners configuration described earlier, and thus we have many options to choose from: Cassandra, Elasticsearch, MySQL, Redis, Slack, SMS, SMTP, and so on. For example, if we want to monitor the entire Salt activity from a HipChat room, this is possible too.

Grains and pillar data is also cached on the master; similarly, the local filesystem is preferred and is the default, but you can choose to store the data in a remote system or using a local in-memory Redis database as well.

SLS files defined under the `file_roots` paths or fetched from external services are also cached, but refreshed when their content has changed in their original location. This optimization is very important when the (proxy) minion and the master are running on separate physical machines (eventually, having poor connectivity between them), as the files are not fetched unless required. For large files, this brings an important improvement in terms of execution speed. The default caching path is under */var/cache/salt/minion* for regular minions, or */var/cache/salt/proxy/<ID>* for proxy minions. This can also be changed via the `cachedir` option.

Understanding Salt logging

Salt will catch and log everything possible from the underlying applications. The logging level can be adjusted with the `log_level` option on the master or minion (each application has its own independent logging process), the possibilities being `garbage`, trace, debug, info, warning, error, or critical—with the caveat that the first three may log sensitive data.

For more granular logging, we can set different levels per module type:

```
log_granular_levels:
  salt.states: warning
  salt.beacon: error
  salt.modules: info
```

Extending Salt

As we hope we have emphasized in this section, every Salt component is pluggable. The extension modules can be placed in a directory with subdirectories for each of Salt's module types, such as *modules*, *states*, *returners*, *output*, and *runners*. The naming convention for subdirectories is to prepend a _ to the module type, so execution modules are defined under *_module*, runners under *_runners*, and output under *output*. The parent directory can be specified with the option extension_modules, or module_dirs—which accepts a list of paths. Alternatively, we can also include it as one of the file_roots paths.

```
extension_modules
  - /etc/salt/extmods
```

For example, a new execution module called *example.py* can be placed under */etc/salt/extmods/_modules*:

```
# -*- coding: utf-8 -*-

def test():
    return {
        'network_programming_with_salt': True
    }
```

To make Salt aware of the new module, we need to resynchronize the modules using the saltutil.sync_all execution function:

```
$ sudo salt vmx1 saltutil.sync_all
vmx1:
    ----------
    beacons:
    clouds:
    engines:
    grains:
    log_handlers:
    modules:
        - modules.example
    output:
    proxymodules:
    renderers:
    returners:
```

```
sdb:
states:
utils:
```

Here you can see `module.example`, which is telling us that the new execution module `example` has been synchronized and is available to be invoked:

```
$ sudo salt vmx1 example.test
vmx1:
    ----------
    network_programming_with_salt:
        True
```

Remember, modules can be used from the CLI or directly within SLS files such as templates:

```
{%- set successful = salt.example.test()['network_programming_with_salt'] -%}
```

Salt Summary

In this section, we covered some of the most important topics to be aware of when just getting started with Salt for network automation. One of the greatest attributes of Salt that we covered was the use of the SLS file. Remember, you have complete control of how to write SLS data files, from using Jinja and YAML (as the defaults), to using Mako and HJSON, to adding in a new or custom templating language or even data format. This allows you to maintain the use of Salt and extend its capabilities according to the environmental requirements, without depending on the official codebase. Another major benefit of Salt is the use of proxy minions. With Salt, you have a natively built-in ability to distribute load between proxy minions that make it a great choice for large and distributed networks.

Event-Driven Network Automation with StackStorm

StackStorm is an open source software project for providing flexible event-driven automation. It is often lumped together with some of the other tools in this chapter, but StackStorm actually wasn't built to replace existing configuration management tools. For instance, many popular workflows in StackStorm actually leverage tools like Ansible for performing configuration management tasks.

The best way to think about StackStorm is that it fits in the sweet spot between configuration management (or general automation) and monitoring. It aims to provide a set of primitives for allowing the user to describe the tasks that should take place in response to certain events. For this reason, StackStorm can be thought of as the IFTTT (if-this-then-that) of IT infrastructure.

In many areas of IT, we usually respond to problems or outages manually. One very popular use case for StackStorm is the concept of auto-remediation, which is the idea of attempting to resolve issues without any human intervention. Naturally, if you're just getting started, there's not a magical button you can press to automatically fix problems. However, auto-remediation is the idea that after you've fixed a problem manually, you should commit that same procedure as some sort of automated workflow, reducing the number of manual tasks over time. StackStorm aims to allow you to do just that.

The design of StackStorm is meant to work well with infrastructure-as-code practices. These practices take the approach that your infrastructure can be described using text files (such as YAML files and Jinja templates we've used in many other places in this book), and that these files can and should be managed in the same way that software developers manage source code for applications.

In StackStorm, nearly everything is described using YAML files. As we go through the following examples, keep this paradigm in mind, and remember that it's always a good idea to use version control and automated testing for the files we use to manage our infrastructure.

In the following section, we'll explore some of the basic StackStorm concepts you'll need to understand in order to get started. You'll find that many of the concepts within StackStorm embrace infrastructure-as-code—everything in StackStorm is defined using plain-text files. So you can (and should) manage everything in StackStorm using the concepts we learned in Chapter 8.

StackStorm Concepts

There are a number of concepts we'll need to familiarize ourselves with in order to use StackStorm, as shown in Figure 9-4. Together, they form a set of tools that make event-driven automation possible.

First, *actions* are conceptually closest to the functionality offered by some of the other tools discussed in this chapter. They're where the actual work gets done. They're logically distinct bits of code that perform tasks like making API calls and executing scripts. They're the atomic building blocks of the "automation" part of event-driven automation.

From there, we want to talk about *workflows*. Workflows are a way to stitch actions together coherently to accomplish your business logic. You may start a workflow by running a few actions to gather some additional data from your infrastructure, then use that data to make decisions about which actions you should run in order to fix a problem. Workflows are available in StackStorm in two forms. The simplest format is ActionChains, which are a rudimentary way to "chain" actions together. The second format is Mistral, which is an OpenStack project with its own workflow definition that comes bundled with StackStorm, and it is much more flexible.

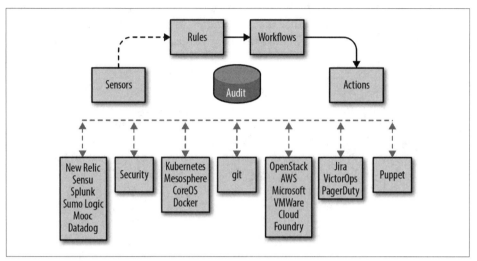

Figure 9-4. StackStorm concepts

Now that we have actions and workflows to do the work on our behalf, we'll want to bring these concepts into the world of "event-driven" automation. For this, we use *sensors* and *triggers*. You can think of sensors as little bits of Python code whose sole purpose is to gather data about your infrastructure. Note that these aren't agents that you deploy to endpoints like servers or network devices; rather, sensors run within StackStorm itself, and usually connect programmatically to external entities like monitoring or management systems, or in some cases, discrete nodes like virtual machines or network devices, in order to gather the information they need. However, this data is meaningless unless we have a way of recognizing what an "event" is. For that, sensors can also define triggers, which fire when something meaningful has occurred as indicated by the data being brought in by the sensor. For instance, the `napalm.LLDPNeighborDecrease` trigger notifies StackStorm when a given network device experiences a reduction in LLDP neighbors.

The crux of event-driven automation with StackStorm comes in the form of *rules*. Rules are the StackStorm equivalent of "if-this-then-that"—they're a way to connect incoming triggers to actions or workflows that respond to events. You may want to execute a workflow that pushes a new configuration to a network device when the `napalm.LLDPNeighborDecrease` trigger fires; this automated response would be defined in a rule.

Finally, it's worth mentioning that all of these concepts are distributed in StackStorm via *packs*. Packs are the atomic unit of distribution for all manner of extensibility in StackStorm—sensors, rules, workflows, and actions are all defined with text files, and those files are placed in a pack so they can be referenced. For instance, the `napalm.LLDPNeighborDecrease` sensor is in the `napalm` pack. Not all packs are installed by default, but there are CLI commands for easily installing new packs from the StackStorm Exchange. For instance, to download the `napalm` pack, you would simply run:

```
st2 pack install napalm
```

This will make all of the actions, workflows, sensors, or rules present in the `napalm` pack available to you in your instance of StackStorm.

Now that we have the basic concepts in mind, let's talk about how StackStorm works under the covers.

StackStorm Architecture

StackStorm is not really one component, but several microservices that work together to make event-driven automation possible (see Figure 9-5). The distributed nature of StackStorm was designed so that each component could scale independently as needs change. This also allows each function to be more resilient in a failure scenario.

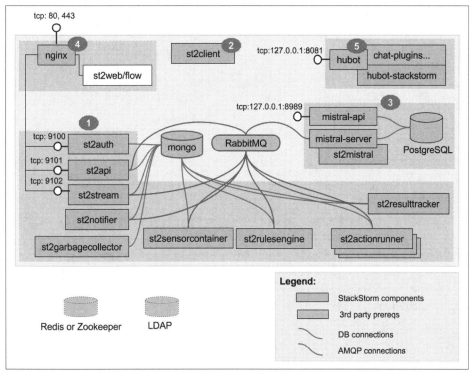

Figure 9-5. StackStorm components

For instance, if you know you will require a lot of horsepower for your workflows, but won't be watching for that many events in order to kick them off, you may want to spin up some additional st2actionrunner components to handle the load. If you wanted to handle a large number of events you would scale the st2sensorcontainer component in the same way.

Note that none of these components are "agents"; this does not mean you need to install any of these components on the rest of your infrastructure. Everything you see in Figure 9-5 is still self-contained within the servers or instances running Stack-Storm.

One component in particular is worth talking about—st2web. This is just a handy name for the web UI that comes with StackStorm (see Figure 9-6).

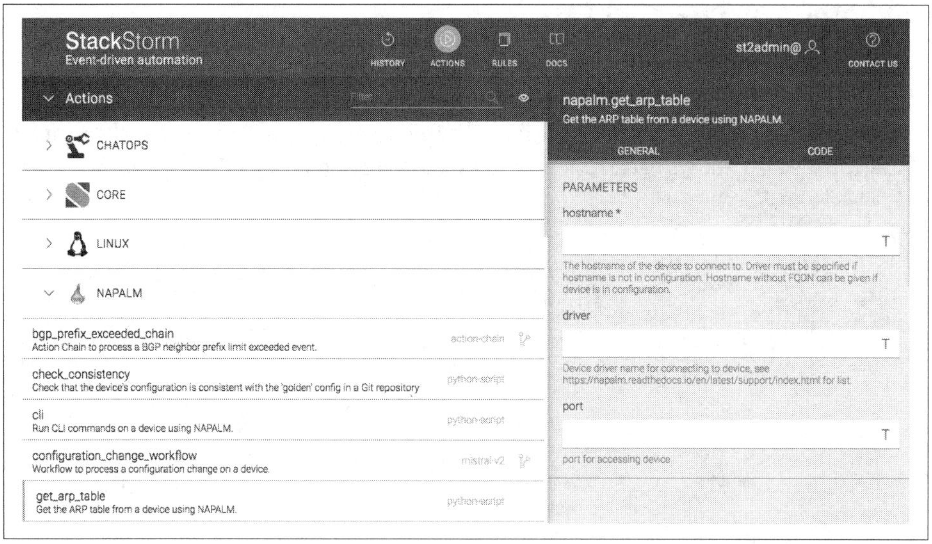

Figure 9-6. StackStorm web UI

You can use this web UI to do almost anything in StackStorm. So, if you're just getting used to the idea of working in the bash shell, this may be a more friendly option. The examples we'll use in this chapter will use the StackStorm CLI, as it is a bit clearer for our purposes.

Actions and Workflows

Now that we have the concepts and high-level architecture down, we should move into some practical examples of everything we've learned thus far.

StackStorm is very powerful, and as a result, there's a lot to discuss. Rather than cram this section full of examples for everything you could possibly want to know, we'll give an overview of the important details. For everything else, bookmark the StackStorm documentation (*https://docs.stackstorm.com*) and refer to that for much more detailed explanations, code snippets, and more.

In addition, StackStorm has a very active Slack community (sign up for free at *https://stackstorm.com/?#community*), and it's the best place to get questions or concerns answered.

You may wish to follow along—and to that end, you should check out the "st2vagrant" repository (*https://github.com/StackStorm/st2vagrant*). There, you'll find a Vagrantfile and some scripts for easily spinning up a single-instance deployment of StackStorm.

Vagrant is described in detail in the next chapter, Chapter 10.

Let's start with something simple, like running a single `echo` command to print "Hello World." For this we'll use the `core.local` action, which allows us to execute any command we'd otherwise run directly in bash.

A variety of backends can be leveraged within actions to actually perform the work. For instance, `core.local` happens to simply pass a value to the bash shell, but an action may use a Python or bash script to drive more complicated logic.

StackStorm comes with its own command-line interface: the `st2` command. One subcommand available to use is the `st2 run` command, which allows us to directly run actions or workflows without having to mess with sensors or rules.

We can run `st2 run core.local -h` to see what parameters are required by that action without actually running it:

```
vagrant@st2vagrant:~$ st2 run core.local echo -h

Action that executes an arbitrary Linux command on the localhost.

Required Parameters:
    cmd
        Arbitrary Linux command to be executed on the local host.
        Type: string
```

```
Optional Parameters:
    cwd
        Working directory where the command will be executed in
        Type: string

    env
        Environment variables which will be available to the command(e.g.
        key1=val1,key2=val2)
        Type: object

    kwarg_op
        Operator to use in front of keyword args i.e. "--" or "-".
        Type: string
        Default: --

    timeout
        Action timeout in seconds. Action will get killed if it doesn't finish
        in timeout seconds.
        Type: integer
        Default: 60
```

As shown in the previous example, the core.local action requires a single positional parameter—namely, the command you wish the action to execute (which in our case is the echo command):

```
vagrant@st2vagrant:~$ st2 run core.local echo "Hello World!"
.
id: 59598d2bc4da5f0506c24981
status: succeeded
parameters:
  cmd: echo Hello World!
result:
  failed: false
  return_code: 0
  stderr: ''
  stdout: Hello World!
  succeeded: true
```

The output shows that our command succeeded, and that stdout contains the string we passed to echo.

Now that we're comfortable with the command line, we can look at something a bit more relevant to network automation. Assuming we've installed the napalm pack using the st2 pack install napalm command shown previously, we can use st2 actions list to view all the actions available to us in this pack:

```
vagrant@st2vagrant:~$ st2 action list --pack=napalm
+------------------------------------+
| ref                                |
+------------------------------------+
| napalm.bgp_prefix_exceeded_chain   |
```

```
| napalm.check_consistency          |
| napalm.cli                        |
| napalm.configuration_change_workflow |
| napalm.get_arp_table              |
| napalm.get_bgp_config             |
| napalm.get_bgp_neighbors          |
| napalm.get_bgp_neighbors_detail   |
| napalm.get_config                 |
| napalm.get_environment            |
| napalm.get_facts                  |
| napalm.get_firewall_policies      |
| napalm.get_interfaces             |
| napalm.get_lldp_neighbors         |
| napalm.get_log                    |
| napalm.get_mac_address_table      |
| napalm.get_network_instances      |
| napalm.get_ntp                    |
| napalm.get_optics                 |
| napalm.get_probes_config          |
| napalm.get_probes_results         |
| napalm.get_route_to               |
| napalm.get_snmp_information        |
| napalm.interface_down_workflow    |
| napalm.loadconfig                 |
| napalm.ping                       |
| napalm.traceroute                 |
+-----------------------------------+
```

In order to use this pack, we need to configure it so that the pack is able to understand how to reach our network devices and how to authenticate to them. All packs are configured with YAML files located at */opt/stackstorm/configs/*, so this pack's configuration will be located at */opt/stackstorm/configs/napalm.yaml*. A minimal configuration is shown here:

```
---
html_table_class: napalm
config_repo: https://github.com/StackStorm/vsrx-configs.git

credentials:
  local:
    username: root
    password: Juniper

devices:
- hostname: vsrx01
  driver: junos
  credentials: local
```

In this configuration, we have a single device with a hostname vsrx01, using the local credentials, resulting in a username root and a password Juniper.

When we make changes to the configuration, it's important to ensure StackStorm is aware of those changes by reloading them. The st2ctl utility is useful for doing this:

```
vagrant@st2vagrant:~$ st2ctl reload --register-configs
Registering content...[flags = --config-file /etc/st2/st2.conf --register-configs]
2017-07-03 01:49:44,941 INFO [-] Connecting to database "st2" @ "0.0.0.0:27017" as
user "stackstorm".
2017-07-03 01:49:45,056 INFO [-] ================================================
2017-07-03 01:49:45,056 INFO [-] ############## Registering configs ##############
2017-07-03 01:49:45,056 INFO [-] ================================================
2017-07-03 01:49:45,181 INFO [-] Registered 1 configs.
##### st2 components status #####
st2actionrunner PID: 1007
st2actionrunner PID: 1053
st2api PID: 891
st2api PID: 1286
st2stream PID: 893
st2stream PID: 1288
st2auth PID: 874
st2auth PID: 1287
st2garbagecollector PID: 872
st2notifier PID: 884
st2resultstracker PID: 879
st2rulesengine PID: 888
st2sensorcontainer PID: 864
st2chatops PID: 881
mistral-server PID: 1032
mistral-api PID: 987
mistral-api PID: 2703
mistral-api PID: 2706
```

At the time of this writing all actions in the napalm pack require at least one argument, namely hostname. This lets the action know which device in the pack configuration you intend to work with.

Now, we should be able to run NAPALM actions. The napalm.get_facts action will retrieve facts about our network device:

```
vagrant@st2vagrant:~$ st2 run napalm.get_facts hostname=vsrx01
..
id: 5959a495c4da5f0506c2498a
status: succeeded
parameters:
  hostname: vsrx01
result:
  exit_code: 0
  result:
    raw:
      fqdn: vsrx01
```

```
      hostname: vsrx01
      interface_list:
      - ge-0/0/0
      - ge-0/0/1
      - ge-0/0/2
      - ge-0/0/3
      model: FIREFLY-PERIMETER
      os_version: 12.1X47-D15.4
      serial_number: da12e84e2e72
      uptime: 240
      vendor: Juniper
   stderr: ''
   stdout: ''
```

Here, we're able to see some useful information about our device, like the vendor and the list of interfaces present.

Actions by design are really intended to perform a single task well. However, in the real world, our day-to-day tasks in infrastructure rarely take the form of a single task. Usually, the work we do is accomplished over several discrete tasks, and includes some decision making along the way.

For instance, if we notice a router has gone offline, we might want to gather information from its peers. We might want to perform cable checks. For other issues, there may be an entirely different set of tasks required. As discussed previously, workflows allow us to use actions in more interesting ways by allowing us to commit all of these complicated decisions into a text file as if it were source code.

For the sake of brevity, we'll only cover one of the workflow options in StackStorm—specifically, Mistral. Mistral is an OpenStack project that provides two main things:

- A standardized YAML-based language for defining workflows
- Open source software for receiving and processing workflow execution requests

 When you install StackStorm using the instructions in the documentation, Mistral is installed and runs alongside the other StackStorm processes.

Let's look at a simple example of a Mistral workflow so you can become familiar with how it works.

```
---
version: '2.0'

examples.mistral-basic:
    description: A basic workflow that runs an arbitrary linux command.
```

```
    type: direct
    input:
        - cmd
    output:
        stddout: "{{ _.cmd }}"
    tasks:
        task1:
            action: core.local cmd="{{ _.cmd }}"
            publish:
                stdout: "{{ task('task1').result.stdout }}"
```

This workflow has a few important focus points:

- `input` is where we declare the parameters for the workflow. These are published within the workflow as named variables, which can be used in other tasks.

- `output` controls which values are published from the workflow when it finishes.

- `tasks` contains a list of tasks. In this simple example, we have only one: `task1`. Note that this task not only references the action we want to run in that task (namely `core.local`) but also contains a key, `publish`, which assigns the values of `stdout` and `stderr` to similarly named variables (you may have noticed it's using small Jinja snippets to do this). Note also that `stdout` is being passed to `output` so we can see the result when the workflow finishes.

Workflows are executed in the same way we executed our actions earlier. As mentioned previously, the actual work being done by actions can take the form of a bash or Python script, a simple shell command, or in this case, a Mistral workflow. We can use `st2 run` once more, taking care to pass in the required `cmd` parameter, which the workflow passes into the familiar `core.local` action:

```
vagrant@st2vagrant:~$ st2 run examples.mistral-basic cmd="echo Hello, Mistral!"
.
id: 595ad9c3c4da5f0521ea906c
action.ref: examples.mistral-basic
parameters:
  cmd: echo Hello, Mistral!
status: succeeded
result_task: task1
result:
  failed: false
  return_code: 0
  stderr: ''
  stdout: Hello, Mistral!
  succeeded: true
start_timestamp: 2017-07-03T23:56:51.069066Z
end_timestamp: 2017-07-03T23:56:52.442155Z
+-------------------------+-------------------------+-------+------------+
| id                      | status                  | task  | action     |
+-------------------------+-------------------------+-------+------------+
| 595ad9c3c4da5f0521ea906f | succeeded (0s elapsed) | task1 | core.local |
+-------------------------+-------------------------+-------+------------+
```

This output is a bit different from our last example. Any time you run an action, StackStorm produces an action "execution." This execution represents everything about how that action ran. You'll notice in this output as well as the previous examples that each time we call st2 run, an execution ID is produced. In the output for our Mistral workflow, this is true, but we also see a table of child executions. These child executions are the tasks in our workflow.

For a more network-centric example, let's look at one of the Mistral workflows in the napalm pack (modified for brevity):

```yaml
---
version: '2.0'

napalm.interface_down_workflow:

  input:
    - hostname
    - interface

  type: direct

  tasks:

    show_interface:
      action: "napalm.get_interfaces"
      input:
        hostname: "{{ _.hostname }}"
        interface: "{{ _.interface }}"
      on-success: "show_interface_counters"

    show_interface_counters:
      action: "napalm.get_interfaces"
      input:
        hostname: "{{ _.hostname }}"
        interface: "{{ _.interface }}"
        counters: true
      on-success: "show_log"

    show_log:
      action: "napalm.get_log"
      input:
        hostname: "{{ _.hostname }}"
        lastlines: 10
```

You'll notice the first two tasks use the on-success keyword to control which task runs next (if the statement's enclosing task results in a successful status, that is).

Running this workflow results in some familiar output, showing three executions, one for each of the tasks in our workflow:

```
vagrant@st2vagrant:~$ st2 run napalm.interface_down_workflow hostname=vsrx01
interface="ge-0/0/1"
......
id: 595adf58c4da5f0521ea90a0
action.ref: napalm.interface_down_workflow
parameters:
  hostname: vsrx01
  interface: ge-0/0/1
status: succeeded
start_timestamp: 2017-07-04T00:20:40.895706Z
end_timestamp: 2017-07-04T00:20:52.735536Z
+--------------------------+-----------+-------------------------+-----------------------+
| id                       | status    | task                    | action                |
+--------------------------+-----------+-------------------------+-----------------------+
| 595adf59c4da5f0521ea90a3 | succeeded | show_interface          | napalm.get_interfaces |
| 595adf5cc4da5f0521ea90a5 | succeeded | show_interface_counters | napalm.get_interfaces |
| 595adf5fc4da5f0521ea90a7 | succeeded | show_log                | napalm.get_log        |
+--------------------------+-----------+-------------------------+-----------------------+
```

We can use st2 execution get <*id*> to view the result of one of these executions:

```
vagrant@st2vagrant:~$ st2 execution get 595adf5cc4da5f0521ea90a5
id: 595adf5cc4da5f0521ea90a5
status: succeeded (3s elapsed)
parameters:
  counters: true
  hostname: vsrx01
  interface: ge-0/0/1
result:
  exit_code: 0
  result:
    raw:
      name: ge-0/0/1
      rx_broadcast_packets: 0
      rx_discards: 0
      rx_errors: 0
      rx_multicast_packets: 0
      rx_octets: 0
      rx_unicast_packets: 0
      tx_broadcast_packets: 0
      tx_discards: 0
      tx_errors: 0
      tx_multicast_packets: 0
      tx_octets: 0
      tx_unicast_packets: 0
  stderr: ''
  stdout: ''
```

Finally, we can use some basic branching logic in Mistral to make some more advanced decisions within the workflow. The following example is a slightly modified version of the previous example, but with a new task added at the beginning:

```
---
version: '2.0'

napalm.interface_down_workflow:

  input:
    - hostname
    - interface
    - skip_show_interface

  type: direct

  tasks:

    decide_task:
      action: "core.noop"
      on-success:
      - show_interface: "{{ _.skip_show_interface != True }}"
      - show_interface_counters: "{{ _.skip_show_interface == True }}"

    show_interface:
      action: "napalm.get_interfaces"
      input:
        hostname: "{{ _.hostname }}"
        interface: "{{ _.interface }}"
      on-success: "show_interface_counters"

    show_interface_counters:
      action: "napalm.get_interfaces"
      input:
        hostname: "{{ _.hostname }}"
        interface: "{{ _.interface }}"
        counters: true
      on-success: "show_log"

    show_log:
      action: "napalm.get_log"
      input:
        hostname: "{{ _.hostname }}"
        lastlines: 10
```

The `core.noop` action essentially does nothing. This is a common way of making early decisions in a Mistral workflow. The value of the `on-success` key for this task is a list instead of a simple string indicating the next task. In this case, the conditions listed in each list item will determine the next task to run. We can pass `skip_show_interface` into the workflow, and see that `show_interface` does not run.

```
vagrant@st2vagrant:~$ st2 run napalm.interface_down_workflow hostname=vsrx01
interface="ge-0/0/1" skip_show_interface=True
....
id: 595b4a7ec4da5f0521ea90b4
action.ref: napalm.interface_down_workflow
parameters:
```

```
    hostname: vsrx01
    interface: ge-0/0/1
    skip_show_interface: true
status: succeeded
start_timestamp: 2017-07-04T07:57:50.606796Z
end_timestamp: 2017-07-04T07:57:58.032456Z
+---------------------------+-----------+----------------------------+-----------------------+
| id                        | status    | task                       | action                |
+---------------------------+-----------+----------------------------+-----------------------+
| 595b4a7ec4da5f0521ea90b7  | succeeded | decide_task                | core.noop             |
| 595b4a7fc4da5f0521ea90b9  | succeeded | show_interface_counters    | napalm.get_interfaces |
| 595b4a81c4da5f0521ea90bb  | succeeded | show_log                   | napalm.get_log        |
+---------------------------+-----------+----------------------------+-----------------------+
```

There's a lot more you can do with actions and workflows, but this will be enough to get you started.

Sensors and Triggers

Actions and workflows are useful in their own right, but in order to enable event-driven automation, we need to gather information about our infrastructure and recognize when actionable events happen. This is accomplished through sensors and triggers. Sensors are little bits of Python code that bring external data into StackStorm —for instance, by periodically pollling REST APIs or subscribing to message queues.

 StackStorm also allows you to configure incoming webhooks (*https://docs.stackstorm.com/webhooks.html*), which allows external systems to "push" events to StackStorm (sensors provide more of a "pull" model of integration).

Sensors are the preferred integration method since they offer a more granular and tighter integration, but webhooks offer a simple integration mechanism that allows you to get data into StackStorm quickly. This can be helpful when working with systems that don't yet have a sensor built for them, or that only offer outgoing webhooks as an integration mechanism.

We can see the sensors available on the system using `st2 sensor list` (using the `pack` flag to focus on the `napalm` pack for brevity):

```
vagrant@st2vagrant:~$ st2 sensor list --pack=napalm
+---------------------------+--------+-------------------------------------------+---------+
| ref                       | pack   | description                               | enabled |
+---------------------------+--------+-------------------------------------------+---------+
| napalm.NapalmLLDPSensor   | napalm | Sensor that uses NAPALM to retrieve LLDP  | True    |
|                           |        | information from network devices          |         |
+---------------------------+--------+-------------------------------------------+---------+
```

This particular sensor periodically queries each of the devices in our configuration file for the LLDP neighbor table. It will keep track of the number of LLDP neighbors active for each device.

As mentioned previously, triggers are the way that StackStorm knows an "event" has occurred. For instance, if the LLDP neighbor count stays the same, we don't need to do anything. However, if that number changes, that's an actionable event. For our example, we have two triggers, one representing a neighbor increase, and the other a neighbor decrease:

```
vagrant@st2vagrant:~$ st2 trigger list --pack=napalm
+------------------------------+--------+---------------------------------------------------+
| ref                          | pack   | description                                       |
+------------------------------+--------+---------------------------------------------------+
| napalm.LLDPNeighborDecrease  | napalm | Trigger which occurs when a device's LLDP neighbors |
|                              |        | decrease                                          |
| napalm.LLDPNeighborIncrease  | napalm | Trigger which occurs when a device's LLDP neighbors |
|                              |        | increase                                          |
+------------------------------+--------+---------------------------------------------------+
```

The code that implements our LLDP sensor is responsible for determining when the neighbor count has changed and firing the appropriate trigger.

Let's see if we can cause one of these triggers to fire. We'll log in to our network device and confirm that we can see at least one LLDP neighbor:

```
root@vsrx01> show lldp neighbors
Local Interface    Parent Interface    Chassis Id         Port info      System Name
ge-0/0/1.0         -                   4c:96:14:10:01:00  ge-0/0/2.0     vsrx02
```

Since we are seeing a neighbor on ge-0/0/1, we can shut that interface to clear it from the table.

```
root@vsrx01# set interfaces ge-0/0/1 unit 0 disable

[edit]
root@vsrx01# commit
commit complete
```

This particular sensor periodically provides some useful log messages about the neighbor count.

> The log file for all sensor activity is usually located at /var/log/st2/st2sensorcontainer.log but can be located elsewhere via configuration.

```
2017-07-04 23:54:16,134 139956844022352 INFO lldp_sensor [-] vsrx01 LLDP neighbors
STAYED at 1
2017-07-04 23:54:22,732 139956844022352 INFO lldp_sensor [-] vsrx01 LLDP neighbors
STAYED at 1
2017-07-04 23:54:28,701 139956844022352 INFO lldp_sensor [-] vsrx01 LLDP neighbors
went DOWN to 0
2017-07-04 23:54:34,748 139956844022352 INFO lldp_sensor [-] vsrx01 LLDP neighbors
STAYED at 0
```

We can see that the sensor knew that the neighbor count was staying constant at 1, until it decreased to 0, and stayed there.

However, as we've discussed, the trigger is the important part. We can query Stack-Storm for a list of "trigger instances," which are specific occurrences that a trigger was fired. Each time a neighbor count decreases for a device, the `napalm.LLDPNeighborDecrease` trigger should fire. We can see that this has indeed happened:

```
vagrant@st2vagrant:~$ st2 trigger-instance list --trigger=napalm.LLDPNeighborDecrease
+--------------------------+--------------------------------+-----------------+-----------+
| id                       | trigger                        | occurrence_time | status    |
+--------------------------+--------------------------------+-----------------+-----------+
| 595c2ab4c4da5f035af38903 | napalm.LLDPNeighborDecrease    | < truncated >   | processed |
+--------------------------+--------------------------------+-----------------+-----------+
```

Finally, in the same way we retrieved details for action executions, we can use the ID for this trigger instance to see the details (payload) of this particular event:

```
vagrant@st2vagrant:~$ st2 trigger-instance get 595c2ab4c4da5f035af38903
+-----------------+--------------------------------------------------------+
| Property        | Value                                                  |
+-----------------+--------------------------------------------------------+
| id              | 595c2ab4c4da5f035af38903                               |
| trigger         | napalm.LLDPNeighborDecrease                            |
| occurrence_time | 2017-07-04T23:54:28.713000Z                            |
| payload         | {                                                      |
|                 |     "device": "vsrx01",                                |
|                 |     "timestamp": "2017-07-04 23:54:28.701351",         |
|                 |     "oldpeers": 1,                                      |
|                 |     "newpeers": 0                                       |
|                 | }                                                      |
| status          | processed                                              |
+-----------------+--------------------------------------------------------+
```

This will come in handy as we discuss rules in the next section.

Rules

We finally arrive at the crux of everything we've learned thus far. To recap, actions allow us to perform bread-and-butter automation. Sensors and triggers represent "events" in StackStorm. Now to perform event-driven automation, we need a way to tie events from triggers to actions or workflows. That's where rules come in.

Rules are defined (much like a lot of other things in StackStorm) in YAML files. The plain-English version of a rule might be: "When *X* happens, do *Y*." In our case, *X* is a trigger instance, and *Y* is an action or workflow.

One of the simplest examples of a rule is the ability to run an `echo` every few seconds. There's a special trigger in StackStorm called `core.st2.IntervalTimer` that allows us to treat the passage of a certain amount of time as an actionable event:

```
---
name: sample_rule_with_timer
pack: "examples"
description: Sample rule using an Interval Timer.
```

```
enabled: true

trigger:
  parameters:
    delta: 5
    unit: seconds
  type: core.st2.IntervalTimer

criteria: {}

action:
  parameters:
    cmd: echo "{{trigger.executed_at}}"
  ref: core.local
```

There are three main parts to every rule:

trigger

This section specifies the name of the trigger we want to watch for (in this case, core.st2.IntervalTimer) as well as any parameters that trigger requires.

criteria

This will further restrict which trigger instances will match this rule. Since nothing is specified here, all instances of core.st2.IntervalTimer will fire this rule.

action

Here we specify the action or workflow we want to fire, as well as any parameters it requires. As long as a trigger instance is seen that matches the other two sections, this action or workflow will execute.

```
vagrant@st2vagrant:~$ st2 execution list -a id action.ref context.user status
+--------------------------------+--------------------+--------------+-----------------------+
| id                             | action.ref         | context.user | status                |
+--------------------------------+--------------------+--------------+-----------------------+
|   595c3093c4da5f035af38bb0     | core.local         | stanley      | succeeded (1s elapsed) |
|   595c3098c4da5f035af38bb6     | core.local         | stanley      | succeeded (1s elapsed) |
|   595c309dc4da5f035af38bbc     | core.local         | stanley      | succeeded (1s elapsed) |
+--------------------------------+--------------------+--------------+-----------------------+
vagrant@st2vagrant:~$ st2 execution get 595c309dc4da5f035af38bbc
id: 595c309dc4da5f035af38bbc
status: succeeded (1s elapsed)
parameters:
  cmd: echo "2017-07-05 00:19:41.779821+00:00"
result:
  failed: false
  return_code: 0
  stderr: ''
  stdout: '2017-07-05 00:19:41.779821+00:00'
  succeeded: true
```

A dead giveaway that these executions were fired by our rule is that the user that executed them is the built-in user stanley, instead of the user we're logged in with (in this case, st2admin).

We can use a rule to notify us via Slack when our LLDP neighbor count decreases:

```
---
name: "lldp_notify"
pack: "napalm"
enabled: true
description: "Notify of LLDP Neighbor Decrease"

trigger:
  type: "napalm.LLDPNeighborDecrease"
  parameters: {}

criteria: {}

action:
  ref: slack.post_message
  parameters:
    message: "WARNING: {{trigger.device}}'s LLDP Neighbors just went DOWN to
      {{trigger.newpeers}} (was {{ trigger.oldpeers }})""
    channel: '#general'
```

In the previous example, we're watching for all instances of the trigger napalm.LLDPNeighborDecrease. When one occurs, the slack.post_message action is called to post a message to slack (notice that fields in this trigger's payloads like device and newpeers are referenced to add context to the message).

We could, of course, go further than simple notifications. Let's say the number of LLDP neighbors decreased because someone logged on to our device and accidentally shut one of the interfaces (like we did in the section on triggers). We'd probably push a config like this to bring the interface back online:

```
interfaces {
    ge-0/0/1 {
        unit 0 {
            enable;
        }
    }
}
```

Instead of simply raising a notification, we could react to this event by automatically pushing this configuration using the napalm pack's loadconfig action:

```
---
name: "lldp_remediate"
pack: "napalm"
enabled: true
description: "Bring interface back up when LLDP neighbor count decreases"

trigger:
  type: "napalm.LLDPNeighborDecrease"
  parameters: {}
```

```
criteria: {}

action:
  ref: napalm.loadconfig
  parameters:
    hostname: "{{ trigger.device }}"
    config_file: /vagrant/remediation_config.txt
```

As discussed previously, running workflows is functionally very similar to running actions. You may have a full workflow for doing troubleshooting, auto-remediation, notifications, or a combination of these. Rules can execute full-blown workflows, or simple actions.

StackStorm Summary

There's a lot more to StackStorm, but these core concepts will get you started down the road of auto-remediation and event-driven network automation. The idea behind StackStorm is to give you the tools that allow you to put processes in place that react autonomously to infrastructure events, in the same way that you would manually, but in a more reliable fashion.

For more information on StackStorm, the best place to visit is the project's documentation (*https://docs.stackstorm.com/*), as well as the free Slack channel (*https://stackstorm.com/?#community*), where there's almost always someone on hand ready to answer any questions.

Summary

In this chapter, we discussed how some automation tools—like Ansible, Salt, and StackStorm—can be put to work in a network automation use case. We provided examples for using the products for network automation, and we discussed the advantages and disadvantages of each product along the way.

## CHAPTER 10

Continuous Integration

In this chapter, we are going to change direction a little bit. Up until now, this book has provided details on specific tools and technologies that you can learn, all for the purpose of applying them toward network automation. However, it would be improper to assume that network automation is all about shiny new tools—in fact, that's only one piece of the bigger picture.

This chapter is going to instead focus much more on optimizing the processes around network management and operations. Armed with knowledge of the specific tools and technologies mentioned in previous chapters, you can use this chapter as a guide for using those tools to solve the *real*, challenging problems that network operators at any scale are facing. This chapter will answer questions like:

- How can I use network automation to produce a more stable, more available network?
- How can I help the network move as quickly as the rest of the business demands, without compromising on availability?
- What kind of software or tools can I use to help me implement better processes around my network?

Networking touches *every* other area of IT, and any outages, policy changes, or impediments to efficient process will impact any technology connected to the network. In modern times, these impacts are felt by every other technology discipline. This has caused the rest of IT and the business at large to view the network as something that should "get out of the way" and "just work." These days, the network is called upon to be always accessible, and be more flexible at a more rapid pace than ever before, ensuring it support any service or application the business requires.

The reality is there is no magic bullet here; to accomplish these goals takes discipline, and it requires a disruption of your existing processes and communication silos. It also takes a significant amount of work, learning, and new tools. That work may seem like you're just adding more complexity, but it will pay off in the long run by adding both stability and speed to your network operations processes.

One common underlying theme is the removal of humans from the direct control path of the network. You would be right to be skeptical of this idea, since we've talked about automating humans out of a job for a long time. However, removal of humans from direct control is not the same thing as removing humans entirely. Today, humans maintain direct control over the network by forming a manual, human pipeline for making changes to the network, as illustrated in Figure 10-1.

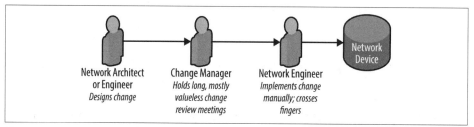

Figure 10-1. Humans in direct path of network

This technique has proven to be slow and arduous, while also not providing much, if any, additional reliability to making changes on the network. This method mostly just gets in the way, while providing the illusion of safety around making changes.

When we talk about removing humans from the direct path, we're talking about Continuous Integration—that is, automating the discrete tasks that should be taking place when we are managing infrastructure change, and freeing technical resources to sit above that pipeline, improving it and making it more efficient (Figure 10-2).

As a result of this fundamental shift toward Continuous Integration, we can actually introduce real protections against human error in network operations instead of the "Change Management Theater" that we've relied on historically.

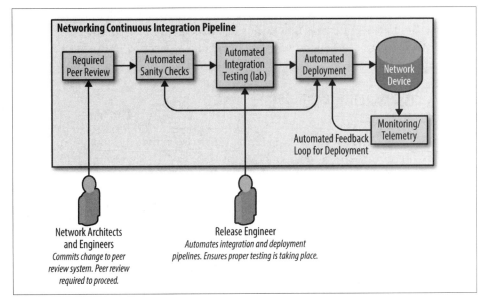

Figure 10-2. *Automated change with Continuous Integration*

Important Prerequisites

To maximize your success in using the concepts in this chapter, there are a few things to keep in mind.

Simple Is Better

One of the best things you can do to enable your network for network automation has nothing to do with learning to code or using a hot new automation tool—it's all about your network design. Stay away from snowflakes, and strive to deploy network services in a cookie-cutter fashion.

In other words, you may decide you want to deploy network configurations driven by templates. If each of your network devices has a unique configuration with a wide variety of features, it's going to be fairly difficult to build templates for a large group of devices.

 Network configuration templates were discussed in detail in Chapter 6.

The more thought you put into the consistency of network design, the less work you'll have to do when it comes time to automate the network. Often this means staying away from vendor-specific features, or bypassing embedded features entirely and implementing network services right at the compute layer.

People, Process, and Technology

In the previous chapters, we've discussed a lot of great technologies and tools, but there are a lot more serious challenges facing the network industry today—challenges of process and of working with other IT teams that may not share your primary skill set.

Many of the chapters in this book address specific technologies and tools that you can use to build efficient systems for network automation. There are a multitude of technologies that can be used for purposes of automation—many of which may be new to many network engineers, and it's important to be aware of them. It's also important to improve and change the ways that we communicate with other areas of IT and the business at large—which we discuss in Chapter 11.

In this chapter, however, we're going to discuss some process enhancements that software developers have used for quite some time to improve the way they make changes to applications. The ultimate goal is to make such changes quickly, and push them into production while minimizing the risk of negative impact. There are many important lessons here that can be learned by the network engineering community, especially when considering network automation.

Learn to Code

First, you don't have to be a software developer to leverage the concepts in this chapter. In fact, this chapter primarily exists to convey that message. However, you will likely find that no one tool (or even set of tools) will solve all your problems.

It's likely that you'll have to fill in some gaps in your Continuous Integration journey by writing some sort of custom solution, like a script. Use this as an opportunity to broaden your skill set. As discussed in Chapter 4, Python is a great language to start with, as it's simple enough to learn quickly and robust enough to solve a lot of complex problems.

Introduction to Continuous Integration

Before we dive into how Continuous Integration (CI) is useful within a network automation context, let's first talk about its origins, and how it provides value to software development teams.

First, when we talk about implementing CI, we're looking to accomplish two primary objectives:

Move faster
> Be able to respond to the changing needs of the business more quickly.

Improve reliability
> Learn from old lessons, and improve quality and stability of the overall system.

Before CI, changes to software were often made in large batches and sometimes it took months for developers to see their features make it into production. This made for incredibly long feedback loops, and if there were any serious issues, or new features/requirements, it took a very long time for issues to be addressed. This inefficiency meant not only that new features took much longer to get developed, but also that software quality suffered.

Naturally, it would be great if developers could simply make changes and push them directly to production, right? It would certainly solve the speed problem—and developers would certainly be able to see the results of their changes more quickly. However, as you might expect, this is incredibly risky. In this model, it's very easy to introduce bugs into production, which could seriously impact the bottom line for many businesses.

Continuous Integration (when combined with Continuous Deployment, which we'll explore later in this chapter) is the best of both worlds. In this model, we're pushing changes to production very quickly—but we're doing so within a context that tests and validates these changes, to be more confident that they're not going to cause problems when they're manifested in production.

In the sections to come, we're going to discuss some of the components of and concepts related to Continuous Integration, and then look at how we can apply these concepts to our network automation journey.

Basics of Continuous Integration

In short, Continuous Integration is all about being able to merge changes to a source code repository at any time. A team of developers, no matter when they're working, can "integrate" changes to some shared repository at any time because there are tools in place that allow the team to know—in an automated fashion—that those changes are not going to break the functionality of the overall system.

You might have heard the term *pipeline* used when discussing CI. This is used because CI is not one particular technology, but usually a suite of different tools and technologies used together to accomplish the goal. Changes to a codebase flow through these tools in some sort of predetermined way, which forms a *CI pipeline*. All changes must go through this pipeline in its entirety before moving on to deployment (Figure 10-3).

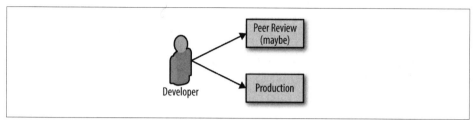

Figure 10-3. Deploying software directly to production

The diagram in Figure 10-3 should look very familiar. Network engineers around the world do this all the time. Maybe they're not deploying software, but what they *are* deploying is a critical change to infrastructure that tends to have a higher "blast radius" than most other infrastructure changes. Logging in to an SSH session to a router to make some config changes is no less risky than editing the source code of an application live in production.

In contrast, Continuous Integration offers only one place where a human can push changes, and that's the CI pipeline—specifically the very first part of the pipeline known as *peer review*. This is the first in a long line of automated steps such as automated testing and sanity checks. In order for changes to make it into production, they *must* go through this pipeline without exception (Figure 10-4).

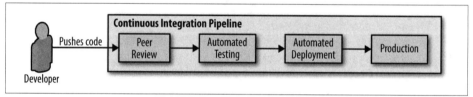

Figure 10-4. Deploying software to a Continuous Integration pipeline

Again, the point of CI is to increase speed while also maintaining (or improving) stability. It does so by creating a single point of entry for making any changes. It becomes nonoptional to change your infrastructure without subjecting that change to a suite of tests that ensure it undergoes to technical peer review, as well as prevent old mistakes from being repeated.

Some organizations hire specialists called *release engineers* to manage the Continuous Integration pipeline. They're skilled with tools like Git, testing tools, build servers, and peer review systems. They maintain the integrity of the pipeline so the developers don't have to. Ultimately, their goal is to automate the process from the laptop to production (thus, "release" engineer).

It's not always easy to get head count for a dedicated release engineer, but if you can, and if your team is large enough to warrant it, it's nice to have.

We've talked about the basics of Continuous Integration, so now let's dive into some of the components and related concepts and technologies you might encounter along the way.

Continuous Delivery

Continuous Delivery (CD) is another term you may have heard as closely related to CI. Continuous Delivery is the idea that the software team is continuously providing software that is able to be deployed into production; they are *delivering* working software in the form of an always-deployable codebase.

Continuous Deployment tends to imply that you're always pushing new code to production immediately. The industry has lately been using the term *Continuous Delivery* instead. This term generally means that your code is always in a condition where it *could* be deployed at any time, but doesn't have to be. Your organization may still wish to keep deployments on a set schedule, such as on a nightly or weekly basis.

Continuous Integration is fairly easy to apply to network automation (as we'll see in upcoming sections), but Continuous Delivery requires a bit more thought. The rest of this chapter may blur the lines between CI and CD with respect to network automation, so keep in mind a few things:

- *What* am I deploying?
- *To what/whom* am I deploying it?

These are important questions to address because they determine your delivery model. For instance, some network teams may perform all their automation with in-house Python applications. This is fairly simple since they are essentially a software development shop within the infrastructure team.

On the other hand is the canonical network automation example: provide some kind of configuration artifact (say, some YAML file) into a Git repository, and have the

CI/CD pipeline take it through some basic sanity checks before finally calling it with a tool like Ansible, resulting in actual and immediate changes to network devices in production. This may work for some organizations, but this is analogous to a software development team deploying each and every software patch to production immediately—and this is not always desired.

Consider, perhaps, a "staging" environment to which these changes can be continuously delivered, and whenever the business requires that those changes are finally deployed to production, they can be moved from staging, where (hopefully) they've been tested. At the time this chapter was written, many network vendors have heard our demands for providing virtual images of their platforms, so this is much easier to do than it used to be.

> While all of these virtual appliances work great for testing automation, not all are actually meant to carry production network traffic. Please refer to your vendor's documentation for clarity on this.

You also need to think about rollback procedures. Are you periodically taking the configurations that are in your "production" Git repository and using them to overwrite the current "production" configurations, or at least making comparisons between the two? If you're not, even if you roll back the repository, the production "deployment" of those configurations may not get rolled back. What will be the impact, based on whether you're using Ansible or Puppet, or maybe some custom Python programs, if you roll back the Git repository? You need to own that layer of your software stack and understand how your tools and software will react (if at all) when your production configurations get rolled back.

The truth is, you'll likely have to address the Continuous Delivery question on your own. What works for one organization probably won't work for yours, due to the large number of tools and languages available for solving network automation problems. However, this chapter should at least provide some starting points, and ideas for how to properly deliver changes to your network in an automated fashion.

Test-Driven Development

It's also important to discuss yet another software development paradigm that has seen a growing amount of adoption—Test-Driven Development (TDD).

Let's say you're working as a software developer and you've been tasked with creating a new feature in your software project. Naturally, you might first gather some basic requirements, put together a minimal design, and then move forward with building the feature (Figure 10-5). We'll even say that you're on board with Continuous Integration, so you will then build some unit tests that validate the functionality that you've built. Unfortunately, it doesn't always happen this way. In reality, building tests after the feature has been built is often difficult to justify, or at the very least, deemed less important than the feature itself.

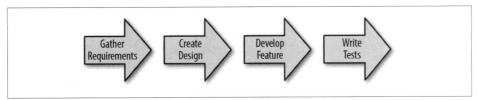

Figure 10-5. Software development life cycle before test-driven development

In practice, this can easily lead to the accumulation of "technical debt." In other words, if you don't build your tests first, there's always a temptation to not build them immediately after you develop the desired feature, or to not build them at all. This inevitably leads to gaps in test coverage, and on large projects, this gap only increases over time.

Test-driven development turns this idea on its head. When using TDD, after going through requirements gathering and putting together a basic design, you would *first* write a test for that feature, before the feature is even implemented (Figure 10-6). Naturally, this means the test would fail, since there's no code to test against. So, the final validation of this feature is to write code that passes that test (or tests).

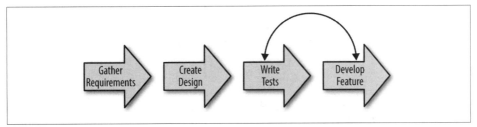

Figure 10-6. Software development life cycle after test-driven development

Why use a test-driven approach? The most immediate benefit is the reduction of technical debt—if the tests are built before the feature, then there's no temptation to let test coverage fall behind while the shiny new features take priority. However, there's also a bit of a conceptual difference. By writing tests first, the developer must have a strong grasp on how their software is being used—since they're writing tests to do just that. This is widely believed to have a positive influence on software quality.

When you apply these concepts to network automation, you begin to realize numerous parallels. The network is as much of a business resource as the applications that flow on top of it. Therefore, it's important to have adequate testing in place that not only validates any changes made on the network, but also helps warn of any problems ahead of time (capacity planning). Are you gathering detailed statistics about the applications flowing on your network? Not just what the SNMP service on your network devices are telling you—but from the perspective of the applications themselves? It's important as network engineers to learn the lesson that TDD is teaching software developers: the use case matters. User experience matters.

The point of bringing up TDD in this chapter is twofold. We want to remember two things whether leveraging existing network automation tools, or writing our own software:

- We care enough about the quality of our network automation system, our network's uptime, and the positive experience of our users and applications to ensure our system is properly—not minimally—tested.

- Testing is so important that it should be done before you automate a single thing on your network. With the software available today, and the increasingly lower barrier to entry for these tools to nondevelopers, there really is no excuse for not doing this.

 We'll see a lot more detail about *how* to do this testing in a future section of this chapter, in case those two points seem a little far-fetched. For now, just keep those two points in mind—they are crucial for the success of any network automation effort.

By adopting a methodology similar to TDD, we are not only helping to put the applications first, but we're also building a repeatable process by which we can constantly be *sure* that our network is serving the needs of the application, despite changes to configuration or environment. Later in this chapter we'll discuss some specific tools and technologies that we can use to accomplish these goals.

Why Continuous Integration for Networking?

So far, we've discussed ideas like Continuous Integration as well as test-driven development, and how those concepts have provided value to software development teams. From now on, however, we'll be applying concepts like these exclusively to our network automation journey.

Why are we doing this? What value could Continuous Integration or test-driven development have to network engineers? Remember the goals of Continuous Integration:

Move faster
    Be able to respond to the changing needs of the business more quickly

Improve reliability
   Learn from old lessons, and improve quality and stability of the overall system

These goals, which have driven results for more stable software and more agile development teams, can also help us to create a *more* reliable network—not less. Automation that compromises on either of these two goals is pointless.

"CI for networking" means a lot of the same things as the canonical software example—creating a single point where changes to network infrastructure are performed, where testing and reviewing those changes is automated and nonoptional.

For a long time, we've thought about and administered our networks as black boxes that happen to be connected to each other, and this mindset isn't very conducive to the practices and concepts implemented in CI. So the first thing to do is start to think about your network as a pool of resources and fluid configurations—a system with ever-changing environments and requirements.

This is the driving idea behind the "infrastructure as code" movement—maintaining the state and configuration of your infrastructure with the same processes developers use to manage source code.

A Continuous Integration Pipeline for Networking

At this point, we've discussed a lot of the high-level concepts and theories behind Continuous Integration, but now it's time to put these concepts into practice. In this section, we'll go through a few practical examples and tools for helping us achieve the goals we've discussed within the context of network automation.

While reading the following examples, keep these tips in mind:

- The tools used in this section are just examples. In every category, there are choices beyond what's presented here. It is encouraged that you evaluate the tools available in each category and determine if they fit your needs.

- This section comes after the previous section for a reason. Implementing these tools without fixing the bad process that has plagued many organizations for years will accomplish nothing.

It's also worth noting that these tools can be configured in a variety of ways. Only one approach will be presented in this section, so remember the fundamental concepts here, and adopt the right configuration to realize the same benefits within your organization.

There are five main components to our Continuous Integration pipeline for networking:

- Peer review
- Build automation
- Deployment tools
- Test/dev/staging environment
- Testing tools and test-driven network automation

To illustrate the concepts in this chapter, we'll use a project called Templatizer, which renders Jinja templates into network device configurations based on data found in YAML data files. Many of the examples will center on the Templatizer Git repository hosted on our private Git server.

Figure 10-7 will serve as a useful illustrative example for our Continuous Integration journey.

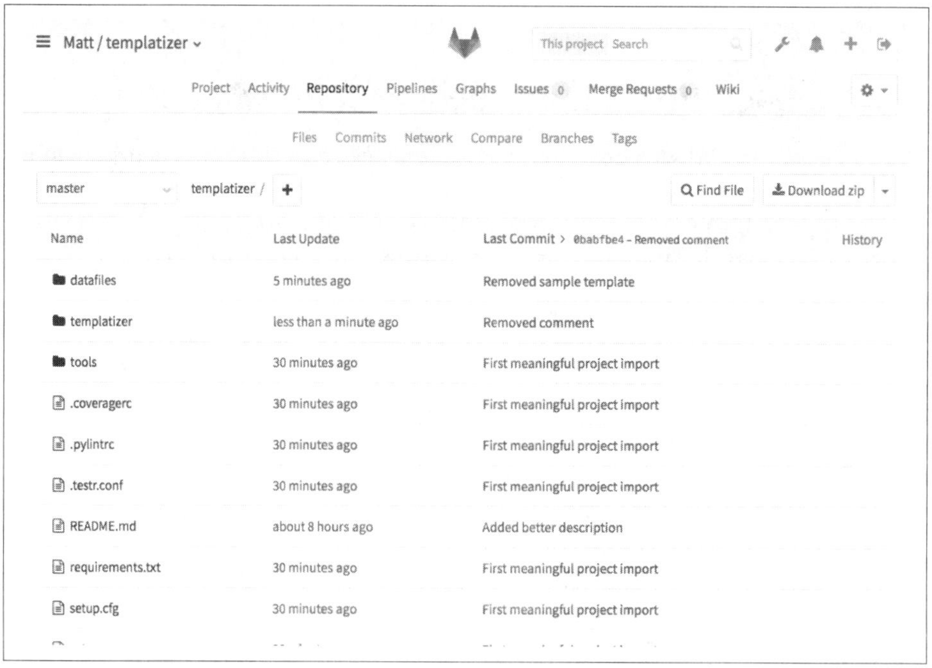

Figure 10-7. Templatizer project

Peer Review

When we talk about peer review in a traditional software sense, we're typically talking about source code for an application. A developer will submit a patch containing some diffs to some source code files, that patch will be posted to the code review system in some way, and a reviewer (or reviewers) will look at the patch and provide comments or approval.

When adapting this portion of the pipeline for network automation, we're not that far off from this example. Several other chapters in this book, like Chapters 5 and 6, have advocated an "infrastructure-as-code" approach with network automation, where any and all relevant configuration information is treated in the same way a developer would treat source code. In our case, instead of Java code, we might have YAML files or Jinja templates. They're all just text files, and we can run automated tests on them just the same.

We're going to be building on the knowledge we gained about version control in Chapter 8 by using Git to not only control the versions of our various configuration artifacts like YAML files, but also leverage the first stage of this pipeline—peer review—to get an additional pair of eyes on our change to make sure we're doing the right thing.

If you've maintained any form of production IT infrastructure, you've likely taken part in Change Approval Board (CAB) meetings. Perhaps you were responsible for filling out a form where you describe the configuration change you want to make, and then attending long conference calls to say a few quick words that were carefully constructed to appease the approvers and get them out of your way. This process has deep roots in modern IT, but it doesn't do much to *actually* minimize risk, or provide transparency between related technical teams. This is the old way of doing things.

When we talk about using Continuous Integration for networking, we start with the idea of peer review, and it might seem similar to what was just described, but there are some fundamental differences. In CI, if you want to make the change, you simply cut a new branch in Git, and *make the change*. By having our configurations performed in a Git repository that is part of a CI pipeline, we don't have to ask for permission before doing the work in a branch, because that work is not actually pushed through production until it has been reviewed and merged to master.

This new model has some very attractive benefits. With respect to peer review, there is now no need to "describe" the change you want to make, and hope you get it right when it comes time to implement—now, the description of the change is the same as the change itself. There is no ambiguity about what you're going to do because it's displayed right in the peer review system being used. In order to put your change into production, the approver(s) will simply merge your working branch into master.

When it comes to code review platforms, we have a few options. Here is a non-exhaustive list:

GitHub

Very popular SaaS offering for reviewing and displaying source code (enterprise edition also available for a cost).

GitLab

Community edition is open source and free to download and run behind your firewall. There is also a tiered SaaS offering, as well as a closed-source enterprise edition.

Gerrit

Open source, complicated, but lots of integrations available, and a popular choice for many open source projects.

All three options leverage Git for the actual version control portion (and Git is therefore the way that you will interface with them when submitting code) but on top of Git, they implement a fairly unique code review workflow. For instance, with GitHub, you can submit additional changes by simply pushing more commits to the same branch, but with Gerrit, the submitter must always work with the same commit (meaning additional changes require the --amend flag to be used).

We'll be using GitLab throughout this chapter, primarily because it offers a lot for free, and we don't have to fuss around with setup too much. Know, however, that the other systems may work out better for you.

 At this point, you should be familiar with not only Jinja templates and YAML files, but also how to work with a Git repository. Our example assumes the Templatizer project has already been cloned to the local filesystem, and we're ready to do some work.

As an illustrative example, we'll add some Jinja templates and YAML files so the Templatizer project is able to create configurations for network device interfaces. We'll start by creating a new Git branch for committing our changes:

```
~$ git checkout -b "add-interface-template"

Switched to a new branch 'add-interface-template'
```

We're on a branch that is only on our machine (we haven't run git push yet) and it's on a non-master branch. So we simply make the change. No waiting for approval before we get started—we do the work first, and let the work speak for itself when the time comes for approval.

After we've added the template and YAML file, Git should notify us that two new files are present but untracked:

```
~$ git status

On branch add-interface-template
Untracked files:
  (use "git add <file>..." to include in what will be committed)

    datafiles/interfaces.yml
    templatizer/templates/interfaces.j2

nothing added to commit but untracked files present (use "git add" to track)
```

We need only make a commit and push to our origin remote, which in this case is the GitLab repository shown earlier:

```
~$ git add datafiles/ templatizer/

~$ git commit -s -m "Added template and datafile for device interfaces"
[add-interface-template 4121bfa] Added template and datafile for device interfaces
 2 files changed, 10 insertions(+)
 create mode 100644 datafiles/interfaces.yml
 create mode 100644 templatizer/templates/interfaces.j2

~$ git push origin add-interface-template
Counting objects: 7, done.
Delta compression using up to 8 threads.
Compressing objects: 100% (7/7), done.
Writing objects: 100% (7/7), 718 bytes | 0 bytes/s, done.
Total 7 (delta 2), reused 0 (delta 0)
To http://gitlab/Matt/templatizer.git
 * [new branch]      add-interface-template -> add-interface-template
```

The next step is to log in to our code review system (GitLab) and initiate the step that would kick off a peer review. Every code review system has its own workflow, but ultimately they all accomplish the same thing. For instance, Gerrit uses terminology like *change* and *patchset*, and GitHub uses *pull requests*. In short, these tools are a way of saying, "I have a change, and I'd like it to be merged into the main branch" (usually master).

GitLab uses a concept very similar to GitHub pull requests called *merge requests*. Now that we've pushed our changes to a branch, we can specify in the merge request creation wizard that we'd like to merge the commit we made on "add-interface-template" to the master branch, which is considered "stable" for this project (Figure 10-8).

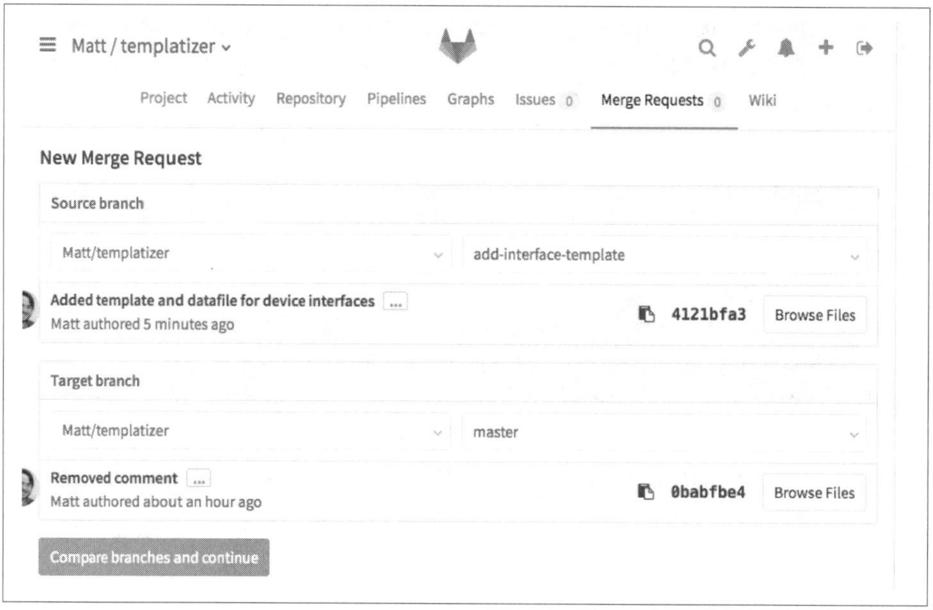

Figure 10-8. Creating a merge request

After we click through to the follow-up confirmation screen, our merge request is created. Keep in mind that this is still just that—a request. There has still been zero impact to the master branch, and as a result, the current "stable" version of the Templatizer project. This is just a proposal that we've made, and will serve as a point of reference for the upcoming peer review.

So the next step is to get our merge request reviewed by someone in authority. This part of the workflow can differ based on the culture of the team, as well as the review platform. Some teams restrict access to the master branch so that only certain senior members can accept merge requests, while other teams use the honor system and ask that each merge request is reviewed by at least one other team member. A common convention is to refrain from merging any changes until someone gives a "+1," which is a way of saying, "From my perspective, this change is ready to be merged." This may happen right away, or a reviewer may have some comments or pointers before they're ready to give their +1.

Our imaginary teammate Fred is on hand to review our Templatizer change, and we can engage him any number of ways. Most code review tools have a way of "adding" a reviewer, which should notify them by email, or you can message them directly. Either way, Figure 10-9 shows what Fred will see when reviewing our change in GitLab.

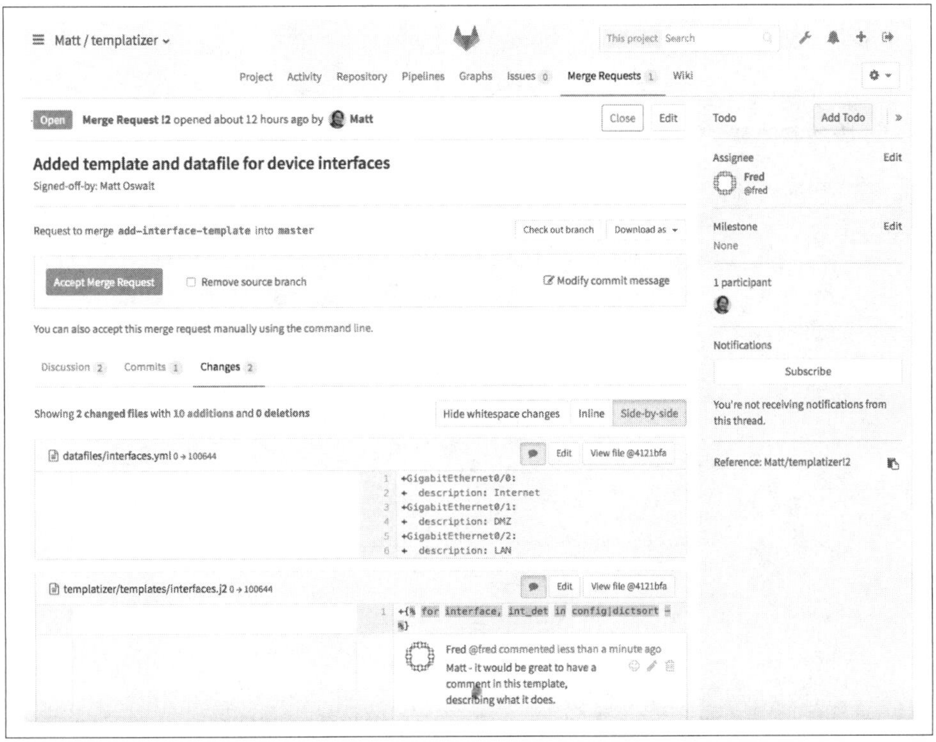

Figure 10-9. Fred providing comments to merge request

As you can see, Fred left a message indicating he felt we should add a comment to our template, explaining how it works. It's not uncommon for a change to go through multiple iterations before being merged, and most platforms have facilities for this. With GitLab, we only need to add another commit to this branch and push to GitLab, and the new commit will be added to this merge request. Fred can easily see these additional changes, and once he is satisfied that this change is ready to be merged, he can do so.

Figure 10-10 shows us how GitLab can track this entire event stream for anyone that may want to see the status of this change.

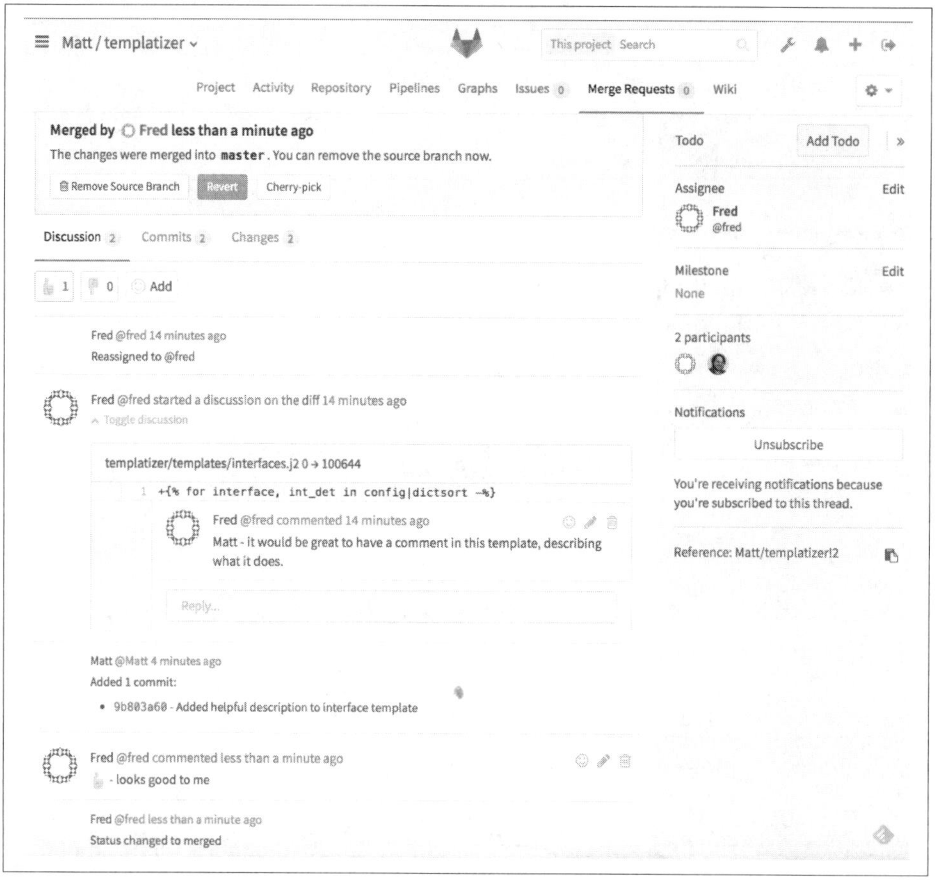

Figure 10-10. Change accepted and merged

Build Automation

Next up is an extremely important topic, *build automation*. This term largely stems from the use of Continuous Integration tooling as a way of automatically compiling or installing software in order to test it. For instance, a program written in C must be compiled before it can be run in a test environment.

We may not necessarily be compiling software in our pipeline, but we can reuse many of the tasks that software developers will want to automatically perform on every proposed change to the repository. For instance, a pipeline for a Python project may perform some static code analysis to ensure the code conforms to Python's style guide, PEP8. In a network automation context, we may only be making changes to YAML files, but we can perform similar checks to automate some of the simple stuff that we don't want human reviewers to deal with, including verifying that the file is in fact valid YAML (ensuring indentation is correct)!

This is the crux of what makes build automation so valuable. Before even bothering a human reviewer, there are a number of things we can automatically do to ensure that the reviewer is providing useful comments:

- Static code analysis (checking for proper syntax and adherence to any style guides)
- Unit testing (unit tests, parsing of data files or templates, etc.)
- Integration testing (does this change break any existing functionality in the whole system?)

With these out of the way, the reviewer can leave comments like "this needs to be more readable," instead of "add a space here." For this reason, these automated steps usually take place immediately when a change is submitted (our merge request from the previous example), and a reviewer is only engaged when these checks pass.

This process saves time for both the submitter and the reviewer, since the submitter gets close to immediate feedback if their change breaks something, and the reviewer knows that if a change passes these basic tests, they won't be wasting their time with simple comments. It also produces repeatable, more stable changes to network automation efforts—when a bug is discovered, it can be added to these automated tests to ensure it doesn't happen again.

As expected, there are a number of platforms that provide this kind of functionality. One very popular choice is Jenkins, which is an open source build server with a multitude of integrations and capabilities. For our example, we're going to stick with GitLab, since it offers all of the features we need for these examples, and they're all bundled into the single piece of software. In addition, much of the actual automation can be done by scripts in the repository itself, keeping the dependence on the actual build server to a minimum, and providing for a lot of transparency for anyone working with the repository.

Let's say we make a minor change to our new *interfaces.yml* file, and Fred reviews it. Everything looks good to him, so he gives a +1 and merges the change to the master branch (Figure 10-11).

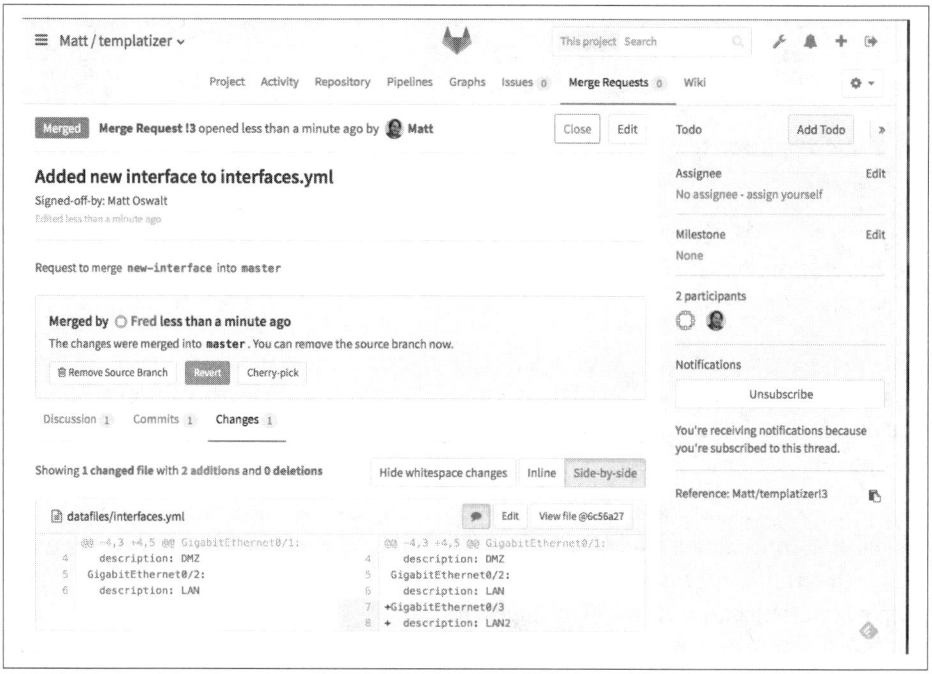

Figure 10-11. Minor change to YAML

However, we have a problem. This change produces invalid YAML, which shows when we try to run our Templatizer program:

```
File "/Users/mierdin/Code/Python/templatizer/lib/python2.7/site-packages/yaml/scanner.py", line 289,
  in stale_possible_simple_keys "could not found expected ':'", self.get_mark())
yaml.scanner.ScannerError: while scanning a simple key
  in "datafiles/interfaces.yml", line 7, column 1
could not found expected ':'
  in "datafiles/interfaces.yml", line 8, column 14
```

This was a very minor change, but Fred is still a human being and overlooks typos like this, just as Matt did. In larger changes, where multiple files undergo multiple changes, this can be an even more common occurrence.

On the other hand, it should be trivial to write a script that checks for this error, and provides feedback to our build system. If we can do this, and configure our automated build system to check for this on all future patches, we should avoid this problem in the future:

```python
#!/usr/bin/env python

import os
import sys
import yaml

# YAML_DIR is the location of the directory where the YAML files are kept
YAML_DIR = "%s/../datafiles/" % os.path.dirname(os.path.abspath(__file__))

# Let's loop over the YAML files and try to load them
for filename in os.listdir(YAML_DIR):
    yaml_file = "%s%s" % (YAML_DIR, filename)

    if os.path.isfile(yaml_file) and ".yml" in yaml_file:
        try:
            with open(yaml_file) as yamlfile:
                configdata = yaml.load(yamlfile)

            # If there was a problem importing the YAML, we can print
            # an error message, and quit with a non-zero error code
            # (which will trigger our CI system to indicate failure)
        except Exception:
            print("%s failed YAML import" % yaml_file)
            sys.exit(1)

sys.exit(0)
```

This is a highly simplified example. There are several libraries that can allow you to do much more detailed validation. Check out pyk walify for more detailed YAML validation (not just syntax, but the presence of expected values).

Once we've committed that script to our *tools* directory in the repo, since we're running GitLab we also need to modify the CI configuration file *.gitlab-ci.yml*:

```yaml
test:
  script:
  - cd tools/ && python validate_yaml.py
```

Now, GitLab will run this script every time a change is proposed. Now that this validator script is in place, let's take a look at what Fred sees now, when Matt proposes another change with invalid YAML (Figure 10-12):

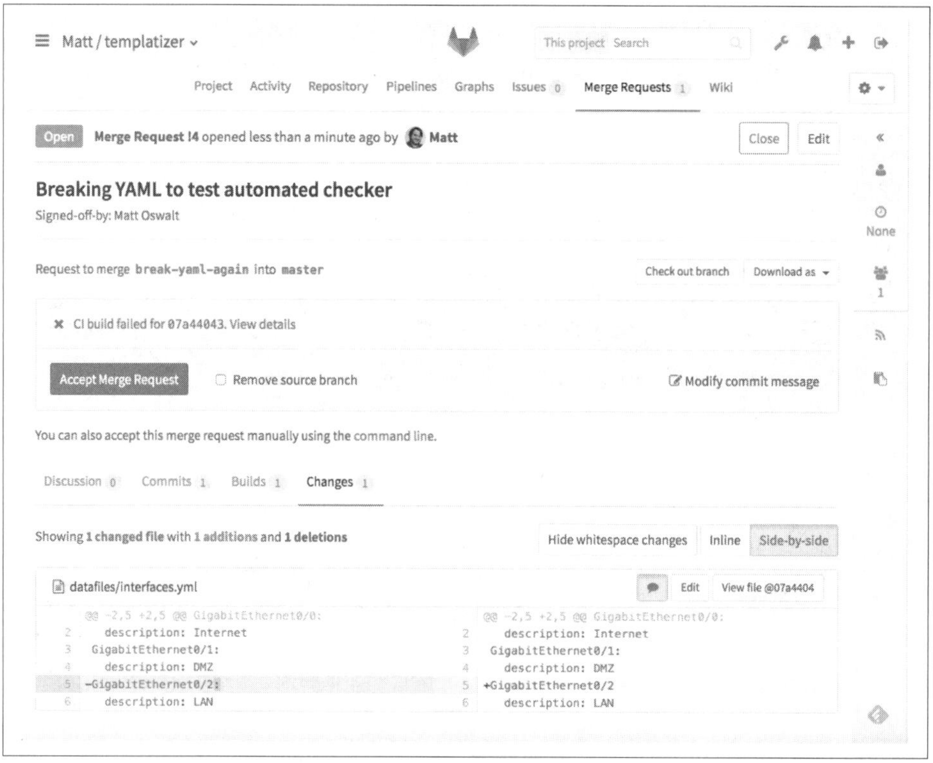

Figure 10-12. CI build failed due to invalid YAML

Both Matt and Fred are able to plainly see that there was a problem during automated testing. They can also click through to see details about what happened, including a full console log that shows the output of the script, indicating which file had the issue (Figure 10-13).

Figure 10-13. YAML validation script output

This is just one example in a multitude of possibilities with respect to automated validation and testing. Templatizer is also a Python project, so we can explore some of the tooling present in that ecosystem to run some Python-specific validation and testing as part of this CI pipeline. For instance, Tox is a popular tool for doing all kinds of automated testing within a Python project. The OpenStack community uses Tox to really simplify the CI process, by summarizing a slew of tasks within a small list of commands:

```
test:
  script:
  - cd tools/ && python validate_yaml.py
  - tox -epep8  # Checks for PEP8 compliance with Python files
  - tox -epy27  # Runs unit tests
  - tox -ecover # Checks for unit test coverage
```

Again, all of these commands must pass without error in order to "pass" the build process. When a reviewer receives a merge request that shows that these checks were passed, they know it's ready for a real review.

This part of the pipeline is crucial and is a great way to keep the workflow efficient, while also helping to ensure that past mistakes are not repeated. Here are some additional ideas that may be useful at this stage in the pipeline—explore each in your own journey toward network automation:

- Unit testing any code (e.g., Python)
- Integration testing to ensure any code is able to interoperate with other projects and APIs
- Syntax and style validation (both source code as well as data formats like YAML)

Test/Dev/Staging Environment

After some basic automated testing of simple things like syntax or style, it's usually desirable to run more "real-world" testing on the changes we make to our repository. In the case of Templatizer, we might want to actually render real configurations using the Jinja templates and YAML files against virtual devices that mimic the real production devices we'd like to eventually target. There are a number of ways to do this, and we'll discuss some of them here.

One interesting solution, if you're just looking to do some small-scale testing on your laptop, is Vagrant. Vagrant is a tool developed by HashiCorp to make management of virtual machines easier. The configuration for this environment is contained within a file called a Vagrantfile. This is a plain-text file that's easy to place in a Git repository, and useful for ensuring that anyone working on a repository can spin up identical virtual environments. Virtual images can also be automatically downloaded from a predetermined location, reducing the need for users to put together their own images. If configured properly, a user needs only to type `vagrant up` into a shell and the environment will be instantiated automatically.

This has useful implications for software developers (a Vagrantfile can be configured to spin up identical development environments for all developers working on a code-base), but network engineers can also use Vagrant to spin up multi-vendor lab topologies. For instance, Juniper makes their Junos images publicly available to be used with Vagrant.

We can devise a Vagrantfile that constructs a simple three-node topology:

```
Vagrant.configure(2) do |config|

  # NOTE - by the time this book was released, this image was quite old.
  # Please refer to Juniper documentation on the appropriate image to use.
  config.vm.box = "juniper/ffp-12.1X47-D15.4-packetmode"
  config.vm.box_version = "0.2.0"

  config.vm.define "vsrx01" do |vsrx01|
    vsrx01.vm.host_name = "vsrx01"
    vsrx01.vm.network "private_network",
                ip: "192.168.12.11",
                virtualbox__intnet: "01-to-02"
    vsrx01.vm.network "private_network",
                ip: "192.168.31.11",
                virtualbox__intnet: "03-to-01"
  end

  config.vm.define "vsrx02" do |vsrx02|
    vsrx02.vm.host_name = "vsrx02"
    vsrx02.vm.network "private_network",
                ip: "192.168.23.12",
                virtualbox__intnet: "02-to-03"
    vsrx02.vm.network "private_network",
                ip: "192.168.12.12",
                virtualbox__intnet: "01-to-02"
  end

  config.vm.define "vsrx03" do |vsrx03|
    vsrx03.vm.host_name = "vsrx03"
    vsrx03.vm.network "private_network",
                ip: "192.168.31.13",
                virtualbox__intnet: "03-to-01"
    vsrx03.vm.network "private_network",
                ip: "192.168.23.13",
                virtualbox__intnet: "02-to-03"
  end
end
```

In the directory where this Vagrantfile is located, we need only run `vagrant up`, a Junos image will be downloaded, and three virtual Junos routers will be started and connected as described. We can immediately log in to any one of these devices quite easily:

```
~$ vagrant up vsrx01
Bringing machine 'vsrx01' up with 'virtualbox' provider...
==> vsrx01: Checking if box 'juniper/ffp-12.1X47-D15.4-packetmode' is up to date...
==> vsrx01: Clearing any previously set forwarded ports...
==> vsrx01: Clearing any previously set network interfaces...
==> vsrx01: Preparing network interfaces based on configuration...
    vsrx01: Adapter 1: nat
    vsrx01: Adapter 2: intnet
    vsrx01: Adapter 3: intnet
==> vsrx01: Forwarding ports...
    vsrx01: 22 (guest) => 2222 (host) (adapter 1)
==> vsrx01: Booting VM...
==> vsrx01: Waiting for machine to boot. This may take a few minutes...
    vsrx01: SSH address: 127.0.0.1:2222
    vsrx01: SSH username: root
    vsrx01: SSH auth method: private key
==> vsrx01: Machine booted and ready!
==> vsrx01: Checking for guest additions in VM...
    vsrx01: No guest additions were detected on the base box for this VM! Guest
    vsrx01: additions are required for forwarded ports, shared folders, host only
    vsrx01: networking, and more. If SSH fails on this machine, please install
    vsrx01: the guest additions and repackage the box to continue.
    vsrx01:
    vsrx01: This is not an error message; everything may continue to work properly,
    vsrx01: in which case you may ignore this message.
==> vsrx01: Setting hostname...
==> vsrx01: Configuring and enabling network interfaces...
==> vsrx01: Machine already provisioned. Run `vagrant provision` or use the `--provision`
==> vsrx01: flag to force provisioning. Provisioners marked to run always will still run.

[output omitted for similar output from vsrx02 and vsrx03...]

~$ vagrant ssh vsrx01
--- JUNOS 12.1X47-D15.4 built 2014-11-12 02:13:59 UTC
root@vsrx01% cli
root@vsrx01> show version
Hostname: vsrx01
Model: firefly-perimeter
JUNOS Software Release [12.1X47-D15.4]
```

Provided there are sufficient resources present on your machine to run the topology, and that the images you need are available, there are a multitude of ways this can be used for testing network changes. This is fairly unprecedented—network vendors have historically been very slow to provide free-to-use virtual images of their platforms. However, more and more vendors are starting to do just that.

To bring this back to Continuous Integration and automated testing, this concept could be very useful for validating our changes. For instance, if you made a change to our Templatizer repository that we would like to test before rolling into production, we could render one of these templates and automatically deploy that configuration change to a virtual topology provisioned by Vagrant. Even if you're just looking to test something out on your laptop, Vagrant remains an increasingly useful tool for evaluating network platforms.

It's also possible to run a virtual environment in the public or private cloud. For instance, if your organization is running an OpenStack deployment, many of these virtual network devices can be run as virtual machines in OpenStack. You could even automate their deployment using OpenStack Heat templates. Alternatively, companies like Network to Code (*http://networktocode.com/*) provide workflow automation with their On Demand Labs platform (*https://labs.networktocode.com*) for network engineers to leverage public cloud resources to run these virtual topologies. These methods are useful if you want the same topology to be accessible by multiple engineers, all the time.

 Disclosure: Jason Edelman, one of the authors of this book, is the founder of Network to Code.

Many of these options can be automated using many of the same tools that you would use to automate the "real thing," and it's important that you consistently use the same tooling between your test and production environments, otherwise the testing is pointless. For instance, if your goal is to use a virtual environment to test the deployment of a configuration change using Ansible, construct a virtual topology that mimics your production infrastructure as closely as possible, then run through the same Ansible workflow in both the test environment and production. This gives you greater confidence that if it worked in test, it will work in production.

Test environments are one of the key components that force organizations to seriously consider a dedicated engineer for maintaining them. To do this right, test environments need to be carefully maintained, so that they're not a tremendous bottleneck to the rest of the pipeline, and that they are an adequate simulation of the real network environment.

Deployment Tools

Earlier in the chapter, we discussed the importance of understanding *what* you're deploying in a Continuous Integration/Continuous Delivery pipeline. One reason for this is that it has a big impact on the tools you use to actually deploy the changes you make.

For instance, if you're writing some Python code to automate some tasks around your network, you should consider treating it like a full-fledged software project. Regardless of the size, production code is production code. A small script is as likely to have bugs as a large web application.

In addition to the very important testing and peer review discussed earlier, you may find it useful to explore the delivery mechanisms that software developers are starting to use. If your organization uses cloud platforms like OpenStack, you may be able to leverage the available APIs to automatically deploy your changes at the end of the CI pipeline.

It's also becoming increasingly popular to deploy software in Docker containers. You could instruct your CI pipeline to automatically build a Docker image once a new change is reviewed and merged. This image can be deployed to a Docker Swarm or Kubernetes cluster in production.

On the other hand, sometimes we're not deploying custom software—sometimes our Git repositories are used simply to store configuration artifacts like YAML or Jinja templates. This is common for network automation efforts that use configuration management tools like Ansible to push network device configurations onto the infrastructure. However, while the method of deployment may differ between network engineers and software developers, Continuous Integration plays a vital role (Figure 10-14).

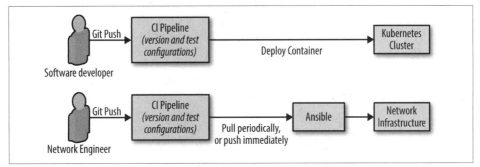

Figure 10-14. A comparison of development and networking CI pipelines

In this case, it's important to understand how these configurations are going to be used in production, as well as how rollbacks will be handled. This is an important idea not only for deciding how Ansible will actually run in production, but also how the configuration templates themselves are constructed. For instance, you might consider running an Ansible playbook to deploy some configuration templates onto a set of network devices every time a new change is merged to the master branch—but what impact will that have on the configuration? Will the configuration always be overwritten? If so, will that overwrite a crucial part of the configuration that you didn't intend?

Some vendors provide tools to assist with this. For instance, when pushing an XML-based configuration to a Junos device, you can use the `operation` flag with a value of `"replace"` to specify that you want to replace an entire section of configuration. The following example shows a Jinja template for a Junos configuration that uses this option:

```
<configuration>
  <protocols>
    <bgp operation="replace">
      {% for groupname, grouplist in bgp.groups.iteritems() %}
      <group>
        <name>{{ groupname }}</name>
        <type>external</type>
        {% for neighbor in grouplist %}
        <neighbor>
          <name>{{ neighbor.addr }}</name>
          <peer-as>{{ neighbor.as }}</peer-as>
        </neighbor>
        {% endfor %}
      </group>
      {% endfor %}
    </bgp>
  </protocols>
</configuration>
```

Unfortunately, not all vendors allow for this, but in this particular case, you could simply overwrite entire sections of configuration for each new patch in the CI pipeline, to ensure that "what it should be" (WISB) always equals "what it really is" (WIRI).

This is another area where there is no silver bullet. The answer to the deployment question depends largely on what you are deploying, and how often. It's best to first settle on a strategy for network automation; decide if you want to invest in some developers and write more formalized software, or if you want to leverage existing open source or commercial tools to deploy simple scripts and templates. This will guide you toward the appropriate deployment model.

Above all, however, deployment should *never* take place until the aforementioned concepts like peer review and automated testing have taken place. A network automation effort that does not prioritize quality and stability above all is doomed to failure.

Testing Tools and Test-Driven Network Automation

Earlier in this chapter, we talked a lot about the influence that test-driven development can have on network automation. In that section, we discussed how important it was to go beyond the traditional network statistics that we use as network engineers and leverage additional tools and metrics more useful for determining application and user experience. These metrics can be used before and after each change to truly determine the health of the network and its configuration (Figure 10-15).

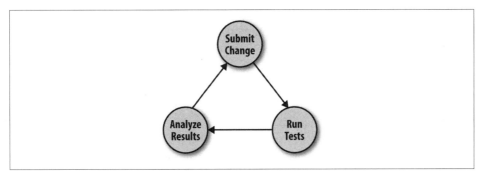

Figure 10-15. Continuously testing automated changes

Unfortunately, after several decades, the tools available for determining application experience or troubleshooting on the network haven't improved or evolved very much. These days, troubleshooting a network problem is typically relegated to one of only a handful of tools like ping, traceroute, iperf, and whatever your network management platform is able to poll via SNMP.

Largely, these tools are insufficient even from a network engineer's perspective, let alone the fact that they provide minimal visibility into application performance, which is why we run networks in the first place. However, thanks to the rise of open source, and offerings like GitHub that make open source software much easier to consume, this is starting to change.

One area that is ripe for improvement, especially within network infrastructure, is the ability to gather detailed telemetry in a flexible and scalable way. Currently, network engineers are limited to what SNMP can provide, which has a few shortcomings. SNMP is a monitoring tool that is not only limited to network infrastructure itself, but even then only exposes a subset of available data points within those devices.

The main problem here is that we're ignoring a lot of really valuable context available outside the network itself. Using frameworks like Intel's Snap (*https://github.com/ intelsdi-x/snap*), we can constantly and intelligently gather telemetry about infrastructure elements that rely on the network, like application servers, clusters, containers, and more. If we make a change on the network that adversely affects one of these entities, we can see that in the available telemetry, and perhaps automatically roll back those changes based on a set threshold.

An additional, complementary approach is to actively test the network and application infrastructure using tools like ToDD (*https://github.com/toddproject/todd*), which provides a mechanism to perform network testing like ping, http, port scanning, and bandwidth testing in a fully distributed manner. ToDD also aggregates reported data in a single JSON document so you can make decisions on the resulting test data, regardless of scale. It's important to test application-level performance (not just "ping") and to also test at a scale comparable to peak real-world activity.

The ToDD project was started by one of the authors of this book—Matt Oswalt.

Tools like these can provide additional visibility during failover testing, such as the simulation of a data center failure. Failover testing is an under-appreciated activity when it comes to network infrastructure. Often, it's hard to get the approval to run such a test, and in the rare cases where such approval is obtained, it's even more difficult to determine how the network and the connected applications are performing. Using these and other tools, we can gather a baseline of what "normal" application performance looks like, and by running the same tests after a failover, we can have greater confidence that we have sufficient capacity to keep the business running.

These are just a few examples—the point is that open source software is no longer just an elite club only for software developers. These days, there is no excuse not to at least consider using tools like these to fill in some of the huge gaps in existing monitoring strategies—specifically the lack of application-level visibility into network performance.

Summary

These days, chances are good that your organization has some kind of in-house software development shop. Reach out to those teams and ask about their processes. If they're using Continuous Integration, there's a chance that they'd be willing to let you leverage some of their existing tooling to accomplish similar goals with network automation. As mentioned previously, a dedicated release engineer can help greatly with management of the pipeline itself.

In this chapter we talked about a lot of process improvements (as well as some tooling to help enforce these processes), but the real linchpin to all of this transformative change is a culture that understands the costs and benefits of this approach. We'll talk a lot more about this in Chapter 11. If you don't have buy-in from the business to make these improvements, they will not last.

It's also important to remember that a big part of CI/CD is continuously learning. Continuously challenge the status quo, and ask yourself if the current model of managing and monitoring your network is *really* sufficient. Application requirements change often, so the answer to this question is often "no." Try to stay plugged in to the application and software development communities so you can get ahead of these requirements and build a pipeline that can respond to these changes quickly.

## CHAPTER 11

Building a Culture for Network Automation

The network industry is heavily product-driven, perhaps more than nearly any other technology discipline. Very rarely do we hear about "revolutionary" new IT processes or stories of how an organization won against its competitors because of its great IT team; it's always the shiny new hardware or software products that grab the headlines.

However, new products—even "revolutionary" ones—don't solve business problems on their own. The advent of x86 virtualization technologies is arguably one of the biggest disruptions we've ever seen in IT, yet 10 years later despite this disruption, we're still taking weeks or even months to provision virtual machines. Clearly, our problems aren't limited to the technology we use. Maybe we need a change in our culture as well. That's what this chapter is about—why a good culture is a crucial, foundational element for network automation, and how to get there.

It's also easy to over-rotate on topics of culture and think that it's the sole cause of all of our problems. The reality is that we need a balance of good people, good process, and good technology in order to win. The cultural change discussed in this chapter is all about satisfying our desire to get things done and work on a team of similarly minded individuals.

In this chapter you won't read about how many hugs your engineers should be giving per day, or why it's important for a company to have an indoor trampoline to keep engineers happy. This chapter will take a different view on the subject of "culture," and you'll find that it all revolves around one very simple idea: people want to work with other people that give a crap about what they do.

If you're in a position where you're looking to keep things pretty consistent career-wise and not looking to make major changes, this chapter probably won't mean much to you. However, if you picked up this book, and read this far (kudos, by the way), it's quite likely you're looking to improve, even a little bit. You're not quite happy with the status quo. You want to be an agent for change in your organization, and on a personal note, you want to "level up" your technical skill set.

To that end, we'll discuss three topics in particular:

- Organizational strategy and flexibility
- Embracing failure
- Skills and education

Organizational Strategy and Flexibility

The first thing you need to address is your team and its place within the organization. If your team isn't right, all of the other topics in this book will collapse under weight.

Transforming an Old-World Organization

Enterprise IT is not known for its ability to be on the cutting edge. Traditionally, the technology stack in an IT shop can lag behind by 5, or sometimes even 10 years, compared to what technology leaders are doing or thinking about. This trend isn't totally unwarranted; the cutting edge got its name for a reason. However, there's also a lot of bad or outdated reasoning for why an IT shop might use a "legacy" technology stack.

Automation encounters this hurdle all the time. There are often concerns from folks who want to automate but just can't convince anyone else in their organization to take even the first steps. Or (and this is often worse because of the "bad reputation" it creates) someone started doing basic automation, it went wrong, and it took down a revenue-generating system.

Unfortunately, there's no easy answer to this. Each organization has its own battle scars and unique history. However, one potential answer can be found in a great book, *How to Win Friends and Influence People*. In it, Dale Carnegie hands down several nuggets of wisdom that are useful for life in general—but one theme that's present in many places in the book is the need to see things from others' perspective. To (heavily) paraphrase:

> You can't get anyone to do anything they don't want to do. So you have to make them want to do it.

We'll discuss this a bit more in the next section, but in short, the business has to want the automation or in-house scripting. This cannot be some science project that upper management only finds out about when things go wrong.

Even if you start the right way, by communicating your automation strategy to the business, there will be opposition. Change always brings out the antibodies. It would be strange if it didn't at least make someone feel uncomfortable. The important thing is to remember why you're doing this—it's not because automation is cool (even though it is), it's for the tangible, measurable benefits it can provide to your business.

Another very important point is the need to do things slowly, building good, lasting engineering habits, and to set the right expectations from the beginning. Automation is not unlike healthy weight loss. Anyone that has been able to lose weight and keep it off will tell you it's not about fad diets, it's about fundamentals like eating the right things, in the right portions, and exercising. Short-term gains are not nearly as important as building healthy habits over the long term. Fad diets may show some short-term success, and they're certainly flashy, but they aren't meant to provide any lasting benefits or success.

Similarly, automation is incremental. If your organization is focused on putting together an "automation" or "DevOps" team, the effort is already doomed to failure. Automation is one of those things that needs buy-in across silos, and needs to grow organically over time. It is for this reason that those organizations that already heavily automate usually don't really call it anything special. It's just "modern operations."

 Some organizations have had success with a temporary "virtual" team assembled from members of various IT disciplines, who are tasked with bringing automation into the organization. This can be helpful to get started, but don't lose sight of the fact that the ultimate goal is to improve operations across the entire organization, not to have a team dedicated to automation so the rest of the organization doesn't have to worry about it.

To recap, don't try to boil the ocean or try to formally define everything you'll need to automate in the next century. Just get started. Start small, and automate the simple stuff, even if it involves writing a few scripts and running them with cron, or focusing on automated troubleshooting initially. You'll find there's a lot more to do once you've simply gotten started, and you'll have a lot more confidence to keep it up.

The Importance of Executive Buy-in

Again, it is very important that automation is done with a well-communicated purpose and strategy. That purpose has to focus on delivering value to the business—whether it's better uptime, security, or just responding more quickly to changing business needs. Those metrics should already be tracked, and if you're thinking about starting automation without these, you have the order wrong. The very first thing you should be addressing is how well you are communicating your short- and long-term technology goals with the business.

Once this is addressed, there are some very tangible benefits you'll realize once starting down the automation path. First, any additional head count that's needed for automation will be an easier pill to swallow. A very common complaint among engineers struggling to get automation started in their organization is the lack of resources to do it. With proper communication with the business, it will be widely understood that the cost of a bit of additional head count would pale in comparison to ongoing outages resulting from either totally manual processes, or half-baked automation tooling that was written by an overworked engineer.

However, the single most important reason to have frequent, quality communication regarding automation with the business leadership is that when things go wrong—and they will—you won't find yourself ripping out all those new tools and processes, but rather working forward to fix them. We'll discuss this later in the chapter, but one of the reasons the hyper-scale web companies like Facebook and Google talk about embracing failure is because they ensure they learn from their failures, and strive to ensure they don't encounter the same problems twice. Each failure is an opportunity to grow. Getting the business on board with this plan from the get-go will make sure that any failures are not only learned from, but planned for.

As an illustrative example, GitLab (the SaaS version of the software we used in Chapter 10) famously had a significant outage in January 2017. Not only did the service go down, but restoring the service took 18 hours due to a series of previously undetected failures in their backup procedures. Rather than shut the doors and try to figure out what went wrong in private, GitLab published a Google Doc outlining everything they knew, and exposed it publicly so users could see what was going on. They even live-streamed their work to bring the service back online. Once the service was available again, they published an extremely thorough blog post outlining not only what went wrong and how they fixed it, but also what they're putting into place to ensure this event doesn't happen again. This went a long way to assure customers that GitLab was serious about their service and that they were interested in learning from mistakes.

The bottom line is that failures will happen and that automation doesn't obviate the need for proper architectural design. Establishing a contract of transparency and frequent communication with the business leadership will help get the time and tools you need to build a proper foundation for an automation initiative.

Build Versus Buy

With all of IT becoming embroiled in the "open source movement," it's easy to get caught up in the hype. "Stop buying everything from vendors, and build everything yourself using open source software," right? Unfortunately, this sentiment differs from reality.

Despite what the analysts might have you believe, big organizations like Facebook or Google—known for their automation chops—don't build everything from scratch. At every part of their technology stack, they make compromises on what's economical for them to "build" versus "buy off the shelf." For instance, they may build their own servers for their huge data centers, but they don't fabricate every single component from its base elements. They still have to buy something—they've just made the decision to go deeper into that stack. In contrast, they may find it perfectly acceptable to go with a canned solution from Cisco for their corporate wireless connectivity.

The point here is that everyone has to make this decision for themselves. It is likely that you are not at the scale of Facebook or Google, and therefore you won't get the same benefits of building your own servers that they do, but it's also very possible that you could benefit from taking on a bit more of the pie than you traditionally have.

A good rule of thumb to follow in Enterprise IT is that you can buy your way into 80% of the features you need. Vendors can't cater to every enterprise (try as they might), so they have to spread their engineering across their entire customer base and put out products that are good enough for the immediate use cases. This means that the technology stack you acquire in this way will leave about 20% of your specific use case unaddressed. Traditionally, Enterprise IT has just simply accepted this—but they don't have to.

Even basic scripting can help fill in this remaining 20% feature gap. For instance, you may have a wireless controller that doesn't generate reports the way you want. Instead of waiting for months/years for your vendor to change their UI (which may never happen), perhaps investigate if the controller comes with an API. Maybe you could write a Python script to retrieve this data and use a graphics library to generate some nice visuals for you. Note that this doesn't mean you're a software developer now—it's simply knowing enough about scripting that you have an alternative to waiting years for your vendor to respond to your feature request.

Each side of the "Build versus Buy" paradigm tends to have its own traits (Figure 11-1). Organizations that choose to go with a commercial, off-the-shelf solution in one area tend to rely on external resources for support, whereas a technology stack that's built in-house tends to keep the support model in-house as well, which relies much more heavily on promoting self-sufficient expertise in that area.

Build	Buy
- Supported by internal teams	- Support contracts
- Assembled from small components	- Pre-built, vendor-validated solutions
- Open source	- Commercial/closed source

Figure 11-1. Build versus Buy

However, no technology decision is so binary. A good way of looking at the "Build versus Buy" paradigm—as with many other concepts in this chapter—is as a spectrum. No organization builds everything from scratch. Each technology team must figure out the right mix for their business. In reality, each organization will have a combination of these two strategies.

Embracing Failure

It's easy to become jaded against hyper-scale web companies talking about "failing fast," and "embracing failure." It does sound a bit absurd, doesn't it? There are usually serious financial penalties associated with failure at the infrastructure layer, so it's no wonder these ideas are met with a bit of resistance.

However, this resistance is often born out of a misunderstanding of the principle behind these catchphrases. The point of "embracing failure" isn't that failure is awesome. It's not. However, as bad as failure is, repeated failure is far worse. The idea behind "failing fast" is to never fail the same way twice. Go in with the assumption that failure will happen (because it will) and have a game plan for how you'll learn from it. The reason it may appear that some of the web-scale companies are excited about failure is because with the processes and the culture they have, it usually represents a failure they've not yet seen, so they get to work on a new problem. They get to modify or build their systems in a way to account for that failure.

So, for the rest of us, the idea of embracing failure is not so different. The idea is to learn from failure, whether it's an outage caused by a bug in the technology you already use, or someone fat-fingering an automation workflow or script and bringing down a data center. Failure happens with or without automation; the key is to understand and plan how your organization is going to react to it.

 This is why automated testing is so important. Putting this into place means that testing is not optional when changes are made—they're literally part of how the change goes into production. Your automated tests are the machine-language version of the lessons you've learned in the past. We discussed automated testing in Chapter 10.

In a previous section, we talked about the importance of obtaining buy-in from the business, and this is a big reason for doing just that. Failure is a natural part of IT regardless of where you are on the automation spectrum. Getting buy-in from the business can turn conversations about ripping out those "scripts gone wild" into conversations about learning from a failure and ensuring it doesn't happen twice. Hold proper postmortems and be clear about where the problem occurred, bringing data to the conversation and being analytical rather than assigning blame. Failure isn't always a sign that you're doing the wrong thing, it can also be a sign that your technology stack or skill sets are maturing and experiencing growing pains. Include "what if" scenarios in both your architectural discussions as well as when coordinating resources and goals with the business. Build failure planning into everything you do, so there are no surprises when everyone has to rush to the network operations center (NOC) to fix something.

Failure is also a really common reason automation breaks down and organizations revert to manual processes. It may happen very subtly. Especially in network automation, when things go wrong, it's tempting to circumvent the automation and log directly into infrastructure nodes, as you did before the automation was in place. Depending on how much automation is in place, this may literally be the only way to fix the problem, so this isn't always a bad thing.

However, a good litmus test for the "automation health" of an organization is what that organization does to the automation after the failure. The healthiest organizations immediately work to modify the automation so the failure doesn't occur again. We should learn from examples like the previously discussed outage at GitLab, who started working immediately after fixing the problem to ensure it never happened again. Software development teams do this often; when a bug is discovered in software, the bug is fixed, but a unit test is also created to re-create the parameters that caused the bug, to ensure that the bug is not reintroduced in the future (known as a regression).

Failure happens. Learn from it, and use a process that helps ensure you don't make the same mistake twice.

Skills and Education

Having the right skills has always been important in IT, especially if you want to differentiate yourself. This is certainly going to become even more critical as the pace of change continues to accelerate and you find your favorite technology stack being outdated by something new.

If you're reading this book, congratulations—you've already taken a great first step in the right direction. The chapters of this book were written to the IT professional who's looking for something "more," who isn't content with the traditional vendor-centric, coin-operated model of the past few decades.

We'll dive into a few specific areas of focus for enhancing your IT education and bringing your skill set into the next generation.

Learn What You Don't Know

One of the most common reactions when we have conversations with peers or customers about what kind of things they can do to get started with automation is: "I didn't even know that was possible!"

Indeed, working in IT can have a tendency to keep one in a bubble: constantly hearing different versions of the same message, and working on mostly the same things. This is one of the most dangerous scenarios for a technologist, because it's worse than simply not knowing another technical discipline. In this scenario, you don't know what you don't know. It might never have occurred to you that you could use Python to talk to that switch in your broom closet, because those conversations just never made it into your world. If you stay in your bubble, you will have no idea what's out there and will have difficulty growing as a technologist.

Fortunately, preventing this is easy. Frequently go outside your comfort zone. Jump into some kind of environment that operates outside your current "bubble." There are an absolute multitude of technologies that may be interesting to you, and you may not ever even find out about them until you challenge yourself to explore a new area.

This has tremendous value to you in your own career development, but it also essentially brings fresh ideas into your organization. This benefit isn't always tangible, as evidenced by how difficult it can be to get approval to go to conferences, especially conferences that are outside your technical discipline. If you're in a position where you're in charge of deciding which conferences to invest in, realize that this is one of the least expensive ways to get fresh ideas into your own organization.

In short, go outside your comfort zone. Things don't change that much in Enterprise IT, because our culture is very focused on and attached to IT vendors. These vendors have a vested interest in keeping things constant; rapid change doesn't fit their sales model. One thing we can do to fight this is to stop getting all our ideas and guidance from vendors. Instead of going to your vendor's big week-long marketing festival, maybe go to some smaller meet-ups, like your local network operator group. Or maybe check out some conferences outside your skill set entirely, like a developer or automation conference.

Focus on Fundamentals

In any technical discipline, we always hear new terms like "digital transformation" and "software defined" to describe the latest shiny new technology to enter the market. These terms give you a sense that you're falling behind in the technology realm, and that buying the latest product (physical or virtual) will bring you back to the cutting edge.

In truth, most of us actually are a bit behind the times when it comes to technology. Especially in Enterprise IT, the technology stack can lag 5, 10, or maybe even more years behind what's considered the cutting-edge stuff that folks in Silicon Valley are working with. However, buying the latest shiny product from your vendor never has and never will solve this problem for you. If this were the case, we would have solved this a long time ago. The real reason for stagnation in technology is an underinvestment in people and skill sets outside the traditional vendor-driven messaging we, at times, blindly follow.

This book has focused primarily on vendor-agnostic skill sets, processes, and culture for a reason—technology doesn't really change that much. Speeds and feeds get bigger and better, and the industry can tend to go in strange directions at times, but it's always a pendulum. Old patterns become new again, and the fundamental technology in use at the lowest level is usually the same. The TCP/IP you've known and loved from your earliest CCNA days is still very relevant in the latest Software Defined Networking products. The latest wireless products still reduce down to RF at their core.

This is one of the lessons that infrastructure professionals can learn from software developers. In general terms, infrastructure professionals don't "build" as much as they "operate," whereas software developers are accustomed to thinking like builders. To that end, software development is less of a skill than it is a collection of microskills. Just like a painter learns things like brush technique and the science of mixing colors, software developers pick up languages, tools, algorithms, and hardware knowledge, with the understanding that they will all become useful some day when the next big project calls for them.

These days, especially with the increasing importance of open source software in IT, the need for systems or computer science fundamentals has never been higher. Learn about Linux. Explore a programming language. These fundamentals will help lead you to understanding more about what we've taken for granted in IT for so long. New IT products come out all the time, but they all run on hardware and software. So, whether you're looking to make an entrance to a new discipline, or get deeper within your current one, focusing on the fundamentals is the best way to stay relevant across the vast yet shallow changes in the IT stack over the long term.

Certifications?

Inevitably, we must answer the ever-popular question: "What is the value of IT certifications in the era of automation?" It's an intriguing question, especially since it cannot be answered identically for everyone, as each one of us is at a different place in our IT career.

Certifications carry with them an implication that you know the material covered. So, while there are problems with IT certifications today, there's no denying that there's an interesting trade-off worth investigating. The certification will somewhat inflexibly define your capabilities in that area, but it's something concrete and well recognized by employers. Without certifications, you'd have to start every interview from scratch and prove to your potential employer that you know what you're talking about. Certifications are a good way to short-circuit this, and certainly, if you're new in IT, this is a very useful tool to have.

However, there are some limitations to what certifications bring to you. The value of this short circuit decreases over time as you gather more experience. In addition, certifications often serve the vendor first, so they won't get you 100% coverage of everything you might want to know. You may find it useful to rely more on certifications at the beginning of your career, and as you gain experience, you can dive deeper into fundamentals, relying less on vendors to prove to employers what you know.

If you focus on the fundamentals, IT certifications become much more of a tactical tool than a career-defining education path. Certifications are perfectly fine for cutting through the initial stages of a hiring process, and for some employers, certifications are a requirement. However, understanding the fundamentals will not only help you win in an interview, it will also ensure that you continue to climb the technical ladder as the winds of IT change.

Won't Automation Take My Job?!

One of the most common questions about automation is: "What will happen to my job?" Indeed, there's a widespread belief that automation will mean a reduction in head count. After all, if a machine can do my job, who will pay me to do it manually?

This idea seems to be predicated on a few incorrect assumptions. The first of these is that automation is somehow an instantaneous, night/day difference, which is never the case. Automation is always incremental, and imperfect at every layer. You solve the easiest problems first, and gradually move up the stack to bigger problems. You occasionally go back and improve what you wrote last year.

Another incorrect assumption is that once automation is in place, there will be nothing left to do. This is also incorrect, not only because of the first reason given in the previous paragraph, but also because automation unlocks new capabilities you didn't have before. It's true that automation does eliminate the need for a warm-blooded human being to fill a certain role, but doing so creates new challenges that simply didn't exist before, and those people should be reallocated to deal with the new problems. So while a certain role might be replaced by automation, there are always new opportunities opening up further up the stack.

So in a "post-automation" organization, it's clear that roles and responsibilities will change. You still need good, well-trained people, they'll just need to be reallocated to take on new challenges uncovered through the introduction of automation.

Summary

Hopefully this chapter has highlighted one very important truth: movements like DevOps aren't just about new technology or tools, but they're also not all about process, or even culture. DevOps is about all three working together. You have to approach your organization and your people with a systems mindset, in the same way you might approach a technology problem. DevOps is about optimizing a human system and improving communication so that all three pillars of IT are working in harmony. Proper communication is extremely critical. You will not have success if you don't understand how the business works. Nor will you have success if you are not able to communicate the value of what you're doing.

Many of the thoughts shared in this chapter stem from the belief that, while society often likes to break every issue down into a binary, absolute choice between two polar opposites, the reality is often much more like a spectrum. This is very true in IT as well. What works for one organization may not work for you. It is up to you to take the pragmatic approach and really think about the problems you're trying to solve. Don't simply rely on IT analysts or big web-scale companies to make your strategic technology decisions for you.

Finally, the journey you need to undergo can't possibly be contained in a single chapter (or even a whole book). You need to get involved with other communities of people that have already made this journey, so you can learn from their mistakes. One great resource for this is the Slack team for "Network to Code" (sign up for free at *http://slack.networktocode.com/*). There, you'll find over 50 channels focused on various topics related to infrastructure automation, broken down by vendor or open source project. Especially if you're new to automation, this is an extremely good place to get started.

In conclusion, be the automator—not the automated.

Advanced Networking in Linux

In Chapter 3, we discussed some basic Linux networking concepts. In this appendix, we'll use the building blocks from Chapter 3 as a basis for discussing a few advanced Linux networking concepts and configurations.

The topics we'll cover in this appendix include:

- Using macvlan interfaces
- Networking virtual machines (VMs)
- Working with network namespaces
- Networking Linux containers
- Using Open vSwitch (OVS)

Many of these topics could be books on their own! Thus, our focus in discussing these topics won't be to provide comprehensive, in-depth coverage; instead, we'll focus on providing enough information for you to understand where these topics fit into the overall networking picture as well as the basics of how to install, configure, or manage these networking configurations.

We'll start with using macvlan interfaces.

Using macvlan Interfaces

The *macvlan interface* is sort of like the reverse of a VLAN interface, which we discussed in Chapter 3. VLAN interfaces allow a single physical interface to communicate in multiple VLANs (broadcast domains) simultaneously; you can think of this as a "many (networks) to one (physical interface)" arrangement. Contrast that to mac vlan interfaces, which allow you to create multiple logical interfaces on a single broadcast domain—a "one (network) to many (logical interfaces)" arrangement. Each macvlan logical interface will have its own Media Access Control (MAC) address, and will only be able to see traffic destined for its MAC address. (One macvlan interface can't snoop on another macvlan interface's traffic, in other words.)

This may sound a bit esoteric, but there are at least a couple of use cases where this functionality can come in handy—let's explore those first.

Use Cases for macvlan Interfaces

Currently, macvlan interfaces have a couple use cases:

- If you're consolidating hosts and want to preserve the MAC address and IP address of hosts being retired, you can re-create those interfaces as macvlan interfaces on the new hosts. This will allow services to continue without any changes, even though the services are now running on a different host.

- You may also wish to use macvlan interfaces instead of a traditional Linux bridge in cases where you don't need the full functionality of the Linux bridge. We'll look at a couple examples of this, one in the next section and one later in the appendix.

Armed with this context of how macvlan interfaces could be used, we can dig into some of the technical details of working with macvlan interfaces.

Creating, Configuring, and Deleting macvlan Interfaces

To create a macvlan interface, you'll once again turn to the ip command—specifically, the ip link command. The generic syntax for the command to add a macvlan interface is ip link add link *parent-device macvlan-device* type macvlan.

Breaking that command down a bit:

- The *parent-device* is the physical interface with which the new macvlan interface should be associated. You may also see this referred to as the *lower device*.

- The *macvlan-device* is the name to be given to the new macvlan logical interface. Unlike with VLAN interfaces, there is no established naming convention.

So, let's say you wanted to create a macvlan interface on a CentOS system, and the new logical interface should be linked to the physical interface named ens33. The command would look like this:

```
[vagrant@centos ~]$ ip link add link ens33 macvlan0 type macvlan
[vagrant@centos ~]$
```

If you wanted to create the macvlan interface with a specific MAC address (the previous command uses an auto-generated MAC address), then insert **address** *desired-MAC-address* between the macvlan device name and the type macvlan statement.

Once you've created the interface, you can verify that the interface was created using ip link list, and the -d parameter—which exposed additional information about VLAN interfaces—will expose additional information about macvlan interfaces:

```
[vagrant@centos ~]$ ip -d link list macvlan0
6: macvlan0@ens33: <BROADCAST,MULTICAST> mtu 1500 qdisc noop state DOWN mode DEFAULT
    link/ether b6:73:dc:60:a3:10 brd ff:ff:ff:ff:ff:ff promiscuity 0
    macvlan  mode vepa
```

Note the macvlan mode vepa on the last line; this indicates the current mode of the macvlan device. A mode of vepa indicates that the Linux host expects the upstream switch to support 802.1Qbg, which—as of this writing—was fairly limited. Other modes are available; in addition to vepa, you can use bridge, private, and passthru. The bridge mode is *probably* what you'll want in most cases, and you can set the mode either when the interface is created or later.

To set the mode when the interface is created:

```
[vagrant@centos ~]$ ip link add link ens33 macvlan0 type macvlan mode bridge
[vagrant@centos ~]$
```

Or, if you need to set the mode after the interface has been created, use ip link set:

```
[vagrant@centos ~]$ ip link set macvlan0 type macvlan mode bridge
[vagrant@centos ~]$ ip -d link list macvlan0
6: macvlan0@ens33: <BROADCAST,MULTICAST> mtu 1500 qdisc noop state DOWN mode DEFAULT
    link/ether b6:73:dc:60:a3:10 brd ff:ff:ff:ff:ff:ff promiscuity 0
    macvlan  mode bridge
[vagrant@centos ~]$
```

As with almost all other kinds of interfaces, you'll still need to enable the interface (set the state to up) and assign an IP address for the interface to be fully functional:

```
[vagrant@centos ~]$ ip link set macvlan0 up
[vagrant@centos ~]$ ip addr add 192.168.100.112/24 dev macvlan0
[vagrant@centos ~]$
```

To delete a macvlan interface, first disable it with ip link set, then delete it with ip link delete:

```
[vagrant@centos ~]$ ip link set macvlan0 down
[vagrant@centos ~]$ ip link delete macvlan0
[vagrant@centos ~]$
```

So how does one make macvlan interface configurations persistent? By default, RHEL/Fedora/CentOS systems (as of the time of writing) did not have a means whereby you could use a per-interface configuration file in */etc/sysconfig/network-*

scripts to create persistent macvlan interface configurations. There are workarounds for this; for example, we found at least one GitHub repository (*https://github.com/larsks/initscripts-macvlan*) that has scripts to make this possible.

On Debian/Ubuntu systems, there is a workaround that leverages the `pre-up` functionality in network configuration stanzas to run other commands before bringing up the network interface. This configuration, for example, would create a persistent macvlan interface associated with the eth2 physical interface:

```
auto macvlan0
iface macvlan0 inet static
  address 192.168.100.110/24
  pre-up ip link add link eth2 macvlan0 type macvlan
```

Networking Virtual Machines

Providing networking for VMs running on a Linux-based hypervisor is a topic that could be a book unto itself, but in this section we're going to attempt to tackle a couple of high-level configurations that should cover the majority of the implementations you're likely to encounter in the real world. To help keep the amount of material we need to cover manageable, we'll limit our discussion in this section to using the KVM hypervisor (as opposed to Xen or another Linux-based solution) and generally only with the Libvirt virtualization API. There are, of course, other hypervisors, other tools, and other configurations; unfortunately, we can't cover all possible combinations here.

The two VM networking configurations we'll discuss are:

- Networking VMs using a Linux bridge
- Networking VMs using macvtap interfaces

Let's start by looking at using a Linux bridge.

Using a Bridge

Bridging VMs onto a physical network via one (or more) of the Linux host's physical interfaces is a very common use case for the Linux bridge. In fact, it was one of the examples we used in Chapter 3 when we first introduced bridging in Linux. In this section, we'll take a slightly more detailed look at how this works.

When you are networking VMs using a bridge with KVM and Libvirt, several different components come into play:

- A Linux bridge (naturally)
- A Libvirt virtual network that tells Libvirt which Linux bridge to use

- A virtual network interface
- A KVM guest domain (the word *domain* is used to refer to a VM running on KVM)

Let's see how all these pieces fit together.

Generally, one of the first things you'd do is use Libvirt to create a virtual network by defining it via some XML. (If you're not familiar with XML, no problem; refer to Chapter 5.) A virtual network is an abstraction used by Libvirt to refer to a specific underlying networking configuration. The underlying network configuration could be a bridge (as in this case), or it could be some other configuration (as we'll see in the next section).

Libvirt uses XML for the definitions of its abstractions, including virtual networks. The following XML code would create a virtual network named network-br0 that references a Linux bridge named br0. Note that it's up to the system administrator to create br0 and associate a physical interface with the bridge, using the procedures and commands outlined in Chapter 3.

```
<network>
  <name>network-br0</name>
  <forward mode="bridge"/>
  <bridge name="br0"/>
</network>
```

To tell a KVM domain to use this virtual network, you'd configure its domain XML to look something like this (we're only showing you the networking-relevant portion of the domain's XML definition, and not all possible options are included):

```
<interface type="network">
  <source network="network-br0"/>
</interface>
```

In this case, we're telling Libvirt (via this XML definition for a guest domain) to reference the Libvirt network named network-br0. This Libvirt network, in turn, references the Linux bridge named br0. The advantage of using the virtual network abstraction is that we could switch the underlying network bridge from br0 to br1 by simply modifying the virtual network definition. We wouldn't have to modify any of the VMs because they reference the virtual network.

With this configuration in place, when the guest domain is started KVM and Libvirt will automatically create a virtual network interface (a TAP device) and attach it to the bridge specified by the Libvirt virtual network definition (in this case, br0). The guest domain will have its own network interface, which will be associated by the hypervisor with the TAP device. This creates a "chain" of connectivity: the guest's eth0 is connected to the TAP device, which is connected to the bridge, which is connected to the physical interface and the network beyond.

Libvirt automates almost all of this for you, which can make it a bit more difficult to observe it in action. It's possible, though, to manually set all this up so that you can see how the pieces fit together. The next few paragraphs will walk you through the steps required to manually bridge a VM onto a network. We don't recommend this for any sort of production use, but it can be useful as a learning exercise to better understand what's happening "behind the scenes" with KVM and Libvirt.

First, you'll want to create the Linux bridge and attach a physical interface to the bridge. Assuming that eth1 is the interface you want to attach to the bridge, you'd run commands like these:

```
vagrant@trusty:~$ ip link add name br0 type bridge
vagrant@trusty:~$ ip link set br0 up
vagrant@trusty:~$ ip link set eth1 master br0
vagrant@trusty:~$ ip link set eth1 up
vagrant@trusty:~$
```

Note that whether you are manually attaching VMs to a bridge or using Libvirt, you would still have to use the various ip commands to create the Linux bridge and attach one (or more) interfaces. Note that the interfaces you attach to the bridge could be VLAN interfaces!

Next, you'd want to create the TAP device using a new command we haven't shown you yet: the ip tuntap command. The generic form of the command to add a TAP device is **ip tuntap add** *dev-name* **mode tap**. If we wanted to use the name tap0 for the TAP device to which we'll connect our VM, we run these commands:

```
vagrant@trusty:~$ ip tuntap add tap0 mode tap
vagrant@trusty:~$ ip link set tap0 up
vagrant@trusty:~$ ip -d link list tap0
5: tap0: <NO-CARRIER,BROADCAST,MULTICAST,UP> mtu 1500 qdisc pfifo_fast state DOWN
    mode DEFAULT group default qlen 500
    link/ether 7e:28:d5:99:ca:ab brd ff:ff:ff:ff:ff:ff promiscuity 0
    tun
vagrant@trusty:~$
```

The first command creates the TAP device, the second command enables the link, and the third command verifies the status of the device. The output of the third command tells you the interface is enabled but not connected to anything (note the NO-CARRIER in the output).

Next, add the TAP device to the existing bridge, then verify using the bridge link command:

```
vagrant@trusty:~$ ip link set tap0 master br0
vagrant@trusty:~$ bridge link list
3: eth1 state UP : <BROADCAST,MULTICAST,UP,LOWER_UP> mtu 1500 master br0 state
```

```
forwarding priority 32 cost 4
5: tap0 state DOWN : <NO-CARRIER,BROADCAST,MULTICAST,UP> mtu 1500 master br0 state
disabled priority 32 cost 100
vagrant@trusty:~$
```

The final step is to launch a virtual machine and attach it to the TAP device. We won't go into any great detail on the command used here, if for no other reason than we think it's unlikely you'll need it in real-world usage (you're far more likely to use the virsh command that comes with Libvirt). Note that the command is line-wrapped with backslashes here to make it more readable.

```
vagrant@trusty:~$ qemu-system-x86_64 -enable-kvm -hda cirros-01.qcow2 \
-net nic -net tap,ifname=tap0,script=no,downscript=no -vnc :1 &
[1] 866
vagrant@trusty:~$
```

This will boot a KVM domain in the background. If you now run ip -d link list tap0, you'll see that the TAP device is active (note that bridge link list would also show you the TAP device is up and active):

```
vagrant@trusty:~$ ip -d link list tap0
5: tap0: <BROADCAST,MULTICAST,UP,LOWER_UP> mtu 1500 qdisc pfifo_fast master br0
    state UP mode DEFAULT group default qlen 500
    link/ether 7e:28:d5:99:ca:ab brd ff:ff:ff:ff:ff:ff promiscuity 1
    tun
    bridge_slave
vagrant@trusty:~$
```

If you have a DHCP server running on the network segment to which the KVM host's eth1 is connected, then your KVM guest domain should obtain an IP address and be reachable from other systems on the same subnet.

Again, let us reiterate that you *don't* have to perform all the manual steps we outlined here to use bridged networking with KVM and Libvirt. We included the manual steps here to help you better understand all the various pieces that are involved. KVM and Libvirt automate the majority of these steps.

Also, now that we've covered VLAN interfaces we can point out that you can also use VLAN interfaces in a bridge. This might be one way of bridging different VMs on a single Linux hypervisor onto different VLANs—create a bridge for each VLAN, add a VLAN interface to each bridge, and then attach VMs to that bridge.

While using a bridge is one (very common) way to provide networking for VMs, it's by far not the only way. Later in this appendix in "Using Open vSwitch" on page 519, we'll talk about how to use Open vSwitch (OVS) to provide networking for VMs. First, though, let's take a look at another way of providing network connectivity to VMs: macvtap interfaces.

Using macvtap Interfaces

In "Using macvlan Interfaces" on page 501 we showed you how to use macvlan interfaces to configure a Linux system with multiple network identities on a single physical interface. A close relative (it uses the same Linux kernel driver) of the macvlan
interface is the macvtap interface, which allows us to use these multiple identities to
provide network connectivity for VMs.

To use macvtap interfaces with KVM and Libvirt, you'd again first start with defining
a Libvirt virtual network that references macvtap interfaces. This snippet of XML
would allow you to define a virtual network named macvtap-net that leverages macvtap interfaces running in bridge mode and is associated with the eth1 physical interface:

```
<network>
  <name>macvtap-net</name>
  <forward mode="bridge">
    <interface dev="eth1"/>
  </forward>
</network>
```

Just as when we use a bridge with KVM and Libvirt, the domain XML configuration
then needs to only reference the Libvirt network:

```
<interface type="network">
  <source network="macvtap-net"/>
</interface>
```

When you start/launch a VM using Libvirt, it will automatically create a macvtap
interface on the associated physical interface. You can verify this by running ip link
list; you should see a macvtap interface in the output.

One interesting side effect, if you will, of using macvtap interfaces is that the MAC
address seen inside the guest domain will be the same as the MAC address used by
the macvtap interface. For example, here's the output of ip link list eth0 from
within a guest domain when using a macvtap interface:

```
2: eth0: <BROADCAST,MULTICAST,UP,LOWER_UP> mtu 1500 qdisc pfifo_fast qlen 1000
    link/ether 52:54:00:9c:51:74 brd ff:ff:ff:ff:ff:ff
```

For comparison, here's the output of ip link list macvtap0 on the host system,
where macvtap0 is the macvtap interface created by Libvirt when the guest domain
was launched:

```
5: macvtap0@eth1: <BROADCAST,MULTICAST,UP,LOWER_UP> mtu 1500 qdisc pfifo_fast state
    UNKNOWN mode DEFAULT group default qlen 500
    link/ether 52:54:00:9c:51:74 brd ff:ff:ff:ff:ff:ff
```

This direct correlation between the MAC address inside the guest and the MAC address outside the guest may simplify some troubleshooting and/or information gathering efforts.

We're going to discuss one other way of providing networking for VMs (using Open vSwitch), but before we do that we're going to take a slight detour into a couple other advanced Linux networking topics.

Working with Network Namespaces

Network namespaces in Linux are a way to support multiple separate routing tables and multiple separate iptables configurations, and to "scope" or limit network interfaces to a particular namespace. They are probably most closely related to Virtual Routing and Forwarding (VRF) instances in the networking world, but are used in a variety of ways. One notable way we'll discuss later is in conjunction with Linux containers.

 While network namespaces can be used to create VRF instances, there is separate work going on the Linux kernel community right now to build "proper" VRF functionality into Linux. This proposed VRF functionality would provide additional logical Layer 3 separation within a namespace. It's still too early yet to see where this will lead, but we wanted you to know about it nevertheless.

Every Linux system comes with a default network namespace, and this is the namespace where you (as the user) can see the routing table, iptables configuration, and network interfaces. However, as we'll show in this section, it's possible to create non-default network namespaces, and to assign network interfaces to these non-default network namespaces for a variety of purposes.

We'll start by examining some use cases for network namespaces; this will help provide context on how they might be used.

Use Cases for Network Namespaces

So what sort of use cases exist for network namespaces? There are a few that spring to mind:

Per-process routing
> Running a process in its own network namespace allows you to do configure routing on a per-process basis.

Enabling VRF configurations
> We mentioned at the start of this section that network namespaces were probably most closely related to VRF instances in the networking world, so it's only natural

that enabling VRF-like configurations would be a prime use case for network namespaces.

Support for overlapping IP address spaces
You might also use network namespaces to provide support for overlapping IP address spaces, where the same address (or address range) might be used for different purposes and have different meanings. In the bigger picture, you'd probably need to combine this with overlay networking and/or network address translation (NAT) in order to fully support such a use case.

Let's continue our discussion of network namespaces by looking at how to create (and remove) non-default network namespaces.

Creating and Removing Network Namespaces

Creating a network namespace is really pretty straightforward. The tool of choice is again the `ip` command from the `iproute2` package, this time using the `netns` set of subcommands.

To create a network namespace, the syntax for the command is **ip netns add** *namespace-name*. As an example, let's say that you wanted to create a namespace called `blue`:

```
[vagrant@centos ~]$ ip netns add blue
[vagrant@centos ~]$
```

Note there's no feedback for a successful command; to verify the namespace was added, you'll need to use `ip netns list`:

```
[vagrant@centos ~]$ ip netns list
blue
[vagrant@centos ~]$
```

Deleting network namespaces is equally straightforward:

```
[vagrant@centos ~]$ ip netns del blue
[vagrant@centos ~]$ ip netns list
[vagrant@centos ~]$
```

The lack of output from the `ip netns list` command indicates there are no network namespaces other than the "default" namespace in which all networking objects normally reside.

While adding and deleting namespaces is (somewhat) interesting, the real value lies in actually *using* network namespaces. To do that, we'll first need to look at how to assign interfaces to a particular namespace.

Placing Interfaces in a Network Namespace

By default, all of the networking-related objects and configurations belong to the "default" network namespace (also known as "netns 0"). Also by default, a newly created network namespace contains no network interfaces. Thus, a newly created network namespace has *no* network connectivity to anything: not to the default namespace, not to the outside world, not to *anything*. To fix that, you need to place an interface into the namespace.

To place an interface into a namespace, use the `ip link` command (obviously this command assumes that the `blue` namespace has already been created):

```
vagrant@jessie:~$ ip link set eth1 netns blue
vagrant@jessie:~$
```

As you can tell from this example, the general syntax to place an interface into a network namespace is `ip link set` *interface-name* `netns` *namespace-name*.

Once you place an interface into a namespace, it disappears from the default namespace. This makes sense, because an interface can exist in only a single namespace at any given time. For example, consider Figures A-1 and A-2. Figure A-1 shows the output of `ip link list` on a CentOS 7 system with two physical interfaces (ens32 and ens33).

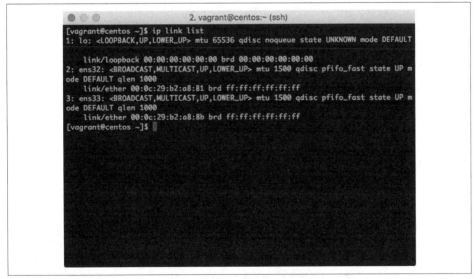

Figure A-1. Listing of interfaces before we assign an interface to a namespace

Now look at Figure A-2, which shows the output of `ip link list` on the same CentOS 7 system *after* one of the physical interfaces has been moved to a different network namespace.

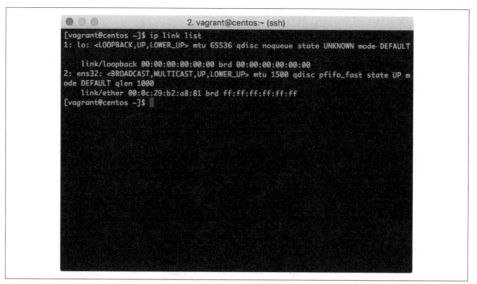

Figure A-2. Listing of interfaces after we assign an interface to a namespace

As you can see, the interface has disappeared from the default namespace.

Although we've only shown you examples that assign a physical interface to a namespace, you're not limited to physical interfaces. Suppose you wanted to assign a VLAN interface to a namespace:

```
[vagrant@centos ~]$ ip link set ens33.150 netns blue
[vagrant@centos ~]$
```

Or suppose you want to assign a macvlan interface to a particular namespace:

```
[vagrant@centos ~]$ ip link set macvlan0 netns red
[vagrant@centos ~]$
```

This gives you a great deal of flexibility in how you connect network namespaces to the outside world.

Regardless of the type of interface, the command to assign it to a namespace remains the same: **ip link set** *interface-name* **netns** *namespace-name*. And regardless of the type of interface, once it is assigned to a namespace it disappears from the default namespace. To work with any interface assigned to a non-default namespace, you need to run commands within the context of the namespace in which it resides. In other words, you're going to need to execute commands *inside* a particular namespace.

Executing Commands in a Network Namespace

To execute a command in the context of a specific network namespace, you'll need to use the ip netns exec command. The general syntax for this command is **ip netns exec** *namespace-name command*. Let's look at a few examples.

In the previous section, we used the ip link set command to assign the eth1 interface on a Debian 8.x system into the blue namespace. If we now want to be able to see that interface, we'll combine ip netns exec (to execute a command inside a particular namespace) with ip link list (to show us the list of network interfaces), like this:

```
vagrant@jessie:~$ ip netns exec blue ip link list
1: lo: <LOOPBACK> mtu 65536 qdisc noop state DOWN mode DEFAULT group default
    link/loopback 00:00:00:00:00:00 brd 00:00:00:00:00:00
3: eth1: <BROADCAST,MULTICAST> mtu 1500 qdisc noop state DOWN mode DEFAULT group
    default qlen 1000
    link/ether 00:0c:29:7d:38:9d brd ff:ff:ff:ff:ff:ff
vagrant@jessie:~$
```

We can see from this output that the eth1 interface exists inside the blue namespace, but is currently disabled (note state DOWN in the output). To enable this interface:

```
vagrant@jessie:~$ ip netns exec blue ip link set eth1 up
vagrant@jessie:~$ ip netns exec blue ip link list eth1
3: eth1: <BROADCAST,MULTICAST,UP,LOWER_UP> mtu 1500 qdisc pfifo_fast state UP
    mode DEFAULT group default qlen 1000
    link/ether 00:0c:29:7d:38:9d brd ff:ff:ff:ff:ff:ff
vagrant@jessie:~$
```

Now the interface is up, and we could assign an IP address and check the namespace's routing table:

```
vagrant@jessie:~$ ip netns exec blue ip addr add 192.168.100.10/24 dev eth1
vagrant@jessie:~$ ip netns exec blue ip route list
192.168.100.0/24 dev eth1  proto kernel  scope link  src 192.168.100.11
vagrant@jessie:~$
```

To prove that the namespaces are separate—in other words, that the IP configuration within the blue namespace does not affect the default namespace—run the ip route list command in the default namespace as follows:

```
vagrant@jessie:~$ ip route list
default via 192.168.70.2 dev eth0
192.168.70.0/24 dev eth0  proto kernel  scope link  src 192.168.70.242
vagrant@jessie:~$
```

The IP configuration and associated route linked to eth1 no longer affect the default namespace, only the blue namespace where the interface is assigned. (We'll leave it as an exercise for the readers to check the routing table in the blue namespace.)

Now that we have an interface that is assigned to a namespace, is enabled, and has an IP address configured, we can test connectivity from that specific namespace to the outside world using `ip netns exec` and the ubiquitous `ping` command:

```
vagrant@jessie:~$ ip netns exec blue ping -c 4 192.168.100.100
```

Throughout all these examples we're showing, you may have noticed that we keep having to type `ip netns exec` in front of commands in order to execute them in a particular namespace. Here, you may find leveraging bash's alias functionality—the ability to create commands that reference other commands—to be extraordinarily helpful. For example, you could define the alias `nsblue` to execute commands inside the `blue` network namespace:

```
vagrant@trusty:~$ alias nsblue="ip netns exec blue"
vagrant@trusty:~$
```

With this alias defined, you can now just type `nsblue` instead of `ip netns exec blue` when you want to execute commands inside the `blue` network namespace.

```
vagrant@trusty:~$ nsblue ip link list
3: eth1: <BROADCAST,MULTICAST,UP,LOWER_UP> mtu 1500 qdisc pfifo_fast state UP
    mode DEFAULT group default qlen 1000
    link/ether 00:0c:29:7d:38:9d brd ff:ff:ff:ff:ff:ff
vagrant@trusty:~$
```

Although these examples show physical interfaces being assigned to a network namespace, remember that you can assign just about any type of interface—physical interfaces, VLAN interfaces, or macvlan interfaces—to a network namespace. When you assign one of these types of interfaces to a network namespace, though, you're connecting that namespace to the outside world (a particular VLAN if you're using a VLAN interface, for example). What if you wanted to connect this new namespace with the default namespace? This is where veth (virtual Ethernet) pairs come into play.

Connecting Network Namespaces with veth Pairs

Virtual Ethernet pairs (more commonly known as *veth pairs*) are a special kind of logical interface supported by the Linux kernel. Because of the way veth pairs work they always come in pairs: traffic entering one interface in the pair comes out the other interface in the pair. Like other types of interfaces, one member of a veth pair can be assigned to a non-default network namespace—thus enabling users to *connect* network namespaces to each other.

Let's take a quick look at how this works. First, you'll create the veth pair using the `ip` command. The syntax for the command is **ip link add** *veth-name* **type veth peer name** *veth-peer*. If you wanted to create a veth pair named veth0 and veth1, then the command would look like this:

```
vagrant@trusty:~$ ip link add veth0 type veth peer name veth1
vagrant@trusty:~$ ip -d link list veth0
5: veth0: <BROADCAST,MULTICAST> mtu 1500 qdisc noop state DOWN mode DEFAULT group
    default qlen 1000
    link/ether f6:67:c0:f8:75:7d brd ff:ff:ff:ff:ff:ff promiscuity 0
    veth
vagrant@trusty:~$
```

Any traffic that enters either member of the veth pair will exit the other member of the veth pair. So, if we place veth1 into a network namespace, then traffic that enters veth1 in whatever namespace we place it will exit veth0 in the default namespace, thus connecting the two namespaces together.

In the following set of commands, we'll create a network namespace called green, then place veth1 into that namespace. We'll then use ip netns exec to configure veth1, and then test connectivity between the two namespaces.

```
vagrant@trusty:~$ ip netns add green
vagrant@trusty:~$ ip link set veth1 netns green
vagrant@trusty:~$ ip netns exec green ip addr add 10.0.3.1/24 dev veth1
vagrant@trusty:~$ ip netns exec green ip link set veth1 up
vagrant@trusty:~$ ip addr add 10.0.3.2/24 dev veth0
vagrant@trusty:~$ ip link set veth0 up
vagrant@trusty:~$ ping -c 4 10.0.3.1
PING 10.0.3.1 (10.0.3.1) 56(84) bytes of data.
64 bytes from 10.0.3.1: icmp_seq=1 ttl=64 time=0.046 ms
64 bytes from 10.0.3.1: icmp_seq=2 ttl=64 time=0.078 ms
64 bytes from 10.0.3.1: icmp_seq=3 ttl=64 time=0.066 ms
64 bytes from 10.0.3.1: icmp_seq=4 ttl=64 time=0.077 ms

--- 10.0.3.1 ping statistics ---
4 packets transmitted, 4 received, 0% packet loss, time 3002ms
rtt min/avg/max/mdev = 0.046/0.066/0.078/0.016 ms
vagrant@trusty:~$
```

So what did we just do here? We already had the veth pair, so we created a namespace named green and placed veth1 into that namespace. We then assigned an IP address to veth1, and enabled the interface. Then, *so that the default namespace had a route to the destination*, we added an IP address to veth0. We then pinged between the two network namespaces.

What if you wanted to connect a network namespace to the outside world using veth pairs? No problem—create the veth pair, place one veth interface in the network namespace, and then put the other veth interface into a bridge with a physical interface. Your network namespace is now bridged to the outside world. (We'll leave it to you to do this as a learning exercise.)

Naturally, we could create more complex topologies, but this gives you an idea of what's possible using veth pairs to connect network namespaces.

In the next section, we'll take a look at a practical application of network namespaces: Linux containers.

Networking Linux Containers

In the previous section, we talked about how network namespaces were a way for Linux to "scope," or limit, network interfaces to a particular subset of the overall system—in other words, to isolate network interfaces in their own little space (a network namespace). The Linux kernel also supports other types of namespaces: a mount namespace, a process namespace, and (in newer kernel versions) a user namespace. In each case, the purpose of the namespace is to scope or limit resources in their own sub-OS. When you combine namespaces with other Linux kernel–level features like control groups (cgroups), you gain the ability to create lightweight sandboxes that isolate processes (or groups of processes) from one another. This is the basis for Linux *containers*, which are a lightweight way of running multiple, isolated processes on a single Linux instance.

Linux containers have been around for a while, but it's only in the last couple of years that the world has really taken notice. This is due in part to the rise of Docker (the open source project), which is one particular model for working with Linux containers. Docker uses namespaces, cgroups, and a layered copy-on-write filesystem combined with an easy-to-use CLI tool to make it extraordinarily easy to create and leverage Linux containers.

If you're interested in more details on Docker, we recommend the O'Reilly book *Using Docker*, by Adrian Mouat.

However, Docker is not the only container game in town. An older (and some might say more mature) approach is known as LXC (which stands for *LinuX* Containers). Docker and LXC leverage the exact same kernel features (namespaces for isolation and cgroups for resource accounting and limiting); where they differ is in how they build their containers and how a user leverages their containers. Each approach has its advantages and disadvantages.

What LXC and Docker do share (in addition to their use of the same underlying Linux kernel constructs) are certain facets of how they do container networking (all these are default settings):

- Both LXC and Docker leverage veth pairs, placing one of the veth interfaces into a network namespace with the container and leaving the peer interface in the default network namespace.

- Both LXC and Docker leverage a Linux bridge to which the veth peer interface in the default namespace is attached. The default LXC bridge is named lxcbr0, whereas the default Docker bridge is named docker0.

- Both LXC and Docker use custom iptables rules to perform network address translation (NAT) for container connectivity.

Aside from the use of iptables, we've discussed all these mechanisms in previous sections, so you should already be familiar with veth interfaces, placing veth interfaces into a network namespace, and using bridges to provide connectivity.

Although you can see that LXC and Docker share a fair number of similarities, there are also quite a few differences, especially in terms of how you configure network settings for each. Let's take a closer look at configuring container networking for both LXC and Docker.

Configuring LXC Networking

LXC stores networking configuration on a per-container basis. On Ubuntu systems (this path may vary from distribution to distribution), the file */var/lib/lxc/<container-name>/config* contains some critical LXC networking configuration options:

- The `lxc.network.type` option controls the networking type for the containers. The default is `veth`, which tells LXC to use veth pairs. You can also specify `macvlan`, which tells LXC to use macvlan interfaces. In the event of using macvlan interfaces, you can use the `lxc.network.macvlan.mode` to set the mode (`private`, `vepa`, `bridge`) of the macvlan interfaces. LXC also supports a value of `vlan`, which means containers will leverage a VLAN interface for connectivity.

- The `lxc.network.link` setting controls the bridge to which the LXC will be connected in the default namespace. By default, this value is `lxcbr0`. Leaving this value blank means that the container won't be connected to a bridge. Later in this appendix in "Using Open vSwitch" on page 519, we'll show you a use case for leaving this setting blank.

- The `lxc.network.veth.pair` option specifies the name of the veth pair that will sit outside the container namespace (the other member of the pair will be moved into the container's network namespace). This lets you control the naming convention used for the veth peer that remains in the default network namespace.

- The `lxc.network.ipv4`, `lxc.network.ipv4.gateway`, `lxc.network.ipv6`, and `lxc.network.ipv6.gateway` settings control IPv4 and IPv6 configuration for the container, respectively.

In short, LXC provides pretty extensive control over how networking is provided for containers.

Configuring Docker Networking

Configuring Docker networking is both simpler and also more complicated than configuring LXC networking. This sounds odd, but allow us to explain.

Prior to the release of Docker 1.9, Docker relied solely upon the use of veth interfaces, a Linux bridge, and a set of iptables rules. Configuring any of these settings involved making changes to the DOCKER_OPTS environment variable one uses when launching the Docker daemon. This is the simple part.

With the release of Docker 1.9, Docker added a pluggable network subsystem that enables multiple types of networks to be created and managed by the Docker daemon. The "old" Docker bridge network is still available, but it was also possible to create multi-host overlay networks, and third-party network plug-ins were supported.

Docker networking changed again with the release of Docker 1.12, which introduced "Swarm mode" and built-in VXLAN multi-host overlay networking. Third-party networking plug-ins needed to be rewritten, which—as of the time of this writing—was still under way.

What's this about ipvlan interfaces?

In this section we've discussed a few different types of logical interfaces: VLAN interfaces, macvlan interfaces, and veth pairs, for example. We haven't discussed *ipvlan interfaces*, which are like macvlan interfaces but are differentiated at Layer 3 using IP addresses instead of at Layer 2 using MAC addresses. The support for ipvlan interfaces is still quite new, though, and ipvlan interfaces really only have a use case in container networking.

Because Docker's multi-host networking functionality is still changing rapidly, we'll focus on the default bridge network that Docker offers. Almost all of the configuration of Docker's default bridge network involves changing the flags passed to the Docker daemon when it is launched, either by modifying the DOCKER_OPTS environment variable or by modifying the file used to launch the daemon. Some of the applicable configuration options include:

- The -b or --bridge option allows you to specify the name of the bridge that Docker should use. You can set this parameter to use a bridge *other* than docker0.

- The --bip parameter allows you to specify the IP address assigned to the bridge interface.

- The `--iptables=true` option enables Docker to automatically add the appropriate iptables rules to perform NAT.

In addition to these daemon-wide settings, some networking options—specifically, exposed ports—are per-container. Exposed ports can be found in two possible places:

- The container's `Dockerfile` may contain one or more ports in an `EXPOSE` statement, which tells the Docker daemon which ports need to be exposed to the outside world. For example, an `EXPOSE 80` statement in a `Dockerfile` tells the Docker daemon to dynamically link a public port on the Docker host to port 80 on the container. The key thing to note there is that the assigned public port is non-deterministic and allocated dynamically by the Docker daemon.
- The command used to launch a container may contain one or more `-p` parameters, which allows the user to *control* the mapping between public ports and container ports. For example, using `-p 80:80` tells the Docker daemon to link the Docker host's port 80 to the container's port 80.

Fortunately, Docker offers a `docker inspect` command, which—when given the ID of a running container—will provide all the information you need about the container's networking configuration. This includes the container's IP address and port mapping.

Having taken a look at networking with Docker and LXC, let's turn our attention to our last major section: using Open vSwitch for networking.

Using Open vSwitch

Open vSwitch (OVS) is an open source, production-quality multi-layer virtual switch designed to run within a hypervisor (although, as we'll see later, OVS has lots of applications besides just using it with a hypervisor). OVS was designed with network automation in mind, built to support programmatic control while still supporting a wide range of management protocols and standards. OVS was also designed from the ground up to support OpenFlow, the seminal SDN protocol, and is considered by many to be *the* definitive reference OpenFlow implementation. OVS is also widely supported: both the Xen and KVM hypervisors support OVS, and at the time of this writing a port of OVS to Hyper-V was nearly complete (it will likely be complete by the time this book makes it to print). Numerous management and orchestration systems, including OpenStack, have support for OVS.

Given its prominent role in the SDN and network automation spaces, it's fully expected that we should provide coverage of OVS in a book on network automation. However, because of the broad swath of features that OVS supports, we'll have to constrain our discussion. As a result, we'll focus on three core areas:

- Installing OVS (discussing OVS on Linux only)
- Configuring OVS
- Connecting workloads to OVS

Let's start at the beginning, and that's installing OVS.

Installing OVS

Due to OVS's architecture—comprising both a userspace daemon as well as a kernel module—the procedure for installing OVS varies depending on your Linux distribution and which version of the OVS kernel module you want to use.

Since version 3.3, the upstream Linux kernel has shipped with an OVS module. To use the upstream kernel module, no further action is required; you need only to install the userspace components. If, on the other hand, you prefer to use the kernel module from the OVS tree (which may be newer than the upstream module and therefore support more features), then you'll need to install and compile a kernel module for the currently running kernel.

 If you'd like to verify whether your Linux kernel supports the upstream OVS kernel module, just run *modprobe openvswitch* (you may need to use sudo if you don't have superuser privileges). If the command reports an error, your kernel doesn't have the OVS upstream module, and you'll need to install a kernel module. Keep in mind, though, that the upstream OVS module has been in the Linux kernel since version 3.3, so virtually *all* modern distributions will have the upstream OVS module available in the kernel.

On Debian 8.x and Ubuntu 14.04, installation packages for both the userspace components and the kernel module are available in the primary repositories. Installation, therefore, is just a matter of using apt-get install:

- To use the upstream kernel module, just install the userspace packages. The names of the userspace components are openvswitch-common and openvswitch-switch.

- To use the kernel module that ships with OVS, also install the openvswitch-datapath-dkms package (and the necessary prerequisites, dkms, make, and libc6-dev).

We stated that Debian 8.x has packages for OVS in the primary repositories, but be aware that, depending on your installation method, the primary repositories may not be enabled. Check your repository configuration in */etc/apt/sources.list* if you are unsure (you can use the cat command to view the configuration, and edit it to enable the primary repositories if necessary).

On RHEL/CentOS/Fedora, the story is—as of this writing—a bit more complicated. RHEL 7.x and CentOS 7.x do not ship with a repository enabled that contains OVS. In order to install OVS, you either have to compile from source, or add a repository that contains OVS packages. One such repository is the OpenStack repository from the CentOS Cloud Special Interest Group (SIG). You can enable this repository by running yum install centos-release-openstack; when that command completes, verify the repository has been added using yum repolist. Fedora, however, ships with OVS packages available in the default Fedora repositories; no additional repositories need to be added or enabled.

To install OVS on RHEL/CentOS/Fedora once you have an available package, it's just a matter of running yum install to install the openvswitch package.

Note that as of this writing RHEL/CentOS/Fedora don't offer a package to install the kernel module from the OVS tree; if you want that kernel module, you'll have to manually compile it and install it. Given that manually compiling and installing a kernel module is a fairly in-depth topic, it's not something we'll discuss here. There are, however, a number of guides available online from various sources.

Once you have OVS installed, we can move on to our next section: configuring OVS.

Configuring OVS

OVS can be configured in a couple of different ways: you can use the OVS-specific command-line tools, or you can leverage OVS integration into the Linux network configuration scripts (*/etc/network/interfaces* on Debian/Linux, */etc/sysconfig/network-scripts* on RHEL/CentOS/Fedora). In this section, we'll focus primarily on the use of the OVS-specific command-line tools. The reason for this is that OVS *doesn't* follow the general Linux convention of needing to edit configuration files in order for a configuration to be persistent.

That's right—changes you make to the OVS configuration using the OVS command-line tools are persistent. OVS maintains its own configuration database, and the OVS command-line tools manipulate that database. When a system is restarted, OVS will reread its configuration from the configuration database; thus, every change you make to OVS using the OVS command-line tool *is* a persistent change. This is a key difference with OVS versus a lot of the other network configurations we discussed in Chapter 3 and in this appendix.

The primary tool you will use to configure OVS is `ovs-vsctl`. Like the `ip` commands we discussed both here and in Chapter 3, the `ovs-vsctl` command has a number of subcommands for various purposes:

- The `show` subcommand simply prints an overview of the configuration database's contents (i.e., prints an overview of OVS's configuration).

- The `add-br` command adds an OVS bridge to the OVS configuration. Any OVS bridge is conceptually and functionally similar to the Linux bridge, but with a vastly expanded set of capabilities.

- The `del-br` command deletes an OVS bridge.

- The `add-port` command adds a port to an OVS bridge. Ports can be physical interfaces (like eth1 or ens33) or logical network interfaces (like a VLAN interface or a veth interface).

- Similarly, the `del-port` command removes a port from an OVS bridge.

There are more commands, but these comprise the bulk of the functionality you'll need to get started with OVS. Let's look at some examples.

Assuming you have OVS installed and running, let's start by creating an OVS bridge. First, we'll show the current configuration (to show that it is empty—that OVS is essentially unconfigured), and then we'll add a bridge and show the configuration again. The syntax for adding a bridge to OVS is **ovs-vsctl add-br** *bridge-name*. Here's the command in action:

```
[vagrant@centos ~]$ ovs-vsctl show
e1b45dda-69fa-4cb1-ad37-23eea2e63052
    ovs_version: "2.4.0"
[vagrant@centos ~]$ ovs-vsctl add-br br0
[vagrant@centos ~]$ ovs-vsctl show
e1b45dda-69fa-4cb1-ad37-23eea2e63052
    Bridge "br0"
        Port "br0"
            Interface "br0"
                type: internal
    ovs_version: "2.4.0"
[vagrant@centos ~]$
```

You now have an OVS bridge—but like a Linux bridge, it doesn't really *do* anything until you add some ports. Let's add the physical ens33 interface to this bridge:

```
[vagrant@centos ~]$ ovs-vsctl add-port br0 ens33
```

As you can see, the syntax for adding a port to a bridge is **ovs-vsctl add-port** *bridge-name port-name*. With one exception that we'll discuss later, the port you're adding to OVS needs to already exist and be recognized by Linux.

Running `ovs-vsctl` show now will show the physical port has been added:

```
[vagrant@centos ~]$ ovs-vsctl show
e1b45dda-69fa-4cb1-ad37-23eea2e63052
    Bridge "br0"
        Port "ens33"
            Interface "ens33"
        Port "br0"
            Interface "br0"
                type: internal
    ovs_version: "2.4.0"
```

To delete a port or a bridge, you'd use the `del-port` or `del-br` commands, respectively:

```
[vagrant@centos ~]$ ovs-vsctl del-port br0 ens33
[vagrant@centos ~]$ ovs-vsctl del-br br0
[vagrant@centos ~]$ ovs-vsctl show
e1b45dda-69fa-4cb1-ad37-23eea2e63052
    ovs_version: "2.4.0"
[vagrant@centos ~]$
```

In addition to the subcommands we've shown you so far, you may also find yourself needing to use the `set` subcommand to set properties or values. For example, to apply a VLAN tag to an OVS port, you'd use the command syntax **ovs-vsctl set port** *port-name tag=value*. Suppose you have a port named vnet0 that represents a VM (this is a scenario we'll discuss shortly in "Using VMs with OVS" on page 527), and you want that VM to be on VLAN 10. You'd use this command:

```
vagrant@trusty:~$ ovs-vsctl set port vnet0 tag=10
vagrant@trusty:~$ ovs-vsctl show
fe63a9ea-f72f-4aa2-b390-42ecbed6deef
    Bridge "br0"
        Port "vnet0"
            tag: 10
            Interface "vnet0"
        Port "br0"
            Interface "br0"
                type: internal
        Port "eth1"
            Interface "eth1"
    ovs_version: "2.0.2"
vagrant@trusty:~$
```

You may also find the `list` subcommand helpful, as it will list all the properties/values associated with a configuration object in the OVS configuration database. If you wanted to see all the configuration values for the vnet0 port, you'd run this command:

```
vagrant@trusty:~$ ovs-vsctl list port vnet0
_uuid               : cc51fc7e-ce14-41c6-9ad6-7b3ae717afa9
bond_downdelay      : 0
```

```
bond_fake_iface    : false
bond_mode          : []
bond_updelay       : 0
external_ids       : {}
fake_bridge        : false
interfaces         : [74e6ede7-1a13-45c1-84d6-f66cbfc5a353]
lacp               : []
mac                : []
name               : "vnet0"
other_config       : {}
qos                : []
statistics         : {}
status             : {}
tag                : 10
trunks             : []
vlan_mode          : []
vagrant@trusty:~$
```

There's obviously much, much more—like creating overlay networks with a protocol like VXLAN or Geneve, working with OpenFlow flows, or setting OVS to use an external controller—but the majority of what you'll do with OVS will involve adding and removing bridges, adding and removing ports, and setting properties on ports.

Let's turn our attention now to putting some of the commands we've shown you in the section to work as we look at connecting various types of workloads to OVS.

Connecting Workloads to OVS

Here we'll use the term *workloads* to refer to any sort of entity that needs network connectivity—this could be a network namespace, a container, a virtual machine (like a KVM guest domain), or the OVS host system itself.

The process for connecting workloads to OVS will vary based on a variety of factors, but it will generally look like this:

- For network namespaces and containers, you'll often use a veth pair to connect a network namespace to OVS.

- For KVM guest domains, attaching to OVS is typically handled via a TAP interface.

- For the host system, you can direct traffic through OVS by using an OVS internal port.

Let's take a look at each of these scenarios in a bit more detail. Refer back to previous sections if you need a refresher on any of the commands used.

Connecting network namespaces with OVS

Recall from our earlier discussion on network namespaces that one way to connect network namespaces is to use a veth pair. One of the veth interfaces is placed in a network namespace (using the `ip link set` command), and the peer interface remains in the primary namespace.

We can use veth pairs with OVS to connect network namespaces to OVS (and thus to any sort of network topology that OVS supports—a physical network or an overlay network). To do this, we'd use the same basic setup we described earlier to bridge a network namespace onto the network.

Assuming you have a network namespace named green, then you'd first create the veth pair, place one of the veth interfaces into the green namespace, and configure the interface in the green namespace:

```
[vagrant@centos ~]$ ip link add veth0 type veth peer name veth1
[vagrant@centos ~]$ ip link set veth1 netns green
[vagrant@centos ~]$ ip netns exec green ip addr add 192.168.100.12/24 dev veth1
[vagrant@centos ~]$ ip netns exec green ip link set veth1 up
[vagrant@centos ~]$ ip link set veth0 up
```

At this point, you have a veth pair (veth0 and veth1), and the veth1 interface has been assigned to the green interface and given an IP address. Both veth interfaces are also up (enabled), so that traffic will flow between them. Now, to connect the green network namespace to OVS, just add veth0 to an OVS bridge. Let's assume you already have an OVS bridge named br0, and that bridge also contains the ens33 physical interface:

```
[vagrant@centos ~]$ ovs-vsctl add-port br0 veth0
[vagrant@centos ~]$ ovs-vsctl show
e1b45dda-69fa-4cb1-ad37-23eea2e63052
    Bridge "br0"
        Port "veth0"
            Interface "veth0"
        Port "br0"
            Interface "br0"
                type: internal
        Port "ens33"
            Interface "ens33"
    ovs_version: "2.4.0"
[vagrant@centos ~]$
```

You can see that we just used the `ovs-vsctl add-port` command, along with the name of the bridge (br0) and the name of the interface to add (veth0). The network namespace is now connected to OVS (in this particular configuration, we've just bridged the network namespace onto the network connected to the ens33 physical interface).

Naturally, once you have a network namespace connected to OVS, it can then take advantage of all of OVS's features. We've only shown you a simple example here.

Now that you've seen one way of using network namespaces with OVS, let's look at a practical example: using containers with OVS.

Using containers with OVS

Because containers leverage network namespaces, a lot of what we discussed in the previous section applies here. The key differences are primarily in the container-specific workflow.

As of this writing, Docker containers did not have a built-in method for connecting containers to OVS for networking. Although Docker uses veth pairs and has the ability to use a Linux bridge, and although OVS has bridges that behave a lot like a Linux bridge, the glue to connect Docker containers to OVS has not yet materialized. However, things are moving very rapidly in this area, and we anticipate that a link between Docker containers and OVS will appear in the very near future.

LXC, on the other hand, has built-in support for OVS. There are at least two ways to accomplish this:

- First, if you're using Libvirt with LXC, you can use a Libvirt virtual network to frontend an OVS bridge. We describe this process in the next section, "Using VMs with OVS" on page 527. The use of a Libvirt virtual network is identical, whether you're using containers or VMs.

- Alternatively, you can configure LXC to use a script to attach one of the veth interfaces to OVS.

Let's take a slightly closer look at that second option. (We're going to narrow our focus during this discussion to cover only LXC on Ubuntu.) We mentioned earlier that, by default, LXC stores container configuration information in */var/lib/lxc/ <container-name>/config*, and it's in this file that you'll find the configuration options necessary to link LXC with OVS for networking. We covered a lot of these configuration options in "Configuring LXC Networking" on page 517, but there's one setting that is particularly applicable in this instance.

- The `lxc.network.script.up` option provides the name of a script that will be run when a container's network interface is set to up (enabled). Here is where you can provide a script that will take the veth pair (whose name is known, since it's controlled by the `lxc.network.veth.pair` directive) and attach it to an OVS bridge. A (simple) sample script might look something like this:

```
#!/bin/bash

BRIDGE="br0"
```

```
ovs-vsctl --may-exist add-br $BRIDGE
ovs-vsctl --if-exists del-port $BRIDGE $5
ovs-vsctl --may-exist add-port $BRIDGE $5
```

The $5 refers to the fifth parameter supplied to the script, which—in this specific case--is the name of the veth interface specified in the lxc.network.veth.pair configuration option. We haven't really discussed the --may-exist or --if-exists options to ovs-vsctl, but their behavior is just as you might expect. The --may-exist option prevents an error if the bridge or port already exists, while the --if-exists option takes an action only if the specified object exists.

Using this sort of configuration, LXC will create the veth pair (naming the interfaces according to the lxc.network.veth.pair configuration directive) and then run this script. The script will take the veth interface and attach it to the specified OVS bridge, and the container now has connectivity to OVS and whatever network topologies OVS is configured to support (bridged or overlay connectivity, for example).

What about using OVS with VMs? In the next section, you'll see that using VMs with OVS is generally also pretty straightforward.

Using VMs with OVS

To keep our discussion manageable, we'll focus (as we have in previous sections) on the KVM hypervisor with Libvirt. This is by no means a limit on OVS's part; it's simply a way for us to keep the amount of material manageable.

In "Networking Virtual Machines" on page 504, we introduced you to the concept of a Libvirt virtual network, which is an abstraction Libvirt uses to refer to lower-level constructs. For the last few years, Libvirt has offered built-in support for OVS, so that Libvirt virtual networks can leverage OVS directly.

The following bit of XML would define an OVS-backed Libvirt virtual network:

```
<network>
  <name>ovs-net</name>
  <forward mode="bridge"/>
  <bridge name="br0"/>
  <virtualport type="openvswitch"/>
</network>
```

You'd then reference this Libvirt virtual network by name in the KVM guest domain's configuration, like the following example (which shows only the networking-relevant portion of the guest domain's configuration):

```
<interface type="network">
  <source network="ovs-net"/>
</interface>
```

When using this sort of configuration, after the KVM guest domain is started you'll see a new interface attached to OVS when you run `ovs-vsctl show`:

```
vagrant@trusty:~$ ovs-vsctl show
fe63a9ea-f72f-4aa2-b390-42ecbed6deef
    Bridge "br0"
        Port "eth1"
            Interface "eth1"
        Port "br0"
            Interface "br0"
                type: internal
        Port "vnet0"
            Interface "vnet0"
    ovs_version: "2.0.2"
vagrant@trusty:~$
```

This is a TAP interface, which you can verify with `ip -d link list vnet0` (note the "tun" in the output, which indicates it is a TUN/TAP device):

```
vagrant@trusty:~$ ip -d link list vnet0
7: vnet0: <BROADCAST,MULTICAST,UP,LOWER_UP> mtu 1500 qdisc pfifo_fast master
    ovs-system state UNKNOWN mode DEFAULT group default qlen 500
    link/ether fe:54:00:19:bc:6f brd ff:ff:ff:ff:ff:ff promiscuity 1
    tun
vagrant@trusty:~$
```

This VM is now bridged onto the physical network attached to eth1, but as with network namespaces you could leverage any of OVS's advanced features with this connection.

So far we've shown you connecting network namespaces, containers, and VMs to OVS. What if we want traffic from the host OVS system itself to flow through OVS? For that, you can use an OVS internal port.

Using OVS internal ports

OVS internal ports allow you to present a logical network interface to the host's TCP/IP stack. In that respect, you can compare OVS internal ports to VLAN interfaces, macvlan interfaces, or veth interfaces—all of these are logical network interfaces. The key difference here is that OVS internal ports *only* exist within the context of a particular OVS configuration.

Let's consider an example. We've shown you how to use an OVS bridge named br0 in the previous two sections. Every OVS bridge comes with a corresponding OVS internal port. You've seen this already, but you may not have noticed it. Consider this output of `ovs-vsctl show`:

```
vagrant@trusty:~$ ovs-vsctl show
fe63a9ea-f72f-4aa2-b390-42ecbed6deef
    Bridge "br0"
        Port "eth1"
```

```
                Interface "eth1"
            Port "br0"
                Interface "br0"
                    type: internal
        ovs_version: "2.0.2"
vagrant@trusty:~$
```

Note that br0 exists as a port, and as an interface with type internal. This is an OVS internal port, and the fact that ip link list shows the interface proves that the host's networking stack recognizes this as a logical network interface.

```
vagrant@trusty:~$ ip link list br0
6: br0: <BROADCAST,UP,LOWER_UP> mtu 1500 qdisc noqueue state UNKNOWN mode DEFAULT
    group default
    link/ether 00:0c:29:7d:38:9d brd ff:ff:ff:ff:ff:ff
vagrant@trusty:~$
```

If you now delete the OVS bridge with ovs-vsctl del-br br0, what happens when we try to use ip link list to view the interface?

```
vagrant@trusty:~$ ip link list br0
Device "br0" does not exist.
vagrant@trusty:~$
```

This is what we mean when we say that an OVS internal port exists only within the context of an OVS configuration. It's not part of the host's network stack configuration; rather, it's part of the OVS configuration. Remove it from OVS, and it is removed from the host's network configuration.

You can use this to influence how the host's networking stack directs traffic. Let's say that you wanted to create a logical network interface that would serve as a tunnel endpoint (TEP) for VXLAN overlay traffic managed by OVS. Here are the commands you'd use to create an OVS internal port (we'll break this down after the example):

```
[vagrant@centos ~]$ ovs-vsctl add-port br0 tep0 -- set interface tep0 type=internal
[vagrant@centos ~]$ ovs-vsctl show
e1b45dda-69fa-4cb1-ad37-23eea2e63052
    Bridge "br0"
        Port "br0"
            Interface "br0"
                type: internal
        Port "ens33"
            Interface "ens33"
        Port "tep0"
            Interface "tep0"
                type: internal
    ovs_version: "2.4.0"
```

The unusual command syntax is needed because OVS expects interfaces to already exist when they are added to OVS. Naturally, tep0 doesn't exist, because we're creating it. So, we use the double-hyphen to tell OVS to link the commands together—thus creating the tep0 port and setting its type to `internal` at the same time.

Note that you *can* split the commands, if you don't mind OVS reporting an error first:

```
[vagrant@centos ~]$ ovs-vsctl add-port br0 tep0
ovs-vsctl: Error detected while setting up 'tep0'. See ovs-vswitchd log for details.
[vagrant@centos ~]$ ovs-vsctl set interface tep0 type=internal
[vagrant@centos ~]$ ovs-vsctl show
e1b45dda-69fa-4cb1-ad37-23eea2e63052
    Bridge "br0"
        Port "br0"
            Interface "br0"
                type: internal
        Port "ens33"
            Interface "ens33"
        Port "tep0"
            Interface "tep0"
                type: internal
    ovs_version: "2.4.0"
[vagrant@centos ~]$
```

Now that the tep0 interface exists, you can configure it like you would any other logical interface. Here, we'll assign an IP address to the tep0 interface and set the interface to up (enabled):

```
[vagrant@centos ~]$ ip link list tep0
10: tep0: <BROADCAST,MULTICAST> mtu 1500 qdisc noop state DOWN mode DEFAULT
    link/ether 9e:da:79:89:c3:6a brd ff:ff:ff:ff:ff:ff
[vagrant@centos ~]$ ip addr add 10.1.1.100/24 dev tep0
[vagrant@centos ~]$ ip link set tep0 up
[vagrant@centos ~]$ ip route list
default via 192.168.70.2 dev ens32  proto static  metric 100
10.1.1.0/24 dev tep0  proto kernel  scope link  src 10.1.1.100
192.168.70.0/24 dev ens32  proto kernel  scope link  src 192.168.70.244
192.168.70.0/24 dev ens32  proto kernel  scope link  src 192.168.70.244  metric
100 [vagrant@centos ~]$
```

Based on the output of the `ip route list` command, you can see that the host's network configuration has been influenced by the configuration of the OVS internal port —this CentOS system now has a new route associated with the IP address assigned to the tep0 interface.

Now let's see if you *really* understand how this configuration works: how does the traffic from tep0 get onto the network? If you said via the ens33 interface, you're exactly right! The OVS internal interface is a logical interface that is bridged onto the physical network via the br0 bridge, which contains the ens33 physical interface. Likewise, inbound traffic bound for 10.1.1.100/24 will enter the system via the ens33 interface.

This just barely scratches the surface of what is possible with OVS, but it should at least give you an idea of the basic concepts that are involved. As we mentioned earlier, OVS is a key part of a number of influential open source projects, so time spent working with OVS will pay off in a number of different areas.

Using NAPALM

NAPALM, *Network Automation and Programmability Abstraction Layer with Multivendor support*, is a Python library that offers a robust set of operations to manage network devices using a common set of Python objects regardless of *how* each operation is performed for a given device type.

While NAPALM has a growing set of features, we're focused on two core primary functions of NAPALM in this section:

- Configuration management
- Retrieving information from network devices

In each of these, note that performing any given operation is the same no matter which vendor or OS you're working with, as long as there is a supported NAPALM driver and feature for the given operation.

NAPALM supports a large quantity of device vendors and uses different APIs to communicate to each of them. For example, Cisco Nexus currently uses NX-API, Arista EOS uses eAPI, Cisco IOS uses SSH, and the Juniper Junos drivers use NETCONF. When evaluating NAPALM, you should be aware of which API is required for the device(s) you're working with.

For more details on supported APIs and devices, as well as greater detail on topics not covered in this appendix, consult the NAPALM documentation (*https://napalm.read thedocs.io/en/latest/*). For now, we'll start by looking at managing configurations with NAPALM.

Understanding Configuration Management in NAPALM

NAPALM offers a different approach to managing device configurations while still allowing for a more traditional approach to configuring devices. The unique approach NAPALM takes is referred to as *declarative configuration management*.

The sole focus with declarative configuration is what you want the device configuration to be. This is in stark contrast to worrying about what it is, and how to go from what it is to what you want it to be. While this is a major benefit and feature of NAPALM, it's actually a by-product of particular features that exist on the actual network devices. A few of these device-centric features include candidate configurations with Juniper, configuration sessions with Arista, and the `config replace` feature with Cisco IOS.

In NAPALM terminology, managing a full configuration in a declarative fashion is a *configuration replace* operation.

For a more traditional mode of operations, NAPALM also offers a *configuration merge* operation—this is the ability to take a partial configuration or just a few device commands and *ensure* they exist on the target network device.

In either case and largely based on the underlying device OS supported, changes only take place if they're needed. You'll get to see this as we walk through a few examples.

We'll get started with performing a configuration replace.

Performing a Configuration Replace

Performing a configuration replace means that we're sending the *full* active configuration on the device, and the goal is to ensure that particular configuration exists on the device. In essence, we are declaring what the configuration should be, not worrying about any "no" or "delete" commands.

Our Arista EOS device, eos-spine1 currently has the following full configuration (minus a few interfaces we removed to shorten it):

```
eos-spine1#show run
! Command: show running-config
! device: eos-spine1 (vEOS, EOS-4.15.2F)
!
! boot system flash:vEOS-lab.swi
!
transceiver qsfp default-mode 4x10G
!
hostname eos-spine1
ip domain-name ntc.com
!
snmp-server community networktocode ro
!
```

```
spanning-tree mode mstp
!
aaa authorization exec default local
!
no aaa root
!
username ntc privilege 15 secret 5 $1$KergS3bl$RFVho/GXf.3bQHhOCbeky1
!
vrf definition MANAGEMENT
   rd 100:100
!
interface Ethernet1
   no switchport
!
interface Ethernet2
   no switchport
!
interface Ethernet3
   no switchport
!
interface Ethernet4
   no switchport
!
...
!
interface Management1
   vrf forwarding MANAGEMENT
   ip address 10.0.0.11/24
!
ip route vrf MANAGEMENT 0.0.0.0/0 10.0.0.2
!
ip routing
ip routing vrf MANAGEMENT
!
router ospf 100
   router-id 100.100.100.100
   network 10.0.0.10/32 area 0.0.0.0
   network 10.0.1.10/32 area 0.0.0.0
   network 10.0.2.10/32 area 0.0.0.0
   network 10.0.3.10/32 area 0.0.0.0
   network 10.0.4.10/32 area 0.0.0.0
   max-lsa 12000
!
management api http-commands
   protocol http
   no shutdown
   vrf MANAGEMENT
      no shutdown
!
management ssh
   vrf MANAGEMENT
      no shutdown
```

```
!
!
end
eos-spine1#
```

In order to perform a configuration replace, we first need to store the configuration we want to deploy locally on our server. We'll save this as *eos-spine1.conf* without making any changes so it's exactly what's on the device.

We're now ready to redeploy this configuration onto the device.

Before you do anything with NAPALM, you need to load the correct driver and instantiate a NAPALM device object.

 You can easily install NAPALM with `pip install napalm`.

```
>>> from napalm import get_network_driver
>>>
>>> driver = get_network_driver('eos')
>>> device = driver('eos-spine1', 'ntc', 'ntc123')
>>>
```

At this point, `device` is a variable that is a NAPALM device object. This object has methods for working with device configurations including performing the configuration replace operation. This operation is executed with the method `load_replace_candidate()`.

```
>>> device.open()   # required to load credentials and connect to device
>>>                 # based on API being used
>>>
>>> device.load_replace_candidate(filename='eos-spine1.conf')
>>>
```

When `load_replace_candidate()` is executed, it is only loading the configuration onto the device. It is *not* making any changes to the running configuration. For Arista, the new configuration is loaded into an active session. You can even view this on the EOS CLI.

```
eos-spine1#show configuration sessions
Maximum number of completed sessions: 1
Maximum number of pending sessions: 5

   Name            State          User      Terminal
   ------------- ------------- ---------- --------
   napalm_574288   pending

eos-spine1#
```

The Arista EOS NAPALM driver uses configuration sessions for the configuration management operations within NAPALM. Note that *how* the methods operate under the covers within NAPALM is in fact different per device driver. As mentioned earlier, Juniper uses candidate configurations, Cisco IOS uses configuration replace, and Cisco NXOS uses checkpoint files for full config replaces. *How* the configuration merge, which we cover next, works *may* differ per device too.

At this point the configuration is loaded into an active EOS session. You could also view the *diffs*, or the commands that'll be applied, with a command on the CLI. For EOS, that command would be `show session-config named napalm_574288 diffs`.

However, more important is the uniform NAPALM method that retrieves the command diffs that'll be applied to the device. You can use the method `compare_con fig()` to see the commands that *will* get applied.

```
>>> diffs = device.compare_config()
>>> print(diffs)

>>>
```

As expected, since we were deploying the same configuration that exists on the device, there aren't any diffs. However, if there were diffs, we could add a conditional check in Python and then commit the configuration to the active running configuration using the NAPALM method `commit_config()`.

```
>>> if diffs:
...     device.commit_config()
...
>>>
```

We'll now walk through an example that actually makes a change. On the EOS device, there is a single community string in the full config file:

```
!
snmp-server community networktocode ro
!
```

We're going to remove that community from *eos-spine1.conf* and replace it with two other commands:

```
!
snmp-server community ntc ro
snmp-server community secret123 rw
!
```

Let's use the same two methods to load the config onto the device and view the diffs.

```
>>> device.load_replace_candidate(filename='eos-spine1.conf')
>>>
```

```
>>> diffs = device.compare_config()
>>> print(diffs)
@@ -7,7 +7,8 @@
 hostname eos-spine1
 ip domain-name ntc.com
 !
-snmp-server community networktocode ro
+snmp-server community ntc ro
+snmp-server community secret123 rw
 !
 spanning-tree mode mstp
 !
>>>
```

Take note of the diff generated and what was in the new configuration file. We did not send any "no" commands to device. Rather, we deployed the full desired configuration and EOS calculated the commands that need to be removed and added in order to apply the configuration. This is a huge difference compared to more traditional approaches to configuration management.

Finally, if the diffs look good, you can apply (or commit) them using the commit_config() method.

```
>>> device.commit_config()
>>>
```

If, for whatever reason, you need to revert to the original configuration, you can use the built-in method rollback().

```
>>> device.rollback()
>>>
```

From a workflow perspective and our examples, we're exactly back to where we started with a configuration that has a single SNMP community string.

We're going to shift now and take a look at only sending a partial configuration to an Arista switch.

Performing a Configuration Merge

Remember at this point, there is only a single community string on the Arista EOS switch.

```
eos-spine1#show run | inc snmp-server
snmp-server community networktocode ro
eos-spine1#
```

It may be difficult to always build (through Jinja templating) and deploy a *full* configuration. It's more realistic for those just starting their automation journey to manage specific features. In this example, we're only worrying about SNMP. Thus, we've created a configuration file called *snmp.conf*.

In *snmp.conf*, we've put only the two community strings that we want to deploy to the device.

```
snmp-server community ntc ro
snmp-server community secret123 rw
```

We're now ready to deploy the commands from this file to the device. In order to do this, we'll use the load_merge_candiate() method. This method is used when you're not sending a full configuration to the device.

```
>>> device.load_merge_candidate(filename='snmp.conf')
>>>
>>> diffs = device.compare_config()
>>>
>>> print(diffs)
@@ -8,6 +8,8 @@
 ip domain-name ntc.com
 !
 snmp-server community networktocode ro
+snmp-server community ntc ro
+snmp-server community secret123 rw
 !
 spanning-tree mode mstp
 !
>>>
```

Take note of the diffs generated. Notice how the existing SNMP community is unchanged. In a configuration merge, the goal is a bit different. It's ensuring the new commands exist, but it will not purge or remove any existing configurations.

While a configuration merge does not purge any commands or specific configuration hierarchy in a declarative fashion, if you know how NAPALM is functioning for a specific device driver, you can use it to your advantage to manage a specific feature in a declarative fashion.

For example, let's manage OSPF using the merge configuration operation. As you saw before, the current configuration for OSPF is as follows.

```
eos-spine1#show run section ospf
router ospf 100
   router-id 100.100.100.100
   network 10.0.0.10/32 area 0.0.0.0
   network 10.0.1.10/32 area 0.0.0.0
   network 10.0.2.10/32 area 0.0.0.0
   network 10.0.3.10/32 area 0.0.0.0
   network 10.0.4.10/32 area 0.0.0.0
   max-lsa 12000
eos-spine1#
```

We've created a configuration file called *ospf.conf* that has the following commands.

```
router ospf 100
   router-id 100.100.100.100
   network 10.0.4.10/32 area 0.0.0.0
   network 10.0.5.10/32 area 0.0.0.0
   max-lsa 12000
```

Let's load these commands to device.

```
>>> device.load_merge_candidate(filename='ospf.conf')
>>>
>>> diffs = device.compare_config()
>>>
>>> print(diffs)
@@ -54,6 +56,7 @@
      network 10.0.2.10/32 area 0.0.0.0
      network 10.0.3.10/32 area 0.0.0.0
      network 10.0.4.10/32 area 0.0.0.0
+     network 10.0.5.10/32 area 0.0.0.0
      max-lsa 12000
   !
  management api http-commands
>>>
```

As you may have expected, there is only one change, which is the additional new network statement.

However, since we know the NAPALM driver for Arista EOS is using configuration sessions (which applies all commands in a session as a single transaction), we can take advantage of that and declaratively manage the full OSPF configuration. Let's see how.

We've now created a new OSPF configuration called *ospf-2.conf*. This is the same configuration as we previously used, but we've simply added the no router ospf 100 commands at the top of the file.

```
no router ospf 100
router ospf 100
   router-id 100.100.100.100
   network 10.0.4.10/32 area 0.0.0.0
   network 10.0.5.10/32 area 0.0.0.0
   max-lsa 12000
```

Let's load this OSPF configuration onto the device and view the diffs.

```
>>> device.load_merge_candidate(filename='ospf-2.conf')
>>>
>>> diffs = device.compare_config()
>>> print(diffs)
@@ -49,11 +51,8 @@
  !
  router ospf 100
     router-id 100.100.100.100
-    network 10.0.0.10/32 area 0.0.0.0
```

```
    -    network 10.0.1.10/32 area 0.0.0.0
    -    network 10.0.2.10/32 area 0.0.0.0
    -    network 10.0.3.10/32 area 0.0.0.0
         network 10.0.4.10/32 area 0.0.0.0
    +    network 10.0.5.10/32 area 0.0.0.0
         max-lsa 12000
     !
    management api http-commands
    >>>
```

You can see that the final configuration for OSPF will end up being exactly what was in the *ospf-2.conf*. We did not need to send N "no" commands to remove the undesired network statements. In this workflow, the OSPF process was *not* removed and readded. There was no drop in OSPF adjacencies. Of course, this is something you'd want to test yourself too.

Retrieving Data with NAPALM

The second major function delivered by NAPALM is the ability to retrieve information from network devices in a uniform fashion. Any data returned with NAPALM is normalized and the same for all devices NAPALM supports.

If you recall, when we looked at various APIs in Chapter 7, each vendor or device returned vendor-specific key-value pairs. The caveat to this is if the device supports vendor-neutral data models such as YANG models from the OpenConfig working group that we mentioned in Chapter 5, which isn't yet too widely adopted by network vendors.

We still have our `device` object instantiated. Let's use the `dir()` function, which we originally introduced way back in Chapter 4, to see the methods that the NAPALM device object supports.

```
>>> dir(device)
[...omitted methods..., 'cli', 'close', 'commit_config', 'compare_config',
compliance_report', 'config_session', 'device', 'discard_config', 'enablepwd',
'get_arp_table', 'get_bgp_config', 'get_bgp_neighbors',
'get_bgp_neighbors_detail', 'get_config', 'get_environment', 'get_facts',
'get_firewall_policies', 'get_interfaces', 'get_interfaces_counters',
'get_interfaces_ip', 'get_lldp_neighbors', 'get_lldp_neighbors_detail',
'get_mac_address_table', 'get_network_instances', 'get_ntp_peers',
'get_ntp_servers', 'get_ntp_stats', 'get_optics', 'get_probes_config',
'get_probes_results', 'get_route_to', 'get_snmp_information', 'get_users',
'hostname', 'is_alive', 'load_merge_candidate', 'load_replace_candidate',
'load_template', 'locked', 'open', 'password', 'ping', 'port', 'profile',
'rollback', 'timeout', 'traceroute', 'transport', 'username']
>>>
```

You'll see the two methods we covered earlier, load_merge_candidate() and load_replace_candidate(), but you'll also see that the majority of methods are get_ methods used to retrieve information from network devices.

We're going to review a few of these now.

The first one we're going to look at is called get_facts(). This is used to retrieve common information from the device, such as OS, uptime, interfaces, vendor, model, hostname, and FQDN.

```
>>> device.get_facts()
{u'os_version': u'4.15.2F-2663444.4152F', u'uptime': 15645,
u'interface_list': [u'Ethernet1', u'Ethernet2', u'Ethernet3', u'Ethernet4',
u'Ethernet5', u'Ethernet6', u'Ethernet7', u'Management1'],
u'vendor': u'Arista', u'serial_number': u'', u'model': u'vEOS',
u'hostname': u'eos-spine1', u'fqdn': u'eos-spine1.ntc.com'}
>>>
```

The great thing about the data that is returned is structured exactly the same no matter which vendor you're using within NAPALM. In this case, NAPALM is normalizing and doing the heavy lifting, making it so you don't need to integrate/translate each vendor you're working with. NAPALM is already doing that for you.

Let's take a look at a few more examples. The get_snmp_information() function retrieves a dictionary that summarizes the SNMP configuration present on a device:

```
>>> device.get_snmp_information()
{u'community': {u'networktocode': {u'mode': u'ro', u'acl': u''}}, u'contact': u'',
u'location': u'', u'chassis_id': u''}
>>>
```

The get_lldp_neighbors() function provides a dictionary that summarizes a list of currently seen LLDP neighbors, on a per-interface basis:

```
>>> device.get_lldp_neighbors()
{u'Ethernet2': [{u'hostname': u'eos-spine2.ntc.com', u'port': u'Ethernet2'}],
u'Ethernet3': [{u'hostname': u'eos-spine2.ntc.com', u'port': u'Ethernet3'}],
u'Ethernet1': [{u'hostname': u'eos-spine2.ntc.com', u'port': u'Ethernet1'}],
u'Ethernet4': [{u'hostname': u'eos-spine2.ntc.com', u'port': u'Ethernet4'}],
u'Management1': [{u'hostname': u'eos-spine2.ntc.com', u'port': u'Management1'},
{u'hostname': u'vmx2', u'port': u'fxp0'}, {u'hostname': u'vmx1', u'port': u'fxp0'},
{u'hostname': u'csr2.ntc.com', u'port': u'Gi1'}, {u'hostname': u'csr1.ntc.com',
u'port': u'Gi1'}]}
>>>
```

Both of these functions return a dictionary. We can create a small script to consume and print the LLDP neighbors dictionary in a human-friendly format:

```
>>> for interface, neighbors in device.get_lldp_neighbors().items():
...     print("INTERFACE: " + interface)
...     print("NEIGHBORS: ")
...     for neighbor in neighbors:
```

```
...            print("  - {}".format(neighbor['hostname']))
...
INTERFACE:  Ethernet2
NEIGHBORS:
  - eos-spine2.ntc.com
INTERFACE:  Ethernet3
NEIGHBORS:
  - eos-spine2.ntc.com
INTERFACE:  Ethernet1
NEIGHBORS:
  - eos-spine2.ntc.com
INTERFACE:  Ethernet4
NEIGHBORS:
  - eos-spine2.ntc.com
INTERFACE:  Management1
NEIGHBORS:
  - eos-spine2.ntc.com
  - vmx2
  - vmx1
  - csr2.ntc.com
  - csr1.ntc.com
>>>
```

There are other NAPALM functions that work in a similar way. Understanding the output format of each of these functions is a good first step to being able to perform further tasks based on the current state of the network.

NAPALM Integrations

NAPALM can be used to build custom Python applications. As you've seen, at its core, it is a Python library. However, due to the openness of NAPALM and extensibility of other open source Python projects, NAPALM is also heavily used within other tools, such as Ansible, Salt, and StackStorm.

Using NAPALM in Ansible

NAPALM integrations in Ansible come in the form of Ansible modules. This was also mentioned in the Ansible section in Chapter 9.

There are two primary Ansible modules that map back to what we discussed in this section with regard to NAPALM managing configuration and retrieving device configurations. They are called `napalm_install_config`, used to perform configuration replace and configuration merge operations, and `napalm_get_facts`, used as a wrapper for any `get_` method supported by NAPALM.

Let's take a look at an example using `napalm_install_config`.

```
- name: DEPLOY CONFIGURATIONS WITH NAPALM
  napalm_install_config:
```

```
hostname: "{{ inventory_hostname }}"
username: "{{ un }}"
password: "{{ pwd }}"
dev_os: "{{ os }}"
config_file: configs/snmp.conf
diff_file: diffs/{{ inventory_hostname }}-snmp.diffs
commit_changes: True
replace_config: False
```

The `napalm_install_config` modules support a number of parameters, several being self-explanatory, including `hostname`, `username`, and `password`. The next few are defined as follows:

dev_os

> OS, device driver of NAPALM for the device being managed (e.g., `eos`, `ios`, `junos`)

config_file

> File that has the configuration commands to be loaded onto the network device

diff_file

> File on the Ansible server that'll have the *diffs* generated from the `compare_con fig()` method

commit_changes

> Boolean value and if `True`, the `commit_config()` method will be executed. You can set it so commands are not applied if you just want to see the diffs.

replace_config

> Boolean value and if `True`, the `load_replace_candidate()` method is executed, else if `False`, the `load_merge_candidate()` method is executed.

If you've properly installed the NAPALM Ansible modules, you can also use the `ansible-doc` utility to see more examples using the NAPALM modules:

```
ntc@ntc:~$ ansible-doc napalm_install_config
# output omitted
ntc@ntc:~$ ansible-doc napalm_get_facts
# output omitted
```

> As we said earlier, we did not cover NAPALM YANG integrations in this section. There are Ansible modules for that as well, which are out of the scope of this book.

Using NAPALM in Salt

Salt is a little different than Ansible when it comes to NAPALM integrations in that everything we showed with regard to Salt in Chapter 9 used NAPALM.

NAPALM is natively integrated to Salt and is the most popular network driver for managing network devices with Salt.

Here are a few of the integrations that you'll find more detail about as you read the Salt section in Chapter 9.

There is a specific proxy minion integration for NAPALM. Here is a sample configuration:

```
proxy:
  proxytype: napalm
  driver: nxos
  fqdn: nxos-spine1.dc.amers
  username: ntc
  password: ntc123
```

Each NAPALM getter maps to one or more specific Salt execution modules that are used to retrieve information from devices.

Retrieve NTP statistics from the device with a minion ID of vmx1:

```
$ sudo salt vmx1 ntp.stats
# output omitted
```

Retrieve the active BGP neighbors from the device with a minion ID of vmx1:

```
$ sudo salt vmx1 bgp.neighbors
# output omitted
```

There is also a state function in Salt called `netconfig.managed` that is performing the configuration replace and merge functions we reviewed earlier.

For example, suppose there was an SLS state file called *ntp.sls* that contained the following:

```
ntp_peers_example:
  netconfig.managed:
    - template_name: salt://ntp_template.j2
    - debug: true
```

You can apply the configuration generated from the template to the device using the `salt` CLI, but the main point as you view the following output is that you can see the diffs. These diffs are the same ones you'd see when using the `compare_config()` method with NAPALM.

```
$ sudo salt vmx1 state.apply ntp
vmx1:
  ----------
```

```
          ID: ntp_peer_example
    Function: netconfig.managed
      Result: True
     Comment: Configuration changed!
     Started: 10:48:16.160777
    Duration: 4331.08 ms
     Changes:
              ----------
              diff:
                  [edit system ntp]
                  +    peer 10.10.10.1;
                  +    peer 10.10.10.3;
                  +    peer 10.10.10.2;
                  -    peer 1.2.3.4;
                  -    peer 5.6.7.8;
              loaded_config:
                  delete system ntp peer 1.2.3.4
                  delete system ntp peer 5.6.7.8
                  set system ntp peer 10.10.10.1
                  set system ntp peer 10.10.10.3
                  set system ntp peer 10.10.10.2

Summary for vmx1
------------
Succeeded: 1 (changed=1)
Failed:    0
------------
Total states run:    1
Total run time:    4.331 s
```

Using NAPALM in StackStorm

As also covered in Chapter 9, there is also a NAPALM integration in StackStorm. The NAPALM integration to StackStorm comes in the form of a StackStorm pack.

Here is a list of actions supported via the StackStorm pack:

```
vagrant@st2vagrant:~$ st2 action list --pack=napalm -a ref
+-------------------------------------+
| ref                                 |
+-------------------------------------+
| napalm.bgp_prefix_exceeded_chain    |
| napalm.check_consistency            |
| napalm.cli                          |
| napalm.configuration_change_workflow |
| napalm.get_arp_table                |
| napalm.get_bgp_config               |
| napalm.get_bgp_neighbors            |
| napalm.get_bgp_neighbors_detail     |
| napalm.get_config                   |
| napalm.get_environment              |
| napalm.get_facts                    |
```

```
| napalm.get_firewall_policies       |
| napalm.get_interfaces              |
| napalm.get_lldp_neighbors          |
| napalm.get_log                     |
| napalm.get_mac_address_table       |
| napalm.get_network_instances       |
| napalm.get_ntp                     |
| napalm.get_optics                  |
| napalm.get_probes_config           |
| napalm.get_probes_results          |
| napalm.get_route_to                |
| napalm.get_snmp_information        |
| napalm.interface_down_workflow     |
| napalm.loadconfig                  |
| napalm.ping                        |
| napalm.traceroute                  |
+------------------------------------+
```

As you can see by now, these map directly back to specific NAPALM device object methods you saw earlier in this section.

And here is how you'd get facts using the StackStorm st2 CLI:

```
vagrant@st2vagrant:~$ st2 run napalm.get_facts hostname=vsrx01
# output omitted
```

You can, of course, use the data in actual StackStorm workflows, which we show in Chapter 9.

Index

Symbols

!= (does not equal to) expression, 107
\# (hash sign), 45, 159
$ (dollar sign), 45
% (modulus operator), 104
* (multiplication operator), 103
--- (triple hyphens), 157
-i parameter, 50
-r parameter, 50, 51
.. (two periods), 46
./ command, 49
/ (root) directory, 43
: (colon), 119
; (semicolon), 101
== (equal to) expression, 107
\n (End of Line) character, 101
{} (curly braces), 100, 171
~ (tilde), 44
… (ellipsis), 157

A

absolute paths, 46
Accept header, 217
Accton, 12
Actions (StackStorm), 439, 442-452
Active Networks, 3
Address Resolution Protocol (ARP), 44
advanced data structures, 156
Ansible
    vs. Ansible Tower, 362
    automating Linux servers, 362
    automating network devices, 363
    benefits of, 398
    check mode, verbosity, and limit, 384
    compliance checks, 390
    configuration templates, 378
    inventory files, 363-370
    Jinja templates, 379
    Linux and, 37
    modules, basics of, 372
    modules, common core network, 377
    modules, config, 383
    modules, debug, 387
    modules, facts, 386
    modules, third-party, 395-398
    network automation using, 377-395
    network configuration files, 381
    overview of, 361
    playbooks, 370-374
    provider parameter, 373
    register task attribute, 388
    report generation, 392-395
    role in device provisioning, 23
    show commands, 388
    using NAPALM in, 396, 543
    variable files, 375-376, 378
    writing data to files, 388
append() method, 109
Application Programming Interfaces (APIs)
    (see also network APIs)
    basics of, 30, 291
    constructing proper requests, 222, 231
    NETCONF, 32, 206-215, 222-231
    RESTful APIs, 33, 202
    Simple Network Management Protocol
        (SNMP), 25, 30, 487
    SSH/Telnet and the CLI, 31
Application Virtual Switch (AVS), 8

configuration templates (see network configuration templates)
contact information, xix
containment (Python), 121
Content-Type header, 217
Continuous Deployment, 465
Continuous Integration (CI)
    basics of, 463-465
    benefits of for networking, 468
    challenges of, 459-462
    CI pipeline for, 469-488
    Continuous Delivery (CD), 465
    goals of, 462
    networking CI pipeline, 460
    prerequisites to adopting, 461
    test-driven development (TDD), 466-468
control plane, 1, 6
controller networking, 15
count() method, 98, 110
cp command, 51, 300
Cumulus Networks, 12, 37
cURL command-line tool, 215-217
curly braces ({}), 100, 171

D
daemons
    in CentOS 7.1, 61
    in Debian GNU/Linux 8.1, 58
    in Ubunto Linux 14.04 LTS, 60
    overview of, 57
    presenting process information to, 62
    showing network connections to, 62
Data Center Network Fabrics, 13
data formats
    defined, xiv, 153, 178
    JSON, 169-173
    overview of, 153-156
    types of data, 155
    XML, 162-169
    YAML, 156-162
data models
    defined, 153, 178
    in JSON, 173
    in XSD, 163-165
    in YAML, 161
    in YANG, 174-178
    key facts of, 174
    language selection, 178
data plane, 1, 6

data retrieval
    data collection example, 25
    push model of, 25
    using NAPALM, 541-543
data types (generic), 155-156
data types (Python)
    boolean values, 104-107
    dictionaries, 113-117
    lists, 107-112
    numbers, 102-104
    overview of, 92
    sets and tuples, 117-119
    strings, 93-102
Debian
    Debian package format, 41
    history of, 41
    working with daemons, 58
debug module (Ansible), 387
declarative configuration, 259-261, 534 (see also configuration management)
DELETE requests, 204
dependencies, defined, 40
deployment tools, 484-486
development environments, 481-484
device APIs, 10
device provisioning, 22-24
DevOps, 498
dictionaries
    accessing and iterating over values, 116
    accessing key-value pairs, 114
    accessing lists of keys and values, 115
    built-in methods of, 114
    converting lists to, 113
    overview of, 113, 156
    removing values from, 115
    updating information in, 115
dict[key], 113
dir() function, 94, 109, 541
directories (see files and directories (Linux))
distributed version control system (DVCS), 312 (see also Git; source control)
Django, 181
dnf (Dandified YUM), 40
Docker, 485, 516, 518, 526
does not equal to != expression, 107
dollar sign ($), 45
double periods (..), 46
dynamic routing protocol, 79

JSON (JavaScript Object Notation)
basics of, 169-171
curly braces, 171
data models in, 173
in Python, 172
JSON Schema, 173
Juniper's Contrail, 9

K

key-value pairs, 156
keys() method, 115
KVM hypervisor, 504, 527

L

len() function, 108
Libvirt virtualization API, 504, 527
limit (Ansible), 384
Linux
applications of, 42
automating servers using Ansible, 362
benefits of understanding, 37
distributions available, 39-42
distributions covered, xvii
file and directory manipulation, 48-54
filesystem navigation, 43-48
history of, 38
interfaces, 62-73
Linux bridge, 79-85, 504-507
macvlan interfaces, 501-504
network namespaces, 509-516
networking Linux containers, 516-519, 526
Open vSwitch (OVS) and, 519-531
package format, 40
routing as a router, 77-79
routing as an end host, 73-77
running programs, 54-57
shebang, 55
shells, 43
Vagrant environments for, 45
virtual machine networking, 504-509
working with daemons, 57-62
lists
accessing individual elements of, 108, 145
appending elements to, 109
built-in methods of, 109
converting to dictionaries, 113
counting objects in, 110
creating, 107
creating empty, 109

inserting elements in, 109
overview of, 156
removing elements from, 111
sorting, 112
load_merge_candiate(), 539, 542
load_replace_candidate(), 536, 542
loops (Jinja), 187-193
loops (Python)
enumerate function, 127
for loop, 124-127
iterating over dictionaries with, 116
overview of, 123
while loop, 123
lower() method, 95
ls utility, 53
LXC (LinuX Containers), 516, 526
LXML library, 162

M

macvlan interfaces
creating, configuring, and deleting, 502
use cases for, 502
vs. VLAN interfaces, 501
macvtap interfaces, 508
Mako, 181
man (manual) command, 51
management information bases (MIBs), 25
mathematical operators, 102-104
McKeown, Nick, 1
merge requests (GitLab), 473
methods (Python), 92
methods, vs. functions, 108 (see also individual methods)
migrations, 26
mkdir (make directory) command, 48
modules (Ansible), 372, 377
modules (Python), 140-142
modules (Salt), 410, 437
modulus operator (%), 104
multiplication operator (*), 103
mv command, 51

N

NAPALM (Network Automation and Programmability Abstraction Layer with Multivendor support)
Ansible modules, 396
benefits of, 533
configuration management in, 534-541

554 | Index

top file (Salt), 405
touch command, 48-50
Tox, 481
tracking changes, 294
Triggers (StackStorm), 440, 452
triple hyphens (---), 157
troubleshooting, 28-30
truth tables, 104
try/except statements, 146
tuple data type, 118, 156
type function, 94, 102
typographical conventions, xviii

U

Ubuntu Linux, 41, 60
update() method, 115
updates, 470
    (see also Continuous Integration (CI))
upper() method, 95
user permissions, 51-54

V

Vagrant, 45, 481-484
values() method, 115
variable files (Ansible), 375-376, 378
VeloCloud, 14
verbosity (Ansible), 384
version control, 293, 471
    (see also source control)
Viptela, 14
Virtual Ethernet pairs (veth pairs), 514
Virtual eXtensible LAN (VxLAN), 9
virtual machines (VMs), 504-509, 527
Virtual Routing and Forwarding (VRF), 509
virtual switching, 8
VLAN interfaces, 70-73
VMware distributed switch (VDS), 8
VMware standard switch (VSS), 8
VMware's NSX, 9

W

web development, templates for, 181
webhooks (StackStorm), 452

which command, 57
while loop, 123
white-box switching, 11-13
whitespace, removing, 97
Wide Area Networking (WAN), 14
Workflows (StackStorm), 439, 442-452
working directory (Git), 297

X

XML (eXtensible Markup Language)
    basics of, 162-163
    benefits of, 162
    data models using XSD, 163-165
    Junos representation, 154
    searching using XQuery, 169
    transforming with XSLT, 165-169
XML Schema Definition (XSD), 163-165
XQuery, 169

Y

YAML (YAML Ain't Markup Language)
    basics of, 156-160
    data models in, 161
    device provisioning example, 23
    double curly braces in, 24
    ellipsis, 157
    hash sign, 159
    three hyphens, 157
    YAML from Python, 160
YANG
    benefits of, 178
    key facts of data models, 174
    leaf statement, 175
    leaf-list statement, 176
    list statement, 176
    overview of, 174-175
    YANG containers, 177
yum (Yellowdog Updater, Modified), 40

Z

zero touch provisioning (ZTP), 15
ZeroMQ, 429

About the Authors

Jason Edelman, CCIE 15394 & VCDX-NV 167, is a born and bred network engineer from the great state of New Jersey. He was the typical "lover of the CLI" or "router jockey." At some point several years ago, he made the decision to focus more on software, development practices, and how they are converging with network engineering. Jason currently runs a boutique consulting firm, Network to Code, helping vendors and end users take advantage of new tools and technologies to reduce their operational inefficiencies. Jason has a Bachelor's of Engineering from Stevens Institute of Technology in New Jersey and still resides locally in the New York City metro area. Jason also writes regularly on his personal blog at *jedelman.com* and can be found on Twitter as @jedelman8 (*https://twitter.com/jedelman8*).

Scott S. Lowe is an engineering architect at VMware, Inc. He currently focuses on cloud computing and network virtualization after having spent a number of years specializing in compute virtualization. Scott has authored a number of technical books on vSphere and OpenStack, and shares technical content regularly on his blog at *blog.scottlowe.org*. He lives in Denver, Colorado, with his wife and the two youngest of their seven kids.

Matt Oswalt is a network software developer, working on the technical and non-technical challenges at the intersection of software development and network infrastructure. He is at his happiest in front of a keyboard, next to a brewing kettle, or wielding his silo-smashing sledgehammer. He publishes his work in this area and more at *keepingitclassless.net*, and on Twitter as @Mierdin (*https://twitter.com/Mierdin*).

Colophon

The animal on the cover of *Network Programmability and Automation* is a gavial crocodile (*Gavialis gangeticus*). This reptile can be found in two countries: India, along the Chambal, Girwa, and Son Rivers; and Nepal, along the Narayani River. The gavial's name originated from the knob of tissue that grows on the tip of the male's snout called a *ghara*, the Hindi word for pot.

The gavial is easily distinguishable from other crocodiles because of its long, slender snout and narrow, sharp teeth. It feeds primarily on small fish and crustaceans. It herds fish toward the shore, and stuns them using an underwater jaw clap. It does not chew its prey, but swallows it whole. This species rarely attacks humans, but with 110 interdigitated teeth, you don't want to get too close.

This crocodile is very long, measuring 13–20 ft (4–6 m). The color ranges from olive green to brown-gray with a light underside. It reaches maturity at 8–12 years. Males use their gharas to vocalize and blow bubbles during mating displays. Females make nests in the sand banks and guard the eggs for 83–94 days, then tend to the hatchlings for several months.

The preferred habitat of the gavial is high-banked rivers with clear, fast-flowing water and deep pools. Since the mid-1900s, the gavial's numbers have declined as much as 98 percent due to hunting for traditional medicine and drastic changes to their fresh-water habitats.

Many of the animals on O'Reilly covers are endangered; all of them are important to the world. To learn more about how you can help, go to *animals.oreilly.com*.

The cover image is from *Braukhaus Lexicon*. The cover fonts are URW Typewriter and Guardian Sans. The text font is Adobe Minion Pro; the heading font is Adobe Myriad Condensed; and the code font is Dalton Maag's Ubuntu Mono.

Learn from experts.
Find the answers you need.

Sign up for a **10-day free trial** to get **unlimited access** to all of the content on Safari, including Learning Paths, interactive tutorials, and curated playlists that draw from thousands of ebooks and training videos on a wide range of topics, including data, design, DevOps, management, business—and much more.

Start your free trial at:
oreilly.com/safari

(No credit card required.)